# THE PROPER STUDY
# OF MANKIND

# THE PROPER STUDY OF MANKIND

## An Anthology of Essays

### ISAIAH BERLIN

Edited by Henry Hardy and Roger Hausheer
Foreword by Noel Annan
Introduction by Roger Hausheer

Know then thyself, presume not God to scan;
The proper study of Mankind is Man.

Alexander Pope, *An Essay on Man*, ii 1

Farrar, Straus and Giroux
New York

Farrar, Straus and Giroux
19 Union Square West, New York 10003

First published in 1997 by Chatto & Windus Limited, United Kingdom
First Farrar, Straus and Giroux edition, 1998

Library of Congress Cataloging-in-Publication Data
Berlin, Isaiah, Sir.
The proper study of mankind : an anthology of essays / Isaiah
Berlin ; edited by Henry Hardy and Roger Hausheer ; with a foreword
by Noel Annan and an introduction by Roger Hausheer. — 1st Farrar,
Straus and Giroux ed.
p. cm.
"First published in 1997 by Chatto & Windus Limited, United
Kingdom"—T.p. verso.
Includes bibliographical references and index.
ISBN 0-374-23750-6 (alk. paper)
1. Human beings. 2. Philosophical anthropology. 3. History—
Philosophy. 4. Political science—Philosophy. I. Hardy, Henry.
II. Hausheer, Roger. III. Title.
B1618.B451H47 1998
192—dc21                                                    97-43470

# CONTENTS

| | |
|---|---|
| *Note to the American edition* | viii |
| *Foreword by Noel Annan* | ix |
| *Editorial preface by Henry Hardy* | xvi |
| *Introduction by Roger Hausheer* | xxiii |

The Pursuit of the Ideal | 1

Philosophical Foundations
The Concept of Scientific History | 17
Does Political Theory Still Exist? | 59

Freedom and Determinism
'From Hope and Fear Set Free' | 91
Historical Inevitability | 119

Political Liberty and Pluralism
Two Concepts of Liberty | 191

History of Ideas
The Counter-Enlightenment | 243
The Originality of Machiavelli | 269
The Divorce between the Sciences and the
   Humanities | 326
Herder and the Enlightenment | 359

Russian Writers
The Hedgehog and the Fox | 436
Herzen and his Memoirs | 499
Conversations with Akhmatova and Pasternak | 525

Romanticism and Nationalism in the Modern Age
The Apotheosis of the Romantic Will | 553
Nationalism: Past Neglect and Present Power | 581

Twentieth-Century Figures
Winston Churchill in 1940 | 605
President Franklin Delano Roosevelt | 628

*Concise bibliography of Isaiah Berlin's writings* | 639
*Index* | 645

## Note to the American edition

Isaiah Berlin died on 5 November 1997. Because the British edition of *The Proper Study of Mankind*, from which this one is derived, was published in February 1997, the author is at times referred to, in the introductory items that follow, in the present tense. Some of these references might perhaps strike the reader of this posthumous American edition as inappropriate. I considered altering them, but decided that to do so would be artificial – especially in my preface, which, after all, bears the date of its composition – and so I left them as they were.

Since I am writing this only five weeks after Isaiah Berlin's death, I shall for a moment allow myself to relax an editor's customary, somewhat formal, manner, and express the hope that this retrospective anthology of the work he published in his lifetime may now fittingly take on an extra role: to serve as a tribute to a man I loved, a friend who, of the human beings I have known, was not only the most remarkable and delightful, but also, in so many ways, the wisest, the surest in judgement, and the best.

11 December 1997                                    HENRY HARDY

# FOREWORD

*Noel Annan*

Isaiah Berlin began his academic career as a philosopher at Oxford and became famous as a historian of ideas. Oxford philosophy is important to him. It rooted him in the English linguistic analytical tradition that descends from Hume, Mill and Russell. That is why when he wrote his account of the two concepts of liberty he was so wary of what is often called 'positive freedom'. When he wrote (in 1958) it was fashionable to expose the fallacies in Mill's *On Liberty* and praise the conception of freedom that T. H. Green, influenced by Hegel and other Continental philosophers, had popularised. Green had argued that when the State interfered and passed laws forbidding pollution or controlling factory machinery, in order to safeguard workers' lives, the State was not curtailing freedom. Yes, a few men might consider that their freedom had been curtailed, but vastly more people would now be free to do things that hitherto they had been unable to do. The sum of freedom would be increased. 'Freedom for an Oxford don', it was said, 'is a very different thing from freedom for an Egyptian peasant.'[1] To accept positive freedom became the hall-mark of the intelligent social democrat.

Berlin denounced this proposition as claptrap. If positive freedom is a valid ideal, then what defence is there against the Marxist claim that the State has the right to inflict terrible punishments upon those who oppose its power to compel individuals to act against what they want to do, on the grounds that they should be contributing to the welfare of the mass of the population? For Berlin the classic English interpretation of liberty is correct. It means not being coerced, not being imprisoned or terrorised. Yes, the Egyptian peasant needs food and medicine, 'but the minimum

[1] p. 196 below.

freedom that he needs today, and the greater degree of freedom that he may need tomorrow, is not some species of freedom peculiar to him, but identical with that of professors, artists and millionaires'.[1] It may well be necessary to sacrifice freedom to prevent misery. But it *is* a sacrifice; and to declare that I am really more free is a perversion of words. It may be that society is more just or prosperous and all sorts of poor people are now able to enjoy holidays abroad or have a decent home. They were free before to enjoy these things but they did not have the money. It is a perversion of language to say that now for the first time they are free.

Perversion of language is not a philosopher's fad. It matters. It matters if we say we are more free when new laws are passed to compel us to wear seat-belts in cars. We may be safer and the law may be admirable, but we are less free. Suppose we follow Rousseau and argue that no one in his right mind would wish to be a slave of ignoble passions. Suppose I am an alcoholic, a slave to the bottle. Would I not welcome being freed from that slavery? Surely my enlightened self would wish to renounce that part of my liberty that enslaves me to the bottle. Few of us are saints. Saints declare, 'In thy service is perfect freedom', renounce worldly vices, and live according to a spiritual rule. But what are we to do with the majority of mankind who are unable to master their sinful passions? Here, says Berlin, the real horror of a purely rational view of life unfolds. For if it can be shown that there is only one correct view of life, people who fail to follow it must be forced to do so. Positive freedom is the road to serfdom.

But there is yet another way of denying that human beings are free agents. Are they not the playthings of fate, caught inescapably by the impersonal forces of history? Historical processes are inevitable and, although statesmen pretend that they have the power to control events, human beings are powerless to do so. Climate, demography, the vagaries of the economy, class structures and political forces overwhelm them. It is the mission of the historian, so this line of reasoning continues, to unmask these impersonal forces. History is not an art, it is a science, 'no more, no less' as the Cambridge historian J. B. Bury said. One of Berlin's longest and most dense articles is deployed against this contention, and in his joust against E. H. Carr, the apologist for Stalin's regime,

[1] p. 197 below.

he was judged to have unhorsed his opponent. To believe in determinism would entail a shattering loss in the concepts with which we discuss morality – praise, blame, regret, forgiveness for instance.

Rooted though Berlin was in the English tradition of philosophy he rejected much that was fashionable among his contemporaries. He thought logical positivism no less disastrous than determinism. The natural sciences were not the paradigm of knowledge. Too much of what we know and value in life is excluded by this way of categorising thought. For what is remarkable about the body of his work is that it recognises how valuable, how challenging, how original were the contributions of the German philosophers in the eighteenth and nineteenth centuries. These were the men who were revolting against the soulless, mechanical ideas of the French Enlightenment. Berlin begged his contemporaries to stop regarding them and their analogues in Russia or Italy – Vico, Herder, Hamann, Herzen and Moses Hess – as benighted romantics.

He has praised them for recognising the passion men and women feel for their homeland, their own specific culture, for their nation or for their community – say, a mining village. These were what gave them their sense of identity. Marx ignored this. Berlin knows how Jews in Eastern Europe felt alienated from the society in which they lived; and from this understanding he perceives how Germans in the eighteenth century felt alienated from a Europe dominated by French culture and sophistication – just as in our times Third World countries are alienated by the Western sense of superiority.

Berlin therefore disagreed with the most powerful voices in philosophy because he did something not all that common among philosophers immediately before and after the War. He read the works of philosophers long dead, indeed of some who would not in Oxford have been called philosophers. He did not convict them of error and contrast them with the truth as we know it today. Nor did he divide them into those who point the way to saner times and those whom tyrants have used to justify their cruelty. What he did was to evoke their vision of life and contrast it with other visions of life. That is not all. He denies that there is any way of proving that one vision is more valid or more justifiable than any other. One might find Joseph de Maistre's analysis of society hateful, but we would be wrong not to realise that it contains some terrible truths, however liberals might shudder at the conclusions Maistre drew from them. Consider Nietzsche. In his works are conclusions which the Nazis tried to translate into political action. But we would be amputating part of our sensibility if we failed to receive Nietzsche's astonishing understanding of a world no longer willing to accept the sanctions of religion as valid. Or consider Carlyle. Set beside his contemporaries, Marx and Tolstoy, he cuts a very poor figure. But he was nearer the truth than Marx and Tolstoy in reminding us that nations and societies need leaders. We do not have to agree with Carlyle when he praises Frederick the Great and Cromwell for the harshness and inhumanity of their decisions. Marx and Tolstoy were wrong to declare that statesmen are so insignificant that they do not influence events. Churchill, Roosevelt and Ben-Gurion had a crucial influence upon the destiny of their countries.

This way of looking at philosophy sustains Berlin's belief in pluralism. 'Pluralism' is a dingy word. Most people accept that there are many groups and interests in society, and a good society arranges for them to tolerate each other's existence: indeed the most powerful of all institutions in society, the State, should make a special effort to give minority interests as much scope as possible. Most people think pluralism is a pragmatic compromise. It does not compel us to abandon our belief in socialism or in the beneficence of the inequality produced by the market economy, or our belief that there is a rule, could we but act upon it, that should govern all our lives. But Berlin means something much more disturbing. He takes the unfashionable view that good ends conflict. Equality and freedom frequently conflict; and to get more of one you have to surrender some part of the other. No one can doubt Berlin's belief in the importance of liberty. But he does not beat a drum-roll for Hayek. Liberty is only one of the good things in life for which he cares. For him equality is also a sacred value, and those who reject equality as a bad dream are unsympathetic to him. He acknowledges that if liberty for the powerful and intelligent means the exploitation of the weak and less gifted, the liberty of the powerful and intelligent should be curtailed. To publish a book in England, however offensive to Moslems, is one thing. But to sell the same book in the old city in Jerusalem with maximum publicity and invite riots and death is another. The need to make distinctions of this kind is the justification of pluralism.

Or consider the plight of Antigone. Sophocles thought she was right to put respect for the corpses of her beloved brothers before

her obligation to the law. ('My nature is to love not to hate.')[1]
Sartre took the opposite view. Or consider spontaneity. It is a
virtue: but we should not expect to find it uppermost in the
abilities of the Cabinet Secretary. Indeed one could argue that
spontaneity is the last quality one wants such a high bureaucrat to
exhibit. Values collide and often cannot be made to run in parallel.
And not only values. Propositions too. Truth is not a unity.

It was on this matter that Berlin dissented from the English
analytic philosophers. The summit of his ambition as a young man
had been to get the group that centred upon Austin and Ayer to
accept some point he had made as original or important. To have
done that would have been to establish something that was true.
True, because the circle's discussions – though most of the points
made were minute distinctions in logic or perception – were
sustained by a great unspoken assumption. The assumption was
that all solutions to all major problems can be found if we try hard
enough. Philosophers accepted as axiomatic that there could be
only one true answer to a question: other answers were errors.
Furthermore, all true answers must be compatible with other true
answers. Truth is a unity. The good life must conform to these
truths which philosophers discovered: otherwise it would not be
good. In the end either we or our successors will discover these
truths. And when we do we shall be able to reorganise society on
rational lines free from superstition, dogma and oppression. Berlin
disagreed; and he praised Machiavelli for being the first major
thinker to deny that this was so. A politician cannot operate
according to the strict morality of personal life.

Is Berlin a relativist? Is he saying that there is no disputing about
tastes, or that we can never understand another culture because we
cannot get inside it? Certainly not. However different we are from
Polynesian islanders or ancient Athenians, the very fact that we can
imagine what it would be like to be one means that comparisons
between cultures are possible. Our ability to recognise virtually
universal values informs every discussion we have about the nature
of man, about sanity, about reason. Is he then an anti-rationalist?
Impossible for one of his training at Oxford. He is opposed to
Oakeshott because he believes reason can be applied to numbers of
social problems and produce results. Reason may diminish the
bruising conflicts between good ends. Peaceful trade-offs are

---

[1] Sophocles, *Antigone*, line 523.

possible, nor are they always fudges. Reason is needed to sort out the conflicting claims of justice, mercy, privation and personal freedom. It is true that every solution creates a new problem, new needs and demands. If children have got greater freedom because their parents fought for it, the children may make such importunate demands for a juster society that they threaten the very freedom their parents fought for. The ideas that liberated one generation become the shackles of the next. In saying this Berlin was reminding us that philosophers alone cannot explain the nature of being: the historian too can enlighten us. The history of ideas is the gateway to self-knowledge. We need it to remind us that people are not an undifferentiated mass to be organised as efficiently as possible. Efficiency and organisation should not be regarded as the ultimate goals in life. They are means, limited means, to enable men and women to live better and happier lives.

No one has ever made ideas come alive more than Isaiah Berlin. This is not strange, because he personifies them. They live because they are the progeny of human beings, and Berlin is a connoisseur of individual men and women. Nothing pleases him more than to praise famous men, such as Churchill or Roosevelt, because they enhance life and show that the impersonal forces of history, or the so-called laws that govern society, can be defied. Men and women of genius change the world. Even obscure scholars, who certainly will not change the world, can add something to the total sum of comedy, idiosyncrasy, perhaps of tragedy, when their special oddity is revealed. Berlin wants us to understand the immense variety of emotions and ideals in the world we inhabit.

That is why, Berlin insists, it is foolish to expect men and women, still more their ideas, to conform to one set of principles. He likes to play games to bring this home to us. In one of his best-known essays, on Tolstoy, he divides thinkers into hedgehogs and foxes – the hedgehogs who 'know one big thing', like Dostoevsky or Aquinas, and the foxes who 'know many things', like Turgenev or Hume – Tolstoy being a natural fox who tried to become a hedgehog. Then again he divides statesmen into those of single principle who try to bend events to their will, like Hitler, Trotsky and de Gaulle, and those who sense how events are moving and how their fellow citizens feel, and find the way to give effect to those feelings, like Lincoln, Bismarck, Lloyd George and Roosevelt. He revels in the difference between human beings. He admires austere remote scholars, but also enjoys ebullient, effervescent scholars who prefer vehemence to reticence, pleasure to authority, who deflate the self-important and the pompous. High spirits have their place in a university as well as *gravitas*. He is not blind to human failings and he dislikes those who are inhuman and insensitive. Indeed some who battle for power and position are evil and sinister. Like Hamlet he stands amazed at 'What a piece of work is a man'; unlike Hamlet he delights in man.

Berlin, then, is hostile to the pretensions of technocrats and revolutionaries. The technocrats driving through their plans against opposition, sublime in their indifference to the ignorant opposition of those for whom they are certain a better future exists, appal him by their lack of humility. The revolutionaries, oblivious to suffering, equally appal him. Sometimes it may be necessary to go to war, assassinate a tyrant, overthrow law and order. But there is an even chance that no improvement will result. One of his favourite quotations, which he uses time and again, is from Kant: 'Out of the crooked timber of humanity no straight thing was ever made.'[1] He recognises that the young may pass him by. The young so often want to fight and suffer to create a nobler society. But, even when set against the most dedicated and pure socialists of my generation, he seems to me to have written the truest and the most moving of all the interpretations of life that my own generation made.

See pp. 16, 241, 603, 642 below.

# EDITORIAL PREFACE

*Henry Hardy*

ISAIAH BERLIN is widely and justifiably regarded as one of the best English essayists of the twentieth century. His enthusiastically acclaimed collections of essays, published during the course of the last quarter of a century, have proved enduringly popular and inspirational. His canvas is broad – from philosophy and the history of thought to portraits of contemporaries, from political ideas to the nineteenth-century Russian intelligentsia. His exemplary lucidity and his rare penetration are familiar to and valued by a very wide readership. The importance of his central ideas is hard to exaggerate.

This anthology is a response to the suggestion that the time is ripe to re-present Berlin's work to a new generation of readers who may not have encountered his previous collections, not all of which are now equally readily available. Our aim has been twofold: to provide within one set of covers a selection from the best of Berlin's published essays, and to exhibit the full range of his work. Though several of the essays are virtually self-selecting by these criteria, the choice of others is closer to being arbitrary, and there will certainly be readers familiar with Berlin's writings who would prefer a somewhat different list of contents. We ourselves omitted some essays only with the greatest reluctance, in the attempt to keep the volume within manageable proportions: 'The Philosophical Ideas of Giambattista Vico', 'European Unity and its Vicissitudes' and 'Fathers and Children' might be picked out for special mention in this connection. We happily allow, then, that adjustments at the margins would have been possible, though we are clear that enough of the central core is here to make this a defensible way of fulfilling the aims which we have set ourselves.

Such a defence is implicit in the introduction. Indeed, I should make clear that, despite my use of the first person plural, it was

Roger Hausheer who took the lead in making the selection. He has made a long and careful study of Berlin's *oeuvre*, and is therefore ideally placed to identify its landmarks, and to provide the new visitor with the overview that follows. The main credit for the generosity and scope of this anthology is his, though we have modified its contents in discussion, and take joint responsibility for the result. Selection and title (the latter being my suggestion) have been graciously approved by the author. The subheadings within the list of contents are meant only as rough signposts, partly to guide those who prefer to read the essays in an order other than that in which they are printed: although the printed order has a certain logic, each essay stands on its own, and it may well be, for example, that some readers will find the rather more abstract essays in the earlier sections easier to approach if read after the more historically concrete studies that follow.

The responsibility for textual editing has been mine, though Roger Hausheer's help, especially with German sources, has been invaluable. Most of the essays have already appeared in collections edited by me (jointly with Aileen Kelly in the case of 'The Hedgehog and the Fox'), and here I have made only minor further corrections, also adding references for previously unreferenced quotations, so far as I could.[1] The three essays that do not fall into this category, since they appeared in volumes published before I became Isaiah Berlin's editor, are 'Historical Inevitability', 'Two Concepts of Liberty' and 'Herder and the Enlightenment': here too I have mostly added references where there were none (as throughout the first two of these pieces) and checked translations and existing references, amending where necessary; I have also broken up some extremely long paragraphs and made a number of (mostly minor, copy-editorial) corrections, but the texts remain, of course, essentially unchanged. The author has added a clarificatory footnote about Herder and relativism on page 390; this also has a bearing on some of the references to relativism in the other pieces. Such overlap between the essays as naturally occurs, given their independent origins, has been left, in order not to damage their individual integrity.

*

[1] Where I have failed, I should be exceedingly grateful to hear from anyone who can supply missing references.

Details of the original publication of the essays are as follows: 'On the Pursuit of the Ideal', an abbreviated version of which was read on 15 February 1988 at the ceremony in Turin at which the author was awarded the first Senator Giovanni Agnelli International Prize 'for the ethical dimension in advanced societies', was published privately by the Agnelli Foundation, and also appeared in the *New York Review of Books*, 17 March 1988; 'The Concept of Scientific History' appeared as 'History and Theory: The Concept of Scientific History' in *History and Theory* 1 (1960); 'Does Political Theory Still Exist?' was published first in French as 'La théorie politique existe-t-elle?' in *Revue française de science politique* 11 (1961), and then in English in Peter Laslett and W. G. Runciman (eds), *Philosophy, Politics and Society*, 2nd Series (Oxford, 1962: Blackwell); ' "From Hope and Fear Set Free" '[1] (the Presidential Address for the 1963–4 Session) appeared in the *Proceedings of the Aristotelian Society* 64 (1964), and is reprinted here by courtesy of the Editor of the Aristotelian Society; 'Historical Inevitability', the first Auguste Comte Memorial Trust Lecture, was delivered on 12 May 1953 at the London School of Economics and Political Science, published by Oxford University Press in London in 1954, and reprinted in revised form in *Four Essays on Liberty* (London and New York, 1969: Oxford University Press); 'Two Concepts of Liberty', the author's Inaugural Lecture as Chichele Professor of Social and Political Theory at Oxford University, was delivered on 31 October 1958, published by the Clarendon Press in Oxford in the same year, and reprinted in revised form in *Four Essays on Liberty*; 'The Counter-Enlightenment' appeared in the *Dictionary of the History of Ideas*, vol. 2 (New York, 1973: Scribner's); 'The Originality of Machiavelli', the first draft of which was read at a meeting of the British section of the Political Studies Association in 1953, was published in a shortened form, as 'The Question of Machiavelli', in the *New York Review of Books*, 4 November 1971, and in full in Myron P. Gilmore (ed.), *Studies on Machiavelli* (Florence, 1972: Sansoni); 'The Divorce between the Sciences and the Humanities' was the second Tykociner Memorial Lecture, published by the University of Illinois in 1974; 'Herder and the Enlightenment', which began life as a lecture delivered to Johns Hopkins University in 1964, appeared in Earl R. Wasserman (ed.), *Aspects of the Eighteenth*

---

[1] The title is a line from Swinburne's *The Garden of Proserpine*.

*Century* (Baltimore, 1965: Johns Hopkins Press), and was reprinted in revised form in *Vico and Herder: Two Studies in the History of Ideas* (London, 1976: Hogarth Press; New York, 1976: Viking); 'The Hedgehog and the Fox' first appeared, in a shorter form, as 'Lev Tolstoy's Historical Scepticism' in *Oxford Slavonic Papers* 2 (1951), and was reissued with additions under its present title in 1953 in London by Weidenfeld and Nicolson and in New York by Simon and Schuster; 'Herzen and his Memoirs' is the introduction to Alexander Herzen, *My Past and Thoughts*, translated by Constance Garnett (London, 1968: Chatto and Windus; New York, 1968: Knopf), and was also published, as 'The Great Amateur', in the *New York Review of Books*, 14 March 1968; 'Conversations with Akhmatova and Pasternak', given as a Bowra Lecture in Oxford on 13 May 1980, appeared in the *New York Review of Books*, 20 November 1980, and is a shorter version of 'Meetings with Russian Writers in 1945 and 1956', which is to be found in *Personal Impressions* (see p. 641 below); 'The Apotheosis of the Romantic Will: The Revolt against the Myth of an Ideal World' was published in an Italian translation in *Lettere italiane* 27 (1975), and first appeared in its original English form in *The Crooked Timber of Humanity* (see p. 642 below); 'Nationalism: Past Neglect and Present Power' appeared as 'El nacionalismo: descuido del pasado y poder actual' in *Diálogos* 14 No 6 (November–December 1978), and under its present title in *Partisan Review* 46 (1979); 'Winston Churchill in 1940', commissioned as a review of the second volume of Churchill's war memoirs, first appeared in 1949 in *Atlantic Monthly* 184 No 3 (as 'Mr Churchill') and *Cornhill Magazine* 981 (as 'Mr Churchill and F.D.R.'), and was reissued in book form in 1964 as *Mr Churchill in 1940* (London: John Murray; Boston/Cambridge: Houghton Mifflin/Riverside Press); 'President Franklin Delano Roosevelt' appeared in 1955 in *Political Quarterly* 26 and, as 'Roosevelt Through European Eyes', in *Atlantic Monthly* 196 No 1. I am grateful to the publishers concerned for allowing these essays to be reprinted. They are drawn from seven previously published collections, as detailed in the concise bibliography at the end of this volume.

As before, I have depended heavily on the expert knowledge of a number of scholars, especially in the search for the sources of quotations that I have not found in the author's notes. Professors F. M. Barnard and H. B. Nisbet have devoted many hours (as has

Roger Hausheer) to helping me with Herder's dismayingly large corpus, and my gratitude for their generosity is especially heartfelt; Professor Hans Dietrich Irmscher and Dr Regine Otto have very kindly solved a number of the problems that remained. Professor T. J. Reed has been a ready help with other German sources, in the face of repeated enquiries, and Dr Andrew Fairbairn (whose patience is also exemplary) mainly but by no means exclusively with quotations from eighteenth-century French authors. Other problems have been solved for me by Edward Acton, J. H. Burns, Terrell Carver, R. F. Christian, Julie Curtis, Timothy Day, John Derry, Paul Foote, Michael Freeden, Patrick Gardiner, Gwen Griffith Dickson, Leofranc Holford-Strevens, David Howells, Michael Inwood, John H. Kautsky, Richard Lebrun, Meira Levinson, Helen McCurdy, David Miller, J. C. O'Flaherty, Bruce Phillips, Leon Pompa, H. T. Mason, David Place, Michael Quinn, Philip Schofield, the late Elisabeth Stopp, J. L. H. Thomas and Ralph Walker.

For other kinds of help I should like to thank Adrian Hale, Librarian of Wolfson College; Marion Maneker of Viking Penguin; Will Sulkin, Jenny Uglow and Rowena Skelton-Wallace at Chatto and Windus; and Pat Utechin, the author's secretary, whose support has been no less indispensable to me this time than on numerous previous occasions. I am grateful to Lord Annan for allowing us to use as a foreword an adapted version of his discussion of Isaiah Berlin in *Our Age* (London, 1990: Weidenfeld and Nicolson; New York, 1990: Random House), and for making the adaptations. Finally I express once more my great gratitude to the benefactors who have financed the Fellowship that has enabled me to undertake my current work on Isaiah Berlin, and to Lord Bullock for being my advocate with them.

November 1996                                    HENRY HARDY
Wolfson College, Oxford


*Note by Roger Hausheer*

To the above I should like to add several expressions of gratitude of my own: to Lord Bullock and Lord Annan for their help and encouragement; to the Master and Fellows of St Catherine's College, Oxford, for electing me to a Visiting Fellowship, in 1994–5; and to the

Leverhulme Trust for a generous Research Award for the same period – all of which enabled me, in the most congenial surroundings, to make a start on an intellectual life of Isaiah Berlin, of which the piece that follows is a small offshoot. And not least to my co-editor for coming to my aid by radically shortening (and on occasion revising) an introduction which, as first drafted, turned out to be too long and too elaborate for the purpose in hand.

ROGER HAUSHEER

# INTRODUCTION

*Roger Hausheer*

IT IS PARADOXICAL that at a time of unprecedented moral and political confusion there should be an upsurge of interest in popular expositions of science, whose subject-matter is fully comprehensible only to a handful of experts. Yet the very realm that matters to us most, and is accessible to all of us in virtue of our humanity, namely that of the human studies, seems not to have captured the popular imagination to the same degree. This is especially regrettable since, largely unnoticed by the general public, an advance in the understanding of human beings has taken place over the past two hundred years whose relevance to present concerns can scarcely be exaggerated. Isaiah Berlin's work forms an indispensable part of this advance, of which it can indeed be seen as a kind of summation.

Berlin has spent most of his long life reflecting on certain central human problems, especially questions of human identity and value, association and organisation, political theory and practice. To no small degree his interest in these issues has arisen from his life. Born in Riga, a Jewish subject of the Russian Tsar, he was a child in Petrograd during the early stages of the Russian Revolution, where he witnessed an episode which filled him with a lasting hatred of violence. Coming to England at the age of eleven, he rapidly adapted to his new environment, and has had a dazzling academic career at Oxford. His origins left him with three major allegiances – Jewish, Russian and English. It was perhaps this early collision in the formation of a supremely intelligent and sensitive man that first stimulated his interest in the cluster of issues that have always preoccupied him. His childhood was disrupted by one of the great political storms of the century, and his early middle life dominated by the Second World War and his work as a political analyst in Washington and Moscow. Also, though he rarely speaks of this, no account of his life can leave out the persecution and loss of many close relatives in the Nazi holocaust and under the Soviet tyranny.

There is therefore an authentic quality in what he says about the great issues of our time which is often lacking in the writings of academics. Again, unlike many intellectuals, Berlin has had close links with public life. His network of connections has made him a privileged observer of, at times an active participant in, some of the major events of the day. His famous wartime dispatches from Washington and his intimate association with Chaim Weizmann during the period leading up to the foundation of the State of Israel are just two of the better-known instances.

There is, besides, his special intellectual temperament, his remarkable ability to enter into and recreate a wide diversity of outlooks. It is his capacity for self-transposition into minds of radically differing temperaments in other times and places that makes him such a perceptive explorer of the modern condition; and his voyage of discovery may come to be seen as an analogue in the mental sphere of those pioneering explorations of the external world which have formed the major triumphs of Western humanity since the Renaissance. He is one of the earliest, most prescient participants in a peculiarly modern predicament in which ever more people are finding they share, namely the clash of cultures and values which permeates our world. In this area there is no contemporary thinker who has more to say to us.

Yet though, as Noel Annan's foreword makes clear, Berlin is justly renowned, his reputation is still one-sided – partly because it has fallen victim to itself: his brilliance as a lecturer and talker and his great gift for friendship sometimes distract attention from his intellectual achievement. To meet him is to know at once why he is so celebrated. But it is a large step from here to immersion in the entire corpus of his writings. Moreover, the sheer scale of his activity in many prima facie unrelated fields has meant that he will be admired by different readers for apparently disconnected parts of his *oeuvre*, with scarcely any realisation that these are all fragments of a total picture.

Again, real obstacles stand in the path of a full reception of his views in all their often subversive originality. To begin with, the influence of scientific patterns of thought on our general outlook has become extremely pervasive; and the overwhelming majority is today uncritically in thrall to more or less crude forms of scientism. This general temper constitutes a major barrier to an understanding of Berlin's achievement, though no thinker has battled more doggedly against it. Furthermore, since a large part of Berlin's attention has been devoted to examining the deepest of structures, the categories which form the ultimate moulds of our experience, his readers face the sheer difficulty of seeing what is so close to them – part of themselves and their perceptual equipment – that it cannot be 'seen' at all, only sensed, gestured at.

There is also the danger of a kind of emotional rejection of some of Berlin's claims. Some of our dearest ideals and beliefs, part of the bedrock of our conception of ourselves, are revealed as less solid and timeless than we had thought, which can be deeply unsettling. In addition, the doctrine of objective pluralism, the core of Berlin's contribution, subverts major rationalist tenets that have held sway for at least two thousand years, and which underlie the political doctrines not just of the great oppressive system-builders but also of even the mildest modern liberals. An important preliminary to understanding Berlin's achievement is to clear away these misapprehensions, dispelling irrational resistance, and tying together the strands of his contribution to our understanding of ourselves as free, creative, self-critical beings. From this standpoint all his essays seem like parts of a single design which is slowly uncovered.

Though in one sense Berlin is a philosopher, concerned to analyse our basic concepts and categories, he is also extremely curious about the huge diversity of human life. His interest in history, literature and the arts, in politics and social life – in every expression of human existence and behaviour – has been wide-ranging. His desire for knowledge for its own sake was a prime motive for his wartime decision to abandon pure philosophy: he wished to know more at the end of his life than at the beginning. And it was not by chance that the cumulative discipline he turned to was the history of ideas. Already while writing on Marx in the 1930s he had encountered the scientific, sociological approach of the French Enlightenment. As an empiricist and believer in rational methods, he was bound to be sympathetic to their desire to sweep away theology and metaphysics, superstition, tradition and blind authority. Why should there not be a science of man on a par with the Newtonian system in physics? Condorcet had spoken of the day when there would be a naturalistic sociology which would study humans as the life sciences study bees and beavers. It was this programme that provided the central intellectual inspiration of the

French Revolution. Yet although the Revolution was a cleansing storm, it did anything but achieve its positive goal of a lasting rational social order. And by the time Berlin was writing his book on Marx, he knew that the most recent heir of the scientistic Enlightenment tradition, the Bolshevik Revolution, had spawned an oppressive dictatorship that overshadowed even the excesses of the French Revolutionary era. Something in the fundamental premisses of this entire approach to the study of society was amiss.

In the course of such reflections Berlin was bound to encounter the whole cohort of thinkers who, from the beginning, had rebelled against this entire outlook. It was to the enemies of the Enlightenment that Berlin turned to gain insight into the foundering of a general tendency with whose overall ambitions he was in total sympathy, but some of whose unexamined assumptions he had begun seriously to doubt.

Among these assumptions is that everything should be studied with objective detachment as mere material which can be exhaustively described, classified or brought under causal laws. For scientific purposes, nothing has an independent life of its own outside the system of laws that govern its behaviour or beyond the classificatory schema into which it falls. The unaccountable, the unpredictable, the undescribable are excluded by a method which is by its very nature deterministic. In the case of physics, for example, which for the Enlightenment was the paradigm of science, things have no purposes – 'final causes' – no inner lives or ideals; there are only causal regularities. No doubt Aristotle had been guilty of anthropomorphism when he attributed final causes to everything, including the universe itself; but the tendency of Enlightenment thinkers was to eliminate purposes altogether. This seemed unduly austere, especially when they came to study man and his works.

More generally, the new scientific world-picture rested upon three cardinal presuppositions common to most systematic Western thought from the time of Plato. These are that the cosmos constitutes a single harmonious whole, whose structure exists independently of any observer; that we can discover what this structure is, and find answers to all our questions, of theory and practice; and that we will then possess a seamless, coherent body of knowledge, in which no proposition can contradict another.

It is against these monolithic dogmas that so much of Berlin's work is directed. At times he attacks them directly, at other times he exposes their shortcomings by examining the ideas of some of their most formidable opponents. He separates the human realm, where freedom, choice and self-conscious purposive action are central, from the world of impersonal forces. His first step is to defend a non-deterministic form of human freedom. ' "From Hope and Fear Set Free" ' represents in this respect a blow struck against one of the central orthodoxies running through the history of Western philosophy.

The question of free will and determinism has preoccupied Berlin all his life. In this essay he takes issue with the ancient doctrine that any increase in knowledge entails an increase in liberty. In its strongest form this view virtually identifies rationality and freedom. The doctrine of classical self-determinism, that true liberty is rational self-direction, Berlin rejects. I cannot be considered free if nothing, including myself and my own nature, can conceivably be other than it is. In that case the notions of freedom and responsibility become otiose.

The next step is taken at the level of collective human life when, in 'Historical Inevitability', Berlin attacks deterministic theories which see history as obeying unalterable laws. Such views are inspired partly by the success of the natural sciences, partly by the deep-rooted belief in teleology according to which all things, like human beings, pursue purposes; and not least by our perennial desire to abdicate responsibility. Berlin exposes all these positions as dogmatic and unempirical. But he also points to a more general argument against determinism which takes us to the very core of his vision of man.

Few modern thinkers have been as aware as Berlin of the central categories that constitute our notion of human beings. We have known since Kant that there is a framework of categories by which our conception of the external world is bounded. We see, think and act in terms of these, and while we can be made aware of them, they cannot themselves be objects of a science. The intensely difficult enquiry that reveals such categories can be extended in two directions. It can be pressed deeper into the realm of subjectivity, revealing its basic structures; and it can explore the historical emergence of some of the deepest presuppositions about what we are as human beings. While Berlin's contribution has lain largely in the latter sphere, what he says about the former is nevertheless of great interest. He is intensely aware of a primordial 'sense of reality' prior to all further thought and rational analysis, including predictive science. The pages where he describes this, particularly in 'Historical Inevitability' and 'The Hedgehog and the Fox', shine with a luminosity rare in modern philosophy. This primitive sense is the root of our conviction that we are free beings in some absolutely non-deterministic sense. So basic is this conviction that our entire moral vocabulary rests upon it: notions such as responsibility, praise, remorse and desert stand or fall with it. We cannot think it away without thinking away so much of our fundamental sense of our humanity that the attempt proves impossible. To seek to explain this unanalysable 'categorial' awareness in scientific terms is like trying to make the base of the mountain balance on its summit: it lies several levels below and beyond the reach of causal concepts.

There are, then, compelling reasons why humans cannot be studied just as natural objects exhaustively explainable by natural science. In 'The Concept of Scientific History' in particular, Berlin shows how history differs from science, and explains why a science of history is conceptually impossible. This essay, together with 'Does Political Theory Still Exist?', suggests a programme for the type of history of ideas that Berlin advocates. Human beings interpret themselves in terms of very general models. Some of these are as old as humanity itself, and so virtually universal; others change, sometimes dramatically, through history. The Western tradition in political thought has seen a succession of such models. As they become antiquated, do too little justice to the altering patterns of experience, they are replaced by others. No model can encompass the whole of experience once and for all: each is exclusive and at best casts light on a portion of human life. But unlike superseded scientific theories, these models retain a permanent value, for each opens its own special doors of self-understanding; and it should be a central concern of historians of ideas in each generation to ask questions of these models and to evaluate their relevance to the unique problems of their own day. Berlin has spent his life engaged in this activity, with some remarkable results.

Virtually all Berlin's work in the history of ideas revolves around what he sees as the greatest revolution in our basic outlook since the Renaissance: the rebellion against monism. The writer whose work, for Berlin, contains the earliest premonitions of this shift is

Machiavelli. He, Berlin tells us, was probably the first to juxtapose starkly two mutually exclusive systems of morality: Christian ethics, which aim at the perfection of the individual life; and those of Republican Rome, which aim at the power and the glory of the body politic. No criteria exist for choosing between these two equally valid systems. It is this, and not Machiavelli's 'Machiavellianism', that has exercised us ever since. It marks the first irreparable fracture in the belief in a single universal structure of values.

Further cracks were opened up by the strange, isolated genius Giambattista Vico. On Berlin's interpretation, Vico was the first to state explicitly that humans do not possess an unalterable essence; that they understand their own works and the world of history which they themselves make in a way in which they cannot understand the world of external nature; that there is a distinction between the knowledge we acquire as agents, from inside, and that which we acquire by observation, from outside; that a culture has a pervasive pattern by which all its products are marked; that all human institutions and creations are forms of self-expression; that permanent standards in art or life are not available and that everything human should be judged in terms of the canons of its own time and place; and that a new variety of knowledge must be added to the two traditional types (deductive and empirical) – a form of knowledge whereby we enter into the mental universe of other ages and peoples by recreative imagination.

The implications for Berlin's own conception of cultural history are apparent: the works of Vico gave birth to the cardinal distinction between the sciences and the humanities. The fatal consequence for monism is that if an unbridgeable gap exists between these two provinces, then a breach has been blown in the dogma that all knowledge must form a seamless whole.

It is in the German world that Berlin sees the revolt against the central Enlightenment dogmas as really taking hold. The *Sturm und Drang* movement railed against all forms of political organisation; and in every sphere of life rejected rules as such. It was the great counter-rationalist J. G. Hamann who first did this consciously. He was against all abstraction. Scientific generalisations had at best an instrumental value: they could not yield unassailable knowledge. True knowledge is given to us only by the senses, and by spontaneous imagination and insight. Everything worth knowing is known by direct perception. Hamann's theory of language, according to which it does not map a pre-existent timeless reality but creates its own world, with the implication that there are as many worlds as languages, has a very modern ring; and had an immense impact on his disciple J. G. Herder.

For Berlin, Herder is of central importance. By uncovering some of the principal categories that have transformed the modern world he made a permanent contribution to human self-understanding. Three novel ideas originate with him: populism, the belief that men can realise themselves fully only as members of an identifiable culture with roots in language, tradition, history; expressionism, the notion that men's works 'are above all voices speaking', forms of communication conveying a total vision of life; and pluralism, the recognition of an indefinite variety of cultures and systems of values, all equally ultimate, and incommensurable with one another, so that the belief in a universally valid path to human fulfilment is rendered incoherent.

After this nothing was the same. From the early 1800s, particularly in the German lands, a new, powerful image bound its spell on the European imagination. Berlin throws light on this in both 'The Counter-Enlightenment' and 'The Apotheosis of the Romantic Will'. Successive German writers went to increasing lengths in their rejection of the notion of objectivity as such, leaving Vico and Herder far behind – not only in the realm of ethics and aesthetics, but also with regard to the very existence of the objective world. A revolutionary shift of categories occurs, whereby the will usurps the function of the intellect, and free creation replaces scientific discovery. Though this began in the artistic sphere, and in private relations between people, it soon overflowed into politics and social life, with catastrophic results.

Here the central figure, for Berlin, is J. G. Fichte, whose philosophy of the absolute ego that creates everything ushered in an epoch. The heroic individual imposing his will on nature or society becomes the dominant model. The notion of the creative, assertive self generating its own values and goals comes to inform many, very diverse, artistic and political movements. This is the birthplace of pragmatism, existentialism, subjectivism, relativism. Knowledge is demoted to the status of handmaid to our practical purposes, and the world itself is but the image cast by our life-projects. Heroism and martyrdom, integrity and authenticity are the values around which lives are henceforth organised. Ends are created, not discovered. The truth or falsehood of an ideal is no longer thought important, or even to be a question at all.

The implications for the idea of nationalism are very great. As a coherent doctrine nationalism first emerges in the pages of Herder, whose arch-enemy was French universalist materialism. Berlin presents Herder's thought as both a rejection of universal rational rules and a German reaction to the condescending attitude of the dominant French. This natural response of wounded pride on the part of a backward people towards a more advanced one is an early case of an attitude which was to become increasingly prevalent in the nineteenth century, and has become a world-wide syndrome today. For Herder the sense of nationhood is benign: but when the free creative self of the German romantics takes on collective forms, as so easily happens, and becomes identified with a nation, or race, or culture, or some other suprapersonal entity, then fights to the death occur. Each separate entity pursues its own independent goals, which it seeks to realise and impose against all comers. Without universal criteria of adjudication, the war of all against all ensues. This is aggressive nationalism with a vengeance, and from here to Fascism and National Socialism is a short step.

No one has grasped this great mutation of ideas more fully than Berlin; and no one has entered into the minds and hearts of some of its major figures with greater empathy. When he writes about Joseph de Maistre, one of the great harbingers of Fascism, he sounds at some moments almost like an apologist. And so evident is his admiration for the obscurantist arch-reactionary Hamann that some might suppose that Berlin himself belongs to the same camp. Nevertheless, he has often repeated that he is a staunch supporter of Enlightenment. What then is his own position?

There are five main ways in which he believes that the underlying assumptions of Western rationalism must be radically modified or abandoned. In the first place, anti-rationalist thinkers have undermined the rationalist faith in a single system of timeless norms. But where the full-blown romantics tended to be subjectivists and relativists, and thereby undermined monism comprehensively, Vico and Herder, each in his own way, subscribed to a form of value pluralism which allowed for the flowering of a vast variety of value systems within a shared human horizon. These systems may conflict with and exclude one another; yet so long as a system is such that we can accept, perhaps only after a great effort of imagination, that it was right for those people in those circumstances – and provided it does not offend against our core sense of what it is to be human – then it must be admitted into the great family of possible moral universes. This is the manifestation at a cultural level of what Berlin has identified as 'objective pluralism', to which, albeit in a sophisticated and evolved form, he himself subscribes.

Secondly, any faith in a single static pattern embracing the whole of mankind is blown to pieces. Pluralism entails that Utopia is not so much unrealisable in practical terms as inconceivable, given the nature of human values. All enterprises based on the search for a perfect society are given the lie by this devastating claim.

Thirdly, in 'Two Concepts of Liberty', which has set the framework for serious discussion of liberty ever since, Berlin used these insights to develop a doctrine of liberty which is both profound and original. In addition to all the standard liberal arguments for individual liberty, he urges that there is one supreme consideration which confers a unique status on 'negative' liberty, the freedom to act without outside interference. In a world where values collide, rational solutions to all political questions are not available. Hence the rule of experts and specialists is in principle impossible, and tragic clashes and agonising choices, far from being a pathological anomaly, are an ineradicable part of the human condition. Each individual must in the end decide for himself. Therefore the maximum freedom from interference consonant with basic social order and justice is most likely to promote human flourishing and avoid frustration and suffering. Hence Berlin's eloquent plea for negative liberty. Hence, too, his cautionary words against the 'positive' liberty of self-mastery which, with the monist claims and collectivist implications that so easily become attached to it, can convert liberty into its opposite – an oppressive tyranny, where everyone is forced into his allotted slot. Totalitarian dictatorships of the left and of the right have made these dangers all too plain in the twentieth century.

Fourthly, in Berlin's view Herder and the romantics brought to light a permanent historical category: the notion of 'belonging' – especially to a nation. Most liberal internationalists have regarded nations and nationalism as a deformation of humanity and not as integral to it. Following Herder, Berlin, virtually alone among liberal thinkers of any stature, has paid serious attention to this phenomenon. In his view Herder, in propounding the conception of 'belonging' which he was the first to make explicit – the deep need of humans for membership of a continuous cultural and historical community rooted in its own territory – discovered a fundamental and unaltering human requirement. If Berlin is right, then the need to acquire and express one's identity through such a community is a universal need just as imperious as the need for food or for shelter: deprivation may not prove immediately fatal, but in the long run it will wreak havoc.

In a world of settled normality, communities would, for Herder, coexist in a state of happy and creative self-absorption, uninvaded by, and untroubled by invidious comparisons with, their neighbours. But this deep human need has enemies of two main types: the universalising tendencies of science and technology; and disruption of the community by invasion, alien rule or expulsion. Any of these can trigger those pathological convulsions of national self-awareness with which the modern world is too familiar. For good or evil, ancient regional and cultural (and racial and religious) identities are resurfacing on every hand.

Finally, Berlin's own approach to acquiring knowledge of human beings has its roots in the anti-rationalist rebellion. He insists on the variety of types of knowledge and of their irreducibility to a single standard, and exposes the harm done by the blind application of a model successful in one area of experience to every aspect of human existence. He makes clear that unthinking imposition upon humans of abstract schemas drawn from alien disciplines has been both the greatest stumbling-block to human self-understanding and one of the greatest sources of suffering. In true empiricist fashion he subjects the Enlightenment tradition to the most devastating test available, namely the ferocious and continuing reaction against it. Here history is the equivalent of the scientist's laboratory. There is no better method for exposing flaws in rationalistic constructions. Wherever these appear to break down before the onslaught, Berlin concedes that the Enlightenment must give ground. Moreover, he wants it to make a virtue of necessity by enriching such key notions as 'man', 'society', 'culture', 'history', 'knowledge' in the light of its defeats. The result is a net increase in our knowledge of what human beings are and can be. His project, therefore, is continuous in spirit with that of the Enlightenment, whatever radical breaks he may make with some of its more rigidly unempirical assumptions.

In particular, it is to the Counter-Enlightenment thinkers that we may trace Berlin's acute sense of those exclusively human forms of knowledge and insight which comprise the greatest and most valued part of our human lives. He has traced the earliest origins of this movement, and worked out some of its most radical conclusions and their relevance to our day. In this sense, is he not both a genealogist and a consummator of that elusive but long-awaited 'Newtonian revolution' in the human studies desiderated by Kant and the thinkers of the Enlightenment? Is it too fanciful to see him as representing the summation of a series of developments which began in the late eighteenth century, passed through the hands of a chain of subsequent thinkers, principally in the German world, and have now come to their richest and most balanced fruition? This process has set upon secure foundations the rational study of man, not just as a physical animal, viewed essentially from outside in naturalistic terms (an approach whose astounding success within its own limits Berlin has often warmly applauded), but as a free, autonomous, unpredictably creative, self-interpreting and self-transforming species, whose proper element is history, and whose nature is revealed, not timelessly once and for all, but in his most basic, all-informing, evolving – and sometimes violently transformed and clashing – concepts and categories. This makes the human studies as autonomous and rationally transparent as they can ever be made, and raises a large arena for human freedom and dignity clear of the destructive incursions of science and technology, and levelling universalist principles generally. That this advance has taken a form inconceivable by the Enlightenment thinkers themselves is just one of the many paradoxes in the history of ideas.

Unlike most political theorists Berlin is not directly engaged in normative political theory, and the attempt to see in him a coherent ideological figure with views on all the issues of his time is misleading. He is not a preacher or a prescriber, a creator or a constructor. He peddles no simple doctrines, and gave up his chair in political theory partly because he felt he had none to purvey. Rather the opposite: he is an observer, an analyst, a describer. His ambition is to know. In this respect, many of his personal views on a whole range of issues are incidental to his major preoccupations. The object of his investigations is the almost endless plurality of total views of the world, and this precludes his espousing any exclusive vision of man and his condition. This is of a piece with his remarkable capacity to deploy a cool impersonality combined with a warm responsiveness, both towards the great, stable visions of the human condition, and to idiosyncrasies of feeling and temperament on the part of individuals. That is the secret of his mental constitution: the intellectual core has the hard clarity of a diamond, while the periphery flames and sparkles with that intense engagement that makes his essays on people so irresistible. His 'Conversations with Akhmatova and Pasternak' and the pieces on Churchill and Roosevelt need no commentary, and will probably lead the reader to want to devour whole his celebrated book of 'personal impressions'.

At the same time Berlin's ideas do carry normative implications. We have seen that he rules out the notion of Utopia as such: this has consequences most movingly stated in 'The Pursuit of the Ideal', and explains the great attraction for Berlin of the nineteenth-century Russian radical Alexander Herzen. In an age stiff with narrow dogmas, Herzen stood out in his belief that the basic, perennial human problems have no solutions. We can only do our best in the situations in which we find ourselves, with no guarantee of success. Indeed, we transform ourselves through the efforts we make to solve the problems of our age and culture, and so create new kinds of humans and new problems. Future problems and needs cannot, in principle, be predicted, still less provided for in advance; in each generation political arrangements must give the fullest possible scope to free choice and creative effort, the opening up of new, unpredictable paths to fulfilment. In Berlin's view there is a form of social and political organisation which has, historically, proved able to provide both the positive social framework for the maximum flourishing of individuals in this sense, as well as the best context for trade-offs between values, and that is the New Deal of Roosevelt. Berlin has always been an enthusiastic New Dealer – a natural allegiance, surely, for an objective pluralist.

Berlin's value pluralism is one of the boldest and most hopeful doctrines to emerge in the recent history of Western thought. It poses a considerable intellectual and imaginative challenge, and this, combined with its refusal of easy answers – its demand, indeed, for a degree of renunciation – may (despite his doubts) make it peculiarly captivating to the moral idealism of the young. It is an outlook at once generous, sober and humane, in whose dry light life is seen to be something enormously worth living despite the absence of absolute guarantees. Permeated by a sense of moral pathos and personal responsibility, it has the potential to fill the vacuum created by the demise of traditional religion and of secular ideologies such as Marxism. It is a powerful promoter of tolerance, understanding and sanity, both among individuals and peoples, and, if its truth must sooner or later be borne in on all societies that have reached a certain level of maturity, we may perhaps entertain the guarded hope that it will come more and more to shape the life of civilised countries everywhere.

However this may be, Berlin has probably given us the most mature reading of human history, and of human nature and its most abiding and fundamental attributes and needs, as well as of the deep changes these undergo through time, that we possess. His thought seems to accord with the actual character of that portion of the world that matters most to us, the entire human realm of thoughts, feelings, aspirations, actions and sufferings. Recent history has afforded abundant confirmation of Berlin's central vision and the concepts and categories that permeate and support it. It will not be surprising if he comes increasingly to be regarded as one of the most significant thinkers of his time.

# THE PROPER STUDY
# OF MANKIND


For Aline

# THE PURSUIT OF THE IDEAL

I

THERE ARE, in my view, two factors that, above all others, have shaped human history in the twentieth century. One is the development of the natural sciences and technology, certainly the greatest success story of our time – to this, great and mounting attention has been paid from all quarters. The other, without doubt, consists in the great ideological storms that have altered the lives of virtually all mankind: the Russian Revolution and its aftermath – totalitarian tyrannies of both right and left and the explosions of nationalism, racism and, in places, religious bigotry which, interestingly enough, not one among the most perceptive social thinkers of the nineteenth century had ever predicted.

When our descendants, in two or three centuries' time (if mankind survives until then), come to look at our age, it is these two phenomena that will, I think, be held to be the outstanding characteristics of our century – the most demanding of explanation and analysis. But it is as well to realise that these great movements began with ideas in people's heads: ideas about what relations between men have been, are, might be and should be; and to realise how they came to be transformed in the name of a vision of some supreme goal in the minds of the leaders, above all of the prophets with armies at their backs. Such ideas are the substance of ethics. Ethical thought consists of the systematic examination of the relations of human beings to each other, the conceptions, interests and ideals from which human ways of treating one another spring, and the systems of value on which such ends of life are based. These beliefs about how life should be lived, what men and women should be and do, are objects of moral enquiry; and when applied to groups and nations, and, indeed, mankind as a whole, are called political philosophy, which is but ethics applied to society.

If we are to hope to understand the often violent world in which we live (and unless we try to understand it, we cannot expect to be able to act rationally in it and on it), we cannot confine our attention to the great impersonal forces, natural and man-made, which act upon us. The goals and motives that guide human action must be looked at in the light of all that we know and understand; their roots and growth, their essence, and above all their validity, must be critically examined with every intellectual resource that we have. This urgent need, apart from the intrinsic value of the discovery of truth about human relationships, makes ethics a field of primary importance. Only barbarians are not curious about where they come from, how they came to be where they are, where they appear to be going, whether they wish to go there, and if so, why, and if not, why not.

The study of the variety of ideas about the views of life that embody such values and such ends is something that I have spent forty years of my long life in trying to make clear to myself. I should like to say something about how I came to become absorbed by this topic, and particularly about a turning-point which altered my thoughts about the heart of it. This will, to some degree, inevitably turn out to be somewhat autobiographical – for this I offer my apologies, but I do not know how else to give an account of it.

## II

When I was young I read *War and Peace* by Tolstoy, much too early. The real impact on me of this great novel came only later, together with that of other Russian writers, both novelists and social thinkers, of the mid-nineteenth century. These writers did much to shape my outlook. It seemed to me, and still does, that the purpose of these writers was not principally to give realistic accounts of the lives and relationships to one another of individuals or social groups or classes, not psychological or social analysis for its own sake – although, of course, the best of them achieved precisely this, incomparably. Their approach seemed to me essentially moral: they were concerned most deeply with what was responsible for injustice, oppression, falsity in human relations, imprisonment whether by stone walls or conformism – unprotesting submission to man-made yokes – moral blindness, egoism, cruelty, humiliation, servility, poverty, helplessness, bitter indignation, despair on the part of so many. In short, they were concerned with the nature of these experiences and their roots in the human condition: the condition of Russia in the first place, but, by implication, of all mankind. And conversely they wished to know what would bring about the opposite of this, a reign of truth, love, honesty, justice, security, personal relations based on the possibility of human dignity, decency, independence, freedom, spiritual fulfilment.

Some, like Tolstoy, found this in the outlook of simple people, unspoiled by civilisation; like Rousseau, he wished to believe that the moral universe of peasants was not unlike that of children, not distorted by the conventions and institutions of civilisation, which sprang from human vices – greed, egoism, spiritual blindness; that the world could be saved if only men saw the truth that lay at their feet; if they but looked, it was to be found in the Christian gospels, the Sermon on the Mount. Others among these Russians put their faith in scientific rationalism, or in social and political revolution founded on a true theory of historical change. Others again looked for answers in the teachings of the Orthodox theology, or in liberal Western democracy, or in a return to ancient Slav values, obscured by the reforms of Peter the Great and his successors.

What was common to all these outlooks was the belief that solutions to the central problems existed, that one could discover them, and, with sufficient selfless effort, realise them on earth. They all believed that the essence of human beings was to be able to choose how to live: societies could be transformed in the light of true ideals believed in with enough fervour and dedication. If, like Tolstoy, they sometimes thought that man was not truly free but determined by factors outside his control, they knew well enough, as he did, that if freedom was an illusion it was one without which one could not live or think. None of this was part of my school curriculum, which consisted of Greek and Latin authors, but it remained with me.

When I became a student at the University of Oxford, I began to read the works of the great philosophers, and found that the major figures, especially in the field of ethical and political thought, believed this too. Socrates thought that if certainty could be established in our knowledge of the external world by rational methods (had not Anaxagoras arrived at the truth that the sun was many times larger than the Peloponnese, however small it looked in the sky?) the same methods would surely yield equal certainty in the field of human behaviour – how to live, what to be. This could be achieved by rational argument. Plato thought that an élite of sages who arrived at such certainty should be given the power of governing others intellectually less well endowed, in obedience to patterns dictated by the correct solutions to personal and social problems. The Stoics thought that the attainment of these solutions was in the power of any man who set himself to live according to reason. Jews, Christians, Muslims (I knew too little about Buddhism) believed that the true answers had been revealed by God to his chosen prophets and saints, and accepted the interpretation of these revealed truths by qualified teachers and the traditions to which they belonged.

The rationalists of the seventeenth century thought that the answers could be found by a species of metaphysical insight, a special application of the light of reason with which all men were endowed. The empiricists of the eighteenth century, impressed by the vast new realms of knowledge opened by the natural sciences based on mathematical techniques, which had driven out so much error, superstition, dogmatic nonsense, asked themselves, like Socrates, why the same methods should not succeed in establishing similar irrefutable laws in the realm of human affairs. With the new methods discovered by natural science, order could be introduced into the social sphere as well – uniformities could be observed, hypotheses formulated and tested by experiment; laws could be based on them, and then laws in specific regions of experience could be seen to be entailed by wider laws; and these in turn to be entailed by still wider laws, and so on upwards, until a great harmonious system, connected by unbreakable logical links and capable of being formulated in precise – that is, mathematical – terms, could be established.

The rational reorganisation of society would put an end to spiritual and intellectual confusion, the reign of prejudice and superstition, blind obedience to unexamined dogmas, and the stupidities and cruelties of the oppressive regimes which such intellectual darkness bred and promoted. All that was wanted was the identification of the principal human needs and discovery of the means of satisfying them. This would create the happy, free, just, virtuous, harmonious world which Condorcet so movingly predicted in his prison cell in 1794. This view lay at the basis of all progressive thought in the nineteenth century, and was at the heart of much of the critical empiricism which I imbibed in Oxford as a student.

III

At some point I realised that what all these views had in common was a Platonic ideal: in the first place that, as in the sciences, all genuine questions must have one true answer and one only, all the rest being necessarily errors; in the second place that there must be a dependable path towards the discovery of these truths; in the third place that the true answers, when found, must necessarily be compatible with one another and form a single whole, for one truth cannot be incompatible with another – that we knew a priori. This kind of omniscience was the solution of the cosmic jigsaw puzzle. In the case of morals, we could then conceive what the perfect life must be, founded as it would be on a correct understanding of the rules that governed the universe.

True, we might never get to this condition of perfect knowledge – we may be too feeble-witted, or too weak or corrupt or sinful, to achieve this. The obstacles, both intellectual and those of external nature, may be too many. Moreover, opinions, as I say, had widely differed about the right path to pursue – some found it in Churches, some in laboratories; some believed in intuition, others in experiment, or in mystical visions, or in mathematical calculation. But even if we could not ourselves reach these true answers, or indeed, the final system that interweaves them all, the answers must exist – else the questions were not real. The answers must be known to someone: perhaps Adam in Paradise knew; perhaps we shall only reach them at the end of days; if men cannot know them, perhaps the angels know; and if not the angels, then God knows. The timeless truths must in principle be knowable.

Some nineteenth-century thinkers – Hegel, Marx – thought it was not quite so simple. There were no timeless truths. There was historical development, continuous change; human horizons altered with each new step in the evolutionary ladder; history was a drama with many acts; it was moved by conflicts of forces, sometimes called dialectical, in the realms of both ideas and reality – conflicts which took the form of wars, revolutions, violent upheavals of nations, classes, cultures, movements. Yet after inevitable setbacks, failures, relapses, returns to barbarism, Condorcet's dream would come true. The drama would have a happy ending – man's reason had achieved triumphs in the past, it could not be held back for ever. Men would no longer be victims of nature or of their own largely irrational societies: reason would triumph;

universal harmonious co-operation, true history, would at last begin.

For if this was not so, do the ideas of progress, of history, have any meaning? Is there not a movement, however tortuous, from ignorance to knowledge, from mythical thought and childish fantasies to perception of reality face to face, to knowledge of true goals, true values as well as truths of fact? Can history be a mere purposeless succession of events, caused by a mixture of material factors and the play of random selection, a tale full of sound and fury signifying nothing? This was unthinkable. The day would dawn when men and women would take their lives in their own hands and not be self-seeking beings or the playthings of blind forces that they did not understand. It was, at the very least, not impossible to conceive what such an earthly paradise could be; and if it was conceivable we could, at any rate, try to march towards it. That has been at the centre of ethical thought from the Greeks to the Christian visionaries of the Middle Ages, from the Renaissance to progressive thought in the last century; and, indeed, is believed by many to this day.

IV

At a certain stage in my reading, I naturally met with the principal works of Machiavelli. They made a deep and lasting impression upon me, and shook my earlier faith. I derived from them not the most obvious teachings – on how to acquire and retain political power, or by what force or guile rulers must act if they are to regenerate their societies, or protect themselves and their States from enemies within or without, or what the principal qualities of rulers on the one hand, and of citizens on the other, must be, if their States are to flourish – but something else. Machiavelli was not a historicist: he thought it possible to restore something like the Roman Republic or Rome of the early Principate. He believed that to do this one needed a ruling class of brave, resourceful, intelligent, gifted men who knew how to seize opportunities and use them, and citizens who were adequately protected, patriotic, proud of their State, epitomes of manly, pagan virtues. That is how Rome rose to power and conquered the world, and it is the absence of this kind of wisdom and vitality and courage in adversity, of the qualities of both lions and foxes, that in the end brought it down.

Decadent States were conquered by vigorous invaders who retained these virtues.

But Machiavelli also sets side by side with this the notion of Christian virtues – humility, acceptance of suffering, unworldliness, the hope of salvation in an afterlife – and he remarks that if, as he plainly himself favours, a State of a Roman type is to be established, these qualities will not promote it: those who live by the precepts of Christian morality are bound to be trampled on by the ruthless pursuit of power on the part of men who alone can re-create and dominate the republic which he wants to see. He does not condemn Christian virtues. He merely points out that the two moralities are incompatible, and he does not recognise an overarching criterion whereby we are enabled to decide the right life for men. The combination of *virtù* and Christian values is for him an impossibility. He simply leaves you to choose – he knows which he himself prefers.

The idea that this planted in my mind was the realisation, which came as something of a shock, that not all the supreme values pursued by mankind now and in the past were necessarily compatible with one another. It undermined my earlier assumption, based on the *philosophia perennis*, that there could be no conflict between true ends, true answers to the central problems of life.

Then I came across Giambattista Vico's *Scienza nuova*. Scarcely anyone in Oxford had then heard of Vico, but there was one philosopher, Robin Collingwood, who had translated Croce's book on Vico, and he urged me to read it. This opened my eyes to something new. Vico seemed to be concerned with the succession of human cultures – every society had, for him, its own vision of reality, of the world in which it lived, and of itself and of its relations to its own past, to nature, to what it strove for. This vision of a society is conveyed by everything that its members do and think and feel – expressed and embodied in the kinds of words, the forms of language that they use, the images, the metaphors, the forms of worship, the institutions that they generate, which embody and convey their image of reality and of their place in it; by which they live. These visions differ with each successive social whole – each has its own gifts, values, modes of creation, incommensurable with one another: each must be understood in its own terms – understood, not necessarily evaluated.

The Homeric Greeks, the master class, Vico tells us, were cruel, barbarous, mean, oppressive to the weak; but they created the *Iliad* and the *Odyssey*, something we cannot do in our more enlightened day. Their great creative masterpieces belong to them, and once the vision of the world changes, the possibility of that type of creation disappears also. We, for our part, have our sciences, our thinkers, our poets, but there is no ladder of ascent from the ancients to the moderns. If this is so, it must be absurd to say that Racine is a better poet than Sophocles, that Bach is a rudimentary Beethoven, that, let us say, the Impressionist painters are the peak which the painters of Florence aspired to but did not reach. The values of these cultures are different, and they are not necessarily compatible with one another. Voltaire, who thought that the values and ideals of the enlightened exceptions in a sea of darkness – of classical Athens, of Florence of the Renaissance, of France in the *grand siècle* and of his own time – were almost identical, was mistaken.[1] Machiavelli's Rome did not, in fact, exist. For Vico there is a plurality of civilisations (repetitive cycles of them, but that is unimportant), each with its own unique pattern. Machiavelli conveyed the idea of two incompatible outlooks; and here were societies the cultures of which were shaped by values, not means to ends but ultimate ends, ends in themselves, which differed, not in all respects – for they were all human – but in some profound, irreconcilable ways, not combinable in any final synthesis.

After this I naturally turned to the German eighteenth-century thinker Johann Gottfried Herder. Vico thought of a succession of civilisations, Herder went further and compared national cultures in many lands and periods, and held that every society had what he called its own centre of gravity, which differed from that of others. If, as he wished, we are to understand Scandinavian sagas or the poetry of the Bible, we must not apply to them the aesthetic criteria of the critics of eighteenth-century Paris. The ways in which men live, think, feel, speak to one another, the clothes they wear, the songs they sing, the gods they worship, the food they eat, the assumptions, customs, habits which are intrinsic to them – it is these that create communities, each of which has its own 'lifestyle'. Communities may resemble each other in many respects, but the

---

[1] Voltaire's conception of enlightenment as being identical in essentials wherever it is attained seems to lead to the inescapable conclusion that, in his view, Byron would have been happy at table with Confucius, and Sophocles would have felt completely at ease in quattrocento Florence, and Seneca in the *salon* of Madame du Deffand or at the court of Frederick the Great.

Greeks differ from Lutheran Germans, the Chinese differ from both; what they strive after and what they fear or worship are scarcely ever similar.

This view has been called cultural or moral relativism – this is what that great scholar, my friend Arnaldo Momigliano, whom I greatly admired, supposed both about Vico and about Herder. He was mistaken. It is not relativism. Members of one culture can, by the force of imaginative insight, understand (what Vico called *entrare*) the values, the ideals, the forms of life of another culture or society, even those remote in time or space. They may find these values unacceptable, but if they open their minds sufficiently they can grasp how one might be a full human being, with whom one could communicate, and at the same time live in the light of values widely different from one's own, but which nevertheless one can see to be values, ends of life, by the realisation of which men could be fulfilled.

'I prefer coffee, you prefer champagne. We have different tastes. There is no more to be said.' That is relativism. But Herder's view, and Vico's, is not that: it is what I should describe as pluralism – that is, the conception that there are many different ends that men may seek and still be fully rational, fully men, capable of understanding each other and sympathising and deriving light from each other, as we derive it from reading Plato or the novels of medieval Japan – worlds, outlooks, very remote from our own. Of course, if we did not have any values in common with these distant figures, each civilisation would be enclosed in its own impenetrable bubble, and we could not understand them at all; this is what Spengler's typology amounts to. Intercommunication between cultures in time and space is possible only because what makes men human is common to them, and acts as a bridge between them. But our values are ours, and theirs are theirs. We are free to criticise the values of other cultures, to condemn them, but we cannot pretend not to understand them at all, or to regard them simply as subjective, the products of creatures in different circumstances with different tastes from our own, which do not speak to us at all.

There is a world of objective values. By this I mean those ends that men pursue for their own sakes, to which other things are means. I am not blind to what the Greeks valued – their values may not be mine, but I can grasp what it would be like to live by their light, I can admire and respect them, and even imagine myself as pursuing them, although I do not – and do not wish to, and perhaps could not if I wished. Forms of life differ. Ends, moral principles, are many. But not infinitely many: they must be within the human horizon. If they are not, then they are outside the human sphere. If I find men who worship trees, not because they are symbols of fertility or because they are divine, with a mysterious life and powers of their own, or because this grove is sacred to Athena – but only because they are made of wood; and if when I ask them why they worship wood they say 'Because it is wood' and give no other answer; then I do not know what they mean. If they are human, they are not beings with whom I can communicate – there is a real barrier. They are not human for me. I cannot even call their values subjective if I cannot conceive what it would be like to pursue such a life.

What is clear is that values can clash – that is why civilisations are incompatible. They can be incompatible between cultures, or groups in the same culture, or between you and me. You believe in always telling the truth, no matter what: I do not, because I believe that it can sometimes be too painful and too destructive. We can discuss each other's point of view, we can try to reach common ground, but in the end what you pursue may not be reconcilable with the ends to which I find that I have dedicated my life. Values may easily clash within the breast of a single individual; and it does not follow that, if they do, some must be true and others false. Justice, rigorous justice, is for some people an absolute value, but it is not compatible with what may be no less ultimate values for them – mercy, compassion – as arises in concrete cases.

Both liberty and equality are among the primary goals pursued by human beings through many centuries; but total liberty for wolves is death to the lambs, total liberty of the powerful, the gifted, is not compatible with the rights to a decent existence of the weak and the less gifted. An artist, in order to create a masterpiece, may lead a life which plunges his family into misery and squalor to which he is indifferent. We may condemn him and declare that the masterpiece should be sacrificed to human needs, or we may take his side – but both attitudes embody values which for some men or women are ultimate, and which are intelligible to us all if we have any sympathy or imagination or understanding of human beings. Equality may demand the restraint of the liberty of those who wish to dominate; liberty – without some modicum of which there is no choice and therefore no possibility of remaining human as we understand the word – may have to be curtailed in order to make room for social welfare, to feed the hungry, to clothe the naked, to shelter the homeless, to leave room for the liberty of others, to allow justice or fairness to be exercised.

Antigone is faced with a dilemma to which Sophocles implied one solution, Sartre offers the opposite, while Hegel proposes 'sublimation' on to some higher level – poor comfort to those who are agonised by dilemmas of this kind. Spontaneity, a marvellous human quality, is not compatible with capacity for organised planning, for the nice calculation of what and how much and where – on which the welfare of society may largely depend. We are all aware of the agonising alternatives in the recent past. Should a man resist a monstrous tyranny at all costs, at the expense of the lives of his parents or his children? Should children be tortured to extract information about dangerous traitors or criminals?

These collisions of values are of the essence of what they are and what we are. If we are told that these contradictions will be solved in some perfect world in which all good things can be harmonised in principle, then we must answer, to those who say this, that the meanings they attach to the names which for us denote the conflicting values are not ours. We must say that the world in which what we see as incompatible values are not in conflict is a world altogether beyond our ken; that principles which are harmonised in this other world are not the principles with which, in our daily lives, we are acquainted; if they are transformed, it is into conceptions not known to us on earth. But it is on earth that we live, and it is here that we must believe and act.

The notion of the perfect whole, the ultimate solution, in which all good things coexist, seems to me to be not merely unattainable – that is a truism – but conceptually incoherent; I do not know what is meant by a harmony of this kind. Some among the Great Goods cannot live together. That is a conceptual truth. We are doomed to choose, and every choice may entail an irreparable loss. Happy are those who live under a discipline which they accept without question, who freely obey the orders of leaders, spiritual or temporal, whose word is fully accepted as unbreakable law; or those who have, by their own methods, arrived at clear and unshakeable convictions about what to do and what to be that brook no possible doubt. I can only say that those who rest on such comfortable beds of dogma are victims of forms of self-induced myopia, blinkers that may make for contentment, but not for understanding of what it is to be human.

V

So much for the theoretical objection, a fatal one, it seems to me, to the notion of the perfect State as the proper goal of our endeavours. But there is in addition a more practical socio-psychological obstacle to this, an obstacle that may be put to those whose simple faith, by which humanity has been nourished for so long, is resistant to philosophical arguments of any kind. It is true that some problems can be solved, some ills cured, in both the individual and social life. We can save men from hunger or misery or injustice, we can rescue men from slavery or imprisonment, and do good – all men have a basic sense of good and evil, no matter what cultures they belong to; but any study of society shows that every solution creates a new situation which breeds its own new needs and problems, new demands. The children have obtained what their parents and grandparents longed for – greater freedom, greater material welfare, a juster society; but the old ills are forgotten, and the children face new problems, brought about by the very solutions of the old ones, and these, even if they can in turn be solved, generate new situations, and with them new requirements – and so on, for ever – and unpredictably.

We cannot legislate for the unknown consequences of consequences of consequences. Marxists tell us that once the fight is won and true history has begun, the new problems that may arise will generate their own solutions, which can be peacefully realised by the united powers of harmonious, classless society. This seems to me a piece of metaphysical optimism for which there is no evidence in historical experience. In a society in which the same goals are universally accepted, problems can be only of means, all soluble by technological methods. That is a society in which the inner life of man, the moral and spiritual and aesthetic imagination, no longer speaks at all. Is it for this that men and women should be destroyed or societies enslaved? Utopias have their value – nothing so wonderfully expands the imaginative horizons of human potentialities – but as guides to conduct they can prove literally fatal. Heraclitus was right, things cannot stand still.

So I conclude that the very notion of a final solution is not only impracticable but, if I am right, and some values cannot but clash, incoherent also. The possibility of a final solution – even if we forget the terrible sense that these words acquired in Hitler's day – turns out to be an illusion; and a very dangerous one. For if one really believes that such a solution is possible, then surely no cost would be too high to obtain it: to make mankind just and happy and creative and harmonious for ever – what could be too high a price to pay for that? To make such an omelette, there is surely no limit to the number of eggs that should be broken – that was the faith of Lenin, of Trotsky, of Mao, for all I know of Pol Pot. Since I know the only true path to the ultimate solution of the problem of society, I know which way to drive the human caravan; and since you are ignorant of what I know, you cannot be allowed to have liberty of choice even within the narrowest limits, if the goal is to be reached. You declare that a given policy will make you happier, or freer, or give you room to breathe; but I know that you are mistaken, I know what you need, what all men need; and if there is resistance based on ignorance or malevolence, then it must be broken and hundreds of thousands may have to perish to make millions happy for all time. What choice have we, who have the knowledge, but to be willing to sacrifice them all?

Some armed prophets seek to save mankind, and some only their own race because of its superior attributes, but whichever the motive, the millions slaughtered in wars or revolutions – gas chambers, gulag, genocide, all the monstrosities for which our century will be remembered – are the price men must pay for the felicity of future generations. If your desire to save mankind is serious, you must harden your heart, and not reckon the cost.

The answer to this was given more than a century ago by the Russian radical Alexander Herzen. In his essay *From the Other Shore*, which is in effect an obituary notice of the revolutions of 1848, he said that a new form of human sacrifice had arisen in his time – of living human beings on the altars of abstractions – nation, Church, party, class, progress, the forces of history – these have all been invoked in his day and in ours: if these demand the slaughter of living human beings, they must be satisfied. These are his words:

> If progress is the goal, for whom are we working? Who is this Moloch who, as the toilers approach him, instead of rewarding them, draws back; and as a consolation to the exhausted and doomed multitudes, shouting 'morituri te salutant', can only give the . . . mocking answer that after their death all will be beautiful on earth. Do you truly wish to condemn the human beings alive today to the sad role . . . of wretched galley-slaves who, up to their knees in mud, drag a barge . . . with . . . 'progress in the future' upon its flag? . . . a goal which is infinitely remote is no goal, only . . . a deception; a goal must be

closer – at the very least the labourer's wage, or pleasure in work performed.[1]

The one thing that we may be sure of is the reality of the sacrifice, the dying and the dead. But the ideal for the sake of which they die remains unrealised. The eggs are broken, and the habit of breaking them grows, but the omelette remains invisible. Sacrifices for short-term goals, coercion, if men's plight is desperate enough and truly requires such measures, may be justified. But holocausts for the sake of distant goals, that is a cruel mockery of all that men hold dear, now and at all times.

## VI

If the old perennial belief in the possibility of realising ultimate harmony is a fallacy, and the position of the thinkers I have appealed to – Machiavelli, Vico, Herder, Herzen – are valid, then, if we allow that Great Goods can collide, that some of them cannot live together, even though others can – in short, that one cannot have everything, in principle as well as in practice – and if human creativity may depend upon a variety of mutually exclusive choices: then, as Chernyshevsky and Lenin once asked, 'What is to be done?' How do we choose between possibilities? What and how much must we sacrifice to what? There is, it seems to me, no clear reply. But the collisions, even if they cannot be avoided, can be softened. Claims can be balanced, compromises can be reached: in concrete situations not every claim is of equal force – so much liberty and so much equality; so much for sharp moral condemnation, and so much for understanding a given human situation; so much for the full force of the law, and so much for the prerogative of mercy; for feeding the hungry, clothing the naked, healing the sick, sheltering the homeless. Priorities, never final and absolute, must be established.

The first public obligation is to avoid extremes of suffering. Revolutions, wars, assassinations, extreme measures may in desperate situations be required. But history teaches us that their consequences are seldom what is anticipated; there is no guarantee, not even, at times, a high enough probability, that such acts will

[1] A. I. Gertsen, *Sobranie sochinenii v tridtsati tomakh* (Moscow, 1954–66), vol. 6, p. 34.

lead to improvement. We may take the risk of drastic action, in personal life or in public policy, but we must always be aware, never forget, that we may be mistaken, that certainty about the effect of such measures invariably leads to avoidable suffering of the innocent. So we must engage in what are called trade-offs – rules, values, principles must yield to each other in varying degrees in specific situations. Utilitarian solutions are sometimes wrong, but, I suspect, more often beneficent. The best that can be done, as a general rule, is to maintain a precarious equilibrium that will prevent the occurrence of desperate situations, of intolerable choices – that is the first requirement for a decent society; one that we can always strive for, in the light of the limited range of our knowledge, and even of our imperfect understanding of individuals and societies. A certain humility in these matters is very necessary.

This may seem a very flat answer, not the kind of thing that the idealistic young would wish, if need be, to fight and suffer for, in the cause of a new and nobler society. And, of course, we must not dramatise the incompatibility of values – there is a great deal of broad agreement among people in different societies over long stretches of time about what is right and wrong, good and evil. Of course traditions, outlooks, attitudes may legitimately differ; general principles may cut across too much human need. The concrete situation is almost everything. There is no escape: we must decide as we decide; moral risk cannot, at times, be avoided. All we can ask for is that none of the relevant factors be ignored, that the purposes we seek to realise should be seen as elements in a total form of life, which can be enhanced or damaged by decisions.

But, in the end, it is not a matter of purely subjective judgement: it is dictated by the forms of life of the society to which one belongs, a society among other societies, with values held in common, whether or not they are in conflict, by the majority of mankind throughout recorded history. There are, if not universal values, at any rate a minimum without which societies could scarcely survive. Few today would wish to defend slavery or ritual murder or Nazi gas chambers or the torture of human beings for the sake of pleasure or profit or even political good – or the duty of children to denounce their parents, which the French and Russian revolutions demanded, or mindless killing. There is no justification for compromise on this. But on the other hand, the search for perfection does seem to me a recipe for bloodshed, no better even if it is demanded by the sincerest of idealists, the purest of heart. No more rigorous moralist than Immanuel Kant has ever lived, but even he said, in a moment of illumination, 'Out of the crooked timber of humanity no straight thing was ever made.'[1] To force people into the neat uniforms demanded by dogmatically believed-in schemes is almost always the road to inhumanity. We can only do what we can: but that we must do, against difficulties.

Of course social or political collisions will take place; the mere conflict of positive values alone makes this unavoidable. Yet they can, I believe, be minimised by promoting and preserving an uneasy equilibrium, which is constantly threatened and in constant need of repair – that alone, I repeat, is the precondition for decent societies and morally acceptable behaviour, otherwise we are bound to lose our way. A little dull as a solution, you will say? Not the stuff of which calls to heroic action by inspired leaders are made? Yet if there is some truth in this view, perhaps that is sufficient. An eminent American philosopher of our day once said, 'There is no a priori reason for supposing that the truth, when it is discovered, will necessarily prove interesting.' It may be enough if it is truth, or even an approximation to it; consequently I do not feel apologetic for advancing this. Truth, said Tolstoy, 'has been, is and will be beautiful'.[2] I do not know if this is so in the realm of ethics, but it seems to me near enough to what most of us wish to believe not to be too lightly set aside.

[1] *Kant's gesammelte Schriften* (Berlin, 1900–  ), vol. 8, p. 23, line 22.
[2] *Sevastopol in May*, chapter 16.

# THE CONCEPT OF SCIENTIFIC HISTORY

HISTORY, according to Aristotle, is an account of what individual human beings have done and suffered. In a still wider sense, history is what historians do. Is history then a natural science, as, let us say, physics or biology or psychology are sciences? And if not, should it seek to be one? And if it fails to be one, what prevents it? Is this due to human error or impotence, or to the nature of the subject, or does the very problem rest on a confusion between the concept of history and that of natural science? These have been questions that have occupied the minds of both philosophers and philosophically minded historians at least since the beginning of the nineteenth century, when men became self-conscious about the purpose and logic of their intellectual activities. But two centuries before that Descartes had already denied to history any claim to be a serious study. Those who accepted the validity of the Cartesian criterion of what constitutes rational method could (and did) ask how they could find the clear and simple elements of which historical judgements were composed, and into which they could be analysed: where were the definitions, the logical transformation rules, the rules of inference, the rigorously deduced conclusions? While the accumulation of this confused amalgam of memories and travellers' tales, fables and chroniclers' stories, moral reflections and gossip might be a harmless pastime, it was beneath the dignity of serious men seeking what alone is worth seeking – the discovery of the truth in accordance with principles and rules which alone guarantee scientific validity.

Ever since this doctrine of what was and what was not a science was enunciated, those who have thought about the nature of historical studies have laboured under the stigma of the Cartesian condemnation. Some have tried to show that history could be made respectable by being assimilated to one of the natural sciences, whose overwhelming success and prestige in the seventeenth and eighteenth centuries held out the promise of rich fruit wherever their methods were applicable; others declared that history was indeed a science, but a science in some different sense, with its own methods and canons, no less exacting, perhaps, than those of the sciences of nature, but resting on foundations different from them; there were those who defiantly declared that history was indeed subjective, impressionistic, incapable of being made rigorous, a branch of literature, or an embodiment of a personal vision – or that of a class, a Church, a nation – a form of self-expression which was, indeed, its pride and justification: it laid no claim to universal and eternal objectivity and preferred to be judged as an interpretation of the past in terms of the demands of the present, or as a philosophy of life, not as a science. Still others have tried to draw distinctions between sociology, which was a true science, and history, which was an art or, perhaps, something altogether *sui generis*, neither a science nor an art, but a discipline with its own structure and purposes, misunderstood by those who tried to draw false analogies between it and other intellectual activities.

In any case, the logic of historical thought and the validity of its credentials are issues that do not preoccupy the minds of the leading logicians of our day. The reasons for this are not far to seek. Nevertheless it remains surprising that philosophers pay more attention to the logic of such natural sciences as mathematical physics, which comparatively few of them know well at first hand, and neglect that of history and the other humane studies, with which in the course of their normal education they tend to be more familiar.

Be that as it may, it is not difficult to see why there has been a strong desire to regard history as a natural science. History purports to deal with facts. The most successful method of identifying, discovering and inferring facts is that of the natural sciences. This is the only region of human experience, at any rate in modern times, in which progress has indubitably been made. It is natural to wish to apply methods successful and authoritative in one sphere to another, where there is far less agreement among specialists. The whole trend of modern empiricism has tended towards such a view. History is an account of what men have done and of what has happened to them. Man is largely, some would say wholly, a three-dimensional object in space and time, subject to natural laws: his bodily wants can be studied empirically as those of other animals. Basic human needs for, say, food or shelter or procreation, and his other biological or physiological requirements, do not seem to have altered greatly through the millennia, and the laws of the interplay of these needs with one another and with the human environment can all in principle be studied by the methods of the biological and, perhaps, psychological sciences. This applies particularly to the results of man's collective activities, unintended by the agent, which, as the Historical School has emphasised since the days of Bossuet and Vico, play a decisive part in influencing his life, and which can surely be explained in purely mechanistic terms as fields of force, or causal or functional correlations of human action and other natural processes. If only we could find a series of natural laws connecting at one end the biological and physiological states and processes of human beings with, at the other, the equally observable patterns of their conduct – their social activities in the wider sense – and so establish a coherent system of regularities, deducible from a comparatively small number of general laws (as Newton, it is held, had so triumphantly done in physics), we should have in our hands a science of human behaviour. Then we could perhaps afford to ignore, or at least treat as secondary, such intermediate phenomena as feelings, thoughts, volitions, of which men's lives seem to themselves to be largely composed, but which do not lend themselves easily to exact measurement. If these data could be regarded as by-products of other, scientifically observable and measurable, processes, then we could predict the publicly observable behaviour of men (what more can a science ask for?) without taking the vaguer and more elusive data of introspection much into account. This would constitute the natural sciences of psychology and sociology, predicted by the materialists of the French Enlightenment, particularly Condillac and Condorcet and their nineteenth-century followers – Comte, Buckle, Spencer, Taine – and many a modern behaviourist, positivist and 'physicalist' since their day.

What kind of science would history constitute? The traditional division of the sciences is into the inductive and the deductive. Unless one claimed acquaintance with a priori propositions or rules, derived not from observation but from knowledge, based on intuition or revelation, of the laws governing the behaviour of men and of their goals, or of the specific purposes of their creator – and few historians since the Middle Ages have openly professed to possess such knowledge – this science could not be wholly deductive. But is it then inductive? It is difficult or impossible to conduct large-scale experiments on human beings, and knowledge must therefore largely rest on observation. However, this disability has not prevented astronomy or geology from becoming a flourishing science, and the mechanists of the eighteenth century confidently looked forward to a time when the application of the methods of the mathematical sciences to human affairs would explode such myths as those of revealed truth, the inner light, a personal deity, an immaterial soul, freedom of the will, and so forth; and so solve all social problems by means of a scientific sociology as clear, exact and capable of predicting future behaviour as, to use Condorcet's phrase, the sciences that study the societies of bees or beavers.[1] In the nineteenth century this claim came to be regarded as too sweeping and too extravagant. It became clear that the methods and concepts of the mechanists were not adequate for dealing with growth and change; the adoption of more complex vitalistic or evolutionary categories and models served to demarcate the procedures of the biological from those of the purely physical sciences; the former seemed clearly more appropriate to the behaviour and development of human beings. In the twentieth century psychology has begun to assume the role that biology had played in the previous century, and its methods and discoveries with regard both to individuals and to groups have in their turn transformed our approach to history.

Why should history have had so long to wait to become a science? Buckle, who believed in the science of history more passionately, perhaps, than any man who ever lived, explained this very simply by the fact that historians were inferior in mental power to the mathematicians and physicists and chemists. He declared that those sciences advanced fastest which in the first instance attracted the attention of the cleverest men, and their successes naturally in their turn attracted other able heads into their service. In other words, if men as gifted as Galileo or Newton, or even Laplace or Faraday, had devoted themselves to dealing with the disordered mass of truth and falsehood that went by the name of history, they could soon have set it to rights and made a firmly

[1] *Oeuvres de Condorcet*, ed. A. Condorcet O'Connor and M. F. Arago (Paris, 1847–9), vol. 1, p. 392.

built, clear and fertile natural science of it.[1] This was a promise held out by those who were, very understandably, hypnotised by the magnificent progress of the natural sciences of their day. Intelligent and sceptical thinkers like Taine and Renan in France, not to speak of really passionate positivists like Comte, and, in some of their writings, Engels and Plekhanov, profoundly believed in this prospect. Their hopes have scarcely been fulfilled. It may be profitable to ask why this is so.

Before an answer to this question is attempted, two further sources of the belief that history can, at least in principle, be transformed into a natural science may be noted. The first is perhaps conveyed best by the metaphors that, at any rate since the nineteenth century, all educated men have tended to use. When we speak of rational as opposed to Utopian policies, we tend to say of the latter that they ignore, or are defeated by, the 'inexorable logic

[1] 'In regard to nature, events apparently the most irregular and capricious have been explained, and have been shown to be in accordance with certain fixed and universal laws. This has been done because men of ability, and, above all, men of patient, untiring thought, have studied natural events with the view of discovering their regularity: and if human events were subjected to a similar treatment, we have every right to expect similar results ... Whoever is at all acquainted with what has been done during the last two centuries, must be aware that every generation demonstrates some events to be regular and predictable, which the preceding generation had declared to be irregular and unpredictable: so that the marked tendency of advancing civilisation is to strengthen our belief in the universality of order, of method, and of law. This being the case, it follows that if any facts, or class of facts, have not yet been reduced to order, we, so far from pronouncing them to be irreducible, should rather be guided by our experience of the past, and should admit the probability that what we now call inexplicable will at some future time be explained. This expectation of discovering regularity in the midst of confusion is so familiar to scientific men, that among the most eminent of them it becomes an article of faith: and if the same expectation is not generally found among historians, it must be ascribed partly to their being of inferior ability to the investigators of nature, and partly to the greater complexity of those social phenomena with which their studies are concerned.

'... The most celebrated historians are manifestly inferior to the most successful cultivators of physical science: no one having devoted himself to history who in point of intellect is at all to be compared with Kepler, Newton, or many others ...

'[Nevertheless] I entertain little doubt that before another century has elapsed, the chain of evidence will be complete, and it will be as rare to find an historian who denies the undeviating regularity of the moral world, as it now is to find a philosopher who denies the regularity of the material world.' Henry Thomas Buckle, *History of Civilization in England* (London, 1857), vol. 1, pp. 6–7 and 31.

of the (historical) facts' or the 'wheels of history', which it is idle to try to stay. We speak of the futility of defying the 'forces of history', or the absurdity of efforts to 'put the clock back' or to 'restore the past'. We speak of the youth, the maturity, the decay of peoples or cultures, of the ebb and flow of social movements, of the rise and fall of nations. Such language serves to convey the idea of an inexorably fixed time-order – the 'river of time' on which we float, and which we must willy-nilly accept; a moving stair which we have not created, but on which we are borne, obeying, as it were, some natural law governing the order and shape of events – in this case, events consisting of, or at any rate affecting, human lives, activities and experiences. Metaphorical and misleading though such uses of words can be, they are pointers to categories and concepts in terms of which we conceive the 'stream of history', namely, as something possessing a certain objective pattern that we ignore at our peril. It is a short step from this to conclude that whatever has a pattern exhibits regularities capable of being expressed in laws; and the systematic interconnection of laws is the content of a natural science.

The second source of this belief lies deeper still. Patterns of growth, or of the march of events, can plausibly be represented as a succession of causes and effects, capable of being systematised by natural science. But sometimes we speak as if something more fundamental than empirical connections (which idealist philosophers call 'mechanical' or 'external' or 'mere brute conjunctions') give their unity to the aspects, or the successive phases, of the existence of the human race on earth. When we say, for instance, that it is absurd to blame Richelieu for not acting like Bismarck because it is obvious that Richelieu could not have acted like a man living in Germany in the nineteenth century; and that conversely Bismarck could not have done what Richelieu accomplished, because the seventeenth century had its own character, very different from the deeds, events, characteristics of the eighteenth century which it uniquely determined, and which in their turn uniquely determined those of the nineteenth; what we are then affirming is that this order is an objective order; that those who do not understand that what is possible in one age and situation may be wholly inconceivable in another fail to understand something universal and fundamental about the only way in which social life, or the human mind, or economic growth, or some other sequence, not merely does, but can, or perhaps must, develop. Similarly, when we say that the proposition that *Hamlet* was written at the court of Genghis Khan in Outer Mongolia is not merely false but absurd; that if someone acquainted with the relevant facts seriously supposes that it could have been written at that time and in that place he is not merely unusually ignorant or mistaken, but out of his mind; that *Hamlet* not merely was not, but could not have been, written there or then – that we can dismiss this hypothesis without discussion – what is it that entitles us to feel so certain? What kind of 'could not' is this 'could not'? Do we rule out propositions asserting possibilities of this kind as being false on scientific, that is, empirical-inductive grounds?

It seems to me that we call them grotesque (and not merely implausible or false) because they conflict, not just with this or that fact or generalisation which we accept, but with presuppositions which are entailed by our whole way of thinking about the world – the basic categories that govern such central concepts of our thought as man, society, history, development, growth, barbarism, maturity, civilisation and the like. These presuppositions may turn out to be false or misleading (as, for example, teleology or deism are considered to have been by positivists or atheists), but they are not refuted by experiment or empirical observation. They are destroyed or transformed by those changes in the total outlook of a man or a milieu or a culture which it is the hardest (and the most important) test of the history of ideas (and, in the end, of history as such) to be able to explain.

What is here involved is a deeply ingrained, widespread, long-lived *Weltanschauung* – the unquestioning (and not necessarily valid) assumption of one particular objective order of events or facts. Sometimes it is a vertical order – succession in time – which makes us realise that the events or institutions of, say, the fourteenth century, because they were what they were, of necessity (however we analyse this sort of necessity), and not just as a matter of fact – contingently – occurred earlier than those of the sixteenth, which were 'shaped', that is, in some sense determined (some would say caused), by them; so that anyone who tries to date the works of Shakespeare before those of Dante, or to omit the fifteenth century altogether, fitting the end of the fourteenth into the beginning of the sixteenth century without a break, can be convicted of suffering from a defect different in kind, not degree, from (and less easily remediable than) ignorance or lack of scientific method. At other times we conceive of the order as

'horizontal'; that is, it underlies the perception of the interconnec-
tions between different aspects of the same stage of culture – the
kinds of assumptions and categories that the anti-mechanistic
German philosophers of culture, Herder and his disciples (and
before them Vico), brought to light. It is this kind of awareness
(the historical sense) that is said to enable us to perceive that a
certain type of legal structure is 'intimately connected' with, or is
part of the same complex as, an economic activity, a moral outlook,
a style of writing or of dancing or of worship; it is by means of this
gift (whatever may be its nature) that we recognise various
manifestations of the human spirit as 'belonging to' this or that
culture or nation or historical period, although these manifestations may be as different from one another as the way in which
men form letters on paper from their system of land tenure.
Without this faculty we should attach no sense to such social-
historical notions as 'the typical', or 'the normal', or 'the discordant', or 'the anachronistic', and consequently we should be unable
to conceive the history of an institution as an intelligible pattern, or
to attribute a work of art to its time and civilisation and milieu, or
indeed to understand or explain how one phase of a civilisation
'generates' or 'determines' another. The sense of what remains
identical or unitary in differences and in change (of which idealist
philosophers have made altogether too much) is also a dominant
factor in giving us our sense of unalterable trends, of the 'one-
directional' flow of history. From this it is easy to pass to the far
more questionable belief that whatever is unalterable is so only
because it obeys laws, and that whatever obeys laws can always be
systematised into a science.

These are among the many factors that have made men crave for
a natural science of history. All seemed ready, particularly in the
nineteenth century, for the formulation of this new, powerful and
illuminating discipline, which would do away with the chaotic
accumulation of facts, conjectures and rules of thumb that had
been treated with such disdain by Descartes and his scientifically-
minded successors. The stage was set, but virtually nothing
materialised. No general laws were formulated – nor even moderately reliable maxims – from which historians could deduce
(together with knowledge of the initial conditions) either what
would happen next, or what had happened in the past. The great
machine which was to rescue them from the tedious labours of
adding fact to fact and of attempting to construct a coherent

account out of their hand-picked material seemed like a plan in the head of a cracked inventor. The immense labour-saving instrument which, when fed with information, would itself order it, deduce the right conclusions, and offer the proper explanations, removing the need for the uncertain, old-fashioned, hand-operated tools with which historians had fumbled their way in the unregenerate past, remained a bogus prospectus, the child of an extravagant imagination, like designs for a perpetual motion machine. Neither psychologists nor sociologists, neither the ambitious Comte nor the more modest Wundt, had been able to create the new mechanism: the 'nomothetic' sciences – the system of laws and rules under which the factual material could be ordered so as to yield new knowledge – remained stillborn.

One of the criteria of a natural science is rightly regarded as being its capacity for prediction; or, in the case of a historical study, retrodiction – filling in gaps in the past for which no direct testimony exists with the aid of extrapolation performed according to relevant rules or laws. A method of this conjectural sort is employed in archaeology or palaeontology where vast gaps in knowledge exist and there is no better – more dependable – avenue to factual truth in the absence of concrete factual evidence. In archaeology we make efforts to link our knowledge of one remote period to our knowledge of another by trying to reconstruct what must, or at least may have, occurred to account for the transition from one stage to the other through many unknown intermediate phases. But this way of filling gaps is commonly regarded as a none too reliable method of discovery of the past, and one to which no one would wish to resort if he could find the more concrete kind of evidence (however the quality and extent of such concreteness is assessed) on which we base knowledge of the historical, as opposed to prehistoric, period of human life; still less as a 'scientific' substitute for it.

What would the structure of such a science be like, supposing that one were able to formulate it? It would, presumably, consist of causal or functional correlations – a system of interrelated general propositions of the type 'Whenever or wherever $\phi$ then or there $\psi$' – variables into which precise dates and places could be fitted; and it would possess two forms, the 'pure' and the 'applied'. The 'pure' sciences of social statics or social dynamics, of which Herbert Spencer perhaps a little too optimistically proclaimed the existence, would then be related to the 'applied' science of history, somewhat as physics is to mechanics, or at least as anatomy applies to the diagnosis of specific cases by a physician. If it existed, such a science would have revolutionised the old empirical, hand-woven history by mechanising it, as astronomy abolished the rules of thumb accumulated by Babylonian star-gazers, or as Newtonian physics transformed older cosmologies. No such science exists. Before we ask why this is so, it would perhaps be profitable to consider some of the more obvious ways in which history, as it has been written until our day, differs from a natural science conceived in this fashion.

Let me begin by noting one conspicuous difference between history and the natural sciences. Whereas in a developed natural science we consider it more rational to put our confidence in general propositions or laws than in specific phenomena (indeed this is part of the definition of rationality), this rule does not seem to operate successfully in history. Let me give the simplest possible kind of example. One of the common-sense generalisations that we regard as most firmly established is that the normal inhabitants of this planet can see the sun rise every morning. Suppose a man were to say that on a given morning he had not, despite repeated attempts, seen the sun rise; and that since one negative instance is, by the rules of our ordinary logic, sufficient to kill a general proposition, he regarded his carefully carried out observation as fatal not merely to the hitherto accepted generalisation about the succession of night and day, but to the entire system of celestial mechanics, and indeed of physics, which purports to reveal the causes of this phenomenon. This startling claim would not normally be regarded as a conclusion to be unhesitatingly accepted. Our first reaction would be to try to construct an *ad hoc* hypothesis to save our system of physics, supported as it is by the most systematic accumulation of controlled observation and deductive reasoning made by men. We should suggest to the objector that perhaps he was not looking at the right portion of the sky; that clouds intervened; that he was distracted; that his eyes were closed; that he was asleep; that he was suffering from a hallucination; that he was using words in unfamiliar senses; that he was lying or joking or insane; we should advance other explanations, any one of which would be compatible with his statement, and yet preserve physical science intact. It would not be rational to jump to the immediate conclusion that if the man, in our considered judgement, had told the truth, the whole of our hard-won physics must be rejected, or even modified. No doubt, if the phenomenon repeated itself, and other men failed to perceive the sun rising under normal conditions, some physical hypotheses, or indeed laws, might have to be drastically altered, or even rejected; perhaps the foundations of our physical sciences would have to be built anew. But we should only embark on this in the last resort. Yet if *per contra* a historian were to attempt to cast doubt on – or explain away – some piece of individual observation of a type not otherwise suspect, say, that Napoleon had been seen in a three-cornered hat at a given moment during the battle of Austerlitz; and if the historian did so solely because he put his faith, for whatever reason, in a theory or law according to which French generals or heads of State never wore three-cornered hats during battles, his method, one can safely assert, would not meet with universal or immediate recognition from his profession. Any procedure designed to discredit the testimony of normally reliable witnesses or documents as, let us say, lies or forgeries, or as being defective at the very point at which the report about Napoleon's hat occurred, would be liable to be regarded as itself suspect, as an attempt to alter the facts to fit a theory.

I have chosen a crude and trivial instance; it would not be difficult to think of more sophisticated examples, where a historian lays himself open to the charge of trying to press the facts into the service of a particular theory. Such historians are accused of being prisoners of their theories; they are accused of being fanatical or cranky or doctrinaire, of misrepresenting or misreading reality to fit in with their obsessions, and the like. Addiction to theory – being doctrinaire – is a term of abuse when applied to historians; it is not an insult if applied to a natural scientist. We are saying nothing derogatory if we say of a natural scientist that he is in the grip of a theory. We may complain if we think that his theory is false, or that he is ignoring relevant evidence, but we do not deplore the fact that he is trying to fit the facts into the pattern of a theory; for that is his business. It is the business of a natural scientist to be a theorist; that is, to formulate doctrines – true rather than false, but, above all, doctrines; for natural science is nothing if it is not a systematic interlacing of theories and doctrines, built up inductively, or by hypothetical-deductive methods, or whatever other method is considered best (logically reputable, rational, publicly testable, fruitful) by the most competent practitioners in the field. It seems clear that whereas in history we tend, more often than not, to attach greater credence to the existence of particular facts than to general hypotheses, however well supported, from which these facts could in theory be deduced, in a natural science the opposite seems more often to be the case: there it is (in cases of conflict) often more rational to rely upon a properly supported general theory – say that of gravitation – than on particular observations. This difference alone, whatever its root, must cast prima facie doubt upon any attempt to draw too close an analogy between the methods of history and those of natural science.

It may be objected at this point that the only logical justification for belief in particular facts must involve general propositions, and therefore always in the end rests on some form of induction. For what other way of justifying beliefs about facts have we? The first of these assertions is true, but the second is not, and their conflation leads to confusion. It needs no deep reflection to realise that all our thought is shot through with general propositions. All thinking involves classification; all classification involves general terms. My very notion of Napoleon or hats or battles involves some general beliefs about the entities which these words denote. Moreover, my reasons for trusting an eye-witness account or a document entail judgements about the reliability of different kinds of testimony, or the range within which the behaviour of individuals is or is not variable, and the like – judgements which are certainly general. But in the first place it is a far cry from the scattered generalisations implicit in the everyday use of words (or ideas) to the systematic structure of even the most rudimentary science;[1] and in the second place I am certain, for example, that I am not at this moment the Emperor of Mars dreaming a dream in which I am a university teacher on the Earth; but I should find it exceedingly hard to justify my certainty by inductive methods that avoid circularity. Most of the certainties on which our lives are founded would scarcely pass this test. The vast majority of the types of reasoning on which our beliefs rest, or by which we should seek to justify them if they were challenged, are not reducible to formal deductive or inductive schemata, or combinations of them. If I am asked what rational grounds I have for supposing that I am not on Mars, or that the Emperor Napoleon

[1] This can be put in another way by saying that the generalisations of history, like those of ordinary thought, are sometimes unconnected; so that a change in the degree of belief in any one of these does not, as in a natural science, *automatically* affect the status of all the others. This is a crucial difference.

existed and was not merely a sun myth, and if in answer to this I try to make explicit the general propositions which entail these conclusions, together with the specific evidence for them, and the evidence for the reliability of this evidence, and the evidence for that evidence in its turn, and so on, I shall not get very far. The web is too complex, the elements too many and not, to say the least, easily isolated and tested one by one; anyone can satisfy himself of this by trying to analyse and state them explicitly. The true reason for accepting the proposition that I live on Earth, and that an Emperor Napoleon I existed, is that to assert their contradictories is to destroy too much of what we take for granted about the present and the past. Any given generalisation may be capable of being tested or refined by inductive or other scientific tests; but we accept the total texture, compounded as it is out of literally countless strands – including both general and particular beliefs – without the possibility, even in principle, of any test for it in its totality. For the total texture is what we begin and end with. There is no Archimedean point outside it whence we can survey the whole of it and pronounce upon it. We can test one part in terms of another, but not the whole, as it were, at one go. When the proposition that the earth was flat was abandoned, this wrought great havoc in the assumptions of common sense; but it could not in principle destroy them all. For in that case nothing would have remained that could be called thinking or criticism.

It is the sense of the general texture of experience – the most rudimentary awareness of such patterns – that constitutes the foundation of knowledge, that is itself not open to inductive or deductive reasoning: for both these methods rest upon it. Any one proposition or set of propositions can be shaken in terms of those that remain fixed; and then these latter in their turn; but not all simultaneously. All my beliefs cannot be overthrown. Even if the ground beneath one of my feet is crumbling, my other foot must rest securely planted, at least for the time being; otherwise there is no possibility of thought or communication. It is this network of our most general assumptions, called common-sense knowledge, that historians to a greater degree than scientists are bound, at least initially, to take for granted: and they must take a good deal of it for granted, since their subject-matter can be detached from it to a far smaller degree than that of natural science.

Let us look at this from another angle. The natural sciences largely consist of logically linked laws about the behaviour of objects in the world. In certain cases these generalisations can be represented in the form of an ideal model – an imaginary entity whose characteristics are by definition what they must be if the entity in question obeys the general laws in question, and can be exhaustively described solely in terms of obeying these laws; that is, it consists of nothing but what instantiates such laws. Such models (or deductive schemata) exhibit most vividly and clearly the laws which we attempt to apply to reality; the objects of the natural world can then be described in terms of the degree of deviation that they exhibit from the ideal model. The degree to which these differences can be systematically described, the simplicity of the models and the range of their application largely determine the success or failure of a given science to perform its task. The electron, the chromosome, the state of perfect competition, the Oedipus complex, the ideal democracy are all such models; they are useful to the degree to which the actual behaviour of real entities in the world can be represented with lesser or greater precision in terms of their deviation from the frictionless behaviour of the perfect model. This is the purpose for which the model is constructed; its usefulness corresponds to the degree to which it fulfils it.

Such a model or deductive schema is not much in evidence in normal historical writing; if only because the general propositions out of which it must be constructed, and which, if they existed, would require precise formulation, turn out to be virtually impossible to specify. The general concepts that are necessarily employed by historians – notions like State or development or revolution or trend of opinion or economic decline or political power – enter into general propositions of far lesser range or dependability (or specifiability) than those that occur in even the least developed natural science worthy of its title. Such historical generalisations turn out too often to be tautological, or vague or inaccurate; 'All power tends to corrupt', 'Every revolution is followed by a reaction', 'Change in the economic structure leads to novel forms of music and painting' will yield, taken with some specified initial conditions – for example 'Cromwell had a great deal of power' or 'A revolution broke out in Russia in 1917' or 'The United States went through a period of radical industrialisation' – scarcely any reliable historical or sociological deductions. What is lacking here is an interconnected tissue of generalisations which an electronic brain could mechanically apply to a situation mechanically specifiable as relevant. What occurs in historical thinking seems much more like the operation of common sense, where we weave together various prima facie logically independent concepts and general propositions, and bring them to bear on a given situation as best we can. The capacity to do this successfully – the ability to 'weave together', 'bring to bear' various concepts – is a skill, an empirical knack (sometimes called judgement) which electronic brains cannot be given by their manufacturers.

At this point we may be told that the mysterious capacity of weighing or assessing a concrete situation, the arts of diagnosis and prognosis (the so-called faculty of judgement) is not unique to history and the other humane studies, or to thinking and decision-making in ordinary life; for in the natural sciences too the capacity for perceiving the relevance of one rather than another theory or concept to the solution of a given problem, and the 'bringing to bear' (sometimes with the most dramatic effect) upon a given body of data of notions sometimes derived from very remote fields, is nothing if not the peculiar skill of a gifted investigator, sometimes amounting to the insight of genius, which techniques or machines cannot in principle be made to replace. This is, of course, true; yet there exists one striking difference between the canons of explanation and logical justification used by the sciences and the humanities that will serve to indicate the difference between them. In a developed work of natural science – say a textbook of physics or biology (I do not refer to speculative or impressionistic discourses which are to be found in scientific treatises) – the links between the propositions are, or should be, logically obvious; the propositions follow from each other; that is to say, the conclusions are seen logically to follow from premises, either with demonstrative certainty, or else with varying degrees of probability which, in the sciences which use statistical methods, should be capable of being estimated with a fair degree of precision. Even if such symbols of inference as 'because', or 'therefore', or 'hence', were omitted, a piece of reasoning in mathematics or physics or any other developed natural science (if it were clearly set out) should be able to exhibit its inner logical structure by the sheer meaning and order of its component propositions. As for the propositions that are stated without argument, these are, or should be, such that, if challenged, their truth or probability could be demonstrated by recognised logical steps from truths established experimentally and accepted by virtually all the relevant specialists. This is very far from being the case in even the best, most convincing, most rigorously argued works of history. No student of the subject can, I think, fail to note the abundance in works of history of such phrases as 'small wonder if', 'it was therefore hardly surprising when', 'the inevitable consequences swiftly followed', 'events took their inexorable course', 'in the circumstances', 'from this it was but a short step to', and most often of all the indispensable, scarcely noticeable and deeply treacherous 'thus', 'whereupon', 'finally' and the like. If these bridges from one set of facts or statements to another were suddenly withdrawn from our textbooks, it is, I think, not too much to say that the transition from one set of statements to the other would become a great deal less smooth: the bald juxtaposition of events or facts would at times be seen to carry no great logical force in itself, and the best constructed cases of some of our best historians (and lawyers) would begin – to minds conditioned by the logical criteria of natural science – to seem less irresistible.

I do not mean to imply that the humanities, and particularly history, take their readers in by a species of confidence trick – by simulating the outer shell, the logical structure, of scientific method without its substance; only that the force of such convenient, and perhaps indispensable, links as 'because' and 'therefore' is not identical in the two spheres; each performing its own legitimate – and parallel – functions, and leading to difficulties only if they are regarded as performing logically identical tasks in both spheres. This point will, I hope, become clearer still if it is further developed.

Let us assume that a historian who is attempting to discover and explain the course of a large historical phenomenon, such as a war or a revolution, is pressed to state those laws and general propositions which alone (at least in theory) could justify his constant use of such logical links as 'hence', 'therefore', 'the unavoidable result was', 'from this there was no turning back' and the rest of his stock-in-trade, what could his answer be? He might hesitantly trot out some general maxims about the influence of environment or a particular state of affairs – a bad harvest, or an inflationary spiral, or a wound to national pride – as it affects men in general or a specific group of human beings in particular; or he might speak about the influence of the interests of this or that class or nation, or the effect of religious convictions or social habits or political traditions. But if he is then pressed about the evidence for these generalisations, and upon marshalling what he can, is then told that no self-respecting natural science would tolerate so vague, unsifted and above all exiguous a body of factual evidence, nor such impressionistic methods of surveying it or deriving conclusions from it, he would not (if he were honest or wise) insist on claiming the authority of the methods of a fully-fledged natural science for his activity.

At this point someone might quite correctly point out to him that not all social sciences are in so deplorable a condition; that, for example, there exist disciplines – economics is perhaps the best known – where something resembling scientific procedure does appear to take place. In economics concepts can, we are assured, be defined with a fair measure of precision: there is here to be found distinct awareness of the differences between definitions, hypotheses and inductive generalisations; or between the empirical evidence and the conclusions drawn from it; or between the model and the reality to which it is applied; or between the fruit of observation and that of extrapolation; and so forth. This is then held up as a model to the unfortunate historian, wandering helplessly in his dark and pathless wood. Yet if he tries to follow such advice, and to apply to his own subject apparatus recommended by either metaphysical or positivist discoverers of historical patterns, his progress is soon arrested.

Attempts to provide history with laws have taken two main directions: all-embracing schemata, and division into specialised disciplines. The first has given us the systems of historiosophers, culminating in the vast edifices of Hegel, Spengler, Toynbee and the like, which turn out to be either too general, vague and occasionally tautological to cast new light on anything in particular, or, when the specific findings of the formulae are tested by exact scholars in the relevant fields, to yield implausible results. The second path leads to monographs about selected aspects of human activity – for example, the history of technology, or of a given science or art or craft or social activity. These do indeed, at their best, satisfy some of the criteria of natural scientists, but only at the expense of leaving out the greater part of what is known of the lives of the human beings whose histories are in this way recorded. In the case of a limited field – say the history of coinage in ancient Syracuse – this is, of course, deliberate and desirable as well as unavoidable; my point is that it is only the deliberate limitation of the field that renders it so.

Any attempt to 'integrate' these isolated strands, treated by the special disciplines, into something approaching (as near as we can make it so) a 'total' description of human experience – of what, in Aristotle's words, 'Alcibiades did and suffered'[1] – comes up against an insurmountable obstacle: that the facts to be fitted into the scientific grid and subsumed under the adopted laws or model (even if public criteria for selecting what is important and relevant from what is trivial and peripheral can be found and employed) are too many, too minute, too fleeting, too blurred at the edges. They criss-cross and penetrate each other at many levels simultaneously, and the attempt to prise them apart, as it were, and pin them down, and classify them, and fit them into their specific compartments, turns out to be impracticable. Wherever efforts to pursue this policy have been pressed with real vehemence – by those who were obsessed with the dominant role of some one factor, as Buckle was by that of climate, or Taine by his trinity of the milieu, the moment and the race, or Marxists by that of base and superstructure and the class struggle – they lead to distortions, and the accounts that result, even when they contain illuminating ideas and *aperçus*, are liable to be rejected as being over-schematised, that is, as exaggerating and omitting too much, as too unfaithful to human life as we know it.

The fact that this is so seems to me of cardinal importance, and to carry a crucial implication. For one of the central differences between such genuine attempts to apply scientific method to human affairs as are embodied in, say, economics or social psychology, and the analogous attempt to apply it in history proper, is this: scientific procedure is directed in the first place to the construction of an ideal model, with which the portion of the real world to be analysed must, as it were, be matched, so that it can be described and analysed in terms of its deviation from the model. But to construct a useful model will be feasible only when it is possible to abstract a sufficient number of sufficiently stable similarities from the things, facts, events of which the real world – the flow of experience – is composed. Only where such recurrences in the real world are frequent enough, and similar enough to be classifiable as so many deviations from the selfsame model, will the idealised model that is compounded of them – the electron, the

---

[1] *Poetics* 1451[b]11.

gene, the economic man – do its job of making it possible for us to extrapolate from the known to the unknown.

It follows from this that the greater the number of similarities[1] that we are able to collect (and the more dissimilarities we are able to ignore) – that is to say, the more successfully we abstract – the simpler our model will be, the narrower will be the range of characteristics to which it will apply, and the more precisely it will apply to it; and, conversely, the greater the variety of objects to which we want our model to apply, the less we shall be able to exclude, and consequently the more complex the model will become, and the less precisely it will fit the rich diversity of objects which it is meant to summarise, and so the less of a model, of a master key, it will necessarily be. A theory festooned with *ad hoc* hypotheses to account for each specific deviation from the norm will, like Ptolemy's epicycles, in the end cease to be useful. Exclusion – neglect of what is beyond the defined frontiers – is entailed in model-building as such. Hence it begins to look as if, given the world as it is,[2] the utility of a theory or a model tends to vary directly as the number of cases, and inversely as the number of characteristics, which it succeeds in covering. Consequently one may, at times, be compelled to choose between the rival rewards of increased extension or intension – between the range of a theory and the richness of its content.

The most rigorous and universal of all models is that of mathematics, because it operates at the level of the highest possible abstraction from natural characteristics. Physics, similarly, ignores deliberately all but the very narrow group of characteristics which material objects possess in common, and its power and scope (and its great triumphs) are directly attributable to its rejection of all but certain selected ubiquitous and recurrent similarities. As we go down the scale, sciences become richer in content and correspondingly less rigorous, less susceptible to quantitative techniques. Economics is a science precisely to the degree to which it can

---

[1] Or at best significant similarities, that is, those in which we are interested.

[2] This is an empirical fact. The world might have been different; if, for example, it possessed fewer characteristics and these coexisted or recurred with much greater uniformity and regularity, the facts of history could more easily be reduced to a natural science or sciences. But human experience would then be altogether different, and not describable in terms of our familiar categories and concepts. The tidier and more uniform such a universe, the less like our own, the less able are we to imagine it or conceive what our experience would be like.

successfully eliminate from consideration those aspects of human activity which are not concerned with production, consumption, exchange, distribution and so on. The attempt to eliminate from the consideration of economists psychological factors, such as, for instance, the springs of human action, or the variety of purposes or states of mind connected with or expressed by them; or to exclude moral or political considerations, such as, for example, the respective values of motives and consequences, or of individual versus group satisfaction – such a procedure is wholly justified so long as its sole aim is to render economics as much of a science as possible: that is to say, an instrument capable of analysis and prediction. If anyone then complains that economics, so conceived, leaves out too much, or fails to solve some of the most fundamental problems of individual and social welfare – among them questions which had originally stimulated this science into existence – one is entitled to reply that the omitted sides of life can be accommodated, and moral, psychological, political, aesthetic, metaphysical questions can perhaps be answered, but only at the price of departing from the rigour and the symmetry – and predictive power – of the models with which economic science operates; that versatility, richness of content, capacity to deal with many categories of problems, adaptability to the complexities of widely varying situations – all this may be purchasable only at the expense of logical simplicity, coherence, economy, width of scope, and, above all, capacity to move from the known to the unknown. These latter characteristics, with which Newtonian physics had, understandably enough, hypnotised the entire intellectual world, can be obtained only by drawing precise frontiers for a given activity and ruthlessly casting out (so far as possible) whatever has not been provided for in this specification. It is for this reason that even in the case of the more descriptive and time-bound (biological and genetic) disciplines, the more general and rigorous the concepts involved and the more 'technical' the approach, the better able they are to use methods similar to those of the physical sciences; the more elastic their concepts and the richer their content, the remoter from a natural science they will be.

If this is true, then there is a good deal in the Comtean classification of the sciences: mathematics, physics, biology, psychology, sociology are indeed rungs in a descending order of comprehensiveness and precision, and in an ascending order of concreteness and detail. General history – the richest of all human studies – shows this very plainly. If I am purely an economic historian, I can probably establish certain generalisations about the behaviour of some commodity – say wool – in some portion of the Middle Ages, for which enough documentary evidence exists to enable me to establish correlations between the production, sale, distribution of wool, and so forth, and certain other related social and economic facts and events. But I am able to do this only by averting my gaze from questions – sometimes very important and fascinating ones – about other characteristics of the wool-producers or wool-merchants; at least I do not attempt to establish measurable correlations between the sources and movements of the bales of wool and the religious and moral and aesthetic attitudes of wool-growers or wool-users, and their political ideals, and their conduct as husbands or citizens or churchmen, all at once. For the model which attempted to deal with all these aspects of life would (as things are) lose in predictive power and the precision of its results, even if the story gained in comprehensiveness, richness, depth and interest. For this reason, I find it useful to employ technical terms (always symptomatic of the fact that a model is at work) in an artificially delimited field – namely that of economic history. The same considerations apply, for example, to the history of technology, or of mathematics, or of clothing, and the like. I construct the model by abstracting; by noting only what, say, industrial techniques, or mathematical methods, or methods of composing music, have in common, and constructing my model out of these common characteristics, however much of general interest I may be leaving out. The more I wish to put in, the more over-weighted and, in due course, cluttered up and shapeless my model is bound to become, until it is scarcely a model at all, for it no longer covers a sufficient number of actual and possible cases in a sufficient variety of places and times. Its utility as a model will steadily diminish.

The proposition that sciences deal with the type, not the individual, was accepted and indeed insisted upon by those philosophical historians, particularly in France, who desired to assimilate their activities to those of scientists. When Renan, or Taine, or Monod preached the necessity of scientific history, they did not merely mean (as I suspect that, for example, Bury did) that historians should seek to be precise, or exercise rigour in observation or reasoning, or apply the findings of the natural sciences to the explanation of human action or experience wherever possible, or that they should grind no axe but that of objective truth, and state it without qualification whatever the moral or social or political consequences. They claimed much more. Taine states this point of view clearly, when he declares that historians work with samples:

> What was there in France in the eighteenth century? Twenty million men ... twenty million threads the criss-crossing of which makes a web. This immense web, with innumerable knots, cannot be grasped clearly in its entirety by anyone's memory or imagination. Indeed all we have is mere fragments ... the historian's sole task is to restore them – he reconstructs the wisps of the threads that he can see so as to connect them with the myriad threads that have vanished ... Fortunately, in the past as now, society included groups, each group consisting of men who were like one another, born in the same condition, moulded by the same education, moved by the same interests, with the same needs, same tastes, same *moeurs*, same culture, same basis to their lives. In seeing one, you have seen all. In every science we study each class of facts by means of chosen samples.

He goes on to say that one must enter into the private life of a man, his beliefs, sentiments, habits, behaviour. Such a sample will give us

> insight into the force and direction of the current that carries forward the whole of his society. The monograph, then, is the historian's best tool: he plunges it into the past like a lancet and draws it out charged with complete and authentic specimens. One understands a period after twenty or thirty such soundings: only they must be carried out and interpreted correctly.[1]

This is characteristic of the high tide of positivist optimism in which truth is mixed with error. No doubt it is true that our only key to understanding a culture or an age is the detailed study of the lives of representative individuals or families or groups. We cannot examine all the acts and thoughts of all (or even a large number) of the human beings alive during the age in question (or any other age): we generalise from samples. We integrate the results of such generalisations into what Taine calls the total 'web'. In 'reconstructing' the 'vanished threads' we make use of chemistry, astronomy,

---

[1] *Discours de M. Taine prononcé à l'Académie française* (Paris, 1880), pp. 24–7.

geology, palaeontology, epigraphy, psychology, every scientific method known to us. But the objective of all this is to understand the relation of parts to wholes, not, as Taine believed, of instance to general law. In a natural science – physics and zoology, economics and sociology – our aim is to construct a model ('the meson', 'the mammal', 'the monopolistic firm', 'the alienated proletarian') which we can apply, with which we can reach out into the unknown past or future with a fair degree of confidence in the result; for the central criterion of whether or not a study is a true science is its capacity to infer the unknown from the known. The process that Taine describes is not this at all; it is reconstruction in terms of a pattern, an interrelated social whole, obtained from 'entering into' individual human lives, provided that they turn out to be 'typical' – that is, significant or characteristic beyond themselves. The recognition of what is characteristic and represen- tative, of what is a 'good' sample suitable for being generalised, and, above all, of how the generalisations fit in with each other – that is the exercise of judgement, a form of thinking dependent on wide experience, memory, imagination, on the sense of 'reality', of what goes with what, which may need constant control by, but is not at all identical with, the capacity for logical reasoning and the construction of laws and scientific models – the capacity for perceiving the relations of particular case to law, instance to general rule, theorems to axioms, not of parts to wholes or fragments to completed patterns. I do not mean that these are incompatible 'faculties' capable of functioning in isolation from each other. Only that the gifts are dissimilar, that the qualitative distinctions and similiarities are not reducible without residue to quantitative ones, that the capacity for perceiving the former is not translatable into models, and that Buckle and Comte and Taine and Engels and their cruder or more extremist modern disciples, when they bandy the word 'scientific', are sometimes blind to this, and so lead men astray.

Let me put this in yet another way. Every student of historiogra- phy knows that many of the major achievements of modern historians come from their practice of certain rules, which the more reflective among them sometimes express in advice to practitioners of this craft. Historical students are told not to pay too much attention to personal factors or heroic and unusual figures in human history. They are told to attend to the lives of ordinary men, or to economic considerations or social factors or irrational impulses or traditional, collective and unconscious springs of action; or not to forget such impersonal, inconspicuous, dull, slowly or imperceptibly altering factors of change as erosion of the soil, or systems of irrigation and drainage, which may be more influential than spectacular victories, or catastrophic events, or acts of genius; they are told not to allow themselves to be carried away by the desire to be entertaining or paradoxical, or over-rationalistic, or to point a moral or demonstrate a theory; and much else of this kind. What justifies such maxims? They do not follow automatically from the rules of the deductive or inductive disciplines; they are not even rules of specialised techniques (like, say, the *a fortiori* principle in rhetoric, or that of *difficilior lectio* in textual criticism). What logical or technical rules can be laid down for determining precisely what, in a given situation, is due to rational or purposive, and what to 'senseless' or irrational, factors, how much to personal action, how much to impersonal forces? If anyone supposes that such rules can be drawn up, let him attempt to do so. It seems plain that such maxims are simply distillations of generalised sagacity – of practical judgement founded on observation, intelligence, imagination, on empirical insight, knowledge of what can and what cannot be, something that resembles a skill or gift more than it does factual knowledge[1] but is not identical with either; a capability of the highest value to action (in this case to mental labour) which scientific techniques can direct, aid, sharpen, criticise, radically correct, but never replace.

All this may be no more than another way of saying something trite but true – that the business of a science is to concentrate on similarities, not differences, to be general, to omit whatever is not relevant to answering the severely delimited questions that it sets itself to ask; while those historians who are concerned with a field wider than the specialised activities of men are interested at least as much in the opposite: in that which differentiates one thing, person, situation, age, pattern of experience, individual or collective, from another. When such historians attempt to account for and explain, say, the French Revolution, the last thing that they seek to do is to concentrate only on those characteristics which the French Revolution has in common with other revolutions, to abstract only common recurrent characteristics, to formulate a law on the basis of them, or at any rate a hypothesis, from which

---

[1] See pp. 43–4 and 52 below.

something about the pattern of all revolutions as such (or, more modestly, all European revolutions), and therefore of this revolution in particular, could in principle be reliably inferred. This, if it were feasible, would be the task of sociology, which would then stand to history as a 'pure' science to its application. The validity of the claim of this type of sociology to the status of a natural science is another story, and not directly related to history, whose tasks are different. The immediate purpose of narrative historians (as has often been repeated), whatever else it may be besides this, is to paint a portrait of a situation or a process, which, like all portraits, seeks to capture the unique patterns and peculiar characteristics of its particular subject; not to be an X-ray which eliminates all but what a great many subjects have in common. This is, by now, a truism, but its bearing on the possibility of transforming history into a natural science has not always been clearly perceived. Two great thinkers understood this, and grappled with the problem: Leibniz and Hegel. Both made heroic efforts to bridge the gulf by such doctrines as those of 'individual essences' and 'concrete universals' – a desperate dialectical attempt to fuse together individuality and universality. The imaginative brilliance of the metaphysical constructions in which the passage of the Rubicon is deducible from the essence of Julius Caesar, or the even more ambitious inevitabilities of the *Phenomenology*, and their failure, serves to indicate the central character of the problem.

One way of appreciating this contrast is by examining two uses of the humble word 'because'. Max Weber, whose discussion of this problem is extraordinarily illuminating, asked himself under what conditions I accept an explanation of a given individual action or attitude as adequate, and whether these conditions are the same as those that are required in the natural sciences – that is to say, he tried to analyse what is meant by rational explanation in these contrasted fields. If I understand him correctly, the type of argument he uses goes somewhat as follows: Supposing that a doctor informs me that his patient recovered from pneumonia because he was injected with penicillin, what rational grounds have I for accepting this 'because'? My belief is rational only if I have rational grounds for believing the general proposition 'Penicillin is effective against pneumonia', a causal proposition established by experiment and observation, which there is no reason to accept unless, in fact, it has been arrived at by valid methods of scientific inference. No amount of general reflection would justify my accepting this general proposition (or its application in a given case) unless I know that it has been or could be experimentally verified. The 'because' in this case indicates a claim that a *de facto* correlation between penicillin and pneumonia has, in fact, been established. I may find this correlation surprising or I may not; this does not affect its reality; scientific investigation – the logic of which, we now think, is hypothetico-deductive – establishes its truth or probability; and this is the end of the matter.

If, on the other hand, I am told, in the course of a historical narrative (or in a work of fiction, or ordinary life) that *x* resented the behaviour of *y*, because *x* was weak and *y* was arrogant and strong; or that *x* forgave the insult he had received from *y*, because he was too fond of *y* to feel aggrieved; and if, having accepted these 'because' statements as adequate explanations of the behaviour of *x* and *y*, I am then challenged to produce the general law which I am leaning on, consciously or not, to 'cover' these cases, what would it be reasonable for me to reply? I may well produce something like 'The weak often resent the arrogant and strong', or 'Human beings forgive insults from those they love.' But supposing I am then asked what concrete evidence I have for the truth of these general propositions, what scientific experiments I or others have per- formed to establish these generalisations, how many observed and tested cases they rest on, I may well be at a loss to answer. Even if I am able to cite examples from my own or others' experience of the attitude of the weak to the strong, or of the behaviour of persons capable of love and friendship, I may be scornfully told by a psychologist – or any other devotee of strict scientific method – that the number of instances I have produced is ludicrously insufficient to be adequate evidence for a generalisation of such scope; that no respectable science would accept these few positive or negative instances, which, moreover, have not been observed under scientific conditions, as a basis for serious claims to formu- late laws; that such procedures are impressionistic, vague, pre- scientific, unworthy to be reckoned as ground for a scientific hypothesis. And I may further be told that what cannot enter a natural science cannot be called fully rational, but only an approxi- mation to it (an 'explanation sketch').

Implicit in this approach is Descartes' criterion, the setting up of the methods of mathematics (or physics) as the standard for all rational thought. Nevertheless, the explanation that I have given in terms of the normal attitude of the weak to the strong, or of friends to one another, would, of course, be accepted by most rational beings (writers and readers of history among them) as an adequate explanation of the behaviour of a given individual in the relevant situation. This kind of explanation may not be admissible in a treatise on natural science, but in dealing with others, or describing their actions, we accept it as being both normal and reasonable; neither as inescapably shallow, or shamefully unexamined, or doubtful, nor as necessarily needing support from the laboratory. We may, of course, in any given case, be mistaken – mistaken about particular facts to be accounted for, about the attitudes of the relevant individuals to one another, or in taking for granted the generalisations implicit in our judgement; these may well be in need of correction from psychologists or sociologists. But because we may be in error in a given instance, it does not follow that this type of explanation is always systematically at fault, and should or could always be replaced by something more searching, more inductive, more like the type of evidence that is alone admitted in, say, biology.

If we probe further and ask why it is that such explanations – such uses of 'because' – are accepted in history, and what is meant by saying that it is rational to accept them, the answer must surely be that what in ordinary life we call adequate explanations often rest not on specific pieces of scientific reasoning, but on our experience in general, on our capacity for understanding the habits of thought and action that are embodied in human attitudes and behaviour, on what is called knowledge of life, sense of reality. If someone tells us 'x forgave y because he loved him' or 'x killed y because he hated him', we accept these propositions easily, because they, and the propositions into which they can be generalised, fit in with our experience, because we claim to know what men are like, not, as a rule, by careful observation of them as psychological specimens (as Taine recommends), or as members of some strange tribe whose behaviour is obscure to us and can only be inferred from (preferably controlled) observation, but because we claim to know (not always justifiably) what – in essentials – a human being is, in particular a human being who belongs to a civilisation not too unlike our own, and consequently one who thinks, wills, feels, acts in a manner which (rightly or wrongly) we assume to be intelligible to us because it sufficiently resembles our own or those of other human beings whose lives are intertwined with our own.

This sort of 'because' is the 'because' neither of induction nor of deduction, but the 'because' of understanding – *Verstehen* – of recognition of a given piece of behaviour as being part and parcel of a pattern of activity which we can follow, which we can remember or imagine, and which we describe in terms of the general laws which cannot possibly all be rendered explicit (still less organised into a system), but without which the texture of normal human life – social or personal – is not conceivable. We make mistakes; we may be shallow, unobservant, naïve, unimaginative, not allow enough for unconscious motives, or unintended consequences, or the play of chance or some other factor; we may project the present into the past or assume uncritically that the basic categories and concepts of our civilisation apply to remote or dissimilar cultures which they do not fit. But although any one explanation, or use of 'because' and 'therefore', may be rejected or shaken for any of these or a hundred other reasons (which scientific discoveries in, say, physics or psychology, running against the complacent assumptions of common sense, may well provide), *all* such explanations cannot be rejected *in toto* in favour of inductive procedures derived from the natural sciences, because that would cut the ground from beneath our feet: the context in which we think, act, expect to be understood or responded to, would be destroyed.

When I understand a sentence which someone utters, my claim to know what he means is not, as a rule, based on an inductively reached conclusion that the statistical probability is that the noises he emits are, in fact, related and expressive in the way that I take them to be – a conclusion derived from a comparison of the sounds he utters with a great many other sounds that a great many other beings have uttered in corresponding situations in the past. This must not be confused with the fact that, if pressed to justify my claim, I could conduct an experiment which would do something to support my belief. Nevertheless, my belief is usually a good deal stronger than that which any process of reasoning that I may perform with a view to bolstering it up would, in a natural science, be held to justify. Yet we do not for this reason regard such claims to understanding as being less rational than scientific convictions, still less as being arbitrary. When I say that I realise that *x* forgave *y* because he loved him or was too good-natured to bear a grudge, what I am ultimately appealing to is my own (or my society's) experience and imagination, my (or my associates') knowledge of what such relationships have been and can be. This knowledge, whether it is my own, or taken by me on trust – accepted uncritically – may often be inadequate, and may lead me to commit blunders – a Freudian or a Marxist may open my eyes to much that I had not yet understood – but if *all* such knowledge were rejected unless it could pass scientific tests, I could not think or act at all.

The world of natural science is the world of the external observer noting as carefully and dispassionately as he can the compresence or succession (or lack of it), or the extent of correlation, of empirical characteristics. In formulating a scientific hypothesis I must, at least in theory, start from the initial assumption that, for all I know, anything might occur next door to, or before or after, or simultaneously with, anything else; nature is full of surprises; I must take as little as possible for granted; it is the business of natural science to establish general laws recording what most often or invariably does occur. But in human affairs, in the interplay of men with one another, of their feelings, thoughts, choices, ideas about the world or each other or themselves, it would be absurd (and, if pushed to extremes, impossible) to start in this manner. I do not start from an ignorance which leaves all doors – or as many of them as possible – open, for here I am not primarily an external observer, but myself an actor; I understand other human beings, and what it is to have motives, feelings, or follow rules, because I am human myself, and because to be active – that is, to want, intend, make plans, speculate, do, react to others self-consciously, be aware of my situation *vis-à-vis* other conscious beings and the non-human environment – is *eo ipso* to be engaged in a constant fitting of fragments of reality into the single all-embracing pattern that I assume to hold for others besides myself, and which I call reality. When, in fact, I am successful in this – when the fragments seem to me to fit – we call this an explanation; when in fact they do fit, I am called rational; if they fit badly, if my sense of harmony is largely a delusion, I am called irrational, fanciful, distraught, silly; if they do not fit at all, I am called mad.

So much for differences in method. But there is also a profound difference of aim between scientific and historical studies. What they seek for is not the same. Let me illustrate this with a simple example. Supposing that we look at an average, unsophisticated European or American school text of modern European history that offers a sample of the kind of elementary historical writing upon which most of us have been brought up. Let us consider the kind of account that one finds (or used to find) in routine works of this type of, say, the causes of the French Revolution. It is not unusual to be told that among them were – to give the headings – (i) the oppression of French peasants by the aristocracy, the Church, the King etc.; (ii) the disordered state of French finances; (iii) the weak character or the stupidity of Louis XVI; (iv) the subversive influence of the writings of Voltaire, the Encyclopaedists, Rousseau and other writers; (v) the mounting frustration of the ambitions of the economically rising French bourgeoisie, barred from its proper share of political power; and so on. One may reasonably protest against the crudity and naïvety of such treatments of history: Tolstoy has provided some very savage and entertaining parodies of it and its practitioners.[1] But if one's main anxiety is to convert history into a science, one's indignation should take a different and much more specific form. One should declare that what is here manifested is a grotesque confusion of categories, an outrage to scientific method. For the analysis of the condition of the peasants belongs to the science of economics, or perhaps of social history; that of French fiscal policy to the science of public finance, which is not primarily a historical study, but one founded (according to some) on timeless principles; the weakness of the King's character or intellect is a matter for individual psychology (or biography); the influence of Voltaire and Rousseau belongs to the history of ideas; the pressure of the middle classes is a sociological topic; and so forth. Each of these disciplines must surely possess its own factual content, methods, canons, concepts, categories, logical structure. To heap them into one, and reel off a list of causes, as if they all belonged to the same level and type, is intellectually scandalous: the rope composed of these wholly heterogeneous strands must at once be unwound; each of the strands must then be treated separately in its proper logical box. Such should be the reaction of someone who takes seriously the proposition that history is, or at any rate should be, a natural science or a combination of such sciences. Yet the truth about history – perhaps the most important truth of all – is that general history is precisely this amalgam, a rich brew composed of apparently disparate ingredients, that we do in fact think of these different causes as factors in a single unitary sequence – the history of the French nation or French society during a particular segment of time – and that although there may be great profit to be gained

[1] See pp. 452–4 below.

from detaching this or that element of a single process for analysis in a specialised laboratory, yet to treat them as if they were genuinely separate, insulated streams which do not compose a single river is a far wilder departure from what we think history to be than the indiscriminate compounding of them into one string of causes, as is done in the simple-minded schoolbooks.

History is what historians do, and what at any rate some historians aim at is to answer those who wish to be told what important changes occurred in French public life between 1789 and 1794, and why they took place. We wish, ideally at any rate, to be presented, if not with a total experience – which is a logical as well as a practical impossibility – at least with something full enough and concrete enough to meet our conception of public life (itself an abstraction, but not a deductive schema, not an artificially constructed model), seen from as many points of view and at as many levels as possible, including as many components, factors, aspects as the widest and deepest knowledge, the greatest analytical power, insight, imagination can present. If we are told that this cannot be achieved by a natural science – that is, by the application of models to reality, because models can only function if their subject-matter is relatively 'thin', consisting as it does of deliberately isolated strands of experience, and not 'thick', that is, not with the texture constituted by the interwoven strands – then history, if it is set on dealing with the compound and not some meticulously selected ingredient of it, as it must be, will, in this sense, not be a science after all. A scientific cast of mind is seldom found together with historical curiosity or historical talent. We can make use of the techniques of the natural sciences to establish dates, order events in time and space, exclude untenable hypotheses and suggest new explanatory factors (as sociology, psychology, economics, medicine have so notably done), but the function of all these techniques, indispensable as they are today, can be no more than ancillary, for they are determined by their specific models, and are consequently 'thin', whereas what the great historians sought to describe and analyse and explain is necessarily 'thick'; that is the essence of history, its purpose, its pride, and its reason for existence.

History, and other accounts of human life, are at times spoken of as being akin to art. What is usually meant is that writing about human life depends to a large extent on descriptive skill, style, lucidity, choice of examples, distribution of emphasis, vividness of characterisation, and the like. But there is a profounder sense in which the historian's activity is an artistic one. Historical explanation is to a large degree arrangement of the discovered facts in patterns which satisfy us because they accord with life – the variety of human experience and activity – as we know it and can imagine it. That is the difference that distinguishes the humane studies – *Geisteswissenschaften* – from those of nature. When these patterns contain central concepts or categories that are ephemeral, or confined to trivial or unfamiliar aspects of human experience, we speak of such explanations as shallow, or inadequate, or eccentric, and find them unsatisfactory on those grounds. When these concepts are of wide scope, permanent, familiar, common to many men and many civilisations, we experience a sense of reality and dependability that derives from this very fact, and regard the explanation as well-founded, serious, satisfactory. On some occasions (seldom enough) the explanation not only involves, but reveals, basic categories of universal import, which, once they are forced upon consciousness, we recognise as underlying all our experience; yet so closely interwoven are they with all that we are and feel, and therefore so totally taken for granted, that to touch them at all is to communicate a shock to the entire system; the shock is one of recognition and one that may upset us, as is liable to happen when something deep-set and fundamental that has lain unquestioned and in darkness is suddenly illuminated or prised out of its frame for closer inspection. When this occurs, and especially when the categories thus uncovered seem applicable to field after field of human activity, without apparent limits – so that we cannot tell how far they may yet extend – we call such explanations profound, fundamental, revolutionary, and those who proffer them – Vico, Kant, Marx, Freud – men of depth of insight and genius.

This kind of historical explanation is related to moral and aesthetic analysis, in so far as it presupposes conceiving of human beings not merely as organisms in space, the regularities of whose behaviour can be described and locked in labour-saving formulae, but as active beings, pursuing ends, shaping their own and others' lives, feeling, reflecting, imagining, creating, in constant interaction and intercommunication with other human beings; in short, engaged in all the forms of experience that we understand because we share in them, and do not view them purely as external observers. This is what is called the inside view: and it renders possible and indeed inescapable explanation whose primary function is not to predict or extrapolate, or even control, but fit the loose and fleeting objects of sense, imagination, intellect into the central succession of patterns that we call normal, and which is the ultimate criterion of reality as against illusion, incoherence, fiction. History is merely the mental projection into the past of this activity of selection and adjustment, the search for coherence and unity, together with the attempt to refine it with all the self-consciousness of which we are capable, by bringing to its aid everything that we conceive to be useful – all the sciences, all the knowledge and skills, and all the theories that we have acquired, from whatever quarter. This, indeed, is why we speak of the importance of allowing for imponderables in forming historical judgement, or of the faculty of judgement that seems mysterious only to those who start from the preconception that their induction, deduction and sense perception are the only legitimate sources of, or at least certified methods justifying claims to, knowledge. Those who, without mystical undertones, insist on the importance of common sense, or knowledge of life, or width of experience, or breadth of sympathy or imagination, or natural wisdom, or 'depth' of insight – all normal and empirical attributes – are suspected of seeming to smuggle in some kind of illicit, metaphysical faculty only because the exercise of these gifts has relatively little value for those who deal with inanimate matter, for physicists or geologists. Capacity for understanding people's characters, knowledge of ways in which they are likely to react to one another, ability to 'enter into' their motives, their principles, the movement of their thoughts and feelings (and this applies no less to the behaviour of masses or to the growth of cultures) – these are the talents that are indispensable to historians, but not (or not to such a degree) to natural scientists. The capacity for knowing which is like knowing someone's character or face is as essential to historians as knowledge of facts. Without sufficient knowledge of facts a historical construction may be no more than a coherent fiction, a work of the romantic imagination; it goes without saying that if its claim to be true is to be sustained, it must be, as the generalisations which it incorporates must in their turn be, tethered to reality by verification of the facts, as in any natural science. Nevertheless, even though in this ultimate sense what is meant by 'real' and 'true' is identical in science, in history and in ordinary life, yet the differences remain as great as the similarities.

This notion of what historians are doing when they are explaining may cast light also upon something that was mentioned earlier;

namely, the idea of the inexorable succession of the stages of development, which made it not merely erroneous but absurd to suppose that *Hamlet* could have been written at the court of Genghis Khan, or that Richelieu could have pursued the policies realised by Bismarck. For this kind of certainty is not something that we derive from a careful inductive investigation of conditions in Outer Mongolia, as opposed to those of Elizabethan England, or of the political relations between the great powers in the nineteenth century as opposed to those in the seventeenth, but from a more fundamental sense of what goes with what. We conceive of historical succession as being akin to that of the growth of the individual personality; to suggest that a child thinks or wills or acts like an old man, or vice versa, is something that we reject on the basis of our own direct experience (I mean by this not introspection, but knowledge of life – something that springs from interaction with others and with the surrounding environment and constitutes the sense of reality). Our conception of a civilisation is analogous to this. We do not feel it necessary to enumerate all the specific ways in which a wild nomad differs from a European of the Renaissance, or ask ourselves why it is that – what inductive evidence we have for the contingent proposition that – the culture of the Renaissance is not merely different from, but represents a more mature phase of human growth than, that of Outer Mongolia two thousand years ago. The proposition that the culture of the Renaissance not merely did not precede, but cannot have preceded, the nomadic stage in the continuous development that we call a single culture, is something bound up so closely with our conception of how men live, of what societies are, of how they develop, indeed of the very meaning of the concept of man, growth, society, that it is logically prior to our investigations and not their goal or product. It is not so much that it stands in no need of justification by their methods or results, as that it is logically absurd to bolster it up in this way. For this reason one might hesitate to call such knowledge empirical, for it is not confirmable or corrigible by the normal empirical methods, in relation to which it functions as base – as a frame of reference. But neither, of course, is it a priori (as Vico and Hegel, who showed original insight into the matter, sometimes imply) if by that is meant that it is obtainable in some special, non-natural way. Recognition of the fundamental categories of human experience differs from both the acquisition of empirical information and deductive reasoning; such categories are logically prior to either, and are least subject to change among the elements that constitute our knowledge. Yet they are not unalterable; and we can ask ourselves to what degree this or that change in them would affect our experience. It is possible, although *ex hypothesi* not easy, to conceive of beings whose fundamental categories of thought or perception radically differ from ours; the greater such differences, the harder it will be for us to communicate with them; or, if the process goes further, to regard them as being human or sentient; or, if the process goes far enough, to conceive of them at all.

It is a corollary of this that one of the difficulties that beset historians and do not plague natural scientists is that of reconstructing what occurred in the past in terms not merely of our own concepts and categories, but also of how such events must have looked to those who participated in or were affected by them – psychological facts that in their turn themselves influenced events. It is difficult enough to develop an adequate consciousness of what we are and what we are at, and how we have arrived where we have done, without also being called upon to make clear to ourselves what such consciousness and self-consciousness must have been like for persons in situations different from our own; yet no less is expected of the true historian. Chemists and physicists are not obliged to investigate the states of mind of Lavoisier or Boyle; still less of the unenlightened mass of men. Mathematicians need not worry themselves with the general outlook of Euclid or Newton. Economists *qua* economists need not grasp the inner vision of Adam Smith or Keynes, still less of their less gifted contemporaries. But it is the inescapable business of the historian who is more than a compiler or the slave of a doctrine or a party to ask himself not merely what occurred (in the sense of publicly observable events), but also how the situation looked to various representative Greeks or Romans, or to Alexander or Julius Caesar, and above all to Thucydides, Tacitus or anonymous medieval chroniclers, or to Englishmen or Germans in the sixteenth century, or Frenchmen in 1789 or Russians in 1917, or to Luther, or Cromwell, or Robespierre or Lenin.

This kind of imaginative projection of ourselves into the past, the attempt to capture concepts and categories that differ from those of the investigator by means of concepts and categories that cannot but be his own, is a task that he can never be sure that he is even beginning to achieve, yet is not permitted to abjure. He seeks to apply scientific tests to his conclusions, but this will take him only a little way. For it is a commonplace by now that the frontiers between fact and interpretation are blurred and shifting, and that what is fact from one perspective is interpretation from another. Even if chemical and palaeographic and archaeological methods yield some hard pebbles of indubitable fact, we cannot evade the task of interpretation, for nothing counts as a historical interpretation unless it attempts to answer the question of how the world must have looked to other individuals or societies if their acts and words are to be taken as the acts and words of human beings neither wholly like ourselves nor so different as not to fit into our common past. Without a capacity for sympathy and imagination beyond any required by a physicist there is no vision of either past or present, neither of others nor of ourselves; but where it is wholly lacking, ordinary thinking – as well as historical thinking – cannot function at all.

The contrast which I am trying to draw is not that between the two permanently opposed but complementary human demands: one for unity and homogeneity, the other for diversity and heterogeneity, which Kant has made so clear.[1] The contrast I mean is one between different types of knowledge. When the Jews are enjoined in the Bible to protect strangers, 'for ye know the heart of a stranger, seeing ye were strangers in the land of Egypt',[2] this knowledge is neither deductive, nor inductive, nor founded on direct inspection, but akin to the 'I know' of 'I know what it is to be hungry and poor', or 'I know how political bodies function', or 'I know what it is to be a Brahmin.' This is neither (to make use of Gilbert Ryle's useful classification) the 'knowing that' which the sciences provide, nor the 'knowing how' which is the possession of a disposition or skill, nor the knowledge of direct perception, acquaintance, memory, but the type of knowledge that an administrator or politician must possess of the men with whom he deals. If the historian (or, for that matter, the contemporary commentator on events) is endowed with this too poorly, if he can fall back only on inductive techniques, then, however accurate his discoveries of fact, they remain those of an antiquarian, a chronicler, at best an archaeologist, but not those of a historian. It is not only erudition

[1] *Critique of Pure Reason*, A654/B682.
[2] Exodus, chapter 23, verse 9.

or belief in theories of human behaviour that enabled Marx or Namier to write history of the first order.

Perhaps some light may be cast on this issue by comparing historical method with that of linguistic or literary scholarship. No scholar could emend a text without a capacity (for which no technique exists) for 'entering into the mind of' another society and age. Electronic brains cannot perform this: they can offer alternative combinations of letters but not choose between them successfully, since the infallible rules for 'programming' have not been formulated. How do gifted scholars in fact arrive at their emendations? They do all that the most exacting natural science would demand: they steep themselves in the material of their authors; they compare, contrast, manipulate combinations like the most accomplished cypher-breakers; they may find it useful to apply statistical and quantitative methods; they formulate hypotheses and test them; all this may well be indispensable but it is not enough. In the end what guides them is a sense (which comes from study of the evidence) of what a given author could, and what he could not, have said; of what fits and what does not fit into the general pattern of his thought. This, let me say again, is not the way in which we demonstrate that penicillin cures pneumonia.

It might be that the deepest chasm which divides historical from scientific studies lies between the outlook of the external observer and that of the actor. It is this that was brought out by the contrast between 'inner' and 'outer' which Vico initiated, and after him the Germans, and is so suspect to modern positivists; between the questions 'How?' or 'What?' or 'When?' on one side, and the questions 'Why?', 'Following what rule?', 'Towards what goal?', 'Springing from what motive?' on the other. It lies in the difference between the category of mere togetherness or succession (the correlations to which all sciences can in the end be reduced), and that of coherence and interpretation; between factual knowledge and understanding. The latter alone makes intelligible that celebrated identity in difference (which the idealist philosophers exaggerated and abused) in virtue of which we conceive of one and the same outlook as being expressed in diverse manifestations, and perceive affinities (that are often difficult and at times impossible to formulate) between the dress of a society and its morals, its system of justice and the character of its poetry, its architecture and its domestic habits, its sciences and its religious symbols. This is Montesquieu's notorious 'spirit' of the laws (or institutions) that belong to a society. Indeed, this alone gives its sense to the very notion of belonging;[1] without it we should not understand what is meant when something is described as belonging to, or as characteristic or typical of, an age or a style or an outlook, nor, conversely, should we know what it is for some interpretation to be anachronistic, what is meant by an incompatibility between a given phenomenon and its alleged context in time; this type of misattribution is different in kind from formal inconsistency, a logical collision of theories or propositions.

A concentrated interest in particular events or persons or situations as such,[2] and not as instances of a generalisation, is a prerequisite of that historical sense which, like a sense of occasion in agents intent on achieving some specific purpose, is sharpened by love or hate or danger; it is this that guides us in understanding, discovering and explaining. When historians assert particular propositions like 'Lenin played a crucial role in making the Russian Revolution', or 'Without Churchill Britain would have been defeated in 1940', the rational grounds for such assertions, whatever their degree of plausibility, are not identical with generalisations of the type 'Such men, in such conditions, usually affect events in this fashion', for which the evidence may be exceedingly feeble; for we do not test the propositions solely – or indeed generally – by their logical links with such general propositions (or explanation sketches), but rather in terms of their coherence with our picture of a specific situation. To analyse this type of knowledge into a finite collection of general and particular, categorical and hypothetical, propositions, is not practicable. Every judgement that we formulate, whether in historical thought or ordinary life, involves general ideas and propositions without which there can be no thought or language. At times some among these generalisations can be clearly stated, and combined into

---

[1] Cf. p. 24 above.

[2] 'There are really only two ways of acquiring knowledge of human affairs' says Ranke: 'through the perception of the particular, or through abstraction ... the former [is the method] of history. There is no other way ...

'Two qualities, I think, are required for the making of the true historian: first he must feel a participation and pleasure in the particular for itself ... Just as one takes delight in flowers without thinking to what genus of Linnaeus ... they belong ... without thinking how the whole manifests itself in the particular.

'Still, this does not suffice; ... while [the historian] reflects on the particular, the development of the world in general will become apparent to him.' In *The Varieties of History*, ed. Fritz Stern (New York, 1956), pp. 58–9.

models; where this occurs, natural sciences arise. But the descriptive and explanatory language of historians, because they seek to record or analyse or account for specific or even unique phenomena as such[1] – as often as not for their own sakes – cannot, for that reason, be reduced without residue to such general formulae, still less to models and their applications. Any attempt to do so will be halted at the outset by the discovery that the subject-matter involves a 'thick' texture of criss-crossing, constantly changing and melting conscious and unconscious beliefs and assumptions some of which it is impossible and all of which it is difficult to formulate, on which, nevertheless, our rational views and rational acts are founded, and, indeed, which they exhibit or articulate. This is the 'web' of which Taine speaks, and it is possible to go only some way (it is impossible to say in advance how far) towards isolating and describing its ingredients if our rationality is challenged. And even if we succeed in making explicit all (which is absurd) or many (which is not practicable) of our general propositions or beliefs, this achievement will not take us much nearer the scientific ideal; for between a collection of generalisations – or unanalysed knots of them – and the construction of a model there still lies difficult or impassable country: the generalisations must exhibit an exceptional degree of constancy and logical connection if this passage is to be negotiated.

What are we to call the faculty which an artist displays in choosing his material for his particular purpose; or which a politician or a publicist needs when he adopts a policy or presents a thesis, the success of which may depend on the degree of his sensitiveness to circumstances and to human characters, and to the specific interplay between them, with which, and upon which, he is working? The *Wirkungszusammenhang*, the general structure or pattern of experience – understanding of this may indeed be useful for the scientist, but it is absolutely indispensable to the historian. Without it, he remains at best a chronicler or technical specialist; at worst a distorter and writer of inferior fiction. He may achieve accuracy, objectivity, lucidity, literary quality, breadth of knowledge, but unless he conveys a recognisable vision of life, and exhibits that sense of what fits into a given situation and what does not which is the ultimate test of sanity, a perception of a social

---

[1] All facts are, of course, unique, those dealt with by natural scientists no less than any others; but it is not their uniqueness that interests scientists.

Gestalt, not, as a rule, capable of being formalised in terms, let us say, of a field theory – unless he possesses a minimal capacity for this, the result is not recognised by us as an account of reality, that is, of what human beings, as we understand the term, could have felt or thought or done.

It was, I think, L. B. Namier who once remarked about historical sense that there was no a priori short-cut to knowledge of the past; what actually happened can be established only by scrupulous empirical investigation, by research in its normal sense. What is meant by historical sense is the knowledge not of what happened, but of what did not happen. When a historian, in attempting to decide what occurred and why, rejects all the infinity of logically open possibilities, the vast majority of which are obviously absurd, and, like a detective, investigates only those possibilities which have at least some initial plausibility, it is this sense of what is plausible – what men, being men, could have done or been – that constitutes the sense of coherence with the patterns of life that I have tried to indicate. Such expressions as plausibility, likelihood, sense of reality, historical sense denote typical qualitative categories which distinguish historical studies, as opposed to the natural sciences that seek to operate on a quantitative basis. This distinction, which originated in Vico and Herder, and was developed by Hegel and (malgré soi) Marx, by Dilthey and Weber, is of fundamental importance.

The gifts that historians need are different from those of natural scientists. The latter must abstract, generalise, idealise, qualify, dissociate normally associated ideas (for nature is full of strange surprises, and as little as possible must be taken for granted), deduce, establish with certainty, reduce everything to the maximum degree of regularity, uniformity, and, so far as possible, to timeless repetitive patterns. Historians cannot ply their trade without a considerable capacity for thinking in general terms; but they need, in addition, peculiar attributes of their own: a capacity for integration, for perceiving qualitative similarities and differences, a sense of the unique fashion in which various factors combine in the particular concrete situation, which must at once be neither so unlike any other situation as to constitute a total break with the continuous flow of human experience, nor yet so stylised and uniform as to be the obvious creature of theory and not made of flesh and blood. The capacities needed are those rather of association than of dissociation, of perceiving the relation of parts to wholes, of particular sounds or colours to the many possible tunes or pictures into which they might enter, of the links that connect individuals viewed and savoured as individuals, and not primarily as instances of types or laws. It is these that Hegel tried to put under the head of the synthesising 'Reason' as opposed to the analytic 'Understanding'; and to provide with a logic of their own. It is the 'logic' that proved incapable of clear formulation or utility: it is this that cannot be incorporated in electronic brains. Such gifts relate as much to practice as to theory; perhaps to practice more directly. A man who lacks common intelligence can be a physicist of genius, but not even a mediocre historian. Some of the characteristics indispensable to (although not, by themselves, sufficient to move) historians are more akin to those needed in active human intercourse than to those found useful in the study or the laboratory or the cloister. The capacity for associating the fruits of experience in a manner that enables its possessors to distinguish, without the benefit of rules, what is central, permanent or universal from what is local, or peripheral, or transient – that is what gives concreteness and plausibility, the breath of life, to historical accounts. Skill in establishing hypotheses by means of observation or memory or inductive procedures, while ultimately indispensable to the discovery of all forms of truth about the world, is not the rarest of the qualities required by historians, nor is the desire to find recurrences and laws itself a symptom of historical talent.

If we ask ourselves which historians have commanded the most lasting admiration, we shall, I think, find that they are neither the most ingenious, nor the most precise, nor even the discoverers of new facts or unsuspected causal connections, but those who (like imaginative writers) present men or societies or situations in many dimensions, at many intersecting levels simultaneously, writers in whose accounts human lives, and their relations both to each other and to the external world, are what (at our most lucid and imaginative) we know that they can be. The gifts that scientists most need are not these: they must be ready to call everything into question, to construct bold hypotheses unrelated to customary empirical procedures, and drive their logical implications as far as they will go, free from control by common sense or too great a fear of departing from what is normal or possible in the world. Only in this way will new truths and relations between them be found – truths which, in psychology or anthropology as well as physics or mathematics, do not depend upon preserving contact with common human experience. In this sense, to say of history that it should approximate to the condition of a science is to ask it to contradict its essence.

It would be generally agreed that the reverse of a grasp of reality is the tendency to fantasy or Utopia. But perhaps there exist more ways than one to defy reality. May it not be that to be unscientific is to defy, for no good logical or empirical reason, established hypotheses and laws; while to be unhistorical is the opposite – to ignore or twist one's view of particular events, persons, predicaments in the name of laws, theories, principles derived from other fields, logical, ethical, metaphysical, scientific, which the nature of the medium renders inapplicable? For what else is it that is done by those theorists who are called fanatical because their faith in a given pattern is not overcome by their sense of reality? For this reason the attempt to construct a discipline which would stand to concrete history as pure to applied, no matter how successful the human sciences may grow to be – even if, as all but obscurantists must hope, they discover genuine, empirically confirmed, laws of individual and collective behaviour – seems an attempt to square the circle. It is not a vain hope for an ideal goal beyond human powers, but a chimera, born of lack of understanding of the nature of natural science, or of history, or of both.

# DOES POLITICAL THEORY STILL EXIST?

I

Is THERE still such a subject as political theory? This query, put with suspicious frequency in English-speaking countries, questions the very credentials of the subject: it suggests that political philosophy, whatever it may have been in the past, is today dead or dying. The principal symptom which seems to support this belief is that no commanding work of political philosophy has appeared in the twentieth century. By a commanding work in the field of general ideas I mean at the very least one that has in a large area converted paradoxes into platitudes or vice versa. This seems to me no more (but also no less) than an adequate criterion of the characteristic in question.

But this is scarcely conclusive evidence. There exist only two good reasons for certifying the demise of a discipline: one is that its central presuppositions, empirical, or metaphysical, or logical, are no longer accepted because they have (with the world of which they were a part) withered away, or because they have been discredited or refuted. The other is that new disciplines have come to perform the work originally undertaken by the older study. These disciplines may have their own limitations, but they exist, they function, and have either inherited or usurped the functions of their predecessors: there is no room left for the ancestor from whom they spring. This is the fate that overtook astrology, alchemy, phrenology (positivists, both old and new, would include theology and metaphysics). The postulates on which these disciplines were based either were destroyed by argument or collapsed for other reasons; consequently they are today regarded merely as instances of systematic delusion.

This type of systematic parricide is, in effect, the history of the natural sciences in their relation to philosophy, and so has a direct bearing upon the question before us. The relevant consideration is this: There exist at least two classes of problems to which men have succeeded in obtaining clear answers. The first have been so formulated that they can (at least in principle, if not always in practice) be answered by observation and by inference from observed data. These determine the domains of natural science and of everyday common sense. Whether I ask simple questions about whether there is any food in the cupboard, or what kind of birds are to be found in Patagonia, or the intentions of an individual, or more complicated ones about the structure of matter, or the behaviour of social classes or international markets, I know that the answer, to have any genuine claim to truth, must rest on someone's observation of what exists or happens in the spatio-temporal world. Some would say 'organised observation'. I should be inclined to agree. But differences on this issue, while they are crucial for the philosophy of science and the theory of knowledge, do not affect my argument. All the generalisations and hypotheses and models with which the most sophisticated sciences work can be established and discredited ultimately only by the data of inspection or introspection.

The second type of question to which we can hope to obtain clear answers is formal. Given certain propositions called axioms, together with rules for deducing other propositions from them, I can proceed by mere calculation. The answers to my questions will be valid or invalid according to whether the rules that I accept without question as part of a given discipline have been correctly used. Such disciplines contain no statements based on observation of fact, and therefore are not nowadays expected to provide information about the universe, whether or not they are used in providing it. Mathematics and formal logic are, of course, the best-known examples of formal sciences of this type, but heraldry, chess, and theories of games in general, are similar applications of the formal methods which govern such disciplines.

The two methods of answering questions may be, very generally, denominated empirical and formal. Among the characteristics of both are at least these:

1 Even if we do not know the answer to a given question, we know what kinds of methods are appropriate in looking for the answer; we know what kinds of answers are relevant to these questions, even if they are not true. If I am asked about the work-ings of the Soviet system of criminal law, or why Kennedy was elected President of the United States, I may not be able to answer

the question, but I know within what region the relevant evidence must lie, and how an expert would use such evidence to obtain the answer; I must be able to state this in very general terms, if only to show that I have understood the question. Similarly, if I am asked for the proof of Fermat's theorem, I may not be able to give it, indeed I may know that no one has yet been able to provide it, but I also know what kinds of demonstration would count as answers to this problem, even though they may be incorrect or inconclusive, and can discriminate these from assertions which are irrelevant to the topic. In other words, in all these cases, even if I do not know the answer, I know where to look for it, or how to identify an authority or expert who knows how to set about looking for it.

2 This means, in effect, that where the concepts are firm, clear and generally accepted, and the methods of reasoning and arriving at conclusions are agreed between men (at least the majority of those who have anything to do with these matters), there and only there is it possible to construct a science, formal or empirical. Wherever this is not the case – where the concepts are vague or too much in dispute, and methods of argument and the minimum qualifications that constitute an expert are not generally agreed, where we find frequent recriminations about what can or what cannot claim to be a law, an established hypothesis, an undisputed truth, and so on – we are at best in the realm of quasi-science. The principal candidates for inclusion in the charmed circle who have not succeeded in passing the required tests are the occupants of the large, rich and central, but unstable, volcanic and misty, region of 'ideologies'. One of the rough and ready tests for finding out which region we are in is whether a set of rules, accepted by the great majority of experts in the subject, and capable of being incorporated in a textbook, can be applied in the field in question. To the degree to which such rules are applicable, a discipline approaches the coveted condition of an accepted science. Psychology, sociology, semantics, logic, perhaps certain branches of economics, are in a no man's land, some nearer to, some further from, the frontier which demarcates, less or more clearly, the territory of the established sciences.

3 But besides these two major categories, there arise questions which fall outside either group. It is not only that we may not know the answers to certain questions, but that we are not clear how to set about trying to answer them – where to look – what would constitute evidence for an answer and what would not.

When I am asked 'Where is the image in the mirror?' or 'Can time stand still?' I am not sure what kind of question it is that is being asked, or whether indeed it makes any sense at all. I am in not much better plight with some traditional questions which have probably been asked since the dawn of thought, such as 'How did the world begin?' and, following that, 'What happened before the beginning?' Some say that these are not legitimate questions; but then what makes them illegitimate? There is something that I am trying to ask; for I am certainly puzzled by something. When I ask 'Why can I not be in two places at once?', 'Why can I not get back into the past?' or, to move to another region, 'What is justice?' or 'Is justice objective and absolute?' or again 'How can we ever be sure that an action is just?', no obvious method of settling these questions lies to hand. One of the surest hallmarks of a philosophical question – for this is what all these questions are – is that we are puzzled from the very outset, that there is no automatic technique, no universally recognised expertise, for dealing with such questions. We discover that we do not feel sure how to set about clearing our minds, finding out the truth, accepting or rejecting earlier answers to these questions. Neither induction (in its widest sense of scientific reasoning), nor direct observation (appropriate to empirical enquiries), nor deduction (demanded by formal problems) seem to be of help. Once we do feel quite clear about how we should proceed, the questions no longer seem philosophical.

The history – and indeed the advance – of human thought (this is perhaps a truism) have, in fact, largely consisted in the gradual shuffling of all the basic questions that men ask into one or the other of two well-organised compartments – the empirical and the formal. Wherever concepts grow firm and clear and acquire universal acceptance, a new science, natural or formal, comes into being. To use a simile that I cannot claim to have invented, philosophy is like a radiant sun that, from time to time, throws off portions of itself; these masses, when they cool down, acquire a firm and recognisable structure of their own and acquire independent careers as tidy and regular planets; but the central sun continues on its path, and does not seem to diminish in mass or radiance. The 'status' and vitality of philosophy is another matter, and seems to be directly connected with the extent to which it deals with issues

that are of concern to the common man. The relation of philosophy to opinion and conduct is a central question of both history
and sociology, too large to be considered here. What concerns us is
that philosophy in one state of development may turn into a
science in the next.

It is no confusion of thought that caused astronomy, for
example, to be regarded as a philosophical discipline in, say, the
time of Scotus Erigena, when its concepts and methods were not
what we should today regard as firm or clear, and the part played
by observation in relation to a priori teleological notions (such as
the yearning of each body to realise the full perfection of its nature)
made it impossible to determine whether the amalgam that went
under the name of the knowledge of celestial bodies was empirical
or formal. As soon as clear concepts and specific techniques
developed, the science of astronomy emerged. In other words,
astronomy in its beginning could not be relegated to either
compartment, even if such compartments as the empirical and the
formal had been clearly distinguished; and it was, of course, part of
the 'philosophical' status of early medieval astronomy that the
civilisation of that time (Marxists would say 'the superstructure')
did not permit the distinction between the two compartments to be
clearly demarcated.

What, therefore, is characteristic of specifically philosophical
questions is that they do not (and some of them perhaps never will)
satisfy conditions required by an independent science, the principal
among which is that the path to their solution must be implicit in
their very formulation. Nevertheless, there are some subjects which
clearly are near the point of taking flight and divorcing themselves
from the main body in which they were born, much as physics and
mathematics and chemistry and biology have done in their day.
One of these is semantics; another is psychology; with one foot,
however reluctantly, they are still sunk in philosophical soil; but
they show signs of a tendency to tear themselves loose and
emancipate themselves, with only historical memories to tell them
of their earlier, more confused, if in some respects richer, years.

II

Among the topics that remain obstinately philosophical, and have,
despite repeated efforts, failed to transform themselves into sciences, are some that in their very essence involve value judgements.

Ethics, aesthetics, criticism explicitly concerned with general ideas, all but the most technical types of history and scholarship, still live at various points of this limbo, unable or unwilling to emerge by either the empirical or the formal door. The mere fact that value judgements are relevant to an intellectual pursuit is clearly not sufficient to disqualify it from being a recognised science. The concept of normal health certainly embodies a valuation, and although there is sufficient universal consensus about what constitutes good health, a normal state, disease and so on, this concept, nevertheless, does not enter as an intrinsic element into sciences such as anatomy, physiology and pathology. Pursuit of health may be the strongest sociological and psychological (and moral) factor in creating and promoting these sciences; it may determine which problems and aspects of the subject have been most ardently attended to; but it is not referred to in the science itself, any more than the uses of history or logic need be mentioned in historical or logical works. If so clear, universally accepted, 'objective' a value as that of a desirable state of health is extruded from the structure of the natural sciences, this fact is even more conspicuous in more controversial fields. The attempts, from Plato to our own day (particularly persistent and numerous in the eighteenth century), to found objective sciences of ethics and aesthetics on the basis of universally accepted values, or of methods of discovering them, have met with little success; relativism, subjectivism, romanticism, scepticism with regard to values keep breaking in.

What, we may ask at this point, is the position of political theory? What are its most typical problems? Are they empirical, or formal, or neither? Do they necessarily entail questions of value? Are they on the way to independent status, or are they by their very nature compelled to remain only an element in some wider body of thought?

Among the problems which form the core of traditional political theory are those, for instance, of the nature of equality, of rights, law, authority, rules. We demand the analysis of these concepts, or ask how these expressions function in our language, or what forms of behaviour they prescribe or forbid and why, or into what system of value or outlook they fit, and in what way. When we ask, what is perhaps the most fundamental of all political questions, 'Why should anyone obey anyone else?', we ask not 'Why do men obey?' – something that empirical psychology, anthropology and sociology might be able to answer – nor yet 'Who obeys whom, when and where, and determined by what causes?', which could perhaps be answered on the basis of evidence drawn from these and similar fields. When we ask why a man should obey, we are asking for the explanation of what is normative in such notions as authority, sovereignty, liberty, and for the justification of their validity in political arguments. These are words in the name of which orders are issued, men are coerced, wars are fought, new societies are created and old ones destroyed – expressions which play as great a part as any in our lives today. What makes such questions prima facie philosophical is the fact that no wide agreement exists on the meaning of some of the concepts involved. There are sharp differences on what constitute valid reasons for actions in these fields; on how the relevant propositions are to be established or even rendered plausible; on who or what constitutes recognised authority for deciding these questions; and there is consequently no consensus on the frontier between valid public criticism and subversion, or between freedom and oppression, and the like. So long as conflicting replies to such questions continue to be given by different schools and thinkers, the prospects of establishing a science in this field, whether empirical or formal, seem remote. Indeed, it seems clear that disagreements about the analysis of value concepts, as often as not, spring from profounder differences, since the notions of, say, rights or justice or liberty will be radically dissimilar for theists and atheists, mechanistic determinists and Christians, Hegelians and empiricists, romantic irrationalists and Marxists, and so forth. It seems no less clear that these differences are not, at least prima facie, either logical or empirical, and have usually and rightly been classified as irreducibly philosophical.

This carries at least one important implication. If we ask the Kantian question 'In what kind of world is political philosophy – the kind of discussion and argument in which it consists – in principle possible?' the answer must be 'Only in a world where ends collide.' In a society dominated by a single goal there could in principle only be arguments about the best means to attain this end – and arguments about means are technical, that is, scientific and empirical in character: they can be settled by experience and observation or whatever other methods are used to discover causes and correlations; they can, at least in principle, be reduced to positive sciences. In such a society no serious questions about political ends or values could arise, only empirical ones about the most effective paths to the goal. And, indeed, something amounting to this was, in effect, asserted by Saint-Simon and Comte; and, on some interpretations of his thought, by Marx also, at any rate after 'prehistory', that is, the class war, is over, and man's true 'history' – the united attack on nature to obtain goods upon whose desirability the whole of society is agreed – has begun. It follows that the only society in which political philosophy in its traditional sense, that is, an enquiry concerned not solely with elucidation of concepts, but with the critical examination of presuppositions and assumptions, and the questioning of the order of priorities and ultimate ends, is possible, is a society in which there is no total acceptance of any single end. There may be a variety of reasons for this: because no single end has been accepted by a sufficient number of persons; because no one end can be regarded as ultimate, since there can, in principle, exist no guarantee that other values may not at some time engage men's reason or their passions; because no unique, final end can be found – inasmuch as men can pursue many distinct ends, none of them means to, or parts of, one another; and so on. Some among these ends may be public or political; nor is there any reason to suppose that all of them must, even in principle, be compatible with one another. Unless political philosophy is confined to the analysis of concepts or expressions, it can be pursued consistently only in a pluralist, or potentially pluralist, society. But since all analysis, however abstract, itself involves a critical approach to the assumptions under analysis, this distinction remains purely academic. Rigid monism is compatible with philosophical analysis only in theory. The plight of philosophy under despotism in our own times provides conclusive concrete evidence for this thesis.

### III

Let me try to make this clearer. If we could construct a society in which it was believed universally (or at least by as many people as believe that the purpose of medicine is to promote or maintain health and are agreed about what constitutes health) that there was only one overriding human purpose: for example, a technocratic society dedicated to the single end of the richest realisation of all human faculties; or a utilitarian society dedicated to the greatest happiness of men; or a Thomist or communist or Platonic or anarchist society, or any other society which is monistic in this sense – then plainly all that would matter would be to find the right roads to the attainment of the universally accepted end.

This statement needs to be qualified in at least two respects. The schema is in the first place artificially over-simplified. In practice, the kind of goal that can command the allegiance of a society – happiness, power, obedience to the divine will, national glory, individual self-realisation, or some other ultimate pattern of life, is so general that it leaves open the question of what kind of lives or conduct incarnate it. No society can be so 'monolithic' that there is no gap between its culminating purpose and the means towards it – a gap filled with secondary ends, penultimate values, which are not means to the final end, but elements in it or expressions of it; and these in their turn incarnate themselves in still more specific purposes at still lower levels, and so on downwards to the particular problem of everyday conduct. 'What is to be done?' is a question which can occur at any level – from the highest to the lowest: doubts and disputes concerning the values involved at any of these levels, and the relationships of these values to one another, can arise at any point.

These questions are not purely technical and empirical, not merely problems about the best means to a given end, nor are they mere questions of logical consistency, that is, formal and deductive; but properly philosophical. To take contemporary examples: What is claimed for integration of blacks and whites in the Southern States of the United States is not that it is a means towards achieving a goal external to itself – social justice or equality – but that it is itself a form of it, a value in the hierarchy of values. Or again 'One man one vote', or the rights of minorities or of colonial territories, are likewise not simply questions of machinery – a particular means of promoting equality which could, in theory, be equally well realised by other means, say by more ingenious voting devices – but, for those who believe in these principles, intrinsic ingredients in the ideal of social equality, and consequently to be pursued as such, and not solely for the sake of their results. It follows that even in a society dominated by a single supreme purpose, questions of what is to be done, especially when the subordinate ends come into conflict, cannot be automatically answered by deductive reasoning from accepted premises, aided by adequate knowledge of facts, as certain thinkers, Aristotle at times, or Bertrand Russell in his middle phase, or a good many Catholic casuists, seem to have assumed.

Moreover, and this is our second qualification, it might well be the case that although the formulae accepted by a society were sacred and immutable, they might carry different – and perhaps incompatible – meanings for different persons and in different situations; philosophical analysis of the relevant concepts might well bring out sharp disagreements. This has been the case conspicuously where the purpose or ideal of a society is expressed in such vague and general terms as the common good, or the fulfilment of the law of God, or rights to life, liberty and the pursuit of happiness, and the like.

Nevertheless, and in spite of these qualifications, the stylised model of a society whose ends are given once and for all, and which is merely concerned with discovery of means, is a useful abstraction. It is useful because it demonstrates that to acknowledge the reality of political questions presupposes a pluralism of values – whether ultimate ones, or on the lower slopes of the hierarchy of values – recognition of which is incompatible with a technocratic or authoritarian, everything-is-either-an-indisputable-end-or-a-means, monistic structure of values. Nor is the monistic situation entirely a figment of theory. In critical situations where deviation from the norm may involve disastrous consequences – in battles, surgical operating rooms, revolutions – the end is wholly concrete, varying interpretations of it are out of place, and all action is conceived as a means towards it alone. It is one of the stratagems of totalitarian regimes to represent all situations as critical emergencies, demanding ruthless elimination of all goals, interpretations, forms of behaviour save for one absolutely specific, concrete, immediate end, binding on everyone, which calls for ends and means so narrow and clearly definable that it is easy to impose sanctions for failing to pursue them.

To find roads is the business of experts. It is therefore reasonable for such a society to put itself into the hands of specialists of tested experience, knowledge, gifts and probity, whose business it is, to use Saint-Simon's simile, to conduct the human caravan to the oasis the reality and desirability of which are recognised by all. In such a society, whatever its other characteristics, we should expect to find intensive study of social causation, especially of what types of political organisation yield the best results, that is, are best at advancing society towards the overriding goal. Political thought in such a society would be fed by all the evidence that can be supplied by the empirical sciences of history, psychology, anthropology, sociology, comparative law, penology, biology, physiology and so forth. The goal (and the best ways of avoiding obstacles to it) may become clearer as the result of careful studies of human thought and behaviour; and its general character must not at any stage be obscure or doubtful; otherwise differences of value judgement will creep into the political sciences as well, and inject what can only be called philosophical issues (or issues of principle) incapable of being resolved by either empirical or formal means. Differences of interpretation of fact – provided these are uncontaminated by disagreements about the ends of life – can be permitted; but if political theory is to be converted into an applied science, what is needed is a single dominant model – like the doctor's model of a healthy body – accepted by the whole, or the greater part, of the society in question. The model will be its 'ideological foundation'. Although such a model is a necessary condition for such a science, it may not, even then, begin to be a sufficient one.

It is at this point that the deep division between the monists and pluralists becomes crucial and conspicuous. On one side stand Platonists and Aristotelians, Stoics and Thomists, positivists and Marxists, and all those who seek to translate political problems into scientific terms. For them human ends are objective: men are what they are, or change in accordance with discoverable laws; and their needs or interests or duties can be established by the correct (naturalistic, or transcendental, or theological) methods. Given that we can penetrate past errors and confusion by true and reliable modes of investigation – metaphysical insight, or the social sciences, or some other dependable instrument – and thereby establish what is good for men and how to effect this, the only unsolved problems will be more or less technical: how to obtain the means for securing these ends, and how to distribute what the technical means provide in the socially and psychologically best manner. This, in the most general terms, is the ideal both of the enlightened atheists of the eighteenth century and the positivists of the nineteenth; of some Marxists of the twentieth, and of those Churches which know the end for which man is made, and know that it is in principle attainable – or at least is such that the road towards it can be discerned – here, below.

On the other side are those who believe in some form of original sin or the impossibility of human perfection, and therefore tend to be sceptical of the empirical attainability of any final solution to the deepest human problems. With them are to be found the sceptics and relativists and also those who believe that the very efforts to solve the problems of one age or culture alter both the men who strive to do so and those for whose benefit the solutions are applied, and thereby create new men and new problems, the character of which cannot today be anticipated, let alone analysed or solved, by men bounded by their own historical horizons. Here too belong the many sects of subjectivists and irrationalists; and in particular those romantic thinkers who hold that ends of action are not discovered, but are created by individuals or cultures or nations as works of art are, so that the answer to the question 'What should we do?' is undiscoverable not because it is beyond our powers to find the answer, but because the question is not one of fact at all, the solution lies not in discovering something which is what it is, whether it is discovered or not – a proposition or formula, an objective good, a principle, a system of values objective or subjective, a relationship between a mind and something non-mental – but resides in action: something which cannot be found, only invented – an act of will or faith or creation obedient to no pre-existent rules or laws or facts. Here too stand those twentieth-century heirs of romanticism, the existentialists, with their belief in the free self-commitment by individuals to actions or forms of life determined by the agent choosing freely; such choice does not take account of objective standards, since these are held to be a form of illusion or 'false consciousness', and the belief in such figments is psychologically traced to fear of freedom – of being abandoned, left to one's own resources – a terror which leads to uncritical acceptance of systems claiming objective authority, spurious theo-logical or metaphysical cosmologies which undertake to guarantee the eternal validity of moral or intellectual rules and principles. Not far from here, too, are fatalists and mystics, as well as those who believe that accident dominates history, and other irrational-ists; but also those indeterminists and those troubled rationalists who doubt the possibility of discovering a fixed human nature obedient to invariant laws; especially those for whom the proposi-tion that the future needs of men and their satisfaction are predictable does not fit into an idea of human nature which entails such concepts as will, choice, effort, purpose, with their presuppo-sition of the perpetual opening of new paths of action – a presupposition which enters into the very definition of what we mean by man. This last is the position adopted by those modern Marxists who, in the face of the cruder and more popular versions of the doctrine, have understood the implications of their own premisses and principles.

IV

Men's beliefs in the sphere of conduct are part of their conception of themselves and others as human beings; and this conception in its turn, whether conscious or not, is intrinsic to their picture of the world. This picture may be complete and coherent, or shadowy or confused, but almost always, and especially in the case of those who have attempted to articulate what they conceive to be the structure of thought or reality, it can be shown to be dominated by one or more models or paradigms: mechanistic, organic, aesthetic, logical, mystical, shaped by the strongest influence of the day – religious, scientific, metaphysical or artistic. This model or paradigm determines the content as well as the form of beliefs and behaviour. A man who, like Aristotle or Thomas Aquinas, believes that all things are definable in terms of their purpose, and that nature is a hierarchy or an ascending pyramid of such purposive entities, is committed to the view that the end of human life consists in self-fulfilment, the character of which must depend on the kind of nature that a man has, and on the place that he occupies in the harmonious activity of the entire universal, self-realising enterprise. It follows that the political philosophy and, more particularly, the diagnosis of political possibilities and purposes of an Aristotelian or a Thomist will *ipso facto* be radically different from that of, let us say, someone who has learned from Hobbes or Spinoza or any modern positivist that there are no purposes in nature, that there are only causal (or functional or statistical) laws, only repetitive cycles of events, which may, however, within limits, be harnessed to fulfil the purposes of men; with the corollary that the pursuit of purposes is itself nothing but a product in the human consciousness of natural processes the laws of which men can neither significantly alter nor account for, if by accounting is meant giving an explanation in terms of the goals of a creator who does not exist, or of a nature of which it is meaningless to say that it pursues purposes – for what is that but to attempt to apply to it a subjective human category, to fall into the fallacy of animism or anthropomorphism?

The case is similar with regard to the issue of freedom and authority. The question 'Why should I obey (rather than do as I like)?' will be (and has been) answered in one way by those who, like Luther, or Bodin, or the Russian Slavophils and many others whose thoughts have been deeply coloured by biblical imagery, conceive of life (although in very different fashions) in terms of the relations of children to their father, and of laws as his commands, where loyalty, obedience, love and the presence of immediate authority are all unquestioned, and surround life from birth to death as real and palpable relationships or agencies. This question will be answered very differently by the followers of, say, Plato or Kant (divided by a whole heaven as these thinkers are), who believe in permanent, impersonal, universal, objective truths, conceived on the model of logical or mathematical or physical laws, by analogy with which their political concepts will be formed. Yet other, and wholly dissimilar, sets of answers will be determined by the great vitalistic conceptions, the model for which is drawn from the facts of growth as conceived in early biology, and for which reality is an organic, qualitative process, not analysable into quantitative units. Other answers again will originate in minds dominated by the image of some central force, thrusting forward in many guises, like some gnostic or Brahmin notion of perpetual self-creation; or be traceable to a concept drawn from artistic activity, in which the universe is seen not as an unconscious quasi-biological process of the spirit or the flesh, but as the endless creation of a demiurge, in which freedom and self-fulfilment lie in the recognition by men of themselves as involved in the purposive process of cosmic creation – a vision fully revealed only to those beings to whom the nature of the world is disclosed, at least fragmentarily, through their own experience as creators (something of this kind emanated from the doctrines of Fichte, Schelling, Carlyle, Nietzsche and other romantic thinkers, as well as Bergson and in places Hegel, and, in his youth, Marx, who were obsessed by aesthetico-biological models). Some among these, anarchists and irrationalists, conceive of reality as freedom from all rules and set ideals – fetters, even when they are self-imposed, upon the free creative spirit – a doctrine of which we have heard, if anything, too much. The model itself may be regarded as the product of historical factors: the social (and psychological) consequences of the development of productive forces, as Marx taught, or the effects in the minds of individuals of purely psychological processes, which Freud and his disciples have investigated. The study of myths, rationalisations, ideologies and obsessive patterns of many kinds has become a great and fertile preoccupation of our time. The fundamental assumption underlying this approach is that the 'ideological' model has not been arrived at by rational methods, but is the product of causal factors; it may disguise itself in rational dress, but, given the historical, or economic, or geographical, or psychological situation, must, in any case, have emerged in one form or another.

For political thinkers, however, the primary question is not that of genesis and conditions of growth, but that of validity and truth: Does the model distort reality? Does it blind us to real differences and similarities and generate other, fictitious, ones? Does it suppress, violate, invent, deceive? In the case of scientific (or common-sense) explanations or hypotheses, the tests of validity include increase in the power of accurate (or more refined) prediction or control of the behaviour of the subject-matter. Is political thought practical and empirical in this sense? Machiavelli and, in differing degrees, Hobbes, Spinoza, Helvétius, Marx at times speak as if this were so. This is one of the interpretations of the famous doctrine of the unity of theory and practice. But is it an adequate account of the purpose or achievements of – to take only the moderns – Locke or Kant or Rousseau or Mill or the liberals, the existentialists, the logical positivists and linguistic analysts and natural law theorists of our own day? And if not, why not?

To return to the notion of models. It is by now a commonplace that the data of observation can be accommodated to almost any theoretical model. Those who are obsessed by one model can accept facts, general propositions, hypotheses and even methods of argument adopted and perfected by those who were dominated by quite a different model. For this reason political theory, if by theories we mean no more than causal or functional hypotheses and explanations designed to account only for what happens – in this case for what men have thought or done or will think or do – can perfectly well be a progressive empirical enquiry, capable of detaching itself from its original metaphysical or ethical foundations, and sufficiently adaptable to preserve through many changes of intellectual climate its own character and development as an independent science. After all, even mathematics, although bound up with – and obstructed by – metaphysics and theology, has nevertheless progressed from the days of the Greeks to our own; so too have the natural sciences, at any rate since the seventeenth century, despite vast upheavals in the general *Weltanschauungen* of the societies in which they were created.

But I should like to say once again that unless political theory is conceived in narrowly sociological terms, it differs from political science or any other empirical enquiry in being concerned with somewhat different fields: namely with such questions as what is specifically human and what is not, and why; whether specific categories, say those of purpose or of belonging to a group or of law, are indispensable to understanding what men are; and so, inevitably, with the source, scope and validity of certain human goals. If this is its task, it cannot, from the very nature of its interests, avoid evaluation; it is thoroughly committed not only to the analysis of, but to conclusions about the validity of, ideas of the good and the bad, the permitted and the forbidden, the harmonious and the discordant which any discussion of liberty or justice or authority or political morality is sooner or later bound to encounter. These central conceptions, moral, political, aesthetic, have altered as the all-inclusive metaphysical models in which they are an essential element have themselves altered. Any change in the central model is a change in the ways in which the data of experience are perceived and interpreted. The degree to which such categories are shot through with evaluation will doubtless depend on their direct connection with human desires and interests. Statements about physical nature can achieve neutrality in this respect; this is more difficult when the data are those of history, and nearly impossible in the case of moral and social life, where the words themselves are inescapably charged with ethical or aesthetic or political content.

To suppose, then, that there have been or could be ages without political philosophy is like supposing that, as there are ages of faith, so there are or could be ages of total disbelief. But this is an absurd notion: there is no human activity without some kind of general outlook. Scepticism, cynicism, refusal to dabble in abstract issues or to question values, hard-boiled opportunism, contempt for theorising, all the varieties of nihilism are, of course, themselves metaphysical and ethical positions, committal attitudes. Whatever else the existentialists have taught us, they have made this fact plain. The idea of a completely *wertfrei* theory (or model) of human action (as contrasted, say, with animal behaviour) rests on a naïve misconception of what objectivity or neutrality in the social studies must be.

V

The notion that a simile or model drawn from one sphere is necessarily misleading when applied to another, and that it is possible to think without such analogies in some direct fashion – 'face to face' with the facts – will not bear criticism. To think is to generalise, to generalise is to compare. To think of one phenomenon or cluster of phenomena is to think in terms of its resemblances to and differences from others. This is by now a hoary platitude. It follows that without parallels and analogies between one sphere and another of thought and action, whether conscious or not, the unity of our experience – our experience itself – would not be possible. All language and thought is, in this sense, necessarily 'metaphorical'. The models, once they are made conscious and explicit, may turn out to be obsolete or misleading. Yet even the most discredited among these models in politics – the social contract, patriarchalism, the organic society and so forth – must have started with some initial validity to have had the influence on thought that they have had.

No analogy powerful enough to govern the concepts of generations of men can have been wholly specious. When Jean Bodin or Herder or the Russian Slavophils or the German sociologist Tönnies transfer the notion of family nexus to political life, they remind us of aspects of relationships between men united by traditional bonds, or bound by common habits and loyalties, which had been misrepresented by the Stoics or Machiavelli or Bentham or Nietzsche or Herbert Spencer. So, too, assimilation of law to a command issued by some constituted authority in any one of the three types of social order distinguished by Max Weber throws some light on the concept of law. Similarly, the social contract is a model which to this day helps to explain something of what it is that men feel to be wrong when a politician pronounces an entire class of the population (say capitalists or blacks) to be outside the community – not entitled to the benefits conferred by the State and its laws. So too Lenin's image of the factory which needs no supervision by coercive policemen after the State has withered away; Maistre's image of the executioner and his victims as the corner-stone of all authority, or of life as a perpetual battlefield in which only terror of supernatural power keeps men from mutual extermination; the State's role as traffic policeman and night-watchman (Lassalle's contemptuous description of the liberal ideal); Locke's analogy of government with trusteeship; the constant use by Burke and the entire romantic movement of metaphors drawn from organic growth and decay; the Soviet model of an army on the march, with its accompanying attributes and values, such as uncritical loyalty, faith in leadership, and military goals such as the need to overtake, destroy, conquer some specified enemy – all these illuminate some types of social experience.

The great distortions, the errors and crimes that have sought their inspiration and justification in such images, are evidence of mechanical extrapolation, or over-enthusiastic application to the whole, of what, at most, explains a sector of life. It is a form of the ancient fallacy of the Ionian philosophers, who wanted a single answer to the question 'What are all things made of?' Everything is not made of water, nor fire, nor is explained by the irresistible march towards the world State or the classless society. The history of thought and culture is, as Hegel showed with great brilliance, a changing pattern of great liberating ideas which inevitably turn into suffocating strait-jackets, and so stimulate their own destruction by new, emancipating, and at the same time enslaving, conceptions. The first step to the understanding of men is the bringing to consciousness of the model or models that dominate and penetrate their thought and action. Like all attempts to make men aware of the categories in which they think, it is a difficult and sometimes painful activity, likely to produce deeply disquieting results. The second task is to analyse the model itself, and this commits the analyst to accepting or modifying or rejecting it, and, in the last case, to providing a more adequate one in its stead.

It is seldom, moreover, that there is only one model that determines our thought; men (or cultures) obsessed by single models are rare, and while they may be more coherent at their strongest, they tend to collapse more violently when, in the end, their concepts are blown up by reality – experienced events, 'inner' or 'outer', that get in the way. Most men wander hither and thither, guided and, at times, hypnotised by more than one model, which they seldom trouble to make consistent, or even fragments of models which themselves form a part of some none too coherent or firm pattern or patterns. To drag them into the light makes it possible to explain them and sometimes to explain them away. The purpose of such analysis is to clarify; but clarification may expose shortcomings and subvert what it describes. That has often and quite justly been charged against political thought, which, at its best, does not disclaim this dangerous power. The ultimate test of the adequacy of the basic pattern by which we think and act is the only test that common sense or the sciences afford, namely, whether it fits in with the general lines on which we think and communicate; and if some among these in turn are called into question, then the final measure is, as it always must be, direct confrontation with the concrete data of observation and introspection which these concepts and categories and habits order and render intelligible. In this sense, political theory, like any other form of thought that deals with the real world, rests on empirical experience, though in what sense of 'empirical' still remains to be discussed.

## VI

When one protests (as we ourselves did above) that the application of such (social or political) models or combinations of overlapping models, which at most hold a part of our experience, causes distortion when applied beyond it, how do we set about justifying this charge? How do we know that the result is distortion? We usually think this because the universal application of a simile or a pattern – say that of the general will, or the organic society, or basic structure and superstructure, or the liberating myth – seems to those who reject it to ignore something that they know directly of human nature and thereby to do violence to what we are, or what we know, by forcing it into the Procrustean bed of some rigid dogma; that is to say, we protest in the name of our own view of what men are, have been, could be.

How do we know these things? How do we know what is and what is not an adequate programme for human beings in given historical circumstances? Is this knowledge sociological, or psychological? Is it empirical at all, or metaphysical and even theological? How do we argue with those whose notions are different from ours? Hume, Helvétius, Condorcet, Comte are clear that such knowledge must be based on empirical data and the methods of the natural sciences; all else is imaginary and worthless.

The temptation to accept this simple solution was (and is) very great. The conflict of the rival explanations (or models) of social and individual life had, by the late eighteenth century, grown to be a scandal. If one examines what answers were offered, let us say, between the death of Newton and the birth of Darwin, to a central political question – why anyone should obey anyone else – the babel of voices is appalling, perhaps the most confused in recorded history. Some said that I should obey those rules or institutions submission to which alone would fulfil my nature, with the rider that my needs and the correct path to their satisfaction were clear only to those privileged observers who grasped at least some part of the great hierarchy of being. Others said that I should obey this or that authority or law because only in that way could I (without aid of experts) fulfil my 'true' nature, or be able to fit into a harmonious whole. Some supposed this whole to be static; others taught that it was dynamic, but could not agree on whether it moved in recurrent cycles, or a straight, or spiral, or irregular evolutionary line, or by a series of oscillations leading to 'dialectical' explosions; or again, whether it was teleological or functional or causally determined.

Some conceived the ultimate universal pattern in mechanistic, others in organic, others still in aesthetic terms. There were those who said that men must obey because they had promised to do so, or others had promised on their behalf; or that they were behaving as if they had promised and this was tantamount to having promised, whether they admitted this or no; or, if this seemed unconvincing, that it were best that they should behave as if they had so promised, since otherwise no one would know where he was and chaos would ensue. Some told men to obey because they would be happier if they did, or because the majority, or all men, would be happier; or because it was God's will that they should obey, or the will of the sovereign, or of the majority, or of the best or wisest, or of history, or of their State, or their race, or their culture, or their Church.

They were told also that they must obey because the natural law laid down that they must do so, but there were differences about how the precepts of natural law were to be discovered, whether by rational or by empirical means, or by intuition, and again, by common men or only by the experts; the experts in their turn were identified by some with natural scientists, by others with specialists in metaphysics or theology, or perhaps in some other discipline – mass psychology, mystical revelation, the laws of history, of economics, of natural evolution, of a new synthesis of all or some of these. Some people supposed that truth in these matters could be discovered by a faculty which they called moral sense, or common sense, or the perception of the fitness of things, or that it consisted in what they had been told by their parents or nurses, or was to be found in accepted views which it was mere perversity to question, or came from one or other of many sources of this sort which Bentham mocks at so gaily and effectively. Some (and perhaps these have always been the majority) felt it to be in some degree subversive to raise such questions at all.

This situation caused justified indignation in a country dominated by free enquiry and its greatest triumph, Newtonian science. Surely this monstrous muddle could be cleared away by the strong new broom of scientific method – a similar chaos had, after all, not so long ago prevailed in the natural sciences too. Galileo and Newton – and the light of reason and experiment – had silenced for ever the idle chatter of the ignoramus, the dark muttering of the metaphysician, the thunder of the preacher, the hysterical shrieks of the obscurantist. All genuine questions were questions of discoverable fact – *calculemus* was to be the motto of the new method;[1] all problems must be so reformulated that inspection of the facts – aided by mathematical techniques – would answer them decisively, with a clear, universally valid, empirical statement of verifiable fact.

VII

Nevertheless, attempts by the *philosophes* of the eighteenth century to turn philosophy, and particularly moral and political philosophy, into an empirical science, into individual and social psychology, did not succeed. They failed over politics because our political notions are part of our conception of what it is to be human, and this is not solely a question of fact, as facts are conceived by the natural sciences; nor the product of conscious reflection upon the specific discoveries of anthropology or sociology or psychology, although all these are relevant and indeed indispensable to an adequate notion of the nature of man in general, or of particular groups of men in particular circumstances. Our conscious idea of man – of how men differ from other entities, of what is human and what is not human, or inhuman – involves the use of some among the basic categories in terms of which we perceive and order and interpret data. To analyse the concept of man is to recognise these categories for what they are. To do this is to realise that they are

[1] Cf. p. 134 below, note 1.

categories, that is, that they are not themselves subjects for scientific hypotheses about the data which they order. The analogy with the sciences which dominates the pre-Kantian thinkers of the eighteenth century – Locke, Hume and Condillac, for example – is a typical misapplication of a model that works in one sphere to a region where it will obscure at least as much as it illuminates.

Let me try to make this more specific. When the theological and metaphysical models of the Middle Ages were swept away by the sciences of the seventeenth and eighteenth centuries, they disappeared largely because they could not compete with new disciplines in describing, predicting, controlling the contents of the external world. To the extent to which man was regarded as an object in material nature the sciences of man – psychology, anthropology, economics, sociology and so on – began to supplant their theologico-metaphysical predecessors. The questions of the philosophers were affected by this: some were answered or rendered obsolete; but some remained unanswered. The new human sciences studied men's actual habits; they promised, and in some cases provided, analyses of what men said, wanted, admired, abhorred; they were prepared to supply empirical evidence for this, or experimental demonstration; but their efforts to solve normative problems were less successful. They tried to reduce questions of value to questions of fact – of what caused what kind of men to feel or behave as they did in various circumstances. But when Kant or Herder or Dostoevsky or Marx duly rejected the Encyclopaedists' answers, the charge against them was not solely that of faulty observation or invalid inference; it was that of a failure to recognise what it is to be a man, that is, failure to take into account the nature of the framework – the basic categories – in terms of which we think and act and assume others to think and act, if communication between us is to work.

In other words, the problem the solutions of which were found insufficient is not in the usual sense empirical, and certainly not formal, but something that is not adequately described by either term. When Rousseau (whether he understood him correctly or not) rejected Hobbes's account of political obligation on the ground that Hobbes seemed to him to explain it by mere fear of superior force, Rousseau claimed not that Hobbes had not seen certain relevant empirical, psychologically discoverable, facts, nor that he had argued incorrectly from what he had seen – but that his account was in conflict with what, in thinking of human beings as human, and distinguishing them, even the most degraded among them, not only in explicit thought, but in our feelings and in our action, from beings that we regard as inhuman or non-human, we all know men to be. His argument is not that the facts used to construct Hobbes's model had gaps in them, but that the model was inadequate in principle; it was inadequate not because this or that psychological or sociological correlation had been missed out, but because it was based on a failure to understand what we mean by motive, purpose, value, personality and the like.

When Kant breaks with the naturalistic tradition, or Marx rejects the political morality of Bentham, or Tolstoy expresses a low opinion of the doctrines of Marx, they are not complaining merely of empirical ignorance or poor logic or insufficient experimental evidence, or internal incoherence. They denounce their adversaries mainly for not understanding what men are and which relationships between them – or between them and outside forces – make them men; they complain of blindness not to the transient aspects of such relations, but to those constant characteristics (such as discrimination of right from good for Kant, or, for Marx, systematic self-transmutation by their own labour) that they regard as fundamental to the notion of man as such. Their criticisms relate to the adequacy of the categories in terms of which we discuss men's ends or duties or interests, the permanent framework in terms of which, not about which, ordinary empirical disagreements can arise.

What are these categories? How do we discover them? If not empirically, then by what means? How universal and unchanging are they? How do they enter into and shape the models and paradigms in terms of which we think and respond? Do we discover what they are by attention to thought, or action, or unconscious processes, and how do we reconcile these various sources of knowledge? These are characteristically philosophical questions, since they are questions about the all but permanent ways in which we think, decide, perceive, judge, and not about the data of experience – the items themselves. The test of the adequate working of the methods, analogies, models which operate in discovering and classifying the behaviour of these empirical data (as natural science and common sense do) is ultimately empirical: it is the degree of their success in forming a coherent and enduring conceptual system.

To apply these models and methods to the framework itself by means of which we perceive and think about them is a major fallacy, by the analysis of which Kant transformed philosophy. In politics it was committed (by Hume and Russell, for example) when enquiry into the empirical characteristics of men was confounded with the analysis of the notion of man (or 'self' or 'observer' or 'moral agent' or 'individual' or 'soul') in terms of which the empirical characteristics were themselves collected and described. Kant supposed these categories to be discoverable a priori. We need not accept this; this was an unwarranted conclusion from the valid perception that there exist central features of our experience that are invariant and omnipresent, or at least much less variable than the vast variety of its empirical characteristics, and for that reason deserve to be distinguished by the name of categories. This is evident enough in the case of the external world: the three-dimensionality of (psychological, common-sense) space, for example, or the solidity of things in it, or the 'irreversibility' of the time-order, are among the most familiar and inalienable kinds of characteristics in terms of which we think and act. Empirical sciences of these properties do not exist, not because they exhibit no regularities – on the contrary they are the very paradigm of the concept of regularity itself – but because they are presupposed in the very language in which we formulate empirical experience. That is why it seems absurd to ask for evidence for their existence, and imaginary examples are enough to exhibit their structure; for they are presupposed in our commonest acts of thought or decision; and where imaginary examples are, for the purpose of an enquiry, as good as, or even better than, empirical data drawn from actual experience, we may be sure that the enquiry is not, in the normal sense, an empirical one. Such permanent features are to be found in the moral and political and social worlds too: less stable and universal, perhaps, than in the physical one, but just as indispensable for any kind of intersubjective communication, and therefore for thought and action. An enquiry that proceeds by examples, and is therefore not scientific, but not formal, that is, deductive, either, is most likely to be philosophical.

There is an ultimate sense, of course, in which such facts as that space has three dimensions, or that men are beings who demand reasons or make choices, are simply given: brute facts and not a priori truths; it is not absurd to suppose that things could have been otherwise. But if they had been (or will one day be) other than they are now, our entire conceptual apparatus – thought, volition, feeling, language – and therefore our very nature, would have been (or will be) different in ways that it is impossible or difficult to describe with the concepts and words available to us as we are today. Political categories (and values) are a part of this all but inescapable web of ways of living, acting and thinking, a network liable to change only as a result of radical changes in reality, or through dissociation from reality on the part of individuals, that is to say, madness.

VIII

The basic categories (with their corresponding concepts) in terms of which we define men – such notions as society, freedom, sense of time and change, suffering, happiness, productivity, good and bad, right and wrong, choice, effort, truth, illusion (to take them wholly at random) – are not matters of induction and hypothesis. To think of someone as a human being is *ipso facto* to bring all these notions into play; so that to say of someone that he is a man, but that choice, or the notion of truth, mean nothing to him, would be eccentric: it would clash with what we mean by 'man' not as a matter of verbal definition (which is alterable at will), but as intrinsic to the way in which we think, and (as a matter of 'brute' fact) evidently cannot but think.

This will hold of values too (among them political ones) in terms of which men are defined. Thus, if I say of someone that he is kind or cruel, loves truth or is indifferent to it, he remains human in either case. But if I find a man to whom it literally makes no difference whether he kicks a pebble or kills his family, since either would be an antidote to *ennui* or inactivity, I shall not be disposed, like consistent relativists, to attribute to him merely a different code of morality from my own or that of most men, or declare that we disagree on essentials, but shall begin to speak of insanity and inhumanity; I shall be inclined to consider him mad, as a man who thinks he is Napoleon is mad; which is a way of saying that I do not regard such a being as being fully a man at all. It is cases of this kind, which seem to make it clear that ability to recognise universal – or almost universal – values enters into our analysis of such fundamental concepts as 'man', 'rational', 'sane', 'natural' – which are usually thought of as descriptive and not evaluative – that lie at the basis of modern translations into empirical terms of the kernel of truth in the old a priori natural law doctrines. It is considerations such as these, urged by neo-Aristotelians and the followers of the later doctrines of Wittgenstein, that have shaken the faith of some devoted empiricists in the complete logical gulf between descriptive statements and statements of value, and have cast doubt on the celebrated distinction derived from Hume.

Extreme cases of this sort are of philosophical importance because they make it clear that such questions are not answered by either empirical observation or formal deduction. Hence those who confine themselves to observations of human behaviour and empirical hypotheses about it – psychologists, sociologists, historians – however profound and original they may be, are not, as such, political theorists, even though they may have much to say that is crucial in the field of political philosophy. That is why we do not consider such dedicated empiricists as the students, say, of the formation and behaviour of parties or élites or classes, or of the methods and consequences of various types of democratic procedure, to be political philosophers or social theorists in the larger sense.

Such men are in the first place students of facts, and aspire to formulate hypotheses and laws, like the natural scientists. Yet as a rule these thinkers cannot go any further: they tend to analyse men's social and political ideas in the light of some overriding belief of their own – for example, that the purpose of all life is or should be the service of God, however interpreted; or on the contrary that it is the pursuit of experimentally discoverable individual or collective satisfaction; or that it lies in the self-realisation of a historical (or psychological or aesthetic) pattern, grasp of which alone can explain men to themselves and give meaning to their thoughts and actions; or, on the contrary, that there exists no human purpose; or that men cannot but seek conflicting ends; or cannot (without ceasing to be human) avoid activities that must end in self-frustration, so that the very notion of a final solution is an absurdity. In so far as it is such fundamental conceptions of man that determine political doctrines (and who will deny that political problems, for example about what men and groups can or should be or do, depend logically and directly on what man's nature is taken to be?), it is clear that those who are governed by these integrating syntheses bring to their study something other than empirical data.

If we examine the models, paradigms, conceptual structures that govern various outlooks, whether consciously or not, and compare the various concepts and categories involved with respect, for example, to their internal consistency or their explanatory force, then what we are engaged upon is not psychology or sociology or logic or epistemology, but moral or social or political theory, or all these at once, depending on whether we confine ourselves to individuals, or to groups, or to the particular types of human arrangements that are classified as political, or deal with them all in one. No amount of careful empirical observation and bold and fruitful hypothesis will explain to us what those men see who see the State as a divine institution, or what their words mean and how they relate to reality; nor what those believe who tell us that the State was sent upon us only for our sins; or those who say that it is a school through which we must go before we are adult and free and can dispense with it; or that it is a work of art; or a utilitarian device; or the incarnation of natural law; or a committee of the ruling class; or the highest stage of the self-developing human spirit; or a piece of criminal folly. But unless we understand (by an effort of imaginative insight such as novelists usually possess in a higher degree than logicians) what notions of man's nature (or absence of them) are incorporated in these political outlooks, what in each case is the dominant model, we shall not understand our own or any human society: neither the conceptions of reason and nature which governed Stoics or Thomists or govern the European Christian Democrats today; nor the very different image at the heart of the holy war of the national-Marxist movements in Africa or in Asia; nor the very different notions that animate the liberal and democratic compromises of the West.

It is by now a platitude to say that understanding human thought and action is in large measure understanding what problems and perplexities they strive with. When these problems, whether empirical or formal, have been conceived in terms of models of reality so ancient, widely accepted and stable that we use them to this day, we understand the problems and difficulties and the attempted solutions without explicit reference to the governing categories; for these, being common to us and to cultures remote from us, do not obtrude themselves on us; stay, as it were, out of sight. In other cases (and this is conspicuously true of politics) the models have not stood still: some of the notions of which they were compounded are no longer familiar. Yet unless we have the knowledge and imagination to transpose ourselves into states of mind dominated by the now discarded or obsolescent model, the thoughts and actions that had them at their centre will remain opaque to us. It is failure to perform this difficult operation that marks much of the history of ideas, and turns it into either a superficial literary exercise, or a dead catalogue of strange, at times almost incomprehensible, errors and confusions.

This may not matter too much in the empirical and formal disciplines, where the test of a belief is, or should be, verification or logical coherence; and where one can accept the latest solutions, and reject the falsified or incoherent solutions of the past without bothering (if one is incurious) to understand why they were ever held. But philosophical doctrines are not established or discredited in this final fashion; for they are concerned with – indeed they owe their existence to – problems that cannot be settled in these ways. They are not concerned with specific facts, but with ways of looking at them; they do not consist of first-order propositions concerning the world. They are second- or higher-order statements about whole classes of descriptions of, or responses to, the world and man's activities in it; and these are in turn determined by models, networks of categories, descriptive, evaluative and hybrids compounded of the two, in which the two functions cannot be disentangled even in thought – categories which, if not eternal and universal, are far more stable and widespread than those of the sciences; sufficiently continuous, indeed, to constitute a common world which we share with medieval and classical thinkers.

Ionian cosmology, the biology of Aristotle, Stoic logic, Arab algebra, Cartesian physics may be of interest to historical specialists, but need not occupy the minds of physicists or biologists or mathematicians who are solely interested in the discovery of new truth. In these studies there is genuine progress: what is past is largely obsolete. But the political philosophy of Plato or Aristotle or Machiavelli, the moral views of the Hebrew prophets or of the Gospels or of the Roman jurists or of the medieval Church – these, whether in the original or in the works of their modern expositors, are incomparably more intelligible and more relevant to our own preoccupations than the sciences of antiquity. The subject-matter of these disciplines – the most general characteristics of men as such, that is, as beings engaged in moral or social or spiritual activities – seems to present problems which preserve a considerable degree of continuity and similarity from one age and culture to another. Methods of dealing with them vary greatly; but none has yet achieved so decisive a victory as to sweep all its rivals into oblivion. The inadequate models of political thought evidently have, by and large, perished and been forgotten; the great illuminating models are still controversial today, stir us still to adherence or criticism or violent indignation.

We might take as examples Karl Popper's denunciation of Plato's political theory or Irving Babbitt's philippics against Rousseau, Simone Weil's violent distaste for the morality of the Old Testament, or the frequent attacks made today on eighteenth-century positivism or 'scientism' in political ethics.[1] Some of the classical constructions are in conflict with one another, but, inasmuch as each rests on a vivid vision of permanent human attributes and is capable of satisfying some enquiring minds in each generation, no matter how different the circumstances of time and place, the models of Plato, or of Aristotle, or of Judaism, Christianity, Kantian liberalism, romanticism, historicism all survive and contend with each other today in a variety of guises. If men or circumstances alter radically, or new empirical knowledge is gained which will revolutionise our conception of man, then certainly some of these edifices will cease to be relevant and will be forgotten like the ethics and metaphysics of the Egyptians or the Incas. But so long as men are as they are, the debate will continue in terms set by these visions and others like them: each will gain or lose in influence as events force this or that aspect of men into prominence. One thing alone is certain, that save to those who understand and even feel what a philosophical question is, how it differs from an empirical or formal question (although this difference need not be explicitly present to the mind, and overlapping or borderline questions are frequent enough), the answers – in this case the main political doctrines of the West – may well seem intellectual fancies, detached philosophical speculations and constructions without much relation to acts or events.

Only those who can to some degree re-enact within themselves the states of mind of men tormented by questions to which these theories claim to be solutions, or at any rate the states of mind of those who may accept the solutions uncritically but would, without them, fall into a state of insecurity and anxiety – only these are capable of grasping what part philosophical views, and especially political doctrines, have played in history, at any rate in the West. The work of the logicians or physicists of the past has

---

[1] What thinker today entertains violent emotions towards the errors of Cartesian physicists or medieval mapmakers?

receded because it has been superseded. But there is something absurd in the suggestion that we reject Plato's political doctrines or Kant's aesthetics or ethics because they have been 'superseded'. This consideration alone should prevent facile assimilation of the two cases. It may be objected to this line of argument that we look upon old ethical or political doctrines as still worth discussion because they are part of our cultural tradition – that if Greek philosophy and biblical ethics had not been an intrinsic element in Western education, they would by now have been as remote from us as early Chinese speculation. But this merely takes the argument a step backwards: it is true that if the general characteristics of our normal experience had altered radically enough – through a revolution in our knowledge or some natural upheaval which altered our reactions – these ancient categories would probably by now have been felt to be as obsolete as those of Hammurabi or the epic of Gilgamesh. That this is not so is doubtless due partly to the fact that our experience is itself organised and 'coloured' by ethical or political categories that we have inherited from our ancestors, ancient spectacles through which we are still looking. But the spectacles would long ago have caused us to blunder and stumble and would have given way to others, or been modified out of recognition as our physical and biological and mathematical spectacles have been, if they had not still performed their task more or less adequately: which argues a certain degree of continuity in at least two millennia of moral and political consciousness.

IX

We may be told that whatever we may maintain about the sources, motives or justification of our beliefs, the content of what adherents of divers philosophies believe tends to be similar if they belong to the same social or economic or cultural milieu or have other – psychological or physiological – characteristics in common. The English philosophers T. H. Green and J. S. Mill preached philosophically contradictory doctrines: Green was a quasi-Hegelian metaphysician, Mill a Humean empiricist, yet their political conclusions were close to one another's; both were humane Victorian liberals with a good deal of sympathy for socialism. This, we shall further be told, was because men are conditioned to believe what they believe by objective historical factors – their social position, or the class structure of their society and their position in it, although their own (erroneous) rationalisation of their beliefs may be as widely different as those of Mill and Green.

So, too, it has been said, the outlook – the 'operational ideas' – of Fascists and Communists display a surprising degree of similarity, given the extreme opposition and incompatibility of the official axioms from which these movements logically start. Hence the plausibility of some of the methods of the 'sociology of knowledge', whether Marxist or Paretian or psychoanalytic, and of the various eclectic forms which, in the hands of Weber, Mannheim and others, this instrument has acquired. Certainly such theorists have cast light on the obscure roots of our beliefs. We may be conditioned to believe what we believe irrationally, by circumstances mainly beyond our control, and perhaps beyond our knowledge too. But whatever may in fact causally determine our beliefs, it would be a gratuitous abdication of our powers of reasoning – based on a confusion of natural science with philosophical enquiry – not to want to know what we believe, and for what reason, what the metaphysical implications of such beliefs are, what their relation is to other types of belief, what criteria of value and truth they involve, and so what reason we have to think them true or valid. Rationality rests on the belief that one can think and act for reasons that one can understand, and not merely as the product of occult causal factors which breed 'ideologies', and cannot, in any case, be altered by their victims. So long as rational curiosity exists – a desire for justification and explanation in terms of motives and reasons, and not only of causes or functional correlations or statistical probabilities – political theory will not wholly perish from the earth, however many of its rivals, such as sociology, philosophical analysis, social psychology, political science, economics, jurisprudence, semantics, may claim to have dispelled its imaginary realm.

It is a strange paradox that political theory should seem to lead so shadowy an existence at a time when, for the first time in history, literally the whole of mankind is violently divided by issues the reality of which is, and has always been, the sole *raison d'être* of this branch of study. But this, we may be sure, is not the end of the story. Neo-Marxism, neo-Thomism, nationalism, historicism, existentialism, anti-essentialist liberalism and socialism, transpositions of doctrines of natural rights and natural law into empirical terms, discoveries made by skilful application of models derived from economic and related techniques to political behaviour, and the collisions, combinations and consequences in action of these ideas, indicate not the death of a great tradition, but, if anything, new and unpredictable developments.

# 'FROM HOPE AND FEAR SET FREE'

DOES KNOWLEDGE always liberate? The view of the classical Greek philosophers, shared by much, though perhaps not all, Christian theology, is that it does. 'And ye shall know the truth, and the truth shall make you free.'[1] Ancient Stoics and most modern rationalists are at one with Christian teaching on this issue. According to this view freedom[2] is the unimpeded fulfilment of my true nature – unimpeded by obstacles whether external or internal. In the case of the passage from which I have quoted, the freedom in question (I follow Festugière's interpretation on this point) is freedom from sin, that is, from false beliefs about God, nature and myself, which obstruct my understanding. The freedom is that of self-realisation or self-direction – the realisation by the individual's own activity of the true purposes of his nature (however such purposes or such natures are defined), which is frustrated by his misconceptions about the world and man's place in it. If to this I add the corollary that I am rational – that is, that I can understand or know (or at least form a correct belief about) why I do what I do, that is, distinguish between acting (which entails making choices, forming intentions, pursuing goals) and merely behaving (that is, being acted upon by causes the operations of which may be unknown to me or unlikely to be affected by my wishes or attitudes) – then it will follow that knowledge of the relevant facts – about the external world, other persons and my own nature – will remove impediments to my policies that are due to ignorance and delusion.

Philosophers (and theologians, dramatists, poets) have differed widely about the character of man's nature and its ends; what kind

[1] Gospel according to St John, chapter 8, verse 32.
[2] I propose to use the words 'freedom' and 'liberty' interchangeably throughout.

and degree of control of the external world is needed in order to achieve fulfilment, complete or partial, of this nature and its ends; whether such a general nature or objective ends exist at all; and where the frontier dividing the external world of matter and non-rational creatures from active agents is to be found. Some thinkers have supposed that such fulfilment was (or had once been, or would one day be) possible on earth, others have denied this. Some maintained that the ends of men were objective and capable of being discovered by special methods of enquiry, but disagreed on what these were: empirical or a priori; intuitive or discursive; scientific or purely reflective; public or private; confined to specially gifted or fortunate enquirers, or in principle open to any man. Others believed that such ends were subjective, or determined by physical or psychological or social factors, which differed widely. Again, Aristotle, for example, supposed that if external conditions were too unfavourable – if a man suffered Priam's misfortunes – this made self-fulfilment, the proper realisation of one's nature, impossible. On the other hand the Stoics and Epicureans held that complete rational self-control could be achieved by a man whatever his external circumstances, since all that he needed was a sufficient degree of detachment from human society and the external world; to this they added the optimistic belief that the degree sufficient for self-fulfilment was in principle perfectly attainable by anyone who consciously sought independence and autonomy, that is, escape from being the plaything of external forces which he could not control.

Among the assumptions that are common to all these views are:

(i) that things and persons possess natures – definite structures independent of whether or not they are known;

(ii) that these natures or structures are governed by universal and unalterable laws;

(iii) that these structures and laws are, at least in principle, all knowable; and that knowledge of them will automatically keep men from stumbling in the dark and dissipating effort on policies which, given the facts – the nature of things and persons and the laws that govern them – are doomed to failure.

According to this doctrine men are not self-directed and therefore not free when their behaviour is caused by misdirected emotions – for example, fears of non-existent entities, or hatreds due not to a rational perception of the true state of affairs but to illusions, fantasies, results of unconscious memories and forgotten wounds. Rationalisations and ideologies, on this view, are false explanations of behaviour the true roots of which are unknown or ignored or misunderstood; and these in their turn breed further illusions, fantasies and forms of irrational and compulsive behaviour. True liberty consists, therefore, in self-direction: a man is free to the degree that the true explanation of his activity lies in the intentions and motives of which he is conscious, and not in some hidden psychological or physiological condition that would have produced the same effect, that is, the same behaviour (posing as choice), whatever explanation or justification the agent attempted to produce. A rational man is free if his behaviour is not mechanical, and springs from motives and is intended to fulfil purposes of which he is, or can at will be, aware; so that it is true to say that having these intentions and purposes is a necessary, if not sufficient, condition for his behaviour. The unfree man is like someone who is drugged or hypnotised: whatever explanations he may himself advance for his behaviour, it remains unaltered by any change in his ostensible, overt motives and policies; we consider him to be in the grip of forces over which he has no control, not free, when it is plain that his behaviour will be predictably the same whatever reasons he advances for it.

To put matters in this way is to identify rationality and freedom, or at least to go a long way towards it. Rational thought is thought the content or, at least, the conclusions of which obey rules and principles and are not merely items in a causal or random sequence; rational behaviour is behaviour which (at least in principle) can be explained by the actor or observer in terms of motives, intentions, choices, reasons, rules, and not solely of natural laws – causal or statistical, or 'organic' or others of the same logical type (whether explanations in terms of motives, reasons and the like and those in terms of causes, probabilities and so on are 'categorially' different and cannot in principle clash or indeed be relevant to one another is of course a crucial question; but I do not wish to raise it here). To call a man a thief is *pro tanto* to attribute rationality to him: to call him a kleptomaniac is to deny it of him. If degrees of a man's freedom directly depend on (or are identical with) the extent of his knowledge of the roots of his behaviour, then a kleptomaniac who knows himself to be one is, to that extent, free; he may be unable to stop stealing or even to try to do so; but his recognition of this, because he is now – so it is maintained – in a position to choose whether to try to resist this compulsion (even if he is bound to fail) or to let it take its course, renders him not merely more rational (which seems indisputable), but more free.

But is this always so? Is awareness of a disposition or causal characteristic on my part identical with – or does it necessarily provide me with – the power to manipulate or alter it? There is, of course, a clear but platitudinous sense in which all knowledge increases freedom in some respect: if I know that I am liable to epileptic fits, or feelings of class consciousness, or the spell-binding effect of certain kinds of music, I can – in some sense of 'can' – plan my life accordingly; whereas if I do not know this, I cannot do so; I gain some increase in power and, to that extent, in freedom. But this knowledge may also decrease my power in some other respect: if I anticipate an epileptic fit or the onset of some painful, or even agreeable, emotion, I may be inhibited from some other free exercise of my power, or be precluded from some other experience – I may be unable to continue to write poetry, or understand the Greek text which I am reading, or think about philosophy, or get up from my chair: I may, in other words, pay for an increase of power and freedom in one region by a loss of them in another. (I propose to return to this point later, in a slightly different context.)[1] Nor am I necessarily rendered able to control my fits of epilepsy or of class consciousness or addiction to Indian music by recognising their incidence. If by knowledge is meant what the classical authors meant by it – knowledge of facts (not knowledge of 'what to do', which may be a disguised way of stating not that something is the case, but a commitment to certain ends or values, or of expressing, not describing, a decision to act in a certain fashion); if, in other words, I claim to have the kind of knowledge about myself that I might have about others, then even though my sources may be better or my certainty greater, such self-knowledge, it seems to me, may or may not add to the sum total of my freedom. The question is empirical: and the answer depends on specific circumstances. From the fact that every gain in knowledge liberates me in some respect, it does not follow, for the reasons given above, that it will necessarily add to the total sum of freedom that I enjoy: it may, by taking with one hand more than it gives with the other, decrease it.

[1] See p. 113 below.

But there is a more radical criticism of this view to be considered. To say that one is free only if one understands oneself (even if this is not a sufficient condition of freedom) presupposes that we have a self to be understood – that there is a structure correctly described as human nature which is what it is, obeys the laws that it does, and is an object of natural study. This has itself been questioned, notably by certain existentialist philosophers. By these it is maintained that far more is a matter of human choice than has usually and complacently been supposed. Since choice involves responsibility, and some human beings at most times, and most human beings at some times, wish to avoid this burden, there is a tendency to look for excuses and alibis. For this reason men tend to attribute too much to the unavoidable operations of natural or social laws – for instance, to the workings of the unconscious mind, or unalterable psychological reflexes, or the laws of social evolution. Critics who belong to this school (which owes much both to Hegel and Marx and to Kierkegaard) say that some notorious impediments to liberty – say, the social pressures of which J. S. Mill made so much – are not objective forces the existence and effects of which are independent of human wishes or activities or alterable only by means not open to isolated individuals – by revolutions or radical reforms that cannot be engineered at the individual's will. What is maintained is the contrary: that I need not be bullied by others or pressed into conformity by schoolmasters or friends or parents; need never be affected in some way that I cannot help by what priests or colleagues or critics or social groups or classes think or do. If I am so affected, it is because I choose it. I am insulted when I am mocked as a hunchback, a Jew, a black, or unnerved by the feeling that I am suspected of being a traitor, only if I choose to accept the opinion – the valuation – of hunchbacks or race or treason of those by whose views and attitudes I am dominated. But I can always choose to ignore or resist this – to snap my fingers at such views and codes and outlooks; and then I am free.

This is the very doctrine, though built on different premisses, of those who drew the portrait of the Stoic sage. If I choose to knuckle under to public sentiment or the values of this or that group or person, the responsibility is mine and not that of outside forces – forces, personal or impersonal, to whose allegedly irresistible influence I attribute my behaviour, attribute it only too eagerly in order to escape blame or self-blame. My behaviour, my character, my personality, according to these critics, is not a mysterious substance or the referent of a pattern of hypothetical general (causal) propositions, but a pattern of choices or of failures to choose which themselves represent a kind of choice to let events take their course, not to assert myself as an active agent. If I am self-critical and face the facts, I may find that I shuffle off my responsibilities too easily.

This applies both in the realms of theory and in those of practical affairs. Thus, if I am a historian, my view of the factors significant in history may well be profoundly affected by my desire to glorify or detract from the reputation of individuals or classes – an act, so it is argued, of free valuation on my part. Once I am aware of this, I can select and judge as I will: 'the facts' never speak – only I, the chooser, the evaluator, the judge, can do so, and do so according to my own sweet will, in accordance with principles, rules, ideals, prejudices, feelings which I can freely view, examine, accept, reject. If I minimise the human cost of a given political or economic policy, in the past or present or future, I shall upon examination often find that I do so because I disapprove of or bear a grudge against the critics or opponents of those who conduct the policy. If I seek to explain away, whether to others or to myself, some unworthy act on my part, on the ground that something – the political or military situation, or my emotion or inner state – was 'too much for me', then I am cheating myself, or others, or both. Action is choice; choice is free commitment to this or that way of behaving, living, and so on; the possibilities are never fewer than two: to do or not to do; be or not be. Hence, to attribute conduct to the unalterable laws of nature is to misdescribe reality: it is not true to experience, verifiably false; and to perpetrate such falsifica-tion – as most philosophers and ordinary men have done and are constantly doing – is to choose to evade responsibility for making choices or failing to make them, to choose to deny that to drift down a current of accepted opinion and behave semi-mechanically is itself a kind of choice – a free act of surrender; this is so because it is always possible, though sometimes painful, to ask myself what it is that I really believe, want, value, what it is that I am doing, living for; and having answered as well as I am able, to continue to act in a given fashion or alter my behaviour.

I do not wish to deny that all this needs saying: that to look on the future as already structured, solid with future facts, is concep-tually fallacious; that the tendency to account both for the whole of our own behaviour and that of others in terms of forces regarded as being too powerful to resist is empirically mistaken, in that it goes beyond what is warranted by the facts. In its extreme form this doctrine does away with determination at one blow: I am determined by my own choices; to believe otherwise – say, in determinism or fatalism or chance – is itself a choice, and a particularly craven one at that. Yet it is surely arguable that this very tendency itself is a symptom of man's specific nature. Such tendencies as looking on the future as unalterable – a symmetrical analogue of the past – or the quest for excuses, escapist fantasies, flights from responsibility, are themselves psychological data. To be self-deceived is *ex hypothesi* something that I cannot have chosen consciously, although I may have consciously chosen to act in a manner likely to produce this result, without shrinking from this consequence. There is a difference between choices and compulsive behaviour, even if the compulsion is itself the result of an earlier uncompelled choice. The illusions from which I suffer determine the field of my choice; self-knowledge – destruction of the illusions – will alter this field, make it more possible for me to choose genuinely rather than suppose that I have chosen something when, in fact, it has (as it were) chosen me. But in the course of distinguishing between true and counterfeit acts of choice (however this is done – however I discover that I have seen through illusions), I nevertheless discover that I have an ineluctable nature. There are certain things that I cannot do. I cannot (logically) remain rational or sane and believe no general propositions, or remain sane and use no general terms; I cannot retain a body and cease to gravitate. I can perhaps in some sense try to do these things, but to be rational entails knowing that I shall fail. My knowledge of my own nature and that of other things and persons, and of the laws that govern them and me, saves my energies from dissipation or misapplication; it exposes bogus claims and excuses; it fixes responsibilities where they belong and dismisses false pleas of impotence as well as false charges against the truly innocent; but it cannot widen the scope of my liberty beyond frontiers determined by factors genuinely and permanently outside my control. To explain these factors is not to explain them away. Increase of knowledge will increase my rationality, and infinite knowledge would make me infinitely rational; it might increase my powers and my freedom: but it cannot make me infinitely free.

To return to the main theme: How does knowledge liberate me?

Let me state the traditional position once again. On the view that I am trying to examine, the classical view which descends to us from Aristotle, from the Stoics, from a great part of Christian theology, and finds its rationalist formulation in the doctrines of Spinoza and his followers both among the German idealists and modern psychologists, knowledge, by uncovering little-recognised and therefore uncontrolled forces that affect my conduct, emancipates me from their despotic force, the greater when they have been concealed and therefore misinterpreted. Why is this so? Because once I have uncovered them, I can seek to direct them, or resist them, or create conditions in which they will be canalised into harmless channels, or turned to use – that is, for the fulfilment of my purposes. Freedom is self-government – whether in politics or in individual life – and anything that increases the control of the self over forces external to it contributes to liberty. Although the frontiers that divide self and personality from 'external' forces, whether in the individual-moral or in the public-social field, are still exceedingly vague – perhaps necessarily so – this Baconian thesis seems valid enough so far as it goes. But its claims are too great. In its classical form it is called the doctrine of self-determination. According to this, freedom consists in playing a part in determining one's own conduct; the greater this part, the greater the freedom. Servitude, or lack of freedom, is being determined by 'external' forces – whether these be physical or psychological; the greater the part played by these forces, the smaller the freedom of the individual. So far, so good. But if it be asked whether the part that I play – my choices, purposes, intentions – might not themselves be determined – caused – to be as they are by 'external' causes, the classical reply seems to be that this does not greatly matter; I am free if and only if I can do as I intended. Whether my state of mind is itself the causal product of something else – physical or psychological, of climate, or blood pressure, or my character – is neither here nor there; it may or may not be so: this, if it is so, may be known or unknown; all that matters, all that those worried about whether a man's acts are free or not wish to know, is whether my behaviour has as a necessary condition my own conscious choice. If it has, I am free in the only sense that any rational being can ask for: whether the choice itself – like the rest of me – is caused or uncaused is not what is at stake; even if it is wholly caused by natural factors, I am no less free.

Anti-determinists have naturally retorted that this merely

pushed the problem a step backwards: the 'self' played its part, indeed, but was itself hopelessly 'determined'. It may be worth going back to the origins of this controversy, for, as often happens, its earliest form is also the clearest. It came up, so far as I can tell, as a consequence of the interest taken by the early Greek Stoics in two, at first unconnected, ideas: that of causation, that is, the conception, new in the fourth century BC, of unbreakable chains of events in which each earlier event acts as a necessary and sufficient cause of the later; and the much older notion of individual moral responsibility. It was perceived as early as the beginning of the next century that there was something paradoxical, and indeed incoherent, in maintaining that men's states of mind, feeling and will as well as their actions were links in unbreakable causal chains, and at the same time that men were responsible, that is, that they could have acted otherwise than in fact they did.

Chrysippus was the first thinker to face this dilemma, which did not seem to trouble Plato or Aristotle, and he invented the solution known as self-determination – the view that so long as men were conceived of as being acted upon by outside forces without being able to resist them, they were as stocks and stones, unfree, and the concept of responsibility was plainly inapplicable to them; if, however, among the factors that determined behaviour was the bending of the will to certain purposes, and if, moreover, such a bending of the will was a necessary (whether or not it was a sufficient) condition of a given action, then they were free: for the act depended on the occurrence of a volition and could not happen without it. Men's acts of will and the characters and dispositions from which, whether or not they were fully aware of it, such acts issued, were intrinsic to action: this is what being free meant.

Critics of this position, Epicureans and sceptics, were not slow to point out that this was but a half-solution. We are told that they maintained that although it might be that the operations of the will were a necessary condition of what could properly be called acts, yet if these operations were themselves links in causal chains, themselves effects of causes 'external' to the choices, decisions and so on, then the notion of responsibility remained as inapplicable as before. One critic[1] called such modified determination *hemidoulia* – 'half-slavery'. I am only half free if I can correctly maintain that I

---

[1] The Cynic Oenamaus.

should not have done $x$ if I had not chosen it, but add that I could not have chosen differently. Given that I have decided on $x$, my action has a motive and not merely a cause; my 'volition' is itself among the causes – indeed, one of the necessary conditions – of my behaviour, and it is this that is meant by calling me or it free. But if the choice or decision is itself determined, and cannot, causally, be other than what it is, then the chain of causality remains unbroken, and, the critics asserted, I should be no more truly free than I am on the most rigidly determinist assumptions.

It is over this issue that the immense discussion about free will that has preoccupied philosophers ever since originally arose. Chrysippus' answer, that all that I can reasonably ask for is that my own character should be among the factors influencing behaviour, is the central core of the classical doctrine of freedom as self-determination. Its proponents stretch in unbroken line from Chrysippus and Cicero to Aquinas, Spinoza, Locke and Leibniz, Hume, Mill, Schopenhauer, Russell, Schlick, Ayer, Nowell-Smith and the majority of the contributors to the subject in our own day. Thus when a recent writer in this chronological order, Richard Hare, in one of his books[1] distinguishes free acts from mere behaviour by saying that a pointer to whether I am free to do $x$ is provided by asking myself whether it makes sense to ask 'Shall I do $x$?' or 'Ought I to do $x$?', he is restating the classical thesis. Hare correctly says that one can ask 'Will I make a mistake?' or 'Will I be wrecked on the sea-shore?' but not 'Shall I make a mistake?' or 'Ought I to be wrecked?'; for to be wrecked or make a mistake cannot be part of a conscious choice or purpose – cannot, in the logical or conceptual sense of the word. And from this he concludes that we distinguish free from unfree behaviour by the presence or absence of whatever it is that makes it intelligible to ask 'Shall I climb the mountain?' but not 'Shall I misunderstand you?' But if, following Carneades, I were to say 'I can indeed ask "Shall I climb the mountain?", but if the answer – and the action – are determined by factors beyond my control, then how does the fact that I pursue purposes, make decisions and so forth liberate me from the causal chain?', this would be regarded as a misconceived enquiry by the Stoics and the entire classical tradition. For if my choice is indispensable to the production of a given effect, then I am not causally determined as, say, a stone or a tree that has no purposes

[1] R. M. Hare, *Freedom and Reason* (Oxford, 1963).

and makes no choices is determined, and that is all that any libertarian can wish to establish.

But no libertarian can in fact accept this. No one genuinely concerned by the problem constituted by the prima facie incompatibility between determinism and freedom to choose between alternatives will settle for saying 'I can do what I choose, but I cannot choose otherwise than as I do.' Self-determination is clearly not the same as mechanical determination. If the determinists are right (and it may well be that they are) then the sort of determination in terms of which human behaviour should be described is not behaviouristic, but precisely Chrysippus' *hemidoulia*. But half a loaf is not the bread that libertarians crave. For if my decisions are wholly determined by antecedent causes, then the mere fact that they are decisions, and the fact that my acts have motives and not only antecedents, do not of themselves provide that line of demarcation between freedom and necessitation, or freedom and its absence, which the ordinary notion of responsibility seems, at least for libertarians, so clearly to entail. It is in this sense that Bacon's followers claim too much.

This may be seen from another angle which will bring us back to the relations of knowledge and liberty. The growth of knowledge increases the range of predictable events, and predictability – inductive or intuitive – despite all that has been said against this position, does not seem compatible with liberty of choice. I may be told that if I say to someone 'I always knew that you would behave with wonderful courage in this situation' the person so complimented will not suppose that his capacity for freedom of choice is being impugned. But that seems to be so only because the word 'knew' is being used, as it were, in a conventionally exaggerated way. When one man says to another 'I know you well: you simply cannot help behaving generously; you could not help it if you tried', the man so addressed may be thought susceptible to flattery, because of the element of complimentary hyperbole in the words 'cannot help' and 'could not ... if you tried'. If the words were intended to be taken literally – if the flatterer meant to be understood as saying 'You can no more help being generous than being old, or ugly, or thinking in English and not in Chinese' – the notion of merit or desert would evaporate, and the compliment would be transformed from a moral into a quasi-aesthetic one.

This may be made clearer if we take a pejorative example: if I were to say of *x* '*x* can no more help being cruel and malicious than a volcano can help erupting – one should not blame him, only deplore his existence or seek to tame him or restrain him as one would a dangerous animal', x might well feel more deeply insulted than if we lectured him on his habits on the assumption that he was free to choose between acting and refraining from acting as he did, free to choose to listen to our homily or pay no attention to it. The mere fact that it is my character that determines my choices and actions does not, if my character itself and its effects are due to ineluctable causes, render me free in the sense that appears to be required by the notions of responsibility or of moral praise and blame. Knowledge of the causes and conditions that determine my choice – knowledge, indeed, that there are such conditions and causes, knowledge that choice is not free (without analysis of this proposition), knowledge that shows that the notion of moral responsibility is wholly compatible with rigorous determinism, and exposes libertarianism as a confusion due to ignorance or error – that kind of knowledge would assimilate our moral views to aesthetic ones, and would lead us to look on heroism or honesty or justice as we now do on beauty or kindness or strength or genius: we praise or congratulate the possessors of the latter qualities with no implication that they could have chosen to own a different set of characteristics.

This world view, if it became generally accepted, would mark a radical shift of categories. If this ever occurs, it will tend to make us think of much of our present moral and legal outlook, and of a great deal of our penal legislation, as so much barbarism founded on ignorance; it will enlarge the scope and depth of our sympathy; it will substitute knowledge and understanding for attribution of responsibility; it will render indignation, and the kind of admiration that is its opposite, irrational and obsolete; it will expose such notions as desert, merit, responsibility, remorse, and perhaps right and wrong too, as incoherent or, at the very least, inapplicable; it will turn praise and blame into purely corrective or educational instruments, or confine them to aesthetic approval or disapproval. All this it will do, and if truth is on its side, it will benefit mankind thereby. But it will not increase the range of our freedom. Knowledge will render us freer only if in fact there is freedom of choice – if on the basis of our knowledge we can behave differently from the way in which we would have behaved without it – can, not must or do – if, that is to say, we can and do behave differently on the basis of our new knowledge, but need not. Where there is no antecedent freedom – and no possibility of it – it cannot be increased. Our new knowledge will increase our rationality, our grasp of truth will deepen our understanding, add to our power, inner harmony, wisdom, effectiveness, but not, necessarily, to our liberty. If we are free to choose, then an increase in our knowledge may tell us what are the limits of this freedom and what expands or contracts it. But only to know that there are facts and laws that I cannot alter does not itself render me able to alter anything: if I have no freedom to begin with, knowledge will not increase it. If everything is governed by natural laws, then it is difficult to see what could be meant by saying that I can 'use' them better on the basis of my knowledge, unless 'can' is not the 'can' of choice – not the 'can' which applies only to situations in which I am correctly described as being able to choose between alternatives, and am not rigorously determined to choose one rather than the other. In other words, if classical determinism is a true view (and the fact that it does not square with our present usage is no argument against it), knowledge of it will not increase liberty – if liberty does not exist, the discovery that it does not exist will not create it. This goes for self-determinism no less than for its most full-blown mechanistic-behaviourist variety.

The clearest exposition of classical self-determinism is probably that given in his *Ethics* by Spinoza. Stuart Hampshire represents him,[1] it seems to me correctly, as maintaining that the fully rational man does not choose his ends, for his ends are given. The better he understands the nature of men and of the world, the more harmonious and successful will his actions be, but no serious problem of choice between equally acceptable alternatives can ever present itself to him, any more than to a mathematician reasoning correctly from true premises to logically unavoidable conclusions. His freedom consists in the fact that he will not be acted upon by causes whose existence he does not know or the nature of whose influence he does not correctly understand. But that is all. Given Spinoza's premises – that the universe is a rational order, and that to understand the rationality of a proposition or an act or an order is, for a rational being, equivalent to accepting or identifying oneself with it (as in the old Stoic notion) – the notion of choice itself turns out to depend upon the deficiencies of knowledge, the

---

[1] Stuart Hampshire, 'Spinoza and the Idea of Freedom', *Proceedings of the British Academy* 46 (1960), 195–215.

degree of ignorance. There is only one correct answer to any problem of conduct, as to any problem of theory. The correct answer having been discovered, the rational man logically cannot but act in accordance with it: the notion of free choice between alternatives no longer has application. He who understands everything understands the reasons which make it as it is and not otherwise, and being rational cannot wish it to be otherwise than as it is. This may be an unattainable (and perhaps even, when thought through, an incoherent) ideal, but it is this conception that underlies the notion that an increase in knowledge is *eo ipso* always an increase in freedom, that is, an escape from being at the mercy of what is not understood. Once something is understood or known (and only then), it is, on this view, conceptually impossible to describe oneself as being at the mercy of it. Unless this maximal rationalist assumption is made, it does not seem to me to follow that more knowledge necessarily entails an increase in the total sum of freedom; it may or may not – this, as I hope to show, is largely an empirical question. To discover that I cannot do what I once believed that I could will render me more rational – I shall not beat my head against stone walls – but it will not necessarily make me freer; there may be stone walls wherever I look; I may myself be a portion of one; a stone myself, only dreaming of being free.

There are two further points to be noted with regard to the relationship of freedom and knowledge:

(*a*) There is the well-known objection, urged principally by Karl Popper, that the idea of total self-knowledge is in principle incoherent, because if I can predict what I shall do in the future, this knowledge itself is an added factor in the situation that may cause me to alter my behaviour accordingly; and the knowledge that this is so is itself an added factor, which may cause me to alter that, and so on *ad infinitum*. Therefore total self-prediction is logically impossible. This may be so: but it is not an argument against determinism as such (nor does Popper so represent it) – only against self-prediction. If *x* can predict the total behaviour of *y*, and *y* predict the total behaviour of *x* (and they do not impart their prophecies to one another), that is all that determinism needs. I cannot be self-consciously spontaneous; therefore I cannot be self-consciously aware of all my states if spontaneity is among them. It does not follow that I can never be spontaneous; nor that, if I am, this state cannot be known to exist while it is occurring, although it cannot be so known to me. For this reason I conclude that, in principle, Popper's argument does not (and is not meant to) refute determinism.

(*b*) Stuart Hampshire, in the course of some recent remarks,[1] advances the view that self-prediction is (logically) impossible. When I say 'I know that I shall do *x*' (as against, for instance, '*x* will happen to me', or 'You will do *x*'), I am not contemplating myself, as I might someone else, and giving tongue to a conjecture about myself and my future acts, as I might be doing about someone else or about the behaviour of an animal – for that would be tantamount (if I understand him rightly) to looking upon myself from outside, as it were, and treating my own acts as mere caused events. In saying that I know that I shall do *x*, I am, on this view, saying that I have decided to do *x*: for to predict that I shall in certain circumstances in fact do *x* or decide to do *x*, with no reference to whether or not I have already decided to do it – to say 'I can tell you now that I shall in fact act in manner *x*, although I am, as a matter of fact, determined to do the very opposite' – does not make sense. Any man who says 'I know myself too well to believe that, whatever I now decide, I shall do anything other than *x* when the circumstances actually arise' is in fact, if I interpret Hampshire's views correctly, saying that he does not really, that is, seriously, propose to set himself against doing *x*, that he does not propose even to try to act otherwise, that he has in fact decided to let events take their course. For no man who has truly decided to try to avoid *x* can, in good faith, predict his own failure to act as he has decided. He may fail to avoid *x*, and he may predict this; but he cannot both decide to try to avoid *x* and predict that he will not even try to do this; for he can always try; and he knows this: he knows that this is what distinguishes him from non-human creatures in nature. To say that he will fail even to try is tantamount to saying that he has decided not to try. In this sense 'I know' means 'I have decided' and cannot in principle be predictive.

That, if I have understood it, is Hampshire's position, and I have a good deal of sympathy with it, for I can see that self-prediction is often an evasive way of disclaiming responsibility for difficult decisions, while deciding in fact to let events take their course, disguising this by attributing responsibility for what occurs to my

[1] Iris Murdoch, S. N. Hampshire, P. L. Gardiner and D. F. Pears, 'Freedom and Knowledge', in D. F. Pears (ed.), *Freedom and the Will* (London, 1963), pp. 80–104.

own allegedly unalterable nature. But I agree with Hampshire's critics in the debate, whom I take to be maintaining that, although the situation he describes may often occur, yet circumstances may exist in which it is possible for me both to say that I am, at this moment, resolved not to do $x$, and at the same time to predict that I shall do $x$, because I am not hopeful that, when the time comes, I shall in fact even so much as try to resist doing $x$. I can, in effect, say 'I know myself well. When the crisis comes, do not rely on me to help you. I may well run away; although I am at this moment genuinely resolved not to be cowardly and to do all I can to stay at your side. My prediction that my resolution will not in fact hold up is based on knowledge of my own character, and not on my present state of mind; my prophecy is not a symptom of bad faith (for I am not, at this moment, vacillating) but, on the contrary, of good faith, of a wish to face the facts. I assure you in all sincerity that my present intention is to be brave and resist. Yet you would run a great risk if you relied too much on my present decision; it would not be fair to conceal my past failures of nerve from you.' I can say this about others, despite the most sincere resolutions on their part, for I can foretell how in fact they will behave; they can equally predict this about me. Despite Hampshire's plausible and tempting argument, I believe that such objective self-knowledge is possible and occurs; and his argument does not therefore appear to me to lessen the force of the determinist thesis. It seems to me that I can, at times, though perhaps not always, place myself, as it were, at an outside vantage-point, and contemplate myself as if I were another human being, and calculate the chances of my sticking to my present resolution with almost the same degree of detachment and reliability as I should have if I were judging the case of someone else with all the impartiality that I could muster. If this is so, then 'I know how I shall act' is not necessarily a statement of decision: it can be purely descriptive. Self-prediction of this kind, provided that it does not claim to be too exact or infallible, and meets Popper's objection, cited above, by remaining tentative, allowing for possible alterations of conduct as a result of the self-prediction itself – seems possible and compatible with determinism.

In other words, I see no reason to suppose that a deterministic doctrine, whether about one's own behaviour or that of others, is in principle incoherent, or incompatible with making choices, provided that these choices are regarded as being themselves no less determined than other phenomena. Such knowledge, or well-founded belief, seems to me to increase the degree of rationality, efficiency, power; the only freedom to which it necessarily contributes is freedom from illusions. But this is not the basic sense of the term about which controversy has been boiling for twenty-two centuries.

I have no wish to enter into the waters of the freewill problem more deeply than I already have. But I should like to repeat what I have indeed said elsewhere, and for which I have been severely taken to task by determinists: that if a great advance were made in psycho-physiology; if, let us suppose, a scientific expert were to hand me a sealed envelope, and ask me to note all my experiences – both introspective and others – for a limited period – say half-an-hour – and write them down as accurately as I could; and if I then did this to the best of my ability, and after this opened the envelope and read the account, which turned out to tally to a striking degree with my log-book of my experience during the last half-hour, I should certainly be shaken; and so I think would others. We should then have to admit, with or without pleasure, that aspects of human behaviour which had been believed to be within the area of the agent's free choice turned out to be subject to discovered causal laws. Our recognition of this might itself alter our behaviour, perhaps for the happier and more harmonious; but this welcome result itself would be a causal product of our new awareness. I cannot see why such discoveries should be considered impossible, or even particularly improbable; they would bring about a major transformation of psychology and sociology; after all, great revolutions have occurred in other sciences in our own day.

The principal difference, however, between previous advances and this imaginary breakthrough (and it is with this surmise that most of my critics have disagreed) is that besides effecting a vast alteration in our empirical knowledge, it would alter our conceptual framework far more radically than the discoveries of the physicists of the seventeenth or twentieth century, or of the biologists of the nineteenth, have changed it. Such a break with the past, in psychology alone, would do great violence to our present concepts and usages. The entire vocabulary of human relations would suffer radical change. Such expressions as 'I should not have done x', 'How could you have chosen x?' and so on, indeed the entire language of the criticism and assessment of one's own and others' conduct, would undergo a sharp transformation, and the expressions we needed both for descriptive and for practical-corrective, deterrent, hortatory purposes (what others would be open to a consistent determinist?) would necessarily be vastly different from the language which we now use.

It seems to me that we should be unwise to underestimate the effect of robbing praise, blame, a good many counterfactual propositions, and the entire network of concepts concerned with freedom, choice, responsibility of much of their present function and meaning. But it is equally important to insist that the fact that such a transformation could occur – or would, at any rate, be required – does not, of course, have any tendency to show that determinism is either true or false; it is merely a consequence which those who accept it as true tend not to recognise sufficiently. I only wish to add that the further issue, whether the truth of determinism is or is not an empirical question, is itself unclear. If so revolutionary an advance in psycho-physiological knowledge were achieved, the need of new concepts to formulate it, and of the consequent modification (to say the least) of concepts in other fields, would itself demonstrate the relative vagueness of the frontiers between the empirical and the conceptual. If these empirical discoveries were made, they might mark a greater revolution in human thought than any that has gone before.

It is idle to speculate on the transformation of language – or of ideas (these are but alternative ways of saying the same thing) – that would be brought about by the triumph of exact knowledge in this field. But would such an advance in knowledge necessarily constitute an overall increase in freedom? Freedom from error, from illusion, fantasy, misdirection of emotions – certainly all these. But is this the central meaning of the word as we commonly use it in philosophy or common speech?

## II

I do not, of course, wish to deny that when we say that a man is free – or freer than he was before – we may be using the word to denote moral freedom, or independence, or self-determination. This concept, as has often been pointed out, is far from clear: the central terms – willing, intention, action, and the related notions – conscience, remorse, guilt, inner versus outer compulsion, and so on – stand in need of analysis, which itself entails a moral psychology that remains unprovided; and in the meanwhile the notion of moral independence – of what is, or should be, independent of what, and how this independence is achieved – remains obscure. Moreover, it seems doubtful whether we should describe a man as being free if his conduct displayed unswerving regularities, issuing (however this is established) from his own thoughts, feelings, acts of will, so that we should be inclined to say that he could not behave otherwise than as he did. Predictability may or may not entail determinism; but if we were in a position to be so well acquainted with a man's character, reactions, outlook that, given a specific situation, we felt sure that we could predict how he would act, better perhaps than he could himself, should we be tempted to describe him as being a typical example of a man morally – or otherwise – free? Should we not think that a phrase used by Patrick Gardiner, a 'prisoner of his personality', described him better?[1] So aptly, indeed, that he might, in certain cases, come to accept it – with regret or satisfaction – himself? A man so hidebound by his own habits and outlook is not the paradigm of human freedom.

The central assumption of common thought and speech seems to me to be that freedom is the principal characteristic that distinguishes man from all that is non-human; that there are degrees of freedom, degrees constituted by the absence of obstacles to the exercise of choice; the choice being regarded as not itself determined by antecedent conditions, at least not as being wholly so determined. It may be that common sense is mistaken in this matter, as in others; but the onus of refutation is on those who disagree. Common sense may not be too well aware of the full variety of such obstacles: they may be physical or psychical, 'inner' and 'outer', or complexes compounded of both elements, difficult and perhaps conceptually impossible to unravel, due to social factors and/or individual ones. Common opinion may oversimplify the issue; but it seems to me to be right about its essence: freedom is to do with the absence of obstacles to action. These obstacles may consist of physical power, whether of nature or of men, that prevents our intentions from being realised: geographical conditions or prison walls, armed men or the threat (deliberately used as a weapon or unintended) of lack of food or shelter or other necessities of life; or again they may be psychological: fears and

[1] op. cit. (p. 105 above, note 1), p. 92.

'complexes', ignorance, error, prejudice, illusions, fantasies, compulsions, neuroses and psychoses – irrational factors of many kinds. Moral freedom – rational self-control – knowledge of what is at stake, and of what is one's motive in acting as one does; independence of the unrecognised influence of other persons or of one's known personal past or that of one's group or culture; destruction of hopes, fears, desires, loves, hatreds, ideals, which will be seen to be groundless once they are inspected and rationally examined – these indeed bring liberation from obstacles, some of the most formidable and insidious in the path of human beings; their full effect, despite the acute but scattered insights of moralists from Plato to Marx and Schopenhauer, is beginning to be understood adequately only in the present century, with the rise of psychoanalysis and the perception of its philosophical implications. It would be absurd to deny the validity of this sense of the concept of freedom, or of its intimate logical dependence on rationality and knowledge. Like all freedom it consists of, or depends on, the removal of obstacles, in this case of psychological impediments to the full use of human powers to whatever ends men choose; but these constitute only one category of such obstacles, however important and hitherto inadequately analysed. To emphasise these to the exclusion of other classes of obstacles, and other better recognised forms of freedom, leads to distortion. Yet it is this, it seems to me, that has been done by those who, from the Stoics to Spinoza, Bradley and Stuart Hampshire, have confined freedom to self-determination.

To be free is to be able to make an unforced choice; and choice entails competing possibilities – at the very least two 'open', unimpeded alternatives. And this, in its turn, may well depend on external circumstances which leave only some paths unblocked. When we speak of the extent of freedom enjoyed by a man or a society, we have in mind, it seems to me, the width or extent of the paths before them, the number of open doors, as it were, and the extent to which they are open. The metaphor is imperfect, for 'number' and 'extent' will not really do. Some doors are much more important than others – the goods to which they lead are far more central in an individual's or society's life. Some doors lead to other open doors, some to closed ones; there is actual and there is potential freedom – depending on how easily some closed doors can be opened, given existing or potential resources, physical or mental. How is one to measure one situation against another? How is one to decide whether a man who is obstructed neither by other persons nor by circumstances from, let us say, the acquisition of adequate security or of material necessities and comforts, but is debarred from free speech and association, is less or more free than one who find its impossible, because of, let us say, the economic policies of his government, to obtain more than the necessities of life, but who possesses greater opportunities of education or of free communication or association with others? Problems of this type will always arise – they are familiar enough in Utilitarian literature, and indeed in all forms of non-totalitarian practical politics. Even if no hard and fast rule can be provided, it still remains the case that the measure of the liberty of a man or a group is, to a large degree, determined by the range of choosable possibilities.

If a man's area of choice, whether 'physical' or 'mental', is narrow, then however contented with it he may be, and however true it may be that the more rational a man is, the clearer the one and only rational path will be to him and the less likely will he be to vacillate between alternatives (a proposition which seems to me to be fallacious), neither of these situations will necessarily make him more free than a man whose range of choice is wider. To remove obstacles by removing desire to enter upon, or even awareness of, the path on which the obstacles lie, may contribute to serenity, contentment, perhaps even wisdom, but not to liberty. Independence of mind – sanity and integration of personality, health and inner harmony – are highly desirable conditions, and they entail the removal of a sufficient number of obstacles to qualify for being regarded, for that reason alone, as a species of freedom – but only one species among others. Someone may say that it is at least unique in this: that this kind of freedom is a necessary condition for all other kinds of freedom – for if I am ignorant, obsessed, irrational, I am thereby blinded to the facts, and a man so blinded is, in effect, as unfree as a man whose possibilities are objectively blocked. But this does not seem to me to be true. If I am ignorant of my rights, or too neurotic (or too poor) to benefit by them, that makes them useless to me; but it does not make them non-existent; a door is closed to a path that leads to other, open, doors. To destroy or lack a condition for freedom (knowledge, money) is not to destroy that freedom itself; for its essence does not lie in its accessibility, although its value may do so. The more avenues men can enter, the broader those avenues, the more avenues that each opens into, the freer they are; the better men know what avenues lie before them, and how open they are, the freer they will know themselves to be. To be free without knowing it may be a bitter irony, but if a man subsequently discovers that doors were open although he did not know it, he will reflect bitterly not about his lack of freedom but about his ignorance. The extent of freedom depends on opportunities of action, not on knowledge of them, although such knowledge may well be an indispensable condition for the use of freedom, and although impediments in the path to it are themselves a deprivation of freedom – of freedom to know. Ignorance blocks paths, and knowledge opens them. But this truism does not entail that freedom implies awareness of freedom, still less that they are identical.

It is worth noting that it is the actual doors that are open that determine the extent of someone's freedom, and not his own preferences. A man is not free merely when there are no obstacles, psychological or otherwise, in the way of his wishes – when he can do as he likes – for in that case a man might be rendered free by altering not his opportunities of action, but his desires and dispositions. If a master can condition his slaves to love their chains he does not thereby prima facie increase their liberty, although he may increase their contentment or at least decrease their misery. Some unscrupulous managers of men have, in the course of history, used religious teachings to make men less discontented with brutal and iniquitous treatment. If such measures work, and there is reason to think that they do so only too often, and if the victims have learnt not to mind their pains and indignities (like Epictetus, for example), then some despotic systems should presumably be described as creators of liberty; for by eliminating distracting temptations, and 'enslaving' wishes and passions, they create (on these assumptions) more liberty than institutions that expand the area of individual or democratic choice and thereby produce the worrying need to select, to determine oneself in one direction rather than another – the terrible burden of the *embarras du choix* (which has itself been taken to be a symptom of irrationality by some thinkers in the rationalist tradition). This ancient fallacy is by now too familiar to need refutation. I only cite it in order to emphasise the crucial distinction between the definition of liberty as nothing but the absence of obstacles to doing as I like (which could presumably be compatible with a very narrow life, narrowed by the influence upon me of personal or impersonal forces, education or law, friend or foe, religious teacher or parent, or even consciously contracted by myself), and liberty as a range of objectively open possibilities, whether these are desired or not, even though it is difficult or impossible to give rules for measuring or comparing degrees of it, or for assessing different situations with regard to it.

There is, of course, a sense, with which all moral philosophers are well acquainted, in which the slave Epictetus is more free than his master or the emperor who forced him to die in exile; or that in which stone walls do not a prison make. Nevertheless, such statements derive their rhetorical force from the fact that there is a more familiar sense in which a slave is the least free of men, and stone walls and iron bars are serious impediments to freedom; nor are moral and physical or political or legal freedoms mere homonyms. Unless some kernel of common meaning – whether a single common characteristic or a 'family resemblance' – is kept in mind, there is the danger that one or other of these senses will be represented as fundamental, and the others will be tortured into conformity with it, or dismissed as trivial or superficial. The most notorious examples of this process are the sophistries whereby various types of compulsion and thought-control are represented as means to, or even as constitutive of, 'true' freedom, or, conversely, liberal political or legal systems are regarded as sufficient means of ensuring not only the freedom of, but opportunities for the use of such freedom by, persons who are too irrational or immature, owing to lack of education or other means of mental development, to understand or benefit by such rules or laws. It is therefore the central meaning of the term, if there is one, that it is important to establish.

There is yet another consideration regarding knowledge and liberty to which I should like to return.[1] It is true that knowledge always, of necessity, opens some doors, but does it never close others? If I am a poet, may it not be that some forms of knowledge will curtail my powers and thereby my liberty too? Let us suppose that I require as a stimulus to my imagination illusions and myths of a certain kind which are provided by the religion in which I have been brought up or to which I have been converted. Let us assume that some honourable rationalist refutes these beliefs, shatters my illusions, dissipates the myths; may it not be that my clear gain in

---

[1] See p. 94 above.

knowledge and rationality is paid for by the diminution or destruction of my powers as a poet? It is easy enough to say that what I have lost is a power that fed on illusions or irrational states and attitudes which the advance of knowledge has destroyed; that some powers are undesirable (like the power of self-deception) and that, in any case, powers are powers and not liberties. It may be said that an increase in knowledge cannot (this would, I think, be claimed as an analytic truth) diminish my freedom; for to know the roots of my activity is to be rescued from servitude to the unknown – from stumbling in a darkness populated with figments which breed fears and irrational conduct. Moreover, it will be said that as a result of the destruction of my idols I have clearly gained in freedom of self-determination; for I can now give a rational justification of my beliefs, and the motives of my actions are clearer to me. But if I am less free to write the kind of poetry that I used to write, is there not now a new obstacle before me? Have not some doors been closed by the opening of others? Whether ignorance is or is not bliss in these circumstances is another question. The question I wish to ask – and one to which I do not know the answer – is whether such absence of knowledge may not be a necessary condition for certain states of mind or emotion in which alone certain impediments to some forms of creative labour are absent. This is an empirical question, but on the answer to it the answer to a larger question depends: whether knowledge never impedes, always increases, the sum total of human freedom.

Again, if I am a singer, self-consciousness – the child of knowledge – may inhibit the spontaneity that may be a necessary condition of my performance, as the growth of culture was thought by Rousseau and others to inhibit the joys of barbarian innocence. It does not matter greatly whether this particular belief is true; the simple uncivilised savage may have known fewer joys than Rousseau supposed; barbarism may not be a state of inno-cence at all. It is enough to allow that there are certain forms of knowledge that have the psychological effect of preventing kinds of self-expression which, on any showing, must be considered as forms of free activity. Reflection may ruin my painting if this depends on not thinking; my knowledge that a disease, for which no cure has been discovered, is destroying me or my friend, may well sap my particular creative capacity, and inhibit me in this or that way; and to be inhibited – whatever its long-term advantages – is not to be rendered more free. It may be replied to this that if I am suffering from a disease and do not know it, I am less free than one who knows, and can at least try to take steps to check it, even if the disease has so far proved to be incurable; that not to diagnose it will certainly lead to dissipation of effort in mistaken directions, and will curtail my freedom by putting me at the mercy of natural forces the character of which, because I do not recognise it, I cannot rationally discount or cope with. This is indeed so. Such knowledge cannot decrease my freedom as a rational being, but it may finish me as an artist. One door opens, and as a result of this another shuts.

Let me take another example. Resistance against vast odds may work only if the odds are not fully known; otherwise it may seem irrational to fight against what, even if it is not known to be irresistible, can be believed with a high degree of probability to be so. For it may be my very ignorance of the odds that creates a situation in which alone I resist successfully. If David had known more about Goliath, if the majority of the inhabitants of Britain had known more about Germany in 1940, if historical probabilities could be reduced to something approaching a reliable guide to action, some achievements might never have taken place. I discover that I suffer from a fatal disease. This discovery makes it possible for me to try to find a cure – which was not possible so long as I was ignorant of the causes of my condition. But supposing that I satisfy myself that the weight of probability is against the discovery of an antidote, that once the poison has entered into the system death must follow; that the pollution of the atmosphere as the result of the discharge of a nuclear weapon cannot be undone. Then what is it that I am now more free to do? I may seek to reconcile myself to what has occurred, not kick against the pricks, arrange my affairs, make my will, refrain from a display of sorrow or indignation inappropriate when facing the inevitable – this is what 'stoicism' or 'taking things philosophically' has historically come to mean. But even if I believe that reality is a rational whole (whatever this may mean), and that any other view of it – for instance, as being equally capable of realising various incompatible possibilities – is an error caused by ignorance, and if I therefore regard everything in it as being necessitated by reason – what I myself should necessarily will it to be as a wholly rational being – the discovery of its structure will not increase my freedom of choice. It will merely set me beyond hope and fear – for these are symptoms of ignorance or fantasy – and beyond choices too, since choosing entails the reality of at least two alternatives, say action and inaction. We are told that the Stoic Posidonius said to the pain that was tormenting him 'Do your worst, pain; nothing that you can do will cause me to hate you.'[1] But Posidonius was a rationalistic determinist: whatever truly is, is as it should be; to wish it to be otherwise is a sign of irrationality; rationality implies that choice – and the freedom defined in terms of its possibility – is an illusion, not widened but killed by true knowledge.

Knowledge increases autonomy both in the sense of Kant, and in that of Spinoza and his followers. I should like to ask once more: is all liberty just that? The advance of knowledge stops men from wasting their resources upon delusive projects. It has stopped us from burning witches or flogging lunatics or predicting the future by listening to oracles or looking at the entrails of animals or the flight of birds. It may yet render many institutions and decisions of the present – legal, political, moral, social – obsolete, by showing them to be as cruel and stupid and incompatible with the pursuit of justice or reason or happiness or truth as we now think the burning of widows or eating the flesh of an enemy to acquire skills. If our powers of prediction, and so our knowledge of the future, become much greater, then, even if they are never complete, this may radically alter our view of what constitutes a person, an act, a choice; and *eo ipso* our language and our picture of the world. This may make our conduct more rational, perhaps more tolerant, charitable, civilised, it may improve it in many ways, but will it increase the area of free choice? For individuals or groups? It will certainly kill some realms of the imagination founded upon non-rational beliefs, and for this it may compensate us by making some of our ends more easily or harmoniously attainable. But who shall say if the balance will necessarily be on the side of wider freedom? Unless one establishes logical equivalences between the notions of freedom, self-determination and self-knowledge in some a priori fashion – as Spinoza and Hegel and their modern followers seek to do – why need this be true? Stuart Hampshire and E. F. Carritt, in dealing with the topic, maintain that, faced with any situation, one can always choose at least between trying to do something and letting things take their course. Always? If it makes sense to say that there is an external world, then to know it, in the descriptive sense of 'know', is not to alter it. As for the other sense of 'know' –

[1] See Cicero, *Tusculan Disputations*, 2. 61.

the pragmatic, in which 'I know what I shall do' is akin to 'I know what to do', and registers not a piece of information but a decision to alter things in a certain way – would it not wither if psycho-physiology advanced far enough? For, in that event, may not my resolution to act or not to act resemble more and more the recommendation of Canute's courtiers?

Knowledge, we are told, extends the boundaries of freedom, and this is an a priori proposition. Is it inconceivable that the growth of knowledge will tend more and more successfully to establish the determinist thesis as an empirical truth, and explain our thoughts and feelings, wishes and decisions, our actions and choices, in terms of invariant, regular, natural successions, to seek to alter which will seem almost as irrational as entertaining a logical fallacy? This was, after all, the programme and the belief of many respected philoso-phers, as different in their outlooks as Spinoza, Holbach, Schopen-hauer, Comte, the behaviourists. Would such a consummation extend the area of freedom? In what sense? Would it not rather render this notion, for want of a contrasting one, altogether otiose, and would not this constitute a novel situation? The 'dissolution' of the concept of freedom would be accompanied by the demise of that sense of 'know' in which we speak not of knowing that, but of knowing what to do, to which Hampshire and Hart have drawn attention; for if all is determined, there is a nothing to choose between, and so nothing to decide. Perhaps those who have said of freedom that it is the recognition of necessity were contemplating this very situation. If so, their notion of freedom is radically different from those who define it in terms of conscious choice and decision.

I wish to make no judgement of value: only to suggest that to say that knowledge is a good is one thing; to say that it is necessarily, in all situations, compatible with, still more that it is on terms of mutual entailment with (or even, as some seem to suppose, is literally identical with), freedom, in most of the senses in which this word is used, is something very different. Perhaps the second assertion is rooted in the optimistic view – which seems to be at the heart of much metaphysical rationalism – that all good things must be compatible, and that therefore freedom, order, knowledge, happiness, a closed future (and an open one?) must be at least compatible, and perhaps even entail one another in a systematic fashion. But this proposition is not self-evidently true, if only on empirical grounds. Indeed, it is perhaps one of the least plausible beliefs ever entertained by profound and influential thinkers.

# HISTORICAL INEVITABILITY

... those vast impersonal forces ...

T. S. Eliot[1]

I

WRITING SOME ten years ago[2] in his place of refuge during the German occupation of northern Italy, Bernard Berenson set down his thoughts on what he called the 'Accidental View of History': they 'led me', he declared, 'far from the doctrine, lapped up in my youth, about the inevitability of events and the Moloch still devouring us today, "historical inevitability". I believe less and less in these more than doubtful and certainly dangerous dogmas, which tend to make us accept whatever happens as irresistible and foolhardy to oppose.'[3] The famous critic's words are particularly timely at a moment when there is, at any rate among philosophers of history, if not among historians, a tendency to return to the ancient view that all that is, is ('objectively viewed') best; that to explain is ('in the last resort') to justify; or that to know all is to forgive all; ringing fallacies (charitably described as half-truths) which have led to special pleading and, indeed, obfuscation of the issue on a heroic scale.

This is the theme on which I should like to speak; but before doing so I must express my gratitude to the Director of this great institution[4] and his colleagues for the honour which they have done me by inviting me to deliver this, the first of the Auguste Comte Memorial Lectures. For, indeed, Comte is worthy of commemoration and praise. He was in his own day a very celebrated thinker, and if his works are today seldom mentioned, at any rate in this country, that is partly due to the fact that he has

---

[1] *Notes towards the Definition of Culture* (London, 1948), p. 88.
[2] This was written in 1953.
[3] Bernard Berenson, *Rumour and Reflection: 1941:1944* (London, 1952), p. 116 (entry dated 11 January 1943).
[4] The London School of Economics and Political Science.

done his work too well. For Comte's views have affected the categories of our thought more deeply than is commonly supposed. Our view of the natural sciences, of the material basis of cultural evolution, of all that we call progressive, rational, enlightened, Western; our view of the relationships of institutions and of public symbolism and ceremonial to the emotional life of individuals and societies, and consequently our view of history itself, owes a good deal to his teaching and his influence. His grotesque pedantry, the unreadable dullness of much of his writing, his vanity, his eccentricity, his solemnity, the pathos of his private life, his dogmatism, his authoritarianism, his philosophical fallacies, all that is bizarre and Utopian in his character and writings, need not blind us to his merits. The father of sociology is by no means the ludicrous figure he is too often represented as being. He understood the role of natural science and the true reasons for its prestige better than most contemporary thinkers. He saw no depth in mere darkness; he demanded evidence; he exposed shams; he denounced intellectual impressionism; he fought many metaphysical and theological mythologies, some of which, but for the blows he struck, might have been with us still; he provided weapons in the war against the enemies of reason, many of which are far from obsolete today. Above all he grasped the central issue of all philosophy – the distinction between words (or thoughts) that are about words, and words (or thoughts) that are about things, and thereby helped to lay the foundation of what is best and most illuminating in modern empiricism; and, of course, he made a great mark on historical thinking. He believed in the application of scientific, that is, naturalistic, canons of explanation in all fields: and saw no reason why they should not apply to relations of human beings as well as relations of things.

This doctrine was not original, and by his time growing somewhat out of date; the writings of Vico had been rediscovered; Herder had transformed the concepts of nation, society and culture; Ranke and Michelet were changing both the art and the science of history. The notion that human history could be turned into a natural science by the extension to human beings of a kind of sociological zoology, analogous to the study of bees and beavers, which Condorcet had so ardently advocated and so confidently prophesied – this simple behaviourism had provoked a reaction against itself. It was seen to be a distortion of the facts, a denial of the evidence of direct experience, a deliberate suppression of much of what we knew about ourselves, our motives, purposes, choices, perpetrated in order to achieve by hook or by crook a single, unitary method in all knowledge. Comte did not commit the enormities of a La Mettrie or a Büchner. He did not say that history was, or was reducible to, a kind of physics; but his conception of sociology pointed in that direction – of one complete and all-embracing pyramid of scientific knowledge; one method; one truth; one scale of rational, 'scientific' values. This naïve craving for unity and symmetry at the expense of experience is with us still.

II

The notion that one can discover large patterns or regularities in the procession of historical events is naturally attractive to those who are impressed by the success of the natural sciences in classifying, correlating, and above all predicting. They consequently seek to extend historical knowledge to fill gaps in the past (and, at times, to build into the limitless gap of the future) by applying 'scientific' method: by setting forth, armed with a metaphysical or empirical system, from such islands of certain, or virtually certain, knowledge of the facts as they claim to possess. And no doubt a great deal has been done, and will be done, in historical as in other fields by arguing from the known to the unknown, or from the little known to the even less known.[1] But

---

[1] I do not wish here to enter into the question of what such procedures are, for example, what is meant by speaking of history as a science – whether the methods of historical discovery are inductive, or 'deductive-hypothetical', or analogical, or to what degree they are or should be similar to the methods of the natural sciences, and to which of these methods, and in which of the natural sciences; for there plainly exists a greater variety of methods and procedures than is usually provided for in textbooks on logic or scientific method. It may be that the methods of historical research are, in at least some respects, unique, and some of them are more unlike than like those of the natural sciences; while others resemble given scientific techniques, particularly when they approach such ancillary enquiries as archaeology or palaeography or physical anthropology. Or again they may depend upon the kind of historical research pursued – and may not be the same in demography as in history, in political history as in the history of art, in the history of technology as in the history of religion. The 'logic' of various human studies has been insufficiently examined, and convincing accounts of its varieties with an adequate range of concrete examples drawn from actual practice are much to be desired.

whatever value the perception of patterns or uniformities may have in stimulating or verifying specific hypotheses about the past or the future, it has played, and is increasingly playing, another and more dubious role in determining the outlook of our time. It has affected not merely ways of observing and describing the activities and characters of human beings, but moral and political and religious attitudes towards them. For among the questions which are bound to arise in any consideration of how and why human beings act and live as they do are questions of human motive and responsibility.

In describing human behaviour it has always been artificial and over-austere to omit questions of the character, purposes and motives of individuals. And in considering these one automatically evaluates not merely the degree and kind of influence of this or that motive or character upon what happens, but also its moral or political quality in terms of whatever scale of values one consciously or semi-consciously accepts in one's thought or action. How did this or that situation arise? Who or what was or is (or will be, or could be) responsible for a war, a revolution, an economic collapse, a renaissance of arts and letters, a discovery or an invention or a spiritual transformation altering the lives of men? It is by now a familiar story that there exist personal and impersonal theories of history. On the one hand, there are theories according to which the lives of entire peoples and societies have been decisively influenced by exceptional individuals[1] – or, alternatively, doctrines according to which what happens occurs as a result not of the wishes and purposes of identifiable individuals, but of those of large numbers of unspecified persons, with the qualification that these collective wishes and goals are not solely or even largely determined by impersonal factors, and are therefore not wholly or even largely deducible from knowledge of natural forces alone, such as environment, or climate, or physical, physiological and psychological processes. On either view, it becomes the

---

[1] Indeed, the very notion of great men, however carefully qualified, however sophisticated, embodies this belief; for this concept, even in its most attenuated form, would be empty unless it were thought that some men played a more decisive role in the course of history than others. The notion of greatness, unlike those of goodness or wickedness or talent or beauty, is not a mere characteristic of individuals in a more or less private context, but is, as we ordinarily use it, directly connected with social effectiveness, the capacity of individuals to alter things radically on a large scale.

business of historians to investigate who wanted what, and when, and where, in what way; how many men avoided or pursued this or that goal, and with what intensity; and, further, to ask under what circumstances such wants or fears have proved effective, and to what extent, and with what consequences.

Against this kind of interpretation, in terms of the purposes and characters of individuals, there is a cluster of views (to which the progress of the natural sciences has given a great and growing prestige) according to which all explanations in terms of human intentions stem from a mixture of vanity and stubborn ignorance. These views rest on the assumption that belief in the importance of the motives is delusive; that the behaviour of men is in fact made what it is by causes largely beyond the control of individuals; for instance by the influence of physical factors or of environment or of custom; or by the 'natural' growth of some larger unit – a race, a nation, a class, a biological species; or (according to some writers) by some entity conceived in even less empirical terms – a 'spiritual organism', a religion, a civilisation, a Hegelian (or Buddhist) World Spirit; entities whose careers or manifestations on earth are the object either of empirical or of metaphysical enquiries, depending on the cosmological outlook of particular thinkers.

Those who incline to this kind of impersonal interpretation of historical change, whether because they believe that it possesses greater scientific value (that is, enables them to predict the future or 'retrodict' the past more successfully or precisely), or because they believe that it embodies some crucial insight into the nature of the universe, are committed by it to tracing the ultimate responsibility for what happens to the acts or behaviour of impersonal or 'trans-personal' or 'super-personal' entities or 'forces' whose evolution is identified with human history. It is true that the more cautious and clear-headed among such theorists try to meet the objections of empirically minded critics by adding, in a footnote or as an afterthought, that, whatever their terminology, they are on no account to be taken to believe that there literally exist such creatures as civilisations or races or spirits of nations living side by side with the individuals who compose them; and they add that they fully realise that all institutions 'in the last analysis' consist of individual men and women, and are not themselves personalities but only convenient devices – idealised models, or types, or labels, or metaphors – different ways of classifying, grouping, explaining or predicting the properties or behaviour of individual human beings in terms of their more important (that is, historically effective) empirical characteristics. Nevertheless these protestations too often turn out to be mere lip-service to principles which those who profess them do not really believe. Such writers seldom write or think as if they took these deflationary caveats over-seriously; and the more candid or naïve among them do not even pretend to subscribe to them. Thus nations or cultures or civilisations, for Schelling or Hegel (and Spengler; and one is inclined, though somewhat hesitantly, to add Toynbee), are certainly not merely convenient collective terms for individuals possessing certain characteristics in common; but seem more 'real' and more 'concrete' than the individuals who compose them. Individuals remain 'abstract' precisely because they are mere 'elements' or 'aspects', 'moments' artificially abstracted for *ad hoc* purposes, and literally without reality (or, at any rate, 'historical' or 'philosophical' or 'real' being) apart from the wholes of which they form a part, much as the colour of a thing, or its shape, or its value are 'elements' or 'attributes' or 'modes' or 'aspects' of concrete objects – isolated for convenience, and thought of as existing independently, on their own, only because of some weakness or confusion in the analysing intellect.

Marx and Marxists are more ambiguous. We cannot be quite sure what to make of such a category as a social 'class' whose emergence and struggles, victories and defeats, condition the lives of individuals, sometimes against, and most often independently of, such individuals' conscious or expressed purposes. Classes are never proclaimed to be literally independent entities: they are constituted by individuals in their (mainly economic) interaction. Yet to seek to explain, or put a moral or political value on, the actions of individuals by examining such individuals one by one, even to the limited extent to which such examination is possible, is considered by Marxists to be not merely impracticable and time-wasting (as indeed it may be), but absurd in a more fundamental sense – because the 'true' (or 'deeper') causes of human behaviour lie not in the specific circumstances of an individual life or in the individual's thoughts or volitions (as a psychologist or biographer or novelist might describe them), but in a pervasive interrelationship between a vast variety of such lives with their natural and man-made environment. Men do as they do, and think as they think, largely as a 'function of' the inevitable evolution of the 'class' as a whole – from which it follows that the history and development of classes can be studied independently of the biographies of their component individuals. It is the 'structure' and the 'evolution' of the class alone that (causally) matters in the end. This is, *mutatis mutandis*, similar to the belief in the primacy of collective patterns held by those who attribute active properties to race or culture, whether they be benevolent internationalists like Herder who thought that different peoples can and should admire, love and assist one another as individuals can and do, because peoples are in some sense individuals (or super-individuals); or by the ferocious champions of national or racial self-assertion and war, like Gobineau or Houston Stewart Chamberlain or Hitler. And the same note, sometimes mild and civilised, sometimes harshly aggressive, is heard in the voices of all those upholders of collectivist mystiques who appeal from individual to tradition, or to the collective consciousness (or 'Unconscious') of a race or a nation or a culture, or, like Carlyle, feel that abstract nouns deserve capital letters, and tell us that Tradition or History (or 'the past', or the species, or 'the masses') is wiser than we, or that the great society of the quick and the dead, of our ancestors and of generations yet unborn, has larger purposes than any single creature, purposes of which our lives are but a puny fragment, and that we belong to this larger unity with the 'deepest' and perhaps least conscious parts of ourselves.[1] There are many versions of this

[1] We are further told that we belong to such wholes and are 'organically' one with them, whether we know it or not; and that we have such significance as we do only to the degree to which we are sensitive to, and identify ourselves with, these unanalysable, imponderable, scarcely explicable relationships; for it is only in so far as we belong to an entity greater than ourselves, and are thereby carriers of 'its' values, instruments of 'its' purposes, living 'its' life, suffering and dying for 'its' richer self-realisation, that we are, or are worth, anything at all. This familiar line of thought should be distinguished from the no less familiar but less ethically charged supposition that men's outlooks and behaviour are largely conditioned by the habits of other past and present members of their society; that the hold of prejudice and tradition is very strong; that there may be inherited characteristics both mental and physical; and that any effort to influence human beings and to judge their conduct must take such non-rational factors into account. For whereas the former view is metaphysical and normative (what Karl Popper calls 'essentialist'), the latter is empirical and descriptive; and while the former is largely found as an element in the kind of ethical or political anti-individualism held by romantic nationalists, Hegelians and other transcendentalists, the latter is a sociological and psychological hypothesis which doubtless carries its own ethical and political implications, but rests its claim on observation of empirical facts, and can be confirmed or refuted or rendered less or more plausible by it. In their

belief, with varying proportions of empiricism and mysticism, 'tender'- and 'tough'-mindedness, optimism and pessimism, collectivism and individualism; but what all such views have in common is the fundamental distinction on which they rest, between, on the one hand, 'real' and 'objective', and, on the other, 'subjective' or 'arbitrary' judgements, based respectively on acceptance or rejection of this ultimately mystical act of self-identification with a reality which transcends empirical experience.

For Bossuet, for Hegel, for Marx,[1] for Spengler (and for almost all thinkers for whom history is 'more' than past events, namely a theodicy) this reality takes on the form of an objective 'march of history'. The process may be thought of as being in time and space or beyond them; as being cyclical or spiral or rectilinear, or as occurring in the form of a peculiar zigzag movement, sometimes called dialectical; as continuous and uniform, or irregular, broken by sudden leaps to 'new levels'; as due to the changing forms of one single 'force', or to conflicting elements locked (as in some ancient myth) in an eternal Pyrrhic struggle; as the history of one deity or 'force' or 'principle', or of several; as being destined to end well or badly; as holding out to human beings the prospect of eternal beatitude, or eternal damnation, or both in turn, or neither. But whatever version of the story is accepted – and it is never a scientific, that is, empirically testable theory, stated in quantitative terms, still less a description of what our eyes see and our ears hear[2] – the moral of it is always one and the same: that we must learn to distinguish the 'real' course of things from the dreams and fancies and 'rationalisations' which we construct unconsciously for our solace or amusement; for these may comfort us for a while, but will betray us cruelly in the end. There is, we are told, a nature of things, and it has a pattern in time: 'Things and actions are what

---

extreme forms these views contradict each other; in their softer and less consistent forms they tend to overlap, and even coalesce.

[1] Or, some prefer to say, Engels.

[2] No one has demonstrated this with more devastating lucidity than Karl Popper. While he seems to me somewhat to underestimate the differences between the methods of natural science and those of history or common sense (Hayek's *The Counter-Revolution of Science* seems, despite some exaggerations, to be more convincing on this topic), he has, in his *The Open Society and its Enemies* and *The Poverty of Historicism*, exposed some of the fallacies of metaphysical 'historicism' with such force and precision, and made so clear its incompatibility with any kind of scientific empiricism, that there is no further excuse for confounding the two.

they are,' said a sober English philosopher over two centuries ago, 'and the consequences of them will be what they will be: why then should we desire to be deceived?'[1]

What, then, must we do to avoid deception? At the very least – if we cannot swallow the notion of super-personal 'spirits' or 'forces' – we must admit that all events occur in discoverable, uniform, unaltering patterns; for if some did not, how could we find the laws of such occurrences? And without universal order – a system of true laws – how could history be 'intelligible'? How could it 'make sense', 'have meaning', be more than a picaresque account of a succession of random episodes, a mere collection (as Descartes, for this very reason, seems to have thought) of old wives' tales? Our values – what we think good and bad, important and trivial, right and wrong, noble and contemptible – all these are conditioned by the place we occupy in the pattern, on the moving stair. We praise and blame, worship and condemn whatever fits or does not fit the interests and needs and ideals that we seek to satisfy – the ends that (being made as we are) we cannot help pursuing – according to our lights, that is, our own perception of our condition, our place in 'Nature'. Such attitudes are held to be 'rational' and 'objective' to the degree to which we perceive this condition accurately, that is, understand where we are in terms of the great world plan, the movement whose regularities we discern as well as our historical sense and knowledge permit. To each condition and generation its own perspectives on the past and future, depending upon where it has arrived, what it has left behind, and whither it is moving; its values depend on this same awareness. To condemn the Greeks or the Romans or the Assyrians or the Aztecs for this or that folly or vice may be not more than to say that what they did or wished or thought conflicts with our own view of life, which may be the true or 'objective' view for the stage which we have reached, and which is perceived less or more clearly according to the depth and accuracy of our understanding of what this stage is, and of the manner in which it is developing. If the Romans and the Aztecs judged differently from us, they may have judged no less well and truly and 'objectively', to the degree to which they understood their own condition and their own very different stage of development. For us to condemn

---

[1] Joseph Butler, *Fifteen Sermons Preached at the Rolls Chapel* (London, 1726), sermon 7, p. 136 [§ 16].

their scale of values is valid enough for our condition, which is the sole frame of reference we have. And if they had known us they might have condemned us as harshly and, because their circumstances and values were what they inevitably were, with equal validity.

According to this view there is nothing, no point of rest outside the general movement, where we or they can take up a stand, no static absolute standards in terms of which things and persons can be finally evaluated. Hence the only attitudes correctly described, and rightly condemned, as relative, subjective and irrational are forms of failure to relate our judgement to our own truest interests, that is, to what will fulfil our natures most fully – to all that the next step in our inevitable development necessarily holds in store. Some thinkers of this school view subjective aberrations with compassion and condone them as temporary attitudes from which the enlightenment of the future will henceforward preserve mankind. Others gloat exultantly or ironically over the inevitable doom of those who misinterpret, and therefore fall foul of, the inexorable march of events. But whether the tone is charitable or sardonic, whether one condemns the errors of foolish individuals or the blind mob, or applauds their inevitable annihilation, this attitude rests on the belief that everything is caused to occur as it does by the machinery of history itself – by the impersonal forces of class, race, culture, History, Reason, the Life-Force, Progress, the Spirit of the Age. Given this organisation of our lives, which we did not create, and cannot alter, it, and it alone, is ultimately responsible for everything. To blame or praise individuals or groups of individuals for acting rightly or wrongly, so far as this entails a suggestion that they are in some sense genuinely free to choose between alternatives, and may therefore be justly and reasonably blamed or praised for choosing as they did and do, is a vast blunder, a return to some primitive or naïve conception of human beings as being able somehow to evade total determination of their lives by forces natural or supernatural, a relapse into a childish animism which the study of the relevant scientific or metaphysical system should swiftly dispel. For if such choices were real, the determined world structure which alone, on this view, makes complete explanation, whether scientific or metaphysical, possible could not exist. And this is ruled out as unthinkable, 'reason rejects it', it is confused, delusive, superficial, a piece of puerile megalomania, pre-scientific, unworthy of civilised men.

The notion that history obeys laws, whether natural or supernatural, that every event of human life is an element in a necessary pattern, has deep metaphysical origins: infatuation with the natural sciences feeds this stream, but is not its sole or, indeed, its principal source. In the first place there is the teleological outlook whose roots reach back to the beginnings of human thought. It occurs in many versions, but what is common to them all is the belief that men, and all living creatures and perhaps inanimate things as well, not merely are as they are, but have functions and pursue purposes. These purposes are either imposed upon them by a creator who has made every person and thing to serve each a specific goal; or else these purposes are not, indeed, imposed by a creator but are, as it were, internal to their possessors, so that every entity has a 'nature' and pursues a specific goal which is 'natural' to it, and the measure of its perfection consists in the degree to which it fulfils it. Evil, vice, imperfection, all the various forms of chaos and error, are, on this view, forms of frustration, impeded efforts to reach such goals, failures due either to misfortune, which puts obstacles in the path of self-fulfilment, or to misdirected attempts to fulfil some goal not 'natural' to the entity in question.

In this cosmology the world of men (and, in some versions, the entire universe) is a single all-inclusive hierarchy; so that to explain why each ingredient of it is as, and where, and when it is, and does what it does, is *eo ipso* to say what its goal is, how far it successfully fulfils it, and what are the relations of co-ordination and subordination between the goals of the various goal-pursuing entities in the harmonious pyramid which they collectively form. If this is a true picture of reality, then historical explanation, like every other form of explanation, must consist, above all, in the attribution to individuals, groups, nations, species of their proper place in the universal pattern. To know the 'cosmic' place of a thing or a person is to say what it is and does, and at the same time why it should be and do as it is and does. Hence to be and to have value, to exist and to have a function (and to fulfil it less or more successfully) are one and the same. The pattern, and it alone, brings into being, and causes to pass away, and confers purpose, that is to say, value and meaning, on all there is. To understand is to perceive patterns. To offer historical explanations is not merely to describe a succession of events, but to make it intelligible; to make intelligible is to reveal the basic pattern – not one of several possible patterns, but the one unique plan which, by being as it is, fulfils only one particular purpose, and consequently is revealed as fitting in a specifiable fashion within the single 'cosmic' overall schema which is the goal of the universe, the goal in virtue of which alone it is a universe at all, and not a chaos of unrelated bits and pieces. The more thoroughly the nature of this purpose is understood, and with it the pattern it entails in the various forms of human activity, the more explanatory or illuminating – the 'deeper' – the activity of the historian will be. Unless an event, or the character of an individual, or the activity of this or that institution or group or historical personage, is explained as a necessary consequence of its place in the pattern (and the larger, that is, the more comprehensive the schema, the more likely it is to be the true one), no explanation – and therefore no historical account – is being provided. The more inevitable an event or an action or a character can be exhibited as being, the better it has been understood, the profounder the researcher's insight, the nearer we are to the one embracing, ultimate truth.

This attitude is profoundly anti-empirical. We attribute purposes to all things and persons not because we have evidence for this hypothesis; for if there were a question of evidence for it, there could in principle be evidence against it; and then some things and events might turn out to have no purpose and therefore, in the sense used above, be incapable of being fitted into the pattern, that is, of being explained at all; but this cannot be, and is rejected in advance, a priori. We are plainly dealing not with an empirical theory but with a metaphysical attitude which takes for granted that to explain a thing – to describe it as it 'truly' is, even to define it more than verbally, that is, superficially – is to discover its purpose. Everything is in principle explicable, for everything has a purpose, although our minds may be too feeble or too distraught to discover in any given case what this purpose is. On such a view to say of things or persons that they exist is to say that they pursue goals; to say that they exist or are real, yet literally lack a purpose, whether imposed from outside or 'inherent' or 'innate', is to say something not false, but literally self-contradictory and therefore meaningless. Teleology is not a theory, or a hypothesis, but a category or a framework in terms of which everything is, or should be, conceived and described.

The influence of this attitude on the writing of history from the epic of Gilgamesh to those enjoyable games of patience which Arnold Toynbee plays with the past and future of mankind – and plays with exhilarating skill and imagination – is too familiar to need emphasis. It enters, however unconsciously, into the thought and language of those who speak of the 'rise' and 'fall' of States or movements or classes or individuals as if they obeyed some irresistible rhythm, a rising or falling wave of some cosmic river, a tidal ebb or flow in human affairs, subject to natural or supernatural laws; as if discoverable regularities had been imposed on individuals or 'super-individuals' by a Manifest Destiny, as if the notion of life as a play were more than a vivid metaphor.[1] To those who use this figure history is a piece – or succession of pieces – comical or tragical, a libretto whose heroes and villains, winners and losers, speak their lines and suffer their fate in accordance with the text conceived in terms of them but not by them; for otherwise nothing could be rightly conceived as tragical or comical; no pattern – no rules – no explanation. Historians, journalists, ordinary men speak in these terms; they have become part and parcel of ordinary speech. Yet to take such metaphors and turns of phrase literally; to believe that such patterns are not invented but intuitively discovered or discerned, that they are not only some among many possible tunes which the same sounds can be made to yield to the musical ear, but are in some sense unique; to think that there exists

---

[1] I do not, of course, wish to imply that metaphors and figures of speech can be dispensed with in ordinary utterance, still less in the sciences; only that the danger of illicit 'reification' – the mistaking of words for things, metaphors for realities – is even greater in this sphere than is usually supposed. The most notorious cases are, of course, those of the State or the Nation, the quasi-personification of which has rightly made philosophers and even plain men uneasy or indignant for over a century. But many other words and usages offer similar dangers. Historical movements exist, and we must be allowed to call them such. Collective acts do occur; societies do rise, flourish, decay, die. Patterns, 'atmospheres', complex interrelationships of men or cultures are what they are, and cannot be analysed away into atomic constituents. Nevertheless, to take such expressions so literally that it becomes natural and normal to attribute to them causal properties, active powers, transcendent properties, demands for human sacrifice, is to be fatally deceived by myths. 'Rhythms' in history occur, but it is a sinister symptom of one's condition to speak of them as 'inexorable'. Cultures possess patterns, and ages spirits; but to explain human actions as their 'inevitable' consequences or expressions is to be a victim of misuse of words. There is no formula which guarantees a successful escape from either the Scylla of populating the world with imaginary powers and dominions, or the Charybdis of reducing everything to the verifiable behaviour of identifiable men and women in precisely denotable places and times. One can do no more than point to the existence of these perils; one must navigate between them as best one can.

*the* pattern, *the* basic rhythm of history – something which both creates and justifies all that there is – that is to take the game too seriously, to see in it a key to reality. Certainly it is to commit oneself to the view that the notion of individual responsibility is, 'in the end', an illusion. No effort, however ingenious, to re-interpret that much-tormented expression will, within a teleologi-cal system, restore its normal meaning to the notion of free choice. The puppets may be conscious and identify themselves happily with the inevitable process in which they play their parts; but it remains inevitable, and they remain marionettes.

Teleology is not, of course, the only metaphysics of history; side by side with it there has persisted a distinction of appearance and reality even more celebrated but of a somewhat different kind. For the teleological thinker all apparent disorder, inexplicable disaster, gratuitous suffering, unintelligible concatenations of random events are due not to the nature of things but to our failure to discover their purpose. Everything that seems useless, discordant, mean, ugly, vicious, distorted is needed, if we but knew it, for the harmony of the whole which only the Creator of the world, or the world itself (if it could become wholly aware of itself and its goals), can know. Total failure is excluded a priori, for at a 'deeper' level all processes will always be seen to culminate in success; and since there must always exist a level 'deeper' than that of any given insight, there is in principle no empirical test of what constitutes 'ultimate' success or failure. Teleology is a form of faith capable of neither confirmation nor refutation by any kind of experience; the notions of evidence, proof, probability and so on are wholly inapplicable to it.

But there is a second, no less time-honoured view according to which it is not goals, less or more dimly discerned, which explain and justify whatever happens, but a timeless, permanent, transcen-dent reality, 'above', or 'outside', or 'beyond'; which is as it is for ever, in perfect, inevitable, self-explaining harmony. Each element of it is necessitated to be what it is by its relations to the other elements and to the whole. If the world does not appear to manifest this, if we do not see actual events and persons as connected with each other by those relations of logical necessity which would make it inconceivable that anything could be other than it is, that is due solely to the failure of our own vision. We are blinded by ignorance, stupidity, passion, and the task of explana-tion in science or in history is the attempt to show the chaos of appearances as an imperfect reflection of the perfect order of reality, so that once more everything falls into its proper place. Explanation is the discovery of the 'underlying' pattern. The ideal is now not a distant prospect beckoning all things and persons towards self-realisation, but a self-consistent, eternal, ultimate 'structure of reality', compresent 'timelessly', as it were, with the confused world of the senses which it casts as a distorted image or a feeble shadow, and of which it is at once the origin, the cause, the explanation and the justification. The relation of this reality to the world of appearances forms the subject-matter of all the departments of true philosophy – of ethics, aesthetics, logic, of the philosophy of history and of law and of politics, according to the 'aspect' of the basic relation that is selected for attention. But under all its various names – form and matter, the one and the many, ends and means, subject and object, order and chaos, change and rest, the perfect and the imperfect, the natural and the artificial, nature and mind – the central issue, that of Reality and Appearance, remains one and the same. To understand truly is to understand it and it alone. It plays the part which the notion of function and purpose plays in teleology. It alone at once explains and justifies.

Finally there is the influence of the natural sciences. At first this seems a paradox: scientific method is surely the very negation of metaphysical speculation. But historically the one is closely interwoven with the other, and, in the field of which I speak, shows important affinities with it, namely, the notion that all that exists is necessarily an object in material nature, and therefore susceptible to explanation by scientific laws. If Newton was able in principle to explain every movement of every particular constituent of physical nature in terms of a small number of laws of great generality, is it not reasonable to suppose that psychological events, which constitute the conscious and unconscious lives of individuals, as well as social facts – the internal relationships and activities and 'experiences' of societies – could be explained by the use of similar methods? It is true that we seem to know a good deal less about the subject-matter of psychology and sociology than about the facts dealt with by physics or chemistry; but is there any objection in principle to the view that a sufficiently scrupulous and imaginative investigation of human beings might, one day, reveal laws capable of yielding predictions as powerful and as precise as those which are now possible in the natural sciences? If psychology and sociology ever attain to their proper stature – and why should they not? – we shall have laws enabling us, at least in theory (for it might still be difficult in practice), to predict (or reconstruct) every detail in the lives of every single human being in the future, present and past. If this is (as surely it is) the theoretical ideal of such sciences as psychology, sociology and anthropology, historical explanations will, if they are successful, simply consist in the application of the laws – the established hypotheses – of these sciences to specific individual situations. There will perhaps be 'pure' psychology, sociology, history, that is, the principles themselves; and there will be their 'application': there will come into being social mathematics, social physics, social engineering, the 'physiology' of every feeling and attitude and inclination, as precise and powerful and useful as their originals in the natural sciences. And indeed this is the very phraseology and the ideal of eighteenth-century rationalists like Holbach and d'Alembert and Condorcet. The metaphysicians are victims of a delusion; nothing in nature is transcendent, nothing purposive; everything is measurable; the day will dawn when, in answer to all the painful problems now besetting us, we shall be able to say with Leibniz, 'calculemus',[1] and return the answers clearly, exactly and conclusively.

What all these concepts – metaphysical and scientific alike – have in common (despite their even vaster differences) is the notion that to explain is to subsume under general formulae, to represent as examples of laws which cover an infinite number of instances; so that with knowledge of all the relevant laws, and of a sufficient range of relevant facts, it will be possible to tell not merely what happens, but also why; for, if the laws have been correctly established, to describe something is, in effect, to assert that it cannot happen otherwise. The question 'Why?' for teleologists means 'In pursuit of what unalterable goal?'; for the non-teleological metaphysical 'realists' it means 'Determined unalterably by what ultimate pattern?'; and for the upholders of the Comtean ideals of social statics and dynamics it means 'Resulting from what causes?' – actual causes which are as they are, whether they might have been otherwise or not. The inevitability of historical processes, of trends, of 'rises' and 'falls', is merely *de facto* for those who believe that the universe obeys only 'natural laws' which make

---

[1] 'Let us calculate': e.g. *Die philosophischen Schriften von Gottfried Wilhelm Leibniz*, ed. C. I. Gerhardt (Berlin, 1875–90), vol. 7, p. 200. Condorcet, in particular, had the same attitude.

it what it is; it is *de jure* as well – the justification as well as the explanation – for those who see such uniformity as not merely something given, brute fact, something unchangeable and unquestionable, but as patterns, plans, purposes, ideals, as thoughts in the mind of a rational Deity or Universal Reason, as goals, as aesthetic, self-fulfilling wholes, as metaphysical rationales, theological otherworldly justifications, as theodicies, which satisfy the craving to know not merely why the world exists, but why it is worthy of existence; and why it is this particular world that exists, rather than some other, or no world at all; the solution being provided in terms of values which are either somehow 'embedded' in the facts themselves or 'determine' them from some 'transcendent' height or depth. All these theories are, in one sense or another, forms of determinism, whether they be teleological, metaphysical, mechanistic, religious, aesthetic or scientific. And one common characteristic of all such outlooks is the implication that the individual's freedom of choice (at any rate here, below) is ultimately an illusion, that the notion that human beings could have chosen otherwise than they did usually rests upon ignorance of facts; with the consequence that any assertion that they should have acted thus or thus, might have avoided this or that, and deserve (and not merely elicit or respond to) praise or blame, approval or condemnation, rests upon the presupposition that some area, at any rate, of their lives is not totally determined by laws, whether metaphysical or theological or expressing the generalised probabilities of the sciences. And this assumption, it is then maintained, is patently false. The advance of knowledge constantly brings new areas of experience under the sway of laws which make systematic inference and prediction possible. Hence we can, if we seek to be rational, praise and condemn, warn and encourage, advocate justice or self-interest, forgive, condone, make resolutions, issue orders, feel justified remorse, only to the degree to which we remain ignorant of the true nature of the world. The more we know, the farther the area of human freedom, and consequently of responsibility, is narrowed. For the omniscient being, who sees why nothing can be otherwise than as it is, the notions of responsibility or guilt, of right and wrong, are necessarily empty; they are a mere measure of ignorance, of adolescent illusion; and the perception of this is the first sign of moral and intellectual maturity.

This doctrine has taken several forms. There are those who believe that moral judgements are groundless because we know too much, and there are those who believe that they are unjustified because we know too little. And again, among the former there are those whose determinism is optimistic and benevolent, and those whose determinism is pessimistic, or else confident of a happy ending yet at the same time indignantly or sardonically malevolent. Some look to history for salvation; others for justice; for vengeance; for annihilation. Among the optimistic are the confident rationalists, in particular the heralds and prophets (from Bacon to modern social theorists) of the natural sciences and of material progress, who maintain that vice and suffering are in the end always the product of ignorance. The foundation of their faith is the conviction that it is possible to find out what all men at all times truly want; and also what they can do and what is for ever beyond their power; and, in the light of this, to invent, discover and adapt means to realisable ends. Weakness and misery, folly and vice, moral and intellectual defects are due to maladjustment. To understand the nature of things is (at the very least) to know what you (and others who, if they are human, will be like you) truly want, and how to get it. All that is bad is due to ignorance of ends or of means; to attain to knowledge of both is the purpose and function of the sciences. The sciences will advance; true ends as well as efficient means will be discovered; knowledge will increase, men will know more, and therefore be wiser and better and happier. Condorcet, whose *Esquisse* is the simplest and most moving statement of this belief, has no doubt that happiness, scientific knowledge, virtue and liberty are bound as 'by an indissoluble chain',[1] while stupidity, vice, injustice and unhappiness are forms of a disease which the advance of science will eliminate for ever; for we are made what we are by natural causes; and when we understand them, this alone will suffice to bring us into harmony with 'Nature'.

Praise and blame are functions of ignorance; we are what we are, like stones and trees, like bees and beavers, and if it is irrational to blame or demand justice from things or animals, climates or soils or wild beasts, when they cause us pain, it is no less irrational to blame the no less determined characters or acts of men. We can regret – and deplore and expose – the depth of human cruelty, injustice and stupidity, and comfort ourselves with the certainty

---

[1] *Esquisse d'un tableau historique des progrès de l'esprit humain*, ed. O. H. Prior and Yvon Belaval (Paris, 1970), p. 228.

that with the rapid progress of our new empirical knowledge this will soon pass away like an evil dream; for progress and education, if not inevitable, are at any rate highly probable. The belief in the possibility (or probability) of happiness as the product of rational organisation unites all the benevolent sages of modern times, from the metaphysicians of the Italian Renaissance to the evolutionary thinkers of the German *Aufklärung*, from the radicals and utilitarians of pre-revolutionary France to the science-worshipping visionaries of the nineteenth and twentieth centuries. It is the heart of all the Utopias from Bacon and Campanella to Lessing and Condorcet, Saint-Simon and Cabet, Fourier and Owen, culminating in the bureaucratic fantasies of Auguste Comte, with his fanatically tidy world of human beings joyfully engaged in fulfilling their functions, each within his own rigorously defined province, in the rationally ordered, totally unalterable hierarchy of the perfect society. These are the benevolent humanitarian prophets – our own age has known not a few of them, from Jules Verne and H. G. Wells and Anatole France and Bernard Shaw to their unnumbered American disciples – generously disposed towards all mankind, genuinely seeking to rescue every living being from its burden of ignorance, sorrow, poverty and humiliating dependence on others.

The other variant of this attitude is a good deal less amiable in tone and in feeling. When Hegel, and after him Marx, describe historical processes, they too assume that human beings and their societies are part and parcel of a wider nature, which Hegel regards as spiritual, and Marx as material, in character. Great social forces are at work of which only the acutest and most gifted individuals are ever aware; the ordinary run of men are blind in varying degrees to that which truly shapes their lives, they worship fetishes and invent childish mythologies, which they dignify with the title of views or theories in order to explain the world in which they live. From time to time the real forces – impersonal and irresistible – which truly govern the world develop to a point where a new historical advance is 'due'. Then (as both Hegel and Marx notoriously believed) the crucial moments of advance are reached; these take the form of violent, cataclysmic leaps, destructive revolutions which, often with fire and sword, establish a new order upon the ruins of the old. Inevitably the foolish, obsolete, purblind, home-made philosophies of the denizens of the old establishment are knocked over and swept away together with their possessors.

For Hegel, and for a good many others, though by no means all, among the philosophers and poets of the romantic movement, history is a perpetual struggle of vast spiritual forces embodied now in institutions – Churches, races, civilisations, empires, national States – now in individuals of more than human stature – 'world-historical figures' – of bold and ruthless genius, towering over, and contemptuous of, their puny contemporaries. For Marx, the struggle is a fight between socially conditioned, organised groups – classes shaped by the struggle for subsistence and survival and consequently for the control of power. There is a sardonic note (inaudible only to their most benevolent and single-hearted followers) in the words of both these thinkers as they contemplate the discomfiture and destruction of the philistines, the ordinary men and women caught in one of the decisive moments of history. Both Hegel and Marx conjure up an image of peaceful and foolish human beings, largely unaware of the part they play in history, building their homes, with touching hope and simplicity, upon the green slopes of what seems to them a peaceful mountainside, trusting in the permanence of their particular way of life, their own economic, social and political order, treating their own values as if they were eternal standards, living, working, fighting without any awareness of the cosmic processes of which their lives are but a passing stage. But the mountain is no ordinary mountain; it is a volcano; and when (as the philosopher always knew that it would) the inevitable eruption comes, their homes and their elaborately tended institutions and their ideals and their ways of life and values will be blown out of existence in the cataclysm which marks the leap from the 'lower' to a 'higher' stage. When this point is reached, the two great prophets of destruction are in their element; they enter into their inheritance; they survey the conflagration with a defiant, almost Byronic, irony and disdain. To be wise is to understand the direction in which the world is inexorably moving, to identify oneself with the rising power which ushers in the new world. Marx – and it is part of his attraction to those of a similar emotional cast – identifies himself exultantly, in his way no less passionately than Nietzsche or Bakunin, with the great force which in its very destructiveness is creative, and is greeted with bewilderment and horror only by those whose values are hopelessly subjective, who listen to their consciences, their feelings, or to what their nurses or teachers tell them, without realising the glories of life in a world which moves from explosion to explosion to fulfil the great cosmic design. When history takes her revenge – and every *enragé* prophet in the nineteenth century looks to her to avenge him against those he hates most – the mean, pathetic, ludicrous, stifling human anthills will be justly pulverised; justly, because what is just and unjust, good and bad, is determined by the goal towards which all creation is tending. Whatever is on the side of victorious reason is just and wise; whatever is on the other side, on the side of the world that is doomed to destruction by the working of the forces of reason, is rightly called foolish, ignorant, subjective, arbitrary, blind; and, if it goes so far as to try to resist the forces that are destined to supplant it, then it – that is to say, the fools and knaves and mediocrities who constitute it – is rightly called retrograde, wicked, obscurantist, perversely hostile to the deepest interests of mankind.

Different though the tone of these forms of determinism may be – whether scientific, humanitarian and optimistic or furious, apocalyptic and exultant – they agree in this: that the world has a direction and is governed by laws, and that the direction and the laws can in some degree be discovered by employing the proper techniques of investigation; and moreover that the working of these laws can only be grasped by those who realise that the lives, characters and acts of individuals, both mental and physical, are governed by the larger 'wholes' to which they belong, and that it is the independent evolution of these 'wholes' that constitutes the so-called 'forces' in terms of whose direction truly 'scientific' (or 'philosophic') history must be formulated. To find the explanation of why given individuals, or groups of them, act or think or feel in one way rather than another, one must first seek to understand the structure, the state of development and the direction of such 'wholes', for example, the social, economic, political, religious institutions to which such individuals belong; once that is known, the behaviour of the individuals (or the most characteristic among them) should become almost logically deducible, and does not constitute a separate problem. Ideas about the identity of these large entities or forces, and their functions, differ from theorist to theorist. Race, colour, Church, nation, class; climate, irrigation, technology, geopolitical situation; civilisation, social structure, the Human Spirit, the Collective Unconscious, to take some of these concepts at random, have all played their parts in theologico-historical systems as the protagonists upon the stage of history. They are represented as the real forces of which individuals are ingredients, at once constitutive, and the most articulate expressions, of this or that phase of them. Those who are more clearly and deeply aware than others of the part which they play, whether willingly or not, to that degree play it more boldly and effectively; these are the natural leaders. Others, led by their own petty personal concerns into ignoring or forgetting that they are parts of a continuous or convulsive pattern of change, are deluded into assuming that (or, at any rate, into acting as if) they and their fellows are stabilised at some fixed level for ever.

What the variants of either of these attitudes entail, like all forms of genuine determinism, is the elimination of the notion of individual responsibility. It is, after all, natural enough for men, whether for practical reasons or because they are given to reflection, to ask who or what is responsible for this or that state of affairs which they view with satisfaction or anxiety, enthusiasm or horror. If the history of the world is due to the operation of identifiable forces other than, and little affected by, free human wills and free choices (whether these occur or not), then the proper explanation of what happens must be given in terms of the evolution of such forces. And there is then a tendency to say that not individuals, but these larger entities, are ultimately 'responsible'. I live at a particular moment of time in the spiritual and social and economic circumstances into which I have been cast: how then can I help choosing and acting as I do? The values in terms of which I conduct my life are the values of my class, or race, or Church, or civilisation, or are part and parcel of my 'station' – my position in the 'social structure'. Nobody denies that it would be stupid as well as cruel to blame me for not being taller than I am, or to regard the colour of my hair or the qualities of my intellect or heart as being due principally to my own free choice; these attributes are as they are through no decision of mine. If I extend this category without limit, then whatever is, is necessary and inevitable. This unlimited extension of necessity, on any of the views described above, becomes intrinsic to the explanation of everything. To blame and praise, consider possible alternative courses of action, accuse or defend historical figures for acting as they do or did, becomes an absurd activity. Admiration and contempt for this or that individual may indeed continue, but it becomes akin to aesthetic judgement. We can eulogise or deplore, feel love or hatred, satisfaction or shame, but we can neither blame nor justify. Alexander, Caesar, Attila, Muhammad, Crom-well, Hitler are like floods and earthquakes, sunsets, oceans, mountains; we may admire or fear them, welcome or curse them, but to denounce or extol their acts is (ultimately) as sensible as addressing sermons to a tree (as Frederick the Great pointed out with his customary pungency in the course of his attack on Holbach's *System of Nature*).[1]

[1] Determinism is, of course, not identical with fatalism, which is only one, and not the most plausible, species of the vast determinist genus. The majority of determinists seem to maintain that such distinctions as those between voluntary behaviour, or between acts and mechanical movements or states, or what a man is and what he is not accountable for, and therefore the very notion of a moral agent, depend on what is or could be affected by individual choice, effort or decision. They hold that I normally praise or blame a man only if, and because, I think that what occurred was (or might at any rate in part be) caused by his choice or the absence of it; and should not praise or blame him if his choices, efforts etc. were conspicuously unable to affect the result that I applaud or deplore; and that this is compatible with the most rigorous determinism, since choice, effort etc. are themselves causally inevitable consequences of identifiable spatio-temporal antecedents. This (in substance the classical 'dissolution' of the problem of free will by the British empiricists – Hobbes, Locke, Hume and their modern followers Russell, Schlick, Ayer, Nowell-Smith, Hampshire etc.) does not seem to me to solve the problem, but merely to push it a step further back. It may be that for legal or other purposes I may define responsibility, moral accountability etc. on some such lines as these. But if I were convinced that although acts of choice, dispositional characteristics etc. did affect what occurred, yet were themselves wholly determined by factors not within the individual's control (including his own motives and springs of action), I should certainly not regard him as morally praiseworthy or blameworthy. In such circumstances the concept of worth and desert, as these terms are now used, would become empty for me.

The same kind of objection seems to me to apply to the connected doctrine that free will is tantamount to capacity for being (causally) affected by praise, blame, persuasion, education etc. Whether the causes that are held completely to determine human action are physical or psychical or of some other kind, and in whatever pattern or proportion they are deemed to occur, if they are truly causes – if their outcomes are thought to be as unalterable as, say, the effects of physical or physiological causes – this of itself seems to me to make the notion of a free choice between alternatives inapplicable. On this view 'I could have acted otherwise' is made to mean 'I could have acted otherwise if I had chosen', i.e. if there were no insuperable obstacle to hinder me (with the rider that my choice may well be affected by praise, social disapproval etc.); but if my choice is itself the result of antecedent causes, I am, in the relevant sense, not free. Freedom to act depends not on absence of only this or that set of fatal obstacles to action – physical or biological, let us say – while other obstacles, e.g. psychological ones – character, habits, 'compulsive' motives etc. – are present; it requires a situation in which no sum total of such causal factors wholly determines the result – in which

To assess degrees of their responsibility, to attribute this or that consequence to their free decision, to set them up as examples or deterrents, to seek to derive lessons from their lives, becomes senseless. We can feel ashamed of our acts or of our states of mind, or of theirs, as a hunchback may be ashamed of his hump; but we cannot feel remorse: for that entails the belief that we not only could have acted otherwise, but also could have freely chosen to do so. These men were what they were; and so are we. They acted as they acted; and so do we. Their behaviour can be explained in terms of whatever fundamental category is to be used, whereby history is reducible to a natural science or a metaphysical or theological schema. So much we can do for them, and, to a more limited degree, for ourselves and our contemporaries. This is all that can be done.

Yet we are adjured, oddly enough, by tough-minded determinists, in the very name of the scientific status of the subject, to avoid bias; regular appeals are made to historians to refrain from sitting in judgement, to remain objective, not to read the values of the present into the past, or of the West into the East; not to admire or condemn ancient Romans for being like or unlike modern Americans; not to denounce the Middle Ages because they failed to practise toleration as it was conceived by Voltaire, nor applaud the Gracchi because we are shocked by the social injustices of our time, or criticise Cicero because of our own experience of lawyers in politics. What are we to make of such exhortations, or of the

there remains some area, however narrow, within which choice is not completely determined. This is the minimal sense of 'can' in this context. Kant's argument that where there is no freedom there is no obligation, where there is no independence of causes there is no responsibility and therefore no desert, and consequently no occasion for praise or reproach, carries conviction. If I can correctly say 'I cannot help choosing thus or thus', I am not free. To say that among the factors which determine the situation are my own character, habits, decisions, choices etc. – which is, of course, conspicuously true – does not alter the case, or render me, in the only relevant sense, free. The feeling of those who have recognised free will as a genuine issue, and are not deceived by the latest efforts to interpret it away, turns out, as so often in the case of major problems which have plagued thoughtful men in every generation, to be sound as against philosophers armed with some all-conquering simple method of sweeping troublesome questions out of sight. Dr Johnson, as in other matters affecting common-sense notions, here, too, seems to have been guided by a sound linguistic sense. It does not, of course, follow that any of the analyses so far provided of the relevant senses of 'can', 'freedom', 'uncaused' etc. is satisfactory. To cut the knot, as Dr Johnson did, is not to untie it.

perpetual pleas to use our imagination or our powers of sympathy or of understanding in order to avoid the injustice that springs from an insufficient grasp of the aims and codes and customs of cultures distant from us in time or space? What meaning has this, save on the assumption that to give moral praise and blame, to seek to be just, is not totally irrational, that human beings deserve justice as stocks or stones do not, and that therefore we must seek to be fair, and not praise and blame arbitrarily, or mistakenly, through ignorance, or prejudice, or lack of imagination? Yet once we transfer responsibility for what happens from the backs of individuals to the casual or teleological operation of institutions or cultures or psychical or physical factors, what can be meant by calling upon our sympathy or sense of history, or sighing after the ideal of total impartiality, which may not indeed be fully attainable, but to which some come nearer than others? Few are accused of biased accounts of geological changes or lack of intuitive sympathy in describing the effect of the Italian climate upon the agriculture of ancient Rome.

To this it may be answered that even if history, like natural science, is satisfaction of curiosity about unalterable processes – merely disfigured by the intrusion of moral judgements – we shall attain a less adequate grasp of even the bare facts unless we have some degree of imaginative insight into ways of life alien, or little known, to us. This is doubtless true; but it does not penetrate to the heart of the objection brought against historians who are accused of prejudice or of colouring their accounts too strongly. It may be (and has doubtless often been said) that Gibbon or Macaulay or Treitschke or Belloc fail to reproduce the facts as we suspect them to have been. To say this is, of course, to accuse the writers of serious inadequacy as historians; but that is not the main gravamen of the charge. It is rather that they are in some sense not merely inaccurate or superficial or incomplete, but that they are unjust; that they are seeking to secure our approval for one side, and, in order to achieve this, unfairly denigrate the other; that in dealing with one side they cite evidence and use methods of inference or presentation which, for no good reason, they deny to the other; and that their motive for doing this derives from their conviction of how men should be, and what they should do; and sometimes also that these convictions spring from views which (judged in terms of the ordinary standards and scales of value which prevail in the societies to which they and we belong) are too narrow; or irrational or inapplicable to the historical period in question; and that because of this they have suppressed or distorted the true facts, as true facts are conceived by the educated society of their, or our, time. We complain, that is to say, not merely of suppression or distortion, but of propagandist aims to which we think this may be due; and to speak of propaganda at all, let alone assume that it can be dangerously effective, is to imply that the notion of injustice is not inoperative, that marks for conduct are, and can properly be, awarded; it is in effect to say that I must either seek not to praise or blame at all, or, if I cannot avoid doing so because I am a human being and my views are inevitably shot through with moral assessments, I should seek to do so justly, with detachment, on the evidence, not blaming men for failing to do the impossible, and not praising them for it either. And this, in its turn, entails belief in individual responsibility – at any rate some degree of it. How great a degree – how wide the realm of possibility, of alternatives freely choosable – will depend on one's reading of nature and history; but it will never be nothing at all.

And yet it is this, it seems to me, that is virtually denied by those historians and sociologists, steeped in metaphysical or scientific determinism, who think it right to say that in (what they are fond of calling) 'the last analysis', everything – or so much of it as makes no difference – boils down to the effects of class, or race, or civilisation, or social structure. Such thinkers seem to me committed to the belief that although we may not be able to plot the exact curve of each individual life with the data at our disposal and the laws we claim to have discovered, yet, in principle, if we were omniscient, we could do so; and that consequently even that minimum residue of value judgement which no amount of conscious self-discipline and self-effacement can wholly eliminate, which colours and is a part of our very choice of historical material, of our emphasis, however tentative, upon some events and persons as being more important or interesting or unusual than others, must be either the result of our own 'ineluctable' conditioning, or else the fruit of our own incurable vanity and ignorance; and in either case remains in practice unavoidable – the price of our human status, part of the imperfection of man; and must be accepted only because it literally cannot be rejected, because men and their outlooks are what they are, and men judge as they do; because they are finite, and forget, or cannot face, the fact that they are so.

This stern conclusion is not, of course, actually accepted by any working historian, or any human being in his non-theoretical moments; even though, paradoxically enough, the arguments by which we are led to such untenable conclusions, by stressing how much narrower is the area of human freedom, and therefore of responsibility, than it was believed to be during the ages of scientific ignorance, have taught many admirable lessons in restraint and humility. But to maintain that, since men are 'determined', history, by which I mean the activity of historians, cannot, strictly speaking, ever be just or unjust but only true or false, wise or stupid, is to expound a noble fallacy, and one that can seldom, if ever, have been acted upon. For its theoretical acceptance, however half-hearted, has led to the drawing of exceedingly civilised consequences, and checked much traditional cruelty and injustice.

III

The proposition that everything that we do and suffer is part of a fixed pattern – that Laplace's observer (supplied with adequate knowledge of facts and laws) could at any moment of historical time describe correctly every past and future event, including those of the 'inner' life, that is, human thoughts, feelings, acts – has often been entertained, and very different implications have been drawn from it; belief in its truth has dismayed some and inspired others. But whether or not determinism is true or even coherent, it seems clear that acceptance of it does not in fact colour the ordinary thoughts of the majority of human beings, including historians, nor even those of natural scientists outside the laboratory. For if it did, the language of the believers would reflect this fact, and be different from that of the rest of us.

There is a class of expressions which we constantly use (and can scarcely do without), like 'You should not (or need not) have done this'; 'Need you have made this terrible mistake?'; 'I could do it, but I would rather not'; 'Why did the King of Ruritania abdicate? Because, unlike the King of Abyssinia, he lacked the strength of will to resist'; '*Must* the Commander-in-Chief be quite so stupid?' Expressions of this type plainly involve the notion of more than the merely logical possibility of the realisation of alternatives other than those which were in fact realised, namely of differences between situations in which individuals can be reasonably regarded as being responsible for their acts, and those in which they can not. For no one will wish to deny that we do often argue about the best among the possible courses of action open to human beings in the present and past and future, in fiction and in dreams; that historians (and detectives and judges and juries) do attempt to establish, as well as they are able, what these possibilities are; that the ways in which these lines are drawn mark the frontiers between reliable and unreliable history; that what is called realism (as opposed to fancy or ignorance of life or Utopian dreams) consists precisely in the placing of what occurred (or might occur) in the context of what could have happened (or could happen) and in the demarcation of this from what could not; that this is what (as I think L. B. Namier once suggested) the sense of history, in the end, comes to; that upon this capacity historical (as well as legal) justice depends; that it alone makes it possible to speak of criticism, or praise and blame, as just or deserved or absurd or unfair; or that this is the sole and obvious reason why accidents, *force majeure* – being unavoidable – are necessarily outside the category of responsibility and consequently beyond the bounds of criticism, of the attribution of praise and blame. The difference between the expected and the exceptional, the difficult and the easy, the normal and the perverse, rests upon the drawing of these same lines.

All this seems too self-evident to argue. It seems superfluous to add that all the discussions of historians about whether a given policy could or could not have been prevented, and what view should therefore be taken of the acts and characters of the actors, are intelligible only on the assumption of the reality of human choices. If determinism were a valid theory of human behaviour, these distinctions would be as inappropriate as the attribution of moral responsibility to the planetary system or the tissues of a living cell. These categories permeate all that we think and feel so pervasively and universally that to think them away, and conceive what and how we should be thinking, feeling and talking without them, or in the framework of their opposites, psychologically greatly strains our capacity – is nearly, if not quite, as impracticable as, let us say, to pretend that we live in a world in which space, time or number in the normal sense no longer exist. We may indeed always argue about specific situations, about whether a given occurrence is best explained as the inevitable effect of antecedent events beyond human control, or on the contrary as due to free human choice; free in the sense not merely that the case would have been altered if we had chosen – tried to act – differently; but that nothing prevented us from so choosing.

It may well be that the growth of science and historical knowledge does in fact tend to show – make probable – that much of what was hitherto attributed to the acts of the unfettered wills of individuals can be satisfactorily explained only by the working of other, 'natural', impersonal factors; that we have, in our ignorance or vanity, extended the realm of human freedom much too far. Yet the very meaning of such terms as 'cause' and 'inevitable' depends on the possibility of contrasting them with at least their imaginary opposites. These alternatives may be improbable; but they must at least be conceivable, if only for the purpose of contrasting them with causal necessities and law-observing uniformities; unless we attach some meaning to the notion of free acts, that is, acts not wholly determined by antecedent events or by the nature and 'dispositional characteristics' of either persons or things, it is difficult to see why we come to distinguish acts to which responsibility is attached from mere segments in a physical, psychical, or psychophysical causal chain of events – a distinction signified (even if all particular applications of it are mistaken) by the cluster of expressions which deal with open alternatives and free choices. Yet it is this distinction that underlies our normal attribution of values, in particular the notion that praise and blame can ever be justly (not merely usefully or effectively) bestowed. If the determinist hypothesis were true, and adequately accounted for the actual world, there is a clear sense in which, despite all the extraordinary casuistry which has been brought to bear to avoid this conclusion, the notion of human responsibility, as ordinarily understood, would no longer apply to any actual, but only to imaginary or conceivable, states of affairs.

I do not here wish to say that determinism is necessarily false, only that we neither speak nor think as if it could be true, and that it is difficult, and perhaps beyond our normal powers, to conceive what our picture of the world would be if we seriously believed it; so that to speak, as some theorists of history (and scientists with a philosophical bent) tend to do, as if one might (in life and not only in the study) accept the determinist hypothesis, and yet continue to think and speak much as we do at present, is to breed intellectual confusion. If the belief in freedom – which rests on the assumption that human beings do occasionally choose, and that their choices are not wholly accounted for by the kind of causal explanations which are accepted in, say, physics or biology – if this is a necessary illusion, it is so deep and so pervasive that it is not felt as such.[1] No doubt we can try to convince ourselves that we are systematically deluded;[2] but unless we attempt to think out the implications of this possibility, and alter our modes of thought and speech to allow for it accordingly, this hypothesis remains hollow; that is, we find it impracticable even to entertain it seriously, if our behaviour is to be taken as evidence of what we can and what we cannot bring ourselves to believe or suppose not merely in theory, but in practice.

My submission is that to make a serious attempt to adapt our thoughts and words to the hypothesis of determinism is a fearful task, as things are now, and have been within recorded history. The changes involved are very radical; our moral and psychological categories are, in the end, more flexible than our physical ones, but not much more so; it is not much easier to begin to think out in real terms, to which behaviour and speech would correspond, what the universe of the genuine determinist would be like, than to think out, with the minimum of indispensable concrete detail (that is, begin to imagine) what it would be like to be in a timeless world, or one with a seventeen-dimensional space. Let those who doubt this try for themselves; the symbols with which we think will hardly lend themselves to the experiment; they, in their turn, are too deeply involved in our normal view of the world, allowing for every difference of period and clime and culture, to be capable of so violent a break. We can, of course, work out the logical implications of any set of internally consistent premisses – logic and mathematics will do any work that is required of them – but

[1] What can and what cannot be done by particular agents in specific circumstances is an empirical question, properly settled, like all such questions, by an appeal to experience. If all acts were causally determined by antecedent conditions which were themselves similarly determined, and so on *ad infinitum*, such investigations would rest on an illusion. As rational beings we should, in that case, make an effort to disillusion ourselves – to cast off the spell of appearances; but we should surely fail. The delusion, if it is one, belongs to the order of what Kant called 'empirically real' and 'transcendentally ideal'. To try to place ourselves outside the categories which govern our empirical ('real') experience is what he regarded as an unintelligible plan of action. This thesis is surely valid, and can be stated without the paraphernalia of the Kantian system.

[2] This desperate effort to remain at once within and without the engulfing dream, to say the unsayable, is irresistible to German metaphysicians of a certain type: e.g. Schopenhauer and Vaihinger.

this is a very different thing from knowing how the result would look 'in practice', what the concrete innovations are; and, since history is not a deductive science (and even sociology becomes progressively less intelligible as it loses touch with its empirical foundations), such hypotheses, being abstract models, pure and unapplied, will be of little use to students of human life. Hence the ancient controversy between free will and determinism, while it remains a genuine problem for theologians and philosophers, need not trouble the thoughts of those whose concern is with empirical matters – the actual lives of human beings in the space and time of normal experience. For practising historians determinism is not, and need not be, a serious issue.

Yet, inapplicable as it may be as a theory of human action, specific forms of the deterministic hypothesis have played an arresting, if limited, role in altering our views of human responsibility. The irrelevance of the general hypothesis to historical studies must not blind us to its importance, touched on above, as a specific corrective to ignorance, prejudice, dogmatism and fantasy on the part of those who judge the behaviour of others. For it is plainly a good thing that we should be reminded by social scientists that the scope of human choice is a good deal more limited than we used to suppose; that the evidence at our disposal shows that many of the acts too often assumed to be within the individual's control are not so – that man is an object in (scientifically predictable) nature to a larger degree than has at times been supposed, that human beings more often than not act as they do because of characteristics due to heredity or physical or social environment or education, or biological or physical characteristics, or the interplay of these factors with each other and with the obscurer factors loosely called psychical characteristics; and that the resultant habits of thought, feeling and expression are, at least in principle, as capable of being classified and made subject to hypotheses and systematic laws as the behaviour of material objects. And this certainly alters our ideas about the limits of freedom and responsibility. If we are told that a given case of stealing is due to kleptomania, we protest that the appropriate treatment is not punishment but a remedy for a disease; and, similarly, if a destructive act or a vicious character is ascribed to a specific psychological or social cause, we decide, if we are convinced that the explanation is valid, that the agent is not responsible for his acts, and consequently deserves therapeutic rather than penal treatment. It is salutary to be reminded of the narrowness of the field within which we can begin to claim to be free; and some would claim that such knowledge is still increasing, and the field still contracting.

Where the frontier between freedom and causal laws is to be determined is a crucial practical issue; knowledge of it is a powerful and indispensable antidote to ignorance and irrationality, and offers us new types of explanation – historical, psychological, sociological, biological – which previous generations have lacked. What we cannot alter, or cannot alter as much as we had supposed, cannot be used as evidence for or against us as free moral agents; it can cause us to feel pride, shame, regret, interest, but not remorse; it can be admired, envied, deplored, enjoyed, feared, wondered at, but not (save in some quasi-aesthetic sense) praised or condemned; our tendency to indignation is curbed, we desist from passing judgement. 'Je ne propose rien, je ne suppose rien, je n'impose rien ... j'expose,' said a French writer proudly, and such *exposition* meant for him the treatment of all events as causal or statistical phenomena, as scientific material, to the exclusion of moral judgement.

Historians of this persuasion, anxious to avoid all personal, above all, all moral, judgements, tend to emphasise the immense predominance of impersonal factors in history, of the physical media in which life is lived, the power of geographical, psychological, social factors which are not, at any rate consciously, man-made, and are often beyond human control. This does tend to check our arrogance, to induce humility by forcing us to admit that our own outlook and scales of value are neither permanent nor universally accepted, that the over-confident, too complacent, moral classifications of past historians and of their societies sprang all too obviously from specific historical conditions, specific forms of ignorance or vainglory, or from particular temperamental traits in the historian (or moralist), or from other causes and circumstances which, from our vantage-point, we perceive to belong to their own place and time, and to have given rise to interpretations which later seem idiosyncratic, smug, shallow, unjust and often grotesque in the light of our own standards of accuracy or objectivity. And, what is even more important, such a line of approach throws doubt upon all attempts to establish a definitive boundary between the individual's free choice and his natural or social necessitation, and does this by bringing to light the egregious blunders of some of those who tried to solve this or that problem in the past, and made mistakes of fact which now, all too plainly, seem due to their (unalterable) milieu, or character, or interests. And this tends to make us ask whether the same might not be equally true of us and our own historical judgements; and so, by suggesting that every generation is 'subjectively' conditioned by its own cultural and psychological peculiarities, leads us to wonder whether it might not be best to avoid all moral judgement, all ascription of responsibility, might not be safest to confine ourselves to impersonal terms, and leave whatever cannot be said in such terms altogether unsaid. Have we learned nothing from the intolerable moral dogmatism and the mechanical classifications of those historians and moralists and politicians whose views are now so dated, so obsolete, and so justly discredited? And, indeed, who are we to make such a parade of our personal opinions, to give such importance to what are no more than symptoms of our own ephemeral outlook? And what right, in any case, have we to sit in judgement on our fellows, whose moral codes are the products of their specific historical environments, as our own are of ours? Is it not better to analyse, to describe, to present the events, and then withdraw and let them 'speak for themselves', refraining from the intolerable presumption of awarding marks, meting out justice, dividing the sheep from the goats according to our own personal criteria, as if these were eternal and not, as in fact they are, neither more nor less valid than those of others with other interests, in other conditions?

Such advice to us (in itself salutary enough) to retain a certain scepticism about our own powers of judgement, especially to beware of ascribing too much authority to our own moral views, comes to us, as I have said, from at least two quarters; from those who think that we know too much, and from those who think that we know too little. We know now, say the former, that we are as we are, and our moral and intellectual criteria are what they are, in virtue of the evolving historical situation. Let me once more mention their varieties. Some among them, who feel sure that the natural sciences will in the end account for everything, explain our behaviour in terms of natural causes. Others, who accept a more metaphysical interpretation of the world, explain it by speaking of invisible powers and dominions, nations, races, cultures; the Spirit of the Age, the 'workings', overt and occult, of 'the Classical Spirit', 'the Renaissance', 'the Medieval Mind', 'the French Revolution', 'the Twentieth Century', conceived as impersonal entities, at once patterns and realities, in terms of whose 'structure' or 'purpose' their elements and expressions – men and institutions – must behave as they do. Still others speak in terms of some teleological procession, or hierarchy, whereby all individuals, countries, institutions, cultures, ages, fulfil their several parts in some cosmic drama, and are what they are in virtue of the part cast for them, but not by them, by the divine Dramatist himself. From this it is not far to the views of those who say that History is wiser than we, that its purposes are unfathomable to us, that we, or some amongst us, are but the means, the instruments, the manifestations, worthy or unworthy, of some vast all-embracing schema of eternal human progress, or of the German Spirit, or of the Proletariat, or of post-Christian civilisation, or of Faustian man, or of Manifest Destiny, or of the American Century, or of some other myth or mystery or abstraction. To know all is to understand all; it is to know why things are and must be as they are; therefore the more we know the more absurd we must think those who suppose that things could have been otherwise, and so fall into the irrational temptation to praise or blame. *Tout comprendre, c'est tout pardonner* is transformed into a mere truism. Any form of moral censure – the accusing finger of historians or publicists or politicians, and indeed the agonies of the private conscience, too – tends, so far as possible, to be explained away as one or other sophisticated version of primitive taboos or psychical tensions or conflicts, now appearing as moral consciousness, now as some other sanction, growing out of, and battening upon, that ignorance which alone generates fallacious beliefs in free will and uncaused choice, doomed to disappear in the growing light of scientific or metaphysical truth.

Or, again, we find that the adherents of a sociological or historical or anthropological metaphysics tend to interpret the sense of mission and dedication, the voice of duty, all forms of inner compulsion of this type, as being an expression within each individual's conscious life of the 'vast impersonal forces' which control it, and which speak 'in us', 'through us', 'to us', for their own inscrutable purposes. To hear is then literally to obey – to be drawn towards the true goal of our 'real' self, or its 'natural' or 'rational' development – that to which we are called in virtue of belonging to this or that class, or nation, or race, or Church, or station in society, or tradition, or age, or culture. The explanation, and in some sense the weight of responsibility, for all human action is (at times with ill-concealed relief) transferred to the broad backs of these vast impersonal forces – institutions or historic trends – better made to bear such burdens than a feeble thinking reed like man, a creature that, with a megalomania scarcely appropriate to his physical and moral frailty, claims, as he too often does, to be responsible for the workings of Nature or of the Spirit; and, flown with his importance, praises and blames, worships and tortures, murders and immortalises other creatures like himself for conceiving, willing or executing policies for which neither he nor they can be remotely responsible; as if flies were to sit in solemn judgement upon each other for causing the revolutions of the sun or the changes of the seasons which affect their lives. But no sooner do we acquire adequate insight into the 'inexorable' and 'inevitable' parts played by all things animate and inanimate in the cosmic process than we are freed from the sense of personal endeavour. Our sense of guilt and of sin, our pangs of remorse and self-condemnation, are automatically dissolved; the tension, the fear of failure and frustration, disappear as we become aware of the elements of a larger 'organic whole' of which we are variously described as limbs or members, or reflections, or emanations, or finite expressions; our sense of freedom and independence, our belief in an area, however circumscribed, in which we can choose to act as we please, falls from us; in its place we are provided with a sense of membership in an ordered system, each with a unique position sacred to himself alone. We are soldiers in an army, and no longer suffer the pains and penalties of solitude; the army is on the march, or goals are set for us, not chosen by us; doubts are stilled by authority. The growth of knowledge brings with it relief from moral burdens, for if powers beyond and above us are at work, it is wild presumption to claim responsibility for their activity or blame ourselves for failing in it. Original sin is thus transferred to an impersonal plane, and acts hitherto regarded as wicked or unjustifiable are seen in a more 'objective' fashion – in a larger context – as part of the process of history which, being responsible for providing us with our scale of values, must not therefore itself be judged in terms of it; and viewed in this new light they turn out no longer wicked but right and good because necessitated by the whole.

This is a doctrine which lies at the heart equally of scientific attempts to explain moral sentiments as psychological or sociological 'residues' or the like, and of the metaphysical vision for which whatever is – 'truly' is – is good. To understand all is to see that nothing could be otherwise than as it is; that all blame, indignation, protest is mere complaint about what seems discordant, about elements which do not seem to fit, about the absence of an intellectually or spiritually satisfying pattern. But this is always evidence only of failure on the part of the observer, of his blindness and ignorance; it can never be an objective assessment of reality, for in reality everything necessarily fits, nothing is superfluous, nothing amiss, every ingredient is 'justified' in being where it is by the demands of the transcendent whole; and all sense of guilt, injustice, ugliness, all resistance or condemnation, is mere proof of (at times unavoidable) lack of vision, misunderstanding, subjective aberration. Vice, pain, folly, maladjustment, all come from failure to understand, from failure, in E. M. Forster's celebrated phrase, to 'connect'.

This is the sermon preached to us by great and noble thinkers of very different outlooks, by Spinoza and Godwin, by Tolstoy and Comte, by mystics and rationalists, theologians and scientific materialists, metaphysicians and dogmatic empiricists, American sociologists, Russian Marxists and German historicists alike. Thus Godwin (and he speaks for many humane and civilised persons) tells us that to understand a human act we must always avoid applying general principles and examine each case in its full individual detail. When we scrupulously examine the texture and pattern of this or that life, we shall not, in our haste and blindness, seek to condemn or to punish; for we shall see why this or that man was caused to act in this or that manner by ignorance or poverty or some other moral or intellectual or physical defect – as (Godwin optimistically supposes) we can always see, if we arm ourselves with sufficient patience, knowledge and sympathy – and we shall then blame him no more than we should an object in nature; and since it is axiomatic that we cannot both act upon our knowledge, and yet regret the result, we can and shall in the end succeed in making men good, just, happy and wise. So, too, Condorcet and Henri de Saint-Simon, and their disciple, Auguste Comte, starting from the opposite conviction – namely that men are not unique or in need, each one of them, of individual treatment, but, no less than inhabitants of the animal, vegetable and mineral kingdoms, belong to types and obey general laws – maintain no less stoutly that once these laws have been discovered (and therefore applied) this will by itself lead to universal felicity. And this conviction has since been echoed by many idealistic liberals and rationalists, technocrats, positivists and believers in the scientific organisation of society; and in very different keys by theocrats, neo-medieval romantics, authoritarians and political mystics of various kinds. This, too, is in substance the morality preached, if not by Marx, then by most of the disciples of Engels and Plekhanov, by Prussian nationalist historians, by Spengler, and by many another thinker who believes that there is a pattern which he has seen but others have not seen, or at least not so clearly seen, and that by this vision men may be saved.

Know and you will not be lost. What it is that we must know differs from thinker to thinker, differs as views of the nature of the world differ. Know the laws of the universe, animate and inanimate, or the principles of growth, or of evolution, or of the rise and fall of civilisations, or the goals towards which all creation tends, or the stages of the Idea, or something less tangible still. Know, in the sense of identifying yourself with it, realising your oneness with it, for, do what you may, you cannot escape from the laws to which you are subject, of whatever kind they may be, 'mechanistic', 'vitalistic', causal, purposive, imposed, transcendent, immanent, or the myriad impalpable strands which bind you to the past – to your land and to the dead, as Barrès declared; to the milieu, the race and the moment, as Taine asserted; to Burke's great society of the dead and living, who have made you what you are; so that the truth in which you believe, the values in terms of which you judge, from the profoundest principles to the most trivial whims, are part and parcel of the historical continuum to which you belong. Tradition or blood or class or human nature or progress or humanity; the *Zeitgeist* or the social structure or the laws of history or the true ends of life; know these – be true to them – and you will be free. From Zeno to Spinoza, from the Gnostics to Leibniz, from Thomas Hobbes to Lenin and Freud, the battle-cry has been essentially the same; the object of knowledge and the methods of discovery have often been violently opposed, but that reality is knowable, and that knowledge and only knowledge liberates, and absolute knowledge liberates absolutely – that is common to many doctrines which are so large and valuable a part of Western civilisation.

To understand is to explain and to explain is to justify. The notion of individual freedom is a delusion. The further we are from omniscience, the wider our notion of our freedom and responsibility and guilt, products of ignorance and fear which populate the unknown with terrifying fictions. Personal freedom is a noble delusion and has had its social value; society might have crumbled without it; it is a necessary instrument – one of the greatest devices of the 'cunning' of Reason or of History, or of whatever other cosmic force we may be invited to worship. But a delusion, however noble, useful, metaphysically justified, historically indispensable, is still a delusion. And so individual responsibility and the perception of the difference between right and wrong choices, between avoidable evil and misfortune, are mere symptoms, evidences of vanity, of our imperfect adjustment, of human inability to face the truth. The more we know, the greater the relief from the burden of choice; we forgive others for what they cannot avoid being, and by the same token we forgive ourselves. In ages in which the choices seem peculiarly agonising, when strongly held ideals cannot be reconciled and collisions cannot be averted, such doctrines seem peculiarly comforting. We escape moral dilemmas by denying their reality; and, by directing our gaze towards the greater wholes, we make them responsible in our place. All we lose is an illusion, and with it the painful and superfluous emotions of guilt and remorse. Freedom notoriously involves responsibility, and it is for many spirits a source of welcome relief to lose the burden of both, not by some ignoble act of surrender, but by daring to contemplate in a calm spirit things as they must be; for this is to be truly philosophical. Thereby we reduce history to a kind of physics; as well blame the galaxy or gamma-rays as Genghis Khan or Hitler. 'To know all is to forgive all' turns out to be, in A. J. Ayer's striking phrase (used in another context), nothing but a dramatised tautology.

IV

We have spoken thus far of the view that we cannot praise or blame because we know – or may one day know, or at any rate could know – too much for that. By a queer paradox the same position is reached by some of those who hold what seems at first the diametrical opposite of this position, that we cannot praise or blame not because we know too much, but because we know too little. Historians imbued with a sense of humility before the scope and difficulties of their task, viewing the magnitude of human claims and the smallness of human knowledge and judgement, warn us sternly against setting up our parochial values as universally valid and applying what may, at most, hold for a small portion of humanity for a brief span in some insignificant corner of the universe to all beings in all places and at all times. Tough-minded realists influenced by Marxism and Christian apologists differ profoundly in outlook, in method, in conclusions, but they are at one in this. The former[1] tell us that the social or economic principles which, for example, Victorian Englishmen accepted as basic and eternal were but the interests of one particular island community at one particular moment of its social and commercial development, and the truths which they so dogmatically bound upon themselves and upon others, and in the name of which they felt justified in acting as they did, were but their own passing economic or political needs and claims masquerading as universal truths, and rang progressively more hollow in the ears of other nations with increasingly opposed interests, as they found themselves frequently the losers in a game where the rules had been invented by the stronger side. Then the day began to dawn when they in their turn acquired sufficient power, and turned the tables, and transformed international morality, albeit unconsciously, to suit themselves. Nothing is absolute, moral rules vary directly as the distribution of power: the prevalent morality is always that of the victors; we cannot pretend to hold the scales of justice even between them and their victims, for we ourselves belong to one side or the other; *ex hypothesi* we cannot see the world from more than one vantage-point at a time. If we insist on judging others in terms of our transient standards we must not protest too much if they, in their turn, judge us in terms of theirs, which sanctimonious persons among us are too swift to denounce for no better reason than that they are not ours.

And some among their Christian opponents, starting from very different assumptions, see men as feeble creatures groping in darkness, knowing but little of how things come about, or what in history inexorably causes what, and how things might have turned out but for this or that scarcely perceptible, all but untraceable, fact or situation. Men, they argue, often seek to do what is right according to their lights, but these lights are dim, and such faint illumination as they give reveals very different aspects of life to

[1] See, for example, the impressive and influential writings of E. H. Carr on the history of our time.

different observers. Thus the English follow their own traditions; the Germans fight for the development of theirs; the Russians to break with their own and those of other nations; and the result is often bloodshed, widespread suffering, the destruction of what is most highly valued in the various cultures which come into violent conflict. Man proposes, but it is cruel and absurd to lay upon him – a fragile creature, born to sorrows – responsibility for many of the disasters that occur. For these are entailed by what, to take a Christian historian of distinction, Herbert Butterfield calls the 'human predicament' itself – wherein we often seem to ourselves virtuous enough, but, being imperfect, and doomed to stay so by Man's original sin, being ignorant, hasty, vainglorious, self-centred, lose our way, do unwitting harm, destroy what we seek to save and strengthen what we seek to destroy. If we understood more, perhaps we could do better, but our intellect is limited. For Butterfield, if I understand him correctly, the 'human predicament' is a product of the complex interaction of innumerable factors, few among them known, fewer still controllable, the greater number scarcely recognised at all. The least that we can do, therefore, is to acknowledge our condition with due humility, and since we are involved in a common darkness, and few of us stumble in it to much greater purpose than others (at least in the perspective of the whole of human history), we should practise understanding and charity. The least we can do as historians, scrupulous to say no more than we are entitled to say, is to suspend judgement; neither praise nor condemn; for the evidence is always insufficient, and the alleged culprits are like swimmers for ever caught in cross-currents and whirlpools beyond their control.

A not dissimilar philosophy is, it seems to me, to be found in the writings of Tolstoy and other pessimists and quietists, both religious and irreligious. For these, particularly the most conservative among them, life is a stream moving in a given direction, or perhaps a tideless ocean stirred by occasional breezes. The number of factors which cause it to be as it is, is very great, but we know only very few of them. To seek to alter things radically in terms of our knowledge is therefore unrealistic, often to the point of absurdity. We cannot resist the central currents, for they are much stronger than we, we can only tack, only trim to the winds and avoid collisions with the great fixed institutions of our world, its physical and biological laws, and the great human establishments with their roots deep in the past – the empires, the Churches, the settled beliefs and habits of mankind. For if we resist these, our small craft will be sunk, and we shall lose our lives to no purpose. Wisdom lies in avoiding situations where we may capsize, in using the winds that blow as skilfully as we can, so that we may last at any rate our own time, preserve the heritage of the past, and not hurry towards a future which will come soon enough, and may be darker even than the gloomy present. On this view it is the human predicament – the disproportion between our vast designs and our feeble means – that is responsible for much of the suffering and injustice of the world. Without help, without divine grace, or one or other form of divine intervention, we shall not, in any case, succeed. Let us then be tolerant and charitable and understanding, and avoid the folly of accusation and counter-accusation which will expose us to the laughter or pity of later generations. Let us seek to discern what we can – some dim outline of a pattern – in the shadows of the past, for even so much is surely difficult enough.

In one important sense, of course, the hard-boiled realists and the Christian pessimists are right. Censoriousness, recrimination, moral or emotional blindness to the ways of life and outlooks and complex predicaments of others, intellectual or ethical fanaticism are vices in the writing of history as in life. No doubt Gibbon and Michelet, Macaulay and Carlyle, Taine and Trotsky (to mention only the eminent dead) do try the patience of those who do not accept their opinions. Nevertheless this corrective to dogmatic partiality, like its opposite, the doctrine of inevitable bias, by shifting responsibility on to human weakness and ignorance, and identifying the human predicament itself as the ultimate central factor in human history, in the end leads us by a different road to the very same position as the doctrine that to know all is to forgive all; only for the latter it substitutes the formula that the less we know, the fewer reasons we can have for just condemnation; for knowledge can lead only to a clearer realisation of how small a part men's wishes or even their unconscious desires play in the life of the universe, and thereby reveals the absurdity of placing any serious responsibility upon the shoulders of individuals, or, for that matter, of classes, or States, or nations.[1]

---

[1] I do not, of course, mean to imply that the great Western moralists, e.g. the philosophers of the medieval Church (and in particular Thomas Aquinas) or those of the Enlightenment, denied moral responsibility; nor that Tolstoy was not agonised by problems raised by it. My thesis is that their determinism committed

Two separate strands of thought are involved in the modern plea for a greater effort at understanding, and the fashionable warnings against censoriousness, moralising, and partisan history. There is, in the first place, the view that individuals and groups always, or at any rate more often than not, aim at what seems to them desirable; but, owing to ignorance, or weakness, or the complexities of the world, which mere human insight and skill cannot adequately understand or control, they feel and act in such a manner that the result is too often disastrous both for themselves and for others, caught in the common human predicament. Yet it is not men's purposes – only the human predicament itself, man's imperfection – that is largely to blame for this. There is, in the second place, the further thesis that in attempting to explain historical situations and to analyse them, to unwind their origins and trace their consequences, and, in the course of this, to fix the responsibility for this or that element in the situation, the historian, however detached, clear-headed, scrupulous, dispassionate he may be, however skilled at imagining himself in other men's shoes, is nevertheless faced with a network of facts so minute, connected by links so many and complex, that his ignorance must always far outweigh his knowledge. Consequently his judgement, particularly his evaluative judgement, must always be founded on insufficient data; and if he succeeds in casting even a little light upon some small corner of the vast and intricate pattern of the past, he has done as well as any human being can ever hope to do. The difficulties of disentangling even a minute portion of the truth are so great that he must, if he is an honest and serious practitioner, soon realise how far he is from being in a position to moralise; consequently to praise and blame, as historians and publicists do so easily and glibly, is presumptuous, foolish, irresponsible, unjust.

This prima facie very humane and convincing thesis[1] is, however, not one but two. It is one thing to say that man proposes, but the consequences are too often beyond his control or powers of prediction or prevention; that since human motives have so seldom had any decisive influence on the actual course of events, they should not play any great part in the accounts of the historian; and that since the historian's business is to discover and describe what

these thinkers to a dilemma which some among them did not face, and none escaped.

[1] Held, unless I have gravely misunderstood his writings, by Herbert Butterfield.

occurred, and how and why, if he allows his moral opinions of men's characters and motives – those least effective of all historical factors – to colour his interpretations, he thereby exaggerates their importance for purely subjective or psychological reasons. For to treat what may be morally significant as *eo ipso* historically influential is to distort the facts. That is one perfectly clear position. Quite distinct from it is the other thesis, namely, that our knowledge is never sufficient to justify us in fixing responsibility, if there is any, where it truly belongs. An omniscient being (if that is a tenable notion) could do so, but we are not omniscient, and our attributions are therefore absurdly presumptuous; to realise this and feel an appropriate degree of humility is the beginning of historical wisdom.

It may well be that both these theses are true. And it may further be that they both spring from the same kind of pessimistic conviction of human weakness, blindness and ineffectiveness both in thought and in action. Nevertheless, these melancholy views are two, not one: the first is an argument from ineffectiveness, the second from ignorance; and either might be true and the other false. Moreover, neither seems to accord with common belief, nor with the common practice either of ordinary men or of ordinary historians; each seems plausible and unplausible in its own way, and each deserves its own defence or refutation. There is, however, at least one implication common to them: in both these doctrines individual responsibility is made to melt away. We may neither applaud nor condemn individuals or groups either because they cannot help themselves (and all knowledge is a growing understanding of precisely this), or conversely because we know too little to know either this or its opposite. But then – this surely follows – neither may we bring charges of moralism or bias against those historians who are prone to praise and blame, for we are all in the same boat together, and no one standard can be called objectively superior to any other. For what, on this view, could 'objective' mean? What standard can we use to measure its degree? It is plain that there can exist no 'super-standard' for the comparison of entire scales of value, which itself derives from no specific set of beliefs, no one specific culture. All such tests must be internal, like the laws of a State that apply only to its own citizens. The case against the notion of historical objectivity is like the case against international law or international morality: that it does not exist. More than this: that the very notion has no meaning, because ultimate standards are what we measure things by, and cannot by definition themselves be measured in terms of anything else.

This is indeed to be hoist by one's own petard. Because all standards are pronounced relative, to condemn bias or moralism in history, and to defend them, turn out themselves to express attitudes which, in the absence of a super-standard, cannot be rationally defended or condemned. All attitudes turn out to be morally neutral; but even this cannot be said, for the contradictory of this proposition cannot be refuted. Hence nothing on this topic can be said at all. This is surely a *reductio ad absurdum* of the entire position. A fatal fallacy must be lurking somewhere in the argument of the anti-moralistic school.[1]

[1] The paradox arising out of general scepticism about historical objectivity may perhaps be put in another fashion. One of the principal reasons for complaining about the moralistic attitude of this or that historian is that his scale of values is thought to distort his judgements, to cause him to pervert the truth. But if we start from the assumption that historians, like other human beings, are wholly conditioned to think as they do by specific material (or immaterial) factors, however incalculable or impalpable, then their so-called bias is, like everything else about their thought, the inevitable consequence of their 'predicament', and so equally are our objections to it – our own ideals of impartiality, our own standards of objective truth in terms of which we condemn, say, nationalistic or woodenly Marxist historians, or other forms of animus or *parti pris*. For what is sauce for the subjective goose must be sauce for the objective gander; if we look at the matter from the vantage-point of a Communist or a chauvinist, our 'objective' attitude is an equal offence against their standards, which are in their own eyes no less self-evident, absolute, valid etc. In this relativistic view the very notion of an absolute standard, presupposing as it does the rejection of all specific vantage-points as such, must, of course, be an absurdity. All complaints about partiality and bias, about moral (or political) propaganda, seem, on this view, beside the point. Whatever does not agree with our views we call misleading, but if this fault is to be called subjectivism, so must the condemnation of it; it ought to follow that no point of view is superior to any other, save in so far as it proceeds from wider knowledge (given that there is a commonly agreed standard for measuring such width). We are what we are, and when and where we are; and when we are historians, we select and emphasise, interpret and evaluate, reconstruct and present facts as we do, each in his own way. Each nation and culture and class does this in its own way – and on this view all that we are doing when we reject this or that historian as a conscious or unconscious propagandist is solely to indicate our own moral or intellectual or historical distance from him; nothing more: we are merely underlining our personal position. And this seems to be a fatal internal contradiction in the views of those who believe in the historical conditioning of historians and yet protest against moralising by them, whether they do so contemptuously like E. H. Carr, or sorrowfully like Herbert Butterfield.

Let us consider the normal thoughts of ordinary men on this topic. In ordinary circumstances we do not feel that we are saying something peculiarly hazardous or questionable if we attempt to assess the value of Cromwell's statesmanship, or if we describe Pasteur as a benefactor of mankind or condemn Hitler's actions. Nor do we feel that we are saying something strange if we maintain that, let us say, Belloc or Macaulay do not seem to apply the same standards of objective truth, or apply them as impartially, as did, let us say, Ranke, or Creighton, or Élie Halévy. In saying this, what are we doing? Are we merely expressing our private approval or disapproval of Cromwell's or Pasteur's or Hitler's character or activities? Are we merely saying that we agree with Ranke's conclusions or Halévy's general tone, that they are more to our taste, please us better (because of our own outlook and temperament) than the tone and conclusions of Macaulay or Belloc? If there is an unmistakable tinge of reproach in our assessment of, say, Cromwell's policies or of Belloc's account of those policies, is that no more than an indication that we are not favourably disposed towards one or other of them, that our moral or intellectual ideals differ from what we take to be theirs, with no indication that we think that they could, and moreover should, have acted differently? And if we do imply that their behaviour might, or should, have been different, is that merely a symptom of our psychological inability to realise that they could not (for no one can) have acted differently, or of an ignorance too deep to entitle us to tell how they could, let alone should, have acted? With the further implication that it would be more civilised not to say such things, but to remember that we may all be equally, or almost equally, deluded, and remember, too, that moral responsibility is a pre-scientific fiction, that with the increase of knowledge and a more scrupulous and appropriate use of language such 'value-charged' expressions, and the false notions of human freedom on which they rest, will, it is to be hoped, finally disappear from the vocabulary of enlightened men, at least in their public utterances? For this seems to me to follow directly from the doctrines outlined above. Determinism, whether benevolent or malevolent, no less than the view that our moral judgements are rendered absurd either because we know too much or because we know too little, seems to point to this. It is a view that in its various forms has been held by many civilised and sensitive thinkers, particularly in the present day. Nevertheless it rests on beliefs about the world and about

human beings which are too difficult to accept; which are unplausible because they render illegitimate certain basic distinctions which
we all draw – distinctions which are inevitably reflected in our
everyday use of words. If such beliefs were true, too much that we
accept without question would turn out to be sensationally false.
Yet these paradoxes are urged upon us, although there is no strong
factual evidence or logical argument to force us to embrace them.

It is part of the same tendency to maintain that, even if total
freedom from moralising is not to be looked for in this world (for
all human beings inevitably live and think by their own varying
moral or aesthetic or religious standards), yet in the writing of
history an effort must be made to repress such tendencies. As
historians it is our duty only to describe and explain, not to
pronounce verdicts. The historian is, we are told, not a judge but a
detective; he provides the evidence, and the reader, who has none
of the professional responsibilities of the expert, can form what
moral conclusions he likes. As a general warning against moralising
history this is, particularly in times of acute partisan emotion,
timely enough. But it must not be interpreted literally. For it
depends upon a false analogy with some among the more exact of
the natural sciences. In these last, objectivity has a specific meaning.
It means that methods and criteria of a less or more precisely
defined kind are being used with scrupulous care; and that
evidence, arguments, conclusions are formulated in the special
terminology invented or employed for the specific purpose of each
science, and that there is no intrusion (or almost none) of irrelevant
considerations or concepts or categories, that is, those specifically
excluded by the canons of the science in question.

I am not sure whether history can usefully be called a science at
all, but certainly it is not a science in this sense. For it employs few,
if any, concepts or categories peculiar to itself. Attempts to
construct special sets of concepts and special techniques for
history[1] have proved sterile, for they either misdescribed – over-
schematised – our experience, or they were felt not to provide
answers to our questions. We can accuse historians of bias, or
inaccuracy, or stupidity, or dishonesty, as we can accuse one
another of these vices in our ordinary daily intercourse; and we can
praise them for the corresponding virtues; and usually with the

[1] As opposed to making profitable use of other disciplines, e.g. sociology or
economics or psychology.

same degree of justice and reason. But just as our ordinary speech would become fantastically distorted by a conscious effort to eliminate from it some basic ingredient – say, everything remotely liable to convey value judgements, our normal, scarcely noticed, moral or psychological attitudes – and just as this is not regarded as indispensable for the preservation of what we should look upon as a normal modicum of objectivity, impartiality and accuracy, so, for the same reason, no such radical remedy is needed for the preservation of a reasonable modicum of these qualities in the writing of history. There is a sense in which a physicist can, to a large degree, speak with different voices as a physicist and as a human being; although even there the line between the two vocabularies is anything but clear or absolute. It is possible that this may in some measure be true of economists or psychologists; it grows progressively less true as we leave mathematical methods behind us, for example, in palaeography, or the history of science or that of the woollen trade; and it comes perilously near an absurdity when demanded of social or political historians, however skilled in the appropriate techniques, however professional, however rigorous. History is not identical with imaginative literature, but it is certainly not free from what, in a natural science, would be rightly condemned as unwarrantably subjective and even, in an empirical sense of the term, intuitive. Except on the assumption that history must deal with human beings purely as material objects in space – must, in short, be behaviourist – its method can scarcely be assimilated to the standards of an exact natural science.[1] The invocation to historians to suppress even that minimal degree of moral or psychological insight and evaluation

[1] That history is in this sense different from physical description is a truth discovered long ago by Vico, and most imaginatively and vividly presented by Herder and his followers, and, despite the exaggerations and extravagances to which it led some nineteenth-century philosophers of history, still remains the greatest contribution of the romantic movement to our knowledge. What was then shown, albeit often in a very misleading and confused fashion, was that to reduce history to a natural science was deliberately to leave out of account what we know to be true, to suppress great portions of our most familiar introspective knowledge, on the altar of a false analogy with the sciences and their mathematical and scientific disciplines. This exhortation to the students of humanity to practise austerities, and commit deliberate acts of self-laceration, that, like Origen, they might escape all temptation to sin (involved in any lapse from 'neutral' protocols of the data of observation), is to render the writing of history (and, it may be added, of sociology) gratuitously sterile.

which is necessarily involved in viewing human beings as creatures with purposes and motives (and not merely as causal factors in the procession of events) seems to me to spring from a confusion of the aims and methods of the humane studies with those of natural science. Purely descriptive, wholly depersonalised history remains, what it has always been, a figment of abstract theory, a violently exaggerated reaction to the cant and vanity of earlier generations.

V

All judgements, certainly all judgements dealing with facts, rest on – embody – generalisations, whether of fact or value or of both, and would make no sense save in terms of such generalisations. This truism, while it does not seem startling in itself, can neverthe-less lead to formidable fallacies. Thus some of the heirs of Descartes who assume that whatever is true must be capable of being (at any rate in principle) stated in the form of scientific (that is, at least quasi-mathematical or mathematically clear) gener-alisations conclude, as Comte and his disciples did, that the generalisations unavoidable in historical judgements must, to be worth anything, be capable of being so formulated, that is, as demonstrable sociological laws; while valuations, if they cannot be stated in such terms, must be relegated to some 'subjective' lumber-room, as 'psychological' odds and ends, expressions of purely personal attitudes, unscientific superfluities, in principle capable of being eliminated altogether, and must certainly be kept out so far as possible from the objective realm in which they have no place. Every science (we are invited to believe) must sooner or later shake itself free of what are at best irrelevances, at worst serious impediments, to clear vision.

This view springs from a very understandable fascination with the morally 'neutral' attitude of natural scientists, and a desire to emulate them in other fields. But it rests on a false analogy. For the generalisations of the historians differ from those of the scientists in that the valuations which they embody, whether moral, political, aesthetic or (as they often suppose) purely historical, are intrinsic, and not, as in the sciences, external, to the subject-matter. If I am a historian and wish to explain the causes of the great French Revolution, I naturally assume or take for granted certain general propositions. Thus I assume that all the ordinarily accepted physical laws of the external world apply. I also assume that all or most men need and consciously seek food, clothing, shelter, some degree of protection for their persons, and facilities for getting their grievances listened to or redressed. Perhaps I assume something more specific, namely, that persons who have acquired a certain degree of wealth or economic power will not be indefinitely content to lack political rights or social status; or that human beings are prey to various passions – greed, envy, lust for power; or that some men are more ambitious, ruthless, cunning or fanatical than others; and so forth. These are the assumptions of common experience; some of them are probably false; some are exaggerated, some confused, or inapplicable to given situations. Few among them are capable of being formulated in the form of hypotheses of natural science; still fewer are testable by crucial experiment, because they are not often sufficiently clear and sharp and precisely defined to be capable of being organised in a formal structure which allows of systematic mutual entailments or exclusions, and consequently of strictly logical or mathematical treatment. More than this: if they do prove capable of such formulation they will lose some of their usefulness; the idealised models of economics (not to speak of those of physics or physiology) will be of limited use in historical research or description. These inexact disciplines depend on a certain measure of concreteness, vagueness, ambiguity, suggestiveness, vividness and so on, embodied in the properties of the language of common sense and of literature and the humanities. Degrees and kinds of precision doubtless depend on the context, the field, the subject-matter; and the rules and methods of algebra lead to absurdities if applied to the art of, say, the novel, which has its own appallingly exacting standards. The precise disciplines of Racine or Proust require as great a degree of genius, and are as creditable to the intellect (as well as to the imagination) of the human race, as those of Newton or Darwin or Hilbert, but these kinds of method (and there is no theoretical limit to their number) are not interchangeable. They may have much or little to learn from each other; Stendhal may have learnt something from the Sensationalists of the eighteenth century, or the *Idéologues* of his own time, or from the *Code Napoléon*. But when Zola seriously contemplated the possibility of a literally 'experimental novel', founded directly on, and controlled by, the results of scientific method and conclusions, the idea remained largely stillborn, as, for similar reasons, the collective novel of the early Russian communist theorists still remains: and that not because we do not (as yet) know a sufficient number of facts (or laws), but because the concepts involved in the worlds described by novelists (or historians) are not the artificially refined concepts of scientific models – the idealised entities in terms of which natural laws are formulated – but a great deal richer in content and less logically simple or streamlined in structure.

Some interplay there is, of course, between a given scientific 'world-picture' and views of life in the normal meaning of this word; the former can give very sharp impulsions to the latter. Writers like H. G. Wells or Aldous Huxley would not have described (or so egregiously misunderstood) both social and individual life as at times they did, had they not been influenced by the natural sciences of their day to an excessive degree. But even such writers as these do not actually deduce anything from scientific generalisations; do not in their writings use any semblance of truly scientific methods; for this cannot be done outside its proper field without total absurdity. The relation of the sciences to historical writing is complex and close: but it is certainly not one of identity or even similarity. Scientific method is indispensable in, say, such disciplines as palaeography, or epigraphy, or archaeology, or economics, or in other activities which are propaedeutic to history, and supply it with evidence, and help to solve specific problems. But what they establish can never suffice to constitute a historical narrative. We select certain events or persons because we believe them to have had a special degree of 'influence' or 'power' or 'importance'. These attributes are not, as a rule, quantitatively measurable, or capable of being symbolised in the terminology of an exact, or even semi-exact, science. Yet they can no more be subtracted or abstracted from the facts – from events or persons – than physical or chronological characteristics; they enter even the driest, barest chronicles of events: it is a truism to say this. And is it so very clear that the most obviously moral categories, the notions of good and bad, right and wrong, so far as they enter into our assessments of societies, individuals, characters, political action, states of mind, are in principle utterly different from such indispensable 'non-moral' categories of value as 'important', 'trivial', 'significant' and so forth? It might perhaps be maintained that views of what is generally regarded as 'important' – the conquests of Alexander or Genghis Khan, or the fall of the Roman Empire, or the French Revolution, or the rise and fall of Hitler – embody relatively more stable assessments than more obviously 'ethical' valuations, or that there would be more general agreement about the fact that the French or Russian Revolutions are 'major' events (in the sense in which the tune which I hummed yesterday afternoon is not) than about whether Robespierre was a good man or a bad one, or whether it was right or wrong to execute the leaders of the National Socialist regime in Germany. And no doubt some concepts and categories are in this sense more universal or more 'stable' than others.[1] But they are not therefore 'objective' in some absolutely clear sense in which ethical notions are not. For our historical language, the words and thoughts with which we attempt to reflect about or describe past events and persons, embody moral concepts and categories – standards both permanent and transient – just as deeply as other notions of value. Our notions of Napoleon or Robespierre as historically important, as worthy of our attention in the sense in which their minor followers are not (as well as the very meaning of terms like 'major' and 'minor'), derive from the fact that the part of the former in forwarding or retarding the interests or the ideals of a great many of their contemporaries (with which our own are bound up) was very considerable; but then so do our 'moral' judgements about them. Where to draw the line – where to exclude judgements as being too subjective to be admitted into an account which we desire to make as 'objective' as possible, that is, as well supported by publicly discoverable, inspectable, comparable facts as we can make it – that is a question for ordinary judgement, that is to say,

---

[1] Such 'stability' is a matter of degree. All our categories are, in theory, subject to change. The physical categories – e.g. the three dimensions and infinite extent of ordinary perceptual space, the irreversibility of temporal processes, the multiplicity and countability of material objects – are perhaps the most fixed. Yet even a shift in these most general characteristics is in principle conceivable. After these come orders and relations of sensible qualities – colours, shapes, tastes etc.; then the uniformities on which the sciences are based – these can be quite easily thought away in fairy tales or scientific romances. The categories of value are more fluid than these; and within them tastes fluctuate more than rules of etiquette, and these more than moral standards. Within each category some concepts seem more liable to change than others. When such differences of degree become so marked as to constitute what are called differences of kind, we tend to speak of the wider and more stable distinctions as 'objective', of the narrower and less stable as the opposite. Nevertheless there is no sharp break, no frontier. The concepts form a continuous series from the 'permanent' standards to fleeting momentary reactions, from 'objective' truths and rules to 'subjective' attitudes, and they criss-cross each other in many dimensions, sometimes at unexpected angles, to perceive, discriminate and describe which can be a mark of genius.

for what passes as such in our society, in our own time and place, among the people to whom we are addressing ourselves, with all the assumptions which are taken for granted, more or less, in normal communication.

Because there is no hard and fast line between 'subjective' and 'objective', it does not follow that there is no line at all; and because judgements of 'importance', normally held to be 'objective', differ in some respects from moral judgements, which are so often suspected of being merely 'subjective', it does not follow that 'moral' is tantamount to 'subjective': that there is some mysterious property in virtue of which those quasi-aesthetic or political judgements which distinguish essential from inessential, or crucial from trivial, are somehow intrinsic to our historical thinking and description. It does not follow that the ethical implications, concerned with responsibility and moral worth, can somehow be sloughed off as if they constituted an external adjunct, a set of subjective emotional attitudes towards a body of commonly accepted, 'hard', publicly inspectable facts; as if these 'facts' were not themselves shot through with such valuations, as if a hard and fast distinction could be made, by historians or anyone else, between what is truly factual and what is a valuation of the facts, in the sense in which such a valuation truly would be an irrelevant and avoidable intrusion in, say, such fields as physics or chemistry (and doubtfully so in economics or sociology), where 'facts' can and should, according to the rules of these sciences, be described, as far as possible, with no moral overtones.

VI

When everything has been said in favour of attributing responsibility for character and action to natural and institutional causes; when everything possible has been done to correct blind or over-simple interpretations of conduct which fix too much responsibility on individuals and their free acts; when in fact there is strong evidence to show that it was difficult or impossible for men to do otherwise than as they did, given their material environment or education or the influence upon them of various 'social pressures'; when every relevant psychological and sociological consideration has been taken into account, every impersonal factor given due weight; after 'hegemonist', nationalist, and other historical heresies have been exposed and refuted; after every effort has been made to induce history to aspire, so far as it can without open absurdity, after the pure, *wertfrei* condition of a science; after all these severities, we continue to praise and to blame. We blame others as we blame ourselves; and the more we know, the more, it may be, are we disposed to blame. Certainly it will surprise us to be told that the better we understand our own actions – our own motives and the circumstances surrounding them – the freer from self-blame we shall inevitably feel. The contrary is surely often true. The more deeply we investigate the course of our own conduct, the more blameworthy our behaviour may seem to us to be, the more remorse we may be disposed to feel; and if this holds for ourselves, it is not reasonable to expect us necessarily, and in all cases, to withhold it from others. Our situations may differ from theirs, but not always so widely as to make all comparisons unfair. We ourselves may be accused unjustly, and so become acutely sensitive to the dangers of unjustly blaming others. But because blame can be unjust and the temptation to utter it too strong, it does not follow that it is never just; and because judgements can be based on ignorance, can spring from violent, or perverse, or silly, or shallow, or unfair notions, it does not follow that the opposites of these qualities do not exist at all; that we are mysteriously doomed to a degree of relativism and subjectivism in history, from which we are no less mysteriously free, or at any rate more free, in our normal daily thought and transactions with one another.

Indeed, the major fallacy of this position must by now be too obvious to need pointing out. We are told that we are creatures of nature or environment, or of history, and that this colours our temperament, our judgements, our principles. Every judgement is relative, every evaluation subjective, made what and as it is by the interplay of the factors of its own time and place, individual or collective. But relative to what? Subjective in contrast with what? Made to conform as it does to some ephemeral pattern as opposed to what conceivable timeless independence of such distorting factors? Relative terms (especially pejoratives) need correlatives, or else they turn out to be without meaning themselves, mere gibes, propagandist phrases designed to throw discredit, and not to describe or analyse. We know what we mean by disparaging a judgement or a method as subjective or biased – we mean that proper methods of weighing evidence have been too far ignored; or that what are normally called facts have been overlooked or suppressed or perverted; or that evidence normally accepted as sufficient to account for the acts of one individual or society is, for no good reason, ignored in some other case similar in all relevant respects; or that canons of interpretation are arbitrarily altered from case to case, that is, without consistency or principle; or that we have reasons for thinking that the historian in question wished to establish certain conclusions for reasons other than those constituted by the evidence, according to canons of valid inference accepted as normal in his day or in ours, and that this has blinded him to the criteria and methods normal in his field for verifying facts and proving conclusions; or all, or any, of these together; or other considerations like them. These are the kinds of ways in which superficiality is, in practice, distinguished from depth, bias from objectivity, perversion of facts from honesty, stupidity from perspicacity, passion and confusion from detachment and lucidity. And if we grasp these rules correctly, we are fully justified in denouncing breaches of them on the part of anyone; why should we not?

But, it may be objected, what of the words such as those we have used so liberally above – 'valid', 'normal', 'proper', 'relevant', 'perverted', 'suppression of facts', 'interpretation' – what do they signify? Is the meaning and use of these crucial terms so very fixed and unambiguous? May not that which is thought relevant or convincing in one generation be regarded as irrelevant in the next? What are unquestioned facts to one historian may, often enough, seem merely a suspicious piece of theorising to another. This is indeed so. Rules for the weighing of evidence do change. The accepted data of one age seem to its remote successors shot through with metaphysical presuppositions so queer as to be scarcely intelligible. All objectivity, we shall again be told, is subjective, is what it is relatively to its own time and place; all veracity, reliability, all the insights and gifts of an intellectually fertile period are such only relatively to their own 'climate of opinion'; nothing is eternal, everything flows.

Yet, frequently as this kind of thing has been said, and plausible as it may seem, it remains in this context mere rhetoric. We do distinguish facts, not indeed sharply from the valuations which enter into their very texture, but from interpretations of them; the borderline may not be distinct, but if I say that Stalin is dead and General Franco still alive, my statement may be accurate or mistaken, but nobody in his senses could, as words are used, take me to be advancing a theory or an interpretation. But if I say that

Stalin exterminated a great many peasant proprietors because in his infancy he had been swaddled by his nurse, and that this made him aggressive, while General Franco did not do so because he did not go through this kind of experience, no one but a very naïve student of the social sciences would take me to be claiming to assert a fact, no matter how many times I begin my sentences with the words 'It is a fact that . . .'. And I shall not readily believe you if you tell me that for Thucydides (or even for some Sumerian scribe) no fundamental distinction existed between relatively 'hard' facts and relatively 'disputable' interpretations. The borderline has, no doubt, always been wide and vague; it may be a shifting frontier; it is affected by the level of generality of the propositions involved; but unless we know where, within certain limits, it lies, we fail to understand descriptive language altogether. The modes of thought of cultures remote from our own are comprehensible to us only to the degree to which we share some, at any rate, of their basic categories; and the distinction between fact and theory is among these. I may dispute whether a given historian is profound or shallow, objective and impartial in his judgements, or borne on the wings of some obsessive hypothesis or overpowering emotion: but what I mean by these contrasted terms will not be utterly different for those who disagree with me, else there would be no argument; and will not, if I can claim to decipher texts at all correctly, be so widely different in different cultures and times and places as to make all communication systematically misleading and delusive. 'Objective', 'true', 'fair' are words of large content, their uses are many, their edges often blurred. Ambiguities and confusions are always possible and often dangerous. Nevertheless such terms do possess meanings, which may, indeed, be fluid, but stay within limits recognised by normal usage, and refer to standards commonly accepted by those who work in relevant fields; and that not merely within one generation or society, but across large stretches of time and space. The mere claim that these crucial terms, these concepts or categories or standards, change in meaning or application, is to assume that such changes can to some degree be traced by methods which themselves are, *pro tanto*, not held liable to such traceable change; for if these change in their turn, then, *ex hypothesi*, they do so in a way scarcely discoverable by us.[1] And if

---

[1] Unless indeed we embark on the extravagant path of formulating and testing the reliability of such methods by methods of methods (at times called the study

not discoverable, then not discountable, and therefore of no use as a stick with which to beat us for our alleged subjectiveness or relativity, our delusions of grandeur and permanence, of the absoluteness of our standards in a world of ceaseless change.

Such charges resemble suggestions, sometimes casually advanced, that life is a dream. We protest that 'everything' cannot be a dream, for then, with nothing to contrast with dreams, the notion of a 'dream' loses all specific reference. We may be told that we shall have an awakening: that is, have an experience in relation to which the recollection of our present lives will be somewhat as remembered dreams now are, when compared to our normal waking experience at present. That may be true; but, as things are, we can have little or no empirical evidence for or against this hypothesis. We are offered an analogy one term of which is hidden from our view; and if we are invited, on the strength of it, to discount the reality of our normal waking life, in terms of another form of experience which is literally not describable and not utterable in terms of our daily experience and normal language – an experience of whose criteria for discriminating between realities and dreams we cannot in principle have any inkling – we may reasonably reply that we do not understand what we are asked to do; that the proposal is quite literally meaningless. Indeed, we may advance the old, but nevertheless sound, platitude that one cannot cast doubt on everything at once, for then nothing is more dubious than anything else, so that there are no standards of comparison and nothing is altered. So too, and for the same reason, we may reject as empty those general warnings which beg us to remember that all norms and criteria, factual, logical, ethical, political, aesthetic, are hopelessly infected by historical or social or some other kind of conditioning; that all are but temporary makeshifts, none are stable or reliable; for time and chance will bear them all away. But if all judgements are thus infected, there is nothing whereby we can discriminate between various degrees of infection, and if everything is relative, subjective, accidental, biased, nothing can be judged to be more so than anything else. If words like 'subjective' and 'relative', 'prejudiced' and 'biased', are terms not of comparison and contrast – if they do not imply the possibility of their own

of methodology), and these by methods of methods of methods; but we shall have to stop somewhere before we lose count of what we are doing: and accept that stage, willy-nilly, as absolute, the home of 'permanent standards'.

opposites, of 'objective' (or at least 'less subjective') or 'unbiased' (or at least 'less biased') – what meaning have they for us? To use them in order to refer to everything whatever, to use them as absolute terms, and not as correlatives, is a rhetorical perversion of their normal sense, a kind of general *memento mori*, an invocation to all of us to remember how weak and ignorant and trivial we are, a stern and virtuous maxim, and merited perhaps, but not a serious doctrine concerned with the question of the attribution of responsibility in history, relevant to any particular group of moralists or statesmen or human beings.

It may, at this stage, be salutary to be reminded once again of the occasions which stimulated respected thinkers to such views. If, moved to indignation by the crudity and lack of scruple of those 'ideological' schools of history which, ignoring all that we know about human beings, paint individuals or classes or societies as heroes and villains, wholly white or unimaginably black, other, more sensitive and honest, historians or philosophers of history protest against this, and warn us about the dangers of moralising, of applying dogmatic standards, we applaud, we subscribe to the protest, yet we must be on our guard lest we protest too much, and, on the plea of curbing excesses, use means which promote some of the diseases of which they purport to be the cure. To blame is always to fail in understanding, say the advocates of toleration; to speak of human responsibility, guilt, crime, wickedness is only a way of saving oneself the effort, the long, patient, subtle or tedious labour, of unravelling the tangled skein of human affairs. It is always open to us, we shall be told, by a feat of imaginative sympathy to place ourselves in the circumstances of an individual or a society; if only we take the trouble to 'reconstruct' the conditions, the intellectual and social and religious 'climate', of another time or place, we shall thereby obtain insight into, or at least a glimpse of, motives and attitudes in terms of which the act we are judging may seem no longer either gratuitous, stupid, wicked or, above all, unintelligible.

These are proper sentiments. It follows that we must, if we are to judge fairly, have adequate evidence before us; possess sufficient imagination, sufficient sense of how institutions develop, how human beings act and think, to enable us to achieve understanding of times and places and characters and predicaments very unlike our own; not let ourselves be blinded by prejudice and passion; make every effort to construct cases for those whom we condemn

– better cases, as Acton said, than they made or could have made for themselves; not look at the past solely through the eyes of the victors; not lean over too far towards the vanquished, as if truth and justice were the monopoly of the martyrs and the minorities; and strive to remain fair even to the big battalions.

All this cannot be gainsaid: it is true, just, relevant, but perhaps hardly startling. And we can add as a corollary: other times, other standards; nothing is absolute or unchanging; time and chance alter all things; and that too would be a set of truisms. Surely it is not necessary to dramatise these simple truths, which are by now, if anything, too familiar, in order to remember that the purposes, the ultimate ends of life, pursued by men are many, even within one culture and generation; that some of these come into conflict, and lead to clashes between societies, parties, individuals, and not least within individuals themselves; and furthermore that the ends of one age and country differ widely from those of other times and other outlooks. And if we understand how conflicts between ends equally ultimate and sacred, but irreconcilable within the breast of even a single human being, or between different men or groups, can lead to tragic and unavoidable collisions, we shall not distort the moral facts by artificially ordering them in terms of some one absolute criterion; recognising that (*pace* the moralists of the eighteenth century) not all good things are necessarily compatible with one another; and shall seek to comprehend the changing ideas of cultures, peoples, classes and individual human beings, without asking which are right, which wrong, at any rate not in terms of some simple home-made dogma. We shall not condemn the Middle Ages simply because they fell short of the moral or intellectual standard of the *révolté* intelligentsia of Paris in the eighteenth century, or denounce these latter because in their turn they earned the disapprobation of moral bigots in England in the nineteenth or in America in the twentieth century. Or, if we do condemn societies or individuals, we shall do so only after taking into account their social and material conditions, their aspirations, codes of value, degrees of progress and reaction, measured in terms of their own situation and outlook; and judge them, when we do (and why in the world should we not?), as we judge anyone or anything: in terms partly of what we like, approve, believe in and think right ourselves, partly of the views of the societies and individuals in question, and of what we think about such views, and of how far we, being what we are, think it natural or desirable to have a wide variety of views; and of what we think of the importance of motives as against that of consequences, or of the value of consequences as against the quality of motives, and so on. We judge as we judge, we take the risks which this entails, we accept correction wherever this seems valid, we go too far, and under pressure we retract. We make hasty generalisations, we prove mistaken, and, if we are honest, we withdraw. We seek to be understanding and just, or we seek to derive practical lessons, or to be amused, and we expose ourselves to praise and blame and criticism and correction and misunderstanding. But in so far as we claim to understand the standards of others, whether members of our own societies or those of distant countries and ages, to grasp what we are told by spokesmen of many different traditions and attitudes, to understand why they think as they think and say what they say, then, so long as these claims are not absurdly false, the 'relativism' and 'subjectivism' of other civilisations do not preclude us from sharing common assumptions, sufficient for some communication with them, for some degree of understanding and being understood.

This common ground is what is correctly called objective – that which enables us to identify other men and other civilisations as human and civilised at all. When this breaks down we do cease to understand, and, *ex hypothesi*, we misjudge; but since by the same hypothesis we cannot be sure how far communication has broken down, how far we are being deluded by historical mirages, we cannot always take steps to avert this or discount its consequences. We seek to understand by putting together as much as we can out of the fragments of the past, make out the best, most plausible cases for persons and ages remote from or unsympathetic or for some reason inaccessible to us; we do our utmost to extend the frontiers of knowledge and imagination; as to what happens beyond all possible frontiers, we cannot tell and consequently cannot care; for it is nothing to us. What we can discern we seek to describe as accurately and fully as possible; as for the darkness which surrounds the field of our vision, it is opaque to us, concerning it our judgements are neither subjective nor objective; what is beyond the horizon of vision cannot disturb us in what we are able to see or seek to know; what we can never know cannot make us doubt or reject that which we do. Some of our judgements are, no doubt, relative and subjective, but others are not; for if none were so, if objectivity were in principle inconceivable, the terms 'subjective' and 'objective', no longer contrasted, would mean nothing; for all correlatives stand and fall together. So much for the secular argument that we must not judge, lest – all standards being relative – we be judged, with the equally fallacious corollary that no individual in history can rightly be pronounced innocent or guilty, for the values in terms of which he is so described are subjective, spring from self-interest or class interest or a passing phase of a culture or from some other such cause; and the verdict has therefore no 'objective' status and no real authority.

And what of the other argument – the *tout comprendre* maxim? It appeals to the world order. If the world follows a fixed design and every element in it is determined by every other, then to understand a fact, a person, a civilisation is to grasp its relationship to the cosmic design, in which it plays a unique part; and to grasp its meaning is to grasp, as we have shown before, its value, its justification, too. To understand the cosmic symphony wholly is to understand the necessity for every note of it; to protest, condemn, complain is merely to show that one has not understood. In its metaphysical form this theory claims to perceive the 'real' design, so that the outer disorder is but a distorted reflection of the universal order – at once the ground and the purpose of all there is – 'within' or 'beyond' or 'beneath'. This is the *philosophia perennis* of Platonists and Aristotelians, Scholastics and Hegelians, Eastern philosophers and contemporary metaphysicians, who distinguish between the harmonious reality which is invisible and the visible chaos of appearances. To understand, to justify, to explain are identical processes.

The empirical versions of this view take the form of belief in some kind of universal sociological causation. Some are optimistic like the theories of Turgot and Comte, emergent evolutionists, scientific Utopians and other convinced believers in the inevitable increase in the quality and variety of human happiness. Alternatively, as in Schopenhauer's version, they may be pessimistic, and hold out the prospect of perpetual suffering which all human efforts to prevent it will only serve to increase. Or they may take a neutral attitude and seek only to establish that there exists an inexorable sequence of cause and effect; that everything, both mental and physical, is subject to discoverable laws; that to understand them is not necessarily to approve, but at least makes it pointless to blame men for not having done better; for there was no other alternative which such men could – causally could – have chosen; so that their historical alibi is unbreakable. We can still, of course, complain in a purely aesthetic fashion. We can complain of ugliness, although we know we cannot alter it; and in the same way we can complain of stupidity, cruelty, cowardice, injustice, and feel anger or shame or despair, while remembering that we cannot put an end to their objects; and in the process of convincing ourselves that we cannot change behaviour, we shall duly cease to speak of cruelty or injustice, but merely of painful or annoying events; and to escape from them we should re-educate ourselves (assuming, inconsistently enough, like many a Greek sage and eighteenth-century radical, that we are free in matters of education, although rigidly conditioned in almost every other respect) to adjust ourselves into conformity with the universe; and, distinguishing what is relatively permanent from what is transient, seek so to form our tastes and views and activities as to fit in with the pattern of things. For if we are unhappy, because we cannot have something we want, we must seek happiness by teaching ourselves to want only what we cannot anyhow avoid. That is the lesson of the Stoics, as it is, less obviously, that of some modern sociologists. Determinism is held to be 'demonstrated' by scientific observation; responsibility is a delusion; praise and blame are subjective attitudes put to flight by the advance of knowledge. To explain is to justify; one cannot complain of what cannot be otherwise; and natural morality – the life of reason – is the morality and the life whose values are identified with the actual march of events, whether it be metaphysically deduced from some intuitive insight into the nature of reality and its ultimate purpose, or established by scientific methods.

But does any ordinary human being, does any practising historian, begin to believe one word of this strange tale?

VII

Two powerful doctrines are at large in contemporary thought, relativism and determinism. The first of these, for all that it is represented as being an antidote to overweening self-confidence, or arrogant dogmatism, or moral self-satisfaction, is nevertheless founded on a fallacious interpretation of experience; the second, for all that its chains are decked with flowers, and despite its parade of noble stoicism and the splendour and vastness of its cosmic design, nevertheless represents the universe as a prison. Relativism opposes to individual protest and belief in moral principles the resignation or the irony of those who have seen many worlds crumble, many ideals turned tawdry or ridiculous by time. Determinism claims to bring us to our senses by showing where the true, the impersonal and unalterable, machinery of life and thought is to be found. The first, when it ceases to be a maxim, or merely a salutary reminder to us of our limitations or of the complexity of the issue, and claims our attention as a serious *Weltanschauung*, rests on the misuse of words, a confusion of ideas, and relies upon a logical fallacy. The second, when it goes beyond indicating specific obstacles to free choice where examinable evidence for this can be adduced, turns out to rest either on a mythology or on a metaphysical dogma. Both have, at times, succeeded in reasoning or frightening men out of their most human moral or political convictions in the name of a deeper and more devastating insight into the nature of things. Yet, perhaps, this is no more than a sign of neurosis and confusion: for neither view seems to be supported by human experience. Why then should either doctrine (but especially determinism) have bound its spell so powerfully on so many otherwise clear and honest minds?

One of the deepest of human desires is to find a unitary pattern in which the whole of experience, past, present and future, actual, possible and unfulfilled, is symmetrically ordered. It is often expressed by saying that once upon a time there was a harmonious unity – 'the unmediated whole of feeling and thought', 'the unity of the knower and the known', of 'the outer and the inner', of subject and object, form and matter, self and not-self; that this was somehow broken; and that the whole of human experience has consisted in an endless effort to reassemble the fragments, to restore the unity, and so to escape or 'transcend' categories – ways of thinking – which split and isolate and 'kill' the living reality, and 'dirempt' us from it. We are told of an endless quest to find an answer to the puzzle, to return to the seamless whole, to the paradise whence we were expelled, or to inherit one which we have still not done enough to earn.

This central conception, whatever its origin or value, is surely at the heart of much metaphysical speculation, of much striving for the unification of the sciences, and of a large proportion of aesthetic and logical, social and historical thought. But whether or not the discovery of a single pattern of experience offers that satisfaction of our reason to which many metaphysicians aspire, and in the name of which they reject empirical science as a mere *de facto* collocation of 'brute' facts – descriptions of events or persons or things not connected by those 'rational' links which alone reason is held to be able to accept – whether or not this lies at the back of so much metaphysics and religion, it does not alter the order of the actual appearances – the empirical scene – with which alone history can properly claim to deal. From the days of Bossuet to those of Hegel and increasingly thereafter, claims have been made, widely varying in degree of generality and confidence, to be able to trace a structure of history (usually *a priori*, for all protests to the contrary), to discover the one and only true pattern into which alone all facts will be found to fit. But this is not, and can never be, accepted by any serious historian who wishes to establish the truth as it is understood by the best critics of his time, working by standards accepted as realistic by his most scrupulous and enlightened fellow workers. For he does not perceive one unique schema as the truth – the only real framework in which alone the facts truly lie; he does not distinguish the one real, cosmic pattern from false ones, as he certainly seeks to distinguish real facts from fiction. The same facts can be arranged in more than one single pattern, seen from several perspectives, displayed in many lights, all of them valid, although some will be more suggestive or fertile in one field than in another, or unify many fields in some illuminating fashion, or, alternatively, bring out disparities and open chasms. Some of these patterns will lie closer than others to the metaphysical or religious outlook of this or that historian or historical thinker. Yet through it all the facts themselves will remain relatively 'hard'. Relatively, but, of course, not absolutely; and, whenever obsession by a given pattern causes a given writer to interpret the facts too artificially, to fill the gaps in his knowledge too smoothly, without sufficient regard to the empirical evidence, other historians will instinctively perceive that some kind of violence is being done to the facts, that the relation between evidence and interpretation is in some way abnormal; and that this is so not because there is doubt about the facts, but because there is an obsessive pattern at work.[1] Freedom from such *idées fixes* – the degree of such freedom – distinguishes true history from the mythology of a given period; for there is no historical thought,

---

[1] Criteria of what is a fact or what constitutes empirical evidence are seldom in grave dispute within a given culture or profession.

properly speaking, save where facts can be distinguished not merely from fiction, but from theory and interpretation, not, it may be, absolutely, but to a lesser or greater degree.

We shall be reminded that there is no sharp break between history and mythology; or history and metaphysics; and that in the same sense there is no sharp line between 'facts' and theories: that no absolute touchstone can in principle be produced; and this is true enough, but from it nothing startling follows. That such differences exist only metaphysicians have disputed; yet history as an independent discipline did, nevertheless, emerge; and that is tantamount to saying that the frontier between facts and cosmic patterns, empirical or metaphysical or theological, indistinct and shifting as it may be, is a genuine concept for all those who take the problems of history seriously. So long as we remain historians the two levels must be kept distinct. The attempt, therefore, to shuffle off responsibility, which, at an empirical level, seems to rest upon this or that historical individual or society, or on a set of opinions held or propagated by one of these, on to some metaphysical machinery which, because it is impersonal, excludes the very idea of moral responsibility, must always be invalid; and the desire to do so may, as often as not, be written down to the wish to escape from an untidy, cruel and above all seemingly purposeless world, into a realm where all is harmonious, clear, intelligible, mounting towards some perfect culmination which satisfies the demands of 'reason', or an aesthetic feeling, or a metaphysical impulse or religious craving; above all, where nothing can be the object of criticism or complaint or condemnation or despair.

The matter is more serious when empirical arguments are advanced for a historical determinism which excludes the notion of personal responsibility. We are here no longer dealing with the metaphysics of history – the theodicies, say, of Schelling or Toynbee – as obvious substitutes for theology. We have before us the great sociological theories of history – the materialistic or scientific interpretations which began with Montesquieu and the *philosophes*, and led to the great schools of the nineteenth century, from the Saint-Simonians and Hegelians to the followers of Comte, Marx, Darwin and the liberal economists; from Freud, Pareto and Sorel to the ideologists of Fascism. Of these Marxism is much the boldest and the most intelligent, but its practitioners, much as they have added to our understanding, have not succeeded in their gallant and powerful attempt to turn history into a science. Arising out of this great movement we have the vast proliferation of anthropological and sociological studies of civilised societies, with their tendency to trace all character and behaviour to the same kind of relatively irrational and unconscious causes as those which are held to have so successfully explained the behaviour of primitive societies; we have witnessed the rebirth of the notion of the 'sociology of knowledge', which suggests that not only our methods but our conclusions and our reasons for believing them, in the entire realm of knowledge, can be shown to be wholly or largely determined by the stage reached in the development of our class or group, or nation or culture, or whatever other unit may be chosen; followed, in due course, by the fusion of these at times unconvincing, but, usually, at least quasi-scientific, doctrines with such non-empirical figments – at times all but personified powers both good and bad – as 'the collectivist spirit', or 'the Myth of the Twentieth Century', or 'the contemporary collapse of values' (sometimes called 'the crisis of faith'), or 'modern man', or 'the last stage of capitalism'.

All these modes of speech have peopled the air with supernatural entities of great power, Neoplatonic and Gnostic spirits, angels and demons who play with us as they will, or, at any rate, make demands on us which, we are told, we ignore at our peril. There has grown up in our modern time a pseudo-sociological mythology which, in the guise of scientific concepts, has developed into a new animism – certainly a more primitive and naïve religion than the traditional European faiths which it seeks to replace.[1] This new cult leads troubled persons to ask such questions as 'Is war inevitable?' or 'Must collectivism triumph?', or 'Is civilisation doomed?' These questions, and the tone in which they are posed, and the way in which they are discussed, imply a belief in the occult presence of vast impersonal entities – wars, collectivism, doom – agencies and forces at large in the world which we have but little power to control or deflect. Sometimes these are said to 'embody themselves' in great men, titanic figures who, because they are at one with their age, achieve superhuman results – Napoleon, Bismarck, Lenin; sometimes in the actions of classes – the great capitalist combines, which work for ends that their

[1] I need hardly add that responsibility (if I may still venture to use this term) for this cannot be placed at the door of the great thinkers who founded modern sociology – Marx, Durkheim, Weber – nor of the rational and scrupulous followers and critics whose work they have inspired.

members scarcely understand themselves, ends towards which their economic and social position 'inevitably' drives them; sometimes in huge inchoate entities called 'the masses', which do the work of history, little knowing of what mighty forces they are the 'creative vehicles'. Wars, revolutions, dictatorships, military and economic transformations are apt to be conceived like the genii of some oriental demonology, djinns which, once set free from the jars in which they have been confined for centuries, become uncontrollable, and capriciously play with the lives of men and nations. It is perhaps not to be wondered at that, with so luxurious a growth of similes and metaphors, many innocent persons nowadays tend to believe that their lives are dominated not merely by relatively stable, easily identifiable, material factors – physical nature and the laws dealt with by the natural sciences; but by even more powerful and sinister, and far less intelligible, factors – the impersonal struggles of classes which members of these classes may not intend, the collision of social forces, the incidences of slumps and booms which, like tides and harvests, can scarcely be controlled by those whose lives depend upon them – above all, by inexorable 'societal' and 'behavioural' patterns, to quote but a few sacred words from the barbarous vocabulary of the new mythologies.

Cowed and humbled by the panoply of the new divinities, men are eager, and seek anxiously, for knowledge and comfort in the sacred books and in the new orders of priesthood which affect to tell them about the attributes and habits of their new masters. And the books and their expositors do speak words of comfort: demand creates supply. Their message is simple and very ancient. In a world where such monsters clash, individual human beings can have but little responsibility for what they do; the discovery of the new, terrifying, impersonal forces may render life infinitely more dangerous, yet if they serve no other purpose, they do, at any rate, divest their victims of all responsibility – from all those moral burdens which men in less enlightened days used to carry with such labour and anguish. So that what we have lost on the swings we make up on the roundabouts: if we lose freedom of choice, at any rate we can no longer blame or be blamed for a world largely out of our control. The terminology of praise and condemnation turns out to be *eo ipso* uncivilised and obscurantist. To record what occurs and why, in impersonal chronicles, as was done by detached and studious monks in other times of violence and strife, is represented as more honourable and more dignified, and more in keeping with the noble humility and integrity of a scholar who in a time of doubt and crisis will at least preserve his soul if he abstains from the easy path of self-indulgence in moral sentiments. Agonising doubts about the conduct of individuals caught in historical crises, and the feeling of hope and despair, guilt, pride and remorse which accompanies such reflections, are taken from us; like soldiers in an army driven by forces too great to resist, we lose those neuroses which spring from the fear of having to choose among alternatives. Where there is no choice there is no anxiety; and a happy release from responsibility. Some human beings have always preferred the peace of imprisonment, a contented security, a sense of having at last found one's proper place in the cosmos, to the painful conflicts and perplexities of the disordered freedom of the world beyond the walls.

Yet this is odd. For the assumptions upon which this kind of determinism has been erected are, when examined, exceedingly unplausible. What are these forces and these inexorable historical laws? What historiographer, what sociologist, can claim as yet to have produced empirical generalisations comparable to the great uniformities of the natural sciences? It is a commonplace to say that sociology still awaits its Newton, but even this seems much too audacious a claim; it has yet to find its Euclid and its Archimedes, before it can begin to dream of a Copernicus. On one side a patient and useful accumulation of facts and analyses, taxonomy, useful comparative studies, cautious and limited hypotheses, still hamstrung by too many exceptions to have any appreciable predictive power;[1] on the other, imposing, sometimes ingenious, theoretical constructions, obscured by picturesque metaphors and a bold mythology, often stimulating to workers in other fields; and between these a vast gap, such as has not existed in historical times between the theories and the factual evidence of the natural sciences. It is idle for sociology to plead that she is still young and has a glorious future. The eponymous hero to honour whose memory these words are being uttered, Auguste Comte, founded it a full hundred years ago, and its great nomothetic

---

[1] And a collection of isolated insights and *aperçus*, like the dubious 'All power either corrupts or intoxicates', or 'Man is a political animal', or 'Der Mensch ist was er ißt.'

conquests are still to come.[1] It has affected other disciplines most fruitfully, notably history, to which it has added a dimension;[2] but it has as yet succeeded in discovering so few laws, or wide generalisations supported by adequate evidence, that its plea to be treated as a natural science can scarcely be entertained, nor are these few poor laws sufficiently revolutionary to make it seem an urgent matter to test their truth. In the great and fertile field of sociology (unlike her more speculative but far more effective younger sister, psychology) the loose generalisations of historically trained minds still, at times, seem more fruitful than their 'scientific' equivalents.

Social determinism is, at least historically, closely bound up with the 'nomothetic' ideals of sociology. And it may, indeed, be a true doctrine. But if it is true, and if we begin to take it seriously, then, indeed, the changes in the whole of our language, our moral terminology, our attitudes toward one another, our views of history, of society and of everything else will be too profound to be even adumbrated. The concepts of praise and blame, innocence and guilt and individual responsibility from which we started are but a small element in the structure which would collapse or disappear. If social and psychological determinism were established as an accepted truth, our world would be transformed more radically than was the teleological world of the classical and medieval ages by the triumphs of mechanistic principles or those of natural selection. Our words – our modes of speech and thought – would be transformed in literally unimaginable ways; the notions of choice, of responsibility, of freedom are so deeply embedded in our outlook that our new life, as creatures in a world genuinely lacking in these concepts, can, I should maintain, be conceived by us only with the greatest difficulty.

But there is, as yet, no need to alarm ourselves unduly. We are speaking only of pseudo-scientific ideals; the reality is not in sight. The evidence for a thoroughgoing determinism is not to hand; and if there is a persistent tendency to believe in it in some theoretical fashion, that is surely due far more to the lure of a 'scientistic' or metaphysical ideal or to a tendency on the part of those who desire

[1] I do not mean to imply that other 'sciences' – e.g. 'political science' or social anthropology – have fared much better in establishing laws; but their claims are more modest.

[2] As well as new methods for testing the validity of old conclusions.

to change society to believe that the stars in their courses are fighting for them. Or it may be due to a longing to lay down moral burdens, or minimise individual responsibility and transfer it to impersonal forces which can be accused of causing all our discontents, rather than to any increase in our powers of critical reflection or improvement in our scientific techniques. Belief in historical determinism of this type is, of course, very widespread, particularly in what I should like to call its 'historiosophical' form, by which I mean metaphysico-theological theories of history, which attract many who have lost their faith in older religious orthodoxies. Yet perhaps this attitude, so prevalent recently, is ebbing; and a contrary trend is discernible today. Our best historians use empirical tests in sifting facts, make microscopic examinations of the evidence, deduce no patterns, and show no false fear in attributing responsibility to individuals. Their specific attributions and analyses may be mistaken, but both they and their readers would rightly reject the notion that their very activity had been superseded and stultified by the advances of sociology, or by some deeper metaphysical insight, like that of oriental star-gazers by the discoveries of the disciples of Kepler.

In their own queer way, some modern existentialists, too, proclaim the crucial importance of individual acts of choice. The condemnation by some among them of all philosophical systems, and of all moral (as of other) doctrines, as equally hollow, simply because they are systems and doctrines, may be invalid; but the more serious of them are no less insistent than Kant upon the reality of human autonomy, that is, upon the reality of free self-commitment to an act or a form of life for what it is in itself. Whether recognition of freedom in this last sense does or does not entitle one logically to preach to others, or judge the past, is another matter; at any rate, it shows a commendable strength of intellect to have seen through the pretensions of those all-explanatory, all-justifying theodicies which promised to assimilate the human sciences to the natural in the quest for a unified schema of all there is.

It needs more than infatuation with a programme to overthrow some of the most deeply rooted moral and intellectual habits of human beings, whether they be plumbers or historians. We are told that it is foolish to judge Charlemagne or Napoleon or Genghis Khan or Hitler or Stalin for their massacres, that it is at most a comment upon ourselves and not upon 'the facts'. Likewise we are told that we should not describe as benefactors of humanity those whom the followers of Comte so faithfully celebrated; or at least that to do so is not our business as historians: because as historians our categories are 'neutral' and differ from the categories we use as ordinary human beings, as those of chemists undeniably do. We are also told that as historians it is our task to describe, let us say, the great revolutions of our own time without so much as hinting that certain individuals involved in them not merely caused, but were responsible for, great misery and destruction – using such words according to the standards not merely of the twentieth century, which is soon over, or of our declining capitalist society, but of the human race at all the times and in all the places in which we have known it; and told that we should practise such austerities out of respect for some imaginary scientific canon which distinguishes between facts and values very sharply, so sharply that it enables us to regard the former as being objective, 'inexorable' and therefore self-justifying, and the latter as merely a subjective gloss upon events – due to the moment, the milieu, the individual temperament – and consequently unworthy of serious scholarship.

To this we can only answer that to accept this doctrine is to do violence to the basic notions of our morality, to misrepresent our sense of our past, and to ignore some among the most general concepts and categories of normal thought. Those who are concerned with human affairs are committed to the use of the moral categories and concepts which normal language incorporates and expresses. Chemists, philologists, logicians, even sociologists with a strong quantitative bias, by using morally neutral technical terms, can avoid these concepts. But historians can scarcely do so. They need not – they are certainly not obliged to – moralise: but neither can they avoid the use of normal language with all its associations and 'built in' moral categories. To seek to avoid this is to adopt another moral outlook, not none at all. The time will come when men will wonder how this strange view, which combines a misunderstanding of the relation of value to fact with cynicism disguised as stern impartiality, can ever have achieved such remarkable fame and influence and respectability. For it is not scientific; nor can its reputation be due entirely to a commendable fear of undue arrogance or philistinism or of too bland and uncritical an imposition of our own dogmas and standards upon others. In part it is due to a genuine misunderstanding of the philosophical implications of the natural sciences, the great prestige of which has been misappropriated by many a fool and impostor since their earliest triumphs. But principally it seems to me to spring from a desire to resign our responsibility, to cease from judging, provided we ourselves are not judged and, above all, are not compelled to judge ourselves; from a desire to flee for refuge to some vast amoral, impersonal, monolithic whole – nature, or history,[1] or class, or race, or the 'harsh realities of our time', or the irresistible evolution of the social structure[2] – that will absorb and integrate us into its limitless, indifferent, neutral texture, which it is senseless to evaluate or criticise, and against which we fight to our certain doom.

This is an image which has often appeared in the history of mankind, always at moments of confusion and inner weakness. It is one of the great alibis, pleaded by those who cannot or do not wish to face the fact of human responsibility, the existence of a limited but nevertheless real area of human freedom, either because they have been too deeply wounded or frightened to wish to return to the traffic of normal life, or because they are filled with moral indignation against the false values and the, to them, repellent moral codes of their own society, or class, or profession, and take up arms against all ethical codes as such, as a dignified means of casting off a morality which is to them, perhaps justifiably, repulsive. Nevertheless, such views, although they may spring from a natural reaction against too much moral rhetoric, are a desperate remedy; those who hold them use history as a method of escape from a world which has, for some reason, grown odious to them, into a fantasy where impersonal entities avenge their grievances and set everything right, to the greater or lesser discomfiture of their persecutors, real and imaginary. And in the course of this they describe the normal lives lived by men in terms which fail to mark the most important psychological and moral distinctions known to us. This they do in the service of an imaginary science; and, like the astrologers and soothsayers whom they have succeeded, cast up their eyes to the clouds, and speak in immense, unsubstantiated images and similes, in deeply misleading metaphors and allegories,

---

[1] 'History has seized us by the throat', Mussolini is reported to have cried on learning of the Allied landing in Sicily. Men could be fought; but once 'History' herself took up arms against one, resistance was vain.

[2] 'The irresistible', Justice Louis Brandeis is said to have remarked, 'is often only that which is not resisted.'

and make use of hypnotic formulae with little regard for experience, or rational argument, or tests of proven reliability. Thereby they throw dust in their own eyes as well as in ours, obstruct our vision of the real world, and further confuse an already sufficiently bewildered public about the relations of morality to politics, and about the nature and methods of the natural sciences and historical studies alike.

# TWO CONCEPTS OF LIBERTY

If men never disagreed about the ends of life, if our ancestors had remained undisturbed in the Garden of Eden, the studies to which the Chichele Chair of Social and Political Theory is dedicated could scarcely have been conceived.[1] For these studies spring from, and thrive on, discord. Someone may question this on the ground that even in a society of saintly anarchists, where no conflicts about ultimate purposes can take place, political problems, for example constitutional or legislative issues, might still arise. But this objection rests on a mistake. Where ends are agreed, the only questions left are those of means, and these are not political but technical, that is to say, capable of being settled by experts or machines, like arguments between engineers or doctors. That is why those who put their faith in some immense, world-transforming phenomenon, like the final triumph of reason or the proletarian revolution, must believe that all political and moral problems can thereby be turned into technological ones. That is the meaning of Engels' famous phrase (paraphrasing Saint-Simon) about 'replacing the government of persons by the administration of things',[2] and the Marxist prophecies about the withering away of the State and the beginning of the true history of humanity. This outlook is called Utopian by those for whom speculation about this condition of perfect social harmony is the play of idle fancy. Nevertheless, a visitor from Mars to any British – or American – university today might perhaps be forgiven if he sustained the impression that its members lived in something very like this

[1] This essay is based on an Inaugural Lecture delivered in 1958.
[2] Engels in *Anti-Dühring* (1877–8): Karl Marx, Friedrich Engels, *Werke* (Berlin, 1956–83), vol. 19, p. 195. Cf. 'Lettres de Henri Saint-Simon à un américain', eighth letter, in *L'industrie* (1817), vol. 1: pp. 182–91 in *Oeuvres de Saint-Simon et d'Enfantin* (Paris, 1865–78), vol. 18.

innocent and idyllic state, for all the serious attention that is paid to fundamental problems of politics by professional philosophers.

Yet this is both surprising and dangerous. Surprising because there has, perhaps, been no time in modern history when so large a number of human beings, in both the East and the West, have had their notions, and indeed their lives, so deeply altered, and in some cases violently upset, by fanatically held social and political doctrines. Dangerous, because when ideas are neglected by those who ought to attend to them – that is to say, those who have been trained to think critically about ideas – they sometimes acquire an unchecked momentum and an irresistible power over multitudes of men that may grow too violent to be affected by rational criticism. Over a hundred years ago, the German poet Heine warned the French not to underestimate the power of ideas: philosophical concepts nurtured in the stillness of a professor's study could destroy a civilisation. He spoke of Kant's *Critique of Pure Reason* as the sword with which German deism had been decapitated, and described the works of Rousseau as the blood-stained weapon which, in the hands of Robespierre, had destroyed the old regime; and prophesied that the romantic faith of Fichte and Schelling would one day be turned, with terrible effect, by their fanatical German followers, against the liberal culture of the West. The facts have not wholly belied this prediction; but if professors can truly wield this fatal power, may it not be that only other professors, or, at least, other thinkers (and not governments or Congressional committees), can alone disarm them?

Our philosophers seem oddly unaware of these devastating effects of their activities. It may be that, intoxicated by their magnificent achievements in more abstract realms, the best among them look with disdain upon a field in which radical discoveries are less likely to be made, and talent for minute analysis is less likely to be rewarded. Yet, despite every effort to separate them, conducted by a blind scholastic pedantry, politics has remained indissolubly intertwined with every other form of philosophical enquiry. To neglect the field of political thought, because its unstable subject-matter, with its blurred edges, is not to be caught by the fixed concepts, abstract models and fine instruments suitable to logic or to linguistic analysis – to demand a unity of method in philosophy, and reject whatever the method cannot successfully manage – is merely to allow oneself to remain at the mercy of primitive and uncriticised political beliefs. It is only a very vulgar historical materialism that denies the power of ideas, and says that ideals are mere material interests in disguise. It may be that, without the pressure of social forces, political ideas are stillborn: what is certain is that these forces, unless they clothe themselves in ideas, remain blind and undirected.

Political theory is a branch of moral philosophy, which starts from the discovery, or application, of moral notions in the sphere of political relations. I do not mean, as I think some Idealist philosophers may have believed, that all historical movements or conflicts between human beings are reducible to movements or conflicts of ideas or spiritual forces, nor even that they are effects (or aspects) of them. But I do mean that to understand such movements or conflicts is, above all, to understand the ideas or attitudes to life involved in them, which alone make such movements a part of human history, and not mere natural events. Political words and notions and acts are not intelligible save in the context of the issues that divide the men who use them. Consequently our own attitudes and activities are likely to remain obscure to us, unless we understand the dominant issues of our own world. The greatest of these is the open war that is being fought between two systems of ideas which return different and conflicting answers to what has long been the central question of politics – the question of obedience and coercion. 'Why should I (or anyone) obey anyone else?' 'Why should I not live as I like?' 'Must I obey?' 'If I disobey, may I be coerced?' 'By whom, and to what degree, and in the name of what, and for the sake of what?'

Upon the answers to the question of the permissible limits of coercion opposed views are held in the world today, each claiming the allegiance of very large numbers of men. It seems to me, therefore, that any aspect of this issue is worthy of examination.

I

To coerce a man is to deprive him of freedom – freedom from what? Almost every moralist in human history has praised freedom. Like happiness and goodness, like nature and reality, it is a term whose meaning is so porous that there is little interpretation that it seems able to resist. I do not propose to discuss either the history of this protean word or the more than two hundred senses of it recorded by historians of ideas. I propose to examine no more than two of these senses – but they are central ones, with a great deal of human history behind them, and, I dare say, still to come. The first of these political senses of freedom or liberty (I shall use both words to mean the same), which (following much precedent) I shall call the 'negative' sense, is involved in the answer to the question 'What is the area within which the subject – a person or group of persons – is or should be left to do or be what he is able to do or be, without interference by other persons?' The second, which I shall call the 'positive' sense, is involved in the answer to the question 'What, or who, is the source of control or interference that can determine someone to do, or be, this rather than that?' The two questions are clearly different, even though the answers to them may overlap.

### The notion of negative freedom

I am normally said to be free to the degree to which no man or body of men interferes with my activity. Political liberty in this sense is simply the area within which a man can act unobstructed by others. If I am prevented by others from doing what I could otherwise do, I am to that degree unfree; and if this area is contracted by other men beyond a certain minimum, I can be described as being coerced, or, it may be, enslaved. Coercion is not, however, a term that covers every form of inability. If I say that I am unable to jump more than ten feet in the air, or cannot read because I am blind, or cannot understand the darker pages of Hegel, it would be eccentric to say that I am to that degree enslaved or coerced. Coercion implies the deliberate interference of other human beings within the area in which I could otherwise act. You lack political liberty or freedom only if you are prevented from attaining a goal by human beings.[1] Mere incapacity to attain a goal is not lack of political freedom.[2] This is brought out by the use of such modern expressions as 'economic freedom' and its counterpart, 'economic slavery'. It is argued, very plausibly, that if a man is too poor to afford something on which there is no legal ban – a loaf of bread, a journey round the world, recourse to the law courts – he is as little free to have it as he would be if it were

---

[1] I do not, of course, mean to imply the truth of the converse.

[2] Helvétius made this point very clearly: 'The free man is the man who is not in irons, not imprisoned in a gaol, nor terrorised like a slave by the fear of punishment.' It is not lack of freedom not to fly like an eagle or swim like a whale. De l'esprit, first discourse, chapter 4.

forbidden him by law. If my poverty were a kind of disease which prevented me from buying bread, or paying for the journey round the world or getting my case heard, as lameness prevents me from running, this inability would not naturally be described as a lack of freedom, least of all political freedom. It is only because I believe that my inability to get a given thing is due to the fact that other human beings have made arrangements whereby I am, whereas others are not, prevented from having enough money with which to pay for it, that I think myself a victim of coercion or slavery. In other words, this use of the term depends on a particular social and economic theory about the causes of my poverty or weakness. If my lack of material means is due to my lack of mental or physical capacity, then I begin to speak of being deprived of freedom (and not simply about poverty) only if I accept the theory.[1] If, in addition, I believe that I am being kept in want by a specific arrangement which I consider unjust or unfair, I speak of economic slavery or oppression. The nature of things does not madden us, only ill will does, said Rousseau.[2] The criterion of oppression is the part that I believe to be played by other human beings, directly or indirectly, with or without the intention of doing so, in frustrating my wishes. By being free in this sense I mean not being interfered with by others. The wider the area of non-interference the wider my freedom.

This is what the classical English political philosophers meant when they used this word.[3] They disagreed about how wide the area could or should be. They supposed that it could not, as things were, be unlimited, because if it were, it would entail a state in which all men could boundlessly interfere with all other men; and this kind of 'natural' freedom would lead to social chaos in which men's minimum needs would not be satisfied; or else the liberties of the weak would be suppressed by the strong. Because they

[1] The Marxist conception of social laws is, of course, the best-known version of this theory, but it forms a large element in some Christian and utilitarian, and all socialist, doctrines.

[2] *Émile*, book 2: p. 320 in *Oeuvres complètes*, ed. Bernard Gagnebin and others (Paris, 1959– ), vol. 4.

[3] 'A free man', said Hobbes, 'is he that . . . is not hindered to do what he has a will to.' *Leviathan*, chapter 21: p. 146 in Richard Tuck's edition (Cambridge, 1991). Law is always a fetter, even if it protects you from being bound in chains that are heavier than those of the law, say some more repressive law or custom, or arbitrary despotism or chaos. Bentham says much the same.

perceived that human purposes and activities do not automatically harmonise with one another, and because (whatever their official doctrines) they put high value on other goals, such as justice, or happiness, or culture, or security, or varying degrees of equality, they were prepared to curtail freedom in the interests of other values and, indeed, of freedom itself. For, without this, it was impossible to create the kind of association that they thought desirable. Consequently, it is assumed by these thinkers that the area of men's free action must be limited by law. But equally it is assumed, especially by such libertarians as Locke and Mill in England, and Constant and Tocqueville in France, that there ought to exist a certain minimum area of personal freedom which must on no account be violated; for if it is overstepped, the individual will find himself in an area too narrow for even that minimum development of his natural faculties which alone makes it possible to pursue, and even to conceive, the various ends which men hold good or right or sacred. It follows that a frontier must be drawn between the area of private life and that of public authority. Where it is to be drawn is a matter of argument, indeed of haggling. Men are largely interdependent, and no man's activity is so completely private as never to obstruct the lives of others in any way. 'Freedom for the pike is death for the minnows';[1] the liberty of some must depend on the restraint of others. Freedom for an Oxford don, others have been known to add, is a very different thing from freedom for an Egyptian peasant.

This proposition derives its force from something that is both true and important, but the phrase itself remains a piece of political claptrap. It is true that to offer political rights, or safeguards against intervention by the State, to men who are half-naked, illiterate, underfed and diseased is to mock their condition; they need medical help or education before they can understand, or make use of, an increase in their freedom. What is freedom to those who cannot make use of it? Without adequate conditions for the use of freedom, what is the value of freedom? First things come first: there are situations in which – to use a saying satirically attributed to the nihilists by Dostoevsky – boots are superior to Pushkin; individual freedom is not everyone's primary need. For freedom is not the mere absence of frustration of whatever kind; this would

---

[1] R. H. Tawney, *Equality* (1931), 3rd ed. (London, 1938), chapter 5, section 2, 'Equality and Liberty', p. 208 (not in previous editions).

inflate the meaning of the word until it meant too much or too little. The Egyptian peasant needs clothes or medicine before, and more than, personal liberty, but the minimum freedom that he needs today, and the greater degree of freedom that he may need tomorrow, is not some species of freedom peculiar to him, but identical with that of professors, artists and millionaires.

What troubles the consciences of Western liberals is, I think, the belief, not that the freedom that men seek differs according to their social or economic conditions, but that the minority who possess it have gained it by exploiting, or, at least, averting their gaze from, the vast majority who do not. They believe, with good reason, that if individual liberty is an ultimate end for human beings, none should be deprived of it by others; least of all that some should enjoy it at the expense of others. Equality of liberty; not to treat others as I should not wish them to treat me; repayment of my debt to those who alone have made possible my liberty or prosperity or enlightenment; justice, in its simplest and most universal sense – these are the foundations of liberal morality. Liberty is not the only goal of men. I can, like the Russian critic Belinsky, say that if others are to be deprived of it – if my brothers are to remain in poverty, squalor and chains – then I do not want it for myself, I reject it with both hands and infinitely prefer to share their fate. But nothing is gained by a confusion of terms. To avoid glaring inequality or widespread misery I am ready to sacrifice some, or all, of my freedom: I may do so willingly and freely; but it is freedom that I am giving up for the sake of justice or equality or the love of my fellow men. I should be guilt-stricken, and rightly so, if I were not, in some circumstances, ready to make this sacrifice. But a sacrifice is not an increase in what is being sacrificed, namely freedom, however great the moral need or the compensation for it. Everything is what it is: liberty is liberty, not equality or fairness or justice or culture, or human happiness or a quiet conscience. If the liberty of myself or my class or nation depends on the misery of a number of other human beings, the system which promotes this is unjust and immoral. But if I curtail or lose my freedom in order to lessen the shame of such inequality, and do not thereby materially increase the individual liberty of others, an absolute loss of liberty occurs. This may be compensated for by a gain in justice or in happiness or in peace, but the loss remains, and it is a confusion of values to say that although my 'liberal', individual freedom may go by the board, some other kind of freedom – 'social' or 'economic' – is increased. Yet it remains true that the freedom of some must at times be curtailed to secure the freedom of others. Upon what principle should this be done? If freedom is a sacred, untouchable value, there can be no such principle. One or other of these conflicting rules or principles must, at any rate in practice, yield: not always for reasons which can be clearly stated, let alone generalised into rules or universal maxims. Still, a practical compromise has to be found.

Philosophers with an optimistic view of human nature and a belief in the possibility of harmonising human interests, such as Locke or Adam Smith or, in some moods, Mill, believed that social harmony and progress were compatible with reserving a large area for private life over which neither the State nor any other authority must be allowed to trespass. Hobbes, and those who agreed with him, especially conservative or reactionary thinkers, argued that if men were to be prevented from destroying one another and making social life a jungle or a wilderness, greater safeguards must be instituted to keep them in their places; he wished correspond-ingly to increase the area of centralised control and decrease that of the individual. But both sides agreed that some portion of human existence must remain independent of the sphere of social control. To invade that preserve, however small, would be despotism. The most eloquent of all defenders of freedom and privacy, Benjamin Constant, who had not forgotten the Jacobin dictatorship, declared that at the very least the liberty of religion, opinion, expression, property must be guaranteed against arbitrary invasion. Jefferson, Burke, Paine, Mill compiled different catalogues of individual liberties, but the argument for keeping authority at bay is always substantially the same. We must preserve a minimum area of personal freedom if we are not to 'degrade or deny our nature'.[1] We cannot remain absolutely free, and must give up some of our liberty to preserve the rest. But total self-surrender is self-defeating. What then must the minimum be? That which a man cannot give up without offending against the essence of his human nature. What is this essence? What are the standards which it entails? This has been, and perhaps always will be, a matter of infinite debate. But whatever the principle in terms of which the area of non-interference is to be drawn, whether it is that of natural law or

[1] Constant, *Principes de politique*, chapter 1: p. 275 in Benjamin Constant, *De la liberté chez les modernes: écrits politiques*, ed. Marcel Gauchet ([Paris], 1980).

natural rights, or of utility, or the pronouncements of a categorical imperative, or the sanctity of the social contract, or any other concept with which men have sought to clarify and justify their convictions, liberty in this sense means liberty *from*; absence of interference beyond the shifting, but always recognisable, frontier. 'The only freedom which deserves the name, is that of pursuing our own good in our own way', said the most celebrated of its champions.[1] If this is so, is compulsion ever justified? Mill had no doubt that it was. Since justice demands that all individuals be entitled to a minimum of freedom, all other individuals were of necessity to be restrained, if need be by force, from depriving anyone of it. Indeed, the whole function of law was the prevention of just such collisions: the State was reduced to what Lassalle contemptuously described as the functions of a night-watchman or traffic policeman.

What made the protection of individual liberty so sacred to Mill? In his famous essay he declares that, unless the individual is left to live as he wishes in 'the part [of his conduct] which merely concerns himself',[2] civilisation cannot advance; the truth will not, for lack of a free market in ideas, come to light; there will be no scope for spontaneity, originality, genius, for mental energy, for moral courage. Society will be crushed by the weight of 'collective mediocrity'.[3] Whatever is rich and diversified will be crushed by the weight of custom, by men's constant tendency to conformity, which breeds only 'withered' capacities, 'pinched and hidebound', 'cramped and dwarfed' human beings. 'Pagan self-assertion' is as worthy as 'Christian self-denial'.[4] 'All errors which [a man] is likely to commit against advice and warning, are far outweighed by the evil of allowing others to constrain him to what they deem his good.'[5] The defence of liberty consists in the 'negative' goal of warding off interference. To threaten a man with persecution unless he submits to a life in which he exercises no choices of his goals; to block before him every door but one, no matter how noble the prospect upon which it opens, or how benevolent the motives of those who arrange this, is to sin against the truth that he

---

[1] J. S. Mill, *On Liberty*, chapter 1: p. 226 in *Collected Works of John Stuart Mill*, ed. J. M. Robson (Toronto/London, 1981–  ), vol. 18.

[2] ibid., p. 224.

[3] ibid., chapter 3, p. 268.

[4] ibid., pp. 265–6.

[5] ibid., chapter 4, p. 277.

is a man, a being with a life of his own to live. This is liberty as it has been conceived by liberals in the modern world from the days of Erasmus (some would say of Occam) to our own. Every plea for civil liberties and individual rights, every protest against exploitation and humiliation, against the encroachment of public authority, or the mass hypnosis of custom or organised propaganda, springs from this individualistic, and much disputed, conception of man.

Three facts about this position may be noted. In the first place Mill confuses two distinct notions. One is that all coercion is, in so far as it frustrates human desires, bad as such, although it may have to be applied to prevent other, greater evils; while non-interference, which is the opposite of coercion, is good as such, although it is not the only good. This is the 'negative' conception of liberty in its classical form. The other is that men should seek to discover the truth, or to develop a certain type of character of which Mill approved – critical, original, imaginative, independent, non-conforming to the point of eccentricity, and so on – and that truth can be found, and such character can be bred, only in conditions of freedom. Both these are liberal views, but they are not identical, and the connection between them is, at best, empirical. No one would argue that truth or freedom of self-expression could flourish where dogma crushes all thought. But the evidence of history tends to show (as, indeed, was argued by James Stephen in his formidable attack on Mill in his *Liberty, Equality, Fraternity*) that integrity, love of truth and fiery individualism grow at least as often in severely disciplined communities, among, for example, the puritan Calvinists of Scotland or New England, or under military discipline, as in more tolerant or indifferent societies; and if this is so, Mill's argument for liberty as a necessary condition for the growth of human genius falls to the ground. If his two goals proved incompatible, Mill would be faced with a cruel dilemma, quite apart from the further difficulties created by the inconsistency of his doctrines with strict utilitarianism, even in his own humane version of it.[1]

---

[1] This is but another illustration of the natural tendency of all but a very few thinkers to believe that all the things they hold good must be intimately connected, or at least compatible, with one another. The history of thought, like the history of nations, is strewn with examples of inconsistent, or at least disparate, elements artificially yoked together in a despotic system, or held together by the danger of some common enemy. In due course the danger passes, and conflicts between the allies arise, which often disrupt the system, sometimes to the great benefit of mankind.

In the second place, the doctrine is comparatively modern. There seems to be scarcely any discussion of individual liberty as a conscious political ideal (as opposed to its actual existence) in the ancient world. Condorcet had already remarked that the notion of individual rights was absent from the legal conceptions of the Romans and Greeks; this seems to hold equally of the Jewish, Chinese and all other ancient civilisations that have since come to light.[1] The domination of this ideal has been the exception rather than the rule, even in the recent history of the West. Nor has liberty in this sense often formed a rallying cry for the great masses of mankind. The desire not to be impinged upon, to be left to oneself, has been a mark of high civilisation on the part of both individuals and communities. The sense of privacy itself, of the area of personal relationships as something sacred in its own right, derives from a conception of freedom which, for all its religious roots, is scarcely older, in its developed state, than the Renaissance or the Reformation.[2] Yet its decline would mark the death of a civilisation, of an entire moral outlook.

The third characteristic of this notion of liberty is of greater importance. It is that liberty in this sense is not incompatible with some kinds of autocracy, or at any rate with the absence of self-government. Liberty in this sense is principally concerned with the area of control, not with its source. Just as a democracy may, in fact, deprive the individual citizen of a great many liberties which he might have in some other form of society, so it is perfectly conceivable that a liberal-minded despot would allow his subjects a large measure of personal freedom. The despot who leaves his subjects a wide area of liberty may be unjust, or encourage the wildest inequalities, care little for order, or virtue, or knowledge; but provided he does not curb their liberty, or at least curbs it less than many other regimes, he meets with Mill's specification.[3]

---

[1] See the valuable discussion of this in Michel Villey, *Leçons d'histoire de la philosophie du droit* (Paris, 1957), which traces the embryo of the notion of subjective rights to Occam.

[2] Christian (and Jewish or Muslim) belief in the absolute authority of divine or natural laws, or in the equality of all men in the sight of God, is very different from belief in freedom to live as one prefers.

[3] Indeed, it is arguable that in the Prussia of Frederick the Great or in the Austria of Joseph II men of imagination, originality and creative genius, and, indeed, minorities of all kinds, were less persecuted and felt the pressure, both of institutions and custom, less heavy upon them than in many an earlier or later democracy.

Freedom in this sense is not, at any rate logically, connected with democracy or self-government. Self-government may, on the whole, provide a better guarantee of the preservation of civil liberties than other regimes, and has been defended as such by libertarians. But there is no necessary connection between individual liberty and democratic rule. The answer to the question 'Who governs me?' is logically distinct from the question 'How far does government interfere with me?' It is in this difference that the great contrast between the two concepts of negative and positive liberty, in the end, consists.[1] For the 'positive' sense of liberty comes to light if we try to answer the question, not 'What am I free to do or be?', but 'By whom am I ruled?' or 'Who is to say what I am, and

---

[1] 'Negative liberty' is something the extent of which, in a given case, it is difficult to estimate. It might, prima facie, seem to depend simply on the power to choose between at any rate two alternatives. Nevertheless, not all choices are equally free, or free at all. If in a totalitarian State I betray my friend under threat of torture, perhaps even if I act from fear of losing my job, I can reasonably say that I did not act freely. Nevertheless, I did, of course, make a choice, and could, at any rate in theory, have chosen to be killed or tortured or imprisoned. The mere existence of alternatives is not, therefore, enough to make my action free (although it may be voluntary) in the normal sense of the word. The extent of my freedom seems to depend on (a) how many possibilities are open to me (although the method of counting these can never be more than impressionistic; possibilities of action are not discrete entities like apples, which can be exhaustively enumerated); (b) how easy or difficult each of these possibilities is to actualise; (c) how important in my plan of life, given my character and circumstances, these possibilities are when compared with each other; (d) how far they are closed and opened by deliberate human acts; (e) what value not merely the agent, but the general sentiment of the society in which he lives, puts on the various possibilities. All these magnitudes must be 'integrated', and a conclusion, necessarily never precise, or indisputable, drawn from this process. It may well be that there are many incommensurable kinds and degrees of freedom, and that they cannot be drawn up on any single scale of magnitude. Moreover, in the case of societies, we are faced by such (logically absurd) questions as 'Would arrangement X increase the liberty of Mr A more than it would that of Messrs B, C and D between them, added together?' The same difficulties arise in applying utilitarian criteria. Nevertheless, provided we do not demand precise measurement, we can give valid reasons for saying that the average subject of the King of Sweden is, on the whole, a good deal freer today [1958] than the average citizen of Spain or Albania. Total patterns of life must be compared directly as wholes, although the method by which we make the comparison, and the truth of the conclusions, are difficult or impossible to demonstrate. But the vagueness of the concepts, and the multiplicity of the criteria involved, are attributes of the subject-matter itself, not of our imperfect methods of measurement, or of incapacity for precise thought.

what I am not, to be or do?' The connection between democracy and individual liberty is a good deal more tenuous than it seemed to many advocates of both. The desire to be governed by myself, or at any rate to participate in the process by which my life is to be controlled, may be as deep a wish as that for a free area for action, and perhaps historically older. But it is not a desire for the same thing. So different is it, indeed, as to have led in the end to the great clash of ideologies that dominates our world. For it is this, the 'positive' conception of liberty, not freedom from, but freedom to – to lead one prescribed form of life – which the adherents of the 'negative' notion represent as being, at times, no better than a specious disguise for brutal tyranny.

## II

### The notion of positive freedom

The 'positive' sense of the word 'liberty' derives from the wish on the part of the individual to be his own master. I wish my life and decisions to depend on myself, not on external forces of whatever kind. I wish to be the instrument of my own, not of other men's, acts of will. I wish to be a subject, not an object; to be moved by reasons, by conscious purposes, which are my own, not by causes which affect me, as it were, from outside. I wish to be somebody, not nobody; a doer – deciding, not being decided for, self-directed and not acted upon by external nature or by other men as if I were a thing, or an animal, or a slave incapable of playing a human role, that is, of conceiving goals and policies of my own and realising them. This is at least part of what I mean when I say that I am rational, and that it is my reason that distinguishes me as a human being from the rest of the world. I wish, above all, to be conscious of myself as a thinking, willing, active being, bearing responsibility for my choices and able to explain them by reference to my own ideas and purposes. I feel free to the degree that I believe this to be true, and enslaved to the degree that I am made to realise that it is not.

The freedom which consists in being one's own master, and the freedom which consists in not being prevented from choosing as I do by other men, may, on the face of it, seem concepts at no great logical distance from each other – no more than negative and positive ways of saying much the same thing. Yet the 'positive' and 'negative' notions of freedom historically developed in divergent directions, not always by logically reputable steps, until, in the end, they came into direct conflict with each other.

One way of making this clear is in terms of the independent momentum which the, initially perhaps quite harmless, metaphor of self-mastery acquired. 'I am my own master'; 'I am slave to no man'; but may I not (as Platonists or Hegelians tend to say) be a slave to nature? Or to my own 'unbridled' passions? Are these not so many species of the identical genus 'slave' – some political or legal, others moral or spiritual? Have not men had the experience of liberating themselves from spiritual slavery, or slavery to nature, and do they not in the course of it become aware, on the one hand, of a self which dominates, and, on the other, of something in them which is brought to heel? This dominant self is then variously identified with reason, with my 'higher nature', with the self which calculates and aims at what will satisfy it in the long run, with my 'real', or 'ideal', or 'autonomous' self, or with my self 'at its best'; which is then contrasted with irrational impulse, uncontrolled desires, my 'lower' nature, the pursuit of immediate pleasures, my 'empirical' or 'heteronomous' self, swept by every gust of desire and passion, needing to be rigidly disciplined if it is ever to rise to the full height of its 'real' nature. Presently the two selves may be represented as divided by an even larger gap; the real self may be conceived as something wider than the individual (as the term is normally understood), as a social 'whole' of which the individual is an element or aspect: a tribe, a race, a Church, a State, the great society of the living and the dead and the yet unborn. This entity is then identified as being the 'true' self which, by imposing its collective, or 'organic', single will upon its recalcitrant 'members', achieves its own, and therefore their, 'higher' freedom. The perils of using organic metaphors to justify the coercion of some men by others in order to raise them to a 'higher' level of freedom have often been pointed out. But what gives such plausibility as it has to this kind of language is that we recognise that it is possible, and at times justifiable, to coerce men in the name of some goal (let us say, justice or public health) which they would, if they were more enlightened, themselves pursue, but do not, because they are blind or ignorant or corrupt. This renders it easy for me to conceive of myself as coercing others for their own sake, in their, not my, interest. I am then claiming that I know what they truly need better than they know it themselves. What, at most, this entails is that they would not resist me if they were rational and as wise as I and understood their interests as I do. But I may go on to claim a good deal more than this. I may declare that they are actually aiming at what in their benighted state they consciously resist, because there exists within them an occult entity – their latent rational will, or their 'true' purpose – and that this entity, although it is belied by all that they overtly feel and do and say, is their 'real' self, of which the poor empirical self in space and time may know nothing or little; and that this inner spirit is the only self that deserves to have its wishes taken into account.[1] Once I take this view, I am in a position to ignore the actual wishes of men or societies, to bully, oppress, torture them in the name, and on behalf, of their 'real' selves, in the secure knowledge that whatever is the true goal of man (happiness, performance of duty, wisdom, a just society, self-fulfilment) must be identical with his freedom – the free choice of his 'true', albeit often submerged and inarticulate, self.

This paradox has been often exposed. It is one thing to say that I know what is good for X, while he himself does not; and even to ignore his wishes for its – and his – sake; and a very different one to say that he has *eo ipso* chosen it, not indeed consciously, not as he seems in everyday life, but in his role as a rational self which his empirical self may not know – the 'real' self which discerns the good, and cannot help choosing it once it is revealed. This monstrous impersonation, which consists in equating what X would choose if he were something he is not, or at least not yet, with what X actually seeks and chooses, is at the heart of all political theories of self-realisation. It is one thing to say that I may be coerced for my own good, which I am too blind to see: this may, on occasion, be for my benefit; indeed it may enlarge the scope of my liberty. It is another to say that if it is my good, then I am not being coerced, for I have willed it, whether I know this or

---

[1] 'The ideal of true freedom is the maximum of power for all members of human society alike to make the best of themselves', said T. H. Green in 1881. *Lecture on Liberal Legislation and Freedom of Contract*: p. 200 in T. H. Green, *Lectures on the Principles of Political Obligation and Other Writings*, ed. Paul Harris and John Morrow (Cambridge, 1986). Apart from the confusion of freedom with equality, this entails that if a man chose some immediate pleasure – which (in whose view?) would not enable him to make the best of himself (what self?) – what he was exercising was not 'true' freedom: and if deprived of it, he would not lose anything that mattered. Green was a genuine liberal: but many a tyrant could use this formula to justify his worst acts of oppression.

not, and am free (or 'truly' free) even while my poor earthly body and foolish mind bitterly reject it, and struggle with the greatest desperation against those who seek, however benevolently, to impose it.

This magical transformation, or sleight of hand (for which William James so justly mocked the Hegelians), can no doubt be perpetrated just as easily with the 'negative' concept of freedom, where the self that should not be interfered with is no longer the individual with his actual wishes and needs as they are normally conceived, but the 'real' man within, identified with the pursuit of some ideal purpose not dreamed of by his empirical self. And, as in the case of the 'positively' free self, this entity may be inflated into some super-personal entity – a State, a class, a nation, or the march of history itself, regarded as a more 'real' subject of attributes than the empirical self. But the 'positive' conception of freedom as self-mastery, with its suggestion of a man divided against himself, has in fact, and as a matter of history, of doctrine and of practice, lent itself more easily to this splitting of personality into two: the transcendent, dominant controller, and the empirical bundle of desires and passions to be disciplined and brought to heel. It is this historical fact that has been influential. This demonstrates (if demonstration of so obvious a truth is needed) that conceptions of freedom directly derive from views of what constitutes a self, a person, a man. Enough manipulation of the definition of man, and freedom can be made to mean whatever the manipulator wishes. Recent history has made it only too clear that the issue is not merely academic.

The consequences of distinguishing between two selves will become even clearer if one considers the two major forms which the desire to be self-directed – directed by one's 'true' self – has historically taken: the first, that of self-abnegation in order to attain independence; the second, that of self-realisation, or total self-identification with a specific principle or ideal in order to attain the selfsame end.

III

*The retreat to the inner citadel*

I am the possessor of reason and will; I conceive ends and I desire to pursue them; but if I am prevented from attaining them I no longer feel master of the situation. I may be prevented by the laws of nature, or by accidents, or the activities of men, or the effect, often undesigned, of human institutions. These forces may be too much for me. What am I to do to avoid being crushed by them? I must liberate myself from desires that I know I cannot realise. I wish to be master of my kingdom, but my frontiers are long and insecure, therefore I contract them in order to reduce or eliminate the vulnerable area. I begin by desiring happiness, or power, or knowledge, or the attainment of some specific object. But I cannot command them. I choose to avoid defeat and waste, and therefore decide to strive for nothing that I cannot be sure to obtain. I determine myself not to desire what is unattainable. The tyrant threatens me with the destruction of my property, with imprisonment, with the exile or death of those I love. But if I no longer feel attached to property, no longer care whether or not I am in prison, if I have killed within myself my natural affections, then he cannot bend me to his will, for all that is left of myself is no longer subject to empirical fears or desires. It is as if I had performed a strategic retreat into an inner citadel – my reason, my soul, my 'noumenal' self – which, do what they may, neither external blind force, nor human malice, can touch. I have withdrawn into myself; there, and there alone, I am secure. It is as if I were to say: 'I have a wound in my leg. There are two methods of freeing myself from pain. One is to heal the wound. But if the cure is too difficult or uncertain, there is another method. I can get rid of the wound by cutting off my leg. If I train myself to want nothing to which the possession of my leg is indispensable, I shall not feel the lack of it.' This is the traditional self-emancipation of ascetics and quietists, of stoics or Buddhist sages, men of various religions or of none, who have fled the world, and escaped the yoke of society or public opinion, by some process of deliberate self-transformation that enables them to care no longer for any of its values, to remain, isolated and independent, on its edges, no longer vulnerable to its weapons.[1] All political isolationism, all economic autarky, every form of autonomy, has in it some element of this attitude. I eliminate the obstacles in my path by abandoning the path; I retreat into my

[1] 'A wise man, though he be a slave, is at liberty, and from this it follows that though a fool rule, he is in slavery', said St Ambrose. It might equally well have been said by Epictetus or Kant. *Corpus Scriptorum Ecclesiasticorum Latinorum*, vol. 82, part 1, ed. Otto Faller (Vienna, 1968), letter 7, § 24 (p. 55).

own sect, my own planned economy, my own deliberately insulated territory, where no voices from outside need be listened to,
and no external forces can have effect. This is a form of the search
for security; but it has also been called the search for personal or
national freedom or independence.

From this doctrine, as it applies to individuals, it is no very
great distance to the conceptions of those who, like Kant, identify
freedom not indeed with the elimination of desires, but with
resistance to them, and control over them. I identify myself with
the controller and escape the slavery of the controlled. I am free
because, and in so far as, I am autonomous. I obey laws, but I have
imposed them on, or found them in, my own uncoerced self.
Freedom is obedience, but, in Rousseau's words, 'obedience to a
law which we prescribe to ourselves',[1] and no man can enslave
himself. Heteronomy is dependence on outside factors, liability to
be a plaything of the external world that I cannot myself fully
control, and which *pro tanto* controls and 'enslaves' me. I am free
only to the degree to which my person is 'fettered' by nothing that
obeys forces over which I have no control; I cannot control the
laws of nature; my free activity must therefore, *ex hypothesi*, be
lifted above the empirical world of causality. This is not the place
in which to discuss the validity of this ancient and famous doctrine;
I only wish to remark that the related notions of freedom as
resistance to (or escape from) unrealisable desire, and as independence of the sphere of causality, have played a central role in politics
no less than in ethics.

For if the essence of men is that they are autonomous beings –
authors of values, of ends in themselves, the ultimate authority of
which consists precisely in the fact that they are willed freely – then
nothing is worse than to treat them as if they were not autonomous, but natural objects, played on by causal influences, creatures
at the mercy of external stimuli, whose choices can be manipulated
by their rulers, whether by threats of force or offers of rewards. To
treat men in this way is to treat them as if they were not self-
determined. 'Nobody may compel me to be happy in his own
way', said Kant. Paternalism is 'the greatest despotism imaginable'.[2] This is so because it is to treat men as if they were not free,

---

[1] *Social Contract*, book 1, chapter 8: p. 365 in *Oeuvres complètes* (op. cit., p. 195
above, note 2), vol. 3; cf. Constant, op. cit. (p. 198 above, note 1), p. 272.

[2] op. cit. (p. 16 above, note 1), vol. 8, p. 290, line 27, and p. 291, line 3.

but human material for me, the benevolent reformer, to mould in accordance with my own, not their, freely adopted purpose. This is, of course, precisely the policy that the early utilitarians recommended. Helvétius (and Bentham) believed not in resisting, but in using, men's tendency to be slaves to their passions; they wished to dangle rewards and punishments before men – the acutest possible form of heteronomy – if by this means the 'slaves' might be made happier.[1] But to manipulate men, to propel them towards goals which you – the social reformer – see, but they may not, is to deny their human essence, to treat them as objects without wills of their own, and therefore to degrade them. That is why to lie to men, or to deceive them, that is, to use them as means for my, not their own, independently conceived ends, even if it is for their own benefit, is, in effect, to treat them as subhuman, to behave as if their ends are less ultimate and sacred than my own. In the name of what can I ever be justified in forcing men to do what they have not willed or consented to? Only in the name of some value higher than themselves. But if, as Kant held, all values are made so by the free acts of men, and called values only so far as they are this, there is no value higher than the individual. Therefore to do this is to coerce men in the name of something less ultimate than themselves – to bend them to my will, or to someone else's particular craving for (his or their) happiness or expediency or security or convenience. I am aiming at something desired (from whatever motive, no matter how noble) by me or my group, to which I am using other men as means. But this is a contradiction of what I know men to be, namely ends in themselves. All forms of tampering with human beings, getting at them, shaping them against their will to your own pattern, all thought-control and conditioning,[2] is, therefore, a denial of that in men which makes them men and their values ultimate.

[1] 'Proletarian coercion, in all its forms, from executions to forced labour, is, paradoxical as it may sound, the method of moulding communist humanity out of the human material of the capitalist period.' These lines by the Bolshevik leader Nikolay Bukharin, especially the term 'human material', vividly convey this attitude. Nikolay Bukharin, *Ekonomika perekhodnogo perioda* [Economics in the Transitional Period] (Moscow, 1920), chapter 10, p. 146.

[2] Kant's psychology, and that of the Stoics and Christians too, assumed that some element in man – the 'inner fastness of his mind' – could be made secure against conditioning. The development of the techniques of hypnosis, 'brainwashing', subliminal suggestion and the like has made this a priori assumption, at least as an empirical hypothesis, less plausible.

Kant's free individual is a transcendent being, beyond the realm of natural causality. But in its empirical form – in which the notion of man is that of ordinary life – this doctrine was the heart of liberal humanism, both moral and political, that was deeply influenced both by Kant and by Rousseau in the eighteenth century. In its a priori version it is a form of secularised Protestant individualism, in which the place of God is taken by the conception of the rational life, and the place of the individual soul which strains towards union with him is replaced by the conception of the individual, endowed with reason, straining to be governed by reason and reason alone, and to depend upon nothing that might deflect or delude him by engaging his irrational nature. Autonomy, not heteronomy: to act and not to be acted upon. The notion of slavery to the passions is – for those who think in these terms – more than a metaphor. To rid myself of fear, or love, or the desire to conform is to liberate myself from the despotism of something which I cannot control. Sophocles, whom Plato reports as saying that old age alone has liberated him from the passion of love – the yoke of a cruel master – is reporting an experience as real as that of liberation from a human tyrant or slave owner. The psychological experience of observing myself yielding to some 'lower' impulse, acting from a motive that I dislike, or of doing something which at the very moment of doing I may detest, and reflecting later that I was 'not myself', or 'not in control of myself', when I did it, belongs to this way of thinking and speaking. I identify myself with my critical and rational moments. The consequences of my acts cannot matter, for they are not in my control; only my motives are. This is the creed of the solitary thinker who has defied the world and emancipated himself from the chains of men and things. In this form the doctrine may seem primarily an ethical creed, and scarcely political at all; nevertheless its political implications are clear, and it enters into the tradition of liberal individualism at least as deeply as the 'negative' concept of freedom.

It is perhaps worth remarking that in its individualistic form the concept of the rational sage who has escaped into the inner fortress of his true self seems to arise when the external world has proved exceptionally arid, cruel or unjust. 'He is truly free', said Rousseau, 'who desires what he can perform, and does what he desires.'[1] In a world where a man seeking happiness or justice or freedom (in

---

[1] op. cit. (p. 195 above, note 2), p. 309.

whatever sense) can do little, because he finds too many avenues of action blocked to him, the temptation to withdraw into himself may become irresistible. It may have been so in Greece, where the Stoic ideal cannot be wholly unconnected with the fall of the independent democracies before centralised Macedonian autocracy. It was so in Rome, for analogous reasons, after the end of the Republic.[1] It arose in Germany in the seventeenth century, during the period of the deepest national degradation of the German States that followed the Thirty Years War, when the character of public life, particularly in the small principalities, forced those who prized the dignity of human life, not for the first or last time, into a kind of inner emigration. The doctrine that maintains that what I cannot have I must teach myself not to desire, that a desire eliminated, or successfully resisted, is as good as a desire satisfied, is a sublime, but, it seems to me, unmistakable, form of the doctrine of sour grapes: what I cannot be sure of, I cannot truly want.

This makes it clear why the definition of negative liberty as the ability to do what one wishes – which is, in effect, the definition adopted by Mill – will not do. If I find that I am able to do little or nothing of what I wish, I need only contract or extinguish my wishes, and I am made free. If the tyrant (or 'hidden persuader') manages to condition his subjects (or customers) into losing their original wishes and embracing ('internalising') the form of life he has invented for them, he will, on this definition, have succeeded in liberating them. He will, no doubt, have made them *feel* free – as Epictetus feels freer than his master (and the proverbial good man is said to feel happy on the rack). But what he has created is the very antithesis of political freedom.

Ascetic self-denial may be a source of integrity or serenity and spiritual strength, but it is difficult to see how it can be called an enlargement of liberty. If I save myself from an adversary by retreating indoors and locking every entrance and exit, I may remain freer than if I had been captured by him, but am I freer than if I had defeated or captured him? If I go too far, contract myself into too small a space, I shall suffocate and die. The logical culmination of the process of destroying everything through which

---

[1] It is not perhaps far-fetched to assume that the quietism of the Eastern sages was, similarly, a response to the despotism of the great auotocracies, and flourished at periods when individuals were apt to be humiliated, or at any rate ignored or ruthlessly managed, by those possessed of the instruments of physical coercion.

I can possibly be wounded is suicide. While I exist in the natural world, I can never be wholly secure. Total liberation in this sense (as Schopenhauer correctly perceived) is conferred only by death.[1]

I find myself in a world in which I meet with obstacles to my will. Those who are wedded to the 'negative' concept of freedom may perhaps be forgiven if they think that self-abnegation is not the only method of overcoming obstacles; that it is also possible to do so by removing them: in the case of non-human objects, by physical action; in the case of human resistance, by force or persuasion, as when I induce somebody to make room for me in his carriage, or conquer a country which threatens the interests of my own. Such acts may be unjust, they may involve violence, cruelty, the enslavement of others, but it can scarcely be denied that thereby the agent is able in the most literal sense to increase his own freedom. It is an irony of history that this truth is repudiated by some of those who practise it most forcibly, men who, even while they conquer power and freedom of action, reject the 'negative' concept of it in favour of its 'positive' counterpart. Their view rules over half our world; let us see upon what metaphysical foundation it rests.

IV

*Self-realisation*

The only true method of attaining freedom, we are told, is by the use of critical reason, the understanding of what is necessary and what is contingent. If I am a schoolboy, all but the simplest truths of mathematics obtrude themselves as obstacles to the free functioning of my mind, as theorems whose necessity I do not understand; they are pronounced to be true by some external authority, and present themselves to me as foreign bodies which I

---

[1] It is worth remarking that those who demanded – and fought for – liberty for the individual or for the nation in France during this period of German quietism did not fall into this attitude. Might this not be precisely because, despite the despotism of the French monarchy and the arrogance and arbitrary behaviour of privileged groups in the French State, France was a proud and powerful nation, where the reality of political power was not beyond the grasp of men of talent, so that withdrawal from battle into some untroubled heaven above it, whence it could be surveyed dispassionately by the self-sufficient philosopher, was not the only way out? The same holds for England in the nineteenth century and well after it, and for the United States today.

am expected mechanically to absorb into my system. But when I understand the functions of the symbols, the axioms, the formation and transformation rules – the logic whereby the conclusions are obtained – and grasp that these things cannot be otherwise, because they appear to follow from the laws that govern the processes of my own reason,[1] then mathematical truths no longer obtrude themselves as external entities forced upon me which I must receive whether I want to or not, but as something which I now freely will in the course of the natural functioning of my own rational activity. For the mathematician, the proof of these theorems is part of the free exercise of his natural reasoning capacity. For the musician, after he has assimilated the pattern of the composer's score, and has made the composer's ends his own, the playing of the music is not obedience to external laws, a compulsion and a barrier to liberty, but a free, unimpeded exercise. The player is not bound to the score as an ox to the plough, or a factory worker to the machine. He has absorbed the score into his own system, has, by understanding it, identified it with himself, has changed it from an impediment to free activity into an element in that activity itself.

What applies to music or mathematics must, we are told, in principle apply to all other obstacles which present themselves as so many lumps of external stuff blocking free self-development. That is the programme of enlightened rationalism from Spinoza to the latest (at times unconscious) disciples of Hegel. *Sapere aude.* What you know, that of which you understand the necessity – the rational necessity – you cannot, while remaining rational, want to be otherwise. For to want something to be other than what it must be is, given the premises – the necessities that govern the world – to be *pro tanto* either ignorant or irrational. Passions, prejudices, fears, neuroses spring from ignorance, and take the form of myths and illusions. To be ruled by myths, whether they spring from the vivid imaginations of unscrupulous charlatans who deceive us in order to exploit us, or from psychological or sociological causes, is a form of heteronomy, of being dominated by outside factors in a direction not necessarily willed by the agent. The scientific determinists of the eighteenth century supposed that the study of the sciences of nature, and the creation of sciences of society on the

---

[1] Or, as some modern theorists maintain, because I have, or could have, invented them for myself, since the rules are man-made.

same model, would make the operation of such causes transparently clear, and thus enable individuals to recognise their own part in the working of a rational world, frustrating only when misunderstood. Knowledge liberates, as Epicurus taught long ago, by automatically eliminating irrational fears and desires.

Herder, Hegel and Marx substituted their own vitalistic models of social life for the older, mechanical, ones, but believed, no less than their opponents, that to understand the world is to be freed. They merely differed from them in stressing the part played by change and growth in what made human beings human. Social life could not be understood by an analogy drawn from mathematics or physics. One must also understand history, that is, the peculiar laws of continuous growth, whether by 'dialectical' conflict or otherwise, that govern individuals and groups in their interplay with each other and with nature. Not to grasp this is, according to these thinkers, to fall into a particular kind of error, namely the belief that human nature is static, that its essential properties are the same everywhere and at all times, that it is governed by unvarying natural laws, whether they are conceived in theological or materialistic terms, which entails the fallacious corollary that a wise lawgiver can, in principle, create a perfectly harmonious society at any time by appropriate education and legislation, because rational men, in all ages and countries, must always demand the same unaltering satisfactions of the same unaltering basic needs. Hegel believed that his contemporaries (and indeed all his predecessors) misunderstood the nature of institutions because they did not understand the laws – the rationally intelligible laws, since they spring from the operation of reason – that create and alter institutions and transform human character and human action. Marx and his disciples maintained that the path of human beings was obstructed not only by natural forces, or the imperfections of their own characters, but, even more, by the workings of their own social institutions, which they had originally created (not always consciously) for certain purposes, but whose functioning they systematically came to misconceive,[1] and which thereupon became obstacles to their creators' progress. Marx offered social and economic hypotheses to account for the inevitability of such misunderstanding, in particular of the illusion that such man-made arrangements were independent forces, as inescapable as the laws of

[1] In practice even more than in theory.

nature. As instances of such pseudo-objective forces, he pointed to the laws of supply and demand, or the institution of property, or the eternal division of society into rich and poor, or owners and workers, as so many unaltering human categories. Not until we had reached a stage at which the spells of these illusions could be broken, that is, until enough men reached a social stage that alone enabled them to understand that these laws and institutions were themselves the work of human minds and hands, historically needed in their day, and later mistaken for inexorable, objective powers, could the old world be destroyed, and more adequate and liberating social machinery substituted.

We are enslaved by despots – institutions or beliefs or neuroses – which can be removed only by being analysed and understood. We are imprisoned by evil spirits which we have ourselves – albeit not consciously – created, and can exorcise them only by becoming conscious and acting appropriately: indeed, for Marx understanding *is* appropriate action. I am free if, and only if, I plan my life in accordance with my own will; plans entail rules; a rule does not oppress me or enslave me if I impose it on myself consciously, or accept it freely, having understood it, whether it was invented by me or by others, provided that it is rational, that is to say, conforms to the necessities of things. To understand why things must be as they must be is to will them to be so. Knowledge liberates not by offering us more open possibilities amongst which we can make our choice, but by preserving us from the frustration of attempting the impossible. To want necessary laws to be other than they are is to be prey to an irrational desire – a desire that what must be X should also be not-X. To go further, and believe these laws to be other than what they necessarily are, is to be insane. That is the metaphysical heart of rationalism. The notion of liberty contained in it is not the 'negative' conception of a field (ideally) without obstacles, a vacuum in which nothing obstructs me, but the notion of self-direction or self-control. I can do what I will with my own. I am a rational being; whatever I can demonstrate to myself as being necessary, as incapable of being otherwise in a rational society – that is, in a society directed by rational minds, towards goals such as a rational being would have – I cannot, being rational, wish to sweep out of my way. I assimilate it into my substance as I do the laws of logic, of mathematics, of physics, the rules of art, the principles that govern everything of which I understand, and therefore will, the rational purpose, by which I can never be thwarted, since I cannot want it to be other than it is.

This is the positive doctrine of liberation by reason. Socialised forms of it, widely disparate and opposed to each other as they are, are at the heart of many of the nationalist, communist, authoritarian, and totalitarian creeds of our day. It may, in the course of its evolution, have wandered far from its rationalist moorings. Nevertheless, it is this freedom that, in democracies and in dictatorships, is argued about, and fought for, in many parts of the earth today. Without attempting to trace the historical evolution of this idea, I should like to comment on some of its vicissitudes.

V

## The Temple of Sarastro

Those who believed in freedom as rational self-direction were bound, sooner or later, to consider how this was to be applied not merely to a man's inner life, but to his relations with other members of his society. Even the most individualistic among them – and Rousseau, Kant and Fichte certainly began as individualists – came at some point to ask themselves whether a rational life not only for the individual, but also for society, was possible, and if so, how it was to be achieved. I wish to be free to live as my rational will (my 'real self') commands, but so must others be. How am I to avoid collisions with their wills? Where is the frontier that lies between my (rationally determined) rights and the identical rights of others? For if I am rational, I cannot deny that what is right for me must, for the same reasons, be right for others who are rational like me. A rational (or free) State would be a State governed by such laws as all rational men would freely accept; that is to say, such laws as they would themselves have enacted had they been asked what, as rational beings, they demanded; hence the frontiers would be such as all rational men would consider to be the right frontiers for rational beings.

But who, in fact, was to determine what these frontiers were? Thinkers of this type argued that if moral and political problems were genuine – as surely they were – they must in principle be soluble; that is to say, there must exist one and only one true solution to any problem. All truths could in principle be discovered by any rational thinker, and demonstrated so clearly that all other rational men could not but accept them; indeed, this was already to a large extent the case in the new natural sciences. On this assumption the problem of political liberty was soluble by establishing a just order that would give to each man all the freedom to which a rational being was entitled. My claim to unfettered freedom can prima facie at times not be reconciled with your equally unqualified claim; but the rational solution of one problem cannot collide with the equally true solution of another, for two truths cannot logically be incompatible; therefore a just order must in principle be discoverable – an order of which the rules make possible correct solutions to all possible problems that could arise in it. This ideal, harmonious state of affairs was sometimes imagined as a Garden of Eden before the Fall of Man, an Eden from which we were expelled, but for which we were still filled with longing; or as a golden age still before us, in which men, having become rational, will no longer be 'other-directed', nor 'alienate' or frustrate one another. In existing societies justice and equality are ideals which still call for some measure of coercion, because the premature lifting of social controls might lead to the oppression of the weaker and the stupider by the stronger or abler or more energetic and unscrupulous. But it is only irrationality on the part of men (according to this doctrine) that leads them to wish to oppress or exploit or humiliate one another. Rational men will respect the principle of reason in each other, and lack all desire to fight or dominate one another. The desire to dominate is itself a symptom of irrationality, and can be explained and cured by rational methods. Spinoza offers one kind of explanation and remedy, Hegel another, Marx a third. Some of these theories may perhaps, to some degree, supplement each other, others are not combinable. But they all assume that in a society of perfectly rational beings the lust for domination over men will be absent or ineffective. The existence of, or cravings for, oppression will be the first symptom that the true solution to the problems of social life has not been reached.

This can be put in another way. Freedom is self-mastery, the elimination of obstacles to my will, whatever these obstacles may be – the resistance of nature, of my ungoverned passions, of irrational institutions, of the opposing wills or behaviour of others. Nature I can, at least in principle, always mould by technical means, and shape to my will. But how am I to treat recalcitrant human beings? I must, if I can, impose my will on them too, 'mould' them to my pattern, cast parts for them in my play. But will this not mean that I alone am free, while they are slaves? They will be so if my plan has nothing to do with their wishes or values, only with my own. But if my plan is fully rational, it will allow for the full development of their 'true' natures, the realisation of their capacities for rational decisions, for 'making the best of themselves' – as a part of the realisation of my own 'true' self. All true solutions to all genuine problems must be compatible: more than this, they must fit into a single whole; for this is what is meant by calling them all rational and the universe harmonious. Each man has his specific character, abilities, aspirations, ends. If I grasp both what these ends and natures are, and how they all relate to one another, I can, at least in principle, if I have the knowledge and the strength, satisfy them all, so long as the nature and the purposes in question are rational. Rationality is knowing things and people for what they are: I must not use stones to make violins, nor try to make born violin-players play flutes. If the universe is governed by reason, then there will be no need for coercion; a correctly planned life for all will coincide with full freedom – the freedom of rational self-direction – for all. This will be so if, and only if, the plan is the true plan – the one unique pattern which alone fulfils the claims of reason. Its laws will be the rules which reason prescribes: they will only seem irksome to those whose reason is dormant, who do not understand the true 'needs' of their own 'real' selves. So long as each player recognises and plays the part set him by reason – the faculty that understands his true nature and discerns his true ends – there can be no conflict. Each man will be a liberated, self-directed actor in the cosmic drama. Thus Spinoza tells us that children, although they are coerced, are not slaves, because they obey orders given in their own interests, and that the subject of a true commonwealth is no slave, because the common interests must include his own.[1] Similarly, Locke says 'Where there is no law there is no freedom', because rational law is a direction to a man's 'proper interests' or 'general good'; and adds that since law of this kind is what 'hedges us in only from bogs and precipices' it 'ill deserves the name of confinement',[2] and speaks of desires to escape from it as being irrational, forms of 'licence', as 'brutish',[3]

---

[1] *Tractatus Theologico-Politicus*, chapter 16: p. 137 in Benedict de Spinoza, *The Political Works*, ed. A. G. Wernham (Oxford, 1958).

[2] *Two Treatises of Government*, second treatise, § 57.

[3] ibid., §§ 6, 163.

and so on. Montesquieu, forgetting his liberal moments, speaks of political liberty as being not permission to do what we want, or even what the law allows, but only 'the power of doing what we ought to will',[1] which Kant virtually repeats. Burke proclaims the individual's 'right' to be restrained in his own interest, because 'the presumed consent of every rational creature is in unison with the predisposed order of things'.[2]

The common assumption of these thinkers (and of many a schoolman before them and Jacobin and Communist after them) is that the rational ends of our 'true' natures must coincide, or be made to coincide, however violently our poor, ignorant, desire-ridden, passionate, empirical selves may cry out against this process. Freedom is not freedom to do what is irrational, or stupid, or wrong. To force empirical selves into the right pattern is no tyranny, but liberation.[3] Rousseau tells me that if I freely surrender all the parts of my life to society, I create an entity which, because it has been built by an equality of sacrifice of all its members, cannot wish to hurt any one of them; in such a society, we are informed, it can be in nobody's interest to damage anyone else. 'In giving myself to all, I give myself to none',[4] and get back as much as I lose, with enough new force to preserve my new gains. Kant tells us that when 'the individual has entirely aban-doned his wild, lawless freedom, to find it again, unimpaired, in a state of dependence according to law', that alone is true freedom, 'for this dependence is the work of my own will acting as a

---

[1] De l'esprit des lois, book 11, chapter 3: p. 205 in Oeuvres complètes de Montesquieu, ed. A. Masson (Paris, 1950–5), vol. 1 A.

[2] Appeal from the Old to the New Whigs (1791): pp. 93–4 in The Works of the Right Honourable Edmund Burke (World's Classics edition), vol. 5 (London, 1907).

[3] On this Bentham seems to me to have said the last word: 'The liberty of doing evil, is it not liberty? If it is not liberty, what is it then? . . . Do we not say that liberty should be taken away from fools, and wicked persons, because they abuse it?' The Works of Jeremy Bentham, ed. John Bowring (Edinburgh, 1843), vol. 1, p. 301. Compare with this the view of the Jacobins in the same period, discussed by Crane Brinton in 'Political Ideas in the Jacobin Clubs', Political Science Quarterly 43 (1928), 249–64, esp. p. 257: 'no man is free in doing evil. To prevent him is to free him.' This view is echoed in almost identical terms by British Idealists at the end of the following century.

[4] Social Contract, book 1, chapter 6: p. 361 in Oeuvres complètes (op. cit., p. 195 above, note 2), vol. 3.

lawgiver'.[1] Liberty, so far from being incompatible with authority, becomes virtually identical with it. This is the thought and language of all the declarations of the rights of man in the eighteenth century, and of all those who look upon society as a design constructed according to the rational laws of the wise lawgiver, or of nature, or of history, or of the Supreme Being. Bentham, almost alone, doggedly went on repeating that the business of laws was not to liberate but to restrain: every law is an infraction of liberty[2] – even if such infraction leads to an increase of the sum of liberty.

If the underlying assumptions had been correct – if the method of solving social problems resembled the way in which solutions to the problems of the natural sciences are found, and if reason were what rationalists said that it was – all this would perhaps follow. In the ideal case, liberty coincides with law: autonomy with authority. A law which forbids me to do what I could not, as a sane being, conceivably wish to do is not a restraint of my freedom. In the ideal society, composed of wholly responsible beings, rules, because I should scarcely be conscious of them, would gradually wither away. Only one social movement was bold enough to render this assumption quite explicit and accept its consequences – that of the Anarchists. But all forms of liberalism founded on a rationalist metaphysics are less or more watered-down versions of this creed.

In due course, the thinkers who bent their energies to the solution of the problem on these lines came to be faced with the question of how in practice men were to be made rational in this way. Clearly they must be educated. For the uneducated are irrational, heteronomous, and need to be coerced, if only to make life tolerable for the rational if they are to live in the same society and not be compelled to withdraw to a desert or some Olympian height. But the uneducated cannot be expected to understand or co-operate with the purposes of their educators. Education, says Fichte, must inevitably work in such a way that 'you will later recognise the reasons for what I am doing now'.[3] Children cannot be expected to understand why they are compelled to go to school,

---

[1] op. cit. (p. 16 above, note 1), vol. 6, p. 316, line 2.

[2] op. cit. (p. 219 above, note 3), ibid.: 'every law is contrary to liberty'.

[3] *Johann Gottlieb Fichte's Sämmtliche Werke*, ed. I. H. Fichte (Berlin, 1845–6), vol. 7, p. 576.

nor the ignorant – that is, for the moment, the majority of mankind – why they are made to obey the laws that will presently make them rational. 'Compulsion is also a kind of education.'[1] You learn the great virtue of obedience to superior persons. If you cannot understand your own interests as a rational being, I cannot be expected to consult you, or abide by your wishes, in the course of making you rational. I must, in the end, force you to be protected against smallpox, even though you may not wish it. Even Mill is prepared to say that I may forcibly prevent a man from crossing a bridge if there is not time to warn him that it is about to collapse, for I know, or am justified in assuming, that he cannot wish to fall into the water. Fichte knows what the uneducated German of his time wishes to be or do better than he can possibly know this for himself. The sage knows you better than you know yourself, for you are the victim of your passions, a slave living a heteronomous life, purblind, unable to understand your true goals. You want to be a human being. It is the aim of the State to satisfy your wish. 'Compulsion is justified by education for future insight.'[2] The reason within me, if it is to triumph, must eliminate and suppress my 'lower' instincts, my passions and desires, which render me a slave; similarly (the fatal transition from individual to social concepts is almost imperceptible) the higher elements in society – the better educated, the more rational, those who 'possess the highest insight of their time and people'[3] – may exercise compulsion to rationalise the irrational section of society. For – so Hegel, Bradley, Bosanquet have often assured us – by obeying the rational man we obey ourselves: not indeed as we are, sunk in our ignorance and our passions, weak creatures afflicted by diseases that need a healer, wards who require a guardian, but as we could be if we were rational; as we could be even now, if only we would listen to the rational element which is, *ex hypothesi*, within every human being who deserves the name.

The philosophers of 'Objective Reason', from the tough, rigidly centralised, 'organic' State of Fichte, to the mild and humane liberalism of T. H. Green, certainly supposed themselves to be fulfilling, and not resisting, the rational demands which, however inchoate, were to be found in the breast of every sentient being.

[1] ibid., p. 574.
[2] ibid., p. 578.
[3] ibid., p. 576.

But I may reject such democratic optimism, and turning away from the teleological determinism of the Hegelians towards some more voluntarist philosophy, conceive the idea of imposing on my society – for its own betterment – a plan of my own, which in my rational wisdom I have elaborated; and which, unless I act on my own, perhaps against the permanent wishes of the vast majority of my fellow citizens, may never come to fruition at all. Or, abandoning the concept of reason altogether, I may conceive myself as an inspired artist, who moulds men into patterns in the light of his unique vision, as painters combine colours or composers sounds; humanity is the raw material upon which I impose my creative will; even though men suffer and die in the process, they are lifted by it to a height to which they could never have risen without my coercive – but creative – violation of their lives. This is the argument used by every dictator, inquisitor and bully who seeks some moral, or even aesthetic, justification for his conduct. I must do for men (or with them) what they cannot do for themselves, and I cannot ask their permission or consent, because they are in no condition to know what is best for them; indeed, what they will permit and accept may mean a life of contemptible mediocrity, or perhaps even their ruin and suicide. Let me quote from the true progenitor of the heroic doctrine, Fichte, once again: 'No one has . . . rights against reason.' 'Man is afraid of subordinating his subjectivity to the laws of reason. He prefers tradition or arbitrariness.'[1] Nevertheless, subordinated he must be.[2] Fichte puts forward the claims of what he called reason; Napoleon, or Carlyle, or romantic authoritarians may worship other values, and see in their establishment by force the only path to 'true' freedom.

The same attitude was pointedly expressed by August Comte, who asked why, if we do not allow free thinking in chemistry or biology, we should allow it in morals or politics.[3] Why indeed? If it makes sense to speak of political truths – assertions of social ends

[1] ibid., pp. 578, 580.

[2] 'To compel men to adopt the right form of government, to impose Right on them by force, is not only the right, but the sacred duty of every man who has both the insight and the power to do so.' ibid., vol. 4, p. 436.

[3] See *Plan des travaux scientifiques nécessaires pour réorganiser la société* (1822): p. 53 in Auguste Comte, *Appendice général du système de politique positive* (Paris, 1854), published as part of vol. 4 of *Système de politique positive* (Paris, 1851–4). [Mill quotes this passage in *Auguste Comte and Positivism*: pp. 301–2 in his *Collected Works* (op. cit., p. 199 above, note 1), vol. 10. H.H.]

which all men, because they are men, must, once they are discovered, agree to be such; and if, as Comte believed, scientific method will in due course reveal them; then what case is there for freedom of opinion or action – at least as an end in itself, and not merely as a stimulating intellectual climate – either for individuals or for groups? Why should any conduct be tolerated that is not authorised by appropriate experts? Comte put bluntly what had been implicit in the rationalist theory of politics from its ancient Greek beginnings. There can, in principle, be only one correct way of life; the wise lead it spontaneously, that is why they are called wise. The unwise must be dragged towards it by all the social means in the power of the wise; for why should demonstrable error be suffered to survive and breed? The immature and untutored must be made to say to themselves: 'Only the truth liberates, and the only way in which I can learn the truth is by doing blindly today, what you, who know it, order me, or coerce me, to do, in the certain knowledge that only thus will I arrive at your clear vision, and be free like you.'

We have wandered indeed from our liberal beginnings. This argument, employed by Fichte in his latest phase, and after him by other defenders of authority, from Victorian schoolmasters and colonial administrators to the latest nationalist or Communist dictator, is precisely what the Stoic and Kantian morality protests against most bitterly in the name of the reason of the free individual following his own inner light. In this way the rationalist argument, with its assumption of the single true solution, has led by steps which, if not logically valid, are historically and psychologically intelligible from an ethical doctrine of individual responsibility and individual self-perfection to an authoritarian State obedient to the directives of an élite of Platonic guardians.

What can have led to so strange a reversal – the transformation of Kant's severe individualism into something close to a pure totalitarian doctrine on the part of thinkers some of whom claimed to be his disciples? This question is not of merely historical interest, for not a few contemporary liberals have gone through the same peculiar evolution. It is true that Kant insisted, following Rousseau, that a capacity for rational self-direction belonged to all men; that there could be no experts in moral matters, since morality was a matter not of specialised knowledge (as the Utilitarians and *philosophes* had maintained), but of the correct use of a universal human faculty; and consequently that what made men free was not acting in certain self-improving ways, which they could be coerced to do, but knowing why they ought to do so, which nobody could do for, or on behalf of, anyone else. But even Kant, when he came to deal with political issues, conceded that no law, provided that it was such that I should, if I were asked, approve it as a rational being, could possibly deprive me of any portion of my rational freedom. With this the door was opened wide to the rule of experts. I cannot consult all men about all enactments all the time. The government cannot be a continuous plebiscite. Moreover, some men are not as well attuned to the voice of their own reason as others: some seem singularly deaf. If I am a legislator or a ruler, I must assume that if the law I impose is rational (and I can consult only my own reason) it will automatically be approved by all the members of my society so far as they are rational beings. For if they disapprove, they must, *pro tanto*, be irrational; then they will need to be repressed by reason: whether their own or mine cannot matter, for the pronouncements of reason must be the same in all minds. I issue my orders and, if you resist, take it upon myself to repress the irrational element in you which opposes reason. My task would be easier if you repressed it in yourself; I try to educate you to do so. But I am responsible for public welfare, I cannot wait until all men are wholly rational. Kant may protest that the essence of the subject's freedom is that he, and he alone, has given himself the order to obey. But this is a counsel of perfection. If you fail to discipline yourself, I must do so for you; and you cannot complain of lack of freedom, for the fact that Kant's rational judge has sent you to prison is evidence that you have not listened to your own inner reason, that, like a child, a savage, an idiot, you are not ripe for self-direction, or permanently incapable of it.[1]

[1] Kant came nearest to asserting the 'negative' ideal of liberty when (in one of his political treatises) he declared that 'The greatest problem of the human race, to the solution of which it is compelled by nature, is the establishment of a civil society universally administering right according to law. It is only in a society which possesses the greatest liberty ... – and also the most exact determination and guarantee of the limits of [the] liberty [of each individual] in order that it may co-exist with the liberty of others – that the highest purpose of nature, which is the development of all her capacities, can be attained in the case of mankind.' 'Idee zu einer allgemeinen Geschichte in weltbürgerlicher Absicht' (1784), in op. cit. (p. 16 above, note 1), vol. 8, p. 22, line 6. Apart from the teleological implications, this formulation does not at first appear very different from orthodox liberalism. The crucial point, however, is how to determine the criterion

If this leads to despotism, albeit by the best or the wisest – to Sarastro's temple in *The Magic Flute* – but still despotism, which turns out to be identical with freedom, can it be that there is something amiss in the premisses of the argument? That the basic assumptions are themselves somewhere at fault? Let me state them once more: first, that all men have one true purpose, and one only, that of rational self-direction; second, that the ends of all rational beings must of necessity fit into a single universal, harmonious pattern, which some men may be able to discern more clearly than others; third, that all conflict, and consequently all tragedy, is due solely to the clash of reason with the irrational or the insufficiently rational – the immature and undeveloped elements in life, whether individual or communal – and that such clashes are, in principle, avoidable, and for wholly rational beings impossible; finally, that when all men have been made rational, they will obey the rational laws of their own natures, which are one and the same in them all, and so be at once wholly law-abiding and wholly free. Can it be that Socrates and the creators of the central Western tradition in ethics and politics who followed him have been mistaken, for more than two millennia, that virtue is not knowledge, nor freedom identical with either? That despite the fact that it rules the lives of

for the 'exact determination and guarantee of the limits' of individual liberty. Most modern liberals, at their most consistent, want a situation in which as many individuals as possible can realise as many of their ends as possible, without assessment of the value of these ends as such, save in so far as they may frustrate the purposes of others. They wish the frontiers between individuals or groups of men to be drawn solely with a view to preventing collisions between human purposes, all of which must be considered to be equally ultimate, uncriticisable ends in themselves. Kant, and the rationalists of his type, do not regard all ends as of equal value. For them the limits of liberty are determined by applying the rules of 'reason', which is much more than the mere generality of rules as such, and is a faculty that creates or reveals a purpose identical in, and for, all men. In the name of reason anything that is non-rational may be condemned, so that the various personal aims which their individual imaginations and idiosyncrasies lead men to pursue – for example, aesthetic and other non-rational kinds of self-fulfilment – may, at least in theory, be ruthlessly suppressed to make way for the demands of reason. The authority of reason and of the duties it lays upon men is identified with individual freedom, on the assumption that only rational ends can be the 'true' objects of a 'free' man's 'real' nature.

I have never, I must own, understood what 'reason' means in this context; and here merely wish to point out that the a priori assumptions of this philosophical psychology are not compatible with empiricism: that is to say, with any doctrine founded on knowledge derived from experience of what men are and seek.

more men than ever before in its long history, not one of the basic assumptions of this famous view is demonstrable, or, perhaps, even true?

## VI

### *The search for status*

There is yet another historically important approach to this topic, which, by confounding liberty with her sisters, equality and fraternity, leads to similarly illiberal conclusions. Ever since the issue was raised towards the end of the eighteenth century, the question of what is meant by 'an individual' has been asked persistently, and with increasing effect. In so far as I live in society, everything that I do inevitably affects, and is affected by, what others do. Even Mill's strenuous effort to mark the distinction between the spheres of private and social life breaks down under examination. Virtually all Mill's critics have pointed out that everything that I do may have results which will harm other human beings. Moreover, I am a social being in a deeper sense than that of interaction with others. For am I not what I am, to some degree, in virtue of what others think and feel me to be? When I ask myself what I am, and answer: an Englishman, a Chinese, a merchant, a man of no importance, a millionaire, a convict – I find upon analysis that to possess these attributes entails being recognised as belonging to a particular group or class by other persons in my society, and that this recognition is part of the meaning of most of the terms that denote some of my most personal and permanent characteristics. I am not disembodied reason. Nor am I Robinson Crusoe, alone upon his island. It is not only that my material life depends upon interaction with other men, or that I am what I am as a result of social forces, but that some, perhaps all, of my ideas about myself, in particular my sense of my own moral and social identity, are intelligible only in terms of the social network in which I am (the metaphor must not be pressed too far) an element.

The lack of freedom about which men or groups complain amounts, as often as not, to the lack of proper recognition. I may be seeking not for what Mill would wish me to seek, namely security from coercion, arbitrary arrest, tyranny, deprivation of certain opportunities of action, or for room within which I am legally accountable to no one for my movements. Equally, I may not be seeking for a rational plan of social life, or the self-perfection of a dispassionate sage. What I may seek to avoid is simply being ignored, or patronised, or despised, or being taken too much for granted – in short, not being treated as an individual, having my uniqueness insufficiently recognised, being classed as a member of some featureless amalgam, a statistical unit without identifiable, specifically human features and purposes of my own. This is the degradation that I am fighting against – I am not seeking equality of legal rights, nor liberty to do as I wish (although I may want these too), but a condition in which I can feel that I am, because I am taken to be, a responsible agent, whose will is taken into consideration because I am entitled to it, even if I am attacked and persecuted for being what I am or choosing as I do.

This is a hankering after status and recognition: 'The poorest he that is in England hath a life to live as the greatest he.'¹ I desire to be understood and recognised, even if this means to be unpopular and disliked. And the only persons who can so recognise me, and thereby give me the sense of being someone, are the members of the society to which, historically, morally, economically, and perhaps ethnically, I feel that I belong.² My individual self is not something which I can detach from my relationship with others, or from those attributes of myself which consist in their attitude towards me. Consequently, when I demand to be liberated from, let us say, the status of political or social dependence, what I demand is an alteration of the attitude towards me of those whose

¹ Thomas Rainborow, speaking at Putney in 1647: p. 301 in *The Clarke Papers: Selections from the Papers of William Clarke*, ed. C. H. Firth, vol. 1 ([London], 1891).

² This has an obvious affinity with Kant's doctrine of human freedom; but it is a socialised and empirical version of it, and therefore almost its opposite. Kant's free man needs no public recognition for his inner freedom. If he is treated as a means to some external purpose, that is a wrong action on the part of his exploiters, but his own 'noumenal' status is untouched, and he is fully free, and fully a man, however he may be treated. The need spoken of here is bound up wholly with the relation that I have with others; I am nothing if I am unrecognised. I cannot ignore the attitude of others with Byronic disdain, fully conscious of my own intrinsic worth and vocation, or escape into my inner life, for I am in my own eyes as others see me. I identify myself with the point of view of my milieu: I feel myself to be somebody or nobody in terms of my position and function in the social whole; this is the most 'heteronomous' condition imaginable.

opinions and behaviour help to determine my own image of myself.

And what is true of the individual is true of groups, social, political, economic, religious, that is, of men conscious of needs and purposes which they have as members of such groups. What oppressed classes or nationalities, as a rule, demand is neither simply unhampered liberty of action for their members, nor, above everything, equality of social or economic opportunity, still less assignment of a place in a frictionless, organic State devised by the rational lawgiver. What they want, as often as not, is simply recognition (of their class or nation, or colour or race) as an independent source of human activity, as an entity with a will of its own, intending to act in accordance with it (whether it is good or legitimate, or not), and not to be ruled, educated, guided, with however light a hand, as being not quite fully human, and therefore not quite fully free.

This gives a far wider than a purely rationalist sense to Kant's remark that paternalism is 'the greatest despotism imaginable'. Paternalism is despotic, not because it is more oppressive than naked, brutal, unenlightened tyranny, nor merely because it ignores the transcendental reason embodied in me, but because it is an insult to my conception of myself as a human being, determined to make my own life in accordance with my own (not necessarily rational or benevolent) purposes, and, above all, entitled to be recognised as such by others. For if I am not so recognised, then I may fail to recognise, I may doubt, my own claim to be a fully independent human being. For what I am is, in large part, determined by what I feel and think; and what I feel and think is determined by the feeling and thought prevailing in the society to which I belong, of which, in Burke's sense, I form not an isolable atom, but an ingredient (to use a perilous but indispensable metaphor) in a social pattern. I may feel unfree in the sense of not being recognised as a self-governing individual human being; but I may feel it also as a member of an unrecognised or insufficiently respected group: then I wish for the emancipation of my entire class, or community, or nation, or race, or profession. So much can I desire this, that I may, in my bitter longing for status, prefer to be bullied and misgoverned by some member of my own race or social class, by whom I am, nevertheless, recognised as a man and a rival – that is as an equal – to being well and tolerantly treated by someone from some higher and remoter group, someone who does not recognise me for what I wish to feel myself to be.

This is the heart of the great cry for recognition on the part of both individuals and groups, and, in our own day, of professions and classes, nations and races. Although I may not get 'negative' liberty at the hands of the members of my own society, yet they are members of my own group; they understand me, as I understand them; and this understanding creates within me the sense of being somebody in the world. It is this desire for reciprocal recognition that leads the most authoritarian democracies to be, at times, consciously preferred by their members to the most enlightened oligarchies, or sometimes causes a member of some newly liberated Asian or African State to complain less today, when he is rudely treated by members of his own race or nation, than when he was governed by some cautious, just, gentle, well-meaning administrator from outside. Unless this phenomenon is grasped, the ideals and behaviour of entire peoples who, in Mill's sense of the word, suffer deprivation of elementary human rights, and who, with every appearance of sincerity, speak of enjoying more freedom than when they possessed a wider measure of these rights, becomes an unintelligible paradox.

Yet it is not with individual liberty, in either the 'negative' or the 'positive' sense of the word, that this desire for status and recognition can easily be identified. It is something no less profoundly needed and passionately fought for by human beings – it is something akin to, but not itself, freedom; although it entails negative freedom for the entire group, it is more closely related to solidarity, fraternity, mutual understanding, need for association on equal terms, all of which are sometimes – but misleadingly – called social freedom. Social and political terms are necessarily vague. The attempt to make the vocabulary of politics too precise may render it useless. But it is no service to the truth to loosen usage beyond necessity. The essence of the notion of liberty, in both the 'positive' and the 'negative' senses, is the holding off of something or someone – of others who trespass on my field or assert their authority over me, or of obsessions, fears, neuroses, irrational forces – intruders and despots of one kind or another. The desire for recognition is a desire for something different: for union, closer understanding, integration of interests, a life of common dependence and common sacrifice. It is only the confusion of desire for liberty with this profound and universal craving for status and understanding, further confounded by being identified with the notion of social self-direction, where the self to be liberated is no longer the individual but the 'social whole', that makes it possible for men, while submitting to the authority of oligarchs or dictators, to claim that this in some sense liberates them.

Much has been written on the fallacy of regarding social groups as being literally persons or selves, whose control and discipline of their members is no more than self-discipline, voluntary self-control which leaves the individual agent free. But even on the 'organic' view, would it be natural or desirable to call the demand for recognition and status a demand for liberty in some third sense? It is true that the group from which recognition is sought must itself have a sufficient measure of 'negative' freedom – from control by any outside authority – otherwise recognition by it will not give the claimant the status he seeks. But is the struggle for higher status, the wish to escape from an inferior position, to be called a struggle for liberty? Is it mere pedantry to confine this word to the main senses discussed above, or are we, as I suspect, in danger of calling any improvement of his social situation favoured by a human being an increase of his liberty, and will this not render this term so vague and distended as to make it virtually useless? And yet we cannot simply dismiss this case as a mere confusion of the notion of freedom with that of status, or solidarity, or fraternity, or equality, or some combination of these. For the craving for status is, in certain respects, very close to the desire to be an independent agent.

We may refuse this goal the title of liberty; yet it would be a shallow view that assumed that analogies between individuals and groups, or organic metaphors, or several senses of the word 'liberty', are mere fallacies, due either to assertions of likeness between entities in respects in which they are unlike, or simple semantic confusion. What is wanted by those who are prepared to barter their own and others' liberty of individual action for the status of their group, and their own status within the group, is not simply a surrender of liberty for the sake of security, of some assured place in a harmonious hierarchy in which all men and all classes know their place, and are prepared to exchange the painful privilege of choosing – 'the burden of freedom' – for the peace and comfort and relative mindlessness of an authoritarian or totalitarian structure. No doubt there are such men and such desires, and no doubt such surrenders of individual liberty can occur, and, indeed, have often occurred. But it is a profound misunderstanding of the temper of our times to assume that this is what makes nationalism or Marxism attractive to nations which have been ruled by alien masters, or to classes whose lives were directed by other classes in a semi-feudal, or some other hierarchically organised, regime. What they seek is more akin to what Mill called 'pagan self-assertion', but in a collective, socialised form. Indeed, much of what he says about his own reasons for desiring liberty – the value that he puts on boldness and non-conformity, on the assertion of the individual's own values in the face of the prevailing opinion, on strong and self-reliant personalities free from the leading-strings of the official lawgivers and instructors of society – has little enough to do with his conception of freedom as non-interference, but a great deal with the desire of men not to have their personalities set at too low a value, assumed to be incapable of autonomous, original, 'authentic' behaviour, even if such behaviour is to be met with opprobrium, or social restrictions, or inhibitive legislation.

This wish to assert the 'personality' of my class, or group or nation, is connected both with the answer to the question 'What is to be the area of authority?' (for the group must not be interfered with by outside masters), and, even more closely, with the answer to the question 'Who is to govern us?' – govern well or badly, liberally or oppressively, but above all 'Who?' And such answers as 'Representatives elected by my own and others' untrammelled choice', or 'All of us gathered together in regular assemblies', or 'The best', or 'The wisest', or 'The nation as embodied in these or those persons or institutions', or 'The divine leader' are answers that are logically, and at times also politically and socially, independent of what extent of 'negative' liberty I demand for my own or my group's activities. Provided the answer to 'Who shall govern me?' is somebody or something which I can represent as 'my own', as something which belongs to me, or to whom I belong, I can, by using words which convey fraternity and solidarity, as well as some part of the connotation of the 'positive' sense of the word 'freedom' (which it is difficult to specify more precisely), describe it as a hybrid form of freedom; at any rate as an ideal which is perhaps more prominent than any other in the world today, yet one which no existing term seems precisely to fit. Those who purchase it at the price of their 'negative', Millian freedom certainly claim to be 'liberated' by this means, in this confused, but ardently felt, sense. 'Whose service is perfect freedom' can in this way be secularised, and the State, or the nation, or the race, or an assembly, or a dictator, or my family or milieu, or I myself, can be substituted for the Deity, without thereby rendering the word 'freedom' wholly meaningless.[1]

No doubt every interpretation of the word 'liberty', however unusual, must include a minimum of what I have called 'negative' liberty. There must be an area within which I am not frustrated. No society literally suppresses all the liberties of its members; a being who is prevented by others from doing anything at all on his own is not a moral agent at all, and could not either legally or morally be regarded as a human being, even if a physiologist or a biologist, or even a psychologist, felt inclined to classify him as a man. But the fathers of liberalism – Mill and Constant – want more than this minimum: they demand a maximum degree of non-interference compatible with the minimum demands of social life. It seems unlikely that this extreme demand for liberty has ever been made by any but a small minority of highly civilised and self-conscious human beings. The bulk of humanity has certainly at most times been prepared to sacrifice this to other goals: security, status, prosperity, power, virtue, rewards in the next world; or justice, equality, fraternity, and many other values which appear wholly, or in part, incompatible with the attainment of the greatest degree of individual liberty, and certainly do not need it as a precondition for their own realisation. It is not a demand for *Lebensraum* for each individual that has stimulated the rebellions and wars of liberation for which men have been ready to die in the past, or, indeed, in the present. Men who have fought for freedom have commonly fought for the right to be governed by themselves or their representatives – sternly governed, if need be, like the

---

[1] This argument should be distinguished from the traditional approach of some of the disciples of Burke or Hegel, who say that, since I am made what I am by society or history, to escape from them is impossible and to attempt it irrational. No doubt I cannot leap out of my skin, or breathe outside my proper element; it is a mere tautology to say that I am what I am, and cannot want to be liberated from my essential characteristics, some of which are social. But it does not follow that all my attributes are intrinsic and inalienable, and that I cannot seek to alter my status within the 'social network', or 'cosmic web', which determines my nature; if this were the case, no meaning could be attached to such words as 'choice' or 'decision' or 'activity'. If they are to mean anything, attempts to protect myself against authority, or even to escape from my 'station and its duties', cannot be excluded as automatically irrational or suicidal.

Spartans, with little individual liberty, but in a manner which allowed them to participate, or at any rate to believe that they were participating, in the legislation and administration of their collective lives. And men who have made revolutions have, as often as not, meant by liberty no more than the conquest of power and authority by a given sect of believers in a doctrine, or by a class, or by some other social group, old or new. Their victories certainly frustrated those whom they ousted, and sometimes repressed, enslaved or exterminated vast numbers of human beings. Yet such revolutionaries have usually felt it necessary to argue that, despite this, they represented the party of liberty, or 'true' liberty, by claiming universality for their ideal, which the 'real selves' of even those who resisted them were also alleged to be seeking, although they were held to have lost the way to the goal, or to have mistaken the goal itself owing to some moral or spiritual blindness. All this has little to do with Mill's notion of liberty as limited only by the danger of doing harm to others. It is the non-recognition of this psychological and political fact (which lurks behind the apparent ambiguity of the term 'liberty') that has, perhaps, blinded some contemporary liberals to the world in which they live. Their plea is clear, their cause is just. But they do not allow for the variety of basic human needs. Nor yet for the ingenuity with which men can prove to their own satisfaction that the road to one ideal also leads to its contrary.

VII

*Liberty and sovereignty*

The French Revolution, like all great revolutions, was, at least in its Jacobin form, just such an eruption of the desire for 'positive' freedom of collective self-direction on the part of a large body of Frenchmen who felt liberated as a nation, even though the result was, for a good many of them, a severe restriction of individual freedoms. Rousseau had spoken exultantly of the fact that the laws of liberty might prove to be more austere than the yoke of tyranny. Tyranny is service to human masters. The law cannot be a tyrant. Rousseau does not mean by liberty the 'negative' freedom of the individual not to be interfered with within a defined area, but the possession by all, and not merely by some, of the fully qualified members of a society of a share in the public power which is entitled to interfere with every aspect of every citizen's life. The liberals of the first half of the nineteenth century correctly foresaw that liberty in this 'positive' sense could easily destroy too many of the 'negative' liberties that they held sacred. They pointed out that the sovereignty of the people could easily destroy that of individuals. Mill explained, patiently and unanswerably, that government by the people was not, in his sense, necessarily freedom at all. For those who govern are not necessarily the same 'people' as those who are governed, and democratic self-government is not the government 'of each by himself', but, at best, 'of each by all the rest'.[1] Mill and his disciples spoke of 'the tyranny of the majority' and of the tyranny of 'the prevailing opinion and feeling',[2] and saw no great difference between that and any other kind of tyranny which encroaches upon men's activities beyond the sacred frontiers of private life.

No one saw the conflict between the two types of liberty better, or expressed it more clearly, than Benjamin Constant. He pointed out that the transference by a successful rising of unlimited authority, commonly called sovereignty, from one set of hands to another does not increase liberty, but merely shifts the burden of slavery. He reasonably asked why a man should deeply care whether he is crushed by a popular government or by a monarch, or even by a set of oppressive laws. He saw that the main problem for those who desire 'negative', individual freedom is not who wields this authority, but how much authority should be placed in any set of hands. For unlimited authority in anybody's grasp was bound, he believed, sooner or later, to destroy somebody. He maintained that usually men protested against this or that set of governors as oppressive, when the real cause of oppression lay in the mere fact of the accumulation of power itself, wherever it might happen to be, since liberty was endangered by the mere existence of absolute authority as such. 'It is not against the arm that one must rail,' he wrote, 'but against the weapon. Some weights are too heavy for the human hand.'[3] Democracy may disarm a given oligarchy, a given privileged individual or set of individuals, but it can still crush individuals as mercilessly as any previous ruler. An equal right to oppress – or interfere – is not equivalent to liberty.

[1] op. cit. (p. 199 above, note 1), p. 219.
[2] ibid., pp. 219–20.
[3] op. cit. (p. 198 above, note 1), p. 270.

Nor does universal consent to loss of liberty somehow miraculously preserve it merely by being universal, or by being consent. If I consent to be oppressed, or acquiesce in my condition with detachment or irony, am I the less oppressed? If I sell myself into slavery, am I the less a slave? If I commit suicide, am I the less dead because I have taken my own life freely? 'Popular government is merely a spasmodic tyranny, monarchy a more centralised despotism.'[1] Constant saw in Rousseau the most dangerous enemy of individual liberty, because he had declared that 'In giving myself to all, I give myself to none.'[2] Constant could not see why, even though the sovereign is 'everybody', it should not oppress one of the 'members' of its indivisible self, if it so decided. I may, of course, prefer to be deprived of my liberties by an assembly, or a family, or a class in which I am a minority. It may give me an opportunity one day of persuading the others to do for me that to which I feel I am entitled. But to be deprived of my liberty at the hands of my family or friends or fellow citizens is to be deprived of it just as effectively. Hobbes was at any rate more candid: he did not pretend that a sovereign does not enslave; he justified this slavery, but at least did not have the effrontery to call it freedom.

Throughout the nineteenth century liberal thinkers maintained that if liberty involved a limit upon the powers of any man to force me to do what I did not, or might not, wish to do, then, whatever the ideal in the name of which I was coerced, I was not free; that the doctrine of absolute sovereignty was a tyrannical doctrine in itself. If I wish to preserve my liberty, it is not enough to say that it must not be violated unless someone or other – the absolute ruler, or the popular assembly, or the King in Parliament, or the judges, or some combination of authorities, or the laws themselves (for the laws may be oppressive) – authorises its violation. I must establish a society in which there must be some frontiers of freedom which nobody should be permitted to cross. Different names or natures may be given to the rules that determine these frontiers: they may be called natural rights, or the word of God, or natural law, or the demands of utility or of the 'permanent interests of man'; I may believe them to be valid a priori, or assert them to be my own ultimate ends, or the ends of my society or culture. What these rules or commandments will have in common is that they are

---

[1] ibid., p. 274.
[2] loc. cit. (p. 219 above, note 4); cf. Constant, ibid., p. 272.

accepted so widely, and are grounded so deeply in the actual nature of men as they have developed through history, as to be, by now, an essential part of what we mean by being a normal human being. Genuine belief in the inviolability of a minimum extent of individual liberty entails some such absolute stand. For it is clear that it has little to hope for from the rule of majorities; democracy as such is logically uncommitted to it, and historically has at times failed to protect it, while remaining faithful to its own principles. Few governments, it has been observed, have found much difficulty in causing their subjects to generate any will that the government wanted. The triumph of despotism is to force the slaves to declare themselves free. It may need no force; the slaves may proclaim their freedom quite sincerely: but they are none the less slaves. Perhaps the chief value for liberals of political – 'positive' – rights, of participating in the government, is as a means for protecting what they hold to be an ultimate value, namely individual – 'negative' – liberty.

But if democracies can, without ceasing to be democratic, suppress freedom, at least as liberals have used the word, what would make a society truly free? For Constant, Mill, Tocqueville, and the liberal tradition to which they belong, no society is free unless it is governed by at any rate two interrelated principles: first, that no power, but only rights, can be regarded as absolute, so that all men, whatever power governs them, have an absolute right to refuse to behave inhumanly; and, second, that there are frontiers, not artificially drawn, within which men should be inviolable, these frontiers being defined in terms of rules so long and widely accepted that their observance has entered into the very conception of what it is to be a normal human being, and, therefore, also of what it is to act inhumanly or insanely; rules of which it would be absurd to say, for example, that they could be abrogated by some formal procedure on the part of some court or sovereign body. When I speak of a man as being normal, a part of what I mean is that he could not break these rules easily, without a qualm of revulsion. It is such rules as these that are broken when a man is declared guilty without trial, or punished under a retroactive law; when children are ordered to denounce their parents, friends to betray one another, soldiers to use methods of barbarism; when men are tortured or murdered, or minorities are massacred because they irritate a majority or a tyrant. Such acts, even if they are made legal by the sovereign, cause horror even in these days, and this springs from the recognition of the moral validity – irrespective of the laws – of some absolute barriers to the imposition of one man's will on another. The freedom of a society, or a class or a group, in this sense of freedom, is measured by the strength of these barriers, and the number and importance of the paths which they keep open for their members – if not for all, for at any rate a great number of them.[1]

This is almost at the opposite pole from the purposes of those who believe in liberty in the 'positive' – self-directive – sense. The former want to curb authority as such. The latter want it placed in their own hands. That is a cardinal issue. These are not two different interpretations of a single concept, but two profoundly divergent and irreconcilable attitudes to the ends of life. It is as well to recognise this, even if in practice it is often necessary to strike a compromise between them. For each of them makes absolute claims. These claims cannot both be fully satisfied. But it is a profound lack of social and moral understanding not to recognise that the satisfaction that each of them seeks is an ultimate value which, both historically and morally, has an equal right to be classed among the deepest interests of mankind.

## VIII

### The One and the Many

One belief, more than any other, is responsible for the slaughter of individuals on the altars of the great historical ideals – justice or progress or the happiness of future generations, or the sacred mission or emancipation of a nation or race or class, or even liberty itself, which demands the sacrifice of individuals for the freedom of society. This is the belief that somewhere, in the past or in the future, in divine revelation or in the mind of an individual thinker, in the pronouncements of history or science, or in the simple heart of an uncorrupted good man, there is a final solution. This ancient faith rests on the conviction that all the positive values in which

---

[1] In Great Britain such legal power is, of course, constitutionally vested in the absolute sovereign – the King in Parliament. What makes this country comparatively free, therefore, is the fact that this theoretically omnipotent entity is restrained by custom or opinion from behaving as such. It is clear that what matters is not the form of these restraints on power – whether they are legal, or moral, or constitutional – but their effectiveness.

men have believed must, in the end, be compatible, and perhaps even entail one another. 'Nature binds truth, happiness and virtue together by an indissoluble chain', said one of the best men who ever lived, and spoke in similar terms of liberty, equality and justice.[1]

But is this true? It is a commonplace that neither political equality nor efficient organisation nor social justice is compatible with more than a modicum of individual liberty, and certainly not with unrestricted *laissez-faire*; that justice and generosity, public and private loyalties, the demands of genius and the claims of society can conflict violently with each other. And it is no great way from that to the generalisation that not all good things are compatible, still less all the ideals of mankind. But somewhere, we shall be told, and in some way, it must be possible for all these values to live together, for unless this is so, the universe is not a cosmos, not a harmony; unless this is so, conflicts of values may be an intrinsic, irremovable element in human life. To admit that the fulfilment of some of our ideals may in principle make the fulfilment of others impossible is to say that the notion of total human fulfilment is a formal contradiction, a metaphysical chimera. For every rationalist metaphysician, from Plato to the last disciples of Hegel or Marx, this abandonment of the notion of a final harmony in which all riddles are solved, all contradictions reconciled, is a piece of crude empiricism, abdication before brute facts, intolerable bankruptcy of reason before things as they are, failure to explain and to justify, to reduce everything to a system, which 'reason' indignantly rejects.

But if we are not armed with an a priori guarantee of the proposition that a total harmony of true values is somewhere to be

---

[1] Condorcet, from whose *Esquisse* these words are quoted (loc. cit.: see p. 136 above, note 1), declares that the task of social science is to show 'by what bonds nature has united the progress of enlightenment with that of liberty, virtue and respect for the natural rights of man; how these ideals, which alone are truly good, yet so often separated from each other that they are even believed to be incompatible, should, on the contrary, become inseparable, as soon as enlightenment has reached a certain level simultaneously among a large number of nations'. He goes on to say that 'Men still preserve the errors of their childhood, of their country and of their age long after having recognised all the truths needed for destroying them.' ibid., pp. 9, 10. Ironically enough, his belief in the need for and possibility of uniting all good things may well be precisely the kind of error he himself so well described.

found – perhaps in some ideal realm the characteristics of which we can, in our finite state, not so much as conceive – we must fall back on the ordinary resources of empirical observation and ordinary human knowledge. And these certainly give us no warrant for supposing (or even understanding what would be meant by saying) that all good things, or all bad things for that matter, are reconcilable with each other. The world that we encounter in ordinary experience is one in which we are faced with choices between ends equally ultimate, and claims equally absolute, the realisation of some of which must inevitably involve the sacrifice of others. Indeed, it is because this is their situation that men place such immense value upon the freedom to choose; for if they had assurance that in some perfect state, realisable by men on earth, no ends pursued by them would ever be in conflict, the necessity and agony of choice would disappear, and with it the central importance of the freedom to choose. Any method of bringing this final state nearer would then seem fully justified, no matter how much freedom were sacrificed to forward its advance.

It is, I have no doubt, some such dogmatic certainty that has been responsible for the deep, serene, unshakeable conviction in the minds of some of the most merciless tyrants and persecutors in history that what they did was fully justified by its purpose. I do not say that the ideal of self-perfection – whether for individuals or nations or Churches or classes – is to be condemned in itself, or that the language which was used in its defence was in all cases the result of a confused or fraudulent use of words, or of moral or intellectual perversity. Indeed, I have tried to show that it is the notion of freedom in its 'positive' sense that is at the heart of the demands for national or social self-direction which animate the most powerful and morally just public movements of our time, and that not to recognise this is to misunderstand the most vital facts and ideas of our age. But equally it seems to me that the belief that some single formula can in principle be found whereby all the diverse ends of men can be harmoniously realised is demonstrably false. If, as I believe, the ends of men are many, and not all of them are in principle compatible with each other, then the possibility of conflict – and of tragedy – can never wholly be eliminated from human life, either personal or social. The necessity of choosing between absolute claims is then an inescapable characteristic of the human condition. This gives its value to freedom as Acton conceived of it – as an end in itself, and not as a temporary need, arising out of our confused notions and irrational and disordered lives, a predicament which a panacea could one day put right.

I do not wish to say that individual freedom is, even in the most liberal societies, the sole, or even the dominant, criterion of social action. We compel children to be educated, and we forbid public executions. These are certainly curbs to freedom. We justify them on the ground that ignorance, or a barbarian upbringing, or cruel pleasures and excitements are worse for us than the amount of restraint needed to repress them. This judgement in turn depends on how we determine good and evil, that is to say, on our moral, religious, intellectual, economic and aesthetic values; which are, in their turn, bound up with our conception of man, and of the basic demands of his nature. In other words, our solution of such problems is based on our vision, by which we are consciously or unconsciously guided, of what constitutes a fulfilled human life, as contrasted with Mill's 'cramped and dwarfed', 'pinched and hidebound' natures. To protest against the laws governing censorship or personal morals as intolerable infringements of personal liberty presupposes a belief that the activities which such laws forbid are fundamental needs of men as men, in a good (or, indeed, any) society. To defend such laws is to hold that these needs are not essential, or that they cannot be satisfied without sacrificing other values which come higher – satisfy deeper needs – than individual freedom, determined by some standard that is not merely subjective, a standard for which some objective status – empirical or a priori – is claimed.

The extent of a man's, or a people's, liberty to choose to live as he or they desire must be weighed against the claims of many other values, of which equality, or justice, or happiness, or security, or public order are perhaps the most obvious examples. For this reason, it cannot be unlimited. We are rightly reminded by R. H. Tawney that the liberty of the strong, whether their strength is physical or economic, must be restrained. This maxim claims respect, not as a consequence of some a priori rule, whereby the respect for the liberty of one man logically entails respect for the liberty of others like him; but simply because respect for the principles of justice, or shame at gross inequality of treatment, is as basic in men as the desire for liberty. That we cannot have everything is a necessary, not a contingent, truth. Burke's plea for the constant need to compensate, to reconcile, to balance; Mill's plea for novel 'experiments in living' with their permanent possibility of error – the knowledge that it is not merely in practice but in principle impossible to reach clear-cut and certain answers, even in an ideal world of wholly good and rational men and wholly clear ideas – may madden those who seek for final solutions and single, all-embracing systems, guaranteed to be eternal. Nevertheless, it is a conclusion that cannot be escaped by those who, with Kant, have learnt the truth that 'Out of the crooked timber of humanity no straight thing was ever made.'[1]

There is little need to stress the fact that monism, and faith in a single criterion, has always proved a deep source of satisfaction both to the intellect and to the emotions. Whether the standard of judgement derives from the vision of some future perfection, as in the minds of the *philosophes* in the eighteenth century and their technocratic successors in our own day, or is rooted in the past – *la terre et les morts* – as maintained by German historicists or French theocrats, or neo-Conservatives in English-speaking countries, it is bound, provided it is inflexible enough, to encounter some unforeseen and unforeseeable human development, which it will not fit; and will then be used to justify the a priori barbarities of Procrustes – the vivisection of actual human societies into some fixed pattern dictated by our fallible understanding of a largely imaginary past or a wholly imaginary future. To preserve our absolute categories or ideals at the expense of human lives offends equally against the principles of science and of history; it is an attitude found in equal measure on the right and left wings in our days, and is not reconcilable with the principles accepted by those who respect the facts.

Pluralism, with the measure of 'negative' liberty that it entails, seems to me a truer and more humane ideal than the goals of those who seek in the great disciplined, authoritarian structures the ideal of 'positive' self-mastery by classes, or peoples, or the whole of mankind. It is truer, because it does, at least, recognise the fact that human goals are many, not all of them commensurable, and in perpetual rivalry with one another. To assume that all values can be graded on one scale, so that it is a mere matter of inspection to determine the highest, seems to me to falsify our knowledge that men are free agents, to represent moral decision as an operation which a slide-rule could, in principle, perform. To say that in some ultimate, all-reconciling, yet realisable synthesis duty *is* interest, or

---

[1] loc. cit. (p. 16 above, note 1).

individual freedom *is* pure democracy or an authoritarian State, is to throw a metaphysical blanket over either self-deceit or deliberate hypocrisy. It is more humane because it does not (as the system-builders do) deprive men, in the name of some remote, or incoherent, ideal, of much that they have found to be indispensable to their life as unpredictably self-transforming human beings.[1] In the end, men choose between ultimate values; they choose as they do because their life and thought are determined by fundamental moral categories and concepts that are, at any rate over large stretches of time and space, a part of their being and thought and sense of their own identity; part of what makes them human.

It may be that the ideal of freedom to choose ends without claiming eternal validity for them, and the pluralism of values connected with this, is only the late fruit of our declining capitalist civilisation: an ideal which remote ages and primitive societies have not recognised, and one which posterity will regard with curiosity, even sympathy, but little comprehension. This may be so; but no sceptical conclusions seem to me to follow. Principles are not less sacred because their duration cannot be guaranteed. Indeed, the very desire for guarantees that our values are eternal and secure in some objective heaven is perhaps only a craving for the certainties of childhood or the absolute values of our primitive past. 'To realise the relative validity of one's convictions', said an admirable writer of our time, 'and yet stand for them unflinchingly is what distinguishes a civilised man from a barbarian.'[2] To demand more than this is perhaps a deep and incurable metaphysical need; but to allow it to determine one's practice is a symptom of an equally deep, and more dangerous, moral and political immaturity.

[1] On this also Bentham seems to me to have spoken well: 'Individual interests are the only real interests . . . Can it be conceived that there are men so absurd as to . . . prefer the man who is not, to him who is; to torment the living, under pretence of promoting the happiness of those who are not born, and who may never be born?' op. cit. (p. 219 above, note 3), p. 321. This is one of the infrequent occasions when Burke agrees with Bentham; for this passage is at the heart of the empirical, as against the metaphysical, view of politics.

[2] Joseph A. Schumpeter, *Capitalism, Socialism, and Democracy* (London, 1943), p. 243.

# THE COUNTER-ENLIGHTENMENT

I

OPPOSITION TO the central ideas of the French Enlightenment, and of its allies and disciples in other European countries, is as old as the movement itself. The proclamation of the autonomy of reason and the methods of the natural sciences, based on observation as the sole reliable method of knowledge, and the consequent rejection of the authority of revelation, sacred writings and their accepted interpreters, tradition, prescription, and every form of non-rational and transcendent source of knowledge, was naturally opposed by the Churches and religious thinkers of many persuasions. But such opposition, largely because of the absence of common ground between them and the philosophers of the Enlightenment, made relatively little headway, save by stimulating repressive steps against the spreading of ideas regarded as dangerous to the authority of Church or State. More formidable was the relativist and sceptical tradition that went back to the ancient world.

The central doctrines of the progressive French thinkers, whatever their disagreements among themselves, rested on the belief, rooted in the ancient doctrine of natural law, that human nature was fundamentally the same in all times and places; that local and historical variations were unimportant compared with the constant central core in terms of which human beings could be defined as a species, like animals, or plants, or minerals; that there were universal human goals; that a logically connected structure of laws and generalisations susceptible of demonstration and verification could be constructed and replace the chaotic amalgam of ignorance, mental laziness, guesswork, superstition, prejudice, dogma, fantasy, and, above all, the 'interested error' maintained by the rulers of mankind and largely responsible for the blunders, vices and misfortunes of humanity. It was further believed that methods similar to those of Newtonian physics, which had achieved such triumphs in the realm of inanimate nature, could be applied with equal success to the fields of ethics, politics and human relationships in general, in which little progress had been made; with the corollary that once this had been effected, it would sweep away irrational and oppressive legal systems and economic policies, the replacement of which by the rule of reason would rescue men from political and moral injustice and misery and set them on the path of wisdom, happiness and virtue.

Against this, there persisted the doctrine that went back to the Greek Sophists, Protagoras, Antiphon and Critias, that beliefs involving value-judgements, and the institutions founded upon them, rested not on discoveries of objective and unalterable natural facts, but on human opinion, which was variable and differed between different societies and at different times; that moral and political values, and in particular justice and social arrangements in general, rested on fluctuating human convention. This was summed up by the Sophist quoted by Aristotle who declared that whereas fire burned both here and in Persia, human institutions change under our very eyes. It seemed to follow that no universal truths, established by scientific methods, that is, truths that anyone could verify by the use of proper methods, anywhere, at any time, could in principle be established in human affairs.

This tradition reasserted itself strongly in the writings of such sixteenth-century sceptics as Cornelius Agrippa, Montaigne and Charron, whose influence is discernible in the sentiments of thinkers and poets in the Elizabethan and Jacobean age. Such scepticism came to the aid of those who denied the claims of the natural sciences or of other universal rational schemas and advocated salvation in pure faith, like the great Protestant reformers and their followers, and the Jansenist wing of the Roman Church. The rationalist belief in a single coherent body of logically deduced conclusions, arrived at by universally valid principles of thought and founded upon carefully sifted data of observation or experiment, was further shaken by sociologically minded thinkers from Bodin to Montesquieu. These writers, using the evidence of both history and the new literature of travel and exploration in newly discovered lands, Asia and the Americas, emphasised the variety of human customs, and especially the influence of dissimilar natural factors, particularly geographical ones, upon the development of different human societies, leading to differences of institutions and outlook, which in their turn generated wide differences of belief and behaviour. This was powerfully reinforced by the revolutionary doctrines of David Hume, especially by his demonstration that no logical links existed between truths of fact and such a priori truths as those of logic or mathematics, a demonstration which tended to weaken or dissolve the hopes of those who, under the influence of Descartes and his followers, thought that a single system of knowledge, embracing all provinces and answering all questions, could be established by unbreakable chains of logical argument from universally valid axioms, not subject to refutation or modification by any experience of an empirical kind.

Nevertheless, no matter how deeply relativity about human values or the interpretation of social, including historical, facts entered the thought of social thinkers of this type, they too retained a common core of conviction that the ultimate ends of all men at all times were, in effect, identical: all men sought the satisfaction of basic physical and biological needs, such as food, shelter, security, and also peace, happiness, justice, the harmonious development of their natural faculties, truth, and, somewhat more vaguely, virtue, moral perfection, and what the Romans had called *humanitas*. Means might differ in cold and hot climates, mountainous countries and flat plains, and no universal formula could fit all cases without Procrustean results, but the ultimate ends were fundamentally similar. Such influential writers as Voltaire, d'Alembert and Condorcet believed that development of the arts and sciences was the most powerful human weapon in attaining these ends, and the sharpest weapon in the fight against ignorance, superstition, fanaticism, oppression and barbarism, which crippled human effort and frustrated men's search for truth and rational self-direction. Rousseau and Mably believed, on the contrary, that the institutions of civilisation were themselves a major factor in the corruption of men and their alienation from nature, from simplicity, purity of heart and the life of natural justice, social equality and spontaneous human feeling; artificial man had imprisoned, enslaved and ruined natural man. Nevertheless, despite profound differences of outlook, there was a wide area of agreement about fundamental points: the reality of natural law (no longer formulated in the language of orthodox Catholic or Protestant doctrine), of eternal principles by following which alone men could become wise, happy, virtuous and free. One set of universal and unalterable principles governed the world for theists, deists and atheists, for optimists and pessimists, puritans, primitivists and believers in progress and the richest fruits of science and culture; these laws governed inanimate and animate nature, facts and events, means and ends, private life and public, all societies, epochs and civilisations; it was solely by departing from them that man fell into crime, vice, misery. Thinkers might differ about what these laws were, or how to discover them, or who were qualified to expound them; that these laws were real, and could be known, whether with certainty, or only probability, remained the central dogma of the entire Enlightenment. It was the attack upon this that constitutes the most formidable reaction against this dominant body of belief.

II

A thinker who might have had a decisive role in this counter-movement, if anyone outside his native country had read him, was the Neapolitan philosopher Giambattista Vico. With extraordinary originality Vico maintained, especially in the last work of his life, the *Scienza nuova*, that the Cartesians were profoundly mistaken about the role of mathematics as the science of sciences; that mathematics was certain only because it was a human invention. It did not, as they supposed, correspond to an objective structure of reality; it was a method and not a body of truths; with its help we could plot regularities – the occurrence of phenomena in the external world – but not discover why they occurred as they did, or to what end. This could be known only to God, for only those who make things can truly know what they are and for what purpose they have been made. Hence we do not, in this sense, know the external world – nature – for we have not made it; only God, who created it, knows it in this fashion. But since men are directly acquainted with human motives, purposes, hopes, fears, which are their own, they can know human affairs as they cannot know nature.

According to Vico, our lives and activities collectively and individually are expressions of our attempts to survive, satisfy our desires, understand each other and the past out of which we emerge. A utilitarian interpretation of the most essential human activities is misleading. They are, in the first place, purely expressive: to sing, to dance, to worship, to speak, to fight, and the institutions which embody these activities, comprise a vision of the world. Language, religious rites, myths, laws, social, religious, juridical institutions, are forms of self-expression, of wishing to convey what one is and strives for; they obey intelligible patterns, and for that reason it is possible to reconstruct the life of other societies, even those remote in time and place and utterly primitive, by asking oneself what kind of framework of human ideas, feelings, acts could have generated the poetry, the monuments, the mythology which were their natural expression. Men grow individually and socially; the world of men who composed the Homeric poems was plainly very different from that of the Hebrews to whom God had spoken through their sacred books, or that of the Roman Republic, or medieval Christianity, or Naples under the Bourbons. Patterns of growth are traceable.

Myths are not, as enlightened thinkers believe, false statements about reality corrected by later rational criticism, nor is poetry mere embellishment of what could equally well be stated in ordinary prose. The myths and poetry of antiquity embody a vision of the world as authentic as that of Greek philosophy, or Roman law, or the poetry and culture of our own enlightened age – earlier, cruder, remote from us, but with its own voice, as we hear it in the *Iliad* or the Twelve Tables, belonging uniquely to its own culture, and with a sublimity which cannot be reproduced by a later, more sophisticated culture. Each culture expresses its own collective experience, each step on the ladder of human development has its own equally authentic means of expression.

Vico's theory of cycles of cultural development became celebrated, but it is not his most original contribution to the understanding of society or history. His revolutionary move is to have denied the doctrine of a timeless natural law the truths of which could have been known in principle to any man, at any time, anywhere. Vico boldly denied this doctrine, which has formed the heart of the Western tradition from Aristotle to our own day. He preached the notion of the uniqueness of cultures, however they might resemble each other in their relationship to their antecedents and successors, and the notion of a single style that pervades all the activities and manifestations of societies of human beings at a particular stage of development. Thereby he laid the foundations at once of comparative cultural anthropology and of comparative historical linguistics, aesthetics, jurisprudence; language, ritual, monuments, and especially mythology, were the sole reliable keys to what later scholars and critics conceived as altering forms of collective consciousness. Such historicism was plainly not compatible with the view that there was only one standard of truth or beauty or goodness, which some cultures or individuals approached more closely than others, and which it was the business of thinkers to establish and men of action to realise. The Homeric poems were an unsurpassable masterpiece, but they could spring only from a brutal, stern, oligarchical, 'heroic' society, and later civilisations, however superior in other respects, did not and could not produce an art necessarily superior to Homer. This doctrine struck a powerful blow at the notion of timeless truths and steady progress, interrupted by occasional periods of retrogression into barbarism, and drew a sharp line between the natural sciences, which dealt with the relatively unaltering nature of the physical world viewed from 'outside', and humane studies, which viewed social evolution from 'inside' by a species of empathetic insight, for which the establishment of texts or dates by scientific criticism was a necessary, but not a sufficient, condition.

Vico's unsystematic works dealt with many other matters, but his importance in the history of the Enlightenment consists in his insistence on the plurality of cultures and on the consequently fallacious character of the idea that there is one and only one structure of reality which the enlightened philosopher can see as it truly is, and which he can (at least in principle) describe in logically perfect language – a vision that has obsessed thinkers from Plato to Leibniz, Condillac, Russell and his more faithful followers. For Vico, men ask different questions of the universe, and their answers are shaped accordingly: such questions, and the symbols or acts that express them, alter or become obsolete in the course of cultural development; to understand the answers one must understand the questions that preoccupy an age or a culture; they are not constant or necessarily more profound because they resemble our own more than others that are less familiar to us. Vico's relativity went further than Montesquieu's. If his view was correct, it was subversive of the very notion of absolute truths and of a perfect society founded on them, not merely in practice but in principle. However, Vico was little read, and how much influence he had had before his *New Science* was revived by Michelet a century after it was written is still uncertain.

If Vico wished to shake the pillars on which the Enlightenment of his times rested, the Königsberg theologian and philosopher J. G. Hamann wished to smash them. Hamann was brought up as a pietist, a member of the most introspective and self-absorbed of all the Lutheran sects, intent upon the direct communion of the individual soul with God, bitterly anti-rationalist, liable to emotional excess, preoccupied with the stern demands of moral obligation and the need for severe self-discipline. The attempt of Frederick the Great in the middle years of the eighteenth century to introduce French culture and a degree of rationalisation, economic and social as well as military, into East Prussia, the most backward part of his provinces, provoked a peculiarly violent reaction in this pious, semi-feudal, traditional Protestant society (which also gave birth to Herder and Kant). Hamann began as a disciple of the Enlightenment, but, after a profound spiritual crisis, turned against it, and published a series of polemical attacks written in a highly idiosyncratic, perversely allusive, contorted, deliberately obscure style, as remote as he could make it from the, to him, detestable elegance, clarity and smooth superficiality of the bland and arrogant French dictators of taste and thought. Hamann's theses rested on the conviction that all truth is particular, never general: that reason is impotent to demonstrate the existence of anything and is an instrument only for conveniently classifying and arranging data in patterns to which nothing in reality corresponds; that to understand is to be communicated with, by men or by God. The universe for him, as for the older German mystical tradition, is itself a kind of language. Things and plants and animals are themselves symbols with which God communicates with his creatures. Everything rests on faith; faith is as basic an organ of acquaintance with reality as the senses. To read the Bible is to hear the voice of God, who speaks in a language which he has given man the grace to understand. Some men are endowed with the gift of understanding his ways, of looking at the universe, which is his book no less than the revelations of the Bible and the fathers and saints of the Church. Only love – for a person or an object – can reveal the true nature of anything. It is not possible to love formulae, general propositions, laws, the abstractions of science, the vast system of concepts and categories – symbols too general to be close to reality – with which the French *lumières* have blinded themselves to concrete reality, to the real experience which only direct acquaintance, especially by the senses, provides.

Hamann glories in the fact that Hume had successfully destroyed the rationalist claim that there is an a priori route to reality, insisting that all knowledge and belief ultimately rest on acquaintance with the data of direct perception. Hume rightly supposes that he could not eat an egg or drink a glass of water if he did not believe in their existence; the data of belief – what Hamann prefers to call faith – rest on grounds and require evidence as little as taste or any other sensation. True knowledge is direct perception of individual entities, and concepts are never, no matter how specific they may be, wholly adequate to the fullness of the individual experience. 'Individuum est ineffabile',[1] wrote Goethe to Lavater in the spirit of Hamann, whom Goethe profoundly admired. The sciences may be of use in practical matters; but no concatenation of concepts will give one an understanding of a man, of a work of art, of what is conveyed by gestures, symbols, verbal and non-verbal, of the style, the spiritual essence, of a human being, a movement, a culture; nor for that matter of the Deity, which speaks to one everywhere if only one has ears to hear and eyes to see. What is real is individual, that is, is what it is in virtue of its uniqueness, its differences from other things, events, thoughts, and not in virtue of what it has in common with them, which is all that the generalising sciences seek to record. 'Passion alone', said Hamann, 'gives to abstractions and hypotheses hands, feet, wings';[2] God speaks to us in poetical words, addressed to the senses, not in abstractions for the learned, and so must anyone who has something to say that matters, who speaks to another person.

Hamann took little interest in theories or speculations about the external world; he cared only for the inner personal life of the individual, and therefore only for art, religious experience, the senses, personal relationships, which the analytic truths of scientific reason seemed to him to reduce to meaningless ciphers. God is a poet, not a mathematician, and it is men who, like Kant, suffer from a 'gnostic hatred of matter'[3] that provide us with endless verbal constructions – words that are taken for concepts, and worse still, concepts that are taken for real things. Scientists invent systems, philosophers rearrange reality into artificial patterns, shut their eyes to reality, and build castles in the air. 'When *data* are given you, why do you need *ficta*?'[4] Systems are mere prisons of the spirit, and they lead not only to distortion in the sphere of

---

[1] Letter to Lavater, *c*.20 September 1780: p. 325, line 7, in *Goethes Briefe* (Hamburg, 1962–7), vol. 1.

[2] Johann Georg Hamann, *Sämtliche Werke*, ed. Joseph Nadler (Vienna, 1949–57) (hereafter in this essay *Werke*), vol. 2, p. 208, line 20.

[3] ibid., vol. 3, p. 285, line 15.

[4] Johann Georg Hamann, *Briefwechsel*, ed. Walther Ziesemer and Arthur Henkel (Wiesbaden and Frankfurt, 1955–79), vol. 6, p. 331, line 22.

knowledge, but to the erection of monstrous bureaucratic machines, built in accordance with the rules that ignore the teeming variety of the living world, the untidy and asymmetrical inner lives of men, and crush them into conformity for the sake of some ideological chimera unrelated to the union of spirit and flesh that constitutes the real world. 'What is this much lauded reason with its universality, infallibility, overweening claims, certainty, self-evidence but an *ens rationis*, a stuffed dummy which the howling superstition of unreason has endowed with divine attributes?'[1] History alone yields concrete truth, and in particular the poets describe their world in the language of passion and inspired imagination. 'The entire treasure of human knowledge and happiness lies in images';[2] that is why the language of primitive man, sensuous and imaginative, is poetical and irrational. 'Poetry is the native language of mankind, and gardening is more ancient than agriculture, painting than writing, song than recitation, proverbs than rational conclusions, barter than trade.'[3] Originality, genius, direct expression, the Bible or Shakespeare fashion the colour, shape, living flesh of the world, which analytical science, revealing only the skeleton, cannot begin to do.

Hamann is first in the line of thinkers who accuse rationalism and scientism of using analysis to distort reality: he is followed by Herder, Jacobi, Möser, who were influenced by Shaftesbury, Young and Burke's anti-intellectualist diatribes, and they, in their turn, were echoed by romantic writers in many lands. The most eloquent spokesman of this attitude is Schelling, whose thought was reproduced vividly by Bergson at the beginning of this century. He is the father of those anti-rationalist thinkers for whom the seamless whole of reality in its unanalysable flow is misrepresented by the static, spatial metaphors of mathematics and the natural sciences. That to dissect is to murder is a romantic pronouncement which is the motto of an entire nineteenth-century movement of which Hamann was a most passionate and implacable forerunner. Scientific dissection leads to cold political dehumanisation, to the strait-jacket of lifeless French rules in which the living body of passionate and poetical Germans is to be held fast by the Solomon of Prussia, Frederick the Great, who knows so much and

---

[1] *Werke*, vol. 3, p. 225, line 3.
[2] ibid., vol. 2, p. 197, line 22.
[3] ibid., line 15.

understands so little. The arch-enemy is Voltaire, whom Herder called a senile child with a corrosive wit in place of human feeling.[1]

The influence of Rousseau, particularly of his early writings, on this movement in Germany, which came to be called *Sturm und Drang*, was profound. Rousseau's impassioned pleas for direct vision and natural feeling, his denunciation of the artificial social roles which civilisation forces men to play against the true ends and needs of their natures, his idealisation of more primitive, spontaneous human societies, his contrast between natural self-expression and the crippling artificiality of social divisions and conventions which rob men of dignity and freedom, and promote privilege, power and arbitrary bullying at one end of the human scale, and humiliating obsequiousness at the other, and so distort all human relations, appealed to Hamann and his followers.

But even Rousseau did not seem to them to go far enough. Despite everything, Rousseau believed in a timeless set of truths which all men could read, for they were engraved on their hearts in letters more durable than bronze, thereby conceding the authority of natural law, a vast, cold, empty abstraction. To Hamann and his followers all rules or precepts are deadly; they may be necessary for the conduct of day-to-day life, but nothing great was ever achieved by following them. English critics were right in supposing that originality entailed breaking rules, that every creative act, every illuminating insight, is obtained by ignoring the rules of despotic legislators. Rules, he declared, are vestal virgins: unless they are violated there will be no issue. Nature is capable of wild fantasy, and it is mere childish presumption to seek to imprison her in the narrow rationalist categories of puny and desiccated philosophers. Nature is a wild dance, and so-called practical men are like sleep-walkers who are secure and successful because they are blind to reality; if they saw reality as it truly is, they might go out of their minds.

Language is the direct expression of the historical life of societies and peoples: 'every court, every school, every profession, every corporation, every sect has its own language';[2] we penetrate the meaning of this language by the passion of 'a friend, an intimate, a

---

[1] *Herder's sämmtliche Werke*, ed. Bernhard Suphan (Berlin, 1877–1913), vol. 5, p. 583.

[2] Hamann, *Werke*, vol. 2, p. 172, line 21.

lover',[1] not by rules, imaginary universal keys which open nothing. The French *philosophes* and their English followers tell us that men seek only to obtain pleasure and avoid pain, but this is absurd. Men seek to live, create, love, hate, eat, drink, worship, sacrifice, understand, and they seek this because they cannot help it. Life is action. It is knowable only by those who look within themselves and perform 'the descent to hell [*Höllenfahrt*] of self-knowledge',[2] as the great founders of pietism – Spener, Francke, Bengel – have taught us. Before a man has liberated himself from the deathly embrace of impersonal, scientific thought which robs all it touches of life and individuality, he cannot understand himself or others, or how or why we come to be what we are.

While Hamann spoke in irregular, isolated flashes of insight, his disciple Herder attempted to construct a coherent system to explain the nature of man and his experience in history. While profoundly interested in the natural sciences and eagerly profiting by their findings, particularly in biology and physiology, and conceding a good deal more to the French than the fanatical Hamann was willing to do, Herder, in that part of his doctrine which entered into the texture of the thought of the movements that he inspired, deliberately aimed against the sociological assumptions of the French Enlightenment. He believed that to understand anything was to understand it in its individuality and development, and that this required the capacity of *Einfühlung* ('feeling into') the outlook, the individual character of an artistic tradition, a literature, a social organisation, a people, a culture, a period of history. To understand the actions of individuals, we must understand the 'organic' structure of the society in terms of which alone the minds and activities and habits of its members can be understood. Like Vico, he believed that to understand a religion, or a work of art, or a national character, one must 'enter into' the unique conditions of its life: those who have been storm-tossed on the waves of the North Sea (as he was during his voyage to the West) can fully understand the songs of the old Skalds as those who have never seen grim northern sailors coping with the elements never will; the Bible can be understood only by those who attempt to enter into the experience of primitive shepherds in the Judaean hills. To grade the merits of cultural wholes, of the legacy of entire traditions, by

[1] ibid., p. 171, line 15.
[2] ibid., p. 164, line 17.

applying a collection of dogmatic rules claiming universal validity, enunciated by the Parisian arbiters of taste, is vanity and blindness. Every culture has its own unique *Schwerpunkt* ('centre of gravity'), and unless we grasp it we cannot understand its character or value. From this springs Herder's passionate concern with the preservation of primitive cultures which have a unique contribution to make, his love of almost every expression of the human spirit, work of the imagination, for simply being what it is. Art, morality, custom, religion, national life grow out of immemorial tradition, are created by entire societies living an integrated communal life. The frontiers and divisions drawn between and within such unitary expressions of collective imaginative response to common experience are nothing but artificial and distorting categorisations by the dull, dogmatic pedants of a later age.

Who are the authors of the songs, the epics, the myths, the temples, the *mores* of the people, the clothes they wear, the language they use? The people itself, the entire soul of which is poured out in all they are and do. Nothing is more barbarous than to ignore or trample on a cultural heritage. Hence Herder's condemnation of the Romans for crushing native civilisations, or of the Church (despite the fact that he was himself a Lutheran clergyman) for forcibly baptising the Balts, and so forcing them into a Christian mould alien to their natural traditions, or British missionaries for doing this to the Indians and other inhabitants of Asia, whose exquisite native cultures were being ruthlessly destroyed by the imposition of alien social systems, religions, forms of education that were not theirs and could only warp their natural development. Herder was no nationalist: he supposed that different cultures could and should flourish fruitfully side by side like so many peaceful flowers in the great human garden; nevertheless, the seeds of nationalism are unmistakably present in his fervid attacks on hollow cosmopolitanism and universalism (with which he charged the French *philosophes*); they grew apace among his aggressive nineteenth-century disciples.

Herder is the greatest inspirer of cultural nationalism among the nationalities oppressed by the Austro-Hungarian, Turkish and Russian empires, and ultimately of direct political nationalism as well, much as he abhorred it, in Austria and Germany and, by infectious reaction, in other lands as well. He rejected the absolute criteria of progress then fashionable in Paris: no culture is a mere means towards another; every human achievement, every human society is to be judged by its own internal standards. In spite of the fact that in later life he attempted to construct a theory of history in which the whole of mankind, in a somewhat vague fashion, is represented as developing towards a common *Humanität* which embraces all men and all the arts and all the sciences, it is his earlier, relativistic passion for the individual essence and flavour of each culture that most profoundly influenced the European imagination. For Voltaire, Diderot, Helvétius, Holbach, Condorcet there is only universal civilisation, of which now one nation, now another, represents the richest flowering. For Herder there is a plurality of incommensurable cultures. To belong to a given community, to be connected with its members by indissoluble and impalpable ties of common language, historical memory, habit, tradition and feeling, is a basic human need no less natural than that for food or drink or security or procreation. One nation can understand and sympathise with the institutions of another only because it knows how much its own mean to itself. Cosmopolitanism is the shedding of all that makes one most human, most oneself. Hence the attack upon what is regarded as the false mechanical model of mankind used by scientifically minded French *philosophes* (Herder makes an exception for Diderot alone, with whose writings, wayward and imaginative and full of sudden insights, he felt a genuine affinity), who understand only machine-like, causal factors, or the arbitrary will of individual kings and legislators and commanders, sometimes wise and virtuous and altruistic, at other times self-interested or corrupt or stupid or vicious. But the forces that shape men are far more complex, and differ from age to age and culture to culture, and cannot be contained in these simple cut and dried formulae. 'I am always frightened when I hear a whole nation or period characterised in a few short words; for what a vast multitude of differences is embraced by the word "nation", or "the Middle Ages", or "ancient and modern times".'[1] Germans can be truly creative only among Germans; Jews only if they are restored to the ancient soil of Palestine. Those who are forcibly pulled up by the roots wither in a foreign environment, when they survive at all: Europeans lose their virtue in America, Icelanders decay in Denmark. Imitation of models (unlike unconscious, unperceived, spontaneous influences by one society on another) leads to artificiality, feeble imitativeness, degraded art and life. Germans

[1] op. cit. (p. 252 above, note 1), vol. 18, p. 56.

must be Germans and not third-rate Frenchmen; life lies in remaining steeped in one's own language, tradition, local feeling; uniformity is death. The tree of (science-dominated) knowledge kills the tree of life.

So, too, Herder's contemporary, Justus Möser, the first historical sociologist, who wrote about the old life of his native region of Osnabrück in western Germany, said that every age has its own style, every war has its own particular tone, the affairs of State have a specific colouring, dress and manner have inner connections with religion and the sciences; that *Zeitstil* and *Volksstil* are everything; that there is a local reason for this or that institution that is not and cannot be universal.[1] Möser maintained that societies and persons could be understood only by means of a total impression, not by isolation of element from element in the manner of analytical chemists; this, he tells us, is what Voltaire had not grasped when he mocked the fact that a law which applied in one German village was contradicted by another in a neighbouring one: it is by such rich variety, founded upon ancient, unbroken tradition, that the tyrannies of uniform systems, such as those of Louis XIV or Frederick the Great, were avoided; it is thus that freedoms were preserved.

Although the influence was not direct, these are the very tones one hears in the works of Burke and many later romantic, vitalistic, intuitionist and irrationalist writers, both conservative and socialist, who defend the value of organic forms of social life. Burke's famous onslaught on the principles of the French revolutionaries was founded upon the selfsame appeal to the myriad strands that bind human beings into a historically hallowed whole, contrasted with the utilitarian model of society as a trading-company held together solely by contractual obligations, the world of 'sophisters, oeconomists, and calculators'[2] who are blind and deaf to the unanalysable relationships that make a family, a tribe, a nation, a movement, any association of human beings held together by something more than a quest for mutual advantage, or by force, or by anything that is not mutual love, loyalty, common history,

---

[1] See the part of the preface to his *Osnabrückische Geschichte* (1768) reprinted as 'Deutsche Geschichte' in *Von Deutscher Art und Kunst* (1773), by Herder and others: esp. p. 157 in the edition of the latter by Edna Purdie (Oxford, 1924).

[2] Edmund Burke, *Reflections on the Revolution in France* (1790): p. 127 in *The Writings and Speeches of Edmund Burke*, ed. Paul Langford (Oxford, 1981– ), vol. 8, *The French Revolution*, ed. L. G. Mitchell (1989).

emotion and outlook. This emphasis in the last half of the eighteenth century on non-rational factors, whether connected with specific religious beliefs or not, which stresses the value of the individual, the peculiar (*das Eigentümliche*), the impalpable, and appeals to ancient historical roots and immemorial custom, to the wisdom of simple, sturdy peasants uncorrupted by the sophistries of subtle 'reasoners', has strongly conservative and, indeed, reactionary implications. Whether stated by the enthusiastic populist Herder with his acute dislike for political coercion, empires, political authority, and all forms of imposed organisation; or by Möser, moderate Hanoverian conservative; or by Lavater, altogether unconcerned with politics; or by Burke, brought up in a different tradition, respectful towards Church and State and the authority of aristocracies and élites sanctified by history – these doctrines clearly constitute a resistance to attempts at a rational reorganisation of society in the name of universal moral and intellectual ideals.

At the same time abhorrence of scientific expertise inspired radical protest in the works of William Blake, of the young Schiller, and of populist writers in eastern Europe. Above all, it contributed to literary turbulence in Germany in the second third of the eighteenth century: the plays of such leaders of the *Sturm und Drang* as Lenz, Klinger, Gerstenberg and Leisewitz are outbursts against every form of organised social or political life. What provoked them may have been the asphyxiating philistinism of the German middle class, or the cruel injustices of the small and stuffy courts of stupid and arbitrary German princelings; but what they attacked with equal violence was the entire tidy ordering of life by the principles of reason and scientific knowledge advocated by the progressive thinkers of France, England and Italy. Lenz regards nature as a wild whirlpool into which a man of feeling and temperament will throw himself if he is to experience the fullness of life; for him, for Schubart and for Leisewitz art and, in particular, literature are passionate forms of self-assertion which look on all acceptance of conventional forms as but 'postponed death'.[1] Nothing is more characteristic of the entire *Sturm und*

---

[1] J. M. R. Lenz, 'Über Götz von Berlichingen': p. 638 in Jakob Michael Reinhold Lenz, *Werke und Briefe in Drei Bänden*, ed. Sigrid Damm (Munich/Vienna, 1987), vol. 2.

*Drang* movement than Herder's cry 'I am not here to think, but to be, feel, live!',[1] or 'Heart! Warmth! Blood! Humanity! Life!'[2] French reasoning is pale and ghostly. It is this that inspired Goethe's reaction in the 1770s to Holbach's *Système de la nature* as a repulsive, 'Cimmerian, corpse-like'[3] treatise, which had no relation to the marvellous, inexhaustibly rich vitality of the Gothic cathedral at Strasbourg, in which, under Herder's guidance, he saw one of the noblest expressions of the German spirit in the Middle Ages, of which the critic of the Augustan age understood nothing. Heinse in his fantasy *Ardinghello und die glückseligen Inseln* leads his central characters, after a bloodstained succession of wild experiences of more than 'Gothic' intensity, to an island where there is total freedom in personal relations, all rules and conventions have finally been flung to the winds, where man in an anarchist-communist society can at last stretch himself to his full stature as a sublime creative artist. The inspiration of this work is a violent, radical individualism, which represents an early form, not unlike the contemporary erotic fantasies of the marquis de Sade, of a craving for escape from imposed rules and laws whether of scientific reason or of political or ecclesiastical authority, royalist or republican, despotic or democratic.

By an odd paradox, it is the profoundly rational, exact, unromantic Kant, with his lifelong hatred of all forms of *Schwärmerei*, who is in part, through exaggeration and distortion of at least one of his doctrines, one of the fathers of this unbridled individualism. Kant's moral doctrines stressed the fact that determinism was not compatible with morality, since only those who are the true authors of their own acts, which they are free to perform or not perform, can be praised or blamed for what they do. Since responsibility entails power of choice, those who cannot freely choose are morally no more accountable than stocks and stones. Thereby Kant initiated a cult of moral autonomy, according to which only those who act and are not acted upon, whose actions spring from a decision of the moral will to be guided by freely adopted principles, if need be against inclination, and not from the inescapable causal pressure of factors beyond their control –

---

[1] op. cit. (p. 252 above, note 1), vol. 29, p. 366.

[2] ibid., vol. 5, p. 538.

[3] *Dichtung und Wahrheit*, book 11: p. 68, line 17, in *Goethes Werke* (Weimar, 1887–1919), vol. 28.

physical, physiological, psychological (such as emotion, desire, habit) – can properly be considered to be free or, indeed, moral agents at all. Kant acknowledged a profound debt to Rousseau, who, particularly in the 'profession of faith of the Savoyard vicar' in the fourth book of his *Émile*, spoke of man as an active being in contrast with the passivity of material nature, a possessor of a will which makes him free to resist the temptations of the senses. 'I am a slave through my vices and free through my remorse'; it is the active will, made known directly by 'conscience', which for Rousseau is 'stronger than reason [i.e. prudential argument] which fights against it', that enables man to choose the good; he acts, if need be, 'against the law of the body', and so makes himself worthy of happiness.[1] But although this doctrine of the will as a capacity not determined by the causal stream is directed against the sensationalist positivism of Helvétius or Condillac, and has an affinity to Kant's free moral will, it does not leave the objective framework of natural law which governs things as well as persons, and prescribes the same immutable, universal goals to all men.

This emphasis upon the will at the expense of contemplative thought and perception, which function within the predetermined grooves of the categories of the mind that man cannot escape, enters deeply into the German conception of moral freedom as entailing resistance to nature and not harmonious collusion with her, overcoming of natural inclination, and rising to Promethean resistance to coercion, whether by things or by men. This, in its turn, led to the rejection of the doctrine that to understand is to accept the view that knowledge demonstrates the rational necessity and therefore the value of what, in his irrational state, may have seemed to man mere obstacles in his path. This conception, opposed as it is to reconciliation with reality, in its later, romantic form favoured the ceaseless fight, at times ending in tragic defeat, against the forces of blind nature, which cares nothing for human ideas, and against the accumulated weight of authority and tradition – the vast incubus of the uncriticised past, made concrete in the oppressive institutions of the present. Thus, when Blake denounces Newton and Locke as the great enemies, it is because he accuses them of seeking to imprison the free human spirit in constricting, intellectual machines; when he says, 'A Robin Red

[1] op. cit. (p. 195 above, note 2), book 4, pp. 584–6.

breast in a Cage / Puts all Heaven in a Rage',[1] the cage is none other than Newtonian physics, which crushes the life out of the free, spontaneous, untrammelled human spirit. 'Art is the Tree of Life ... Science is the Tree of Death';[2] Locke, Newton, the French *raisonneurs*, the reign of cautious, pragmatic respectability and Pitt's police were all, for him, parts of the same nightmare. There is something of this, too, in Schiller's early play *Die Räuber* (written in 1781), where the violent protest of the tragic hero Karl Moor, which ends in failure, crime and death, cannot be averted by mere knowledge, by a better understanding of human nature or of social conditions or of anything else; knowledge is not enough. The Enlightenment doctrine that we can discover what men truly want, and can provide technical means and rules of conduct for their greatest permanent satisfaction, and that this is what leads to wisdom, virtue, happiness, is not compatible with Karl Moor's proud and stormy spirit, which rejects the ideas of his milieu, and will not be assuaged by the reformist gradualism and belief in rational organisation advocated by, say, the *Aufklärung* of the previous generation. 'Law has degraded to a snail's pace what would have been an eagle's flight.'[3] Human nature is no longer conceived of as, in principle, capable of being brought into harmony with the natural world: for Schiller some fatal Rousseauian break between spirit and nature has occurred, a wound has been inflicted on humanity which art seeks to avenge, but knows it cannot fully heal.

Jacobi, a mystical metaphysician deeply influenced by Hamann, cannot reconcile the demands of the soul and the intellect: 'The light is in my heart: as soon as I try to carry it to my intellect, it goes out.'[4] Spinoza was for him the greatest master since Plato of the rational vision of the universe; but for Jacobi this is death in life: it does not answer the burning question of the soul whose homelessness in the chilly world of the intellect only self-surrender to faith in a transcendent God will remedy.

Schelling was perhaps the most eloquent of all the philosophers who represented the universe as the self-development of a primal,

---

[1] 'Auguries of Innocence', line 5: p. 1312 in *William Blake's Writings*, ed. G. E. Bentley, Jr (Oxford, 1978), vol. 2.

[2] 'Laocoon', aphorisms 17, 19: ibid., pp. 665, 666.

[3] *Die Räuber*, act 1, scene 2: p. 21, line 29, in *Schillers Werke*, Nationalausgabe (Weimar, 1943– ), vol. 3.

[4] *Friedrich Heinrich Jacobi's Werke* (Leipzig, 1812–25), vol. 1, p. 367.

non-rational force that can be grasped only by the intuitive powers of men of imaginative genius – poets, philosophers, theologians or statesmen. Nature, a living organism, responds to questions put by the man of genius, while the man of genius responds to the questions put by nature, for they conspire with each other; imaginative insight alone, no matter whose – an artist's, a seer's, a thinker's – becomes conscious of the contours of the future, of which the mere calculating intellect and analytic capacity of the natural scientist or the politician, or any other earthbound empiricist, has no conception. This faith in a peculiar, intuitive, spiritual faculty which goes by various names – reason, understanding, primary imagination – but is always differentiated from the critical analytic intellect favoured by the Enlightenment – the contrast between it and the analytic faculty or method that collects, classifies, experiments, takes to pieces, reassembles, defines, deduces, and establishes probabilities – becomes a commonplace used thereafter by Fichte, Hegel, Wordsworth, Coleridge, Goethe, Carlyle, Schopenhauer and other anti-rationalist thinkers of the nineteenth century, culminating in Bergson and later anti-positivist schools.

This, too, is the source of that stream in the great river of romanticism which looks upon every human activity as a form of individual self-expression, and on art, and indeed every creative activity, as a stamping of a unique personality, individual or collective, conscious or unconscious, upon the matter or the medium in and upon which it functions, seeking to realise values which are themselves not given but generated by the process of creation itself. Hence the denial, both in theory and in practice, of the central doctrine of the Enlightenment, according to which the rules in conformity with which men should live and act and create are pre-established, dictated by nature herself. For Joshua Reynolds, for example, the 'great style' is the realisation of the artist's vision of eternal forms, prototypes beyond the confusions of ordinary experience, which his genius enables him to discern and which he seeks to reproduce, with all the techniques at his command, on his canvas or in marble or bronze. Such mimesis or copying from ideal patterns is, for those who derive from the German tradition of revolt against French classicism, not true creation. Creation is creation of ends as well as means, of values as well as their embodiments; the vision that I seek to translate into colours or sounds is generated by me, and peculiar to me, unlike anything that has ever been, or will be, above all not something that is common to me and other men seeking to realise a common, shared, universal, because rational, ideal. The notion that a work of art (or any other work of man) is created in accordance with rules dictated by objective nature, and therefore binding for all practitioners of it, as Boileau or the abbé Batteux had taught, is rejected *in toto*. Rules may be an aid here or there, but the least spark of genius destroys them, and creates its own practice, which uncreative craftsmen may imitate, and so be saying nothing of their own. I create as I do, whether I am an artist, a philosopher, a statesman, not because the goal that I seek to realise is objectively beautiful, or true, or virtuous, or approved by public opinion, or demanded by majorities or tradition, but because it is my own.

What this creative self may be differs according to doctrine. Some regard it as a transcendent entity to be identified with a cosmic spirit, a divine principle to which finite men aspire as sparks do to the great central flame; others identify it with their own individual, mortal, flesh-and-blood selves, like Byron, or Hugo, or other defiantly romantic writers and painters. Others again identified the creative self with a super-personal 'organism' of which they saw themselves as elements or members – nation, or Church, or culture, or class, or history itself, a mighty force of which they conceived their earthly selves as emanations. Aggressive nationalism, self-identification with the interests of the class, the culture or the race, or the forces of progress – with the wave of a future-directed dynamism of history, something that at once explains and justifies acts which might be abhorred or despised if committed from calculation of selfish advantage or some other mundane motive – this family of political and moral conceptions is so many expressions of a doctrine of self-realisation based on defiant rejection of the central theses of the Enlightenment, according to which what is true, or right, or good, or beautiful can be shown to be valid for all men by the correct application of objective methods of discovery and interpretation, open to anyone to use and verify. In its full romantic guise this attitude is an open declaration of war upon the very heart of the rational and experimental method which Descartes and Galileo had inaugurated, and which for all their doubts and qualifications even such sharp deviationists as Montesquieu, or Hume and Rousseau and Kant, fully and firmly accepted. For the truly ardent opponents of classicism, values are not found but made, not discovered but created; they are to be realised because they are mine, or ours, whatever the nature of the true self is pronounced to be by this or that metaphysical doctrine. The most extravagant of the German romantics, Novalis or Tieck, looked on the universe not as a structure that can be studied or described by whatever methods are most appropriate, but as a perpetual activity of the spirit and of nature, which is the selfsame spirit in a dormant state; of this constant upward movement the man of genius is the most conscious agent, who thus embodies the forward activity that advances the life of the spirit most significantly. While some, like Schelling and Coleridge, conceive this activity as the gradual growth into self-consciousness of the world spirit that is perpetually moving towards self-perfection, others conceive the cosmic process as having no goal, as a purposeless and meaningless movement, which men, because they cannot face this bleak and despair-inducing truth, seek to hide from themselves by constructing comforting illusions in the form of religions that promise rewards in another life, or metaphysical systems that claim to provide rational justification both for what there is in the world and for what men do and can do and should do; or scientific systems that perform the task of appearing to give sense to a process that is, in fact, purposeless, a formless flux which is what it is, a brute fact, signifying nothing. This doctrine, elaborated by Schopenhauer, lies at the root of much modern existentialism and of the cultivation of the absurd in art and thought, as well as of the extremes of egoistic anarchism driven to their furthest lengths by Stirner, and by Nietzsche (in some of his moods), Kierkegaard (Hamann's most brilliant and profound disciple) and modern irrationalists.

The rejection of the central principles of the Enlightenment – universality, objectivity, rationality, the capacity to provide permanent solutions to all genuine problems of life or thought, and (not less important) the accessibility of rational methods to any thinker armed with adequate powers of observation and logical thinking – occurred in various forms, conservative or liberal, reactionary or revolutionary, depending on which systematic order was being attacked. Those, for example, like Adam Müller or Friedrich Schlegel, and, in some moods, Coleridge or Cobbett, to whom the principles of the French Revolution or the Napoleonic organisation came to seem the most fatal obstacles to free human self-expression, adopted conservative or reactionary forms of irrationalism and at times looked back with nostalgia towards some golden past, such as the pre-scientific ages of faith, and tended (not always continuously or consistently) to support clerical and aristocratic resistance to modernisation and the mechanisation of life by industrialism and the new hierarchies of power and authority. Those who looked upon the traditional forces of authority or hierarchical organisation as the most oppressive of social forces – Byron, for example, or George Sand, or, so far as they can be called romantic, Shelley or Büchner – formed the 'left wing' of the romantic revolt. Others despised public life in principle, and occupied themselves with the cultivation of the inner spirit. In all cases the organisation of life by the application of rational or scientific methods, any form of regimentation or conscription of men for utilitarian ends or organised happiness, was regarded as the philistine enemy.

What the entire Enlightenment has in common is denial of the central Christian doctrine of original sin, believing instead that man is born either innocent and good, or morally neutral and malleable by education or environment, or, at worst, deeply defective but capable of radical and indefinite improvement by rational education in favourable circumstances, or by a revolutionary reorganisation of society as demanded, for example, by Rousseau. It is this denial of original sin that the Church condemned most severely in Rousseau's *Émile*, despite its attack on materialism, utilitarianism and atheism. It is the powerful reaffirmation of this Pauline and Augustinian doctrine that is the sharpest single weapon in the root-and-branch attack on the entire Enlightenment by the French counter-revolutionary writers Maistre, Bonald and Chateaubriand, at the turn of the century.

One of the darkest of the reactionary forms of the fight against the Enlightenment, as well as one of the most interesting and influential, is to be found in the doctrines of Joseph de Maistre and his followers and allies, who formed the spearhead of the counter-revolution in the early nineteenth century in Europe. Maistre held the Enlightenment to be one of the most foolish, as well as the most ruinous, forms of social thinking. The conception of man as naturally disposed to benevolence, co-operation and peace, or, at any rate, capable of being shaped in this direction by appropriate education or legislation, is for him shallow and false. The benevolent Dame Nature of Hume, Holbach and Helvétius is an absurd figment. History and zoology are the most reliable guides to nature: they show her to be a field of unceasing slaughter. Men are by nature aggressive and destructive; they rebel over trifles – the change to the Gregorian calendar in the mid-eighteenth century, or Peter the Great's decision to shave the boyars' beards, provoke violent resistance, at times dangerous rebellions. But when men are sent to war, to exterminate beings as innocent as themselves for no purpose that either army can grasp, they go obediently to their deaths and scarcely ever mutiny. When the destructive instinct is evoked men feel exalted and fulfilled. Men do not come together, as the Enlightenment teaches, for mutual co-operation and peaceful happiness; history makes it clear that they are never so united as when given a common altar upon which to immolate themselves. This is so because the desire to sacrifice themselves or others is at least as strong as any pacific or constructive impulse.

Maistre felt that men are by nature evil, self-destructive animals, full of conflicting drives, who do not know what they want, want what they do not want, do not want what they want, and it is only when they are kept under constant control and rigorous discipline by some authoritarian élite – a Church, a State, or some other body from whose decisions there is no appeal – that they can hope to survive and be saved. Reasoning, analysis, criticism shake the foundations and destroy the fabric of society. If the source of authority is declared to be rational, it invites questioning and doubt; but if it is questioned it may be argued away; its authority is undermined by able sophists, and this accelerates the forces of chaos, as in France during the reign of the weak and liberal Louis XVI. If the State is to survive and frustrate the fools and knaves who will always seek to destroy it, the source of authority must be absolute, so terrifying, indeed, that the least attempt to question it must entail immediate and terrible sanctions: only then will men learn to obey it. Without a clear hierarchy of authority – awe-inspiring power – men's incurably destructive instincts will breed chaos and mutual extermination. The supreme power – especially the Church – must never seek to explain or justify itself in rational terms; for what one man can demonstrate, another may be able to refute. Reason is the thinnest of walls against the raging seas of violent emotion: on so insecure a basis no permanent structure can ever be erected. Irrationality, so far from being an obstacle, has historically led to peace, security and strength, and is indispensable to society: it is rational institutions – republics, elective monarchies, democracies, associations founded on the enlightened principles of free love – that collapse soonest; authoritarian Churches, hereditary monarchies and aristocracies, traditional forms of life, like the highly irrational institution of the family, founded on life-long marriage – it is they that persist.

The *philosophes* proposed to rationalise communication by inventing a universal language free from the irrational survivals, the idiosyncratic twists and turns, the capricious peculiarities of existing tongues; if they were to succeed, this would be disastrous, for it is precisely the individual historical development of a language belonging to a people that absorbs, enshrines and encapsulates a vast wealth of half-conscious, half-remembered collective experience. What men call superstition and prejudice are but the crust of custom which by sheer survival has shown itself proof against the ravages and vicissitudes of its long life; to lose it is to lose the shield that protects men's national existence, their spirit, the habits, memories, faith that have made them what they are. The conception of human nature which the radical critics have promulgated and on which their whole house of cards rests is an infantile fantasy. Rousseau asks why it is that man, who was born free, is nevertheless everywhere in chains; Maistre replies, 'This mad pronouncement, *Man is born free*, is the opposite of the truth.'[1] 'It would be equally reasonable', adds the eminent critic Émile Faguet in an essay on Maistre, 'to say that sheep are born carnivorous, and everywhere nibble grass.'[2] Men are not made for freedom, nor for peace. Such freedom and peace as they have had were obtained only under wisely authoritarian governments that have repressed the destructive critical intellect and its socially disintegrating effects. Scientists, intellectuals, lawyers, journalists, democrats, Jansenists, Protestants, Jews, atheists – these are the sleepless enemy that never ceases to gnaw at the vitals of society. The best government the world has ever known was that of the Romans: they were too wise to be scientists themselves; for this purpose they hired the clever, volatile, politically incapable Greeks. Not the luminous intellect, but dark instincts govern man and societies; only élites which understand this, and keep the people from too much secular education, which is bound to make them over-critical and discontented, can give to men as much happiness and justice

---

[1] *Oeuvres complètes de J. de Maistre* (Lyon/Paris, 1884–7), vol. 2, p. 338.
[2] Émile Faguet, *Politiques et moralistes du dix-neuvième siècle*, 1st series (Paris, 1899), p. 41.

and freedom as, in this vale of tears, men can expect to have. But at the back of everything must lurk the potentiality of force, of coercive power.

In a striking image Maistre says that all social order in the end rests upon one man, the executioner. Nobody wishes to associate with this hideous figure, yet on him, so long as men are weak, sinful, unable to control their passions, constantly lured to their doom by evil temptations or foolish dreams, rest all order, all peace, all society. The notion that reason is sufficient to educate or control the passions is ridiculous. When there is a vacuum, power rushes in; even the bloodstained monster Robespierre, a scourge sent by the Lord to punish a country that had departed from the true faith, is more to be admired – because he did hold France together and repelled her enemies, and created armies that, drunk with blood and passion, preserved France – than liberal fumbling and bungling. Louis XIV ignored the clever reasoners of his time, suppressed heresy, and died full of glory in his own bed. Louis XVI played amiably with subversive ideologists who had drunk at the poisoned well of Voltaire, and died on the scaffold. Repression, censorship, absolute sovereignty, judgements from which there is no appeal, these are the only methods of governing creatures whom Maistre described as half men, half beasts, monstrous centaurs at once seeking after God and fighting him, longing to love and create, but in perpetual danger of falling victims to their own blindly destructive drives, held in check by a combination of force and traditional authority and, above all, a faith incarnated in historically hallowed institutions that reason dare not touch.

Nation and race are realities; the artificial creations of constitution-mongers are bound to collapse. 'Nations', said Maistre, 'are born and die like individuals'; they 'have a common soul', especially visible in their language.[1] And since they are individuals, they should endeavour to remain of one race. So too Bonald, his closest intellectual ally, regrets that the French nation has abandoned its ideal of racial purity, thus weakening itself. The question of whether the French are descended from Franks or Gauls, whether their institutions are Roman or German in origin, with the implication that this could dictate a form of life in the present, although it has its roots in political controversies in the sixteenth, seventeenth and early eighteenth centuries, now takes the

[1] op. cit. (p. 266 above, note 1), vol. 1, p. 325.

colour of mystical organicism, which transcends, and is proof against, all forms of discursive reasoning. Natural growth alone is real for Maistre. Only time, only history, can create authority that men can worship and obey: mere military dictatorship, a work of individual human hands, is brutal force without spiritual power; he calls it *bâtonocratie*, and predicts the end of Napoleon.

In similar strain Bonald denounced individualism whether as a social doctrine or an intellectual method of analysing historical phenomena. The inventions of man, he declared, are precarious aids compared to the divinely ordained institutions that penetrate man's very being – language, family, the worship of God. By whom were they invented? Whenever a child is born there are father, mother, family, language, God; this is the basis of all that is genuine and lasting, not the arrangements of men drawn from the world of shopkeepers, with their contracts, or promises, or utility, or material goods. Liberal individualism inspired by the insolent self-confidence of mutinous intellectuals has led to the inhuman competition of bourgeois society, in which the strongest and the fastest win and the weak go to the wall. Only the Church can organise a society in which the ablest are held back so that the whole of society can progress and the weakest and least greedy also reach the goal.

These gloomy doctrines became the inspiration of monarchist politics in France, and together with the notion of romantic heroism and the sharp contrast between creative and uncreative, historic and unhistoric individuals and nations, duly inspired nationalism, imperialism, and finally, in their most violent and pathological form, Fascist and totalitarian doctrines in the twentieth century.

The failure of the French Revolution to bring about the greater portion of its declared ends marks the end of the French Enlightenment as a movement and a system. Its heirs and the countermovements that, to some degree, they stimulated and affected in their turn, romantic and irrational creeds and movements, political and aesthetic, violent and peaceful, individualist and collective, anarchic and totalitarian, and their impact, belong to another page of history.

# THE ORIGINALITY OF MACHIAVELLI

I

THERE IS something surprising about the sheer number of interpretations of Machiavelli's political opinions. There exist, even
now, over a score of leading theories of how to interpret *The
Prince* and the *Discourses* – apart from a cloud of subsidiary views
and glosses. The bibliography of this is vast and growing faster
than ever.[1] While there may exist no more than the normal extent
of disagreement about the meaning of particular terms or theses
contained in these works, there is a startling degree of divergence
about the central view, the basic political attitude of Machiavelli.

This phenomenon is easier to understand in the case of other
thinkers whose opinions have continued to puzzle or agitate
mankind – Plato, for example, or Rousseau, or Hegel, or Marx. But
then it might be said that Plato wrote in a world and in a language
that we cannot be sure we understand; that Rousseau, Hegel, Marx
were prolific theorists, whose works are scarcely models of clarity
or consistency. But *The Prince* is a short book: its style is usually
described as being singularly lucid, succinct and pungent – a model
of clear Renaissance prose. The *Discourses* are not, as treatises on
politics go, of undue length, and they are equally clear and definite.
Yet there is no consensus about the significance of either; they have
not been absorbed into the texture of traditional political theory;

---

[1] The full list now [1972] contains more than three thousand items. The
bibliographical surveys that I have found most valuable are P. H. Harris,
'Progress in Machiavelli Studies', *Italica* 18 (1941), 1–11; Eric W. Cochrane,
'Machiavelli: 1940–1960', *Journal of Modern History* 33 (1961), 113–36; Felix
Gilbert, *Machiavelli and Guicciardini* (Princeton, 1965); Giuseppe Prezzolini,
*Machiavelli anticristo* (Rome, 1954), trans. into English as *Machiavelli* (New
York, 1967; London, 1968); De Lamar Jensen (ed.), *Machiavelli: Cynic, Patriot, or
Political Scientist?* (Boston, 1960); and Richard C. Clark, 'Machiavelli: Biblio-
graphical Spectrum', *Review of National Literatures* 1 (1970), 93–135.

they continue to arouse passionate feelings; *The Prince* has evidently excited the interest and admiration of some of the most formidable men of action of the last four centuries, especially of our own, men not normally addicted to reading classical texts.

There is evidently something peculiarly disturbing about what Machiavelli said or implied, something that has caused profound and lasting uneasiness. Modern scholars have pointed out certain real or apparent inconsistencies between the (for the most part) republican sentiment of the *Discourses* (and the *Histories*) and the advice to absolute rulers in *The Prince*; indeed there is a difference of tone between the two treatises, as well as chronological puzzles: this raises problems about Machiavelli's character, motives and convictions which for three hundred years and more have formed a rich field of investigation and speculation for literary and linguistic scholars, psychologists and historians.

But it is not this that has shocked Western feeling. Nor can it be only Machiavelli's 'realism' or his advocacy of brutal or unscrupulous or ruthless policies that has so deeply upset so many later thinkers, and driven some of them to explain or explain away his advocacy of force and fraud. The fact that the wicked are seen to flourish or that immoral courses appear to pay has never been very remote from the consciousness of mankind. The Bible, Herodotus, Thucydides, Plato, Aristotle – to take only some of the fundamental works of Western culture – the characters of Jacob or Joshua or David, Samuel's advice to Saul, Thucydides' Melian dialogue or his account of at least one ferocious but rescinded Athenian resolution, the philosophies of Thrasymachus and Callicles, Aristotle's advice to tyrants in the *Politics*, Carneades' speeches to the Roman Senate as described by Cicero, Augustine's view of the secular State from one vantage-point, and Marsilio's from another – all these had cast enough light on political realities to shock the credulous out of uncritical idealism.

The explanation can scarcely lie in Machiavelli's tough-mindedness alone, even though he did perhaps dot the i's and cross the t's more sharply than anyone before him.[1] Even if the initial outcry – the reactions of, say, Pole or Gentillet – is to be so explained, this does not account for the reactions of those acquainted with the

[1] His habit of putting things *troppo assolutamente* had already been noted by Guicciardini. See 'Considerazioni intorno ai *Discorsi* del Machiavelli': book 1, chapter 3, p. 8 in *Scritti politici e ricordi*, ed. Roberto Palmarocchi (Bari, 1933).

views of Hobbes or Spinoza or Hegel or the Jacobins and their heirs. Something else is surely needed to account both for the continuing horror and for the differences among the commentators. The two phenomena may not be unconnected. To indicate the nature of the latter phenomenon let me cite only the best-known rival interpretations of Machiavelli's political views produced since the sixteenth century.

According to Alberico Gentili[1] and Garrett Mattingly,[2] the author of *The Prince* wrote a satire, for he certainly cannot literally have meant what he said. For Spinoza,[3] Rousseau,[4] Ugo Foscolo,[5] Luigi Ricci (who introduces *The Prince* to the readers of The World's Classics)[6] it is a cautionary tale; for whatever else he was, Machiavelli was a passionate patriot, a democrat, a believer in liberty, and *The Prince* must have been intended (Spinoza is particularly clear on this) to warn men of what tyrants could be and do, the better to resist them. Perhaps the author could not write openly with two rival powers – those of the Church and of the Medici – eyeing him with equal (and not unjustified) suspicion. *The Prince* is therefore a satire (though no work seems to me to read less like one).

For A. H. Gilbert[7] it is anything but this – it is a typical piece of its period, a mirror for princes, a genre exercise common enough in the Renaissance and before (and after) it, with very obvious borrowings and 'echoes'; more gifted than most of these, and certainly more hard-boiled (and influential); but not so very different in style, content or intention.

Giuseppe Prezzolini[8] and Hiram Haydn,[9] more plausibly,

---

[1] Alberico Gentili, *De legationibus libri tres* (London, 1585), book 3, chapter 9, pp. 101–2.

[2] Garrett Mattingly, 'Machiavelli's *Prince*: Political Science or Political Satire?', *American Scholar* 27 (1958), 482–91.

[3] *Tractatus politicus*, chapter 5, section 7.

[4] *Social Contract*, book 3, chapter 6, note: p. 1480 in *Oeuvres complètes* (op. cit., p. 195 above, note 2), vol. 3.

[5] *I sepolchri*, 156–8: 'che, temprando lo scettro a' regnatori, / gli allòr ne sfronda, ed alle genti svela / di che lagrime grondi e di che sangue . . .'.

[6] Luigi Ricci, preface to Niccolò Machiavelli, *The Prince* (London, 1903).

[7] Allan H. Gilbert, *Machiavelli's* Prince *and its Forerunners* (Durham, North Carolina, 1938).

[8] op. cit. (p. 269 above, note 1).

[9] Hiram Haydn, *The Counter-Renaissance* (New York, 1950).

regard it as an anti-Christian piece (in this following Fichte and others)[1] and see it as an attack on the Church and all her principles, a defence of the pagan view of life. Giuseppe Toffanin,[2] however, thinks Machiavelli was a Christian, though a somewhat peculiar one, a view from which Roberto Ridolfi,[3] his most distinguished modern biographer, and Leslie Walker (in his English edition of the *Discourses*)[4] do not wholly dissent. Alderisio,[5] indeed, regards him as a sincere Catholic, although he does not go quite so far as Richelieu's agent, Canon Louis Machon, in his *Apology for Machiavelli,*[6] or the anonymous nineteenth-century compiler of *Religious Maxims Faithfully Extracted from the works of Niccolò Machiavelli* (referred to by Ridolfi in the last chapter of his biography).[7]

For Benedetto Croce[8] and all the many scholars who have followed him Machiavelli is an anguished humanist, and one who, so far from seeking to soften the impression made by the crimes that he describes, laments the vices of men which make such wicked courses politically unavoidable – a moralist who 'occasionally experiences moral nausea'[9] in contemplating a world in which political ends can be achieved only by means that are morally evil, and thereby the man who divorced the province of politics from that of ethics. But for the Swiss scholars Walder, Kaegi and von

[1] e.g. the Spaniards Pedro de Ribadeneira, *Tratado de la religión* (Madrid, 1595), and Claudio Clemente (pseudonym of Juan Eusebio Nieremberg), *El machiavelismo degollado* (Alcalá, 1637).

[2] Giuseppe Toffanin, *La fine dell'umanesimo* (Turin, 1920).

[3] Roberto Ridolfi, *Vita di Niccolò Machiavelli* (Rome, 1954), trans. by Cecil Grayson as *The Life of Niccolò Machiavelli* (London and Chicago, 1963).

[4] *The Discourses of Niccolò Machiavelli*, trans. and ed. Leslie J. Walker (London, 1950).

[5] Felice Alderisio, *Machiavelli: l'Arte dello Stato nell'azione e negli scritti* (Turin, 1930).

[6] As quoted by Prezzolini, op. cit. (p. 269 above, note 1), English version, p. 231.

[7] op. cit. (note 3 above), English version, p. 235.

[8] Croce ascribes to Machiavelli 'un'austera e dolorosa coscienza morale', *Elementi di politica* (Bari, 1925), p. 62. The idea that Machiavelli actually wishes to denounce naked power politics – what Gerhard Ritter in a volume of that name has called *Die Dämonie der Macht* – goes back to the sixteenth century (see L. Burd's still unsuperseded edition of *The Prince* (Oxford, 1891), pp. 31 ff.).

[9] op. cit. (note 8 above), p. 66; see Cochrane's comment, op. cit. (p. 269 above, note 1), p. 115, note 9.

Muralt[1] he is a peace-loving humanist, who believed in order, stability, pleasure in life, in the disciplining of the aggressive elements of our nature into the kind of civilised harmony that he found in its finest form among the well-armed Swiss democracies of his own time.[2]

For the neo-stoic Justus Lipsius and a century later for Algarotti (in 1759) and Alfieri[3] (in 1786) he was a passionate patriot, who saw in Cesare Borgia the man who, if he had lived, might have liberated Italy from the barbarous French and Spaniards and Austrians who were trampling over her and had reduced her to misery and poverty, decadence and chaos. Garrett Mattingly[4] could not credit this because it was obvious to him, and he did not doubt that it must have been no less obvious to Machiavelli, that Cesare was incompetent, a mountebank, a squalid failure; while Eric Vögelin seems to suggest that it is not Cesare, but (of all men) Tamerlane who was hovering before Machiavelli's fancy-laden gaze.[5]

For Cassirer,[6] Renaudet,[7] Olschki[8] and Keith Hancock,[9] Machiavelli is a cold technician, ethically and politically uncommitted, an objective analyst of politics, a morally neutral scientist, who (Karl Schmid[10] tells us) anticipated Galileo in applying inductive methods to social and historical material, and had no moral interest in the use made of his technical discoveries – equally ready to place them at the disposal of liberators and despots, good men and

---

[1] For references see Cochrane, ibid., p. 118, note 19.

[2] 'The Swiss are most free [liberissimi] because the best armed [armatissimi].' The Prince, chapter 12.

[3] Vittorio Alfieri, Del principe e delle lettere, book 2, chapter 9: pp. 172–3 in Opere, vol. 4, ed. Alessandro Donati (Bari, 1927).

[4] op. cit. (p. 271 above, note 2).

[5] Eric Vögelin, 'Machiavelli's Prince: Background and Formation', Review of Politics 13 (1951), 142–68.

[6] Ernst Cassirer, The Myth of the State (London and New Haven, Connecticut, 1946), chapter 12.

[7] Augustin Renaudet, Machiavel: étude d'histoire des doctrines politiques ([Paris], 1942).

[8] Leonardo Olschki, Machiavelli the Scientist (Berkeley, California, 1945).

[9] W. K. Hancock, 'Machiavelli in Modern Dress: An Enquiry into Historical Method', History 20 (1935–6), 97–115.

[10] Karl Schmid, 'Machiavelli', in Rudolf Stadelmann (ed.), Grosse Geschichts-denker (Tübingen/Stuttgart, 1949); see the illuminating review of Leonard von Muralt, Machiavellis Staatsgedanke (Basel, 1945), by A. P. d'Entrèves, English Historical Review 62 (1947), 96–9.

scoundrels. Renaudet describes his method as 'purely positivist', Cassirer, as concerned with 'political statics'. For Federico Chabod, though, he is not coldly calculating at all, but passionate to the point of unrealism;[1] Ridolfi, too, speaks of *il grande appassionato*,[2] and de Caprariis[3] thinks him positively visionary.

For Herder he is, above all, a marvellous mirror of his age, a man sensitive to the contours of his time, who faithfully described what others did not admit or recognise, an inexhaustible mine of acute contemporary observation; and this is accepted by Ranke and Macaulay, Burd and, in our day, Gennaro Sasso.[4] For Fichte he is a man of deep insight into the real historical (or super-historical) forces that mould men and transform their morality – in particular, a man who rejected Christian principles for those of reason, political unity and centralisation. For Hegel he is the man of genius who saw the need for uniting a chaotic collection of small and feeble principalities into a coherent whole; his specific nostrums may excite disgust, but they are accidents due to the conditions of their own time, now long past; yet, however obsolete his precepts, he understood something more important – the demands of his own age – that the hour had struck for the birth of the modern, centralised, political State, for the formation of which he 'established the truly necessary fundamental principles'.[5]

[1] In his original article of 1925 – 'Del "Principe" di Niccolò Machiavelli', *Nuova rivista storica* 9 (1925), 35–71, 189–216, 437–73; repr. as a book (Milan/Rome/Naples, 1926) – Chabod develops Croce's view in a direction closer to the conclusions of this article. See the English collection of Chabod's essays on Machiavelli, *Machiavelli and the Renaissance*, trans. David Moore, introduction by A. P. d'Entrèves (London, 1958), pp. 30–125 ('*The Prince*: Myth and Reality'), and *Scritti su Machiavelli* (Turin, 1964), pp. 29–135.

[2] op. cit. (p. 272 above, note 3), Italian version, p. 364.

[3] Vittorio de Caprariis, review of Renaudet, op. cit. (p. 273 above, note 7), *Rivista storica italiana* 60 (1948), 287–9.

[4] Gennaro Sasso, *Niccolò Machiavelli* (Naples, 1958).

[5] If Machiavelli's *Prince* is viewed in its historical context – of a divided, invaded, humiliated Italy – it emerges not as a disinterested 'summary of moral and political principles, appropriate to all situations and therefore to none', but 'as a most magnificent and true conception on the part of a man of genuine political genius, a man of the greatest and noblest mind' (*Die Verfassung Deutschlands*, in *Schriften zur Politik und Rechtsphilosophie* (*Sämtliche Werke*, ed. Georg Lasson, vol. 7), 2nd ed. (Leipzig, 1923), p. 113). See p. 135 of the same work for Hegel's defence of 'die Gewalt eines Eroberers' conceived as a unifier of German lands. He regarded Machiavelli as a forerunner in an analogous Italian situation.

The thesis that Machiavelli was above all an Italian and a patriot, speaking principally to his own generation, and if not solely to Florentines, at any rate only to Italians, and must be judged solely, or at least mainly, in terms of his historical context, is a position common to Herder and Hegel, Macaulay and Burd, de Sanctis and Oreste Tommasini.[1] Yet for Herbert Butterfield[2] and Raffaello Ramat[3] he suffers from an equal lack of scientific and historical sense. Obsessed by classical authors, his gaze is on an imaginary past; he deduces his political maxims in an unhistorical and a priori manner from dogmatic axioms (according to Lauri Huovinen)[4] – a method that was already becoming obsolete at the time in which he was writing; in this respect his slavish imitation of antiquity is judged to be inferior to the historical sense and sagacious judge-

---

[1] Especially Tommasini in his huge compendium, *La vita e gli scritti di Niccolò Machiavelli nella loro relazione col machiavellismo* (vol. 1, Rome/Turin/Florence, 1883; vol. 2, Rome, 1911). In this connection Ernst Cassirer makes the valid and relevant point that to value – or justify – Machiavelli's opinions solely as a mirror of their times is one thing; to maintain that he was himself consciously addressing only his own countrymen and, if Burd is to be believed, not even all of them, is a very different one, and entails a false view of him and the civilisation to which he belonged. The Renaissance did not view itself in historical perspective. Machiavelli was looking for – and thought that he had found – timeless, universal truths about social behaviour. It is no service either to him or to the truth to deny or ignore the unhistorical assumptions which he shared with all his contemporaries and predecessors. The praise lavished upon him by the German historical school from Herder onwards, including the Marxist Antonio Gramsci, for the gifts in which they saw his strength – his realistic sense of his own times, his insight into the rapidly changing social and political conditions of Italy and Europe in his time, the collapse of feudalism, the rise of the national State, the altering power relationships within the Italian principalities and the like – might have been galling to a man who believed he had discovered eternal verities. He may, like his countryman Columbus, have mistaken the nature of his own achievement. If the historical school (including the Marxists) is right, Machiavelli did not do, and could not have done, what he set out to do. But nothing is gained by supposing he did not set out to do it; and plenty of witnesses from his day to ours would deny Herder's assertion, and maintain that Machiavelli's goal – the discovery of the permanent principles of a political science – was anything but Utopian; and that he came nearer than most to attaining it.

[2] Herbert Butterfield, *The Statecraft of Machiavelli* (London, 1955).

[3] Raffaello Ramat, '*Il Principe*', in *Per la storia dello stile rinascimentale* (Messina/Florence, 1953), pp. 75–118.

[4] Lauri Huovinen, *Das Bild vom Menschen im politischen Denken Niccolò Machiavellis* (*Annales Academiae Scientiarum Fennicae*, series B, vol. 74 (Helsinki, 1951), No 2).

ment of his friend Guicciardini (so much for the discovery in him of inklings of modern scientific method).

For Bacon[1] (as for Spinoza, and later for Lassalle) he is above all the supreme realist and avoider of Utopian fantasies. Boccalini[2] is shocked by him, but cannot deny the accuracy or importance of his observations; so is Meinecke,[3] for whom he is the father of *Staatsräson*, with which he plunged a dagger into the body politic of the West, inflicting a wound which only Hegel would know how to heal (this is Meinecke's optimistic verdict in the 1920s, apparently withdrawn after the Second World War).

For König[4] he is not a tough-minded realist or cynic at all, but an aesthete seeking to escape from the chaotic and squalid world of the decadent Italy of his time into a dream of pure art, a man not interested in practice who painted an ideal political landscape; much (if I understand this view correctly) as Piero della Francesca painted an ideal city; *The Prince* is to be read as an idyll in the best neo-classical, neo-pastoral, Renaissance style (yet De Sanctis in the second volume of his *History of Italian Literature* denies it a place in the humanist tradition on account of Machiavelli's hostility to imaginative visions).

---

[1] 'We are much beholden to Machiavelli and other writers of that class, who openly and unfeignedly declare and describe what men do, and not what they ought to do.' Bacon goes on to qualify this by explaining that to know the good one must investigate the evil, and ends by calling such approaches 'corrupt wisdom' (*De augmentis*, book 7, chapter 2, and book 8, chapter 2: quoted from *The Works of Francis Bacon*, ed. J. Spedding and others (London, 1857–74), vol. 5, pp. 17 and 76). Compare Machiavelli's aphorism in a letter to Guicciardini, No 179 in Niccolò Machiavelli, *Lettere familiari*, ed. Edoardo Alvisi (Florence, 1883): 'io credo che questo sarebbe il vero modo ad andare in Paradiso, imparare la via dell'Inferno per fuggirla'. A. P. d'Entrèves kindly drew my attention to this characteristic passage; so far as I know there is no reason for supposing that Bacon had any knowledge of it. Nor, it may be, had T. S. Eliot when he wrote 'Lord Morley ... intimates that Machiavelli ... saw only half of the truth about human nature. What Machiavelli did not see about human nature is the myth of human goodness which for liberal thought replaces the belief in Divine Grace' ('Niccolò Machiavelli', in *For Lancelot Andrewes* (London, 1970), p. 50).

[2] Traiano Boccalini, *Ragguagli di Parnaso*, centuria prima, No 89.

[3] Friedrich Meinecke, *Die Idee der Staatsräson in der neueren Geschichte*, 2nd ed. (Munich/Berlin, 1927), trans. by Douglas Scott as *Machiavellism* (London, 1957).

[4] René König, *Niccolo Machiavelli: Zur Krisenanalyse einer Zeitenwende* (Erlenbach-Zurich, 1941).

For Renzo Sereno[1] it is a fantasy indeed, but of a bitterly frustrated man, and its dedication is the 'desperate plea'[2] of a victim of 'Fortune's great and steady malice'.[3] A psychoanalytic interpretation of one queer episode in Machiavelli's life is offered in support of his thesis.

For Macaulay Machiavelli is a political pragmatist and a patriot who cared most of all for the independence of Florence, and acclaimed any form of rule that would ensure it.[4] Marx calls the *History of Florence* a 'masterpiece', and Engels (in the *Dialectics of Nature*) speaks of Machiavelli as one of the 'giants' of the Enlightenment, a man free from *petit-bourgeois* outlook. Soviet criticism is more ambivalent.[5]

For the restorers of the short-lived Florentine republic he was evidently nothing but a venal and treacherous toady, anxious to serve any master, who had unsuccessfully tried to flatter the Medici in the hope of gaining their favour. George Sabine (in his well-

---

[1] Renzo Sereno, 'A Falsification by Machiavelli', *Renaissance News* 12 (1959), 159–67.

[2] ibid., p. 166.

[3] *The Prince*, dedication (trans. by Allan Gilbert in Machiavelli, *The Chief Works and Others*, 3 vols (Durham, North Carolina, 1965), vol. 1, p. 11: all quotations in this essay from Machiavelli's writings are given in this version, unless otherwise stated).

[4] For an extended modern development of this, see Judith Janoska-Bendl, 'Niccolò Machiavelli: Politik ohne Ideologie', *Archiv für Kulturgeschichte* 40 (1958), 315–45.

[5] The only extended treatment of Machiavelli by a prominent Bolshevik intellectual known to me is in Kamenev's short-lived introduction to the Russian translation of *The Prince* (Moscow, 1934), reprinted in English as 'Preface to Machiavelli', *New Left Review* No 15 (May–June 1962), 39–42. This unswervingly follows the full historicist-sociological approach criticised by Cassirer. Machiavelli is described as an active publicist, preoccupied by the 'mechanism of the struggles for power' within and between the Italian principalities, a sociologist who gave a masterly analysis of the 'sociological' jungle that preceded the formation of a 'powerful, national, essentially bourgeois' Italian State. His almost 'dialectical' grasp of the realities of power, and freedom from metaphysical and theological fantasies, establish him as a worthy forerunner of Marx, Engels, Lenin and Stalin. These opinions were brought up at Kamenev's trial and pilloried by Vyshinsky, the prosecutor. See on this Chimen Abramsky, 'Kamenev's Last Essay', *New Left Review* No 15 (May–June 1962), 34–8; and, on the peculiar fate of Machiavelli in Russia, Jan Malarczyk, *Politicheskoe uchenia Makiavelli v Rossii, v russkoi dorevolyutsionnoi i sovetskoi istoriografii* (*Annales Universitatis Mariae Curie-Sklodkowska*, vol. 6, No 1, section G, 1959 (Lubin, 1960)).

known textbook)[1] views him as an anti-metaphysical empiricist, a Hume or Popper before his time, free from obscurantist, theological and metaphysical preconceptions. For Antonio Gramsci[2] he is above all a revolutionary innovator who directs his shafts against the obsolescent feudal aristocracy and papacy and their mercenaries; his *Prince* is a myth which signifies the dictatorship of new, progressive forces: ultimately the coming role of the masses and of the need for the emergence of new politically realistic leaders – *The Prince* is 'an anthropomorphic symbol' of the hegemony of the 'collective will'.

Like Jakob Burckhardt[3] and Friedrich Meinecke,[4] C. J. Friedrich[5] and Charles Singleton[6] maintain that he has a developed conception of the State as a work of art; the great men who have founded or maintain human associations are conceived as analogous to artists whose aim is beauty, and whose essential qualification is understanding of their material – they are moulders of men, as sculptors are moulders of marble or clay.[7] Politics, in this view, leaves the realm of ethics, and approaches that of aesthetics. Singleton argues that Machiavelli's originality consists in his view of political action as a form of what Aristotle called 'making' – the goal of which is a non-moral artefact, an object of beauty or use external to man (in this case a particular arrangement of human affairs) – and not of 'doing' (where Aristotle and Aquinas had placed it), the goal of which is internal and moral, not the creation of an object, but a particular kind – the right way – of living or being.

This position is not distant from that of Villari, Croce and others, inasmuch as it ascribes to Machiavelli the divorce of politics from ethics. Singleton transfers Machiavelli's conception of politics to the region of art, which is conceived as being amoral.

---

[1] George H. Sabine, *A History of Political Theory* (London, 1951).

[2] Antonio Gramsci, *Note sul Machiavelli*, in *Opere*, vol. 5 (Turin, 1949).

[3] Jakob Burckhardt, *The Civilization of the Renaissance in Italy*, trans. S. G. C. Middlemore (London, 1929), part 1, chapter 7, pp. 104 ff.

[4] op. cit. (p. 276 above, note 3).

[5] C. J. Friedrich, *Constitutional Reason of State* (Providence, Rhode Island, 1957).

[6] Charles S. Singleton, 'The Perspective of Art', *Kenyon Review* 15 (1953), 169–89.

[7] See Joseph Kraft, 'Truth and Poetry in Machiavelli', *Journal of Modern History* 23 (1951), 109–21.

Croce gives it an independent status of its own: of politics for politics' sake.

But the commonest view of him, at least as a political thinker, is still that of most Elizabethans, dramatists and scholars alike, for whom he is a man inspired by the Devil to lead good men to their doom, the great subverter, the teacher of evil, *le docteur de la scélératesse*, the inspirer of St Bartholomew's Eve, the original of Iago. This is the 'murderous Machiavel' of the famous four-hundred-odd references in Elizabethan literature.[1] His name adds a new ingredient to the more ancient figure of Old Nick. For the Jesuits he is 'the devil's partner in crime', 'a dishonourable writer and an unbeliever', and *The Prince* is, in Bertrand Russell's words, 'a handbook for gangsters' (compare with this Mussolini's description of it as a *'vade mecum* for statesmen', a view tacitly shared, perhaps, by other heads of State). This is the view common to Protestants and Catholics, Gentillet and François Hotman, Cardinal Pole, Bodin and Frederick the Great, followed by the authors of all the many anti-Machiavels, among the latest of whom are Jacques Maritain[2] and Leo Strauss.[3]

There is prima facie something strange about so violent a disparity of judgements.[4] What other thinker has presented so

[1] Edward Meyer, *Machiavelli and the Elizabethan Drama* (Weimar, 1897). See on this Christopher Morris, 'Machiavelli's Reputation in Tudor England', *Il pensiero politico* 2 (1969), 416–33, especially p. 423. See also Mario Praz, 'Machiavelli and the Elizabethans', *Proceedings of the British Academy* 13 (1928), 49–97; Napoleone Orsini, 'Elizabethan Manuscript Translations of Machiavelli's *Prince*', *Journal of the Warburg Institute* 1 (1937–8), 166–9; Felix Raab, *The English Face of Machiavelli* (London, 1964; Toronto, 1965); J. G. A. Pocock, 'Machiavelli, Harrington and English Political Ideologies in the Eighteenth Century', in *Politics, Language and Time* (London, 1972), pp. 104–47; and, most famous of all, Wyndham Lewis, *The Lion and the Fox* (London, 1951). Zera S. Fink in *The Classical Republicans* (Evanston, 1945), J. G. A. Pocock and Felix Raab stress his positive influence in seventeenth-century England, with Bacon and Harrington at the head of his admirers.

[2] Jacques Maritain, 'The End of Machiavellianism', *Review of Politics* 4 (1942), 1–33.

[3] Leo Strauss, *Thoughts on Machiavelli* (Glencoe, Illinois, 1958).

[4] One of the best and liveliest accounts of the mass of conflicting theories about *The Prince* is provided by E. W. Cochrane in the article cited above on p. 269, note 1, to which this catalogue owes a great deal. For earlier conflicts see Pasquale Villari's standard and in some ways still unsuperseded *The Life and Times of Niccolò Machiavelli*, trans. Linda Villari (London, 1898), and the earlier works cited by him, e.g. Robert von Mohl, 'Die Machiavelli-Literatur', in *Die*

many facets to the students of his ideas? What other writer – and he not even a recognised philosopher – has caused his readers to disagree about his purposes so deeply and so widely? Yet, I must repeat, Machiavelli does not write obscurely; nearly all his interpreters praise him for his terse, dry, clear prose.

What is it that has proved so arresting to so many? Let me deal with some obvious answers. It is no doubt astonishing to find a thinker so free from what we have been taught to regard as being the normal intellectual assumptions of his age. Machiavelli does not so much as mention natural law, the basic category in terms of which (or rather the many varieties of which) Christians and pagans, teleologists and materialists, jurists, theologians and philosophers, before and indeed for many decades after him, discussed the very topics to which he applied his mind. He was of course not a philosopher or a jurist: nevertheless he was a political expert, a well-read man of letters. The influence of the old Stoic-Christian doctrine was not, by his time, what it had once been in Italy, especially among the early humanists. Still, having set himself to generalise about the behaviour of men in society in a novel fashion, Machiavelli might have been expected, if not to refute or reject explicitly, at least to deliver a glancing blow at some of the assumptions which, he clearly thinks, have led so many to their doom. He does, after all, tell us that his path has never before been trodden by any man, and this, in his case, is no mere cliché: there is, therefore, something extraordinary in the fact that he completely ignores the concepts and categories – the routine paraphernalia – in terms of which the best-known thinkers and scholars of his day were accustomed to express themselves. And, indeed, Gentillet in his *Contre-Machiavel* denounces him precisely for this. Only Marsilio before him had dared do this: and Neville Figgis thinks it a dramatic break with the past.[1]

The absence of Christian psychology and theology – sin, grace, redemption, salvation – need cause less surprise: few contemporary humanists speak in such terms. The medieval heritage has grown very thin. But, and this is more noteworthy, there is no trace of Platonic or Aristotelian teleology, no reference to any ideal order,

*Geschichte und Literatur der Staatswissenschaften* (Erlangen, 1855–8), vol. 3, pp. 519–91), and J. F. Christius, *De Nicolao Machiavelli libri tres* (Leipzig, 1731). For later works see above, p. 269, note 1.

[1] John Neville Figgis, *Studies of Political Thought from Gerson to Grotius*, 2nd ed. (Cambridge, 1916).

to any doctrine of man's place in nature in the great chain of being, with which the Renaissance thinkers are deeply concerned – which, say, Ficino or Pico or Poggio virtually take for granted. There is nothing here of what Popper has called 'essentialism', a priori certainty directly revealed to reason or intuition about the unalterable development of men or social groups in certain directions, in pursuit of goals implanted in them by God or by nature. The method and the tone are empirical. Even Machiavelli's theory of historical cycles is not metaphysically guaranteed.

As for religion, it is for him not much more than a socially indispensable instrument, so much utilitarian cement: the criterion of the worth of a religion is its role as a promoter of solidarity and cohesion – he anticipates Saint-Simon and Durkheim in stressing its crucial social importance. The great founders of religions are among the men he most greatly admires. Some varieties of religion (for example, Roman paganism) are good for societies, since they make them strong or spirited; others on the contrary (for example, Christian meekness and unworldliness) cause decay or disintegration. The weakening of religious ties is a part of general decadence and corruption: there is no need for a religion to rest on truth, provided that it is socially effective.[1] Hence his veneration of those who set their societies on sound spiritual foundations – Moses, Numa, Lycurgus.

There is no serious assumption of the existence of God and divine law; whatever our author's private convictions, an atheist can read Machiavelli with perfect intellectual comfort. Nor is there piety towards authority, or prescription – nor any interest in the role of the individual conscience, or in any other metaphysical or theological issue. The only freedom he recognises is political freedom, freedom from arbitrary despotic rule, that is, republicanism, and the freedom of one State from control by other States, or rather of the city or *patria*, for 'State' may be a premature term in this connection.[2]

---

[1] *Discourses* i 12.

[2] See on this much-discussed issue the relevant theses of J. H. Whitfield in *Machiavelli* (Oxford, 1947), especially pp. 93–5, and J. H. Hexter in '*Il principe* and *lo stato*', *Studies in the Renaissance* 4 (1957), 113–35, and the opposed views of Fredi Chiapelli in *Studi sul linguaggio del Machiavelli* (Florence, 1952), pp. 59–73, Francesco Ercole in *La politica di Machiavelli* (Rome, 1926) and Felix Gilbert, op. cit. (p. 269 above, note 1), pp. 328–30. For an earlier version of Gilbert's anti-Ercole thesis see his 'The Concept of Nationalism in Machiavelli's

There is no notion of the rights of, or obligation to, corporations or non-political establishments, sacred or secular – the need for absolute centralised power (if not for sovereignty) is taken for granted. There is scarcely any historical sense: men are much the same everywhere, and at all times, and what has served well for the ancients – their rules of medicine, or warfare, or statecraft – will surely also work for the moderns. Tradition is valued chiefly as a source of social stability. Since there is no far-off divine event to which creation moves and no Platonic ideal for societies or individuals, there is no notion of progress, either material or spiritual. The assumption is that the blessings of the classical age can be restored (if fortune is not too unpropitious) by enough knowledge and will, by *virtù* on the part of a leader, and by appropriately trained and bravely and skilfully led citizens. There are no intimations of an irrevocably determined flow of events; neither *fortuna* nor *necessità* dominates the whole of existence; there are no absolute values which men ignore or deny to their inevitable doom.

It is, no doubt, this freedom from even such relics of the traditional metaphysics of history as linger on in the works of even such perfectly secular humanists as Egidio and Pontano, not to mention earlier authors of 'mirrors for princes', as well as Machiavelli's constant concern with the concrete and practical issues of his day, and not any mysterious presentiment of the coming scientific revolution, that gives him so modern a flavour. Yet it is plainly not these characteristics that have proved so deeply fascinating and horrifying to his readers from his day to our own. 'Machiavelli's doctrine', wrote Meinecke, 'was a sword thrust in the body politic of Western humanity, causing it to cry out and to struggle against itself.'[1]

What was it that was so upsetting in the views of Machiavelli? What was the 'dagger' and the 'unhealed wound' of which Meinecke speaks, 'the most violent mutilation suffered by the human practical intellect'[2] which Maritain so eloquently

*Prince', Studies in the Renaissance* 1 (1954), 38–48. H. C. Dowdall goes further and seems to maintain that it is, in effect, by inventing the word 'State' that Machiavelli founded modern political science: 'The Word "State"', *Law Quarterly Review* 39 (1923), 98–125.

[1] op. cit. (p. 276 above, note 3), English version, p. 49.

[2] op. cit. (p. 279 above, note 2), p. 3.

denounced? If it is not Machiavelli's (ruthless, but scarcely original) realism, nor his (relatively original, but by the eighteenth century pretty widespread) empiricism that proves so shocking during all these centuries, what was it?

'*Nothing*,' says one of his commentators:[1] *The Prince* is a mere tabulation of types of government and rulers, and of methods of maintaining them. It is this and no more. All the 'feeling and controversy' occasioned by it evidently rest on an almost universal misreading of an exceptionally clear, morally neutral text.

I cite this not uncommon view for fairness's sake. My own answer to the question will be clear if before offering it I state (in however brief and over-simplified a form) what I believe Machiavelli's positive beliefs to have been.

## II

Like the Roman writers whose ideals were constantly before his mind, like Cicero and Livy, Machiavelli believed that what men – at any rate superior men – sought was the fulfilment and the glory that come from the creation and maintenance by common endeavour of a strong and well-governed social whole. Only those will accomplish this who know the relevant facts. If you make mistakes and live in a state of delusion you will fail in whatever you undertake, for reality misunderstood – or, worse still, ignored or scorned – will always defeat you in the end. We can achieve what we want only if we understand firstly ourselves, and then the nature of the material with which we work.

Our first task, therefore, is the acquisition of such knowledge. This, for Machiavelli, was mainly psychological and sociological: the best source of information is a mixture of shrewd observation of contemporary reality together with whatever wisdom may be gleaned from the best observers of the past, in particular the great minds of antiquity, the sages whose company (as he says in his celebrated letter to Vettori) he seeks when he gets away from the trivial occupations of his daily life; these noble spirits, in their humanity, treat him kindly and yield answers to his questions; it is they who have taught him that men are in need of firm and energetic civil government. Different men pursue different ends,

[1] Jeffrey Pulver, *Machiavelli: The Man, His Work, and His Times* (London, 1937), p. 227.

and for each pursuit need an appropriate skill. Sculptors, doctors, soldiers, architects, statesmen, lovers, adventurers each pursue their own particular goals. To make it possible for them to do so, governments are needed, for there is no hidden hand which brings all these human activities into natural harmony. (This kind of approach is wholly typical of the humanism of Machiavelli's country and his time.) Men need rulers because they require someone to order human groups governed by diverse interests and bring them security, stability, above all protection against enemies, to establish social institutions which alone enable men to satisfy their needs and aspirations. They will never attain to this unless they are individually and socially healthy; only an adequate education can make them physically and mentally sturdy, vigorous, ambitious and energetic enough for effective co-operation in the pursuit of order, power, glory, success.

Techniques of government exist – of that he has no doubt – although the facts, and therefore the methods of dealing with them, may look different to a ruler and to his subjects. This is a matter of perspective: 'those who draw maps of countries put themselves low down on the plains to observe the nature of mountains . . . and to observe that of low places put themselves high up on mountain tops'.[1] What is certain is that unless there is a firm hand at the helm, the ship of State will founder. Human society will collapse into chaos and squalor unless a competent specialist directs it; and although Machiavelli himself gives reasons for preferring freedom and republican rule, there are situations in which a strong prince (the Duke of Valentino, even a Medici, if his plea had any sincerity to it) is preferable to a weak republic.

All this Aristotle and the later Stoics would have endorsed. But from the fact that there is such a thing as an art of government, indispensable to the attainment of goals that men in fact seek, it does not follow that Machiavelli did not care to what uses it was applied, and merely produced a handbook of scientific political 'directives' that was morally neutral, *wertfrei*. For he makes it all too plain what it is that he himself desires.

Men must be studied in their behaviour as well as in their professions. There is no a priori route to the knowledge of the human material with which a ruler must deal. There is, no doubt, an unchanging human nature the range of whose response to

---

[1] *The Prince*, dedication.

changing situations can be determined (there is no trace in Machiavelli's thought of any notion of systematic evolution or of the individual or society as a self-transforming entity); one can obtain this knowledge only by empirical observation. Men are not as they are described by those who idealise them – Christians or other Utopians – nor by those who want them to be widely different from what in fact they are and always have been and cannot help being. Men (at least his own countrymen for and about whom he was writing) seem to him for the most part to be 'ungrateful, wanton, false and dissimulating, cowardly and greedy . . . arrogant and mean, their natural impulse is to be insolent when their affairs are prospering and abjectly servile when adversity hits them'.[1] They care little for liberty – the name means more to them than the reality – and they place it well below security, property or desire for revenge. These last the ruler can provide to a reasonable degree. Men are easily corrupted, and difficult to cure. They respond both to fear and to love, to the cruel Hannibal and to the just and humane Scipio. If these emotions cannot be combined, fear is the more reliable: provided always that it does not turn to hate, which destroys the minimum of respect that subjects must retain for those who govern them.

Society is, normally, a battlefield in which there are conflicts between and within groups. These conflicts can be controlled only by the judicious use of both persuasion and force. How is this done? As in medicine, architecture or the art of war, we can obtain systematic knowledge of the required technique if only we will look at the practice (and the theory) of the most successful societies we know, namely those of classical times.

Machiavelli's theories are certainly not based on the scientific principles of the seventeenth century. He lived a hundred years before Galileo and Bacon, and his method is a mixture of rules of thumb, observation, historical knowledge and general sagacity, somewhat like the empirical medicine of the pre-scientific world. He abounds in precepts, in useful maxims, practical hints, scattered reflections, especially historical parallels, even though he claims to have discovered general laws, eternally valid *regole generali*. An example of a triumph or a failure in the ancient world, a striking

---

[1] This celebrated passage from the seventeenth chapter of *The Prince* is here given in Prezzolini's vivid rendering: see his 'The Christian Roots of Machiavelli's Moral Pessimism', *Review of National Literatures* 1 (1970), 26–37 at p. 27.

saying by an ancient author, carries more weight with him (as Butterfield and Ramat correctly note) than historical analysis of the type that was becoming common even in his own day, and of which Guicciardini was a master.

Above all he warns one to be on one's guard against those who do not look at men as they are, and see them through spectacles coloured by their hopes and wishes, their loves and hatreds, in terms of an idealised model of man as they want him to be, and not as he is and was and will be. Honest reformers, however worthy their ideals, like the worthy leader of the Florentine Republic, Piero Soderini, whom Machiavelli served, or the far more gifted Savonarola (towards whom his attitude oscillates sharply), foundered and caused the ruin of others, largely because they substituted what should be for what is; because at some point they fell into unrealism.

They were men of a very different quality. Savonarola had a strong will, whereas Soderini was, in Machiavelli's view, small-minded and indecisive. But what they had in common was an inadequate grasp of how to use power. At the crucial moment they both showed their lack of a sense of *verità effettuale* in politics, of what works in practice, of real power, of the big battalions. Machiavelli's texts contain frequent warnings against unreliable sources of information, émigrés for example, whose minds are distorted by their wishes and cannot attain to an objective view of the facts, and others whose reason (this is a humanist common-place) is darkened by the passions that distort their vision.

What has led and will lead such statesmen to their doom? Often enough only their ideals. What is wrong with ideals? That they cannot be attained. How does one know this? This is one of the foundations upon which Machiavelli's claim to be a thinker of the first order ultimately rests. Machiavelli has a clear vision of the society which he wishes to see realised on earth, or, if this sounds too grandiose for so concrete and applied a thinker, the society which he wishes to see attained in his own country, perhaps even in his own lifetime; at any rate within the predictable future. He knows that such an order can be created, because it, or something sufficiently close to it, has been realised in Italy in the past, or in other countries – the Swiss or German cities for example, or the great centralised States in his own time. It is not merely that he wishes to create or restore such an order in Italy, but that he sees in it the most desirable condition that can, as both history and observation teach, be attained by men.

The data of observation are drawn mainly from contemporary Italy; as for history, it is for him what had been recorded by the great historians, the writers whom he most admires, Romans, Greeks, the authors of the Old Testament. Where have men risen to their full height? In Periclean Athens, and in the greatest period of human history – the Roman Republic before its decline, when Rome ruled the world. But he thinks well, too, of the reigns of the 'good' emperors, from Nerva to Marcus Aurelius. He does not feel that he needs to demonstrate that these were golden hours in the life of humanity; this, he believes, must be self-evident to anyone who contemplates these epochs and compares them with the bad periods – the last years of the Roman Republic, the collapse that followed, the barbarian invasion, the medieval darkness (although he may not have thought of it in these terms), the divisions of Italy, the weakness, the poverty, the misery, the defencelessness of the faction-ridden Italian principalities of his own day before the trampling armies of the great, well-organised national States of the north and the west.

He does not trouble to argue this at length: it seems to him perfectly obvious (as it must have done to most men of his age) that Italy was both materially and morally in a bad way. He did not need to explain what he meant by vice, corruption, weakness, lives unworthy of human beings. A good society is a society that enjoys stability, internal harmony, security, justice, a sense of power and of splendour, like Athens in its best days, like Sparta, like the kingdoms of David and Solomon, like Venice as it used to be, but, above all, like the Roman Republic. 'Truly it is a marvellous thing to consider to what greatness Athens came in the space of a hundred years after she freed herself from the tyranny of Pisistratus. But above all, it is very marvellous to observe what greatness Rome came to after she freed herself from her kings.'[1]

The reason for this is that there were men in these societies who knew how to make cities great. How did they do it? By developing certain faculties in men, of inner moral strength, magnanimity, vigour, vitality, generosity, loyalty, above all public spirit, civic sense, dedication to the security, power, glory, expansion of the

[1] *Discourses* ii 2.

*patria*. The ancients developed these qualities by all kinds of means, among which were dazzling shows and bloodstained sacrifices that excited men's senses and aroused their martial prowess, and especially by the kind of legislation and education that promoted the pagan virtues. Power, magnificence, pride, austerity, pursuit of glory, vigour, discipline, *antiqua virtus* – this is what makes States great. Agesilaus and Timoleon, Brutus and Scipio are his heroes; not Pisistratus or Julius Caesar, who extinguished republican regimes and destroyed their spirit by exploiting human weaknesses. But there is no need to stay within Graeco-Roman confines: Moses and Cyrus are as deserving of respect as Theseus and Romulus – stern, sagacious and incorruptible men who founded nations and were rightly honoured by them.

What was done once can be done again. Machiavelli does not believe in the irreversibility of the historical process or the uniqueness of each of its phases. The glories of antiquity can be revived if only men vigorous and gifted and realistic enough can be mobilised for the purpose. In order to cure degenerate populations of their diseases, these founders of new States or Churches may be compelled to have recourse to ruthless measures, force and fraud, guile, cruelty, treachery, the slaughter of the innocent, surgical measures that are needed to restore a decayed body to a condition of health. And, indeed, these qualities may be needed even after a society has been restored to health; for men are weak and foolish and perpetually liable to lapse from the standards that alone can preserve them on the required height. Hence they must be kept in proper condition by measures that will certainly offend against current morality. But if they offend against this morality, in what sense can they be said to be justified? This seems to me to be the nodal point of Machiavelli's entire conception. In one sense they can be justified, and in another not; these senses must be distinguished more clearly than he found it necessary to do, for he was not a philosopher, and did not set himself the task of examining, or even spelling out, the implications of his own ideas.

Let me try to make this clearer. It is commonly said, especially by those who follow Croce, that Machiavelli divided politics from morals – that he recommended, as politically necessary, courses which common opinion morally condemns: for example, treading over corpses for the benefit of the State. Leaving aside the question of what was his conception of the State, and whether he in fact possessed one,[1] it seems to me that this is a false antithesis. For Machiavelli the ends which he advocates are those to which he thinks wise human beings, who understand reality, will dedicate their lives. Ultimate ends in this sense, whether or not they are those of the Judaeo-Christian tradition, are what is usually meant by moral values.

What Machiavelli distinguishes is not specifically moral from specifically political values;[2] what he achieves is not the emancipation of politics from ethics or religion, which Croce and many other commentators regard as his crowning achievement; what he institutes is something that cuts deeper still – a differentiation between two incompatible ideals of life, and therefore two moralities. One is the morality of the pagan world: its values are courage, vigour, fortitude in adversity, public achievement, order, discipline, happiness, strength, justice, above all assertion of one's proper claims and the knowledge and power needed to secure their satisfaction; that which for a Renaissance reader Pericles had seen embodied in his ideal Athens, Livy had found in the old Roman Republic, that of which Tacitus and Juvenal lamented the decay and death in their own time. These seem to Machiavelli the best hours of mankind and, Renaissance humanist that he is, he wishes to restore them.

Against this moral universe (moral or ethical no less in Croce's than in the traditional sense, that is, embodying ultimate human ends however these are conceived) stands in the first and foremost place Christian morality. The ideals of Christianity are charity, mercy, sacrifice, love of God, forgiveness of enemies, contempt for the goods of this world, faith in the life hereafter, belief in the salvation of the individual soul as being of incomparable value – higher than, indeed wholly incommensurable with, any social or political or other terrestrial goal, any economic or military or aesthetic consideration. Machiavelli lays it down that out of men who believe in such ideals, and practise them, no satisfactory human community, in his Roman sense, can in principle be constructed. It is not simply a question of the unattainability of an ideal because of human imperfection, original sin, or bad luck, or

---

[1] See p. 281 above, note 2.

[2] For which he is commended by de Sanctis, and (as Prezzolini points out, op. cit., p. 269 above, note 1) condemned by Maurice Joly in the famous *Dialogue aux enfers entre Machiavel et Montesquieu* (Brussels, 1864), which served as the original of the forged *Protocols of the Learned Elders of Zion* (London, 1920).

ignorance, or insufficiency of material means. It is not, in other words, the inability in practice on the part of ordinary human beings to rise to a sufficiently high level of Christian virtue (which may, indeed, be the inescapable lot of sinful men on earth) that makes it, for him, impracticable to establish, even to seek after, the good Christian State. It is the very opposite: Machiavelli is convinced that what are commonly thought of as the central Christian virtues, whatever their intrinsic value, are insuperable obstacles to the building of the kind of society that he wishes to see; a society which, moreover, he assumes that it is natural for all normal men to want – the kind of community that, in his view, satisfies men's permanent desires and interests.

If human beings were different from what they are, perhaps they could create an ideal Christian society. But he is clear that human beings would in that event have to differ too greatly from men as they have always been; and it is surely idle to build for, or discuss the prospects of, beings who can never be on earth; such talk is beside the point, and only breeds dreams and fatal delusions. What ought to be done must be defined in terms of what is practicable, not imaginary; statecraft is concerned with action within the limits of human possibility, however wide; men can be changed, but not to a fantastic degree. To advocate ideal measures, suitable only for angels, as previous political writers seem to him too often to have done, is visionary and irresponsible and leads to ruin.

It is important to realise that Machiavelli does not wish to deny that what Christians call good is, in fact, good, that what they call virtue and vice are in fact virtue and vice. Unlike Hobbes or Spinoza (or eighteenth-century *philosophes* or, for that matter, the first Stoics), who try to define (or redefine) moral notions in such a way as to fit in with the kind of community that, in their view, rational men must, if they are consistent, wish to build, Machiavelli does not fly in the face of common notions – the traditional, accepted moral vocabulary of mankind. He does not say or imply (as various radical philosophical reformers have done) that humility, kindness, unworldliness, faith in God, sanctity, Christian love, unwavering truthfulness, compassion are bad or unimportant attributes; or that cruelty, bad faith, power politics, sacrifice of innocent men to social needs, and so on are good ones.

But if history, and the insights of wise statesmen, especially in the ancient world, verified as they have been in practice (*verità effettuale*), are to guide us, it will be seen that it is in fact impossible to combine Christian virtues, for example meekness or the search for spiritual salvation, with a satisfactory, stable, vigorous, strong society on earth. Consequently a man must choose. To choose to lead a Christian life is to condemn oneself to political impotence: to being used and crushed by powerful, ambitious, clever, unscrupulous men; if one wishes to build a glorious community like those of Athens or Rome at their best, then one must abandon Christian education and substitute one better suited to the purpose.

Machiavelli is not a philosopher and does not deal in abstractions, but what his thesis comes to is of central concern to political theory: that it is a fact, which men will not face, that these two goals – both, evidently, capable of being believed in by human beings (and, we may add, of raising them to sublime heights) – are not compatible with one another. What usually happens, in his view, is that since men cannot bring themselves resolutely to follow either of these paths wherever they may lead ('men take certain middle ways that are very injurious; indeed, they are unable to be altogether good or altogether bad'),[1] they try to effect compromises, vacillate, fall between two stools, and end in weakness and failure.

Anything that leads to political ineffectiveness is condemned by him. In a famous passage in the *Discourses* he says that Christian faith has made men 'weak', easy prey to 'wicked men', since they 'think more about enduring their injuries than about avenging them'.[2] The general effect of Christian teaching has been to crush men's civic spirit, and make them endure humiliations uncomplainingly, so that destroyers and despots encounter too little resistance. Hence Christianity is in this respect compared unfavourably with Roman religion, which made men stronger and more 'ferocious'.

Machiavelli modifies this judgement on Christianity in at least two passages in the *Discourses*. In the first he observes that Christianity has had this unfortunate effect only because it was misinterpreted in a spirit of *ozio* – quietism or indolence – for there is surely nothing in Christianity which forbids 'the betterment and the defence of our country'.[3] In the second passage he declares that 'If religion of this sort had been kept up among the princes of Christendom, in the form in which its giver founded it, Christian

[1] *Discourses* i 26.
[2] ibid. ii 2.
[3] ibid.

States and republics would be more united, much more happy than they are',[1] but the decadent Christianity of the Church of Rome has had the opposite effect – the papacy has destroyed 'all piety and all religion' in Italy, and her unity too.

Even if these passages are taken literally, and are not viewed as pieces of minimum lip-service to avert clerical censorship or persecution, what they assert is that if the Church had developed a patriotic and thoroughly militant outlook, on the lines of Roman *antiqua virtus*, and had made men virile, stern, devout and public-spirited, it would have produced more satisfactory social consequences. What it has done is to lead, on the one hand, to corruption and political division – the fault of the papacy – and, on the other, to other-worldliness and meek endurance of suffering on earth for the sake of the eternal life beyond the grave. It is this last strain that dissolves the social fabric and helps bullies and oppressors.

In his political attack on the Church of Rome, shared by Guicciardini and others in his time, Machiavelli might have found enthusiastic allies in the Reformation (there is no evidence, so far as I know, that news of the 'monks' quarrel' had ever reached his ears). His demand for a Christianity which did not put the blessings of a pure conscience and faith in heaven above earthly success, and exalted love of glory and self-assertion above meekness and resignation, might have been more difficult to meet. Machiavelli finds nothing to criticise in pagan Roman religion at its most vigorous; he demands a similar religion – not necessarily wholly unchristian, but muscular enough to be, for practical purposes, no less effective. It does not seem unreasonable to conclude from this (as Fichte[2] and Prezzolini[3] tell us) that he is an implacable critic of truly Christian institutions, rather than their champion. In this he is followed by all those later thinkers who share with him either his conception of man and his natural needs (eighteenth-century materialists, Nietzsche, social Darwinists) or (like Rousseau and some nineteenth-century positivists) his civic ideals.

It is important to note that Machiavelli does not formally condemn Christian morality, or the approved values of his own

[1] ibid. i 12.

[2] *Johann Gottlieb Fichte's nachgelassene Werke*, ed. I. H. Fichte (Bonn, 1834–5), vol. 3, pp. 411–13.

[3] op. cit. (p. 269 above, note 1), English version, p. 43.

society. Unlike systematic moralists such as Hobbes or Spinoza he does not attempt to redefine terms to conform with an egoistic rationalism, so that such Christian virtues as, say, pity, humility, self-sacrifice, obedience are shown to be weaknesses or vices. He transposes nothing: the things men call good are indeed good. Words like *buono*, *cattivo*, *onesto*, *inumano* and so forth are used by him as they were in the common speech of his time, and indeed of our own. He merely says that the practice of these virtues makes it impossible to build a society which, once it is contemplated, in the pages of history or by the political imagination, will surely awaken in us – in any man – a great longing.

One of the crucial passages is to be found in the tenth chapter of the first book of the *Discourses*: he is distinguishing between the good and the bad Roman emperors on the lines of Tacitus or Dio, and adds 'if a prince is of human birth, he will be frightened away from any imitation of wicked times and will be fired with an immense eagerness [*immenso desiderio*] to follow the ways of good ones' – 'good' in some non-Christian sense, evidently. Whitfield thinks that he is not pessimistic or cynical. Perhaps not cynical – that is a fine point: the line between cynicism (and indeed pessimism too) and an unflinching realism is at times not easy to draw. But Machiavelli is not, in the usual sense of the word, hopeful. Yet, like every humanist thinker from his own day to ours, he believes that if only the truth were known – the real truth, not the fairy tales of shallow moralists – it would help to make men understand themselves and make them go farther.

He believes also that the qualities that men need in order to revive these *buoni tempi* are not compatible with those that are urged upon them by Christian education. He does not seek to correct the Christian conception of a good man. He does not say that saints are not saints, or that honourable behaviour is not honourable or to be admired; only that this type of goodness cannot, at least in its traditionally accepted forms, create or maintain a strong, secure and vigorous society, that it is in fact fatal to it. He points out that in our world men who pursue such ideals are bound to be defeated and to lead other people to ruin, since their view of the world is not founded upon the truth, at least not upon *verità effettuale* – the truth that is tested by success and experience – which (however cruel) is always, in the end, less destructive than the other (however noble).

If the two passages mentioned above[1] are to be taken literally, Christianity, at least in theory, could have taken a form not incompatible with the qualities that he celebrates; but, not surprisingly, he does not pursue this line of thought. History took another turn. The idea of such a Christian commonwealth – if he gave it a serious thought – must have seemed to him as Utopian as a world in which all or even most men are good. Christian principles have weakened men's civic virtues. Speculation on the form that Christianity might have taken, or could, in unlikely circumstances, still take, can for him only be an idle (and dangerous) pastime.

Christians as he knew them in history and his own experience, that is, men who in their practice actually follow Christian precepts, are good men, but if they govern States in the light of such principles they lead them to destruction. Like Prince Myshkin in Dostoevsky's *The Idiot*, like the well-meaning *Gonfalonieri* of the Florentine Republic, like Savonarola, they are bound to be defeated by the realists (the Medici or the Pope or King Ferdinand of Spain) who understand how to create lasting institutions; build them, if need be, on the bones of innocent victims. I should like to emphasise again that he does not explicitly condemn Christian morality: he merely points out that it is, at least in rulers (but to some degree in subjects too), incompatible with those social ends which he thinks it natural and wise for men to seek. One can save one's soul, or one can found or maintain or serve a great and glorious State; but not always both at once.

This is a vast and eloquent development of Aristotle's *obiter dictum* in the *Politics* that a good man may not be identical with a good citizen (even though Aristotle was not thinking in terms of spiritual salvation). Machiavelli does not explicitly rate either way of life above the other. When he says 'hate is incurred as much by means of good deeds as of bad',[2] he means by 'good deeds' what any man brought up to live by Christian values means. Again, when he says that good faith, integrity are 'praiseworthy'[3] even if they end in failure, he means by 'praiseworthy' that it is right to praise them, for of course what is good (in the ordinary sense) *is* good. When he praises the 'chastity, affability, courtesy and

---

[1] p. 291, note 3, and p. 292, note 1.
[2] *The Prince*, chapter 19.
[3] ibid., chapter 18.

liberality"[1] of Scipio or Cyrus or Timoleon, or even the 'goodness' of the Medici Pope Leo X, he speaks (whether he is sincere or not) in terms of values that are common to Cicero and Dante, to Erasmus and to us. In the famous fifteenth chapter of *The Prince* he says that liberality, mercy, honour, humanity, frankness, chastity, religion, and so forth, are indeed virtues, and a life lived in the exercise of these virtues would be successful if men were all good. But they are not; and it is idle to hope that they will become so. We must take men as we find them, and seek to improve them along possible, not impossible, lines.

This may involve the benefactors of men – the founders, educators, legislators, rulers – in terrible cruelties. 'I am aware that everyone will admit that it would be most praiseworthy for a prince to exhibit such of the above-mentioned qualities as are considered good. But because no ruler can possess or fully practise them, on account of human conditions that do not permit it',[2] he must at times behave very differently in order to compass his ends. Moses and Theseus, Romulus and Cyrus all killed; what they created lasted, and was glorious; 'any man who under all conditions insists on making it his business to be good will surely be destroyed among so many who are not good. Hence a prince . . . must acquire the power to be not good, and understand when to use it and when not to use it, in accord with necessity.'[3] 'If all men were good, this maxim [to break faith if interest dictates] would not be good, but . . . they are bad.'[4] Force and guile must be met with force and guile.

The qualities of the lion and the fox are not in themselves morally admirable, but if a combination of these qualities will alone preserve the city from destruction, then these are the qualities that leaders must cultivate. They must do this not simply to serve their own interest, that is, because this is how one can become a leader, although whether men become leaders or not is a matter of indifference to the author – but because human societies in fact stand in need of leadership, and cannot become what they should be, save by the effective pursuit of power, of stability, *virtù*, greatness. These can be attained when men are led by Scipios and

[1] ibid., chapter 14.
[2] ibid., chapter 15.
[3] ibid.
[4] ibid., chapter 18.

Timoleons or, if times are bad, men of more ruthless character. Hannibal was cruel, and cruelty is not a laudable quality, but if a sound society can be built only by conquest, and if cruelty is necessary to it, then it must not be evaded.

Machiavelli is not sadistic; he does not gloat on the need to employ ruthlessness or fraud for creating or maintaining the kind of society that he admires and recommends. His most savage examples and precepts apply only to situations in which the population is thoroughly corrupt, and needs violent measures to restore it to health, for example where a new prince takes over, or a revolution against a bad prince must be made effective. Where a society is relatively sound, or the rule is traditional and hereditary and supported by public sentiment, it would be quite wrong to practise violence for violence's sake, since its results would be destructive of social order, when the purpose of government is to create order, harmony, strength. If you are a lion and a fox you can afford virtue – chastity, affability, mercy, humanity, liberality, honour – as Agesilaus and Timoleon, Camillus, Scipio and Marcus did. But if circumstances are adverse, if you find yourself surrounded by treason, what can you do but emulate Philip and Hannibal and Severus?

Mere lust for power is destructive: Pisistratus, Dionysius, Caesar were tyrants and did harm. Agathocles, the tyrant of Syracuse, who gained power by killing his fellow citizens, betraying his friends, being 'without fidelity, without mercy, without religion', went too far, and so did not gain glory; 'his outrageous cruelty and inhumanity together with his countless wicked acts'[1] led to success, but since so much vice was not needed for it, he is excluded from the pantheon; so is the savage Oliverotto da Fermo, his modern counterpart, killed by Cesare Borgia. Still, to be altogether without these qualities guarantees failure; and that makes impossible the only conditions in which Machiavelli believed that normal men could successfully develop. Saints might not need them; anchorites could perhaps practise their virtues in the desert; martyrs will obtain their reward hereafter; but Machiavelli is plainly not interested in these ways of life and does not discuss them. He is a writer about government; he is interested in public affairs; in security, independence, success, glory, strength, vigour, felicity on earth, not in heaven; in the present and future as well as

[1] *The Prince*, chapter 8.

the past; in the real world, not an imaginary one. And for this, given unalterable human limitations, the code preached by the Christian Church, if it is taken seriously, will not do. Machiavelli, we are often told, was not concerned with morals. The most influential of all modern interpretations – that of Benedetto Croce, followed to some extent by Chabod, Russo and others – is that Machiavelli, in Cochrane's words:

> did not deny the validity of Christian morality, and he did not pretend that a crime required by political necessity was any less a crime. Rather he discovered . . . that this morality simply did not hold in political affairs and that any policy based on the assumption that it did would end in disaster. His factual, objective description of contemporary political practices, then, is a sign not of cynicism or of detachment, but of anguish.[1]

This account, it seems to me, contains two basic misinterpretations. The first is that the clash is one between 'Christian morality' and 'political necessity'. The implication is that there is an incompatibility between, on the one hand, morality – the region of ultimate values sought after for their own sakes, values recognition of which alone enables us to speak of 'crimes' or morally to justify and condemn anything; and, on the other, politics – the art of adapting means to ends, the region of technical skills, of what Kant was to call 'hypothetical imperatives', which take the form 'If you want to achieve $x$ do $y$ (for example, betray a friend, kill an innocent man)', without necessarily asking whether $x$ is itself intrinsically desirable or not. This is the heart of the divorce of politics from ethics which Croce and many others attribute to Machiavelli. But this seems to me to rest on a mistake.

If ethics is confined to, let us say, Stoic, or Christian or Kantian, or even some types of utilitarian ethics, where the source and criterion of value is the word of God, or eternal reason, or some inner sense or knowledge of good and evil, of right or wrong, voices which speak directly to individual consciousness with absolute authority, this might have been tenable. But there exists an equally time-honoured ethics, that of the Greek *polis*, of which Aristotle provided the clearest exposition. Since men are beings made by nature to live in communities, their communal purposes are the ultimate values from which the rest are derived, or with

---

[1] op. cit. (p. 269 above, note 1), p. 115.

which their ends as individuals are identified. Politics – the art of living in a *polis* – is not an activity which can be dispensed with by those who prefer private life: it is not like seafaring or sculpture, which those who do not wish to do so need not undertake. Political conduct is intrinsic to being a human being at a certain stage of civilisation, and what it demands is intrinsic to living a successful human life.

Ethics so conceived – the code of conduct of, or the ideal to be pursued by, the individual – cannot be known save by understanding the purpose and character of his *polis*: still less be capable of being divorced from it, even in thought. This is the kind of pre-Christian morality which Machiavelli takes for granted. 'It is well known', says Benedetto Croce,[1] 'that Machiavelli discovered the necessity and the autonomy of politics, politics which is beyond moral good and evil, which has its own laws against which it is futile to rebel, which cannot be exorcised and banished from the world with holy water.' Beyond good and evil in some non-Aristotelian, religious or liberal-Kantian sense; but not beyond the good and evil of those communities, ancient or modern, whose sacred values are social through and through. The arts of colonisation or of mass murder (let us say) may also have their 'own laws against which it is futile to rebel' for those who wish to practise them successfully. But if or when these laws collide with those of morality, it is possible and indeed morally imperative to abandon such activities.

But if Aristotle and Machiavelli are right about what men are (and should be – and Machiavelli's ideal is, particularly in the *Discourses*, drawn in vivid colours), political activity is intrinsic to human nature, and while individuals here and there may opt out, the mass of mankind cannot do so; and its communal life determines the moral duties of its members. Hence in opposing the 'laws of politics' to 'good and evil' Machiavelli is not contrasting two 'autonomous' spheres of acting – the 'political' and the 'moral': he is contrasting his own 'political' ethics with another conception of it which governs the lives of persons who are of no interest to him. He is indeed rejecting one morality – the Christian – but not in favour of something that cannot be described as a morality at all, but only as a game of skill, an activity called

[1] op. cit. (p. 272 above, note 8), p. 60.

political, which is not concerned with ultimate human ends, and is therefore not ethical at all.

He is indeed rejecting Christian ethics, but in favour of another system, another moral universe – the world of Pericles or of Scipio, or even of the Duke of Valentino, a society geared to ends just as ultimate as the Christian faith, a society in which men fight and are ready to die for (public) ends which they pursue for their own sakes. They are choosing not a realm of means (called politics) as opposed to a realm of ends (called morals), but opt for a rival (Roman or classical) morality, an alternative realm of ends. In other words the conflict is between two moralities, Christian and pagan (or, as some wish to call it, aesthetic), not between autonomous realms of morals and politics.

Nor is this a mere question of nomenclature, unless politics is conceived as being concerned not (as it usually is) with means, skills, methods, techniques, 'know-how', Croce's *pratica* (whether or not governed by unbreakable rules of its own), but with an independent kingdom of ends of its own, sought for their own sake, a substitute for ethics.[1] When Machiavelli said (in a letter to Francesco Vettori) that he loved his native city more than his own soul, he revealed his basic moral beliefs, a position with which Croce does not credit him.[2]

The second thesis in this connection which seems to me mistaken is the idea that Machiavelli viewed the crimes of his society with anguish. (Chabod in his excellent study, unlike Croce and some Croceans, does not insist on this.) This entails that he accepts the dire necessities of the *raison d'état* with reluctance, because he sees no alternative. But there is no evidence for this: there is no trace of agony in his political works, any more than in his plays or letters.

The pagan world that Machiavelli prefers is built on recognition of the need for systematic guile and force by rulers, and he seems to think it natural and not at all exceptional or morally agonising that they should employ these weapons wherever they are needed. Nor is the distinction he draws that between the rulers and the ruled. The subjects or citizens must be Romans too: they do not

---

[1] Meinecke, Prezzolini (op. cit., p. 269 above, note 1, English version, p. 432) and Ernesto Landi, 'The Political Philosophy of Machiavelli', trans. Maurice Cranston, *History Today* 14 (1964), 550–5, seem to me to approach this position most closely.

[2] Benedetto Croce, 'Per un detto del Machiavelli', *La critica* 28 (1930), 310–12.

need the *virtù* of the rulers, but if they also cheat, Machiavelli's maxims will not work; they must be poor, militarised, honest and obedient; if they lead Christian lives, they will accept too uncomplainingly the rule of mere bullies and scoundrels. No sound republic can be built of such materials as these. Theseus and Romulus, Moses and Cyrus did not preach humility to their subjects, or a view of this world as but a temporary resting-place.

But it is the first misinterpretation that goes deepest, that which represents Machiavelli as caring little or nothing for moral issues. This is surely not borne out by his own language. Anyone whose thought revolves round central concepts such as the good and the bad, the corrupt and the pure, has an ethical scale in mind in terms of which he gives moral praise and blame. Machiavelli's values are not Christian, but they are moral values.

On this crucial point Hans Baron's criticism of the Croce-Russo thesis[1] seems to me correct. Against the view that for Machiavelli politics were beyond moral criticism Baron cites some of the passionately patriotic, republican and libertarian passages in the *Discourses* in which the (moral) qualities of the citizens of a republic are favourably compared with those of the subjects of a despotic prince. The last chapter of *The Prince* is scarcely the work of a detached, morally neutral observer, or of a self-absorbed man, preoccupied with his own inner personal problems, who looks on public life 'with anguish' as the graveyard of moral principles. Like Aristotle's or Cicero's, Machiavelli's morality was social and not individual: but it is a morality no less than theirs, not an amoral region, beyond good or evil.

It does not, of course, follow that he was not often fascinated by the technique of political life as such. The advice given equally to conspirators and their enemies, the professional appraisal of the methods of Oliverotto or Sforza or Baglioni, spring from typical humanist curiosity, the search for an applied science of politics, fascination by knowledge for its own sake, whatever the implications. But the moral ideal, that of the citizen of the Roman Republic, is never far away. Political skills are valued solely as means – for their effectiveness in recreating conditions in which sick men recover their health and can flourish. And this is precisely what Aristotle would have called the moral end proper to man.

[1] Hans Baron, 'Machiavelli: the Republican Citizen and the Author of "The Prince"', *English Historical Review* 76 (1961), 217–53, *passim.*

This leaves still with us the thorny problem of the relation of *The Prince* to the *Discourses*. But whatever the disparities, the central strain which runs through both is one and the same. The vision – the dream – typical of many writers who see themselves as tough-minded realists – of the strong, united, effective, morally regenerated, splendid and victorious *patria*, whether it is saved by the *virtù* of one man or many – remains central and constant. Political judgements, attitudes to individuals or States, to *fortuna*, and *necessità*, evaluation of methods, degree of optimism, the fundamental mood – these vary between one work and another, perhaps within the same exposition. But the basic values, the ultimate end – Machiavelli's beatific vision – does not vary.

His vision is social and political. Hence the traditional view of him as simply a specialist on how to get the better of others, a vulgar cynic who says that Sunday-school precepts are all very well, but in a world full of evil men you too must lie, kill and so on if you are to get somewhere, is incorrect. The philosophy summarised by 'Eat or be eaten, beat or be beaten' – the kind of worldly wisdom to be found in, say, Mazzei[1] or Giovanni Morelli,[2] with whom he has been compared – is not what is central in him. Machiavelli is not specially concerned with the opportunism of ambitious individuals; the ideal before his eyes is a shining vision of Florence or of Italy; in this respect he is a typically impassioned humanist of the Renaissance, save that his ideal is not artistic or cultural but political, unless the State – or regenerated Italy – is considered, in Burckhardt's sense, as an artistic goal. This is very different from mere advocacy of tough-mindedness as such, or of a realism irrespective of its goal.

Machiavelli's values, I should like to repeat, are not instrumental but moral and ultimate, and he calls for great sacrifices in their name. For them he rejects the rival scale – the Christian principles of *ozio* and meekness – not, indeed, as being defective in itself, but as inapplicable to the conditions of real life; and real life for him means not merely (as is sometimes alleged) life as it was lived around him in Italy – the crimes, hypocrisies, brutalities, follies of Florence, Rome, Venice, Milan. This is not the touchstone of reality. His purpose is not to leave unchanged or to reproduce this

[1] Ser Lapo Mazzei, *Lettere di un notaro a un mercante del secolo XIV*, ed. Cesare Guasti (Florence, 1880).

[2] Giovanni di Pagolo Morelli, *Ricordi*, ed. Vittore Branca (Florence, 1956).

kind of life, but to lift it to a new plane, to rescue Italy from squalor and slavery, to restore her to health and sanity.

The moral ideal for which he thinks no sacrifice too great – the welfare of the *patria* – is for him the highest form of social existence attainable by man; but attainable, not unattainable; not a world outside the limits of human capacity, given human beings as we know them, that is, creatures compounded out of those emotional, intellectual and physical properties of which history and observation provide examples. He asks for men improved but not transfigured, not superhuman; not for a world of ideal beings unknown on this earth, who, even if they could be created, could not be called human.

If you object to the political methods recommended because they seem to you morally detestable, if you refuse to embark upon them because they are, to use Ritter's word, *erschreckend*, too frightening, Machiavelli has no answer, no argument. In that case you are perfectly entitled to lead a morally good life, be a private citizen (or a monk), seek some corner of your own. But, in that event, you must not make yourself responsible for the lives of others or expect good fortune; in a material sense you must expect to be ignored or destroyed.

In other words you can opt out of the public world, but in that case he has nothing to say to you, for it is to the public world and to the men in it that he addresses himself. This is expressed most clearly in his notorious advice to the victor who has to hold down a conquered province. He advises a clean sweep: new governors, new titles, new powers and new men; he should

> make the rich poor, the poor rich, as David did when he became king: 'the poor he filled with good things and the rich he sent away empty'. Besides this, he should build new cities, overthrow those already built, change the inhabitants from one place to another; and in short he should leave nothing in that province untouched, and make sure that no rank or position or office or wealth is held by anyone who does not acknowledge it as from you.[1]

He should take Philip of Macedon as his model, who 'grew in these ways until he became lord of Greece'.

Now Philip's historian informs us – Machiavelli goes on to say – that he transferred the inhabitants from one province to another 'as

---

[1] *Discourses* i 26.

herdsmen transfer their herds' from one place to another. Doubtless, Machiavelli continues:

> These methods are very cruel, and enemies to all government not
> merely Christian but human, and any man ought to avoid them and
> prefer to live a private life rather than to be a king who brings such
> ruin on men. Notwithstanding, a ruler who does not wish to take that
> first good way of lawful government, if he wishes to maintain himself,
> must enter upon this evil one. But men take certain middle ways that
> are very injurious; indeed, they are unable to be altogether good or
> altogether bad.[1]

This is plain enough. There are two worlds, that of personal
morality and that of public organisation. There are two ethical
codes, both ultimate; not two 'autonomous' regions, one of
'ethics', another of 'politics', but two (for him) exhaustive alternatives between two conflicting systems of value. If a man chooses
the 'first good way', he must, presumably, give up all hope of
Athens and Rome, of a noble and glorious society in which human
beings can thrive and grow strong, proud, wise and productive;
indeed, they must abandon all hope of a tolerable life on earth: for
men cannot live outside society; they will not survive collectively if
they are led by men who (like Soderini) are influenced by the first,
'private' morality; they will not be able to realise their minimal
goals as men; they will end in a state of moral, not merely political,
degradation. But if a man chooses, as Machiavelli himself has done,
the second course, then he must suppress his private qualms, if he
has any, for it is certain that those who are too squeamish during
the remaking of a society, or even during the pursuit and maintenance of its power and glory, will go to the wall. Whoever has
chosen to make an omelette cannot do so without breaking eggs.

Machiavelli is sometimes accused of too much relish at the
prospect of breaking eggs – almost for its own sake. This is unjust.
He thinks these ruthless methods are necessary – necessary as
means to provide good results, good in terms not of a Christian,
but of a secular, humanistic, naturalistic, morality. His most
shocking examples show this. The most famous, perhaps, is that of
Giovanpaolo Baglioni, who caught Julius II during one of his
campaigns, and let him escape, when in Machiavelli's view he might
have destroyed him and his cardinals and thereby committed a

[1] ibid.

crime 'the greatness of which would have transcended every infamy, every peril that could have resulted from it'.[1]

Like Frederick the Great (who called Machiavelli 'the enemy of mankind' and followed his advice),[2] Machiavelli is, in effect, saying 'Le vin est tiré: il faut le boire.' Once you embark on a plan for the transformation of a society you must carry it through no matter at what cost: to fumble, to retreat, to be overcome by scruples – this is to betray your chosen cause. To be a physician is to be a professional, ready to burn, to cauterise, to amputate; if that is what the disease requires, then to stop half-way because of personal qualms, or some rule unrelated to your art and its technique, is a sign of muddle and weakness, and will always give you the worst of both worlds. And there are at least two worlds: each of them has much, indeed everything, to be said for it; but they are two and not one. One must learn to choose between them, and having chosen, not look back.

There is more than one world, and more than one set of virtues: confusion between them is disastrous. One of the chief illusions caused by ignoring this is the Platonic-Hebraic-Christian view that virtuous rulers create virtuous men. This according to Machiavelli is not true. Generosity is a virtue, but not in princes. A generous prince will ruin the citizens by taxing them too heavily, a mean prince (and Machiavelli does not say that meanness is a good quality in private men) will save the purses of the citizens and so add to public welfare. A kind ruler – and kindness is a virtue – may let intriguers and stronger characters dominate him, and so cause chaos and corruption.

Other writers of 'mirrors for princes' are also rich in such maxims, but they do not draw the implications; Machiavelli's use of such generalisations is not theirs; he is not moralising at large, but illustrating a specific thesis: that the nature of men dictates a public morality which is different from, and may come into collision with, the virtues of men who profess to believe in, and try to act by, Christian precepts. These may not be wholly unrealisable in quiet times, in private life. But they lead to ruin outside this. The analogy between a State and people and an individual is a fallacy: 'a State and a people are governed in a different way from an

---

[1] ibid. i 27.

[2] It is still not clear how much of this Frederick owed to his mentor Voltaire.

individual';[1] 'not individual good but common good is what makes cities great'.[2]

One may disagree with this. One may argue that the greatness, glory and wealth of a State are hollow ideals, or detestable, if the citizens are oppressed and treated as mere means to the grandeur of the whole. Like Christian thinkers, or like Constant and the liberals, or like Sismondi and the theorists of the Welfare State, one may prefer a State in which citizens are prosperous even though the public treasury is poor, in which government is neither centralised nor omnipotent, nor, perhaps, sovereign at all, but the citizens enjoy a wide degree of individual freedom; one may contrast this favourably with the great authoritarian concentrations of power built by Alexander or Frederick the Great or Napoleon, or the great autocrats of the twentieth century.

If so, one is simply contradicting Machiavelli's thesis: he sees no merit in such loose political textures. They cannot last. Men cannot long survive in such conditions. He is convinced that States which have lost the appetite for power are doomed to decadence and are likely to be destroyed by their more vigorous and better-armed neighbours; and Vico and modern 'realistic' thinkers have echoed this.

Machiavelli is possessed by a clear, intense, narrow vision of a society in which human talents can be made to contribute to a powerful and splendid whole. He prefers republican rule in which the interests of the rulers do not conflict with those of the ruled. But (as Macaulay perceived) he prefers a well-governed principate to a decadent republic; and the qualities he admires and thinks capable of being welded into – indeed, indispensable to – a durable society are not different in *The Prince* and the *Discourses*: energy, boldness, practical skill, imagination, vitality, self-discipline, shrewdness, public spirit, good fortune, *antiqua virtus*, *virtù* – firmness in adversity, strength of character, as celebrated by Xenophon or Livy. All his more shocking maxims – those responsible for the 'murd'rous Machiavel' of the Elizabethan stage

---

[1] 'una repubblica e un popolo si governa altrimenti che un privato', *Legazioni all'Imperatore*, quoted by Burd, op. cit. (p. 272 above, note 8), p. 298, note 17.

[2] *Discourses* ii 2. This echoes Francesco Patrizi's 'aliae sunt regis virtutes, aliae privatorum' in *De regno et regis institutione*, quoted by Felix Gilbert in 'The Humanist Concept of the Prince and *The Prince* of Machiavelli', *Journal of Modern History* 11 (1939), 449–83 at p. 464, note 34.

– are descriptions of methods of realising this single end: the classical, humanistic and patriotic vision that dominates him.

Let me cite a round dozen of his most notoriously wicked pieces of advice to princes. You must employ terrorism or kindness, as the case dictates. Severity is usually more effective, but humanity, in some situations, brings better fruit. You may excite fear but not hatred, for hatred will destroy you in the end. It is best to keep men poor and on a permanent war footing, for this will be an antidote to the two great enemies of active obedience – ambition and boredom – and the ruled will then feel in constant need of great men to lead them (the twentieth century offers us only too much evidence for this sharp insight). Competition – divisions between classes – in a society is desirable, for it generates energy and ambition in the right degree.

Religion must be promoted even though it may be false, provided it is of a kind which preserves social solidarity and promotes manly virtues, as Christianity has historically failed to do. When you confer benefits (he says, following Aristotle), do so yourself; but if dirty work is to be done, let others do it, for then they, not the prince, will be blamed, and the prince can gain favour by duly cutting off their heads; for men prefer vengeance and security to liberty. Do what you must do in any case, but try to represent it as a special favour to the people. If you must commit a crime do not advertise it beforehand, since otherwise your enemies may destroy you before you destroy them. If your action must be drastic, do it in one fell swoop, not in agonising stages. Do not be surrounded by over-powerful servants – victorious generals are best got rid of, otherwise they may get rid of you.

You may be violent and use your power to overawe, but you must not break your own laws, for that destroys confidence and disintegrates the social texture. Men should be either caressed or annihilated; appeasement and neutralism are always fatal. Excellent plans without arms are not enough or else Florence would still be a republic. Rulers must live in the constant expectation of war. Success creates more devotion than an amiable character; remember the fate of Pertinax, Savonarola, Soderini. Severus was unscrupulous and cruel, Ferdinand of Spain is treacherous and crafty: but by practising the arts of both the lion and the fox they escaped both snares and wolves. Men will be false to you unless you compel them to be true by creating circumstances in which falsehood will not pay. And so on.

These examples are typical of 'the devil's partner'. Now and then doubts assail our author: he wonders whether a man high-minded enough to labour to create a State admirable by Roman standards will be tough enough to use the violent and wicked means prescribed; and, conversely, whether a sufficiently ruthless and brutal man will be disinterested enough to compass the public good which alone justifies the evil means. Yet Moses and Theseus, Romulus and Cyrus combined these properties.[1] What has been once, can be again: the implication is optimistic.

All these maxims have one property in common: they are designed to create or resurrect or maintain an order which will satisfy what the author conceives as men's most permanent interests. Machiavelli's values may be erroneous, dangerous, odious; but he is in earnest. He is not cynical. The end is always the same: a State conceived after the analogy of Periclean Athens, or Sparta, but above all the Roman Republic. Such an end, for which men naturally crave (of this he thinks that history and observation provide conclusive evidence), 'excuses' any means; in judging means, look only to the end: if the State goes under, all is lost. Hence the famous paragraph in the forty-first chapter of the third book of the *Discourses* where he says, 'when it is absolutely a question of the safety of one's country, there must be no consideration of just or unjust, of merciful or cruel, of praiseworthy or disgraceful; instead, setting aside every scruple, one must follow to the utmost any plan that will save her life and keep her liberty'. The French have reasoned thus: and the 'majesty of their king and the power of their kingdom' have come from it. Romulus could not have founded Rome without killing Remus. Brutus would not have preserved the Republic if he had not killed his sons. Moses and Theseus, Romulus, Cyrus and the liberators of Athens had to destroy in order to build. Such conduct, so far from being condemned, is held up to admiration by the classical historians and the Bible. Machiavelli is their admirer and faithful spokesman.

What is there, then, about his words, about his tone, which has caused such tremors among his readers? Not, indeed, in his own lifetime – there was a delayed reaction of some quarter of a century, but after that it becomes one of continuous and mounting horror. Fichte, Hegel, Treitschke 'reinterpreted' his doctrines and

---

[1] Hugh Trevor-Roper has drawn my attention to the irony of the fact that the heroes of this supreme realist are all, wholly or in part, mythical.

assimilated them to their own views. But the sense of horror was not thereby greatly mitigated. It is evident that the effect of the shock which he administered was not a temporary one: it has lasted almost to our own day.

Leaving aside the historical problem of why there was no immediate contemporary criticism, let us consider the continuous discomfort caused to its readers during the four centuries that have passed since *The Prince* was placed upon the Index. The great originality and the tragic implications of Machiavelli's theses seem to me to reside in their relation to a Christian civilisation. It was all very well to live by the light of pagan ideals in pagan times; but to preach paganism more than a thousand years after the triumph of Christianity was to do so after the loss of innocence – and to be forcing men to make a conscious choice. The choice is painful because it is a choice between two entire worlds. Men have lived in both, and fought and died to preserve them against each other. Machiavelli has opted for one of them, and he is prepared to commit crimes for its sake.

In killing, deceiving, betraying, Machiavelli's princes and republicans are doing evil things, not condonable in terms of common morality. It is Machiavelli's great merit that he does not deny this.[1] Marsilio, Hobbes, Spinoza, and, in their own fashion, Hegel and Marx, did try to deny it. So did many a defender of the *raison d'état*, imperialist and populist, Catholic and Protestant. These thinkers argue for a single moral system: and seek to show that the morality which justifies, and indeed demands, such deeds, is continuous with, and a more rational form of, the confused ethical beliefs of the uninstructed morality which forbids them absolutely.

From the vantage-point of the great social objectives in the name of which these (prima facie wicked) acts are to be performed, they will be seen (so the argument goes) as no longer wicked, but as rational – demanded by the very nature of things – by the common good, or man's true ends, or the dialectic of history – condemned only by those who cannot or will not see a large enough segment of the logical, or theological, or metaphysical, or historical pattern; misjudged, denounced only by the spiritually blind or short-sighted. At worst, these 'crimes' are discords demanded by the

---

[1] This is recognised by Jacques Maritain – see his *Moral Philosophy* (London, 1964), p. 199 – who conceded that Machiavelli 'never called evil good or good evil'. *Machtpolitik* is shown to be what it is: the party with the big battalions; it does not claim that the Lord is on its side: no *Dei gesta per Francos*.

larger harmony, and therefore, to those who hear this harmony, no longer discordant.

Machiavelli is not a defender of any such abstract theory. It does not occur to him to employ such casuistry. He is transparently honest and clear. In choosing the life of a statesman, or even the life of a citizen with enough civic sense to want his State to be as successful and as splendid as possible, you commit yourself to rejection of Christian behaviour.[1] It may be that Christians are right about the well-being of the individual soul, taken outside the social or political context. But the well-being of the State is not the same as the well-being of the individual – they 'are governed in a different way'. You will have made your choice: the only crimes are weakness, cowardice, stupidity, which may cause you to draw back in mid-stream and fail.

Compromise with current morality leads to bungling, which is always despicable, and when practised by statesmen involves men in ruin. The end 'excuses' the means, however horrible these may be in terms of even pagan ethics, if it is (in terms of the ideals of Thucydides or Polybius, Cicero or Livy) lofty enough. Brutus was right to kill his children: he saved Rome. Soderini did not have the stomach to perpetrate such deeds and ruined Florence. Savonarola, who had sound ideas about austerity and moral strength and corruption, perished because he did not realise that an unarmed prophet will always go to the gallows.

If one can produce the right results by using the devotion and affection of men, let this be done by all means. There is no value in causing suffering as such. But if one cannot, then Moses, Romulus, Theseus, Cyrus are the exemplars, and fear must be employed. There is no sinister Satanism in Machiavelli, nothing of Dostoevsky's great sinner, pursuing evil for evil's sake. To Dostoevsky's famous question 'Is everything permitted?' Machiavelli (who for Dostoevsky would surely have been an atheist) answers 'Yes, if the end – that is, the pursuit of a society's basic interests in a specific situation – cannot be realised in any other way.'

This position has not been properly understood by some of those who claim to be not unsympathetic to Machiavelli. Figgis, for

---

[1] At the risk of exhausting the patience of the reader, I must repeat that this is a conflict not of pagan statecraft with Christian morals, but of pagan morals (indissolubly connected with social life and inconceivable without it) with Christian ethics, which, whatever its implication for politics, can be stated independently of it, as, e.g., Aristotle's or Hegel's ethics cannot.

example,[1] thinks that he permanently suspended 'the *habeas corpus* acts of the whole human race', that is to say, that he advocated methods of terrorism because for him the situation was always critical, always desperate, so that he confused ordinary political principles with rules needed, if at all, only in extreme cases.

Others – perhaps the majority of his interpreters – look on him as the originator or at least a defender of what later came to be called 'raison d'état', 'Staatsräson', 'ragion di stato' – the justification of immoral acts when undertaken on behalf of the State in exceptional circumstances. More than one scholar has pointed out, reasonably enough, that the notion that desperate cases require desperate remedies – that 'necessity knows no law' – is to be found not only in antiquity but equally in Aquinas and Dante and other medieval writers long before Bellarmino or Machiavelli.

These parallels seem to me to rest on a deep but characteristic misunderstanding of Machiavelli's thesis. He is not saying that while in normal situations current morality – that is, the Christian or semi-Christian code of ethics – should prevail, yet abnormal conditions can occur such that the entire social structure in which alone this code can function becomes jeopardised, and that in emergencies of this kind acts which are usually regarded as wicked, and rightly forbidden, are justified.

This is the position of, among others, those who think that all morality ultimately rests on the existence of certain institutions – say Roman Catholics who regard the existence of the Church and the papacy as indispensable to Christianity, or nationalists who see in the political power of a nation the sole source of spiritual life. Such persons maintain that extreme and 'frightful' measures needed for protecting the State or the Church or the national culture in moments of acute crisis may be justified, since the ruin of these institutions may fatally damage the indispensable framework of all other values. This is a doctrine in terms of which both Catholics and Protestants, both conservatives and Communists, have defended enormities which freeze the blood of ordinary men.

But this is not Machiavelli's position. For the defenders of the *raison d'état* the sole justification of these measures is that they are exceptional – that they are needed to preserve a system the purpose of which is precisely to preclude the need for such odious

[1] op. cit. (p. 280 above, note 1), p. 76.

measures, so that such steps are justified only because they will end the situations that render them necessary. But for Machiavelli these measures are, in a sense, themselves quite normal. No doubt they are called for only by extreme need; yet political life tends to generate a good many such needs, of varying degrees of 'extremity'; hence Baglioni, who shied away from the logical consequences of his own policies, was clearly unfit to rule.

The notion of *raison d'état* entails a conflict of values which may be agonising to morally good and sensitive men. For Machiavelli there is no conflict. Public life has its own morality, to which Christian principles (or any absolute personal values) tend to be a gratuitous obstacle. This life has its own standards; it does not require perpetual terror; but it approves, or at least permits, the use of force where it is needed to promote the ends of political society.

Sheldon Wolin[1] seems to me right in insisting that Machiavelli believes in a permanent 'economy of violence' – the need for a consistent reserve of force always in the background to keep things going in such a way that the virtues admired by him and by the classical thinkers to whom he appeals can be protected and allowed to flower. Men brought up within a community in which such force, or its possibility, is used rightly, will live the happy lives of Greeks or Romans during their finest hours. They will be characterised by vitality, genius, variety, pride, power, success (Machiavelli scarcely ever speaks of arts or sciences); but it will not, in any clear sense, be a Christian commonwealth. The moral conflict which this situation raises will trouble only those who are not prepared to abandon either course: those who assume that the two incompatible lives are in fact reconcilable.

But to Machiavelli the claims of the official morality are scarcely worth discussing; they are not translatable into social practice: 'If all men were good . . .', but he feels sure that men can never be improved beyond the point at which considerations of power are relevant. If morals relate to human conduct, and men are by nature social, Christian morality cannot be a guide for normal social existence. It remained for someone to state this. Machiavelli did so.

One is obliged to choose: and in choosing one form of life, give up the other. That is the central point. If Machiavelli is right, if it is in principle (or in fact: the frontier seems dim) impossible to be morally good and do one's duty as this was conceived by common

---

[1] Sheldon S. Wolin, *Politics and Vision* (London, 1960), pp. 220–4.

European, and especially Christian, ethics, and at the same time build Sparta or Periclean Athens or the Rome of the Republic or even of the Antonines, then a conclusion of the first importance follows: that the belief that the correct, objectively valid solution to the question of how men should live can in principle be discovered is itself in principle not true. This was a truly *erschreckend* proposition. Let me try to put it in its proper context.

One of the deepest assumptions of Western political thought is the doctrine, scarcely questioned during its long ascendancy, that there exists some single principle which not only regulates the course of the sun and the stars, but prescribes their proper behaviour to all animate creatures. Animals and sub-rational beings of all kinds follow it by instinct; higher beings attain to consciousness of it, and are free to abandon it, but only to their doom. This doctrine, in one version or another, has dominated European thought since Plato; it has appeared in many forms, and has generated many similes and allegories; at its centre is the vision of an impersonal nature or reason or cosmic purpose, or of a divine Creator whose power has endowed all things and creatures each with a specific function; these functions are elements in a single harmonious whole, and are intelligible in terms of it alone.

This was often expressed by images taken from architecture: of a great edifice of which each part fits uniquely in the total structure; or from the human body as an all-embracing organic whole; or from the life of society as a great hierarchy, with God as the *ens realissimum* at the summit of two parallel systems – the feudal order and the natural order – stretching downwards from him, and reaching upwards to him, obedient to his will. Or it is seen as the Great Chain of Being, the Platonic-Christian analogue of the world-tree Yggdrasil, which links time and space and all that they contain. Or it has been represented by an analogy drawn from music, as an orchestra in which each instrument or group of instruments has its own tune to play in the infinitely rich polyphonic score. When, after the seventeenth century, harmonic metaphors replaced polyphonic images, the instruments were no longer conceived as playing specific melodies, but as producing sounds which, although they might not be wholly intelligible to any given group of players (and might even sound discordant or superfluous if taken in isolation), yet contributed to the total pattern perceptible only from a loftier standpoint.

The idea of the world and of human society as a single

intelligible structure is at the root of all the many various versions of natural law – the mathematical harmonies of the Pythagoreans, the logical ladder of Platonic Forms, the genetic-logical pattern of Aristotle, the divine *Logos* of the Stoics and the Christian Churches and of their secularised offshoots. The advance of the natural sciences generated more empirically conceived versions of this image as well as anthropomorphic similes: of Dame Nature as an adjuster of conflicting tendencies (as in Hume or Adam Smith), of Mistress Nature as the teacher of the best way to happiness (as in the works of some French Encyclopaedists), of nature as embodied in the actual customs or habits of organised social wholes; biological, aesthetic, psychological similes have reflected the dominant ideas of an age.

This unifying monistic pattern is at the very heart of the traditional rationalism, religious and atheistic, metaphysical and scientific, transcendental and naturalistic, that has been characteristic of Western civilisation. It is this rock, upon which Western beliefs and lives had been founded, that Machiavelli seems, in effect, to have split open. So great a reversal cannot, of course, be due to the acts of a single individual. It could scarcely have taken place in a stable social and moral order; many beside him, ancient sceptics, medieval nominalists and secularists, Renaissance humanists, doubtless supplied their share of the dynamite. The purpose of this essay is to suggest that it was Machiavelli who lit the fatal fuse.

If to ask what are the ends of life is to ask a real question, it must be capable of being correctly answered. To claim rationality in matters of conduct was to claim that correct and final solutions to such questions can in principle be found. When such solutions were discussed in earlier periods, it was normally assumed that the perfect society could be conceived, at least in outline; for otherwise what standard could one use to condemn existing arrangements as imperfect? It might not be realisable here, below. Men were too ignorant or too weak or too vicious to create it. Or it was said (by some materialistic thinkers in the centuries following *The Prince*) that it was technical means that were lacking, that no one had yet discovered methods of overcoming the material obstacles to the golden age; that we were not technologically or educationally or morally sufficiently advanced. But it was never said that there was something incoherent in the very notion itself.

Plato and the Stoics, the Hebrew prophets and Christian medieval thinkers, and the writers of Utopias from More onward had a vision of what it was that men fell short of; they claimed, as it were, to be able to measure the gap between the reality and the ideal. But if Machiavelli is right, this tradition – the central current of Western thought – is fallacious. If his position is valid then it is impossible to construct even the notion of such a perfect society, for there exist at least two sets of virtues – let us call them the Christian and the pagan – which are not merely in practice, but in principle, incompatible.

If men practise Christian humility, they cannot also be inspired by the burning ambitions of the great classical founders of cultures and religions; if their gaze is centred upon the world beyond – if their ideas are infected by even lip-service to such an outlook – they will not be likely to give all that they have to an attempt to build a perfect city. If suffering and sacrifice and martyrdom are not always evil and inescapable necessities but may be of supreme value in themselves, then the glorious victories over fortune which go to the bold, the impetuous and the young might be neither won nor thought worth winning. If spiritual goods alone are worth striving for, then of how much value is the study of *necessità* – of the laws that govern nature and human lives – by the manipulation of which men might accomplish unheard-of things in the arts and the sciences and the organisation of social lives?

To abandon the pursuit of secular goals may lead to disintegration and a new barbarism; but even if this is so, is it the worst that could happen? Whatever the differences between Plato and Aristotle, or of either of these thinkers from the Sophists and Epicureans or the other Greek schools of the fourth and later centuries, they and their disciples, the European rationalists and empiricists of the modern age, were agreed that the study of reality by minds undeluded by appearances could reveal the correct ends to be pursued by men – that which would make men free and happy, strong and rational.

Some thought that there was a single end for all men in all circumstances, or different ends for men of different kinds or in dissimilar historical environments. Objectivists and universalists were opposed by relativists and subjectivists, metaphysicians by empiricists, theists by atheists. There was profound disagreement about moral issues; but what none of these thinkers, not even the sceptics, had suggested was that there might exist ends – ends in themselves in terms of which alone everything else was justified – which were equally ultimate, but incompatible with one another, that there might exist no single universal overarching standard that would enable a man to choose rationally between them. This was indeed a profoundly upsetting conclusion. It entailed that if men wished to live and act consistently, and understand what goals they were pursuing, they were obliged to examine their moral values. What if they found that they were compelled to make a choice between two incommensurable systems, to choose as they did without the aid of an infallible measuring-rod which certified one form of life as being superior to all others and could be used to demonstrate this to the satisfaction of all rational men? Is it, perhaps, this awful truth, implicit in Machiavelli's exposition, that has upset the moral consciousness of men, and has haunted their minds so permanently and obsessively ever since?

Machiavelli did not himself propound it. There was no problem and no agony for him; he shows no trace of scepticism or relativism; he chose his side, and took little interest in the values that this choice ignored or flouted. The conflict between his scale of values and that of conventional morality clearly did not (*pace* Croce and the other defenders of the 'anguished humanist' inter-pretation) seem to worry Machiavelli himself. It upset only those who came after him, and were not prepared, on the one hand, to abandon their own moral values (Christian or humanist) together with the entire way of thought and action of which these were a part; nor, on the other hand, to deny the validity of, at any rate, much of Machiavelli's analysis of the political facts, and the (largely pagan) values and outlook that went with it, embodied in the social structure which he painted so brilliantly and convincingly.

Whenever a thinker, however distant from us in time or culture, still stirs passion, enthusiasm or indignation, or any kind of intense debate, it is generally the case that he has propounded a thesis which upsets some deeply established *idée reçue*, a thesis which those who wish to cling to the old conviction nevertheless find it hard or impossible to dismiss or refute. This is the case with Plato, Hobbes, Rousseau, Marx. I should like to suggest that it is Machiavelli's juxtaposition of the two outlooks – the two incom-patible moral worlds, as it were – in the minds of his readers, and the collision and acute moral discomfort which follow, that, over the years, has been responsible for the desperate efforts to interpret his doctrines away, to represent him as a cynical and therefore ultimately shallow defender of power politics, or as a diabolist, or as a patriot prescribing for particularly desperate situations which seldom arise, or as a mere time-server, or as an embittered political failure, or as nothing more than a mouthpiece of truths we have always known but did not like to utter, or again as the enlightened translator of universally accepted ancient social principles into empirical terms, or as a crypto-republican satirist (a descendant of Juvenal, a forerunner of Orwell); or as a cold scientist, a mere political technologist free from moral implications; or as a typical Renaissance publicist practising a now obsolete genre; or in any of the numerous other roles that have been and are still being cast for him.

Machiavelli may have possessed some, at any rate, of these attributes, but concentration on one or other of them as constituting his essential, 'true' character seems to me to stem from reluctance to face, still more discuss, the uncomfortable truth which Machiavelli had, unintentionally, almost casually, uncovered; namely, that not all ultimate values are necessarily compatible with one another – that there might be a conceptual (what used to be called 'philosophical') and not merely a material obstacle to the notion of the single ultimate solution which, if it were only realised, would establish the perfect society.

III

Yet if no such solution can, even in principle, be formulated, then all political and, indeed, moral problems are thereby transformed. This is not a division of politics from ethics. It is the uncovering of the possibility of more than one system of values, with no criterion common to the systems whereby a rational choice can be made between them. This is not the rejection of Christianity for paganism (although Machiavelli clearly preferred the latter), nor of paganism for Christianity (which, at least in its historical form, he thought incompatible with the basic needs of normal men), but the setting of them side by side, with the implicit invitation to men to choose either a good, virtuous, private life, or a good, successful, social existence, but not both.

What has been shown by Machiavelli, who is often (like Nietzsche) congratulated for tearing off hypocritical masks, brutally revealing the truth, and so on, is not that men profess one thing and do another (although no doubt he shows this too), but that when they assume that the two ideals are compatible, or perhaps are even one and the same ideal, and do not allow this assumption to be questioned, they are guilty of bad faith (as the existentialists call it, or of 'false consciousness', to use a Marxist formula), which their actual behaviour exhibits. Machiavelli calls the bluff not just of official morality – the hypocrisies of ordinary life – but of one of the foundations of the central Western philosophical tradition, the belief in the ultimate compatibility of all genuine values. His own withers are unwrung. He has made his choice. He seems wholly unworried by, indeed scarcely aware of, parting company with traditional Western morality.

But the question that his writings have dramatised, if not for himself, then for others in the centuries that followed, is this: what reason have we for supposing that justice and mercy, humility and *virtù*, happiness and knowledge, glory and liberty, magnificence and sanctity, will always coincide, or indeed be compatible at all? Poetic justice is, after all, so called not because it does, but because it does not, as a rule, occur in the prose of ordinary life, where, *ex hypothesi*, a very different kind of justice operates: 'a State and a people are governed in a different way from an individual'. Hence what talk can there be of indestructible rights, in either the medieval or the liberal sense? The wise man must eliminate fantasies from his own head, and should seek to dispel them from the heads of others; or, if they are too resistant, he should at least, as Pareto or Dostoevsky's Grand Inquisitor recommended, exploit them as a means to a viable society.

The march of world history stands outside virtue, vice and justice, said Hegel.[1] If for 'the march of history' you substitute 'a well-governed *patria*', and interpret Hegel's notion of virtue as it is understood by Christians or ordinary men, then Machiavelli is one of the earliest proponents of this doctrine. Like all great innovators, he is not without ancestry. But the names of Palmieri and Pontano, and even of Carneades and Sextus Empiricus, have left little mark on European thought.

Croce has rightly insisted that Machiavelli is not detached or cynical or irresponsible. His patriotism, his republicanism, his commitment are not in doubt. He suffered for his convictions. He thought continually about Florence and Italy, and of how to save them. Yet it is not his character, nor his plays, his poetry, his histories, his diplomatic or political activities, that have gained him

---

[1] See Georg Willhelm Friedrich Hegel, *Sämtliche Werke*, ed. Hermann Glockner (Stuttgart, 1927–51), vol. 7, p. 448.

his unique fame.[1] Nor can this be due only to his psychological or sociological imagination. His psychology is often excessively primitive. He scarcely seems to allow for the bare possibility of sustained and genuine altruism; he refuses to consider the motives of men who are prepared to fight against enormous odds, who ignore *necessità* and are prepared to lose their lives in a hopeless cause.

His distrust of unworldly attitudes, absolute principles divorced from empirical observation, is fanatically strong – almost romantic in its violence; the vision of the great prince playing upon human beings like an instrument intoxicates him. He assumes that different societies must always be at war with each other, since they have differing purposes. He sees history as an endless process of cutthroat competition, in which the only goal that rational men can have is to succeed in the eyes of their contemporaries and of posterity. He is good at bringing fantasies down to earth, but he assumes, as Mill was to complain about Bentham, that this is enough. He allows too little to the ideal impulses of men. He has no historical sense and little sense of economics. He has no inkling of the technological progress which is about to transform political and social life, and in particular the art of war. He does not understand how individuals, communities or cultures develop and transform themselves. Like Hobbes, he assumes that the argument or motive for self-preservation automatically outweighs all others.

He tells men above all not to be fools: to follow a principle when this may involve you in ruin is absurd, at least if judged by worldly standards; other standards he mentions respectfully, but takes no interest in them: those who adopt them are not likely to create

---

[1] The moral of his best comedy, *Mandragola*, seems to me close to that of the political tracts: that the ethical doctrines professed by the characters are wholly at variance with what they do to attain their various ends. Virtually every one of them in the end obtains what he wants; if Callimaco had resisted temptation or the lady he seduces had been smitten with remorse, or Fra Timoteo attempted to practise the maxims of the Fathers and the Schoolmen with which he liberally seasons his speeches, this could not have occurred. But all turns out for the best, though not from the point of view of accepted morality. If the play castigates hypocrisy and stupidity, the standpoint is that not of virtue but of candid hedonism. The notion that Callimaco is a kind of prince in private life, successful in creating and maintaining his own world by the correct use of guile and fraud, the exercise of *virtù*, a bold challenge to *fortuna*, and so on, seems plausible. For this see Henry Paolucci, Introduction to Niccolò Machiavelli, *Mandragola*, trans. Anne and Henry Paolucci (New York, 1957).

anything that will perpetuate their name. His Romans are no more real than the stylised figures in his brilliant comedies. His human beings have so little inner life or capacity for co-operation or social solidarity that, as in the case of Hobbes's not dissimilar creatures, it is difficult to see how they could develop enough reciprocal confidence to create a lasting social whole, even under the perpetual shadow of carefully regulated violence.

Few would deny that Machiavelli's writings, more particularly *The Prince*, have scandalised mankind more deeply and continuously than any other political treatise. The reason for this, let me say again, is not the discovery that politics is the play of power – that political relationships between and within independent communities involve the use of force and fraud, and are unrelated to the principles professed by the players. That knowledge is as old as conscious thought about politics – certainly as old as Thucydides and Plato. Nor is it merely caused by the examples that he offers of success in acquiring or holding power – the descriptions of the massacre at Sinigaglia or the behaviour of Agathocles or Oliverotto da Fermo are no more or less horrifying than similar stories in Tacitus or Guicciardini. The proposition that crime can pay is nothing new in Western historiography.

Nor is it merely his recommendation of ruthless measures that so upsets his readers: Aristotle had long ago allowed that exceptional situations might arise, that principles and rules could not be rigidly applied to all situations; the advice to rulers in the *Politics* is tough-minded enough; Cicero is aware that critical situations demand exceptional measures – *ratio publicae utilitatis*, *ratio status*, were familiar in the thought of the Middle Ages. 'Necessity knows no law' is a Thomist sentiment:[1] Pierre d'Auvergne says much the same. Harrington said this in the following century, and Hume applauded him.

These opinions were not thought original by these, or perhaps any, thinkers. Machiavelli did not originate, nor did he make much use of, the notion of *raison d'état*. He stressed will, boldness,

---

[1] It has older origins (cf. p. 310 above). The familiar legal proverb 'Necessitas non habet legem' appears, for example, as a gloss by Accursius on Justinian's *Digest* 1. 10. 1. 1 ('De officiis consulis', gloss on 'expedire'): sig. cI^r in his commentary on the *Digestum vetus* (Venice, 1477). But Publilius Syrus in the first century BC includes the same idea in one of his apophthegms, 'Necessitas dat legem non ipsa accipit': *Sententiae* 444 in *Minor Latin Poets*, ed. and trans. J. Wight Duff and Arnold M. Duff (London/Cambridge, Mass., 1934). H.H.

address, at the expense of the rules laid down by calm *ragione*, to which his colleagues in the *Pratiche Fiorentine*, and perhaps the Oricellari Gardens, may have appealed. So did Leon Battista Alberti when he declared that *fortuna* crushes only the weak and propertyless; so did contemporary poets; so, too, in his own fashion, did Pico della Mirandola in his great apostrophe to the powers of man, who, unlike the angels, can transform himself into any shape – the ardent image which lies at the heart of European humanism in the north as well as the Mediterranean.

Far more original, as has often been noted, is Machiavelli's divorce of political behaviour as a field of study from the theological world-picture in terms of which this topic is discussed before him (even by Marsilio) and after him. Yet it is not his secularism, however audacious in his own day, that could have disturbed the contemporaries of Voltaire or Bentham or their successors. What shocked them is something different.

Machiavelli's cardinal achievement is, let me repeat, his uncovering of an insoluble dilemma, the planting of a permanent question mark in the path of posterity. It stems from his *de facto* recognition that ends equally ultimate, equally sacred, may contradict each other, that entire systems of value may come into collision without possibility of rational arbitration, and that this happens not merely in exceptional circumstances, as a result of abnormality or accident or error – the clash of Antigone and Creon or in the story of Tristan – but (this was surely new) as part of the normal human situation.

For those who look on such collisions as rare, exceptional and disastrous, the choice to be made is necessarily an agonising experience for which, as a rational being, one cannot prepare (since no rules apply). But for Machiavelli, at least of *The Prince*, the *Discourses, Mandragola*, there is no agony. One chooses as one chooses because one knows what one wants, and is ready to pay the price. One chooses classical civilisation rather than the Theban desert, Rome and not Jerusalem, whatever the priests may say, because such is one's nature, and – he is no existentialist or romantic individualist *avant la parole* – because it is that of men in general, at all times, everywhere. If others prefer solitude or martyrdom, he shrugs his shoulders. Such men are not for him. He has nothing to say to them, nothing to argue with them about. All that matters to him and those who agree with him is that such men be not allowed to meddle with politics or education or any of the cardinal factors in human life; their outlook unfits them for such tasks.

I do not mean that Machiavelli explicitly asserts that there is a pluralism or even a dualism of values between which conscious choices must be made. But this follows from the contrasts he draws between the conduct he admires and that which he condemns. He seems to take for granted the obvious superiority of classical civic virtue and brushes aside Christian values, as well as conventional morality, with a disparaging or patronising sentence or two, or smooth words about the misinterpretation of Christianity.[1] This worries or infuriates those who disagree with him the more because it goes against their convictions without seeming to be aware of doing so – and recommends wicked courses as obviously the most sensible, something that only fools or visionaries will reject.

If what Machiavelli believed is true, this undermines one major assumption of Western thought: namely that somewhere in the

---

[1] e.g. in the passages from the *Discourses* cited above, or when he says, 'I believe the greatest good to be done and the most pleasing to God is that which one does to one's native city': *A Discourse on Remodelling the Government of Florence* (Gilbert, op. cit. (p. 277 above, note 3), vol. 1, pp. 113–14). This sentiment is by no means unique in Machiavelli's works: but, leaving aside his wish to flatter Leo X, or the liability of all authors to fall into the clichés of their own time, are we to suppose that Machiavelli means us to think that when Philip of Macedon transplanted populations in a manner that (unavoidable as it is said to have been) caused even Machiavelli a qualm, what Philip did, provided it was good for Macedon, was pleasing to God and, *per contra*, that Giovanpaolo Baglioni's failure to kill the Pope and the Curia was displeasing to him? Such a notion of the Deity is, to say the least, remote from that of the New Testament. Are the needs of the *patria* automatically identical with the will of the Almighty? Are those who permit themselves to doubt this in danger of heresy? Machiavelli may at times have been represented as too Machiavellian; but to suppose that he believed that the claims of God and of Caesar were perfectly reconcilable reduces his central thesis to absurdity. Yet of course this does not prove that he lacked all Christian sentiment: the *Esortazione alla penitenza* composed in the last year of his life (if it is genuine and not a later forgery) may well be wholly sincere, as Ridolfi and Alderisio believe; Capponi may have exaggerated the extent to which he 'drove religion from his heart', even though 'it was not wholly extinct in his thought' (Gino Capponi, *Storia della repubblica di Firenze* (Florence, 1888), vol. 3, p. 191). The point is that there is scarcely any trace of such *états d'âme* in his political writings, with which alone we are concerned. There is an interesting discussion of this by Giuseppe Prezzolini in his already cited article (p. 285 above, note 1), in which this attitude is traced to Augustine, and Croce's thesis is, by implication, controverted.

past or the future, in this world or the next, in the church or the laboratory, in the speculations of the metaphysician or the findings of the social scientist, or in the uncorrupted heart of the simple good man, there is to be found the final solution of the question of how men should live. If this is false (and if more than one equally valid answer to the question can be returned, then it is false) the idea of the sole true, objective, universal human ideal crumbles. The very search for it becomes not merely Utopian in practice, but conceptually incoherent.

One can surely see how this might seem unfaceable to men – believers or atheists, empiricists or apriorists – brought up on the opposite assumptions. Nothing could well be more upsetting to those brought up in a monistic religious or, at any rate, moral, social or political system than a breach in it. This is the dagger of which Meinecke speaks, with which Machiavelli inflicted the wound that has never healed; even though Felix Gilbert is right in thinking that he did not bear the scars of it himself. For he remained a monist, albeit a pagan one.

Machiavelli was doubtless guilty of much confusion and exaggeration. He confused the proposition that ultimate ideals may be incompatible with the very different proposition that the more conventional human ideals – founded on ideas of natural law, brotherly love, and human goodness – were unrealisable and that those who acted on the opposite assumptions were fools, and at times dangerous ones; and he attributed this dubious proposition to antiquity, and believed that it was verified by history. The first of these assertions strikes at the root of all doctrines which believe in the possibility of attaining, or at least formulating, final solutions; the second is empirical, commonplace, and not self-evident. The two propositions are not, in any case, identical or logically connected.

Moreover he exaggerated wildly: the idealised types of the Periclean Greek or the Roman of the old Republic may be irreconcilable with the ideal citizen of a Christian commonwealth (supposing such were conceivable), but in practice – above all in history, to which our author went for illustrations if not for evidence – pure types seldom obtain: mixtures and compounds and compromises and forms of communal life that do not fit into easy classifications, but which neither Christians, nor liberal humanists, nor Machiavelli would be compelled by their beliefs to reject, can be conceived without too much intellectual difficulty. Still, to attack and inflict lasting damage on a central assumption of an entire civilisation is an achievement of the first order.

Machiavelli does not affirm this dualism. He merely takes for granted the superiority of Roman *antiqua virtus* (which may be maddening to those who do not) over the Christian life as taught by the Church. He utters a few casual words about what Christianity might have become, but does not expect it to change its actual character. There he leaves the matter. Anyone who believes in Christian morality, and regards the Christian commonwealth as its embodiment, but at the same time largely accepts the validity of Machiavelli's political and psychological analysis and does not reject the secular heritage of Rome – a man in this predicament is faced with a dilemma which, if Machiavelli is right, is not merely unsolved but insoluble. This is the Gordian knot which, according to Vanini and Leibniz, the author of *The Prince* had tied – a knot which can be cut but not undone.[1] Hence the efforts to dilute his doctrines, or interpret them in such a way as to remove their sting.

After Machiavelli, doubt is liable to infect all monistic constructions. The sense of certainty that there is somewhere a hidden treasure – the final solution to our ills – and that some path must lead to it (for, in principle, it must be discoverable); or else, to alter the image, the conviction that the fragments constituted by our beliefs and habits are all pieces of a jigsaw puzzle, which (since there is an a priori guarantee for this) can, in principle, be solved, so that it is only because of lack of skill or stupidity or bad fortune that we have not so far succeeded in discovering the solution, whereby all interests will be brought into harmony – this fundamental belief of Western political thought has been severely shaken. Surely, in an age that looks for certainties, this is sufficient to account for the unending efforts, more numerous today than ever, to explain *The Prince* and the *Discourses*, or to explain them away?

This is the negative implication. There is also one that is positive, and might have surprised and perhaps displeased Machiavelli. So long as only one ideal is the true goal, it will always seem to men that no means can be too difficult, no price too high, to do whatever is required to realise the ultimate goal. Such certainty is

---

[1] Vanini is quoted by Prezzolini, op. cit. (p. 269 above, note 1), English version, pp. 222–3; Leibniz references ibid., p. 335.

one of the great justifications of fanaticism, compulsion, persecution. But if not all values are compatible with one another, and choices must be made for no better reason than that each value is what it is, and we choose it for what it is, and not because it can be shown on some single scale to be higher than another; if we choose forms of life because we believe in them, because we take them for granted, or, upon examination, find that we are morally unprepared to live in any other way (though others choose differently); if rationality and calculation can be applied only to means or subordinate ends, but never to ultimate ends; then a picture emerges different from that constructed round the ancient principle that there is only one good for men.

If there is only one solution to the puzzle, then the only problems are firstly how to find it, then how to realise it, and finally how to convert others to the solution by persuasion or by force. But if this is not so (Machiavelli contrasts two ways of life, but there could be, and, save for fanatical monists, there obviously are, more than two), then the path is open to empiricism, pluralism, toleration, compromise. Toleration is historically the product of the realisation of the irreconcilability of equally dogmatic faiths, and the practical improbability of complete victory of one over the other. Those who wished to survive realised that they had to tolerate error. They gradually came to see merits in diversity, and so became sceptical about definitive solutions in human affairs.

But it is one thing to accept something in practice, another to justify it rationally. Machiavelli's 'scandalous' writings begin the latter process. This was a major turning-point, and its intellectual consequences, wholly unintended by its originator, were, by a fortunate irony of history (which some call its dialectic), the bases of the very liberalism that Machiavelli would surely have condemned as feeble and characterless, lacking in single-minded pursuit of power, in splendour, in organisation, in *virtù*, in power to discipline unruly men against huge odds into one energetic whole. Yet he is, in spite of himself, one of the makers of pluralism, and of its – to him – perilous acceptance of toleration.

By breaking the original unity he helped to cause men to become aware of the necessity of having to make agonising choices between incompatible alternatives in public and in private life (for the two could not, it became obvious, be genuinely kept distinct). His achievement is of the first order, if only because the dilemma has never given men peace since it came to light (it remains unsolved, but we have learnt to live with it). Men had, no doubt, in practice, often enough experienced the conflict which Machiavelli made explicit. He converted its expression from a paradox into something approaching a commonplace.

The sword of which Meinecke spoke has not lost its edge: the wound has not healed. To know the worst is not always to be liberated from its consequences; nevertheless it is preferable to ignorance. It is this painful truth that Machiavelli forced on our attention, not by formulating it explicitly, but perhaps the more effectively by relegating much uncriticised traditional morality to the realm of Utopia. This is what, at any rate, I should like to suggest. Where more than twenty interpretations hold the field, the addition of one more cannot be deemed an impertinence. At worst it will be no more than yet another attempt to solve the problem, now more than four centuries old, of which Croce at the end of his long life spoke as 'Una questione che forse non si chiuderà mai: la questione del Machiavelli'.[1]

---

[1] *Quaderni della 'Critica'* 5 No 14 (July 1949), 1–9.

# THE DIVORCE BETWEEN
# THE SCIENCES AND THE HUMANITIES

I

MY SUBJECT is the relation of the natural sciences to the humanities: more particularly, a growing tension between them; and especially the moment when, it seems to me, the great divorce between them, which had been brewing for some time, became clear for all who had eyes to see. It was not a divorce between 'two cultures': there have been many cultures in the history of mankind, and their variety has little or nothing to do with the differences between the natural sciences and the humanities. I have tried but altogether failed to grasp what is meant by describing these two great fields of human enquiry as cultures; but they do seem to have been concerned with somewhat different issues, and those who have worked and are working in them have pursued different aims and methods – a fact which, for better or for worse, became explicit in the eighteenth century.

I begin with a tradition in which many eminent scientists today still stand: the tradition of those who believe that it is possible to make steady progress in the entire sphere of human knowledge; that methods and goals are, or should be, ultimately identical throughout this sphere; that the path to progress has been, as often as not – or perhaps a good deal more often – blocked by ignorance, fantasy, prejudice, superstition and other forms of unreason; that we have in our day reached a stage when the achievements of the natural sciences are such that it is possible to derive their structure from a single integrated set of clear principles or rules which, if correctly applied, make possible indefinite further progress in the unravelling of the mysteries of nature.

The approach is in line with a central tradition in Western thought which extends back at least as far as Plato. It appears to me to rest on at least three basic assumptions: (*a*) that every genuine question has one true answer and one only: all the others being false. Unless this is so, the question cannot be a real question –

there is a confusion in it somewhere. This position, which has been made explicit by modern empiricist philosophers, is entailed no less firmly by the views of their theological and metaphysical predecessors, against whom they have been engaged in long and uncompromising warfare. (*b*) The method which leads to correct solutions to all genuine problems is rational in character; and is, in essence, if not in detailed application, identical in all fields. (*c*) These solutions, whether or not they are discovered, are true universally, eternally and immutably: true for all times, places and men: as in the old definition of natural law, they are 'quod ubique, quod semper, quod ab omnibus creditum est'.[1]

Opinions within this tradition have, of course, differed about where the answers were to be sought: some thought they could be discovered only by specialists trained in, let us say, Plato's dialectical method, or Aristotle's more empirical types of investigation; or in the methods of various schools of Sophists, or of the thinkers who trace their descent from Socrates. Others held that such truths were more accessible to men of pure and innocent soul, whose understanding had not been corrupted by philosophic subtleties or the sophistication of civilisation or destructive social institutions, as, for example, Rousseau and Tolstoy at times maintained. There were those, especially in the seventeenth century, who believed that the only true path was that of systems based on rational insight (of which mathematical reasoning offered the perfect example), which yielded a priori truths; others put their faith in hypotheses confirmed or falsified by controlled observation and experiment; still others preferred to rely on what seemed to them plain common sense – *le bon sens* – reinforced by careful observation, experiment, scientific method, but not replaceable by the sciences; and men have pointed to other roads to truth. What is common to all thinkers of this type is the belief that there is only one true method or combination of methods: and that what cannot be answered by it, cannot be answered at all. The implication of this position is that the world is a single system which can be described and explained by the use of rational methods; with the practical corollary that if man's life is to be organised at all, and not left to chaos and the play of uncontrolled nature and chance, then it can be organised only in the light of such principles and laws.

It is not surprising that this view was most strongly held and

[1] Vincent of Lérins, *Commonitorium* 2. 3.

most influential in the hour of the greatest triumph of the natural sciences – surely a major, if not the major, achievement of the human mind: and especially, therefore, in the seventeenth century in Western Europe. From Descartes and Bacon and the followers of Galileo and Newton, from Voltaire and the Encyclopaedists to Saint-Simon and Comte and Buckle, and, in our own century, H. G. Wells and Bernal and Skinner and the Viennese positivists, with their ideal of a unified system of all the sciences, natural and humane, this has been the programme of the modern Enlightenment; and it has played a decisive role in the social, legal and technological organisation of our world. This was perhaps bound sooner or later to provoke a reaction from those who felt that constructions of reason and science, of a single all-embracing system, whether it claimed to explain the nature of things, or to go further and dictate, in the light of this, what one should do and be and believe, were in some way constricting – an obstacle to their own vision of the world, chains on their imagination or feeling or will, a barrier to spiritual or political liberty.

This is not the first occasion on which this phenomenon occurred: the domination of the philosophical schools of Athens in the Hellenistic period was attended by a noticeable increase in mystery cults and other forms of occultism and emotionalism in which non-rational elements in the human spirit sought an outlet. There was the great Christian revolt against the great organised legal systems, whether of the Jews or the Romans; there were medieval antinomian rebellions against the scholastic establishment and the authority of the Church – movements of this kind from the Cathars to the anabaptists are evidence enough of this; the Reformation was preceded and followed by the rise of powerful mystical and irrationalist currents. I will not dwell on more recent manifestations of this – in the German *Sturm und Drang*, in the romanticism of the early nineteenth century, in Carlyle and Kierkegaard and Nietzsche and the vast spectrum of modern irrationalism both on the right and on the left.

It is not, however, with this that I intend to deal, but with the critical attack upon the total claim of the new scientific method to dominate the entire field of human knowledge, whether in its metaphysical – a priori – or empirical-probabilistic forms. This attack, whether its causes were psychological or social (and I am inclined to think that they were, at least in part, due to a reaction on the part of humanists, especially the inward-looking, antimaterialistic Christians among them, against the all-conquering advance of the physical sciences), was itself based on rational argument, and in due course led to the great divorce between the natural sciences and the humanities – *Naturwissenschaft* and *Geisteswissenschaft* – a divorce the validity of which has been challenged ever since and remains a central and highly controversial issue to this day.

As everyone knows, the great triumphs of natural science in the seventeenth century gave the proponents of the scientific method immense prestige. The great liberators of the age were Descartes and Bacon, who carried opposition to the authority of tradition, faith, dogma or prescription into every realm of knowledge and opinion, armed with weapons used during the Renaissance and, indeed, earlier. Although there was much cautious avoidance of open defiance of Christian belief, the general thrust of the new movement was to bring everything before the bar of reason: the cruder forgeries and misinterpretations of texts, on which lawyers and clerics had rested their claims, had been exposed by humanists in Italy and Protestant reformers in France; appeals to the authority of the Bible, or Aristotle, or Roman law, had met with a good deal of acutely argued resistance based both on learning and on critical methods. Descartes made an epoch with his attempt to systematise these methods – notably in his *Discourse on Method* and its application in his *Meditations* – his two most popular and influential philosophical treatises. Spinoza's *Treatise on the Improvement of the Understanding*, his quasi-geometrical method in the *Ethics*, and the severely rationalist assumptions and rigorous logic in his political works and his criticisms of the Old Testament, had carried the war further into the enemy's camp. Bacon and Spinoza, in their different ways, sought to remove obstacles to clear, rational thinking. Bacon exposed what he considered the chief sources of delusion: 'idols' of 'the tribe', 'the cave', 'the market-place' and 'the theatre'[1] – effects, in his view, of the uncritical acceptance of the evidence of the senses, of one's own predilections, of misunderstanding of words, of confusions bred by the speculative fantasies of philosophers, and the like. Spinoza stressed the degree to which emotions clouded reason, and led to groundless fears and hatreds which led to destructive practice; from

---

[1] *Novum organum* I. 39.

Valla to Locke and Berkeley there were frequent warnings and examples of fallacies and confusions due to the misuse of language.

The general, if not the universal, tendency of the new philosophy was to declare that if the human mind can be cleared of dogma, prejudice and cant, of the organised obscurities and Aristotelian patter of the schoolmen, then nature will at last be seen in the full symmetry and harmony of its elements, which can be described, analysed and represented by a logically appropriate language – the language of the mathematical and physical sciences. Leibniz seems to have believed not only in the possibility of constructing a logically perfect language, which would reflect the structure of reality, but in something not unlike a general science of discovery. His views spread far beyond philosophical or scientific circles – indeed, theoretical knowledge was still conceived as one undivided realm; the frontiers between philosophy, science, criticism, theology were not sharply drawn. There were invasions and counter-invasions; grammar, rhetoric, jurisprudence, philosophy made forays into the fields of historical learning and natural knowledge, and were attacked by them in turn. The new rationalism spread into the creative arts. Just as the Royal Society in England formally set itself against the use of metaphor and other forms of rhetorical speech, and demanded language that was plain and literal and precise, so there was in France at this time a corresponding avoidance of metaphor, embellishment and highly coloured expression in, for example, the plays of Racine or Molière, in the verse of La Fontaine and Boileau, writers who dominated the European scene; and because such luxuriance was held to flourish in Italy, Italian literature was duly denounced in France for the impurity of its style. The new method sought to eliminate everything that could not be justified by the systematic use of rational methods, above all the fictions of the metaphysicians, the mystics, the poets; what were myth and legend but falsehoods with which primitive and barbarous societies were gulled during their early, helpless childhood? At best, they were fanciful or distorted accounts of real events or persons. Even the Catholic Church was influenced by the prevailing scientific temper, and the great archival labours of the Bollandists and Maurists were conducted in a semi-scientific spirit.[1]

[1] M. H. Fisch has correctly pointed out that the dissolution of monasteries had released a mass of documentary evidence which had not hitherto been available,

It was natural enough that history was one of the earliest victims of what might be called the positivist character of the new scientific movement. Scepticism about historical veracity was no new thing: ignorance and fantasy, as well as malicious invention, had been attributed to Herodotus by Plutarch; and these charges against narrative history had been repeated at intervals by those who preferred certainty to conjecture. The sixteenth century in particular, perhaps as a result of the mobilisation of history in the religious wars by the various factions, saw a rise of scepticism and doubt: Cornelius Agrippa, in 1531, dwells on the carelessness and contradictions of historians, and their shameless inventions to cover up their ignorance or fill gaps in knowledge where there is no available evidence; on the absurdity of idealising the characters of the main actors in the story; he speaks of the distortion of facts as being due to the historians' passions – wishes, hatreds and fears, desire to please a patron, patriotic motives, national pride – Plutarch glorified the Greeks in comparison with the Romans, and in his own day polemical writers extolled the virtues of Gauls over Franks, and vice versa. How can truth emerge in these conditions? In the same vein Patrizi, at the turn of the century, declares that all history ultimately rests on eye-witness evidence: and argues that those who are present are likely to be involved in the issues, and are therefore liable to be partisan; while those who can afford to be objective because they are neutral and uninvolved are unlikely to see the evidence jealously preserved by the partisans, and have to depend upon the biased accounts of the interested parties.

Such Pyrrhonism grows with the century: it is characteristic of Montaigne, Charron, La Mothe le Vayer, and of course, later in the century, in a more extreme form, of Pierre Bayle, to take but a few examples. So long as history is regarded as a school of virtue, the purpose of which is to celebrate the good and expose the wicked, to show the unaltering character of human nature at all times, everywhere, to be simply moral and political philosophy teaching by examples, it may not matter greatly whether such history is accurate or not. But once a desire for truth for its own sake asserts itself, something more novel is born: the desire to create an advancing science, to accumulate knowledge, to know more than our predecessors and to be aware of this; which leads to the

and this contributed to the fact that the Church, in repelling attacks on her historical claims, had recourse to weapons of historical research.

realisation that this can be achieved only if the reputable practitioners in the field recognise the validity of the same principles and methods and can test each other's conclusions, as has been (and is) the case in physics or mathematics or astronomy and in all the new sciences. It is this new outlook that made the claims of history to be a province of knowledge seem so precarious.

Much of the most formidable attack came from Descartes. His views are well known: true science rests on axiomatic premisses, from which, by the use of rational rules, irrefutable conclusions can be drawn: this is how we proceed in geometry, in algebra, in physics. Where are the axioms, the transformation rules, the inescapable conclusions in historical writing? The progress of true knowledge is the discovery of eternal, unalterable, universal truths: every generation of seekers after truth stands on the shoulders of its predecessors and begins where these others left off, and adds to the growing sum of human knowledge. This is plainly not the case in historical writing, or indeed in the field of the humanities in general. Where, in this province, is the single, ever-mounting edifice of science? A schoolboy today knows more geometry than Pythagoras: what do the greatest classical scholars of our time know about ancient Rome that was not known to Cicero's servant-girl? What have they added to her store? What, then, is the use of all these learned labours? Descartes implies that he does not wish to prevent men from indulging in this pastime – they may find it agreeable enough to while away their leisure in these ways – it is no worse, he says, than learning some quaint dialect, say, Swiss or bas-Breton; but it is not an occupation for anyone seriously concerned with increasing knowledge. Malebranche dismisses history as gossip; this is echoed by other Cartesians; even Leibniz, who composed a sizeable historical work himself, gives a conventional defence of history as a means of satisfying curiosity about origins of families or States, and as a school of morals. Its inferiority to mathematics, and philosophy founded on the mathematical and natural sciences and the other discoveries of pure reason, must be obvious to all thinking men.

These attitudes did not, of course, kill historical studies. Methods of scholarship had advanced greatly since the middle of the fifteenth century, especially by the use made of antiquities. Monuments, legal documents, manuscripts, coins, medals, works of art, literature, buildings, inscriptions, popular ballads, legends could be employed as aids to, and sometimes even substitutes for, unreliable narrative history. The great jurists of the sixteenth century, Budé, Alciati, Cujas, Dumoulin, Hotman, Baudouin and their disciples, and in the following century Coke and Matthew Hale in England, Vranck in the Low Countries, de Gregorio in Italy and Sparre in Sweden, performed major labours of reconstructing legal texts, both Roman and medieval. The school of universal historians in France – Pasquier, Le Roy, Le Caron, Vignier, La Popelinière, and, indeed, the polymath Bodin – originated at least the conception of cultural history;[1] and were followed in the seventeenth century by writers like the abbé de Saint-Réal, Dufresnoy, Charles Sorel, *Père* Gabriel Daniel, and, of course, Boulainvilliers and Fénelon. These early outlines of cultural history, and in particular the growing awareness of the differences rather than the similarities between different societies, ages, civilisations, were a novel development, which, in due course, revolutionised historical notions. Nevertheless, their proponents showed a greater propensity for denouncing useless erudition, and for making up programmes of what historians should do, than for indicating precise methods of performing these tasks or, indeed, performing them. Much of this was meta-history, or theories of history, rather than concrete historical writing. Moreover, the scientific model (or 'paradigm') which dominated the century, with its strong implication that only that which was quantifiable, or at any rate measurable – that to which in principle mathematical methods were applicable – was real, strongly reinforced the old conviction that to every question there was only one true answer, universal, eternal, unchangeable; it was, or appeared to be, so in mathematics, physics, mechanics and astronomy, and soon would be in chemistry and botany and zoology and other natural sciences; with the corollary that the most reliable criterion of objective truth was logical demonstration, or measurement, or at least approximations to this.

Spinoza's political theory is a good example of this approach: he supposes that the rational answer to the question of what is the best government for men is in principle discoverable by anyone, anywhere, in any circumstances. If men have not discovered these timeless solutions before, this must be due to weakness, or the

[1] Phrases like 'les saisons et mutations de moeurs d'un peuple', or 'la complexion et humour' of a nation, or 'façons de vivre', or 'forme de vivre', 'la police' or 'les motifs, les opinions et les pensées des hommes', 'le génie du siècle, des opinions, des moeurs, des idées dominantes', 'les passions qui conduisaient les hommes' were very common throughout the sixteenth and seventeenth centuries.

clouding of reason by emotion, or perhaps bad luck: the truths of which he supposed himself to be giving a rational demonstration could presumably have been discovered and applied by human reason at any time, so that mankind might have been spared many evils. Hobbes, an empiricist, but equally dominated by a scientific model, presupposes this also. The notion of time, change, historical development does not impinge upon these views. Furthermore, such truths, when discovered, must add to human welfare. Consequently the motive for the search is not curiosity, or desire to know the truth as such, so much as utilitarian – the promotion of a better life on earth by making man more rational and therefore wiser, more just, virtuous and happy. The ends of man are given: given by God or nature. Reason, freed from its trammels, will discover what they are: all that is necessary is to find the right means for their attainment.

This is the ideal from Francis Bacon to H. G. Wells and Julian Huxley and many of those who, in our day, believe in moral and political arrangements based on a scientific theory of sociology and psychology. The most famous figure in this entire movement, not in that of science itself, but of the application of its discoveries to the lives of men – certainly its most gifted propagandist – was Voltaire. Its earliest and strongest opponent was the Neapolitan philosopher Giambattista Vico. The contrast between their views may serve to throw light upon the radical difference of attitudes which brought about a crucial parting of the ways.

II

Voltaire is the central figure of the Enlightenment, because he accepted its basic principles and used all his incomparable wit and energy and literary skill and brilliant malice to propagate these principles and spread havoc in the enemy's camp. Ridicule kills more surely than savage indignation: and Voltaire probably did more for the triumph of civilised values than any writer who ever lived. What were these principles? Let me repeat the formula once more: there are eternal, timeless truths, identical in all the spheres of human activity – moral and political, social and economic, scientific and artistic; and there is only one way of recognising them: by means of reason, which Voltaire interpreted not as the deductive method of logic or mathematics, which was too abstract and unrelated to the facts and needs of daily life, but as *le bon sens*, good sense, which, while it may not lead to absolute certainty, attains to a degree of verisimilitude or probability quite sufficient for human affairs, for public and private life. Not many men are fully armed with this excellent faculty, for the majority appear to be incurably stupid; but those few who do possess it are responsible for the finest hours of mankind. All that is of value in the past are these fine hours: from acquaintance with them alone we can learn how to make men good, that is, sane, rational, tolerant, or, at any rate, less savage and stupid and cruel; how to enact laws and governments which will promote justice, beauty, freedom and happiness and diminish brutality, fanaticism, oppression, with which the greater part of human history is filled.

The task of modern historians is therefore plain: to describe and celebrate these moments of high culture and contrast them with the surrounding darkness – the barbarous ages of faith, fanaticism, folly, error and vice. In order to do this historians must give more attention than the ancients to 'customs, laws, manners, commerce, finance, agriculture, population':[1] and also, trade, industry, colonisation and the development of taste. This is far more important than accounts of wars, treaties, political institutions, conquerors, dynastic tables, public affairs, to which historians have attached far too much significance hitherto. Madame du Châtelet, Voltaire tells us, said to him: 'What is the point for a Frenchwoman like me . . . of knowing that in Sweden Égil succeeded King Haquin; or that Ottoman was the son of Ortogul?'[2] She was perfectly right: the purpose of the work which he wrote ostensibly for the illumination of this lady (the famous *Essai sur les moeurs*) is, therefore, not 'to know in which year one prince who doesn't deserve to be remembered succeeded another barbarian prince of some uncouth nation'.[3] 'I wish to show how human societies came into existence, how domestic life was lived, what arts were cultivated, rather than tell once again the old story of disasters and misfortunes . . . those familiar examples of human malice and depravity.'[4] He intends to recount the achievement of 'the human spirit in the most

---

[1] 'Histoire' in *Dictionnaire philosophique*: p. 365 in *Oeuvres complètes de Voltaire*, [ed. Louis Moland] (Paris, 1877–85) (hereafter M), vol. 19. Subsequent references to Voltaire, unless otherwise stated, are to this edition, by volume and page, thus: M xix 365.

[2] Preface to *Essai sur l'histoire universelle*, vol. 3 (1754): M xxiv 41.

[3] *Essai sur les moeurs*, 'Avant-propos': M xi 157.

[4] ibid., chapter 81: M xii 53.

enlightened of ages',[1] for only that is worthy of mention which is worthy of posterity.

History is an arid desert with few oases. There are only four great ages in the West in which human beings rose to their full stature and created civilisations of which they can be proud: the age of Alexander, in which he includes the classical age of Athens; the age of Augustus, in which he includes the Roman Republic and the Empire at their best; Florence during the Renaissance; and the age of Louis XIV in France. Voltaire assumes throughout that these are élitist civilisations, imposed by enlightened oligarchies on the masses, for the latter lack reason and courage, want only to be amused and deceived, and so are naturally prey to religion, that is, for him, to abominable superstitions. Only governments can 'raise or lower the level of nations'.[2]

The basic assumption is, of course, that the goals pursued in these four great cultures are ultimately the same: truth, light are the same everywhere, it is only error that has myriad forms. Moreover, it is absurd to confine enquiry to Europe and that portion of the Near East whence sprang little but the cruelties, fanaticism and nonsensical beliefs of the Jews and the Christians who, whatever Bossuet may seek to demonstrate, were and remain enemies of truth and progress and toleration. It is absurd to ignore the great and peaceful kingdom of China, governed by enlightened Mandarins, or India, or Chaldaea and other parts of the world which only the absurd vanity of Christian Europe excludes from the orbit of history. The purpose of history is to impart instructive truths, not to satisfy idle curiosity, and this can be done only by studying the peaks of human achievement, not the valleys. The historian should not peddle fables, like Herodotus, who is like an old woman telling stories to children, but teach us our duties without seeming to do so, by painting for posterity not the acts of a single man but the progress of the human spirit in the most enlightened ages. 'If you have no more to tell us than that one barbarian succeeded another barbarian on the banks of the Oxus or the Iaxartes, what use are you to the public?'[3] Why should we be interested in the fact that 'Quancum succeeded Kincum, and

---

[1] *Siècle de Louis XIV*, Introduction: M xiv 155.

[2] Letter to Maurice Pilavoine, 23 April 1760.

[3] op. cit. (p. 335 above, note 1), p. 367.

Kicum succeeded Quancum'?[1] We do not wish to know about the life of Louis the Fat, or Louis the Obstinate, or even the barbarous Shakespeare and the tedious Milton: but about the achievements of Galileo, Newton, Tasso, Addison; who wants to know about Shalmaneser or Mardokempad? Historians must not clutter the minds of their readers with accounts of religious wars or other stupidities that degrade mankind, unless it be to show them how low human beings can sink: accounts of Philip II of Spain, or Christian of Denmark, are cautionary tales to warn mankind of the dangers of tyranny; or if, like Voltaire himself, one does write a lively and entertaining biography of Charles XII of Sweden, it is for the sole end of pointing out to men the dangers of a life of reckless adventure. What *is* worth knowing is why the Emperor Charles V did not profit more by his capture of King Francis I of France; or what the value of sound finance was to Elizabeth of England, or Henry IV or Louis XIV in France, or the importance of the *dirigiste* policy of Colbert compared with that of Sully. As for horrors, they too are to be detailed if we are to avoid another St Bartholomew's Eve or another Cromwell.

The task of the historian, he says again and again, is to recount the achievements of those regrettably rare periods when the arts and sciences flourished and nature was made to yield the necessities, comforts and pleasures of man. Meinecke rightly described Voltaire as 'the banker of the Enlightenment', the keeper of its achievements, a kind of scorer in the contest of light against darkness, reason and civilisation against barbarism and religion, Athens and the Rome of the virtuous Caesars against Jerusalem and the Rome of the Popes, Julian the Apostate versus the horrible Gregory of Nazianzus. But how are we to tell what actually happened in the past? Has not Pierre Bayle thrown terrible doubts on the authenticity of particular reports of facts, and shown how unreliable and contradictory historical evidence can be? This may be so, but it is not particular facts that matter, according to Voltaire, so much as the general character of an age or a culture. The acts of single men are of small importance, and individual character is too difficult to elucidate: when we can scarcely tell even what the true character of Mazarin was like, how can we possibly do this for the ancients? Soul, character, dominant motives – all that sort of thing is an impenetrable chaos which can never be

[1] *Essai sur les moeurs*, chapter 195: M xiii 162.

firmly grasped. Whoever, after centuries, would disentangle this chaos simply creates more.

How, then, are we to recover the past? By the light of natural reason – *le bon sens*. Anything not in keeping with natural science, with reason, with the nature [*trempe*] of the human heart is false – why bother with the ravings of savages and the inventions of knaves? We know that monuments are 'historical lies' and that there is not a single temple or college of priests, not a single feast in the Church, that does not originate in some idiocy. The human heart is the same everywhere; and good sense is enough to detect the truth.

*Le bon sens* served Voltaire well: it enabled him to discredit much clerical propaganda and a good many naïve and pedantic absurdities. But it also told him that the empires of Babylon and Assyria could not possibly have coexisted next door to each other in so confined a space; that accounts of temple prostitutes were obvious nonsense; that Cyrus and Croesus were fictional beings; that Themistocles could not possibly have died of drinking ox-blood; that Belus and Ninus could not have been Babylonian kings, for '-us' is not a Babylonian ending; that Xerxes did not flog the Hellespont. The Flood is an absurd fable: as for the shells found on tops of mountains, these may well have dropped from the hats of pilgrims. On the other hand, he found no difficulty at all in accepting the reality of satyrs, fauns, the Minotaur, Zeus, Theseus, Hercules, or the journey of Bacchus to India, and he happily accepted a forged Indian classic, the *Ezour-Veidam*. Yet Voltaire undoubtedly expanded the area of proper historical interest beyond politics, wars, great men, by insisting on the need to describe how men travelled, lived, slept, dressed, wrote, their social and economic and artistic activities. Jacques Coeur was more important than Joan of Arc. He complains that Pufendorf, who has had access to the State archives of Sweden, has told us nothing about the natural resources of that country, the causes of its poverty, what part it played in the Gothic invasions of the Roman Empire; these are novel and important demands. Voltaire denounced Europocentrism; he sketched the need for social, economic, cultural history, which, even though he did not himself realise his programme (his own histories are marvellously readable but largely anecdotal in character – there is no real attempt at synthesis), stimulated the interest of his successors in a wider field. At the same time he devalued the historical nature of history, for his interests are moral, aesthetic, social: as a *philosophe* he is part moralist, part tourist and *feuilletoniste*, and wholly a journalist, albeit of incomparable genius. He does not recognise, even as a cultural historian – or cataloguer – the multiplicity and relativity of values at different times and places, or the genetic dimension in history: the notion of change and growth is largely alien to him. For Voltaire there are only bright ages and dark, and the dark are due to the crimes, follies and misfortunes of men. In this respect he is a good deal less historical than some of his predecessors in the Renaissance. He looks on history, in a loose fashion, as an accumulation of facts, casually connected, the purpose of which is to show men under what conditions those central purposes which nature has implanted in the heart of every man can best be realised: who are the enemies of progress, and how they are to be routed. Thereby Voltaire probably did more than anyone else to determine the entire direction of the Enlightenment: Hume and Gibbon are possessed by the same spirit.

Not until the reaction against the classification of all human experience in terms of absolute and timeless values – a reaction which first began in Switzerland and England among critics and historians of Greek and Hebrew literature, and, penetrating to Germany, created the great intellectual revolution of which Herder was the most influential apostle – did history, as we understand it today, come into its own. Nevertheless, it is to Voltaire, Fontenelle and Montesquieu (who, contrary to the accepted view of him, was no less convinced of the absolute and timeless nature of ultimate human ends, however much means and methods might vary from clime to clime) that we owe the more scientific branches of later historical writing: economic history, the history of science and technology, historical sociology, demography, all the provinces of the knowledge of the past which owe their existence to statistical and other quantitative techniques. But the history of civilisation which Voltaire supposed himself to be initiating was in the end created by the Germans, who looked on him as the arch-enemy of all that they held dear.

Yet even before the Counter-Enlightenment of the Swiss and the English and the Germans, a new conception of the study of history came into being. It was anti-Voltairean in character, and its author was an obscure Neapolitan of whom Voltaire had almost certainly never heard: and, if he had, would have treated with disdain.

III

Giambattista Vico was born in Naples in 1668 and lived there or in its environs until his death in 1744. Throughout his long life he was little known, the very exemplar of a lonely thinker. He was educated by priests, worked for some years as a private tutor, became a minor professor of rhetoric at the University of Naples, and after many years of composing inscriptions, Latin eulogies and laudatory biographies for the rich and the great in order to supplement his meagre income, was rewarded in the last years of his life by being appointed official historiographer to the Austrian Viceroy of Naples.

He was steeped in the literature of humanism, in the classical authors and antiquities, and especially in Roman law. His mind was not analytical or scientific but literary and intuitive. Naples under Spanish and Austrian rulers was not in the vanguard of the new scientific movement; although experimental scientists were at work there, so were the Church and the Inquisition. If anything, the Kingdom of the Two Sicilies was something of a backwater, and Vico, by inclination a religious humanist with a rich historical imagination, was not in sympathy with the great scientific material-ist movement that was determined to sweep away the last relics of the scholastic metaphysics. Nevertheless, in his youth, he fell under the sway of the new currents of thought: he read Lucretius, and the Epicurean conception of gradual human development from primi-tive, semi-bestial beginnings remained with him, despite his Chris-tian faith, all his life. Influenced by the all-powerful Cartesian movement, he began by believing mathematics to be the queen of the sciences. But evidently something in him rebelled against this. In 1709, at the age of forty, in an inaugural lecture, with which professors in the University of Naples were obliged to start each academic year, he published a passionate defence of humanist education: men's minds (*ingenia*) were shaped by the language – the words and the images – which they inherited, no less than their minds, in turn, shaped their modes of expression; the search after a plain, neutral style, like the attempt to train the young exclusively in the dry light of the Cartesian analytic method, tended to rob them of imaginative power. Vico defended the rich, traditional Italian 'rhetoric', inherited from the great humanists of the Renais-sance, against the austere and deflationary style of the French rationalist science-influenced modernists.

Evidently he continued to brood on the two contrasted methods, for in the following year he arrived at a truly startling conclusion: mathematics was indeed, as had always been claimed for it, a discipline which led to wholly clear, irrefutable propositions of universal validity. But this was so not because the language of mathematics was a reflection of the basic and unalterable structure of reality, as thinkers since the days of Plato or even Pythagoras had maintained: it was so because mathematics was not a reflection of anything. Mathematics was not a discovery but a human invention: starting from definitions and axioms of their own choosing, mathematicians could, by means of rules of which they or other men were authors, arrive at conclusions that did indeed logically follow, because the man-made rules, definitions and axioms saw to it that they did so. Mathematics was a kind of game (although Vico did not call it that), in which the counters and the rules were man-made; the moves and their implications were indeed certain, but at the cost of describing nothing – a play of abstractions controlled by their creators. Once this system was applied to the natural world – for instance, as in physics or mechanics – it yielded important truths, but inasmuch as nature had not been invented by men, and had its own characteristics and could not, like symbols, be freely manipulated, the conclusions became less clear, no longer wholly knowable. Mathematics was not a system of laws which governed reality, but a system of rules, in terms of which it was useful to generalise about, analyse and predict, the behaviour of things in space.

Here Vico made use of an ancient scholastic proposition at least as old as St Augustine: that one could know fully only what one had oneself made. A man could understand fully his own intellectual or poetical construction, a work of art or a plan, because he had himself made it, and it was therefore transparent to him: everything in it had been created by his intellect and his imagination. Indeed, Hobbes had asserted as much in the case of political constitutions. But the world – nature – had not been made by men: therefore only God, who had made it, could know it through and through. Mathematics seemed so marvellous an achievement precisely because it was wholly man's own work – the nearest to divine creation that man could attain to. And there were those in the Renaissance who spoke of art, too, in this fashion, and said that the artist was a creator, *quasi deus*, of an imaginary world created alongside the real world, and the artist, the god who had created it, knew it through and through. But about the world of external nature there was something opaque: men could describe it, could tell how it behaved in different situations and relationships, could offer hypotheses about the behaviour of its constituents – physical bodies and the like; but they could not tell why – for what reason – it was as it was, and behaved as it did: only he who made it, namely God, knew that – men had only an outside view, as it were, of what went on on the stage of nature. Men could know 'from the inside' only what they had made themselves and nothing else. The greater the man-made element in any object of knowledge, the more transparent to human vision it will be; the greater the ingredient of external nature, the more opaque and impenetrable to human understanding. There was an impassable gulf between the man-made and the natural: the constructed and the given. All provinces of knowledge could be classified along this scale of relative intelligibility.

Ten years later Vico took a radical step: there existed a field of knowledge besides that of the most obviously man-made constructions – works of art, or political schemes, or legal systems, and, indeed, all rule-determined disciplines – which men could know from within: human history; for it, too, was made by men. Human history did not consist merely of things and events and their compresences and sequences (including those of human organisms viewed as natural objects) as the external world did; it was the story of human activities, of what men did and thought and suffered, of what they strove for, aimed at, accepted, rejected, conceived, imagined, of what their feelings were directed at. It was concerned, therefore, with motives, purposes, hopes, fears, loves and hatreds, jealousies, ambitions, outlooks and visions of reality; with the ways of seeing, and ways of acting and creating, of individuals and groups. These activities we knew directly, because we were involved in them as actors, not spectators. There was a sense, therefore, in which we knew more about ourselves than we knew about the external world; when we studied, let us say, Roman law, or Roman institutions, we were not contemplating objects in nature, of whose purposes, or whether they had any, we could know nothing. We had to ask ourselves what these Romans were at, what they strove to do, how they lived and thought, what kind of relationship with other men they were anxious to promote or frustrate. We could not ask this about natural objects: it was idle to ask what cows or trees or stones, or molecules or cells, were *at*: we had no reason to suppose that they pursued purposes; or, if they did, we could not know what they were; since we had not made them, we could have no God-like 'inside' view of what ends, if any, they pursued or had been created to fulfil. There was, therefore, a clear sense in which our knowledge was superior, at least in kind, about intentional behaviour – that is, action – to our knowledge of the movement or position of bodies in space, the field of the magnificent triumphs of seventeenth-century science. What was opaque to us when we contemplated the external world was, if not wholly transparent, yet surely far more so when we contemplated ourselves. It was therefore a perverse kind of self-denial to apply the rules and laws of physics or of the other natural sciences to the world of mind and will and feeling; for by doing this we would be gratuitously debarring ourselves from much that we could know.

If anthropomorphism was falsely to endow the inanimate world with human minds and wills, there was presumably a world which it was proper to endow with precisely these attributes, namely, the world of man. Consequently, a natural science of men treated as purely natural entities, on a par with rivers and plants and stones, rested on a cardinal error. With regard to ourselves we were privileged observers with an 'inside' view: to ignore it in favour of the ideal of a unified science of all there is, a single, universal method of investigation, was to insist on wilful ignorance in the name of a materialist dogma of what could alone be known. We know what is meant by action, purpose, effort to achieve something or to understand something – we know these things through direct consciousness of them. We possess self-awareness. Can we also tell what others are at? Vico never directly tells us how this is achieved, but seems to take it for granted that solipsism needs no refutation; and, moreover, that we communicate with others because we can and do grasp in some direct fashion, less or more successfully, the purpose and meaning of their words, their gestures, their signs and symbols; for if there were no communication, there would be no language, no society, no humanity. But even if this applies to the present and the living, does it also apply to the past? Can we grasp the acts, the thoughts, the attitudes, the beliefs, explicit and implicit, the worlds of thought and feeling of societies dead and gone? If so, how is this achieved? Vico's answer to this problem is perhaps the boldest and most original of his ideas.

He declared that there were three great doors that lead into the past: language; myths; and rites, that is, institutional behaviour. We speak of metaphorical ways of expression. The aesthetic theorists of his day (Vico tells us) regard this simply as so much embellishment, a heightened form of speech used by poets as a deliberate device to give us pleasure or move us in particular ways, or ingenious ways of conveying important truths.[1] This rests on the assumption that what is expressed metaphorically could, at least in principle, be as well expressed in plain, literal prose, although this might be tedious and not give us the pleasure caused by poetic speech. But, Vico maintains, if you read primitive utterances (Latin antiquities, which he knew best, provide him with the majority of his examples) you will soon realise that what we call metaphorical speech is the natural mode of expression of these early men. When we say that our blood is boiling, this may for us be a conventional metaphor for anger, but for primitive man anger literally resembled the sensation of blood boiling within him; when we speak of the teeth of ploughs, or the mouths of rivers, or the lips of vases, these are dead metaphors or, at best, deliberate artifice intended to produce a certain effect upon the listener or reader. But to our remote ancestors ploughs actually appeared to have teeth; rivers, which for them were semi-animate, had mouths: land was endowed with necks and tongues, metals and minerals with veins, the earth had bowels, oaks had hearts, skies smiled and frowned, winds raged, the whole of nature was alive and active. Gradually, as human experience changed, this, once natural, speech, which Vico

[1] So Fontenelle, whose influence was inferior only to Voltaire's, identifies progress in the arts (as in everything else) with increase in order, clarity, precision, *netteté*, whose purest expression is geometry – the Cartesian method which cannot but improve whatever it touches, in every province of knowledge and creation. Mythology for him, as for Voltaire, is the product of savagery and ignorance. He is suspicious of all metaphor, but especially of *images fabuleuses*, which spring from a 'totally false and ridiculous' conception of things – their use can only help to disseminate error. Poets in primitive times employed mythological language ornamentally, but also as a stratagem to represent themselves as directly inspired by the gods; modern writers should at least use *images spirituelles* – personified abstractions – about, say, time, space, deity, images which speak to reason, not to irrational feeling. The intellectual power, courage, humanity and unswerving pursuit of truth with which the *lumières* of the age fought against nonsense and obscurantism in theory and barbarous cruelties in practice need not blind us to the vices of their virtues, delusions which have exacted their own terrible price. (See Fontenelle's 'Sur la poésie en général': the quoted phrase is on p. 560 in his *Oeuvres complètes* (Paris, 1989– ), vol. 5.)

calls poetical, lingered on as turns of phrase in common speech whose origin had been forgotten or at least were no longer felt, or as conventions and ornament used by sophisticated versifiers. Forms of speech express specific kinds of vision; there is no universal, 'literal' speech which denotes a timeless reality. Before 'poetical' language, men used hieroglyphs and ideograms which convey a vision of the world very different from our own – Vico declares that men sang before they spoke, spoke in verse before they spoke in prose, as is made plain by the study of the kinds of signs and symbols that they used, and the types of use they made of them.

The task before those who wish to grasp what kinds of lives have in the past been led in societies different from their own is to understand their worlds: that is, to conceive what kind of vision of the world men who used a particular kind of language must have had for this type of language to be a natural expression of it. The difficulty of this task is brought home most forcibly by the mythological language which Vico cites. The Roman poet says 'Jovis omnia plena.'[1] What does this mean? Jove – Jupiter – is to us the father of the gods, a bearded thunderer, but the word also means sky or air. How can 'everything' be 'full' of a bearded thunderer, or the father of the gods? Yet this, evidently, is how men spoke. We must therefore ask ourselves what the world must have been like for those to whom such use of language, which is almost meaningless to us, made sense. What could be meant by speaking of Cybele as an enormous woman, and also, at the same time, as the whole of the earth, of Neptune as a bearded marine deity wielding a trident, and also as all the seas and oceans of the world? Thus Heracles is a demigod who slew the Hydra, but is at the same time the Athenian and Spartan and Argive and Theban Heracles; he is many and also one; Ceres is a female deity but also all the corn in the world.

It is a very strange world that we must try, as it were, to transpose ourselves into, and Vico warns us that it is only with the most agonising effort that we can even attempt to enter the mentality of the primitive savages of whose vision of reality these myths and legends are records. Yet it can, to some degree, be

---

[1] Vergil, *Eclogues* 3. 60; cf. Aratus, *Phainomena* 2–4; quoted in *The New Science of Giambattista Vico*, trans. Thomas Goddard Bergin and Max Harold Fisch, revised ed. (New York, 1968), paragraph 379. Subsequent references to the *New Science* are to this edition, thus: NS 379.

achieved, for we possess a faculty that he calls *fantasia* – imagination – with which it is possible to 'enter' minds very different from our own.

How is this done? The nearest we can come to grasping Vico's thought is his parallel between the growth of a species and the growth of the individual: just as we are able to recollect the experiences of childhood (and in our day psychoanalysis has probed further than this), so it must be possible to recapture to some degree the early collective experience of our race, even though this may require terrible effort. This is based on the parallel between the macrocosm and the individual microcosm – phylogenesis resembling ontogenesis, an idea which dates back at least to the Renaissance. There is an analogy between the growth of an individual and that of a people. If I can recollect what it was to have been a child, I shall have some inkling of what it was to have belonged to a primitive culture. Judging others by analogy with what I am now will not do: if animism is the false attribution of human characteristics to natural objects, a similar fallacy is involved in attributing to primitives our own sophisticated notions; memory, not analogy, seems closer to the required faculty of imaginative understanding – *fantasia* – whereby we reconstruct the human past.

The categories of experience of different generations of men differ; but they proceed in a fixed order which Vico thinks he can reconstruct by asking the right questions of the evidence before us. We must ask what kind of experience is presupposed by, renders intelligible, a particular use of symbols (that is, language), what particular vision is embodied in myths, in religious rites, in inscriptions, in the monuments of the past. The answers will enable us to trace human growth and development, to visualise, 'enter into' the minds of men creating their world by effort, by work, by struggle. Each phase of this process conveys, indeed communicates, its experience in its own characteristic forms – in hieroglyphs, in primitive song, in myths and legends, in dances and laws, in ceremonial and elaborate religious rites, which to Voltaire or Holbach or d'Alembert were merely obsolete relics of a barbarous past or a mass of obscurantist hocus-pocus. The development of social consciousness and activity is traceable (Vico maintains) also in the evolution of etymology and syntax, which reflects successive phases of social life, and develops *pari passu* with them. Poetry is not conscious embellishment invented by sophisticated writers, nor is it secret wisdom in mnemonic form – it is a direct form of self-expression of our remote ancestors, collective and communal; Homer is the voice not of an individual poet but of the entire Greek people. This notion, in this specific formulation of it, was destined to have a rich flowering in the theories of Winckelmann and Herder, who, when they first developed their ideas, had not, so far as one can tell, so much as heard of Vico.

As for the unaltering character of basic human nature – the central concept of the Western tradition from the Greeks to Aquinas, from the Renaissance to Grotius, Spinoza, Locke – this could not be so, for man's creations – language, myth, ritual – tell a different story. The first men were savage brutes, cave-dwellers who used 'mute'[1] signs – gestures and then hieroglyphs. The first peal of thunder filled them with terror. Awe – a sense of a power greater than themselves brooding over them – awakened in them. They gathered together for self-protection; there follows the 'age of the gods' or *patres*, stern heads of primitive human tribes. Outside their fortifications there is no security: men attacked by other men stronger than themselves seek protection and are given it by the 'fathers' at the price of becoming slaves or clients. This marks the 'heroic' age of oligarchies, of harsh and avaricious masters, users of 'poetic' speech, ruling over slaves and serfs. There comes a moment when these last revolt, extort concessions, particularly with regard to marriage and burial rites, which are the oldest forms of human institution. They cause their new rites to be recorded – this constitutes the earliest form of law. This, in turn, generates prose, which leads to argument and rhetoric, and so to questioning, to philosophy, scepticism, egalitarian democracy, and, in the end, the subversion of the simple piety, solidarity and deference to authority of primitive societies, to their atomisation and disintegration, to destructive egoism and alienation,[2] and ultimate collapse, unless some Augustus restores authority and order, or an earlier, more primitive and vigorous tribe, with still unexhausted energies and firm discipline, falls upon it and subjugates it; if this does not happen, there is a total breakdown. The primitive life in caves begins again, and so the entire cycle repeats

---

[1] NS 401, 434.

[2] The passage in Vico's *New Science* describing the end of a decadent civilisation is worth quoting: 'no matter how great the throng and press of their bodies, [men] live like wild beasts in a deep solitude of spirit and will, scarcely any two being able to agree since each follows his own pleasure or caprice'. (NS 1106).

itself once more, *corsi e ricorsi*, from the barbarism of savage life to the second barbarism of decay.

There is no progress from the imperfect towards perfection, for the very notion of perfection entails an absolute criterion of value; there is only intelligible change. The stages are not mechanically caused each by its predecessor, but can be seen to flow from the new needs created by the satisfaction of the old ones in the unceasing self-creation and self-transformation of perpetually active men. In this process, war between the classes, in Vico's schema, plays a central role. Here again, Vico draws heavily on mythology. Voltaire tells us that myths are the ravings of savages and the inventions of knaves, or at best harmless fancies conjured up by poets to charm their readers. For Vico they are, as often as not, far-reaching images of past social conflicts out of which many diverse cultures grew. He is an ingenious and imaginative historical materialist: Cadmus, Ariadne, Pegasus, Apollo, Mars, Heracles, all symbolise various turning points in the history of social change.[1] What to the rational thought of a later age seemed bizarre combinations of attributes – Cybele, who is both a woman and the

---

[1] For instance, the story of Theseus and Ariadne is concerned with early seafaring life: the Minotaur represents the pirates who abduct Athenians in ships, for the bull is a characteristic ancient emblem on a ship's prow, and piracy was held in high honour by both the Greeks and the ancient Germans. Ariadne is the art of seafaring, the thread is a symbol of navigation, and the labyrinth is the Aegean Sea. Alternatively, the Minotaur is a half-caste child, a foreigner come to Crete – an early emblem of racial conflict. Cadmus is primitive man, and his slaying of the serpent is the clearing of the vast forest. He sows the serpent's teeth in the ground – the teeth are the teeth of a plough, the stones he casts about him are the clods of earth which the oligarchy of heroes retain against the land-hungry serfs; the furrows are the orders of feudal society; the armed men who spring up from the teeth are heroes, but they fight, not each other, as the myth relates (here Vico decides to 'correct' the evidence), but the robbers and vagabonds who threaten the lives of the settled farmers. The wounding of Mars by Minerva is the defeat of the plebeians by the patricians. In the case of Pegasus, wings represent the sky, the sky represents the birds, flight yields the all-important auspices. Wings plus a horse is equivalent to horse-riding nobles with the right of taking auspices, and therefore authority over the people, and soon such myths represent powers, institutions, and often embody radical changes in the social order; mythological creatures like Draco – a serpent found in China and Egypt too – or Heracles, or Aeneas (whose descent to Avernus is, of course, a symbol of sowing), are not for Vico historical persons, but, like Pythagoras and Solon, are viewed by him as mere symbols of political structures, and not to be fitted into any chronological framework.

earth, horses with wings, centaurs, dryads and the like – are in reality efforts by our ancestors to combine certain functions, or ideas, in a single concrete image. Vico calls such entities 'imaginative universals',[1] images compounded of incompatible characteristics, for which their descendants, who think in concepts and not in sensuous terms, have substituted an abstract phraseology. The transformation of the denotations of particular words and their modifications can also, for Vico, open windows on to the evolution of social structures. This is because language tells us 'the histories of the institutions signified by the words'.[2] Thus the career of the word 'lex' tells us that life in 'the great forest of the earth'[3] was followed by life in huts, and after that villages, cities, academies.[4]

Vico's particular attributions are at times wholly implausible or wild. But this matters less than the fact that he conceived the idea of applying to the accumulated antiquities of the human race a species of Kant's transcendental method, that is, an attempt to conceive what the experience of a particular society must have been like for this or that myth, or mode of worship, or language, or building, to be their characteristic expression. This opened new doors. It discredited the idea of some static spiritual kernel of timeless and unchanging 'human nature'. It reinforced the old Epicurean-Lucretian notion of a process of slow growth from

[1] NS 209, 381, 933.

[2] NS 354.

[3] NS *passim*, e.g. 13, 195, 301, 369, 736, 1097.

[4] NS 239–40. This is a good example of Vico's freely roaming historical imagination: he groups together 'lex' (acorn), 'ilex', 'aquilex', 'legumen' and 'legere' as typical 'sylvan' words, plainly drawn from life in the forest, which then came to mean quite different activities and objects. At first, 'lex' 'must have meant a collection of acorns'. 'Ilex' is 'oak', 'for the oak produces the acorns by which the swine are drawn together' (so, too, 'aquilex' means 'collector of waters'). '*Lex* was next a collection of vegetables, from which the latter were called *legumina*. Later on, at a time when vulgar letters had not yet been invented for writing down the laws, *lex* by a necessity of civil nature must have meant a collection of citizens, or the public parliament; so that the presence of the people was the *lex*, or "law", that solemnised the wills that were made *calatis comitiis*, in the presence of the assembled *comitia*. Finally, collecting letters, and making, as it were, a sheaf of them for each word, was called *legere*, reading.' This is a characteristically fanciful piece of genetic sociological philology; yet in due course this socio-linguistic approach led to rich and important branches of the humanities in the form of historical jurisprudence, social anthropology, comparative religion and the like, particularly in their relations with the genetic and historical aspects of linguistic theory.

savage beginnings. There is no timeless, unalterable concept of justice or property or freedom or rights – these values alter as the social structure of which they are a part alters, and the objects created by mind and imagination in which these values are embodied alter from phase to phase. All talk of the matchless wisdom of the ancients is therefore a ludicrous fantasy: the ancients were frightening savages, *orribili bestioni*,[1] roaming the great forest of the earth, creatures remote from us. There is no omnipresent natural law: the lists of absolute principles spelt out by the Stoics or Isidore of Seville or Thomas Aquinas or Grotius were neither explicitly present in the minds, nor implicit in the acts, of the barbarous early fathers, even of the Homeric heroes. The rational egoists of Hobbes, Locke or Spinoza are arbitrary and unhistorical; if men had been as they are depicted by these thinkers, their history becomes unintelligible.

Each stage of civilisation generates its own art, its own form of sensibility and imagination. Later forms are neither better nor worse than earlier, but simply different, to be judged each as the expression of its own particular culture. How can early men, whose signs were 'mute',[2] who spoke with their bodies, who sang before they spoke (as, Vico adds, stammerers still do),[3] be judged by the criteria of our own sophisticated culture? At a time when the great French arbiters of taste believed in an absolute standard of artistic excellence and knew that the verse of Racine and Corneille (or, indeed, Voltaire) was superior to anything by the shapeless Shakespeare or the unreadable Milton, or, before them, the bizarre Dante, and perhaps the work of the ancients too, Vico maintained that the Homeric poems were a sublime expression of a society dominated by the ambition, avarice and cruelty of its ruling class; for only a society of this kind could have produced this vision of life. Later ages may have perfected other aids to existence, but they cannot create the *Iliad*, which embodies the modes of thought and expression and emotion of one particular kind of way of life; these men literally saw what we do not see.

The new history is to be the account of the succession and variety of men's experience and activity, of their continuous self-transformation from one culture to another. This leads to a bold

[1] NS 374.
[2] loc. cit. (p. 347 above, note 1).
[3] NS 225–30, 461.

relativism, and kills, among other things, the notion of progress in the arts, whereby later cultures are necessarily improvements on, or retrogressions from, earlier ages, each measured by its distance from some fixed, immutable ideal, in terms of which all beauty, knowledge, virtue must be judged. The famous quarrel between the ancients and the moderns can have no sense for Vico: every artistic tradition is intelligible only to those who grasp its own rules, the conventions that are internal to it, an 'organic' part of its own changing pattern of the categories of thought and feeling. The notion of anachronism, even if others had some inkling of it, is rendered central by him. Vico tells us that Polybius once said that it was a misfortune for mankind that it was priests and not philosophers who had presided over its birth; how much error and cruelty would have been spared it but for these mendacious charlatans.[1] Lucretius passionately reiterated this charge. To those who live after Vico, it is as if one were to suggest that Shakespeare could have written his plays at the court of Genghis Khan, or Mozart composed in ancient Sparta. Vico goes far beyond Bodin and Montaigne and Montesquieu:[2] they (and Voltaire) may have

[1] This is in fact based on a misreading of Polybius' text, but it furnished Vico with an occasion for his historicist thesis: and even though Polybius did not commit this fallacy, it forms a strand in the tradition of the Enlightenment against which Vico rebelled.

[2] The difference of the earlier and later attitudes is brought out by the interest in myths and fables on the part of, say, Bodin and Bacon and even Montesquieu on the one hand, and Vico on the other. The former thinkers do not think of myths and fables as inventions of lying priests or merely results of 'human weakness' (to use Voltaire's phrase), but they look to antiquities of this kind for information about the *moeurs* and *façons de vivre* in early or remote societies for the express purpose of discovering whether there are historical lessons to be learned with relevance to their own times and circumstances. Even though temperamentally they may have been intensely curious about other societies, and collected these facts for their own sakes, the ostensible motive was certainly ultilitarian – they wished to improve human life. Vico looks at myths as evidence of the different categories in which experience was organised – spectacles, unfamiliar to us, through which early man and remote peoples looked at the world in which they lived: the purpose is to understand whence we come, how we came to be where we are, how much or how little of the past we still carry with us. His approach is genetic, for it is only through its genesis, reconstructed by *fantasia*, guided by rules which he thinks he has discovered, that anything can be truly understood: not by some intuition of timeless essences, or empirical description or analysis of an object's present state. This marks a genuine turning-point in the conception of history and society.

believed in different social *esprits*, but not in successive stages of historical evolution, each phase of which has its own modes of vision, forms of expression, whether one calls them art or science or religion. The idea of the cumulative growth of knowledge, a single corpus governed by single, universal criteria, so that what one generation of scientists has established, another generation need not repeat, does not fit this pattern at all. This marks the great break between the notion of positive knowledge and that of understanding.

Vico does not deny the utility of the latest scientific techniques in establishing facts. He claims no intuitive or metaphysical faculty which can dispense with empirical investigation. Tests for the authenticity of documents and other evidence, for dating, for chronological order, for establishing who did or suffered what and when and where, whether we are dealing with individuals or classes or societies, for establishing bare facts, the newly established scientific methods of investigation, may well be indispensable. The same applies to the investigation of impersonal factors – geographical or environmental or social – to the study of natural resources, fauna, flora, social structure, colonisation, commerce, finance; here we must use the methods of science, which establish the kind of probability of which Bodin and Voltaire spoke, and every historian who uses sociological and statistical methods has done ever since. With all this Vico has no quarrel. What, then, is novel in his conception of history, over which he tells us he spent twenty years of continuous labour?

It is, I think, this: that to understand history is to understand what men made of the world in which they found themselves, what they demanded of it, what their felt needs, aims, ideals were. He seeks to recover their vision of it, he asks what wants, what questions, what aspirations determined a society's view of reality; and he thinks that he has created a new method which will reveal to him the categories in terms of which men thought and acted and changed themselves and their worlds. This kind of knowledge is not knowledge of facts or of logical truths, provided by observation or the sciences or deductive reasoning; nor is it knowledge of how to do things; nor the knowledge provided by faith, based on divine revelation, in which Vico professed belief. It is more like the knowledge we claim of a friend, of his character, of his ways of thought or action, the intuitive sense of the nuances of personality or feeling or ideas which Montaigne describes so well, and which Montesquieu took into account.

To do this, one must possess imaginative power of a high degree, such as artists and, in particular, novelists require. And even this will not get us far in grasping ways of life too remote from us and unlike our own. Yet even then we need not totally despair, for what we are seeking to understand is men – human beings endowed, as we are, with minds and purposes and inner lives – their works cannot be wholly unintelligible to us, unlike the impenetrable content of non-human nature. Without this power of what he describes as 'entering into' minds and situations the past will remain a dead collection of objects in a museum for us.

This sort of knowledge, not thought of in Descartes' philosophy, is based on the fact that we do know what men are, what action is, what it is to have intentions, motives, to seek to understand and interpret, in order to make ourselves at home in the non-human world, what Hegel called *Bei-sich-selbst-seyn*.[1] The most famous passage in the *New Science* expresses this central insight most vividly:

> ... in the night of thick darkness enveloping the earliest antiquity, so remote from ourselves, there shines the eternal and never failing light of a truth beyond all question: that the world of civil society has certainly been made by men, and that its principles are therefore to be found within the modifications of our own human mind. Whoever reflects on this cannot but marvel that the philosophers should have bent all their energies to the study of the world of nature, which, since God made it, he alone knows; and that they should have neglected the study of the world of nations, or civil world, which, since men had made it, men could come to know.[2]

Men have made their civil world – that is, their civilisation and institutions – but, as Marx was later to point out, not out of 'whole cloth', not out of infinitely malleable material; the external world, men's own physical and psychical constitution, play their part. This does not concern Vico: he is interested only in the human contribution: and when he speaks of the unintended consequences of men's actions, which they have not deliberately 'made', he

[1] op. cit. (p. 317 above, note 1), vol. 11, p. 44.
[2] NS 331.

attributes them to Providence, which guides men for their ultimate benefit in its own inscrutable way. That too, then, like nature, is outside man's conscious control. But what he means is that what one generation of men have experienced and done and embodied in their works, another generation can grasp, although, it may be, with difficulty and imperfectly. For this one must possess a developed *fantasia* – Vico's term for imaginative insight, which he accuses the French theorists of undervaluing. This is the capacity for conceiving more than one way of categorising reality, like the ability to understand what it is to be an artist, a revolutionary, a traitor, to know what it is to be poor, to wield authority, to be a child, a prisoner, a barbarian. Without some ability to get into the skin of others, the human condition, history, what characterises one period or culture as against others, cannot be understood. The successive patterns of civilisation differ from other temporal processes – say, geological – by the fact that it is men – ourselves – who play a crucial part in creating them. This lies at the heart of the art or science of attribution: to tell what goes with one form of life and not with another cannot be achieved solely by inductive methods.

Let me give an example of Vico's method: he is arguing that the story that the Romans borrowed the Twelve Tables (the original Roman code of laws) from the Athens of Solon's day cannot be true; for it is not possible for such barbarians as the Romans must have been in Solon's time to have known where Athens was, or that it possessed a code that might be of value to them. Moreover, even on the improbable assumption that these early Romans knew that there was a more civilised or better organised society to the south-east of them (even though the barbarous tribes of early Rome could scarcely have entertained, however inchoately, such notions as civilisation or a city-state), they could not have translated Attic words into idiomatic Latin without a trace of Greek influence on it, or used, for example, such a word as *auctoritas*, for which no Greek equivalent existed.

This kind of argument rests not on an accumulation of empirical evidence about human behaviour in many times and places, upon which sociological generalisations can be made to rest. Such notions as advanced culture, and what distinguishes it from barbarism, are for Vico not static concepts, but describe stages in the growth of self-awareness in individuals and societies, differences between the concepts and categories in use at one stage of growth from those that shape another, and the genesis of one from another, to understand which ultimately stems from understanding what childhood and maturity are. In the early fifteenth century, the Italian humanist Bruni had declared that whatever was said in Greek could equally well be said in Latin too. This is precisely what Vico denies, as the example of *auctoritas* shows. There is no immutable structure of experience, to reflect which a perfect language could be invented, and into which imperfect approximations to such a language could be transposed. The language of so-called primitives is not an imperfect rendering of what later generations will express more accurately: it embodies its own unique vision of the world, which can be grasped, but not translated totally into the language of another culture. One culture is not a less perfect version of another: winter is not a rudimentary spring; summer is not an undeveloped autumn.

The worlds of Homer or the Bible, or the Kalevala, cannot be understood at all if they are judged in terms of the absolute criteria of Voltaire or Helvétius or Buckle, and given marks according to their distance from the highest reaches of human civilisation, as exemplified in Voltaire's *musée imaginaire*, where the four great ages of man hang side by side as aspects of the single, selfsame peak of human attainment. To say this is a truism which I may be thought to have laboured far too long: it was not a truism in the early eighteenth century. The very notion that the task of historians was not merely to establish facts and give causal explanations for them, but to examine what a situation meant to those involved in it, what their outlook was, by what rules they were guided, what 'absolute presuppositions' (as Collingwood called them)[1] were entailed in what they (but not other societies, other cultures) said or did – all that is certainly novel and profoundly foreign to the thought of the *philosophes* and scientists of Paris. It coloured the thoughts of those who first reacted against the French Enlightenment, critics and historians of national literatures, in Switzerland, in England, in Germany – Bodmer and Breitinger and von Muralt, Hebrew scholars like Lowth, and the Homeric critics like Blackwell, social and cultural thinkers like Young and Adam Ferguson, Hamann and Möser and Herder. After them came the great generation of classical scholars, Wolf and Niebuhr and Boeckh,

[1] R. G. Collingwood, *An Essay on Metaphysics* (Oxford, 1940), *passim*, esp. chapter 5.

who transformed the study of the ancient world, and whose work had a decisive influence on Burckhardt and Dilthey and their successors in the twentieth century. From these origins came comparative philology and comparative anthropology, comparative jurisprudence and religion and literature, comparative histories of art and civilisation and ideas: the fields in which not merely knowledge of facts and events, but understanding – *Einfühlung*, empathy – is required.

The use of informed imagination about, and insight into, systems of value, conceptions of life of entire societies, is not required in mathematics or physics, geology or zoology, or – though some would deny this – in economic history or even sociology if it is conceived and practised as a strictly natural science. This statement is intentionally extreme, intended to emphasise the gap that opened between natural science and the humanities as the result of a new attitude to the human past. No doubt in practice there is a great overlap between impersonal history as it is conceived by, say, Condorcet or Buckle or Marx, who believed that human society could be studied by a human science in principle analogous to that which tells us about the behaviour of 'bees or beavers' (to use Condorcet's analogy),[1] contrasted with the history of what men believed in and lived by, the life of the spirit, blindness to which Coleridge and Carlyle imputed to the utilitarians, and Acton to Buckle (in his famous attack upon him), and Croce to the positivists. Vico began this schism: after that there was a parting of the ways. The specific and unique versus the repetitive and the universal, the concrete versus the abstract, perpetual movement versus rest, the inner versus the outer, quality versus quantity, culture-bound versus timeless principles, mental strife and self-transformation as a permanent condition of man versus the possibility (and desirability) of peace, order, final harmony and the satisfaction of all rational human wishes – these are some of the aspects of the contrast.[2]

---

[1] loc. cit. (p. 20 above, note 1).

[2] Erich Auerbach seems to me to have put this with eloquence and precision: 'When people realise that epochs and societies are not to be judged in terms of a pattern concept of what is desirable absolutely speaking but rather in every case in terms of their own premises; when people reckon among such premises not only natural factors like climate and soil but also the intellectual and historical factors; when, in other words, they come to develop a sense of historical dynamics, of the incomparability of historical phenomena . . . so that each epoch appears as a whole

These conceptions of their subject-matter and method, which are by now taken for granted by historians of literature, of ideas, of art, of law, and by historians of science too, and most of all by historians and sociologists of culture influenced by this tradition, are not as a rule, and do not need to be, consciously present to the minds of natural scientists themselves. Yet, before the eighteenth century, there was, so far as I know, no sense of this contrast. Distinctions between the vast realm of philosophy – natural and metaphysical – theology, history, rhetoric, jurisprudence, were not too sharply drawn; there were disputes about method in the Renaissance, but the great cleavage between the provinces of natural science and the humanities was, for the first time, made, or at least revealed, for better or for worse, by Giambattista Vico. Thereby he started a great debate of which the end is not in sight.

Where did his central insight originate? Did the idea of what a culture is, and what it is to understand it in its unity and variety, and its likeness, but, above all, its unlikeness, to other cultures, which undermines the doctrine of the identity of civilisation and scientific progress conceived as the cumulative growth of knowledge – did this spring fully armed like Pallas Athene out of his head? Who, before 1725, had had such thoughts? How did they percolate – if, indeed, they ever did – to Hamann and Herder in Germany, some of whose ideas are strikingly similar? These are problems on which, even now, not enough research has been done by historians of ideas. Yet, fascinating as they are, their solution seems to me to be less important than the central discoveries themselves; most of all, the notion that the only way of achieving any degree of self-understanding is by systematically retracing our steps, historically, psychologically and, above all, anthropologically, through the stages of social growth that follow empirically

whose character is reflected in each of its manifestations; when, finally, they accept the conviction that the meaning of events cannot be grasped in abstract and general forms of cognition and that the material needed to understand it must not be sought exclusively in the upper strata of society and in major political events but also in art, economy, material and intellectual culture, in the depths of the workaday world and its men and women, because it is only there that one can grasp what is unique, what is animated by inner forces, and what, in both a more concrete and a more profound sense, is universally valid ...'. *Mimesis* (1946), trans. Willard R. Trask (Princeton, 1953), p. 391. I know of no better formulation of the difference between history as science and history as a form of self-knowledge incapable of ever becoming fully organised, and to be achieved – as Vico warned us – only 'with great effort' (NS 338).

discoverable patterns, or, if that is too absolute a term, trends or tendencies with whose workings we are acquainted in our own mental life, but moving to no single, universal goal; each a world on its own, yet having enough in common with its successors, with whom it forms a continuous line of recognisably human experience, not to be unintelligible to their inhabitants. Only in this fashion, if Vico is right, can we hope to understand the unity of human history – the links that connect our own 'magnificent times' to our squalid beginnings in 'the great forest of the earth'.[1]

[1] NS 123; and see p. 349 above, note 3.

# HERDER AND THE ENLIGHTENMENT

We live in a world we ourselves create.[1]

## I

HERDER'S fame rests on the fact that he is the father of the related notions of nationalism, historicism and the *Volksgeist*, one of the leaders of the romantic revolt against classicism, rationalism and faith in the omnipotence of scientific method – in short, the most formidable of the adversaries of the French *philosophes* and their German disciples. Whereas they – or at least the best known among them, d'Alembert, Helvétius, Holbach and, with qualifications, Voltaire and Diderot, Wolff and Reimarus – believed that reality was ordered in terms of universal, timeless, objective, unalterable laws which rational investigation could discover, Herder maintained that every activity, situation, historical period or civilisation possessed a unique character of its own; so that the attempt to reduce such phenomena to combinations of uniform elements, and to describe or analyse them in terms of universal rules, tended to obliterate precisely those crucial differences which constituted the specific quality of the object under study, whether in nature or in history. To the notions of universal laws, absolute principles, final truths, eternal models and standards in ethics or aesthetics, physics or mathematics, he opposed a radical distinction between the method appropriate to the study of physical nature and that called for by the changing and developing spirit of man.

[1] References for quotations from Herder are to *Herder's sämmtliche Werke*, ed. Bernhard Suphan (Berlin, 1877–1913), by volume and page, thus: viii 252, the reference for this quotation. My thanks are due to Professors Burton Feldman and Robert D. Richardson, Roy Pascal, and F. M. Barnard for the use of their renderings of texts by Herder quoted in this essay. My debt to Professor Barnard's *Herder on Social and Political Culture* (Cambridge, 1969) is particularly great: some of his renderings are reproduced verbatim, others in a form somewhat altered by me. To Professor Barnard I also owe a number of other quotations and references.

He is credited with having put new life into the notion of social patterns, social growth, the vital importance of considering qualitative as well as quantitative factors – the impalpable and the imponderable, which the concepts of natural science ignore or deny. Preoccupied with the mysteries of the creative process, whether in individuals or groups, he launched (so we are told) a general attack on rationalism with its tendency to generalise, abstract, assimilate the dissimilar, unify the disparate; and, above all, on its avowed purpose, to create a corpus of systematic knowledge which in principle would be capable of answering all intelligible questions – the idea of a unified science of all there is. In the course of this propaganda against rationalism, scientific method and the universal authority of intelligible laws, he is held to have stimulated the growth of particularism, nationalism and literary, religious and political irrationalism, and thereby to have played a major role in transforming human thought and action in the generation that followed.

This account, which is to be found in some of the best-known monographs on Herder's thought, is broadly true, but oversimplified. His views did have a profound and revolutionary effect upon later thought and practice. He has been praised by some as the champion of faith against reason, poetical and historical imagination against the mechanical application of rules, insight against logic, life against death; by others he has been classed with confused, or retrograde, or irrationalist thinkers who misunderstood what they had learned from the Enlightenment, and fed the stream of German chauvinism and obscurantism; still others have sought to find common ground between him and Comte, or Darwin, or Wagner, or modern sociologists.

It is not my purpose in this study to pronounce directly upon these questions, although I am inclined to think that the extent of his acquaintance with, and fidelity to, the natural sciences of his day has often been seriously underestimated. He was fascinated and influenced by the findings of the sciences no less than Goethe, and, like him, thought that false general inferences were often drawn from them. Herder, was, all his life, a sharp and remorseless critic of the Encyclopaedists, but he accepted, indeed he acclaimed, the scientific theories on which they based their social and ethical doctrines; he merely thought that these conclusions could not follow from the newly established laws of physics or biology, since they plainly contradicted what any sensitive observer, since the beginning of social self-consciousness, knew to be true of human experience and activity.[1] But it is not Herder's attitude to the natural science of his day that I propose to discuss. I wish to confine myself, so far as possible (and at times it is not), to what is truly original in Herder's views, and by no means to all of this: in particular I shall try to examine three cardinal ideas in the rich welter of his thought, ideas which have had great influence for two centuries and are novel, important and interesting in themselves. These ideas, which go against the main stream of the thought of his time, I have called *populism, expressionism* and *pluralism*.[2]

Let me begin by conceding the most obvious of Herder's debts to other thinkers.[3] Herder's thesis that the proper subject of the historical sciences is the life of communities and not the exploits of individuals – statesmen, soldiers, kings, dynasties, adventurers and other famous men – had been stated by Voltaire and Hume and Montesquieu, by Schlözer and Gatterer, and before them by French writers on history in the sixteenth and early seventeenth centuries, and with incomparable imagination and originality by Vico. There is, so far as I know, no conclusive evidence that Herder had read Vico's *Scienza nuova* until at least twenty years after his own theory of history had been formed; but if he had not read

---

[1] On this see the excellent studies by H. B. Nisbet, *Herder and the Philosophy and History of Science* (Cambridge, 1970), and by G. A. Wells, *Herder and After: A Study of the Development of Sociology* (The Hague, 1959).

[2] I shall necessarily have to omit much else that is relevant and interesting: for example, Herder's dominant influence on romanticism, vitalism and existentialism, and, above all, on social psychology, which he all but founded; as well as the use made of his imprecise, often inconsistent, but always many-faceted and stimulating thought by such writers as the Schlegels and Jakob Grimm (especially in their philological excursions), Savigny (who applied to law Herder's notion of organic national growth), Görres (whose nationalism is rooted in, even if it distorts, Herder's vision), Hegel (whose concepts of becoming and of the growth and personality of impersonal institutions begin their lives in Herder's pages), as well as historical geographers, social anthropologists, philosophers of language and of history, and historical writers in the nineteenth and twentieth centuries. My principal reason for choosing the three ideas on which I intend to concentrate is that they are conceptions of the first order of originality and historical importance, the origins and properties of which have not received sufficient notice. My purpose is to do justice to Herder's originality rather than his influence.

[3] The best discussion of this topic known to me occurs in Max Rouché's excellent introduction to his edition and French translation of Herder's *Auch eine Philosophie der Geschichte* (Paris, n.d.), pp. 92–105.

Vico he had heard of him, and probably read Wegelin, and Cesarotti's Homeric commentaries. Moreover, the idea that great poets expressed the mind and experience of their societies, and were their truest spokesmen, was widespread during Herder's formative years. Shaftesbury celebrated artists as the inspired voices of their times, von Muralt, Bodmer and Breitinger in Switzerland placed Shakespeare and Milton and the old German Minnesingers far above the idols of the French Enlightenment. Bodmer corresponded on these topics with Vico's devoted admirer, Count Pietro Calepio;[1] the battle between literary historicism and the neo-classicism of Paris and its German followers was in full swing in Herder's youth. This may perhaps be sufficient to account for the striking resemblance between the views of Vico and Herder, and obviate the long and desperate search for more direct lines. In any case the notion of cultural patterns was far from new in his day, as the ironical title of his early *Yet Another Philosophy of History* was meant to emphasise. The case for it had been presented effectively, if in somewhat general terms, by his arch-enemy Voltaire in the celebrated *Essai sur les moeurs* and elsewhere.

So, too, the notion that the variety of civilisations is, to a large degree, determined by differences of physical and geographical factors – referred to by the general name of 'climate' – had become, since Montesquieu, a commonplace. It occurs, before Montesquieu, in the thought of Bodin, Saint-Evremond, the abbé Dubos and their followers.

As for the dangers of cultural arrogance – the tendency to judge ancient societies in terms of modern values – this had been made a central issue by Herder's older contemporary Lessing (even though Lessing may well have been influenced by him). Nor had anyone written more pungently than Voltaire against the European habit of dismissing as inferior remote civilisations, such as that of China, which he had extolled in order to expose the ridiculous vanity, exclusiveness and fanaticism of the 'barbarous' Judaeo-Christian outlook that recognised no values besides its own. The fact that Herder turned this weapon against Voltaire himself, and accused him of a narrowly *dix-huitième* and Parisian point of view, does not alter the fact that the head and source of all opposition to

---

[1] There is an illuminating discussion of this in Carlo Antoni's *Lo storicismo* (Turin, 1957).

Europocentrism was the Patriarch himself. Voltaire had praised ancient Egypt, and Winckelmann the Greeks; Boulainvilliers had spoken of the superiority of the Northern nations, and so had Mallet in his celebrated history of Denmark; Beat Ludwig von Muralt in his *Letters on the English and the French*, had, as early as 1725, drawn a contrast between the independent spirit of the Swiss and English, particularly English writers, and the conventional mannerisms of the French; Hurd, Millar and, after them, Justus Möser sang the praises of medieval Europe at the very height of the contemptuous dismissal of the Dark Ages by Voltaire and the *Encyclopédie*. They were, it is true, a minority, and, while Justus Möser's paeans to the free life of the ancient Saxons before they were so brutally civilised by Charlemagne may have been influenced by Herder, they were not created by him.

There was new emphasis on cultural differences, and protest against the authority of timeless general laws and rules. The notorious lack of historical sense that made Racine and Corneille represent classical or exotic oriental personages in the clothes and with the manners of the courtiers of Louis XIV was adversely commented on by Dubos and successfully satirised by Saint-Evremond. At the other end of the scale, some German pietists, Arnold and Zinzendorf among others, laid great stress on the proposition that every religion had a unique insight peculiar to itself, and Arnold based on this belief a bold and passionate plea for toleration of deviations from Lutheran orthodoxy, and even of heresies and unbelief.

The notion of the spirit of a nation or a culture had been central not only to Vico and Montesquieu, but to the famous publicist Friedrich Karl von Moser, whom Herder read and knew, to Bodmer and Breitinger, to Hamann and to Zimmermann. Bolingbroke had spoken of the division of men into nationalities as being deeply rooted in Nature herself. By the middle of the century there were plenty of Celtomaniacs and Gothomaniacs – notably Irishmen and Scotsmen who, even without the aid of Ossian, praised the virtues of Gaelic or Germanic tribes and represented them as being morally and socially superior not only to ancient Greeks or Romans, but still more to the decadent civilisation of modern Latin and Mediterranean peoples. Rousseau's celebrated letter to the Poles, advising them to resist forcible assimilation by Russia by stubbornly clinging to their national customs and characteristics, unacceptable as this was to the cosmopolitanism of his time, exhibits the same spirit.

As for the notion of society as an organism, with which Burke and Herder made such play, it was by this time very old indeed. The use of organic metaphors is at least as old as Aristotle; nobody had used them more lavishly than medieval writers; they are the heart and centre of John of Salisbury's political tracts, and are a weapon consciously used by Hooker and Pascal against the new scientific-mechanical conceptions. There was certainly nothing novel in this notion; it represents, on the contrary, if anything, a deliberate return to older views of social life. This is no less true of Burke, who was equally prone to the use of analogies drawn from the new biological sciences; I know of no evidence that Burke had read or heard of Justus Möser's or Herder's ideas.

Differences of ideals – of what made men and societies happy – had been illustrated vividly by Adam Ferguson in his highly original *Essay on the History of Civil Society*, which Herder had read.[1]

In his general explanation of events in naturalistic terms, whether geophysical or biological, Herder adopted the normal approach of the followers of Locke, Helvétius and the Encyclopaedists, and indeed of the entire Enlightenment. Unlike his teacher Hamann, Herder was decisively influenced by the findings of natural science; he gave them a vitalistic interpretation, though not the mystical or theosophical one favoured by Hemsterhuis, Lavater and other 'intuitivists'.

The ancient notion of a single great cosmic force of nature, embodied in finite, dynamic centres, had been given new life by Leibniz and was common to all his disciples.

So, too, the idea of a divine plan realised in human history had passed in uninterrupted succession from the Old Testament and its Jewish interpreters to the Christian Fathers, and then to the classical formulation of Bossuet.

Parallels between primitive peoples remote from one another in time and space – Homeric Greeks and early Romans on the one hand, and Red Indians or Germanic tribes on the other – had been put forward by Fontenelle and by the French Jesuit, *Père* Lafitau;

---

[1] Harold Laski's description of Ferguson as a 'pinchbeck Montesquieu' throws light only on the quality of Laski's critical judgement, in this instance probably a mere echo of Leslie Stephen. Harold J. Laski, *Political Thought in England: From Locke to Bentham* (New York and London, 1920), p. 174.

the protagonists of this approach in the early years of the century, especially English writers such as Blackwell and the Wartons, owed much to these speculations. It had become part and parcel of Homeric scholarship, which flourished both in England and, under the impulsion of Vico, in Italy. Certainly Cesarotti had perceived the wider implications of this kind of approach to literature for comparative philology and anthropology; and when Diderot in the *Encyclopédie*, in the course of a general article devoted to Greek philosophy, dismissed Homer as 'a theologian, philosopher and poet', quoting the view of a 'well-known man' that he was unlikely to be read much in the future,[1] this was a characteristically partisan *boutade*, in the spirit of Descartes and Pierre Bayle, against reverence for the past and dreary erudition, a belated echo of the battle of the ancients and the moderns. Nor was the Bible itself, which Vico had not dared to touch, left unmolested. Philosophical and historical criticism of the text, which had begun with Spinoza and *Père* Simon in the previous century, had been carried on cautiously – despite some opposition from Christian orthodoxy, both Catholic and Protestant – with strict regard to the rules of secular scholarship. Astruc in France, Lowth in England, and after them Michaelis in Germany (and Denmark), treated the Bible as a monument of oriental literature composed at various dates. Everyone knows of Gibbon's debt to Mosheim's coldly secular treatment of early Christian ecclesiastical history. Herder, who was not a trained researcher, had plenty to lean upon.

The same is true of Herder's linguistic patriotism. The defence of the German language had been vigorously taken up by Martin Opitz in the early years of the seventeenth century, and had since then formed part of the conscious programme of theologians, men of letters, and philosophers. Mencke, Horneck, Moscherosch, Logau and Gryphius are names that may not mean a great deal to English readers today; but in the two centuries that followed the Reformation they fought with stubbornness and success under Luther's banner against both Latin and French; and more famous men, Pufendorf and Leibniz, Thomasius and Wolff, Hamann and Lessing, were also engaged in this campaign that had begun long

---

[1] Diderot in the *Encyclopédie*, s.v. 'Grecs (philosophie des)', p. 908, col. 1. Diderot does at least protest that the view he quotes 'shows a lack of philosophy and taste'.

before. Once again, Herder began with something that had by that time become established as a traditional German attitude.

As for the famous reversal of values – the triumph of the concrete over the abstract; the sharp turn towards the immediate, the given, the experienced, and, above all, away from abstractions, theories, generalisations and stylised patterns; and the restoration of quality to its old status above quantity, and of the immediate data of the senses to their primacy over the primary qualities of physics – it is in this cause that Hamann made his name. It formed the basis of Lavater's 'physiognomical' researches; it was at least as old as Shaftesbury; it is pertinent to the works of the young Burke.

The reaction against the reorganisation of knowledge and society by the application of rationalist and scientific principles was in full swing by the time Herder came upon the scene. Rousseau had struck against it in 1750 with his first *Discourse*. Seven years later his moralising and reactionary letter to d'Alembert denouncing the stage had marked a total break with the party of the *philosophes*, as both sides swiftly recognised. In Germany this mood was strongly reinforced by the inward-looking tradition of the pietist movement. The human solidarity and mutual respect of these small groups, inspired by their burning Protestant faith; their belief in the unadorned truth, in the power of goodness, in the inner light; their contempt for outward forms; their rigid sense of duty and discipline; their perpetual self-examination; their obsession with the presence of evil, which at times took hysterical or sadistic forms and generated a good deal of unctuous hypocrisy; and above all their preoccupation with the life of the spirit, which alone liberated men from the bonds of the flesh and of nature – all these strains are very strong in those who were brought up in this stern atmosphere, and particularly in the East Prussians, Knutzen, Hamann, Herder, Kant. Although a great intellectual gulf divides Kant from Herder, they share a common element: a craving for spiritual self-determination as against half-conscious drifting along the streams of uncriticised dogma (whether theological or scientific), for moral independence (whether of individuals or groups), and above all for moral salvation.

If Herder had done no more than create a genuine synthesis out of these attitudes and doctrines, and built with them, if not a system, at any rate a coherent *Weltanschauung* destined to have a decisive influence on the literature and thought of his country, this alone would have been a high enough achievement to earn for him a unique place in the history of civilisation. Invention is not everything. If one were called upon to show what is strictly original in the individual doctrines of Locke or Rousseau, Bentham or Marx, Aquinas, or even Hegel, one could, without much difficulty, trace virtually all their doctrines to antecedent 'sources'. Yet this does not derogate from the originality and genius of these thinkers. 'Small change for a napoleon is not a napoleon.' It is not, however, my purpose to evaluate the work of Herder as a whole, but only to consider certain authentically *sui generis* doctrines which he originated; to discuss them not only for the sake of historical justice, but also as views that are peculiarly relevant and interesting in our own time. Herder's final claim need not rest upon what was, if I am right, most original in his thought. For his vast general influence has sometimes, paradoxically, served to overshadow that which he, virtually alone, launched upon the world.

## II

Let me return to the three topics of this study, namely:

1 *Populism*: the belief in the value of belonging to a group or a culture, which, for Herder at least, is not political, and is indeed, to some degree, anti-political, different from, and even opposed to, nationalism.

2 *Expressionism*:[1] the doctrine that human activity in general, and art in particular, express the entire personality of the individual or the group, and are intelligible only to the degree to which they do so. Still more specifically, expressionism claims that all the works of men are above all voices speaking, are not objects detached from their makers, are part of a living process of communication between persons and not independently existing entities, beautiful or ugly, interesting or boring, upon which external observers may direct the cool and dispassionate gaze with which scientists – or anyone not given to pantheism or mysticism – look on objects in nature. This is connected with the further notions that every form of human self-expression is in some sense

---

[1] I use this term in its widest, most generic sense, with no specific reference to the expressionist painters, writers and composers of the early decades of the twentieth century.

artistic, and that self-expression is part of the essence of human beings as such; which in turn entail such distinctions as those between integral and divided, or committed and uncommitted (that is, unfulfilled), lives; and thence lead to the concept of various hindrances, human and non-human, to the self-realisation which is the richest and most harmonious form of self-expression that all creatures, whether or not they are aware of it, live for.

3 *Pluralism*: the belief not merely in the multiplicity, but in the incommensurability, of the values of different cultures and societies, and, in addition, in the incompatibility of equally valid ideals, together with the implied revolutionary corollary that the classical notions of an ideal man and of an ideal society are intrinsically incoherent and meaningless.

Each of these three theses is relatively novel; all are incompatible with the central moral, historical and aesthetic doctrines of the Enlightenment. They are not independent of each other. Everything in the illimitable, varied and exceedingly rich panorama which Herder's works present is interwoven. Indeed, the notion of unity in difference, still more that of differences in unity, the tension of the one and the many, is his obsessive *idée maîtresse*. Hence the recurrence through all his discussions of a constant theme: the 'organic' oneness of personality with the form of life that it leads, the empirical and metaphysical unity of the physical and the mental, of intellect, will, feeling, imagination, language, action – distinctions and classifications that he regarded as at best superficial, at worst profoundly misleading. Hence the stress on the unity of thought and feeling, of theory and practice, of the public and the private, and his single-minded, life-long and heroic effort to see the universe as a single process.

The celebrated words with which he opens his most famous and ambitious work, *Ideas about the Philosophy of History of Mankind* – 'Our earth is a star among stars'[1] – are very characteristic. There follow chapters on geology, climate, mineral, vegetable and animal life, and lessons in physical geography, until, at last, man is reached. There is a corresponding attempt to link all the arts and all the sciences, to represent religious, artistic, social, political, economic, biological, philosophical experience as facets of one activity; and since the pattern is one, fact and value are not divided (*pace* Hume

[1] xiii 13.

and Kant, with whose works Herder was only too familiar). To understand a thing was, for him, to see how it could be viewed as it was viewed, assessed as it was assessed, valued as it was valued, in a given context, by a particular culture or tradition. To grasp what a belief, a piece of ritual, a myth, a poem or a linguistic usage meant to a Homeric Greek, a Livonian peasant, an ancient Hebrew, an American Indian, what part it played in his life, was for Herder to be able not merely to give a scientific or common-sense explanation, but to give a reason for or justification of the activity in question, or at least to go a long way towards this. For to explain human experiences or attitudes is to be able to transpose oneself by sympathetic imagination into the situation of the human beings who are to be 'explained'; and this amounts to understanding and communicating the coherence of a particular way of life, feeling, action; and thereby the validity of the given act or action, the part it plays in the life and outlook which are 'natural' in the situation. Explanation and justification, reference to causes and to purposes, to the visible and the invisible, statements of fact and their assessment in terms of the historical standards of value relevant to them, melt into one another, and seem to Herder to belong to a single type, and not several types, of thinking. Herder is one of the originators of the secular doctrine of the unity of fact and value, theory and practice, 'is' and 'ought', intellectual judgement and emotional commitment, thought and action.

The sharpest critics of Herder have always conceded the power and breadth of his imagination. He did have an astonishing capacity for conceiving a great variety of actual and possible societies in the past and the present, and an unexampled warmth of sympathy for them all. He was inspired by the possibility of reconstructing forms of life as such, and he delighted in bringing out their individual shape, the fullness of human experience embodied in them: the odder, the more extraordinary a culture or an individual, the better pleased he was. He can hardly condemn anything that displays colour or uniqueness: Indians, Americans and Persians, Greece and Palestine, Arminius and Machiavelli, Shakespeare and Savonarola seem to him equally fascinating. He deeply hates the forces that make for uniformity, for the assimilation, whether in life or in the books of historians, of one culture or way of life to another. He conscientiously looks for uniformities, but what fascinates him is the exception. He condemns the erection of walls between one genus and another; but he seeks for the greatest possible number of distinctions of species within a genus, and of individuals within the species. Hamann had preached to him the need to preserve sensitiveness to specific historical and cultural phenomena, to avoid becoming deadened by the passion for classification and generalisation demanded by networks of tidy concepts, a fatal tendency which he attributed to the natural sciences and their slaves, the Frenchmen who wished to transform everything by the application of scientific method. Like Hamann, Herder preserved his childlike impressionability – his capacity to react spontaneously to the jagged, irregular, not always describable data provided by the senses, by imagination, by religious revelation, by history, by art. He did not hasten to refer them to their appropriate cases in the museum of concepts; he was penetrated through and through by the new spirit of empiricism, of the sacredness of facts. Not so much as Hamann, but more than even Lessing and Diderot, and incomparably more than such official materialists and 'sensualists' as Condillac or Helvétius, Herder avoided the temptation to reduce the heterogeneous flow of experience to homogeneous units, to label them and fit them into theoretical frameworks in order to be able to predict and control them. The notorious luxuriance and formlessness of his ideas is due at least as much to his sense of the complexity of the facts themselves as to a naturally rhapsodical and turbid mind. As a writer he is exuberant and disordered, but not obscure or vague. Even at his most rapt he is not somnambulistic or self-intoxicated; he does not, even in his most lyrical moments, fly from the facts to an ideal heaven, like the German metaphysical poets of his time, Gleim or Uz or Klopstock or even Goethe on occasions. Great scientists and philosophers have often made their impact by violently exaggerating their original insights. But Herder cannot let go of what he sees, feels, hears, learns. His sense of the texture of reality is concrete, while his analytical powers are feeble. The three original theses which form the subject of this study display this again and again, and have consequently often been a source of irritation to tidier, clearer, logically more gifted thinkers.

III

Let me begin with Herder's populism, or his idea of what it is to belong to a group. Everyone seems agreed that Herder began as a typical, almost routine, defender of the great ideas of eighteenth-century enlightenment, that is, as a humanitarian, a cosmopolitan and a pacifist. Later, so it seems to be assumed, he moved towards a more reactionary position, the subordination of reason and intellect to nationalism, Gallophobia, intuition, uncritical faith and belief in tradition. Was this not, after all, the evolution in some degree of other thinkers of his and the succeeding generation in Germany? Almost without exception, they began by welcoming the French Revolution rapturously, planting trees of liberty, and denouncing as obsolete and brutally oppressive the rule of the three hundred German princes, until, horrified by the Terror and wounded by the military humiliation of Germany by the armies of Revolutionary France and, still more, those of Napoleon, they turned into patriots, reactionaries and romantic irrationalists. Was not this the path pursued by Fichte (above all Fichte), Görres, Novalis and the Schlegels, Schleiermacher and Tieck, Gentz and Schelling, and to some degree even by the great libertarian Schiller? Were not Goethe and Humboldt (and Georg Forster, though he died before the reaction set in) almost alone in their unswerving fidelity to reason, toleration and the unity of mankind, in their freedom from nationalism, and, in common with Kant and Hegel, in their loathing for all forms of collective emotional afflatus? Is it not reasonable to assume that this process of retreat from reason took place in Herder too? True, he died before the most crushing defeats had been inflicted by Napoleon on the German armies and princes; yet was it not the case that Herder began as a cosmopolitan and ended as a nationalist? Here too, then, so it would seem, wounded national pride, and perhaps age and the cooling of youthful Utopianism, had had their inescapable effect. Yet this view seems to me untenable. Whatever may have been the evolution of Fichte or Friedrich Schlegel, Herder's form of nationalism remained unaltered throughout his life. His national feeling was not political and never became so, nor did he abandon or modify the peculiar brand of universalism with which he had begun, whether or not the two tendencies were consistent (the least of his concerns), throughout his long and voluminous intellectual activity.

As early as 1765, in an address composed in Riga (where at the age of twenty-one he occupied the post of a Lutheran preacher in that officially Russian city) in answer to the question 'Have we still a republic and a fatherland like the Ancients?',[1] Herder declared

[1] i 13–28.

that this was no longer the case. In Greece the strength and the glory of the *polis* were the supreme goals of all free men. Religion, morals, tradition – every aspect of human activity stemmed from, and was directed to, maintaining the city, and any danger to it was a danger to all that these men were and lived by; if it fell, everything fell with it. But then, he went on to say, Christianity came and the horizons of mankind became immeasurably wider. Christianity, he explained, is a universal religion: it embraces all men and all peoples; it transcends all local and temporary loyalties in the worship of what is universal and eternal.

This thesis was highly characteristic of the Christian humanism of the German *Aufklärung*, and, despite all that has been said to the contrary, Herder never abandoned this point of view. His central belief was expressed towards the end of his life in words similar to those of his early writings: 'To brag of one's country is the stupidest form of boastfulness . . . What is a nation? A great wild garden full of bad plants and good; vices and follies mingle with virtues and merit. What Don Quixote will break a lance for this Dulcinea?'[1] Patriotism was one thing, nationalism another: an innocent attachment to family, language, one's own city, one's own country, its traditions, is not to be condemned. But he goes on to say that aggressive nationalism is detestable in all its manifestations, and wars are mere crimes.[2] This is so because all large wars are essentially civil wars, since men are brothers, and wars are a form of abominable fratricide. 'One fatherland ranged against another in bloody battle is the worst barbarism in the human vocabulary.'[3] A year later he adds: 'We can be nobler heroes than Achilles, loftier patriots than Horatius Cocles.'[4] These views can scarcely be due merely to the fact, by which they are sometimes explained, that political nationalism would have been too unrealistic an outlook in a feeble and divided country governed by several hundred hereditary despots; so that even to look for it there demonstrates a lack of historical sense. Yet the Italians, who were no less divided and politically impotent, had developed a distinct craving for political unification which dated back at least to Machiavelli, even though the prevailing social and political conditions in Italy were not so very unlike those of eighteenth-century Germany.

[1] xvii 211.
[2] See xvii 230 ff.
[3] xvii 319.
[4] xviii 86.

Herder's attitude is clearly the normal enlightened attitude of his time; the point, however, is that he did not abandon it. He believed in kinship, social solidarity, *Volkstum*, nationhood, but to the end of his life he detested and denounced every form of centralisation, coercion and conquest, which were embodied and symbolised both for him, and for his teacher Hamann, in the accursed State. Nature creates nations, not States.[1] The State is an instrument of happiness for a group, not for men as such.[2] There is nothing against which he thunders more eloquently than imperialism – the crushing of one community by another, the elimination of local cultures trampled under the jackboot of some conqueror. He vies with Justus Möser in his tenderness towards long-lived traditions and institutions embodied in particular forms of life that have created unity and continuity in a human community. He cares nothing for *virtù* in the Renaissance sense of the term. Alexander the Great, Julius Caesar, Charlemagne are not heroes for him. The basis of the State is conquest, the history of States is the history of violence, a bloodstained story of aggression. The state is Ixion's wheel and calls for meaningless self-immolation. Why should hundreds suffer hunger and cold to satisfy the whim of a crowned madman, or the dreams bred by the fancy of a *philosophe*?[3]

This may be directed specifically at Frederick the Great and his French advisers, but the import of it is universal. All rule of men over fellow men is unnatural. True human relations are those of father and son, husband and wife, sons, brothers, friends, men; these terms express natural relations which make people happy. All that the State has given us is contradictions and conquests, and, perhaps worst of all, dehumanisation.[4] What pleasure is there in being 'a blind cog in a machine'?[5] God has divided the world by mountains and oceans in order to prevent some fearful Nimrod from conquering the whole. The *Ideen* anticipate socialist historians in representing the history of conquerors as the history of

---

[1] xiii 339–41, 375.

[2] xiii 340.

[3] ibid.

[4] e.g. xiii 341: 'Millions of people on the globe live without States ... Father and mother, man and wife, child and brother, friend and man – these are natural relationships through which we become happy; what the State can give us is an artificial contrivance; unfortunately it can also deprive us of something far more essential – rob us of ourselves.'

[5] xiii 340.

man-hunters. Despite his vow to look with a sympathetic, or at least impartial, eye upon all cultures and all nations, he cannot bring himself to forgive Rome for crushing the cultures of the peoples it had conquered, not even that of Carthage. There may be merit in efficiency and unity, but it is for him more than offset by the tragedy of the destruction; that is, by the evil of the barbarous disregard of so many spontaneous, natural forms of human self-expression: 'Whom nature separated by language, customs, character, let no man artificially join together by chemistry.'[1] This is what the Romans tried to do and how the whole Roman Empire was held together. And its 'Holy' successor was no better – it was an unnatural monster, an absurd clamping together of disparate cultures, 'a lion's head with a dragon's tail, an eagle's wing, a bear's paw, ["glued together"] in one unpatriotic structure of a State'.[2] The Jews, 'parasitic' money-lenders now,[3] were at least not self-worshippers; they are praised for not having made Palestine the source and centre of the world, for not having idealised their ancestors, and for not deriving their genealogy from gods and demigods (it is this last that has enabled them to survive the Diaspora).[4] Empires, especially multi-national ones (a 'wild mingling of various tribes and peoples under one sceptre'),[5] rest on force; they have feet of clay and must collapse. Theocracies that are founded upon some non-political principle, a spiritual or religious force – China or Egypt, for example, to take only non-Christian faiths – have proved correspondingly more durable. The sword of

---

[1] xviii 206.

[2] xiii 385.

[3] xiv 67; cf. xiv 283–4.

[4] Herder was fascinated by the survival of the Jews; he looked upon them as a most excellent example of a *Volk* with its own distinct character (x 139). 'Moses bound the heart of his people to their native soil' (xii 115). Land, common language, tradition, sense of kinship, common law as a freely accepted 'covenant' – all these interwoven factors, together with the bond created by their sacred literature, enabled the Jews to retain their identity in dispersion – but especially the fact that their eyes remained focused upon their original geographical home (xii 115, viii 355, xvii 312) – historical continuity, not race, is what counts (xii 107). This is what creates historical individuality (xii 123, xxxii 207). On this entire subject, and especially the view of the 'Jewish problem', not as religious, but national and political, needing what later came to be known as the Zionist solution, see the interesting article by F. M. Barnard, 'Herder and Israel', *Jewish Social Studies* 28 (1966), 25–33. See also the same author's 'The Hebrews and Herder's Political Creed', *Modern Language Review* 54 (1959), 533–46.

[5] xiii 384.

the spirit is better than mere brute force: not even the acutest poverty, the deepest squalor, still less ambition and love of power, entitle men to have recourse to violence. Like Möser, Herder laments the fact that the Germans are poor, hungry and despised; that Luther's widow had to beg for help from the King of Denmark; that Kepler died of hunger; that men of German speech have been scattered and exiled to England, America, Russia, Transylvania; that gifted artists and inventors are compelled to leave their country and lavish their gifts upon foreigners; that Hessians are sold and bought like Negro slaves while their families starve and perish. Nevertheless, conquest is not the answer. He dwelt on the folly and cruelties of imperialism all his life.

In his first essay on the philosophy of history (*Auch eine Philosophie*, of 1774) he speaks of Roman conquerors as a compound of blood, lust and sinister vices.[1] For the next two decades, and, indeed, in the last years of his life, he continues to denounce the inhumanity of colonial rule, ancient and modern: 'Foreign peoples were judged [by Rome] in terms of customs unknown to them';[2] imposed by violence, this distorted the character of the conquered until 'the Roman eagle ... pecked out their eyes, devoured their innards, and covered [their] wretched corpses with its feeble wings'.[3] It was not a happy day when the bloody tyranny of Rome became united with Christianity.[4] Rome ruined Greece, and the Teutonic Knights and recently converted Poles exterminated the Prussians and enslaved the poor Balts and peaceful Slavs.

> Can you name a land [he asks in his *Letters on the Advancement of Mankind* (1793–7)] where Europeans have entered without defiling themselves for ever before defenceless, trusting mankind, by the unjust word, greedy deceit, crushing oppression, diseases, fatal gifts they have brought? Our part of the earth should be called not the wisest, but the most arrogant, aggressive, money-minded: what it has given these people is not civilisation but the destruction of the rudiments of their own cultures wherever they could achieve this.[5]

This is what the English have done in Ireland, in the Scottish Highlands, and Europeans have done in their colonies, the natives

---

[1] v 508; cf. v 515.
[2] xiv 201.
[3] ibid.
[4] xiv 202.
[5] xviii 222–3; cf. xiv 410.

of which have 'developed a passion for fire-water', whereby they were considered 'ripe for conversion to our faith'.[1] In 1802, in his periodical *Adrastea*, he imagines a conversation between an Asian and a European; in the course of it the Asian (an Indian) says:

> 'Tell me, have you still not lost the habit of trying to convert to your faith peoples whose property you steal, whom you rob, enslave, murder, deprive of their land and their State, to whom your customs seem revolting? Supposing that one of them came to your country, and with an insolent air pronounced absurd all that is most sacred to you – your laws, your religion, your wisdom, your institutions, and so on, what would you do to such a man?' 'Oh, but that is quite a different matter,' replied the European, 'we have power, ships, money, cannon, *culture.*'[2]

On this topic Herder remained uncompromising and passionate: ' "Why are you pouring water over my head?" asked a dying slave of a Christian missionary. "So that you can go to Heaven." "I do not want to go to a heaven where there are white men," he replied, and turned on his side and died.'[3] By this means Europeans are engaged in forging the chains with which other peoples will bind them.[4] Herder is as certain as Karl Marx that those who oppress and exploit others and force their own institutions on others are acting as their own grave-diggers – that one day their victims will rise against them and use their catchwords, their methods and ideals to crush them.

The German mission is not to conquer; it is to be a nation of thinkers and educators. This is their true glory.[5] Sacrifice – self-sacrifice – not the domination of one man over another, is the proper end of man. Herder sets his face against everything that is predatory, against the use of force in any cause but that of self-defence. The Crusades, no matter how Christian in inspiration, are hateful to him, since they conquered and crushed other human

[1] v 546.
[2] xxiii 498.
[3] xviii 224.
[4] v 579.
[5] The most eloquent statement of Herder's conception of the German's earthly miseries and spiritual task is to be found in his epistle in verse, *German National Glory*, written in the 1790s, but effectively first published, posthumously, in 1812 (xviii 208–16), when the mood of many of his countrymen, whipped into a frenzy of nationalism by Jahn, Arndt, Körner and Görres, was wholly different.

communities. Yet consent for him is a false basis of society, for consent is ultimately a form of yielding, however rational or voluntary, to strength, whereas human relations must rest upon respect, affection, kinship, equality, not fear or prudence and utilitarian calculation. It is when religions forget the ends of man and turn into empty, mechanical cults that they develop into a source of unintelligible mystification and their ceremonies decay into a recital of dead formulae, while the priests, who no longer understand their own faith, become instruments of other forces – in particular of the State and the men who control it. For him, as for Nietzsche, the State is the coldest of all cold monsters. Nothing in the whole of human history is more hateful to him than Churches and priests who are instruments of political power; of these he speaks with the same voice as Voltaire or Holbach; as for the State (he says in words that could have been Rousseau's), it robs men of themselves.[1] The State becomes a drug with the help of which men seek to forget themselves, a self-generated method of escaping from the need to live, create and choose. Furthermore, the sheer exercise of bureaucratic activity is a form of self-intoxication, and he speaks of it as a kind of opium by which men are metamorphosed into mechanical functionaries. Profound differences, both personal and literary, came to divide Herder from Goethe and Schiller, but when, in their jointly written *Xenien*, they say

> Deutschland? aber wo liegt es? Ich weiß das Land nicht zu finden
> Wo das Gelehrte beginnt, hört das Politische auf.

and

> Zur Nation euch zu bilden, ihr hoffet es, Deutsche, vergebens,
> Bildet, ihr könnt es, dafür freyer zu Menschen euch aus.

they speak for Herder too.[2] The State is the substitution of machinery for life, a prospect, and a reality, that frightened him no less than it did Rousseau.

What then is the right life for men? They should live in natural units, that is, in societies united by a common culture. Nature, moreover, does not make some nations intrinsically superior to others. Whatever the qualities of the ancient Germans, to look on them, for this reason, as the European people chosen by God, to

---

[1] see p. 373 above, note 4.

[2] *Xenien* 95–6, 'Das deutsche Reich' and 'Deutscher Nationalcharakter': pp. 320–1 in *Schillers Werke* (op. cit., p. 260 above, note 3), vol. 1.

which he has, in virtue of its native ability, accorded the right to own the entire world and to be served by other peoples – that would be the ignoble vanity of barbarians.[1] There is no *Favorit-volk*.[2] A nation is made what it is by 'climate',[3] education, relations with its neighbours, and other changeable and empirical factors, and not by an impalpable inner essence or an unalterable factor such as race or colour. All this, said late in his life, is the pure milk of the doctrine of the Enlightenment. Herder protests, not without a certain malicious satisfaction (as Hamann also did, with equally ironical pleasure), that the great liberal Kant in his *Anthropologie* emphasised race and colour too much. He is equally indignant about Kant's proposition that 'man is an animal who needs a master';[4] he replies, 'Turn the sentence round: the man who needs a master is an animal; as soon as he becomes human, he no longer needs a master.'[5] He also denounces Kant's philosophy of history, according to which it is the vices of mankind – desire for power and mastery over the scarce resources of the earth – that stimulate competition, struggle, and thereby progress, with the corollary that the sufferings of the individual are indispensable to the improvement of the species (a doctrine that was destined to reach its richest development in Hegel, and in another form in Spencer's evolutionary doctrine and the vagaries of social Darwinism). Herder repudiates these doctrines in the pure spirit of liberal, individualist, Weimar cosmopolitanism. Indeed, the perception that cruel and sinister implications are contained in any doctrine that preaches the sacrifice of individuals on the altar of vast abstractions – the human species, society, civilisation, progress (later thinkers were to say race, State, class and a chosen élite) – has its true beginnings here.

Kant's unconcealed lack of sympathy for Herder's sweeping and imprecise generalisations, and his complaints that these were never supported by either adequate evidence or rigorous argument, may

[1] xvii 212.

[2] xviii 247; cf. xviii 248, where Herder says there must be 'no order of rank . . . The Negro is as much entitled to think the white man degenerate . . . as the white man is to think of the Negro as a black beast.'

[3] See iv 204–5, xiii 265–73.

[4] op. cit. (p. 16 above, note 1), vol. 8, p. 23, line 5. But see also Kant's 'Beantwortung der Frage: Was ist Aufklärung?' (ibid., pp. 33–42) and Herder's letter to Hamann of 14 February 1785.

[5] xiii 383.

in part account for Herder's deliberate choice of the famous champion of the inexorable voice of duty, the moral equality of men, and the infinite value of the individual as the butt of his own passionate anti-racialism and anti-imperialism and of his defence of the right of all men and nations to develop along their own, self-chosen, lines. Variety does not, for Herder, entail conflict. He does not see why one community absorbed in the development of its own native talent should not respect a similar activity on the part of others. The Kant of the *Grundlegung* or the *Zum ewigen Frieden* might have agreed; but the Kant of the *Anthropologie* and the other essays on universal history evidently did not. Kant drew a sharp line of division between, on the one hand, individual morality, universal, absolute, free from internal conflict, based on a transcendent rationality wholly unconnected with nature and history and empirical reality, and, on the other, the disharmonies of the processes of nature, the aim of which was the preservation of the species, and the promotion of progress by competition and strife. Herder would have none of this. He found such dualism totally unintelligible. The hard and fast distinctions between orders of experience, mental and corporeal faculties, reason and imagination, the world of sense and the worlds of understanding or the ethical will or a priori knowledge seemed to him so many artificial partitions, 'wooden walls',[1] built by philosophers, to which nothing corresponded in reality. His world is organic, dynamic and unitary: every ingredient of it is at once unique and interwoven with every other by an infinite variety of relationships which, in the end, cannot be analysed or even fully described. 'Similarities, classes, orders, stages', he wrote in 1775, 'are only ... houses of cards in a game. The creator of all things does not see as a man sees. He knows no classes; each thing resembles only itself.'[2] 'I am not sure that I know what "material" and "immaterial" mean. I do not believe that nature erected iron walls between these terms ... I cannot see them anywhere.'[3] He is anxious not to lose any part of reality, not to obliterate or elide or smooth out irregularities in order to fit them into a system, get them neatly covered by a general formula. He inherits from his teacher Hamann the desire to

[1] viii 315.
[2] ibid.
[3] viii 193.

seize the whole in its fullness, in all its peculiar, complex, historically changing manifestations (this is what fascinated and permanently influenced the young Goethe when they met in 1770), and goes a good deal further than Montesquieu, who raised the banner of revolt against the *grands simplificateurs*.[1] The springs of life are mysterious, hidden from those who lack the sense of the inwardness of the spirit of a society, an age, a movement – a sensibility killed by the dissection practised by French *lumières* and their academic German imitators. Like Hamann he is convinced that clarity, rigour, acuteness of analysis, rational, orderly arrangement, whether in theory or practice, can be bought at too high a price. In this sense he is the profoundest critic of the Enlightenment, as formidable as Burke, or Maistre, but free from their reactionary prejudices and hatred of equality and fraternity.

IV

As for Herder's doctrine of expression, it is for him profoundly connected with the ways in which and by which men live. What determines the units in which it is 'natural' for men to live? Despite his tendency to look upon the family and patriarchal institutions as the basic forms of human association, Herder does not explicitly affirm Aristotle's (and Rousseau's) doctrine that a 'natural' or satisfactory human society is constituted only by small human groups in which men can know each other face to face and where (in Aristotle's phrase) one herald can be heard by all. Human groups, large and small, are products of climate, geography, physical and biological needs, and similar factors; they are made one by common traditions and common memories, of which the principal link and vehicle – indeed, more than vehicle, the very incarnation – is language. 'Has a nation . . . anything more precious than the language of its fathers? In it dwells its entire world of tradition, history, religion, principles of existence; its whole heart

---

[1] See, e.g., *De l'esprit des lois*, book 24, chapter 18: p. 290 in op. cit. (p. 219 above, note 1), vol. 1 B. The phrase 'grand simplificateur' and the word 'simplificateur' itself were coined by Sainte-Beuve to describe Benjamin Franklin in 'Franklin à Passy' (29 November 1852): p. 181 in C.-A. Sainte-Beuve, *Causeries du lundi* (Paris, [1926–42]), vol. 7. (The equally familiar 'terribles simplificateurs' was coined by Jacob Burckhardt in a letter of 24 July 1889 to Friedrich von Preen.) H.H.

and soul."[1] It is so because men necessarily think in words or other symbols, since to think is to use symbols; and their feelings and attitudes to life are, he maintains (as Vico did before him), incorporated in symbolic forms – worship, poetry, ritual. This is so whether what they seek are pleasures or necessities: the dance, the hunt – primitive forms of social solidarity expressed and preserved by myth and formalised representation – in fact, the entire network of belief and behaviour that binds men to one another can be explained only in terms of common, public symbolism, in particular by language.

Herder had derived from Hamann his notion that words and ideas are one. Men do not think, as it were, in thoughts and ideas and then look for words in which to 'clothe' them, as one looks for a glove to fit a fully formed hand. Hamann taught that to think was to use symbols, and that to deny this was not so much false as unintelligible, because without symbolism one was led fallaciously to divide the aspects of a single experience into separate entities – the fatal doctrine of Descartes, who spoke of mind and body, thought and its object, matter and mind, as though they were independent existents. Such distinctions as we draw between thought and feeling (and their 'objects'), physical sensation and intellectual or moral or aesthetic awareness are, according to Hamann (where one can understand him), an attempt to draw attention now to this, now to that facet of a single experience; a tendency which, pushed too far, tends to separate and abstract one facet from another, and, pushed further still, to lead to the invention of imaginary abstract objects, or idealised entities – to transform reality into a collection of artificial figments. This springs from a craving for tidy scientific classification, but it distorts the facts, congeals the continuous flow of the living sense of nature and of God into dead fragments, and kills the sources of the true sense of reality – the imagination, consciousness of divine revelation, direct acquaintance with reality, obtained through the senses, which men unspoiled by the logic and metaphysics of rationalism always have.

Hamann was a Christian touched by mysticism: he looked upon the world, upon nature and history, as the speech of God to man; God's words were hieroglyphs, often tormentingly dark, or they were allegories, or they were symbols which opened doors to the

[1] xvii 58.

vision of the truth, which, if only men saw and heard aright, answered the questions of their heads and hearts.[1] Hamann was not himself a visionary. He had had no special revelation; but when, in the midst of an acute spiritual crisis, he turned to the Bible, he was overwhelmed by the realisation that the history of the Jews embodied a universal, trans-historical truth: for it symbolised his own – and every man's – painful quest for God. Men were made in God's image, but as Hamann's pietist ancestors had taught, man was sinful and weak, he stumbled and fell and rose again as he sought to hear the voice of his father and master, the Christ within him and without, who alone could make him whole. Man was healed only by surrendering himself to the unity of life, by allowing his entire being – spirit and flesh, mind, will, and above all senses – to take in that which God was saying to him directly in Holy Writ, and also signified by means of the working of nature and by the pattern of human history. Nature and history were symbols, cryptograms, of the Logos, to be read by those who were not perverted by metaphysical subtleties. Sin was denial of divine grace and of what God had given men: passions, desires, love, a sense of joy in every manifestation of life, of sensuous nature, of creation and procreation in all forms. The existence of this reality could not, indeed, be proved. Hume was right: no facts or events can be demonstrated to exist by reason. Yet we accept them because we cannot help it, because it is animal faith in the external world, given in sense perception, which alone makes it possible for us to think or act at all. God, the world of the senses, the meanings of words – all are directly given and intimately present to any man if only he will let himself see, hear, be.

Herder remained free from mysticism. It was Hamann's rejection of rationalist analyses, and his unabashed sensualism and empiricism, as well as his simple Christian faith, that influenced Herder, and not the peculiar mystical nominalism which led Hamann to seek to understand God's hidden purposes in the occult significance of the individual Hebrew or Greek words of Holy Writ. Hamann's doctrine of language – that language alone was the central organ of all understanding and all purposive action, that men's fundamental activity was to speak to others (to men or

[1] The sources of this view in Christian mysticism and Neoplatonism, and its form in other philosophical systems – for instance, that of Berkeley – have not as yet been sufficiently investigated.

God or themselves), and that only through language could individuals, or groups, and the meanings that they embodied in poetry or ritual, or in the network of human institutions and ways of life, be understood – this great revelation became an article of faith for Herder. To understand men was to understand what they meant, intended, or wished to communicate. Creation is communication. During the great debate in the eighteenth century about the origins of human speech he acquired a European reputation by saying that language was neither a sudden miraculous gift of God, as Süssmilch and other orthodox Christian writers maintained, nor a deliberate invention of particular men at a specific moment of time, a tool for the improvement of life, like the wheel or the compass, as the French scientists – Maupertuis and Condillac – came near to saying, and Monboddo explicitly maintained. Language was a natural growth, no more and no less mysterious than any other form of natural development, and one which, if one believed in a creative God, was divine, inasmuch as God had given man a nature capable of mental activity; the power of generating symbols, of communication, of intentionality, was intrinsic to its development.

At other times, recalled, perhaps by Hamann, to his beliefs as a Lutheran clergyman – he was, after all, the clerical head of the Grand Duchy of Weimar – Herder recanted and conceded that language was indeed implanted in, or taught to, man by God, by a specific creative act. But he could not rest in his belief. How could creatures not spiritually developed enough to use language suddenly come to be capable of doing so? And what is it to be spiritually developed, if not to be capable of thought (that is, the use of symbols, whether images or gestures or words)? Defying the strict Lutherans, towards the end of his life Herder returned openly to the belief that language was an essential part of the natural process of the growth of consciousness, indeed, of human solidarity, which rests on communication between men; for to be fully human is to think, and to think is to communicate; society and man are equally inconceivable without one another. Hence 'Reason pure and simple without language is on earth a Utopia.'[1] Herder means that it is inconceivable rather than improbable. Words, by connecting passions with things, the present with the past, and by making possible memory and imagination, create family, society, literature, history. He declares that to speak and

[1] xiii 357.

think in words is to swim in an inherited stream of images and words; we must accept these media on trust: we cannot create them.[1] The notion of a wholly solitary – as opposed to an artificially self-isolated – man is to him as unintelligible as it is to Aristotle or to some linguistic philosophers of our own time. Mere contemplation yields no truth; it is only life, that is, action with or against others, that does this. For Herder man is shaped by, and must be defined in terms of, his association with others.

We can purify and reform a language, but we cannot create one out of nothing; for to create a language is to think, and to think is to use language. This circle cannot be broken. The relation of particular words or groups of words to specific things is not logically or metaphysically necessary, but causal or conventional. Particular words are used in communicating particular experiences as a result either of natural influences – environmental factors – collectively called 'climate', after Montesquieu; or of psychological ones; or of mere chance; or of the decisions of human beings, who, acquiring some terms by 'natural' means (in some pre-rational state), invent others as they please, arbitrarily. That is why the doctrine of real essences – the Wolffian plan of discovering the truth by the analysis of concepts – is a chimera. Locke was right: we have no insight into 'essences'. Only experience can tell us if the expression x in a particular text means the same as the expression y. The dogmatic certainty of fanatical sectarians about what this or that sacred text must mean is therefore irrational and groundless. Knowledge of philology – the historical development of languages – alone yields the story of changing uses and meanings. Herder is anti-mechanistic: but he is an empiricist, in direct descent from Occam and the English naturalists. Only assiduous historical research, sympathetic insight into the purpose of the speaker, a grasp of the machinery of communication whereby human beings understand each other, whether directly, or across the centuries, can bridge the chasms between different, yet never wholly divorced, civilisations. Language expresses the collective experience of the group.[2]

Has a nation anything more precious? From a study of native literatures

---

[1] See esp. xiii 362.
[2] See, e.g., xi 225, xvii 59, xviii 346, xxx 8.

we learn to know ages and peoples more deeply than along the deceptive, desolate path of their political and military history. In the latter we seldom see more than the manner in which a people was ruled, how it let itself be slaughtered; in the former we learn how it thought, what it wished and craved for, how it took its pleasures, how it was led by its teachers or its inclinations.[1]

Hence Herder's stress on the importance of genetic studies and the history of language, and hence, too, the great impulsion that he gave to studies of comparative linguistics, comparative anthropology and ethnology, and above all to the great philological movement that became the pride of German scholarship towards the end of his life and in the century that followed. His own efforts in this direction were no less suggestive or speculative than those of Vico. After declaring, in language borrowed from Lavater, that the 'physiognomy of languages'[2] is all-important, he insisted, for example, that the languages which preserved genders (such as Russian, with which he came into contact during his Riga years) implied a vision of a world different from the world of those whose languages are sexless; so too did particular uses of pronouns. He insisted that verbs – connected with action – came before nouns, connected with contemplation of objects; that active nations employ different linguistic modes from passive ones; that nuances of language are pointers to differing forms of experience (*Weltanschauungen*). Logic for him is only an abstraction from languages living or dead. There is no 'deep' logical structure presupposed by all forms of rational thought; in his *Sprachphilosophie*, logic is an approximation to what is common in isomorphic languages, which themselves point to a high degree of similarity in the experiences of their users. Anthropology, not metaphysics or logic, whether Aristotelian or Leibnizian or Kantian, is for Herder the key to the understanding of human beings and of their world. It is the history of language that most clearly and continuously reveals such phenomena as social growth – the cycles of infancy, youth, maturity, decay – that are common to individuals and nations.

The relation of language to thought, although in a sense they are one, is an ambivalent one. At any rate, the art of writing, the incorporation of thought in permanent forms, while it creates the possibility of a continuity of social self-awareness, and makes

[1] xviii 137.
[2] xiii 363.

accessible his own and other worlds to an individual, also arrests and kills. What has been put down in writing is incapable of that living process of constant adaptation and change, of the constant expression of the unanalysable and unseizable flow of actual experience, which language, if it is to communicate fully, must possess. Language alone makes experience possible, but it also freezes it. Hamann spoke of the valley of dry bones which only 'a prophet'[1] (such as Socrates, St Paul, Luther, and perhaps himself) could cover with flesh. Herder speaks of corpses – forms of linguistic petrifaction – against which, in due course, men revolt. The history of linguistic revolutions is the history of the succession of cultures, the true revolutions in the history of the human race. Was there once a language common to all men? He does not wish to assert this. On the one hand, he clings to the notion of one world, one basic human personality, the 'organic' interrelation of everything; he insists on the folly and danger of abstraction, of fragmentation, of splitting the human personality into separate faculties, as not only Wolff but Kant, too, had done in their psychologies and in their strict division of body from soul, nature from spirit, the empirical from the a priori, the historical from the eternal. Yet he is a Christian, too, and he is committed to the Aristotelian and biblical doctrine of natural kinds. Man is unique; Lord Monboddo and the naturalists must be mistaken. That, no doubt, is why language had to be a direct gift of God, and not the product of a gradual process of emergence of rational beings out of some pre-rational state of nature – from the animal kingdom and subhuman forms of sentience, or even from insentience.[2] The contradiction is never reconciled.

The only identification that Herder never abandons is that of thought and action, language and activity. Poetry, particularly early epic poetry, is for him pure activity. He was taken in by Ossian, like many of his contemporaries. It is probably from these poems rather than from Homer – although he speaks of the Homeric poems as improvisations, not a dead artefact – that he derives his notion of poetry as activity. Poetry, particularly among early peoples, is, he maintains, magical in character; it is not cool description of nature or of anything else: it is a spur to action for

[1] op. cit. (p. 250 above, note 2), vol. 2, p. 176, line 13.
[2] G. A. Wells, op. cit. (p. 361 above, note 1), p. 43, advances this view, which seems to me very illuminating.

heroes, hunters, lovers; it stimulates and directs. It is not to be savoured by the scholar in his armchair, but is intelligible only to those who have placed themselves in situations similar to the conditions in which such words sprang into existence. During his voyage from Riga to Nantes, he observed the sailors during rough seas. These dour men under a savage discipline, who lived in terror of, and in constant intimate contact with, the elements which they sought to dominate, resurrected for him the dark world of Skalds and Vikings and the Eddas,[1] a world scarcely intelligible to tranquil philologists in their studies or detached literary epicures who turn over the pages idly, without the power to re-create the world of which these works are the vision and the voice. Words, rhythms, actions are aspects of a single experience. These are commonplaces today, but (despite Vico) they were far from being such in Herder's time.

'The more savage, that is, the more alive and freedom-loving a people is (for that is the simple meaning of the word), the more savage, that is, alive, free, sensuous, lyrically active, its songs must be, if it has songs', he wrote in 1773.[2] He compares 'the living presentness of the imagery' of such songs with songs 'written for paper'. 'These arrows of a savage Apollo pierce hearts and carry souls and memories with them.'[3] 'All unpolished peoples sing and act; they sing about what they do and thus sing histories. Their songs are the archives of their people, the treasury of their science and religion ... a picture of their domestic life in joy and in sorrow, by bridal bed and graveside ... Here everyone portrays himself and appears as he is.'[4] Language, content, tone tell us more about the outlook, beliefs, origins, history, mingling of nations than travellers' tales. Then artifice begins. When the words were divorced from music, when the poet began to write 'slowly, in order to be read',[5] art may have gained, but there was a loss of magic, of 'miraculous power'.[6] What do our modern critics, the 'counters of syllables', 'specialists in scansion', masters of dead

---

[1] See below, pp. 403–4.
[2] v 164.
[3] ibid.
[4] ix 532. This quotation, and those earlier in this paragraph, are based on the translations in Burton Feldman and Robert D. Richardson (eds), *The Rise of Modern Mythology 1680–1860* (Bloomington/London, 1972), pp. 229–30.
[5] viii 412.
[6] See viii 390.

learning, know of all this? 'Heart! Warmth! Blood! Humanity! Life!'[1] 'I feel! I am!'[2] These are Herder's mottoes; no wonder that the poets of the *Sturm und Drang* recognised themselves in his writings.

He dreams of a visit to the Northern seas reading 'the story of Utal and Ninetuma in sight of the very island where it all took place'. His voyage to France, which took him past the shores of Scandinavia and England, transported him: 'This was a living and creative Nature, between the deeps of sea and sky',[3] very different from the world in which he was living, where 'we scarcely see or feel, only reflect and reason',[4] in which poets invent imaginary passions and qualities of soul unknown to them or anyone, and compare verses about objects about which one cannot think or feel or imagine anything at all. He feels a kindred spirit in the English scholar Robert Wood, who gazed upon the ruins of Troy, a volume of Homer in hand.[5] He must go to the Scottish Highlands, to see the places described by the great Ossian himself and 'hear the living songs of a living people'.[6] After all, 'The Greeks, too, were once ... savages, and in the best period of their flowering far more of nature remained in them than can be descried by the narrow gaze of a scholiast or a classical scholar.' Homer goes back to ancient sagas, Tyrtaeus to ballads, Arion and Orpheus are 'noble Greek shamans', Sappho's songs are like nothing so much as the songs of a Livonian girl of our own time.[7] Our scholars and translators have no inkling of this. Consider the translation of a Lapp song by the minor poet Christian Ewald Kleist:

> I would willingly give up for this song a dozen of Kleist's imitations. Do not be surprised [he writes to his fiancée Caroline], that a Laplandic youth who knew neither school nor writing, and scarcely knows God, sings better than Major Kleist. After all, the Lapp improvised his song while he was gliding with his reindeer over the snow, and time dragged so slowly on the way to Lake Orra where his beloved lived.[8]

[1] v 538.
[2] viii 96.
[3] v 169.
[4] v 183.
[5] v 169.
[6] v 167.
[7] ix 534.
[8] Letter to Caroline Flachsland, 2 January 1771.

Swiss and English scholars had celebrated Homer, Dante, Shakespeare, Milton. Hurd, Young, Percy, Lowth and Blackwell revived the study of ancient poetry. Enthusiasm for the achievements of the collective genius of primitive societies, under the impulsion of Rousseau, was transformed into a European movement by Herder's passionate advocacy.

All genuine expressions of experience are valid. They differ because lives differ: perhaps because the earth's axis is inclined by twenty-four degrees. This generates different geophysical 'climates', different experiences, different societies. Anything that seems to Herder authentic delights him. He has his preferences: he prefers the Greeks, the Germans and the Hebrews to the Romans, the ancient Egyptians or the Frenchmen of his own time or of the previous century. But, at least in theory, he is prepared to defend them all; he wishes and thinks he is able to penetrate – 'feel himself'[1] (*Einfühlen* is his invention, a hundred years before Lipps or Dilthey or Croce) – into their essence, grasp what it must be like to live, contemplate goals, act and react, think, imagine in the unique ways dictated by their circumstances, and so grasp the patterns of life in terms of which alone such groups are to be defined. The central concept here is that of natural growth, biological, emotional, intellectual. Nature *is* growth – what Bodmer and Breitinger had spoken of, perhaps echoing Vico's *nascimento*, as *Naturwüchsigkeit* – spontaneous natural growth, not the static 'true nature' of Boileau's aesthetics, or Batteux's *la belle nature*, which the artist must learn to discern and reveal from the welter of mere experience.

Everything that is natural is valuable. The notion (for example, the Marquis de Sade's) that vices or decadence or aggression are not less natural than the rich and harmonious development of all human potentialities is not allowed for. In this respect Herder is a true child of the Enlightenment at its most naïve as well as at its most imaginative and penetrating. Arthur Lovejoy was surely right when he included Herder among the thinkers (perhaps the majority in the West) who identified the 'must' of natural laws that caused things to be as they are, and governed the world inexorably, with the 'ought' of the normative rules, derived, apparently, from the selfsame nature, obedience to which alone conducts men towards happiness and virtue and wisdom. But this consensus has

[1] v 503.

its limits. Herder sharply differs from the central thought of the French Enlightenment, and that not only in the respects that all his commentators have noted.

What is usually stressed is, in the first place, his relativism,[1] his admiration of every authentic culture for being what it is, his insistence that outlooks and civilisations must be understood from within, in terms of their own stages of development, purposes and outlooks; and in the second place his sharp repudiation of that central strain in Cartesian rationalism which regards only what is universal, eternal, unalterable, governed by rigorously logical relationships – only the subject-matter of mathematics, logic, physics and the other natural sciences – as true knowledge.

But Herder rebelled against the *Aufklärung* in an even profounder way, by rejecting the very notion of impassable barriers in nature or experience – barriers between types of consciousness or faculties or ideas or natural objects. What repels him equally in such deeply disparate thinkers as Descartes and Kant and the French *philosophes* is their common insistence on rigid divisions between 'faculties' and types of experience, which they seem to him to have introduced merely to make it possible to classify and generalise. He admires Leibniz more than Kant: he recognises the logical gulf between mathematical truths and those of fact, but he regards the former (probably following Hume) as tautologies, statements unconcerned with nature.[2] He is a thoroughgoing empiricist in matters of epistemology. Kant's transcendental categories, which claim to determine experience a priori, seem to him a monstrous conflation of analytic and synthetic: he rejects the 'synthetic a priori' as a hideous confusion.[3] Reality for

---

[1] At various points in this essay I describe Herder as a relativist. Although the general tenor of my remarks makes it clear, I hope, in what sense I use this term, what I say has led to some misunderstanding of my views (see, for example, Arnaldo Momigliano, 'On the Pioneer Trail', *New York Review of Books*, 11 November 1976, 33–8). I have attempted to clarify my position in an article entitled 'Alleged Relativism in Eighteenth-Century European Thought', reprinted in one of my collections of essays, *The Crooked Timber of Humanity* (London, 1990; New York, 1991). Essentially, in the present study of Herder I sometimes use 'relativism' not to mean a species of ethical or epistemological subjectivism, as the term has very often been understood, but to refer to what I have elsewhere identified, I hope more perspicuously, as objective pluralism, free from any taint of subjectivism. I.B. 1996.

[2] xxi 36.

[3] xxi 38.

him admits of no a priori laws; Kant's attempt to distinguish contingent from necessary judgements about experience seems to him to be far more misleading than the distinction between intuited necessities and observed contingencies out of which Spinoza and Leibniz built their systems. Categories, rigorous distinctions of kinds of truth about the nature of reality – like the similar distinctions drawn between words and concepts – distort judgement not only in epistemology and logic, but in politics and ethics and the arts, and indeed all regions of experience. All activities, he insists, express the whole and undivided man whom Descartes and Kant, in their several ways, have done their best to carve up into compartments with their faculty psychology of 'reason', 'imagination', 'intuition', 'feeling', 'will'.[1] He declares that he knows of no criteria for distinguishing such Kantian faculties as *Erkennen, Empfinden, Wollen* – they are indissolubly united in the organic personality of living men.

The attack on Kant in the *Metakritik* of 1799 merely summarises a lifelong attitude. The black-and-white terms these neo-scholastics use to describe man – an inexhaustibly complex organisation – seem to Herder wilfully absolute and arbitrary. Instead, for example, of asking themselves how free men are, free from or for what, and where and when, and in what respects, or what renders them more or less free, these thinkers dogmatically pronounce man to be free, wholly free in some absolute sense, as against animals who are wholly mechanical, or at least wholly lack freedom. They speak of man as distinguished by his possession of reason (not as being less or more rational), and define him in terms

---

[1] According to Herder the soul evolves a pattern from the chaos of things by which it is surrounded, and so 'creates by its own inner power a one out of the many, which belongs to it alone' (xiii 182); cf. xv 532 and H. B. Nisbet, op. cit. (p. 361 above, note 1), p. 63. That the creation of integrated wholes out of discrete data is the fundamental organising activity of human nature is a belief that is central to Herder's entire social and moral outlook: for him all creative activity, conscious and unconscious, generates and is, in turn, determined by its own unique *Gestalt*, whereby every individual and group strives to perceive, understand, act, create, live. This is the idea which dominates his conception of social structure and development, of the nature of an identifiable civilisation, and, indeed, of what men live by (see v 103–5). Nisbet seems to me entirely justified in describing Herder as a forerunner of gestalt psychology. On this see also Martin Schütze's articles, 'Herder's Psychology', *Monist* 35 (1925), 507–54, and 'The Fundamental Ideas in Herder's Thought', *Modern Philology* 18 (1920–1), 65–78, 289–302; 19 (1921–2), 113–30, 361–82; 21 (1923–4), 29–48, 113–32.

of selected properties that one must either possess wholly or not possess at all; they describe him in terms of sharp, artificial dichotomies that arbitrarily break up the interwoven, continuous, at times irregular, fluid, shapeless, often unanalysable, but always perceptible, dynamic, teeming, boundless, eternal multiplicity of nature,[1] and so provide distorting lenses both to philosophers and historians. Attempts to bring manifestations so complex and so various under some general law, whether by philosophers seeking knowledge, or by statesmen seeking to organise and govern, seemed to Herder no better than a search for the lowest common denominator – for what may be least characteristic and important in the lives of men – and, therefore, as making for shallowness in theory and a tendency to impose a crippling uniformity in practice. Herder is one of the earliest opponents of uniformity as the enemy of life and freedom.

One of the central doctrines of the Western tradition, at any rate since Plato, has maintained that the good is one, while evil has many faces; there is one true answer to every real question, but many false ones. Even Aristotle, for whom Plato's ideal of an unchanging, wholly unified society is too rigid, since it does not allow for the variety of human characters and wishes, merely reports this as a fact, not as something desirable in itself. The central current in ethics and politics, as well as metaphysics and theology and the sciences, is cast in a monist mould: it seeks to bring the many into a coherent, systematic unity. Herder is an early and passionate champion of variety: uniformity maims and kills. The 'ferment' of the Middle Ages did at least, he wrote in 1774, 'hold at bay the devouring jaws of despotism' whose tendency is

to crush everything into deadly uniformity. Now is it better, is it healthier and more beneficent for mankind to produce only the lifeless cogs of a huge, wooden, thoughtless machine, or to rouse and activate lively energies? Even if institutions are not perfect, even if men are not always honest, even if there is some disorder and a good deal of disagreement, it is still preferable to a state of affairs in which men are forced to rot and decay during their own lifetime.[2]

Even Montesquieu, so widely praised for his novel sense of the

[1] See xiii 194.
[2] v 516.

differences between societies and of the 'spirit' that animates their laws and institutions, has tried to press these teeming varieties of human life and culture into the strait-jacket of three basic types: 'three wretched generalisations! ... the history of all times and peoples, whose succession forms the great, living work of God, reduced to ruins, divided neatly into three heaps ... Oh, Montesquieu!'[1]

All regionalists, all defenders of the local against the universal, all champions of deeply rooted forms of life, both reactionary and progressive, both genuine humanists and obscurantist opponents of scientific advance, owe something, whether they know it or not, to the doctrines which Herder (with a far wider and more magnificent sweep than Möser or Burke or Ferguson) introduced into European thought. Vico might have achieved something of this. But he was (and is) not read; as Savigny remarked, he came into his own too late to have a decisive influence.

However much lip-service Herder may have paid to 'natural kinds', in general he conceived of nature as a unity in which the *Kräfte* – the mysterious, dynamic, purpose-seeking forces the interplay of which constitutes all movement and growth – flow into each other, clash, combine, coalesce. These forces are not causal and mechanical as in Descartes; nor insulated from each other as in the *Monadology* of Leibniz; his notion of them owes more to Neoplatonic and Renaissance mysticism, and, perhaps, to Erigena's *natura naturans* than to the sciences of his time. For Herder reality is a kind of symbiosis of these *Kräfte* (whose character remains obscure) with an environment that is conceived in somewhat static terms; if the environment is altered too abruptly, the result is some kind of collapse.

Herder found more and more evidence for this. Transplanted flowers decay in unsympathetic climates; so do human beings. Greenlanders do not thrive in Denmark. Africans are miserable and decay in Europe. Europeans become debilitated in America. Conquest crushes, and emigration sometimes leads to enfeeblement – lack of vital force, the flattening out of human beings, and a sad uniformity. The *Ideen* is full of such examples. Like Fourier after him, Herder believed in the complete realisability of all potentialities ('All that can be, is; all that can come into being, will come

[1] v 566.

into being; if not today, then tomorrow'),[1] since everything fits somewhere. Only artificiality is destructive, in life as in art. Marriages of convenience, coldly entered into, ruin children, and are worse for them than pure animality. The patriarchs at times exercised severe and cruel authority: but at least this is more 'natural' – and therefore less harmful – than the artificial reasonings of philosophers. Herder harbours a Rousseau-like suspicion of 'reasoning'. He does not think that Voltaire's desiccated maxims or Wolff's syllogisms are better for children than the stern but natural behaviour of primitive men. Anything is preferable to a system which imposes the ideal of one culture on another and arranges, adjusts, makes for uniform 'physiognomies', as opposed to a condition which is 'natural', in a state of creative disorder, where alone individuality and freedom live and grow. Hence his condemnation of all theories which over-categorise men – into racial types, for example, or social orders – and thereby divide them from each other. Centralisation and *dirigisme* are the enemies: even some degree of inefficiency is preferable to 'a state of affairs in which men are made to rot and decay during their own lifetime'. In the same spirit 'political reform must come from below',[2] since 'even when man abuses his freedom most despicably he is still king; for he can still choose, even if he chooses the worst; he can rule over himself, even if he legislates himself into a beast'.[3] His differences from his fellow opponents of the French *lumières* – Möser, Kant, Rousseau, Burke – are obvious enough.

He condemns the anthropologies which treat men in general and leave the individual drained of too many differentiating characteristics. Even tradition, which otherwise acts as a preservative of the most vital characteristics of human groups, can be a danger when it becomes too mechanical and acts as a narcotic, as it seems to him to have done in Asia, which it put to sleep by eliminating too many of the other ingredients of a healthy life, too many other *Kräfte* that are indispensable to life and activity. This thought is incapable of precise formulation; but, as always with Herder, it is suggestive and has a clear general direction. 'The savage who loves himself, his wife and his child . . . and works for the good of his tribe as for his own . . . is in my view more genuine than that cultivated ghost, the

[1] xiv 86.
[2] xxxii 56.
[3] xiii 147.

... citizen of the world, who, burning with love for all his fellow ghosts, loves a chimera. The savage in his hut has room for any stranger ... the saturated heart of the superfluous cosmopolitan is a home for no one.'[1] He repeats throughout the *Ideen* that originality – freedom of choice and creation – is the divine element in man. When a savage speaks with vigour and precision he is superior to the civilised man who stands on a pedestal built by others.[2] There is much talk in the *Ideen* (this is later echoed by Fichte) about men who live on other men's accounts: they are viewed as 'superfluous cosmopolitans', men whose feelings have been drained away, dehumanised creatures, victims of nature or history, moral or physical cripples, parasites, fettered slaves.

How do men come to lose their humanity? By living on others and by the labour and ideas of others. Herder, in opposition to the primitivists, welcomed invention – the arts and sciences are fruits of the creative powers of man, and through them he rises to the full height of his purposive nature. Inventions as such do not corrupt (in this Herder differs from the Rousseau of the first and second *Discourses*); only if one lives on the inventions of others does one become mechanical and devitalised.[3] Here, too, as in the writings of Mably, Rousseau and Friedrich Karl von Moser,[4] begins that lament, still more characteristic of the following century, and perhaps even more often heard in our own, for the youth that is gone for ever – for the lost virtues of an earlier, more vigorous epoch in the life of mankind. Herder, no less than Mill or Carlyle or Ruskin, speaks with gloom about the triviality and lifelessness of modern men and modern art, in contrast with the full-blooded, doughty, independent human beings of the morning hours of humanity – the creators of the great epics and songs, of an anonymous but more robust age. Before Henri de Saint-Simon he draws a contrast between the creative and the relatively sterile

---

[1] xiii 339.

[2] xiii 371–2.

[3] In his essay on Ossian, Herder speaks of this as the source of the fatal division of labour which creates destructive barriers among men, classes and hierarchies, and the division of spiritual from manual labour which robs men of their humanity. Material progress may march hand in hand with cultural decline; this theme is taken up by Goethe and Schiller and developed by Marx and Marxists. (I owe this point to Professor Roy Pascal.)

[4] Especially in Moser's *Von dem deutschen Nationalgeist*, published in 1765–6, which speaks of the Germans as despised, disregarded, mocked, and preyed upon by everyone.

epochs in the history of culture. Herder has his optimistic moments, when he supposes that a renewal is possible: that if man can only 'cease to be in contradiction with himself' and 'return to himself', and if peoples can only 'find themselves' and learn not to 'think in other people's thoughts',[1] they can recover and revive and create new works of art, in modern terms, as noble and expressive of their true nature as anything that men have created in the past. There is only one course against which Herder sets his face absolutely: that is, any attempt to return to the past. Here there is no salvation. To sigh after the Greeks and wish to return to them, of which he suspects Winckelmann, is absurd and impossible: Winckelmann's idealisation of the Greeks as the originators of art, which among them attained to a sublime height never reached by, say, the Egyptians, is wholly unhistorical and nothing but a terrible delusion.[2]

The dangers to free development are many. In the first place, there is the centralised State; it can rob us of something essential: it can rob us of ourselves. There are foreign cultures that devour German folk-song 'like a cancer'[3] – folk-song that is a response to the deepest human cravings, to collective desires that seek to embody common experiences in symbolic forms not dreamed of in Voltaire's philosophy. There is the more specific danger of foreign languages: I am able to stammer with immense effort in the words of a foreign language; its spirit will evade me. Yet to this we devote the best years of our life![4] But we are not Greeks; we are not Romans; and we cannot become such. To wish to return is to be dominated by a false vision, a crippling illusion as fatal as any for which it attempts to be the cure. Imitation is a terrible curse: human nature is not identical in different parts of the world; the worlds of things and sounds are different. What then must we do?

[1] xiii 160–1. Such phrases are almost verbally exact echoes of sentences in which Hamann deals with what much later came to be called the problem of 'alienation'.

[2] viii 476–7; compare the following (v 565) from *Auch eine Philosophie*: 'There is no country the civilisation of which has been able to take a backward step, and become for the second time what it has once been. The path of destiny is as inflexible as iron ... can today become yesterday? ... You Ptolemies could never again create an Egypt, nor you Hadrians a Greece, nor Julian a Jerusalem.' These cultures have had their day. 'The sword is worn out, the empty scabbard lies in pieces.'

[3] xxv 11.

[4] iv 388–9, xxx 8.

We must seek to be ourselves. 'Let us be characteristic of our nation, language, scene, and let posterity decide whether or not we are classical!'[1] Perhaps Klopstock's *Messias* was less successful than it might have been because it was not 'national' enough.[2] It is here that Herder utters his most ardently nationalist sentiments: 'But now! I cry yet again, my German brothers! But now! The remnants of all living folk-life [*Volksdenkart*] are rolling into the abyss of oblivion ... the light of so-called culture is devouring all about it like a cancer.'[3] 'We speak the words of strangers and they wean us from our own thoughts.'[4] He sees no merit in peasants in wigs, much as Hamann talks of 'false noses'.[5] He appeals to the Germans to know themselves, to understand their place and respect their role in the cosmos, in time and in space.

V

Is this nationalism? In an obvious sense it is. It is anti-French – the voyage to Nantes and Paris (like the later journey to Rome) depressed Herder acutely. He met some of the most distinguished of the *philosophes*, but evidently failed to achieve any degree of communication with them. He suffered that mixture of envy, humiliation, admiration, resentment and defiant pride which backward peoples feel towards advanced ones, members of one social class towards those who belong to a higher rung in the hierarchy. Wounded national feeling – this scarcely needs saying – breeds nationalism, but it is important to realise that Herder's nationalism was never political. If he denounces individualism, he equally detests the State, which coerces and mutilates the free human personality. His social vision is antagonistic to government, power, domination. Louis XIV and Frederick the Great (like Caesar and Charlemagne before them) represent a detestable ideal. Herder does not ask for power and does not wish to assert the superiority

---

[1] ii 57.
[2] v 259; cf. i 268. Rouché, op. cit. (p. 361 above, note 3), p. 98 (cf. ibid., p. 52), is understandably surprised by the spectacle of a Christian clergyman complaining that the central theme of Christian religion is perhaps too foreign a topic for a German poem.
[3] xxv 11.
[4] iv 389.
[5] op. cit. (p. 250 above, note 4), vol. 7, p. 460, line 27.

of his own class or culture or nation. He wishes to create a society in which men, whoever they are, can live full lives, attain to free self-expression, 'be someone'; and he thinks that the less government they have the better. We cannot return to the Greek *polis*. This may, indeed, have been the first stage of a development destined in its later stages to become nationalistic and chauvinistic in the full, aggressive sense. Whether or not this is historically and sociologically true, it is clear that Herder did not himself harbour these sentiments. Even though he seems to have coined the word *Nationalismus*, his conception of a good society is closer to the anarchism of Thoreau or Proudhon or Kropotkin, and to the conception of a culture (*Bildung*) of which such liberals as Goethe and Humboldt were proponents, than to the ideals of Fichte or Hegel or political socialists. For him *die Nation* is not a political entity. He is repelled by the claims of contemporary Celtomaniacs and Teutomaniacs who rhapsodised over the ancient Gaels or Northmen. He celebrates German beginnings because they are part of, and illuminate, his own civilisation, not because German civilisation ranks higher than that of others on some cosmic scale. 'In the works of imagination and feeling the entire soul of the nation reveals itself most freely.'[1] This was developed by Sismondi, Michelet and Mazzini into a full-scale political-cultural doctrine; but Herder stands even closer to the outlook of Ruskin or Lamennais or William Morris, to populists and Christian socialists, and to all of those who, in the present day, are opposed to hierarchies of status or power, or to the influence of manipulators of any kind. He stands with those who protest against mechanisation and vulgarisation rather than with the nationalists of the last hundred years, whether moderate or violent. He favours autarky, but only in personal life; that is, in artistic creation and the rights of natural self-expression. All his invocations of the *Nationalgeist* (an expression probably coined by Freidrich Karl von Moser), and of its many aliases – the *Geist des Volkes, Seele des Volkes, Geist der Nation, Genius des Volkes* and the more empirical *Nationalcharakter*[2] – are intended to stress what is ours, not theirs, even though theirs may intrinsically be more valuable, viewed on some vaster scale.

Herder admits no such scale: cultures are comparable but not

[1] xviii 58.
[2] i 263; ii 160; iii 30; v 185, 217; viii 392; xiii 364; xiv 38, 84; xxv 10; and *passim*.

commensurable; each is what it is, of literally inestimable value in its own society, and consequently to humanity as a whole. Socrates is for him neither the timeless cosmopolitan sage of the Enlightenment, nor Hamann's destroyer of pretentious claims to knowledge whose irony and self-confessed ignorance opened the path to faith and salvation. Socrates is, above all, an Athenian of the fifth century; and that age is over. Aristotle may be more gifted than Leibniz, but Leibniz is ours, Aristotle is not; Shakespeare is ours, other great geniuses, Homer or Moses, are not. Individuality is all; artificial combinations of old and new, native and foreign, lead to false ideas and ruinous practice.[1] Let us follow our own path; let men speak well or ill of our nation, our literature, our language: they are ours, they are ourselves, and let that be enough.[2] Better Germans, whatever they are, than sham Greeks, Frenchmen, Englishmen.[3] But when he says, 'Awake, German nation! Do not let them ravish your Palladium!',[4] declares that fearful storms are coming and warns men not to lie asleep like Jonah in the tempest, and when he tells me to take warning from the terrible example of partitioned Poland,[5] and says, 'Poor, torn, crushed Germany, be hopeful!'[6] and 'Germans, speak German! Spew out the Seine's ugly slime!',[7] it is difficult to avoid the thought that this may indeed have fed the sinister nationalism of Görres and Jahn, Arndt and Treitschke, and their monstrous modern successors. Yet Herder's own sentences refer to purely cultural self-determination; he hates *policirte Nationen*.[8] Nationality for him is purely and strictly a cultural attribute; he believes that people can and should defend their cultural heritage: they need never give in. He almost blames the Jews, despite his passionate addiction to their antiquities, for not preserving a sufficient sense of collective honour and making no effort to return to their home in Palestine, which is the sole place where they can blossom again into a *Nation*. He is interested, not in nationality but in cultures, in worlds, in the total experience of peoples; and the aspects of this experience that he

[1] xiv 227; xv 321; xviii 248.
[2] xviii 160–1.
[3] i 366–7.
[4] xvii 309.
[5] xxix 210.
[6] viii 433.
[7] xxvii 129.
[8] See v 555; cf. v 524.

celebrates are personal relationships, friendship and enmity, attitudes to nature, war and peace, art and science, ways in which
truth, freedom and happiness are pursued, and in particular the
relations of the great civilising leaders to the ungrateful mob. He
fears organisation as such, and, like the early English romantics,
like Young or Thomas and Joseph Warton, he wants to preserve
what is irregular and unique in life and in art, that which no system
can wholly contain.

His attack on political centralisation and intellectual polarisation
springs from the same source. When he imagines the world as a
garden which can contain many flowers, and when he speaks of the
possible and desirable harmony between all the national cultures,
he is not simply ignoring the aggressive potentialities of nation
States or blandly assuming that there is no reason for conflict
between various nationalisms. Rather, he is deeply hostile to the
growth of political, economic, military centralisation, but sees no
reason why culturally autonomous communities need clash. It
may, of course, be unrealistic and unhistorical to suppose that one
kind of autarky need not lead to other and more dangerous kinds.
But it is not the same kind of unrealism as that with which he, and
the Enlightenment generally, are usually charged. His faith is not in
nationalism, collectivism, Teutomania or romantic State-worship,
but in something that is, if anything, incompatible with these
ideals. He is the champion of those mysterious *Kräfte* which are
'living and organic'.[1] For him, as for Shaftesbury (one of those
English thinkers who, like Young and Carlyle, influenced the
Germans far more than his own compatriots), there is, in the end,
only one great creative *Kraft*: 'What is alive in creation is, in all
forms, shapes, channels, one spirit, one single flame.'[2] This is
scarcely an empirical or scientific notion. He sings paeans to the
*Seele des Volkes* which is the social incarnation of the Leibnizian
*vis viva*, 'wonderful, unique ... inexplicable, inextinguishable, and
as old as the *Nation*'.[3] Its most vivid expression is, of course, not
the State, but 'the physiognomy of its speech'.[4]

The point that I wish to stress is that the true heir of this
doctrine is not power politics but what came to be called populism.
It is this that acquired such momentum among the oppressed

[1] xiii 172; cf. xiii 177.
[2] viii 178.
[3] xiv 38.
[4] xiii 364.

people of Eastern Europe, and later spread in Asia and Africa. It inspired not *étatistes* but believers in 'grass roots' – Russian Slavophils and *Narodniks*, Christian Socialists and all those admirers of folk art and of popular traditions whose enthusiasm assumed both serious and ridiculous shapes, still not unfamiliar today. Populism may often have taken reactionary forms and fed the stream of aggressive nationalism; but the form in which Herder held it was democratic and peaceful, not only anti-dynastic and anti-élitist, but deeply anti-political, directed against organised power, whether of nations, classes, races or parties. I have called it populism because this movement, whether in Europe or outside it, seems to me the nearest approximation to Herder's ideal. It is, as a rule, pluralistic, looks on government as an evil, tends, following Rousseau, to identify 'the people' with the poor, the peasants, the common folk, the plebeian masses,[1] uncorrupted by wealth or city life; and, to this day, animates folk enthusiasts and cultural fanatics, egalitarians and agitators for local autonomy, champions of arts and crafts and of simple life, and innocent Utopians of all brands. It is based on belief in loose textures, voluntary associations, natural ties, and is bitterly opposed to armies, bureaucracies, 'closed' societies of any sort.

Historically, populism has, of course, become closely interwoven with real nationalism, and it has, indeed, often provided the soil in which blind xenophobia and irrationalism grew to dangerous heights; and this is no more accidental than the alliances of nationalism with democracy or romanticism or liberalism at various points in the nineteenth century. Nevertheless, it is a historical and moral error to identify the ideology of one period with its consequences at some other, or with its transformation in another context and in combination with other factors. The progeny of Herder in, let us say, England or America are to be found principally among those amateurs who became absorbed in the antiquities and forms of life (ancient and modern) of cultures other than their own, in Asia and Africa or the 'backward' provinces of Europe or America, among professional amateurs and collectors of ancient song and poetry, among enthusiastic and sometimes sentimental devotees of more primitive forms of life in the Balkans or

---

[1] This strain is strong in Herder, particularly in his early years: e.g. 'Philosopher and plebeian, unite in order to be useful!' (xxxii 51), written in 1765, when Herder was twenty-one. There is also his insistence, already quoted, that political reform must always come 'from below' (xxxii 56).

among the Arabs; nostalgic travellers and exiles like Richard Burton, Doughty, Lafcadio Hearn, the English companions of Gandhi or Ibn Saud, cultural autonomists and unpolitical youth movements, as well as serious students and philosophers of language and society.

Perhaps Herder's most characteristic descendants were to be found in Russia, in which he took so abiding an interest. In that country his ideas entered the thought of those critics and creative artists who not merely developed national and pseudo-national forms of their own native art but became passionate champions of all 'natural', 'spontaneous', traditional forms of art and self-expression wherever they manifested themselves. These admirers of ethnic colour and variety as such, Mussorgsky, Stassov, and some of the musicians and painters whom they inspired, so far from supporting authority and repression, stood politically on the left, and felt sympathy for all forms of cultural self-expression, especially on the part of persecuted minorities – Georgians, Poles, Jews, Finns, but also Spaniards, Hungarians and other 'unreconstructed' nations. They denounced, however unjustly and intemperately, such 'organ-grinders' as Rossini and Verdi, or neo-classical schools of painting, for alleged cosmopolitanism, for commercialism, for a tendency to destroy regional or national differences in favour of flat and mechanical forms of life – in short, for rootlessness (a term which afterwards became so sinister and ominous in the mouths of obscurantists and chauvinists), heartlessness, oppression and dehumanisation. All this is typically Herderian.

Something of this kind, too, may have entered Mazzini's ideal of the Young Italy which was to live in harmony and mutual understanding with Young Germany – and the 'Youth' of all nations – once they had thrown away the shackles of oppressive imperialism, of dynastic autocracies, of the denial of the rights of all 'natural' human units, and attained to free self-determination. Such views may have been thoroughly Utopian. But if they were nationalistic, they were so in a sense very different from the later – and pejorative – sense of the word. Populism may have been in part responsible for isolationism, provincialism, suspicion of everything smooth, metropolitan, elegant and socially superior, hatred of the *beau monde* in all its forms; but with this went hostility to centralisation, dogmatism, militarism and self-assertiveness, or, in other words, all that is commonly associated with the full-grown nationalism of the nineteenth century, as well as with deep antipathy to mobs – Herder carefully distinguishes the *Pöbel auf den Gassen* ('the rabble') from the *Volk* (that is, the body of the nation), however this is done[1] – and with a hatred of violence and conquest as strong as any to be found among the other Weimar humanists, Goethe, Wieland and Schiller. The faithful followers of Herder may often have been – and can still be – confused, sentimental, impractical, ineffective and sometimes ridiculous, but not managerial, calculating or brutal. No one made more of this profound contrast than Herder himself.

VI

In this connection it is worth considering Herder's attitude to three great eighteenth-century myths which fed the stream of nineteenth-century nationalism. The first is that of the superiority of a particular tribal culture. His denunciation of patriotic boastfulness – the *Favoritvolk* doctrine – has already been referred to. One of the most quoted sentences from *Yet Another Philosophy of History* tells us that 'Every nation has its own inner centre of happiness, as every sphere its own centre of gravity.'[2] This is what the historian, the critic, the philosopher must grasp, and nothing is more fatal than the attempted assimilation of the *Mittelpunkt* of one culture with those of others. One must 'enter the time, the place, the entire history'[3] of a people; one must 'feel oneself into [*sich hineinfühlen*] everything'.[4] This is what contemporary historians (he is referring specifically to Schlözer) conspicuously fail to do.[5] To understand Hebrew scripture it is not enough, he tells us, to see it as a sublime work of art, and compare its beauties with those of Homer, as the Oxford scholar Robert Lowth had done; we must transport ourselves into a distant land and an earlier age, and read it as the national poem of the Jews, a pastoral and agricultural people, written in ancient, simple, rustic, poetic, not philosophical or abstract, language. 'Be a shepherd among shepherds, a peasant in the midst of an agricultural people, an oriental among the primitive dwellers of the East, if you wish to enjoy these creations in the

[1] xxv 323.
[2] v 509.
[3] v 502.
[4] v 503; cf. ii 118, ii 257, v 536.
[5] v 436–40.

atmosphere of their birth.'[1] Germans are not ancient Hebrews; biblical images are drawn from a world alien to them. When the poet of the Bible speaks of the snows of Lebanon or the pleasant vineyards of Carmel, these are empty words to a German poet.[2] 'The dreadful storms from the sea passing over their land to Arabia were for them thundering steeds bearing the chariot of Jehovah through the clouds.'[3] He says that it would be better for a contemporary poet to sing of electric sparks than copy these Judaean images; for the Bible the rainbow is the footstool of the Lord's house; for the Skalds it is a fiery bridge over which the giants sought to storm heaven.[4] All this is at best only half intelligible to us. The Germans are not biblical Jews, nor are they classical Greeks or Romans either.[5] Every experience is what it is. To understand it is to grasp what it meant to those who expressed it in the monuments through which we try to read it. All understanding is necessarily historical. The *Aufklärer* – Gottsched, Lessing and Moses Mendelssohn – not only lack all historical perspective, they tend to grade, to give marks for moral excellence. Herder, in this (what he would regard as a Spinozan) mood, warns,

---

[1] x 14 (written in 1780–1). This is less than fair to Lowth, who, a good deal earlier than his critic, spoke of biblical verse as words that 'burst forth in sentences pointed, earnest, rapid, and tremulous' and declared that 'we must see all things with their eyes ... we must endeavour ... to read Hebrew as the Hebrews would have read it'. Robert Lowth, *Lectures on the Sacred Poetry of the Hebrews* (1753), trans. from the Latin by G. Gregory (London, 1787), Lectures 1 and 5 (vol. 1, pp. 37 and 113).

[2] i 258–9.

[3] i 264.

[4] ibid.

[5] 'Oh accursed word "classical"! It has transformed Cicero for us into a classical school-rhetorician, Horace and Virgil into classical school-poets, Caesar into a pedant, Livy into a phrasemonger. It is the word "classical" that has divided expression from thought, and thought from the event that has generated it.' This word has become a wall between us and all true education, which would have seen the ancients as living exemplars. 'This word has buried many a genius beneath a heap of words ... crushed him under a millstone of a dead language' (i 412). When a German poet is described as a second Horace, as a new Lucretius, a historian as a second Livy, that is nothing to be proud of; 'but it would be a great, rare, enviable glory for us if one could say about such writers: "This is how Horace, Cicero, Lucretius, Livy would have written if they were writing about this topic, at this particular stage of culture, at this particular time, with this particular purpose, for this particular people, with its particular outlook and its own language"' (i 383).

at any rate in 1774 in *Auch eine Philosophie*, against moral evaluation (prone though he was to it himself, then and later), and urges the critic to understand above all that if one must condemn and praise, this should be done only after an exercise of sympathetic insight – of one's capacity for *Einfühlen* ('empathy').

*Auch eine Philosophie* contains the most eloquent description of the newly discovered sense of history, with its uncanny resemblance to that of Vico, whom, so far as we can tell, Herder did not read until twenty years later:

> How unspeakably difficult it is to convey the particular quality [*Eigenheit*] of an individual human being and how impossible it is to say precisely what distinguishes an individual, his way of feeling and living; how different and how individual [*anders und eigen*] everything becomes once his eyes see it, once his soul grasps it, his heart feels it. How much depth there is in the character of a single people, which, no matter how often observed, and gazed at with curiosity and wonder, nevertheless escapes the word which attempts to capture it, and, even with the word to catch it, is seldom so recognisable as to be universally understood and felt. If this is so, what happens when one tries to master an entire ocean of peoples, times, cultures, countries with one glance, one sentiment, by means of one single word! Words, pale shadow-play! An entire living picture of ways of life, or habits, wants, characteristics of land and sky, must be added, or provided in advance; one must start by feeling sympathy with a nation if one is to feel a single one of its inclinations or acts, or all of them together.[1]

Greece, he continues, was not Athens. It was inhabited and ruled by Athenians, Boeotians, Spartans, Corinthians. Egyptians were traders no less than Phoenicians. Macedon was a conqueror like Rome. The great Greek thinkers had speculative minds as sharp as those of moderns. Yet (Herder repeats in and out of context) they were Egyptians, Romans, Greeks, Macedonians, and *not* inhabitants of our world. Leibniz is ours; Plato is not. Similarity is not identity; one must see both the wood and the trees, although only God can do this completely. All history is an unending conflict between the general idea and the particular; all general ideas are abstractions, dangerous, misleading, and unavoidable. One must seek to see the whole, however unattainable this goal may be. Exceptions and deviations will amaze only those who insist upon

[1] v 502.

forcing an idealised image on the manifold of reality. Hume and Voltaire, Robertson and Schlözer are denounced for using the measuring-rod of their own time. All civilisations are incommensurable.[1] The critic must, so far as he is able, surrender to his author and seek to see with the author's eyes.

Herder disagrees with Diderot's justly celebrated theory of the actor who is inwardly detached from a role when he plays it.[2] The true interpreter must seek to penetrate – lose himself in – the original which he, as it were, recreates, even if he can never wholly achieve this. Genuine translation from one language – that is, way of life – into another is, of course, impossible; no real idiom is literally translatable: the olives sacred to Minerva that grew round the Academy cannot be taken beyond the frontiers of Athens. 'Even when Sparta ravaged Athens, the goddess protected her grove. So no one can take the beauties of our language from us: beauties woven into its texture, glimmering like Phryne's bosom beneath her silken veil.'[3] To translate is – for better or for worse – to create; the translation must be an *Originalarbeit* by a *schöpferisches Genie*;[4] and, of course, because the creator is what he is, and not someone or somewhere else, a great deal is, and must be, lost. Egypt must not be judged by Greek criteria, or by Shaftesbury's modern ones; the schoolboy is not joyless because he takes no pleasure in the avocations of a grown man, nor were the Middle Ages worthless because they do not please Voltaire: there is more in the great ferment of the Dark Ages than the absurdities of Ripuarian or Salic laws. The medieval culture of the West must be seen as a great revolt against the suffocating centralisation of Rome, a 'rewinding of the gigantic, run-down clock'.[5] To denounce or idealise it is equally absurd: 'I am by no means disposed to defend the constant migrations and devastations, the feudal wars, the hordes of monks, the pilgrimages, the crusades. I want only to explain them: to show the spirit that breathed through it all, the ferment of human forces.'[6] This was original enough in 1774. The Middle Ages are not a corridor to the Renaissance, nor is paganism

[1] v 509.
[2] 'Nous sentons, nous; eux, ils observent': *Oeuvres complètes de Diderot*, ed. J. Assézat and Maurice Tourneaux (Paris, 1875–7), vol. 8, p. 368.
[3] ii 44.
[4] i 178.
[5] v 526.
[6] ibid.

an ante-room of Christianity. One culture is never a mere means to another; even if there is a sense in which mankind as a whole is advancing,[1] each of the stages is an end in itself: men are never means to ends beyond themselves. No less than his opponent Kant, he fervently preaches the doctrine that only persons and societies, and almost all of these, are good in themselves – indeed they are all that is good, wholly good, in the world that we know. These maxims, which now (at least in the West) seem so platitudinous, were antinomian heresies in the middle of the eighteenth century in Paris and its intellectual dependencies.

So much for the myth of the Dominant Model. Still bolder was Herder's rejection of the historical myths of the century;[2] of the French myth of classical culture created by the Gallo-Romans, in which lay the true soul of France, and which the barbarians destroyed, and equally of the counter-myth of the superiority of the Frankish conquerors, to which support had been given by Montesquieu, Mallet and Boulainvilliers. Similarly Herder has no truck with the Renaissance myth of the sunlit pagan world killed by the gloomy, pleasure-destroying Christian religion: he uses harsh words about the monks who suppressed the old German songs; but this does not mean that the Middle Ages are the dark haunt of the demons, slaves, diabolical priests and tyrants[3] painted by Voltaire, Gibbon, Hume and, later still, Heine and all the neo-pagans. But neither does he uphold the growing German-Protestant legend of the uncorrupted, fearless, Cheruscan warrior Hermann canonised by Klopstock as Arminius, and then, in the shape of the young Siegfried, placed by Wagner in the German nationalist pantheon. These fantasies offer no avenue of escape. All attempts to flee, whether to modern Paris or to the dark German woods, are condemned by Herder as being equally deluded. Those who, for whatever reason, will not face reality are doomed.

The third great myth of the eighteenth century was that of steady progress, if not inevitable, at least virtually certain; with consequent disparagement of the benighted past, which entailed the view of all earlier centuries as so many steps toward the

---

[1] Herder does not make clear what he means by the progress – *Fortgang* – of mankind: relativism is, on the face of it, incompatible with belief in objective progress. But see the discussion beginning at the foot of this page.

[2] Rouché, op. cit. (p. 361 above, note 3), esp. pp. 17 ff., deals with this far more faithfully than Herder's better known German commentators.

[3] v 486.

superior life of the present and the still more wonderful life of the future. Herder rejects this completely. Each culture is a harmonious lyre – one must merely have the ear to hear its melodies. Those who seek to understand must learn to grasp the respects in which Abraham or Leonidas or Caesar are not men of our time – to see change as it occurs, not in juxtaposed segments which can be detached, compared and awarded marks for merit, for the degree to which they approach our standards of enlightenment. Is there, then, no progress? Are all cultures equally valuable? This is not Herder's view. There is *Fortgang*, but this is not the same as the notion of progress enunciated by, say, Turgot or Condorcet, or, in particular, by Voltaire (for example, in *La Philosophie d'histoire par feu l'abbé Bazin*), against whom, together with the Swiss philosopher of history Iselin, Herder's thunderbolts are specifically directed. Theirs is a shallow, unhistorical delusion. Diversity is everything. This is the central thesis of, to give it its full title, *Auch eine Philosophie der Geschichte zur Bildung der Menschheit*, as of almost all Herder's early writings:

> The general, philosophical, philanthropic temper of our age seeks to extend 'our own ideal' of virtue and happiness to each distant nation, even to the remotest ages in history . . . Those who have thus far taken it upon themselves to explain the centuries of progress have mostly cherished the notion that it must lead to greater virtue and happiness. In support of this they have embroidered or invented facts, played down or suppressed facts that belie it . . . taken words for works, enlightenment for happiness, greater intellectual sophistication for virtue, and so invented the figment of 'the general progressive improvement of the world'.[1]

Others realised that this was a dangerous delusion, and fell into hopeless scepticism like Montaigne, Bayle, Hume, and ultimately even Voltaire and Diderot.

This rests on a misconception of what progress is. It lies in a variety of cultures, incommensurable with each other and incapable of being arranged on some single scale of progress or retrogression. Each society, each culture, develops in its own way. Each age is different, and 'each has the centre of its happiness within itself. The youth is not happier than the innocent, contented child; nor is the peaceful old man less happy than the vigorous man in the

[1] v 511.

prime of life.'[1] The Middle Ages are full of 'abominations, errors, absurdities',[2] but also possess 'something solid, cohesive, noble and majestic'[3] which our age, with its 'enervated coldness ... and human misery',[4] can scarcely understand. 'Light does not nourish men',[5] order and affluence are not enough; still less technical accomplishment 'in the hands of one person, or of a few, who do the thinking' for everyone.[6] There are many ways of life and many truths – to believe that everything is either true or false is a wretched general illusion of our progressive age. True *Fortgang* ('advance') is the development of human beings as integrated wholes and, more particularly, their development as groups – tribes, cultures and communities determined by language and custom, creating out of the totality of their collective experience, and expressing themselves in works of art that are consequently intelligible to common men, and in sciences and crafts and forms of social and political and cultural life that fulfil the cravings (conscious and unconscious) and develop the faculties of a given society, in its interplay with its alterable, but not greatly alterable, natural environment.

> To bind and interrogate this Proteus, which is usually called national character and which shows itself certainly not less in the writings than in the usages and actions of a nation – that is a high and beautiful philosophy. It is practised most surely in poetry; for in the works of ... imagination and feeling the entire soul of the nation reveals itself most freely.[7]

This is what the classical Greeks succeeded in doing so marvellously. Despite all Hamann's anathemas, Herder cannot refrain from expressing his passionate admiration for the culture of Athens – a feeling that he shared with Goethe and Hegel, Hölderlin and Schiller, and, indeed, with the majority of the civilised Germans of his time, romantic and anti-romantic alike. Herder thinks the Greek achievement is in part due to the beauty of nature in Greece,

[1] v 512.
[2] v 527.
[3] v 524.
[4] v 527.
[5] v 525.
[6] v 538.
[7] xviii 58.

a beauty which inspired principles that those fortunate inhabitants (mistakenly but excusably) regarded as objective and universally valid. But there must be no *Favoritvolk*; he hastens to add to the list Kashmiris and Persians, Bokharans and Circassians, who also lived in beautiful natural surroundings, grew handsome themselves and produced beautiful cultures (unlike the Hebrews, whose merits are not aesthetic). The Greeks advanced; they developed their own faculties harmoniously and triumphantly, because nature was propitious and because no great natural accidents arrested this development. But they are not a hallway to the Romans, whose civilisation must be judged in terms of its own internal criteria, its own 'centre of gravity'.

What Herder calls *Fortgang* is the internal development of a culture in its own habitat, towards its own goals; but because there are some qualities that are universal in man, one culture can study, understand and admire another, even though it cannot return to it and will only make itself foolish if it tries. At times Herder speaks like Bossuet: as if history were not an episodic story but a vast drama; as if the finger of God guided the destinies of humanity in some teleological fashion, in a play of which each great cultural epoch was an act. He does not develop this notion, which led Bossuet to see each act as in some degree a link between its predecessor and its successor. More often he speaks as if history were indeed a drama, but one without a dénouement: as if it were like a cosmic symphony of which each movement is significant in itself, and of which, in any case, we cannot hear the whole, for God alone does so. The later movements are not necessarily closer to, or a prefiguring of, some ultimate goal, and, therefore, superior to the earlier movements. Life is not a jigsaw puzzle of which the fragments must fit into some single pattern in terms of which alone they are all intelligible, so that what seems, taken in isolation, irrational or ugly, is seen to be an indispensable ingredient in the great harmonious whole – the world spirit come to full self-consciousness of itself, in Hegel's famous image. Herder believes in the development of each movement of the symphony (each act of the drama) in terms of its own ends, its own values, which are none the worse or less morally valuable because they will pass or be destroyed and be succeeded by others.

There is a general purpose to be achieved by human life on earth, which he calls *Humanität*. This is a notoriously vague term, in Herder and the *Aufklärung* generally, connoting harmonious development of all immortal souls towards universally valid goals: reason, freedom, toleration, mutual love and respect between individuals and societies, as well as physical and spiritual health, finer perceptions, dominion over the earth, the harmonious realisation of all that God has implanted in his noblest work and made in his own image.[1] This is a characteristically all-inclusive, general and optimistic formula of Weimar humanism, which Herder does, indeed, adopt, particularly in his later works, but which he does not seem to have used (for it has no precise connotation) as a universal criterion either of explanation or of value.

He wants above all to be comprehensive and fair. He dislikes Gothic architecture, despite the eloquence on its behalf with which he made so deep an impression on Goethe in Strasbourg; he is repelled by chivalry, by medieval values in general, but he defends them against Voltaire, against caricatures. He placed no great value, particularly towards the end of his life, upon primitivism as such, and in this respect differed from its true admirers in the eighteenth century. Yet colonial subjugation of native populations, ancient and modern, in and outside Europe, is always represented as being morally odious and as a crime against humanity. If paganism requires to be defended against Christian attack, and Homer against Klotz and the *Encyclopédie*, so must Christianity be defended against Holbach, Voltaire and the Sinophiles, and the Chinese and Mongols in their turn against the arrogance of Europeans. The shamans of central Asia, he insists, are not just deceivers; nor are myths simply false statements about reality invented by wicked priests to bamboozle and acquire power over the masses, as Bayle and Voltaire had made the world believe; nor are the inventions of poets merely intended to give pleasure or to instruct. Here he stands with Vico, some time before he read him (one wonders whether he ever more than merely glanced at his work). Shamans express in the form of myth and superstition objects of men's natural wishes – a vision of the world from which poetry naturally springs and which it expresses. Whole worlds are created by such poetry, worlds worthy of man and his creative powers, worlds not commensurable with other worlds, but all equally worthy of our interest and in need of our insight, because they are worlds made by men; by contemplating them we may succeed in grasping what we, in our turn, can be and create. We do

[1] See the remarks on *Humanität* at xiii 154 ff.

this not by learning the lessons of the past (he sometimes says that the past repeats itself, but his central doctrine, in opposition to Hume or Voltaire, is that each page is unique), but rather because the vision of past creation inspires us to find our own centre of gravity, our own *Mittelpunkt* or *Schwerpunkt* or that of the group – nation, region, community – to which we belong.

Without such belonging there is no true creation and no true realisation of human goals. Hence to foist a set of alien values on another *Nation* (as missionaries have done in the Baltic provinces, and are doing, for example, in India) is both ineffective and harmful.[1] Worst of all are those who have no group, because they are exiled or self-exiled, physically or spiritually (for Herder the two are not very different), and are doomed to sterility. Such disintegration seemed to him to threaten the Germans in his own day. Indignantly some of his modern critics point out that he condemned France – the France of the eighteenth and nineteenth centuries! – as being an exhausted society. But whatever his failings as a prophet (and he speaks with many voices, some of them far from distinct and often uttering contradictory sentiments), as a social psychologist he rose above his generation; more clearly than any other writer, he conceived and cast light upon the crucially important social function of 'belonging' – on what it is to belong to a group, a culture, a movement, a form of life. It was a most original achievement.

VII

It is the composer's duty, as a member of society, to speak to and for his fellow human beings.

I believe in roots, in associations, in backgrounds, in personal relationships ... my music now has its roots in where I live and work.

Benjamin Britten[2]

The notion of belonging is at the heart of all Herder's ideas. His doctrine of the unity of theory and practice, like that of his populism, is intelligible only in terms of it. To belong is not a passive condition, but active co-operation, social labour. 'Complete

[1] viii 210; cf. viii 303.
[2] *On Receiving the First Aspen Award* (London, 1964), pp. 12, 21–2.

truth is always only the deed.'[1] Whether one reads the last books of his *Ideas about the Philosophy of History of Mankind*, the earlier treatise *On Hebrew Poetry*, the essays on Shakespeare, Ossian, Homer, the critical 'Groves', or the late *Adrastea* or *Kalligone*, one finds that what dominates them all is the notion that there are central patterns in terms of which each genuine culture – and the human beings who constitute it – can, and indeed must, be identified. For Herder, to be a member of a group is to think and act in a certain way, in the light of particular goals, values, pictures of the world: and to think and act so is to belong to a group. The notions are literally identical. To be a German is to be part of a unique stream of which language is the dominant element, but still only one element among others. He conveys the notion that the ways in which a people – say, the Germans – speak or move, eat or drink, their handwriting, their laws, their music, their social outlook, their dance forms, their theology, have patterns and qualities in common which they do not share, or share to a notably lesser degree, with the similar activities of some other group – the French, the Icelanders, the Arabs, the ancient Greeks. Each of these activities belongs to a cluster which must be grasped as a whole: they illuminate each other. Anyone who studies the speech rhythms, or the history or the architecture, or the physical characteristics of the Germans, will thereby achieve a deeper understanding of German legislation, music, dress. There is a property, not capable of being abstracted and articulated – that which is German in the Germans – which all these diverse activities uniquely evince. Activities like hunting, painting, worship, common to many groups in widely differing times and places, will resemble each other because they belong to the same genus. But the specific quality which each type of activity will show forth will have more in common with generically different activities of the same culture[2] than with specifically similar activities of another culture. Or, at the very least, that which the various activities of the same culture will have in common – the common pervasive pattern in virtue of which they are seen to be elements in one and the same culture – is more important, since it accounts for the characteristics of these activities at a deeper level, than their more superficial

---

[1] 'Die vollständige Wahrheit ist immer nur That,' he wrote in 1774 (viii 261), long before Fichte or Hegel.

[2] This notion is to be found in Hamann.

resemblances to the corresponding activities of other cultures and other human groups. In other words, what German epic poetry has in common with German family life, or German legislation, or German grammar, determines the patterns of these activities – runs through them more deeply – than that which German poetry has in common with Hindu or Hebrew poetry.

This common property is not occult; no special non-empirical faculty is needed to detect it; it is a natural attribute and open to empirical investigation. Despite his theology, his belief in the primacy of religion, and his use of such metaphysical notions as the collective 'soul' and 'spirit', despite the mysterious *Kräfte*, despite occasional lapses into acceptance of the dogma of natural kinds, Herder was far more of an empiricist from the beginning to the end of his life than Leibniz, Kant or even Helvétius. This was obscured by the fact that the following generation of German metaphysicians, whom he influenced, dealt freely in transcendent formulae. Yet in his own day he was at times suspected by the stricter among his fellow churchmen of inclining dangerously toward materialistic heresies. The heart of his empiricism lay in the importance that he attributed to the discovery of patterns in history and nature. It is this directly perceptible, but literally unanalysable, pattern quality, in virtue of which what Germans think or do or say is, as a rule, characteristically and unmistakably German – it is this *Gestalt* quality[1] that, in his view, makes us attribute the doer and the deed, the thinker and the thought, to a specific German culture at a specific stage of its development.

To fit into such a pattern is to belong: it is for this and no other reason that a German exiled from the milieu of his fellow Germans, perhaps a Saxon or a Prussian forced to live elsewhere, will not feel at home there; and whoever does not feel at home cannot create naturally, freely, generously, unselfconsciously, in the manner that Schiller called 'naïve', and that Herder, whether he admits it or not, most admires and believes in. All his talk about the national character, the national genius, the *Volksseele*, the spirit of the people and so forth in the end comes to this alone. His notion of what it is to belong to a family, a sect, a place, a period, a style is the foundation of his populism, and of all the later conscious

---

[1] Since originally writing this, I was glad to find it strongly confirmed by H. B. Nisbet, 'Herder, Goethe, and the Natural "Type"', *Publications of the English Goethe Society* NS 37 (1967), 83–119.

programmes for self-integration or re-integration among men who felt scattered, exiled or alienated. The language in which he speaks of his unfortunate fellow countrymen, driven by poverty or the despotic whims of their masters to Russia or Transylvania or America to become blacks and slaves, is not simply a lament for the material and moral miseries of exile, but is based on the view that to cut men off from their living centre – from the texture to which they naturally belong – or to force them to sit by the rivers of some remote Babylon, and to prostitute their creative faculties for the benefit of strangers, is to degrade, dehumanise, destroy them.[1]

No writer has stressed more vividly the damage done to human beings by being torn from the only conditions in which their history has made it possible for them to live full lives. He insists over and over again that no one milieu or group or way of life is necessarily superior to any other; but it is what it is, and assimilation to a single universal pattern, of laws or language or social structure, as advocated by the French *lumières*, would destroy what is most living and valuable in life and art. Hence the fierce polemic against Voltaire, who, in his *Essai sur les moeurs*, declared that 'Man, generally speaking, was always what he is now',[2] or that morality is the same in all civilised nations.[3] Hence, by definition, it seemed to follow that the rest were barbarous or stupid: Gauls are 'a disgrace to nature'.[4] Hence, too, the attack on Sulzer for demanding a universal philosophical grammar, according to the rules of which one would be enabled to judge of the degree of the perfection of a people's language, and, if need be, correct its rules in the light of the universal rules. Needless to say, this for Herder was both false in principle and the death of poetry and the springs of all creative power. Every group has a right to be happy in its own way. It is terrible arrogance to affirm that, to be happy, everyone should become European.[5] This is so not because, as Voltaire maintained, other cultures may be superior

---

[1] 'No Tyrtaeus', he wrote in 1778, 'will follow our brothers who have been sold to America as soldiers, no Homer will sing of this sad expedition. When religion, people, country are crushed, when these very notions are grown shadowy, the poet's lyre can yield only muted, strangled sounds' (viii 434).

[2] *Oeuvres complètes de Voltaire* (op. cit., p. 335 above, note 1), vol. 11, p. 21.

[3] Cf. *Le philosophe ignorant*, section 31: ibid., vol. 26, pp. 78–9.

[4] ibid., vol. 11, p. 260.

[5] xiii 333–42, esp. 342.

to ours, but simply because they are not comparable. 'No man can convey the character of *his* feeling, or transform my being into his.'[1] 'The Negro is as much entitled to think the white man degenerate . . . as the white man is to think of the Negro as a black beast . . . The civilisation of man is not that of the European; it manifests itself, according to time and place, in every people.'[2] Again, there is no *Favoritvolk*. Herder assumes only that to be fully human, that is, fully creative, one must belong somewhere, to some group or some historical stream, which cannot be defined save in the genetic terms of a tradition, a milieu and a culture, themselves generated by natural forces – the *Klima* (that is, the external world) and physical structure and biological needs which, in interplay with every individual's mind and will, create the dynamic, collective process called society.

This theory entails no mythology. For Herder all groups are ultimately collections of individuals; his use of 'organic' and 'organism' is still wholly metaphorical and not, as in later, more metaphysical thinkers, only half metaphorical. There is no evidence that he conceived of groups as metaphysical 'super-individual' entities or values. For Herder this is no mystique of history, or of a species to which individuals were to be sacrificed, still less of the superior wisdom of the race, or of a particular nation, or even of humanity as a whole. Nevertheless, to understand men is to understand them genetically, in terms of their history, of the one complex of spiritual and physical 'forces' in which they feel free and at home. This notion of being at home, and the corresponding notion of homelessness (nostalgia, he once remarked, is the noblest of all pains) which lies at the heart of his reflections on the emptiness of cosmopolitanism, on the damage done to men by social barriers, oppression by strangers, division, specialisation – like the connected concepts of exploitation and of the alienation of men from each other, and, in the end, from their own true selves – derive from his one central conception. Those who have grasped the notion that men are made miserable not only by poverty, disease, stupidity or the effects of ignorance, but also because they are misfits or outsiders or not spoken to, that liberty and equality are nothing without fraternity; that only those societies are truly

[1] xiii 333–4.
[2] xviii 248–9.

human which may follow a leader but obey no master,[1] are in possession of one of Herder's *idées maîtresses*. His writings radically transformed the notion of relations of men to each other. Hegel's famous definition of freedom as *Bei-sich-selbst-seyn*,[2] as well as his doctrine of *Anerkennung* – reciprocal recognition among men – seem to me to owe much to Herder's teaching. The proposition that man is by nature sociable had been uttered by Aristotle and repeated by Cicero, Aquinas, Hooker, Grotius, Locke and innumerable others. The depth and breadth of Herder's writings on human association and its vicissitudes, the wealth of concrete historical and psychological observation with which he developed the concept of what it is for men to belong to a community, made such formulae seem to be thin abstractions and drove them permanently out of circulation. No serious social theorist after Herder dared advance mechanical clichés of this type in lieu of thought. His vision of society has dominated Western thought; the extent of its influence has not always been recognised, because it has entered too deeply into the texture of ordinary thinking. His immense impact, of which Goethe spoke and to which J. S. Mill bore witness, is due principally to his central thesis – his account of what it is to live and act together – from which the rest of his thought flows, and to which it constantly returns. This idea is at the heart of all populism; and it has entered every subsequent attempt to arrive at truth about society.

## VIII

So much for Herder's specific contribution to the understanding of men and their history. There are two implications of his conception of men that have received little attention from his interpreters. These are, first, his doctrine of the indivisibility of the human personality and, as a corollary of this, his conception of the artist and his expressive role in society; and, secondly, his pluralism and the doctrine of the incompatibility of ultimate human ends.

Herder was, as everyone knows, much occupied with aesthetic questions, and tried to seek out all manifestations of art in their richest and fullest forms. He tended to find them in the creations of the early ages of man. For Herder, art is the expression of men in

[1] cf. p. 378 above.
[2] loc. cit. (p. 353 above, note 1).

society in their fullness. To say that art is expression is to say that it is a voice speaking rather than the production of an object – a poem, a painting, a golden bowl, a symphony, all of which possess their own properties, like objects in nature, independently of the purposes or character or milieu of the men who created them.[1] By the very appropriately called *Stimmen der Völker in Liedern*, and by explicit argument, Herder seeks to demonstrate that all that a man does and says and creates must express, whether he intends it to do so or not, his whole personality; and, since a man is not conceivable outside a group to which, if he is reasonably fortunate, he continues to belong (he retains its characteristics in a mutilated state even if he has been torn from it), conveys also its collective individuality[2] – a culture conceived as a constant flow of thought, feeling, action and expression. Hence he is bitterly opposed to the view, influential in his day as in ours, that the purpose of the artist is to create an object whose merits are independent of the creator's personal qualities or his intentions, conscious or unconscious, or of his social situation.

This is an aesthetic doctrine that reigned long before the doctrine of art for art's sake had been explicitly formulated. The craftsman who makes a golden bowl is entitled, according to this view, to say that it is no business of those who acquire or admire his creation to enquire whether he is himself sincere or calculating, pious or an atheist, a faithful husband, politically sound, a sympathetic boon companion or morally pure. Herder is the true father of the doctrine that it is the artist's mission, above others, to testify in his works to the truth of his own inner experience;[3] from which it follows that any conscious falsification of this experience, from whatever motive – indeed any attempt merely to satisfy the taste of his customers, to titillate their senses, or even to offer them instruction by means that have little to do with his own life or convictions, or to use techniques and skills as a detached exercise, to practise virtuosity for its own sake or for the sake of the pleasure it brings – is a betrayal of his calling.

This was implicit in the artistic movement which came to be

---

[1] A doctrine maintained, so it seemed to Herder, by such despotic Paris arbiters of artistic beauty as the disciples of Boileau – the abbés Dubos, Batteux and the like.

[2] v 502.

[3] But Vico anticipated him: see my *Vico and Herder* (London, 1976), p. 88, note 1.

called *Sturm und Drang*, of which Herder was one of the leaders. To view oneself as a professional who in his works of art plays a role, or performs with a specialised part of himself, while the rest of him is left free to observe the performance; to maintain that one's behaviour as a man – as a father, a Frenchman, a political terrorist – can be wholly detached from one's professional function as a carpenter, doctor, artist – this view, to which Voltaire, if he had considered it, could scarcely have offered any objection, is, for all the writers of the *Sturm und Drang*, a fatal misapprehension and distortion of the nature of man and his relations with other men. Since man is in fact one and not many (and those who are genuinely divided personalities are literally no longer sane), it follows that whether a man be an artist, a politician, a lawyer, a soldier, anything that he does expresses all that he is.

Some among the *Stürmer* remained individualistic – Heinse, for example, or Klinger. But Herder is uncompromisingly hostile to such egomania. The individual, for him, is inescapably a member of some group; consequently all that he does must express, consciously or unconsciously, the aspirations of his group. Hence, if he is conscious of his own acts (and all self-consciousness is embryonic assessment and therefore critical), such awareness, like all true criticism, is inevitably to a high degree social criticism, because it is the nature of human beings to be socially aware: expression is communication. Herder feels that all history shows this to be so. To divide (and not merely to distinguish as facets or aspects of one substance) body and soul, science and craft or art, the individual and society, description and evaluation, philosophical, scientific and historical judgement, empirical and metaphysical statements, as if any of these could be independent of one another, is for Herder false, superficial and misleading.

The body is the image, the expression, of the soul, not its tomb or instrument or enemy. There are no 'iron walls' between body and soul;[1] everything can pass into everything else by the insensible transitions of which Leibniz had spoken in his *Nouveaux Essais*. Once upon a time men 'were all things: poets, philosophers, land surveyors, legislators, musicians, warriors'.[2] In those days there was unity of theory and practice, of man and citizen, a unity that the division of labour destroyed; after that men

[1] viii 193.
[2] viii 261.

became 'half thinkers and half feelers'.[1] There is, he remarks, something amiss about moralists who do not act, epic poets who are unheroic, orators who are not statesmen, and aestheticians who cannot create anything. Once doctrines are accepted uncritically – as dogmatic, unalterable, eternal truths – they become dead formulae, or else their meaning is fearfully distorted. Such ossification and decay lead to nonsense in thought and monstrous behaviour in practice.[2]

This doctrine was destined to have a great flowering, not merely in the application of the concept of alienation in the writings of the young Marx and his friends in their Left-Hegelian phase, and among those who have used these ideas in our own time, but more particularly among pre-Marxist Russian radicals and revolutionaries. No body of men ever believed so devoutly and passionately in the unity of man as the Russian intelligentsia of the last century. These men – at first dissident members of the nobility and gentry, later members of many classes – were united by a burning faith in the right and duty of all men to realise their creative potentialities (physical and spiritual, intellectual and artistic) in the light of the reason and the moral insight with which all men are endowed. What the eighteenth-century French *philosophes* and the German romantics preached, these men sought to practise. Light to them came from the West. And since the number of literate – let alone well-educated – men in Russia was infinitesimal compared to the number who lived in ignorance, misery, hopeless starvation and poverty, it was plainly the first duty of any decent man to give all he could to the effort to lift his brothers to a level where they could lead a human existence.

From this sprang the conception of the intelligentsia as a sacred order called upon by history to dedicate their lives to the discovery and use of all possible means – intellectual and moral, artistic and technological, scientific and educational – in a single-minded effort to discover the truth, realise it in their lives, and with its aid to rescue the hungry and the naked, and make it possible for them to live in freedom and be men once more. Man is one and undivided; whatever he is and does flows from a single centre; but at the same

---

[1] ibid. The celebrated description in the introduction to Karl Marx's *German Ideology* of what a full human life could be seems to be a direct echo of this doctrine.
[2] xiii 195.

time he is as he is within a social web of which he is a constituent; to ignore it is to falsify the nature of man. The famous doctrine that the artist, and above all the writer, has a social obligation to express the nature of the milieu in which he lives, and that he has no right to isolate himself artificially, under the cover of some theory about the need for moral neutrality, or the need for specialisation, the purity of art, or of its specifically aesthetic function – a priestly task that is to be kept uncontaminated, especially by politics – this entire conception, over which such ferocious battles were fought in the following century, stems from Herder's doctrine of the unity of man.

'Everything that a man undertakes, whether it be produced in action or word or anything else, must spring from his whole united powers; all separation of powers is to be repudiated.'[1] This principle of Hamann's, so much admired by Goethe, formed Herder, and became (through Schiller and Friedrich Schlegel) the creed of the Russian radical critics. Whatever a man does, if he is as he should be, will express his entire nature. The worst sin is to mutilate oneself, to suppress this or that side of oneself, in the service of some false aesthetic or political or religious ideal. This is the heart of the revolt against the pruned French garden of the eighteenth century. Blake is a passionate spokesman of this faith no less than Hamann or Herder or Schleiermacher. To understand any creator – any poet or, for that matter, any human being who is not half dead – is to understand his age and nation, his way of life, the society which (like nature in Shaftesbury) 'thinks in him'. Herder says over and over again that the true artist (in the widest sense) creates only out of the fullness of the experience of his whole society, especially out of its memories and antiquities, which shape its collective individuality; and he speaks of Chaucer, Shakespeare, Spenser as being steeped in their national folklore. About this he may be mistaken, but the direction of his thought is clear enough. Poetry – and, indeed, all literature and all art – are the direct expression of uninhibited life. The expression of life may be disciplined, but life itself must not be so. As early poetry was magical, a spur to heroes, hunters, lovers, men of action, a continuation of experience, so, *mutatis mutandis*, it must be so

---

[1] The form of words is Goethe's, in *Dichtung und Wahrheit*, book 12: p. 108, line 25, in op. cit. (p. 258 above, note 3), vol. 28. It is quoted by Roy Pascal on pp. 9–10 and 134 of his *The German Sturm und Drang* (Manchester, 1953), in which he gives an admirable account, the best in English, of this entire movement.

now also. Society may have sadly disintegrated since those days, and Herder concedes that the rhapsodical Klopstock may now be able consciously to express only his own individual, rather than the communal, life; but express he must whatever is in him, and his words will communicate the experience of his society to his fellow men. 'A poet is a creator of a people; he gives it a world to contemplate, he holds its soul in his hand.'[1] He is, of course, to an equal extent created by it.[2] A man lives in a world of which, together with others, he is in some sense the maker. 'We live in a world we ourselves create.'[3] These words of Herder's were destined to be inflated into extravagant metaphysical shapes by Fichte, Schelling, Hegel and the Idealist movement in philosophy; but they are equally at the source of the profoundest sociological insights of Marx and the revolution in the historical outlook that he initiated.[4]

Herder may be regarded as being among the originators of the doctrine of artistic commitment – perhaps with Hamann the earliest thinker consciously to speak (as one would expect of the founder of populism) in terms of the totally *engagé* writer, to see the artist as *ipso facto* committed and not permitted to divide himself into compartments, to separate body from spirit, the secular from the sacred, and, above all, life from art. He believed from the beginning to the end of his life that all men are in some degree artists, and that all artists are, first and last, men – fathers, sons, friends, citizens, fellow worshippers, men united by common action. Hence the purpose of art is not to exist for its own sake (the late *Adrastea* and *Kalligone* are the most ferocious attacks on this doctrine, which he suspected both Kant and Goethe of advancing) or to be utilitarian, or propagandist, or to purvey 'social realism'; still less, of course, should it seek merely to embellish life or invent forms of pleasure or produce artefacts for the market. The artist is a

---

[1] viii 433.

[2] ii 160–1.

[3] viii 252.

[4] It is odd that one of Hamann's most fruitful observations – that the poetry of Livonian peasants in the country round Riga and Mitau, which he knew well, was connected with the rhythms of their daily work – evidently made no impression on his disciple. Herder is fascinated by the intimate relation of action and speech, e.g. in his theory of why it is that (as he supposed) verbs precede nouns in primitive speech, but ignores the influence of work. This was made good much later under Saint-Simonian and Marxist influence.

sacred vessel who is shaped by, and the highest expression of, the spirit of his time and place and society; he is the man who conveys, as far as possible, a total human experience, an entire world. This is the doctrine that, under the impulsion of German romanticism and French socialism, profoundly affected the conception of the artist and his relation to society, and animated Russian critics and writers from the late 1830s until, at any rate, *Doctor Zhivago*. The theory of art as total expression and of the artist as a man who testifies to the truth – as opposed to the concept of him as a purveyor, however gifted and dedicated, or as a priest of an esoteric cult, entered the practice of the great Russian novelists of the nineteenth century, even of such 'pure' writers as Turgenev and Chekhov. Through their works it has had a great, indeed a decisive, influence, not only on the literature and criticism, but on the moral and political ideas and behaviour, of the West, and indeed of the entire world. Consequently, Herder was perhaps not altogether mistaken when he so confidently proclaimed the part to be played by the artist in the world to come.

Whether as an aesthetic critic, or as a philosopher of history, or as a creator of the notion of the non-alienated man, or as the most vehement critic of the classifiers and dividers, Herder (with Hamann) emerges as the originator of the doctrine of the unity of art and life, theory and practice. He is the most eloquent of all the preachers of the restoration of the unbroken human being by the growth of civilisation, *Humanität*, whether by an act of spiritual water-divining whereby the buried stream of the true humanist tradition may be found and continued, or, as Rousseau demanded, by some social transformation that will destroy the shackles that crib and confine men, and will allow them to enter or re-enter the Garden of Eden which they lost when they yielded to the temptation to organise and dominate one another. Once the walls that separate men are knocked down, walls of State or class or race or religion, they will return to themselves and be men and creative once again. The influence of this part of his teaching on the ideas of others, who spoke more articulately and acted with greater political effect, has been very great.[1]

---

[1] Like other passionate propagandists, Herder pleaded for that which he himself conspicuously lacked. As sometimes happens, what the prophet saw before him was a great compensatory fantasy. The vision of the unity of the human personality and its integration into the social organism by 'natural' means was the polar opposite of Herder's own character and conduct. He was, by all

IX

Finally, I come to what is perhaps the most revolutionary of the implications of Herder's position, his famous rejection of absolute values, his pluralism.

Men, according to Herder, truly flourish only in congenial circumstances, that is, where the group to which they belong has achieved a fruitful relationship with the environment by which it is shaped and which in turn it shapes. There the individual is happily integrated into the 'natural community',[1] which grows spontaneously, like a plant, and is not held together by artificial clamps, or soldered together by sheer force, or regulated by laws and regulations invented, whether benevolently or not, by the despot or his bureaucrats. Each of these natural societies contains within itself (in the words of *Yet Another Philosophy of History*) the 'ideal of its own perfection, wholly independent of all comparison with those of others'.[2] If this is so, how must we answer the question, put by men throughout recorded history and settled with such clarity and authority by the great *lumières* of the eighteenth

accounts, a deeply divided, touchy, resentful, bitter, unhappy man in constant need of support and praise, neurotic, pedantic, difficult, suspicious and often insupportable. When he speaks about the 'simple, deep, irreplaceable feeling of being alive' (xiii 337) and compares it with the carefully tended, over-arranged world of, say, the critic Sulzer, he is evidently speaking of an experience which he longed for but must often have lacked. It has frequently been remarked that it is tormented and unbalanced personalities – Rousseau, Nietzsche, D. H. Lawrence – who celebrate with particular passion physical beauty, strength, generosity, spontaneity, above all unbroken unity, harmony and serenity, qualities for which they had an insatiable craving. No man felt less happy in the Prussia of Frederick the Great, or even in the enlightened Weimar of Goethe and Wieland and Schiller, than Herder. Wieland, the most amiable and tolerant of men, found him maddening. Goethe said that he had in him something compulsively vicious – like a vicious horse – a desire to bite and hurt. His ideals seem at times a mirror image of his own frustration.

[1] This is the real community which was later (even before Tönnies) contrasted with the artificial *Gesellschaft*; e.g. Fichte's *Totum* as contrasted with his *Compositum*. But in Herder there are still no explicitly metaphysical overtones: the *Kräfte* realised in communal life – the dynamic forces which he probably derives from Leibniz – are not discovered, nor do they act, in any a priori or transcendent fashion: but neither are they described as being susceptible to scientific tests; their nature, a puzzle to his commentators, evidently did not seem problematic to Herder.

[2] xiv 227.

century, namely: What is the best life for men? And, more particularly: What is the most perfect society?

There is, after all, no dearth of solutions. Every age has provided its own formulae. Some have looked for the solution in sacred books or in revelation or in the words of inspired prophets or the tradition of organised priesthoods; others found it in the rational insight of the skilled metaphysician, or in the combination of scientific observation and experiment, or in the 'natural' good sense of men not 'scribbled over' by philosophers or theologians or perverted by 'interested error'. Still others have found it only in the uncorrupted heart of the simple good man. Some thought that only trained experts could discover great and saving truths; others supposed that on questions of value all sane men were equally well qualified to judge. Some maintained that such truths could be discovered at any time, and that it was mere bad luck that it had taken so long to find the most important among them, or that they had been so easily forgotten. Others held that mankind was subject to the law of growth; and that the truth would not be seen in its fullness until mankind had reached maturity – the age of reason. Some doubted even this, and said men could never attain to such knowledge on earth; or if they did, were too weak to follow it in practice, since such perfection was attainable only by angels, or in the life hereafter. But one assumption was common to all these views: that it was, at any rate in principle, possible to draw some outline of the perfect society or the perfect man, if only to define how far a given society or a given individual fell short of the ideal. This was necessary if one was to be able to compare degrees of imperfection.

But this belief in the final objective answer has not been absolutely universal. Relativists held that different circumstances and temperaments demanded different policies; but, for the most part, even they supposed that, though the routes might differ, the ultimate goal – human happiness, the satisfaction of human wishes – was one and the same. Some sceptical thinkers in the ancient world – Carneades, for example – went further and uttered the disquieting thought that some ultimate values might be incompatible with one another, so that no solution could logically incorporate them all. There was something of this doubt about the logic of the concept of the perfect society not only among the Greeks, but in the Renaissance too, in Pontano, in Montaigne, in Machiavelli, and after them in Leibniz and Rousseau, who thought that no gain could be made without a corresponding loss.[1] Something of this, too, seemed to lie at the heart of the tragedies of Sophocles, Euripides, Shakespeare. Nevertheless, the central stream of the Western tradition was little affected by this fundamental doubt. The central assumption was that problems of value were in principle soluble, and soluble with finality. Whether the solutions could be implemented by imperfect men was another question, a question which did not affect the rationality of the universe. This is the keystone of the classical arch which, after Herder, began to crumble.

If Herder's view of mankind was correct – if Germans in the eighteenth century cannot become Greeks or Romans or ancient Hebrews or simple shepherds, still less all of these together – and if each of the civilisations into which he infuses so much life by his sympathetic *Einfühlen* are widely different, and indeed uncombinable – then how could there exist, even in principle, one universal ideal, valid for all men, at all times, everywhere? The 'physiognomies' of cultures are unique: each presents a wonderful exfoliation of human potentialities in its own time and place and environment. We are forbidden to make judgements of comparative value, for that is measuring the incommensurable; and even though Herder himself may not always be consistent in this respect, since he condemns and praises entire civilisations, his doctrine, at least in his most original works, does not permit this. Nor can it be doubted that he himself made valiant efforts to live up to his earlier principles: for all his dislike of the rigidly centralised Egyptian establishment, or Roman imperialism, or the brutal chivalry of the Middle Ages, or the dogmatism and intolerance of the Catholic Church, he sought to be not merely fair to these civilisations, but to represent them as each realising an ideal of indefeasible validity which, as an expression of a particular manifestation of the human spirit, was valuable in itself, and not as a step to some higher order.

It is this rejection of a central dogma of the Enlightenment, which saw in each civilisation either a stepping-stone to a higher one, or a sad relapse to an earlier and lower one, that gives force, a sense of reality, and persuasive power to his vast panoramic survey. It is true that in the *Ideen* he enunciates the general ideal of *Humanität* towards which man is slowly climbing, and some of Herder's interpreters have faithfully attempted to represent his

[1] See p. 430 below, note 3.

earlier relativism as a phase of his thought which he 'outgrew', or else to reconcile it with his hazy notion of a single progressive movement towards *Humanität*. Thus, Max Rouché thinks that Herder conceives of history as a drama, each act, perhaps each scene, of which can and should be understood and evaluated independently; which does not prevent us from perceiving that, taken together, these episodes constitute a single progressive ascent.[1] Perhaps Herder did come to believe this, or to believe that he believed it. But it remains a vague conception; his skill and imagination, even in the *Ideen*, go into the evocation of the individual cultures and not of the alleged links between them. The whole thrust of the argument, both in such early works as the *Älteste Urkunde des Menschengeschlechts, Von deutscher Art und Kunst, Vom Geist der Ebräischen Poesie*, the *Kritische Wälder*, and in the late and mildly worded *Briefe zu Beförderung der Humanität*, and the *Ideen* itself, not to speak of his classical statement of historical relativism in *Auch eine Philosophie der Geschichte*, is to show and celebrate the uniqueness, the individuality and, above all, the incommensurability with one another of each of the civilisations which he so lovingly describes and defends.[2]

But if all these forms of life are intelligible each in its own terms (the only terms there are), if each is an 'organic' whole, a pattern of ends and means which cannot be resurrected, still less amalgamated, they can scarcely be graded as so many links in a cosmic, objectively knowable, progress, some stages of which are rendered automatically more valuable than others by their relationship – say, proximity to, or mirroring of – the final goal towards which humanity, however uncertainly, is marching. This places Herder's *Weltanschauung*, so far as it is consistent at all, despite all the insights that it shares with them, outside the 'perfectibilian' philosophies of modern times, as remote from the divine tactic of

---

[1] Rouché, op. cit. (p. 361 above, note 3), esp. pp. 9, 48 ff., 62 ff.

[2] Meinecke discusses this in *Die Entstehung des Historismus* (Munich and Berlin, 1936), vol. 2, p. 438 – p. 339 in the translation by J. E. Anderson, *Historism: The Rise of a New Historical Outlook* (London, 1972) – and his conclusions are subjected to penetrating criticism by G. A Wells in 'Herder's Two Philosophies of History', *Journal of the History of Ideas* 21 (1960), 527–37, at 535–6. Despite Wells's strictures, Meinecke's central thesis – that the heart of Herder's doctrines is a systematic relativism – still seems to me, for the reasons given above, to be valid.

Bossuet (or even Burke) as from the doctrine of progress determined by the growth of reason preached by Lessing or Condorcet, or of Voltaire's *bon sens*, or from the ideal of progressive self-understanding and self-emancipation, spiritual or social, Hegelian or Marxist.

If Herder's notion of the equal validity of incommensurable cultures is accepted, the concepts of an ideal State or of an ideal man become incoherent. This is a far more radical denial of the foundations of traditional Western morality than any that Hume ever uttered. Herder's ethical relativism is a doctrine different from that of the Greek sophists or Montesquieu or Burke. These thinkers were agreed, by and large, that what men sought was happiness; they merely pointed out that differences of circumstance and the interplay of environment – 'climate' – with men's nature, conceived as fairly uniform, created different characters and outlooks and, above all, different needs which called for dissimilar institutional means of satisfaction. But they recognised a broad identity or similarity of purpose in all known forms of human activity, universal and timeless goals of men as such, which bound them in a single human species or Great Society. This would, at least in theory, enable a socially imaginative and well-informed universal despot, provided he was enlightened enough, to govern each society with a due regard to its individual needs; and to advance them all towards a final universal harmony, each moving by its own path toward the selfsame purpose – happiness and the rule of wisdom, virtue and justice. This is Lessing's conception, embodied in the famous parable of the three rings in *Nathan the Wise*.[1]

Herder had deep affinities with the *Aufklärung*, and he did write with optimism and eloquence about man's ascent to ideal *Humanität*, and uttered sentiments to which Lessing could have subscribed, no less Goethe. Yet, despite the authority of some excellent scholars,[2] I do not believe that anyone who reads Herder's works with the *Einfühlung* for which he asks, and which he so well describes, will sustain the impression that it is this – the ideal of enlightened Weimar – that fills his mind. He is a rich,

---

[1] It found an unexpected re-incarnation in Mao Tse-tung's celebrated image of the many flowers.

[2] e.g. Rudolf Stadelmann, *Der historische Sinn bei Herder* (Halle/Saale, 1928); Robert Arnold Fritzsche, 'Herder und die Humanität', *Der Morgen* 3 (1927), 402–10); Hermann Vesterling, *Herders Humanitätsprincip* (Halle, 1890).

suggestive, prolix, marvellously imaginative writer, but seldom clear or rigorous or conclusive. His ideas are often confused, sometimes inconsistent, never wholly specific or precise, as, indeed, Kant pointedly complained. As a result, many interpretations can be (and have been) put upon his works. But what lies at the heart of the whole of his thought, what influenced later thinkers, particularly the German romantics and, through them, the entire history of populism, nationalism and individualism, is the theme to which he constantly returns: that one must not judge one culture by the criteria of another; that differing civilisations are different growths, pursue different goals, embody different ways of living, are dominated by different attitudes to life; so that to understand them one must perform an imaginative act of 'empathy' into their essence, understand them 'from within' as far as possible, and see the world through their eyes – be a 'shepherd among shepherds' with the ancient Hebrews,[1] or sail the Northern seas in a tempest and read the Eddas again on board a ship struggling through the Skagerrak.[2]

These widely differing societies and their ideals are not commensurable. Such questions as which of them is the best, or even which one should prefer, which one would judge to be nearer to the universal human ideal, *Humanität*, even subjectively conceived – the pattern most likely to produce man as he should be or as one thinks he should be – are, therefore, for a thinker of this type, in the end, meaningless. 'Not a man, not a country, not a people, not a national history, not a State, is like another. Hence the True, the Beautiful, the Good in them are not similar either.'[3] Herder wrote this in his journal in 1769. The cloven hoof of relativism, or rather pluralism, shows itself even in his most orthodox discussions of universal ideals; for he thinks each image of *Humanität* to be unique and *sui generis*.[4] It is this strain in his thought, and not the language of commonplace universalism which he shares with his age, that struck, and perhaps shocked, the *Aufklärer*, the Kantians, the progressive thinkers of his time. For this goes directly against the notion of steady progress on the part of mankind as a whole, which, despite difficulties and relapses, must, or at least can and

---

[1] See p. 404 above, note 1.
[2] See v 169.
[3] iv 472.
[4] xiv 210.

should, go on; a proposition to which the German no less than the French or Italian Enlightenment was fully committed.[1]

Herder is not a subjectivist. He believes in objective standards of judgement that are derived from understanding the life and purposes of individual societies, and are themselves objective historical structures, and require, on the part of the student, wide and scrupulous scholarship as well as sympathetic imagination. What he rejects is the single overarching standard of values, in terms of which all cultures, characters and acts can be evaluated. Each phenomenon to be investigated presents its own measuring-rod, its own internal constellation of values in the light of which alone 'the facts' can be truly understood. This is much more thoroughgoing than the realisation that man is incapable of complete perfection, which, for instance, Winckelmann allowed,[2] Rousseau lamented, and Kant accepted; or the doctrine that all gains entail some loss.[3] For what is here entailed is that the highest ends for which men have rightly striven and sometimes died are strictly incompatible with one another. Even if it were possible to revive the glories of the past, as those pre-historicist thinkers (Machiavelli or Mably, for instance) thought who called for a return to the heroic virtues of Greece or Rome, we could not revive and unite them all. If we choose to emulate the Greeks, we

---

[1] Among modern thinkers, Herder's relativism most resembles Wyndham Lewis's protest against what he called 'the demon of progress in the arts'. In the tract which bears this title (London, 1954) that acute, if perverse, writer denounced, with characteristically vehement and biting eloquence, the notion that valid universal criteria exist in terms of which it is possible to assert or deny that a work of art of one age is or is not superior to one that belongs to an entirely different tradition. What meaning can be attached to, say, the assertion that Phidias is superior or inferior to Michelangelo or Maillol, or that Goethe or Tolstoy represent an improvement on, or decline from, Homer or Aeschylus or Dante or the Book of Job?

[2] e.g. in his *Geschichte der Kunst des Altertums* (Dresden, 1764), book 4, chapter 2, section 21, where he speaks of 'perfection, for which man is not a suitable vessel'; Herder echoes this almost verbatim (v 498).

[3] op. cit. (p. 134 above, note 1), vol. 3, p. 589; [Henri de] Boulainvilliers, *Histoire de l'ancien gouvernement de la France* (The Hague and Amsterdam, 1727), vol. 1, p. 322; Rousseau in the letter to Mirabeau of 26 July 1767. Herder could have come across this in Wegelin's essay of 1770 on the philosophy of history: see [Jakob von Daniel] Weguelin, 'Sur la philosophie de l'histoire: premier mémoire', *Nouveaux Mémoires de l'Académie royale des sciences et belles-lettres*, 1770 (Berlin, 1772), 361–414.

cannot also emulate the Hebrews; if we model ourselves on the Chinese, whether as they are in reality, or in Voltaire's *opéra bouffe* version, we cannot also be the Florentines of the Renaissance, or the innocent, serene, hospitable savages of eighteenth-century imagination. Even if, *per impossibile*, we could choose among these ideals, which should we select? Since there is no common standard in terms of which to grade them, there can be no final solution to the problem of what men as such should aim at. The proposition that this question can, at least in principle, be answered correctly and finally, which few had seriously doubted since Plato had taken it for granted, is undermined.

Herder, of course, condemns the very wish to resurrect ancient ideals: ideals belong to the form of life which generates them, and are mere historical memories without them: values – ends – live and die with the social wholes of which they form an intrinsic part. Each collective individuality is unique, and has its own aims and standards, which will themselves inevitably be superseded by other goals and values – ethical, social and aesthetic. Each of these systems is objectively valid in its own day, in the course of 'Nature's long year' which brings all things to pass. All cultures are equal in the sight of God, each in its time and place. Ranke said precisely this: his theodicy is a complacent version of Herder's theses, directed equally against those of Hegel and moral scepticism. But if this is so, then the notion of the perfect civilisation in which the ideal human being realises his full potentialities is patently absurd: not merely difficult to formulate, or impossible to realise in practice, but incoherent and unintelligible. This is perhaps the sharpest blow ever delivered against the classical philosophy of the West, to which the notion of perfection – the possibility, at least in principle, of universal, timeless solutions of problems of value – is essential.

The consequences of Herder's doctrines did not make themselves felt immediately. He was thought to be a bold and original thinker, but not a subverter of common moral assumptions. Nor, of course, did he think so himself. The full effect was felt only when the romantic movement, at its most violent, attempted to overthrow the authority both of reason and of dogma on which the old order rested. The extent of its explosive potentialities was not fully realised until the rise of modern anti-rationalist movements – nationalism, Fascism, existentialism, emotivism, and the wars and revolutions made in the name of two among them; that is to say, not until our own time, and perhaps not altogether even today.

X

Herder's works, as might be expected, bristle with contradictions: on the one hand, 'The power which thinks and works in me is in its nature as eternal as that which holds together the sun and the stars ... Wherever and whoever I shall be, I shall be what I am now, a force in a system of forces, a being in the immeasurable harmony of God's world.'[1] Whatever can be, will be. All potentialities will be realised. Herder believes in plenitude, in the great chain of being, in a nature with no barriers. Influenced by the naturalists, by Ritter, by von Haller, he sees man as an animal among animals: man is what he is because of slowly working natural causes, because he walks upright, or because of a cavity in his skull. Yet he also believes, with Aristotle and the Bible, in natural kinds, and in the special act of creation. He believes in a general human essence, a central human character: it is, as Leibniz taught in the *Nouveaux Essais*, like a vein in marble, to be brought out by reason and imagination; men are the Benjamins, the 'darlings of Nature's old age', the peak of the creative process. Yet he also believes that this human essence takes conflicting forms; types differ and the differences are unbridgeable. He makes a curious effort to bring together the monistic notion of the logically rigorous interconnection of all real entities, as in Spinoza's world (although in Herder's case it takes the form of something more flexible and empirical), with the dynamic, self-developing individuated entities of Leibniz.[2] There is a tension between Herder's naturalism and his teleology, his Christianity and his enthusiastic acceptance of the findings of the natural sciences; between, on the one hand, his respect for some, at any rate, of the achievements of the French Encyclopaedists, who believed in quantitative methods and precision and a unified schema of knowledge; and, on the other, his preference for the qualitative approach of Goethe and Schelling and their vitalistic followers. Again, there is a contradiction between his naturalistic determinism, which at times is very

---

[1] xiii 16.

[2] This is developed at length in *God: Some Conversations* (xvi 401–580), in which he defends Spinoza against Jacobi's charges of atheism and pantheism.

strong, and the notion that one can and should resist natural impulses and natural forces;[1] for people who do not resist are overwhelmed. The Jews were crushed by the Romans; their disastrous destiny is ascribed to natural factors; yet he holds that it could have been averted; so, too, the Romans are held to have succumbed to vices which they could have resisted successfully. Herder was not sensitive to the problem of free will as, say, Kant was; there are too many conflicting strains in him. He may have believed, like most self-determinists, that men were free when they did what they chose, but that it was, in some sense, idle to ask whether men were free to choose, since they obviously were not; yet his writings give little evidence that he sought escape in this time-honoured, but hardly satisfactory, 'solution'.[2] Again, there are the separate strands of *Humanität* as a general human ideal (to be realised fully, perhaps, only in the world to come) and the 'Gang Gottes unter die Nationen'[3] – a phrase and a concept which Hegel later appropriated – and, on the other side, his more frequent and characteristic pluralism and relativism. There is noticeable tension between his passion for ancient German tribal life, real or imaginary, as he conceived it – spontaneous, creative and free – and his reluctant admiration for Rome, and even more for the Church, with their universalism and order and capacity for rational organisation. More far-reaching still is the contrast between, on the one hand, his notion of the continuity of overflowing nature, *natura naturans*, the energy that is one in magnetism and electricity, in plants and animals and men, in language and in art – a universal, continuous life-force of which everything is a manifestation, of which laws can be discovered in the form both of the physical sciences of his time, and of biology, psychology and the particular brand of historical geography and anthropology that he favoured – and, on the other hand, the crucial role attributed to the unaccountable leaps of genius, miraculous events, sheer chance, the unanalysable process of true creation, and the consequent impossibility of achieving anything great or lasting

[1] See the magnificent paean to human freedom and man's powers of resistance to nature, xiii 142–50.

[2] *Pace* G. A. Wells, who argues strongly for this interpretation: op. cit. (p. 361 above, note 1), pp. 37–42.

[3] v 565; cf. Georg Wilhelm Friedrich Hegel, *Grundlinien der Philosophie des Rechts* [= *Sämtliche Werke* (op. cit., p. 317 above, note 1), vol. 7] (Stuttgart, 1928), p. 336.

solely by the application of techniques; and, what goes with this, the incommunicability of the central core of what individuates men or cultures and gives them all the colour and force and value they possess, something that is open only to the eye of imaginative intuition, incapable of being reduced to communicable, teachable scientific method. Finally, there is the ban on moralising, but at the same time the impassioned apostrophes to the great moments of human existence, the curses heaped on the enemies of human unity and creativity – the bloodstained conquerors, the ruthless central-isers, the shrivelling of the spirit by narrow and superficial systematisers, with, at the head of them all, the odious Voltaire, with his devitalising ironies and pettiness and lack of insight into what men truly are. All the confusions of his time seem richly reflected in his shapeless, sprawling, but continuously suggestive works.

XI

Herder is in some sense a premonitory symptom, the albatross before the coming storm. The French Revolution was founded on the notion of timeless truths given to the faculty of reason with which all men are endowed. It was dedicated to the creation or restoration of a static and harmonious society, founded on unalter-ing principles, a dream of classical perfection, or, at least, the closest approximation to it feasible on earth. It preached a peaceful universalism and a rational humanitarianism. But its consequences threw into relief the precariousness of human institutions; the disturbing phenomenon of apparently irresistible change; the clash of irreconcilable values and ideas; the insufficiency of simple formulae; the complexity of men and societies; the poetry of action, destruction, heroism, war; the effectiveness of mobs and of great men; the crucial role played by chance; the feebleness of reason before the power of fanatically believed doctrines; the unpredict-ability of events; the part played in history by unintended conse-quences; the ignorance of the workings of the sunken two-thirds of the great human iceberg, of which only the visible portion had been studied by scientists and taken into account by the ideologists of the great Revolution.

   This, too, could be said of the Russian Revolution. Its ideals are too familiar to rehearse; and its results, too, threw doubts, whether justified or not, on the effectiveness of the kind of democracy for which liberals and radicals in the nineteenth century had pleaded; on the ability of rational men to allow for and control the forces of unreason; on revolution as an instrument for the promotion of freedom, a wider culture and social justice. It awakened men forcibly to the effectiveness of resolute conspiracies by disciplined parties; the irrationality of the masses; the weakness of liberal and democratic institutions in the West; the force of nationalist passions. As Durkheim, Pareto and Freud stand to the Russian Revolution – with their views on the uncritical use of such general terms as democracy and liberty, and their theories of the interplay of rational and irrational factors in making for social cohesion and disintegration, ideas which have deeply influenced thought and action in our day – so Herder stands to the events of 1789. The craving for fraternity and for self-expression, and disbelief in the capacity of reason to determine values, dominated the nineteenth century, and even more our own. Herder lived until 1803. He did not attempt to draw the moral of his own doctrines in relation to the fate of Germany or Europe, as Saint-Simon and Hegel and Maistre, in their very different fashions, had attempted to do. Perhaps he died too early in the century. Nevertheless, he, more than any of his contemporaries, sensed the insecurity of the foundations of faith in the Enlightenment held by so many in his time, even while he half accepted it. In this sense, those who thought of him as endowed with special powers – we are told that he was sometimes called a magician and was a model for Goethe's Faust[1] – did him no injustice.

---

[1] e.g. by Günter Jacoby in *Herder als Faust: eine Untersuchung* (Leipzig, 1911). Goethe himself detested such identifications. For a discussion of this see Robert T. Clark, Jr, *Herder: His Life and Thought* (Berkeley and Los Angeles, 1955), pp. 127 ff.

# THE HEDGEHOG AND THE FOX

*An Essay on Tolstoy's View of History*

To the memory of Jasper Ridley

A queer combination of the brain of an English
chemist with the soul of an Indian Buddhist.

E. M. de Vogüé[1]

I

THERE IS a line among the fragments of the Greek poet Archilochus which says: 'The fox knows many things, but the hedgehog
knows one big thing.'[2] Scholars have differed about the correct
interpretation of these dark words, which may mean no more than
that the fox, for all his cunning, is defeated by the hedgehog's one
defence. But, taken figuratively, the words can be made to yield a
sense in which they mark one of the deepest differences which
divide writers and thinkers, and, it may be, human beings in
general. For there exists a great chasm between those, on one side,
who relate everything to a single central vision, one system, less or
more coherent or articulate, in terms of which they understand,
think and feel – a single, universal, organising principle in terms of
which alone all that they are and say has significance – and, on the
other side, those who pursue many ends, often unrelated and even
contradictory, connected, if at all, only in some *de facto* way, for
some psychological or physiological cause, related to no moral or
aesthetic principle. These last lead lives, perform acts and entertain
ideas that are centrifugal rather than centripetal; their thought is
scattered or diffused, moving on many levels, seizing upon the

---

[1] *Le Roman russe* (Paris, 1886), p. 282.

[2] 'πόλλ᾽ οἶδ᾽ ἀλώπηξ, ἀλλ᾽ ἐχῖνος ἓν μέγα.' Archilochus fragment 201 in
M. L. West (ed.), *Iambi et Elegi Graeci*, vol. 1 (Oxford, 1971).

essence of a vast variety of experiences and objects for what they
are in themselves, without, consciously or unconsciously, seeking
to fit them into, or exclude them from, any one unchanging, all-
embracing, sometimes self-contradictory and incomplete, at times
fanatical, unitary inner vision. The first kind of intellectual and
artistic personality belongs to the hedgehogs, the second to the
foxes; and without insisting on a rigid classification, we may,
without too much fear of contradiction, say that, in this sense,
Dante belongs to the first category, Shakespeare to the second;
Plato, Lucretius, Pascal, Hegel, Dostoevsky, Nietzsche, Ibsen,
Proust are, in varying degrees, hedgehogs; Herodotus, Aristotle,
Montaigne, Erasmus, Molière, Goethe, Pushkin, Balzac, Joyce are
foxes.

Of course, like all over-simple classifications of this type, the
dichotomy becomes, if pressed, artificial, scholastic and ultimately
absurd. But if it is not an aid to serious criticism, neither should it
be rejected as being merely superficial or frivolous; like all
distinctions which embody any degree of truth, it offers a point of
view from which to look and compare, a starting-point for genuine
investigation. Thus we have no doubt about the violence of the
contrast between Pushkin and Dostoevsky; and Dostoevsky's
celebrated speech about Pushkin has, for all its eloquence and
depth of feeling, seldom been considered by any perceptive reader
to cast light on the genius of Pushkin, but rather on that of
Dostoevsky himself, precisely because it perversely represents
Pushkin – an arch-fox, the greatest in the nineteenth century – as
being similar to Dostoevsky, who is nothing if not a hedgehog; and
thereby transforms, indeed distorts, Pushkin into a dedicated
prophet, a bearer of a single, universal message which was indeed
the centre of Dostoevsky's own universe, but exceedingly remote
from the many varied provinces of Pushkin's protean genius.
Indeed, it would not be absurd to say that Russian literature is
spanned by these gigantic figures – at one pole Pushkin, at the
other Dostoevsky; and that the characteristics of other Russian
writers can, by those who find it useful or enjoyable to ask that
kind of question, to some degree be determined in relation to these
great opposites. To ask of Gogol, Turgenev, Chekhov, Blok how
they stand in relation to Pushkin and to Dostoevsky leads – or, at
any rate, has led – to fruitful and illuminating criticism. But when
we come to Count Lev Nikolaevich Tolstoy, and ask this of him –
ask whether he belongs to the first category or the second, whether

he is a monist or a pluralist, whether his vision is of one or of many, whether he is of a single substance or compounded of heterogeneous elements – there is no clear or immediate answer. The question does not, somehow, seem wholly appropriate; it seems to breed more darkness than it dispels. Yet it is not lack of information that makes us pause: Tolstoy has told us more about himself and his views and attitudes than any other Russian, more, almost, than any other European, writer; nor can his art be called obscure in any normal sense: his universe has no dark corners, his stories are luminous with the light of day; he has explained them and himself, and argued about them and the methods by which they are constructed, more articulately and with greater force and sanity and lucidity than any other writer. Is he a fox or a hedgehog? What are we to say? Why is the answer so curiously difficult to find? Does he resemble Shakespeare or Pushkin more than Dante or Dostoevsky? Or is he wholly unlike either, and is the question therefore unanswerable because it is absurd? What is the mysterious obstacle with which our enquiry seems faced?

I do not propose in this essay to formulate a reply to this question, since this would involve nothing less than a critical examination of the art and thought of Tolstoy as a whole. I shall confine myself to suggesting that the difficulty may be, at least in part, due to the fact that Tolstoy was himself not unaware of the problem, and did his best to falsify the answer. The hypothesis I wish to offer is that Tolstoy was by nature a fox, but believed in being a hedgehog; that his gifts and achievement are one thing, and his beliefs, and consequently his interpretation of his own achievement, another; and that consequently his ideals have led him, and those whom his genius for persuasion has taken in, into a systematic misinterpretation of what he and others were doing or should be doing. No one can complain that he has left his readers in any doubt as to what he thought about this topic: his views on this subject permeate all his discursive writings – diaries, recorded *obiter dicta*, autobiographical essays and stories, social and religious tracts, literary criticism, letters to private and public correspondents. But the conflict between what he was and what he believed emerges nowhere so clearly as in his view of history, to which some of his most brilliant and most paradoxical pages are devoted. This essay is an attempt to deal with his historical doctrines, and to consider both his motives for holding the views he holds and some of their probable sources. In short, it is an attempt to take Tolstoy's attitude to history as seriously as he himself meant his readers to take it, although for a somewhat different reason – for the light it casts on a single man of genius rather than on the fate of all mankind.

## II

Tolstoy's philosophy of history has, on the whole, not obtained the attention which it deserves, whether as an intrinsically interesting view or as an occurrence in the history of ideas, or even as an element in the development of Tolstoy himself.[1] Those who have treated Tolstoy primarily as a novelist have at times looked upon the historical and philosophical passages scattered through *War and Peace* as so much perverse interruption of the narrative, as a regrettable liability to irrelevant digression characteristic of this great, but excessively opinionated, writer, a lop-sided, home-made metaphysic of small or no intrinsic interest, deeply inartistic and thoroughly foreign to the purpose and structure of the work of art as a whole. Turgenev, who found Tolstoy's personality and art antipathetic, although in later years he freely and generously acknowledged his genius as a writer, led the attack. In letters to Pavel Annenkov,[2] Turgenev speaks of Tolstoy's 'charlatanism', of his historical disquisitions as 'farcical', as 'trickery' which takes in the unwary, injected by an 'autodidact' into his work as an inadequate substitute for genuine knowledge. He hastens to add that Tolstoy does, of course, make up for this by his marvellous artistic genius; and then accuses him of inventing 'a system which seems to solve everything very simply; as, for example, historical fatalism: he mounts his hobby-horse and is off! Only when he touches earth does he, like Antaeus, recover his true strength.'[3] The same note is sounded in the celebrated and touching invocation sent by Turgenev from his death-bed to his old friend and enemy, begging him to cast away his prophet's mantle and return

---

[1] For the purpose of this essay I propose to confine myself almost entirely to the explicit philosophy of history contained in *War and Peace*, and to ignore, for example, *Sevastopol Stories*, *The Cossacks*, the fragments of the unpublished novel on the Decembrists, and Tolstoy's own scattered reflections on this subject except in so far as they bear on views expressed in *War and Peace*.

[2] See E. I. Bogoslovsky, *Turgenev o L. Tolstom* (Tiflis, 1894), p. 41; quoted by P. I. Biryukov, *L. N. Tolstoy: biografiya*, 3rd ed. (Berlin, 1921), vol. 2, pp. 48–9.

[3] ibid.

to his true vocation – that of 'the great writer of the Russian land'.[1] Flaubert, despite his 'shouts of admiration' over passages of *War and Peace*, is equally horrified: 'il se répète et il philosophise',[2] he writes in a letter to Turgenev, who had sent him the French version of the masterpiece then almost unknown outside Russia. In the same strain Belinsky's intimate friend and correspondent, the philosophical tea-merchant Vasily Botkin, who was well disposed to Tolstoy, writes to the poet Afanasy Fet:

> Literary specialists . . . find that the intellectual element of the novel is very weak, the philosophy of history is trivial and superficial, the denial of the decisive influence of individual personalities on events is nothing but a lot of mystical subtlety, but apart from this the artistic gift of the author is beyond dispute – yesterday I gave a dinner and Tyutchev was here, and I am repeating what everybody said.[3]

Contemporary historians and military specialists, at least one of whom had himself fought in 1812,[4] indignantly complained of inaccuracies of fact; and since then damning evidence has been adduced of falsification of historical detail by the author of *War and Peace*,[5] done apparently with deliberate intent, in full knowledge of the available original sources and in the known absence of any counter-evidence – falsification perpetrated, it seems, in the interests not so much of an artistic as of an 'ideological' purpose.

This consensus of historical and aesthetic criticism seems to have set the tone for nearly all later appraisals of the 'ideological' content of *War and Peace*. Shelgunov at least honoured it with a direct attack for its social quietism, which he called the 'philosophy of the swamp'; others for the most part either politely ignored it, or

[1] Letter to Tolstoy of 11 July 1883.
[2] 'He repeats himself and he philosophises.' Gustave Flaubert, *Lettres inédites à Tourguéneff* (Monaco, 1946), p. 218.
[3] A. A. Fet, *Moi vospominaniya* (Moscow, 1890), part 2, p. 175.
[4] See the severe strictures of A. Vitmer, a very respectable military historian, in his *1812 god v 'Voine i mire'* (St Petersburg, 1869), and the tones of mounting indignation in the contemporary critical notices of A. S. Norov, A. P. Pyatkovsky and S. Navalikhin. The first served in the campaign of 1812 and, despite some errors of fact, makes criticisms of substance. The last two are, as literary critics, almost worthless, but they seem to have taken the trouble to verify some of the relevant facts.
[5] See V. B. Shklovsky, *Mater'yal i stil' v romane L'va Tolstogo 'Voina i mir'* (Moscow, 1928), *passim*, but particularly chapters 7 and 8. See below, p. 457.

treated it as a characteristic aberration which they put down to a combination of the well-known Russian tendency to preach (and thereby ruin works of art) with the half-baked infatuation with general ideas characteristic of young intellectuals in countries remote from centres of civilisation. 'It is fortunate for us that the author is a better artist than thinker,' said the critic Dmitry Akhsharumov,[1] and for more than three-quarters of a century this sentiment has been echoed by most of the critics of Tolstoy, both Russian and foreign, both pre-revolutionary and Soviet, both 'reactionary' and 'progressive', by most of those who look on him primarily as a writer and an artist, and of those to whom he is a prophet and a teacher, or a martyr, or a social influence, or a sociological or psychological 'case'. Tolstoy's theory of history is of equally little interest to Vogüé and Merezhkovsky, to Stefan Zweig and Percy Lubbock, to Biryukov and E. J. Simmons, not to speak of lesser men. Historians of Russian thought[2] tend to label this aspect of Tolstoy as 'fatalism', and move on to the more interesting historical theories of Leontiev or Danilevsky. Critics endowed with more caution or humility do not go as far as this, but treat the 'philosophy' with nervous respect; even Derrick Leon, who treats Tolstoy's views of this period with greater care than the majority of his biographers, after giving a painstaking account of Tolstoy's reflections on the forces which dominate history, particularly of the second section of the long epilogue which follows the end of the narrative portion of *War and Peace*, proceeds to follow Aylmer Maude in making no attempt either to assess the theory or to relate it to the rest of Tolstoy's life or thought; and even so much as this is almost unique.[3] Those, again,

---

[1] *Razbor 'Voiny i mira'* (St Petersburg, 1868), pp. 1–4.

[2] e.g. Professors Il'in, Yakovenko, Zenkovsky and others.

[3] Honourable exceptions to this are provided by the writings of the Russian writers N. I. Kareev and B. M. Eikhenbaum, as well as those of the French scholars E. Haumant and Albert Sorel. Of monographs devoted to this subject I know of only two of any worth. The first, 'Filosofiya istorii L. N. Tolstogo', by V. N. Pertsev, in *'Voina i mir': sbornik pamyati L. N. Tolstogo*, ed. V. P. Obninsky and T. I. Polner (Moscow, 1912), after taking Tolstoy mildly to task for obscurities, exaggerations and inconsistencies, swiftly retreats into innocuous generalities. The other, 'Filosofiya istorii v romane L. N. Tolstogo, "Voina i mir"', by M. M. Rubinshtein, in *Russkaya mysl'* (July 1911), 78–103, is much more laboured, but in the end seems to me to establish nothing at all. (Very different is Arnold Bennett's judgement, of which I learnt since writing this: 'The last part of the Epilogue is full of good ideas the johnny can't work out. And

who are mainly interested in Tolstoy as a prophet and a teacher concentrate on the later doctrines of the master, held after his conversion, when he had ceased to regard himself primarily as a writer and had established himself as a teacher of mankind, an object of veneration and pilgrimage. Tolstoy's life is normally represented as falling into two distinct parts: first comes the author of immortal masterpieces, later the prophet of personal and social regeneration; first the aristocratic writer, the difficult, somewhat unapproachable, troubled novelist of genius; then the sage – dogmatic, perverse, exaggerated, but wielding a vast influence, particularly in his own country – a world institution of unique importance. From time to time attempts are made to trace his later period to its roots in his earlier phase, which is felt to be full of presentiments of the later life of self-renunciation; it is this later period which is regarded as important; there are philosophical, theological, ethical, psychological, political, economic studies of the later Tolstoy in all his aspects.

And yet there is surely a paradox here. Tolstoy's interest in history and the problem of historical truth was passionate, almost obsessive, both before and during the writing of *War and Peace*. No one who reads his journals and letters, or indeed *War and Peace* itself, can doubt that the author himself, at any rate, regarded this problem as the heart of the entire matter – the central issue round which the novel is built. 'Charlatanism', 'superficiality', 'intellectual feebleness' – surely Tolstoy is the last writer to whom these epithets seem applicable: bias, perversity, arrogance, perhaps; self-deception, lack of restraint, possibly; moral or spiritual inadequacy – of this he was better aware than his enemies; but failure of intellect, lack of critical power, a tendency to emptiness, liability to ride off on some patently absurd, superficial doctrine to the detriment of realistic description or analysis of life, infatuation with some fashionable theory which Botkin or Fet can easily see through, although Tolstoy, alas, cannot – these charges seem grotesquely unplausible. No man in his senses, during this century at any rate, would ever dream of denying Tolstoy's intellectual

of course, in the phrase of critics, would have been better left out. So it would; only Tolstoy couldn't leave it out. It was what he wrote the book for.' *The Journals of Arnold Bennett*, ed. Newman Flower, 3 vols (London, 1932–3), vol. 2, 1911–21, p. 62.) As for the inevitable efforts to relate Tolstoy's historical views to those of various latter-day Marxists – Kautsky, Lenin, Stalin etc. – they belong to the curiosities of politics or theology rather than to those of literature.

power, his appalling capacity to penetrate any conventional disguise, that corrosive scepticism in virtue of which Prince Vyazemsky tarred *War and Peace* with the brush of *netovshchina* (negativism)[1] – an early version of that nihilism which Vogüé and Albert Sorel later quite naturally attribute to him. Something is surely amiss here: Tolstoy's violently unhistorical and indeed anti-historical rejection of all efforts to explain or justify human action or character in terms of social or individual growth, or 'roots' in the past; this side by side with an absorbed and lifelong interest in history, leading to artistic and philosophical results which provoked such queerly disparaging comments from ordinarily sane and sympathetic critics – surely there is something here which deserves attention.

III

Tolstoy's interest in history began early in his life. It seems to have arisen not from interest in the past as such, but from the desire to penetrate to first causes, to understand how and why things happen as they do and not otherwise, from discontent with those current explanations which do not explain, and leave the mind dissatisfied, from a tendency to doubt and place under suspicion and, if need be, reject whatever does not fully answer the question, to go to the root of every matter, at whatever cost. This remained Tolstoy's attitude throughout his entire life, and is scarcely a symptom either of 'trickery' or of 'superficiality'. With it went an incurable love of the concrete, the empirical, the verifiable, and an instinctive distrust of the abstract, the impalpable, the supernatural – in short an early tendency to a scientific and positivist approach, unfriendly to romanticism, abstract formulations, metaphysics. Always and in every situation he looked for 'hard' facts – for what could be grasped and verified by the normal intellect, uncorrupted by intricate theories divorced from tangible realities, or by otherworldly mysteries, theological, poetical and metaphysical alike. He was tormented by the ultimate problems which face young men in every generation – about good and evil, the origin and purpose of the universe and its inhabitants, the causes of all that happens; but the answers provided by theologians and metaphysicians struck him as absurd, if only because of the words in which they were

---

[1] P. A. Vyazemsky, 'Vospominaniya o 1812 god', *Russkii arkhiv* 7 (1869), columns 181–92, 01–016 [*sic*], esp. columns 185–7.

formulated – words which bore no apparent reference to the everyday world of ordinary common sense to which he clung obstinately, even before he became aware of what he was doing, as being alone real. History, only history, only the sum of the concrete events in time and space – the sum of the actual experience of actual men and women in their relation to one another and to an actual three-dimensional, empirically experienced, physical environment – this alone contained the truth, the material out of which genuine answers – answers needing for their apprehension no special sense or faculties which normal human beings did not possess – might be constructed.

This, of course, was the spirit of empirical enquiry which animated the great anti-theological and anti-metaphysical thinkers of the eighteenth century, and Tolstoy's realism and inability to be taken in by shadows made him their natural disciple before he had learnt of their doctrines. Like M. Jourdain, he spoke prose long before he knew it, and remained an enemy of transcendentalism from the beginning to the end of his life. He grew up during the heyday of the Hegelian philosophy, which sought to explain all things in terms of historical development, but conceived this process as being ultimately not susceptible to the methods of empirical investigation. The historicism of his time doubtless influenced the young Tolstoy as it did all enquiring persons of his time; but the metaphysical content he rejected instinctively, and in one of his letters he described Hegel's writings as unintelligible gibberish interspersed with platitudes. History alone – the sum of empirically discoverable data – held the key to the mystery of why what happened happened as it did and not otherwise; and only history, consequently, could throw light on the fundamental ethical problems which obsessed him as they did every Russian thinker in the nineteenth century. What is to be done? How should one live? Why are we here? What must we be and do? The study of historical connections and the demand for empirical answers to these *proklyatye voprosy*[1] became fused into one in Tolstoy's

---

[1] 'Accursed questions' – a phrase which became a cliché in nineteenth-century Russia for those central moral and social issues of which every honest man, in particular every writer, must sooner or later become aware, and then be faced with the choice of either entering the struggle or turning his back upon his fellow men, conscious of his responsibility for what he was doing. [Although 'voprosy' was widely used by the 1830s to refer to these issues, it seems that the specific phrase 'proklyatye voprosy' was coined in 1858 by Mikhail L. Mikhailov when he

mind, as his early diaries and letters show very vividly.

In his early diaries we find references to his attempts to compare Catherine the Great's *Nakaz*[1] with the passages in Montesquieu on which she professed to have founded it.[2] He reads Hume and Thiers[3] as well as Rousseau, Sterne and Dickens.[4] He is obsessed by the thought that philosophical principles can only be understood in their concrete expression in history.[5] 'To write the genuine history of present-day Europe: there is an aim for the whole of one's life.'[6] Or again: 'The leaves of a tree delight us more than the roots',[7] with the implication that this is nevertheless a superficial view of the world. But side by side with this there is the beginning of an acute sense of disappointment, a feeling that history, as it is written by historians, makes claims which it cannot satisfy, because like metaphysical philosophy it pretends to be something it is not – namely a science capable of arriving at conclusions which are certain. Since men cannot solve philosophical questions by the principles of reason they try to do so historically. But history is 'one of the most backward of sciences – a science which has lost its proper aim'.[8] The reason for this is that history will not, because it cannot, solve the great questions which have tormented men in every generation. In the course of seeking to answer these questions men accumulate a knowledge of facts as they succeed each other in time: but this is a mere by-product, a kind of 'side issue' which – and this is a mistake – is studied as an

used it to render 'die verdammten Fragen' in his translation of Heine's poem 'Zum Lazarus' (1853/4): see 'Stikhotvoreniya Geine', *Sovremennik* 1858 No 3, p. 125; and p. 225 in *Heinrich Heines Sämtliche Werke*, ed. Oskar Walzel (Leipzig, 1911–20), vol. 3. Alternatively, Mikhailov may have been capitalising on the fact that an existing Russian expression fitted Heine's words like a glove, but I have not yet seen an earlier published use of it. H.H.]

[1] Instructions to her legislative experts.

[2] L. N. Tolstoy, *Polnoe sobranie sochinenii* (Moscow/Leningrad, 1928–64), vol. 46, pp. 4–28 (18–26 March 1847).

[3] ibid., pp. 97, 113, 114, 117, 123–4, 127 (20 March to 27 June 1852).

[4] ibid., pp. 126, 127, 130, 132–4, 167, 176, 249; 82, 110; 140 (126–76: 24 June 1852 to 28 September 1853; 249: 'Journal of daily tasks', 3 March 1847; 82, 110: 10 August 1851, 14 April 1852).

[5] ibid., p. 123 (11 June 1852).

[6] ibid., pp. 141–2 (22 September 1852).

[7] ibid., vol. 1, p. 222.

[8] ibid.

end in itself. Again, 'history will never reveal to us what connections there are, and at what times, between science, art and morality, between good and evil, religion and the civic virtues. What it *will* tell us (and that incorrectly) is where the Huns came from, where they lived, who laid the foundations of their power, etc.'[1] According to his friend Nazariev, Tolstoy said to him in the winter of 1846: 'History is nothing but a collection of fables and useless trifles, cluttered up with a mass of unnecessary figures and proper names. The death of Igor, the snake which bit Oleg – what is all this but old wives' tales? Who wants to know that Ivan's second marriage, to Temryuk's daughter, occurred on 21 August 1562, whereas his fourth, to Anna Alekseevna Koltovskaya, occurred in 1572 ...?'[2]

History does not reveal causes; it presents only a blank succession of unexplained events. 'Everything is forced into a standard mould invented by the historians: Tsar Ivan the Terrible, on whom Professor Ivanov is lecturing at the moment, after 1560 suddenly becomes transformed from a wise and virtuous man into a mad and cruel tyrant. How? Why? – You mustn't even ask ...'[3] And half a century later, in 1908, he declares to Gusev: 'History would be an excellent thing if only it were true.'[4] The proposition that history could (and should) be made scientific is a commonplace in the nineteenth century; but the number of those who interpreted the term 'science' as meaning natural science, and then asked themselves whether history could be transformed into a science in this specific sense, is not great. The most uncompromising policy was that of Auguste Comte, who, following his master, Saint-Simon, tried to turn history into sociology, with what fantastic consequences we need not here relate. Karl Marx was perhaps, of all thinkers, the man who took this programme most seriously; and made the bravest, if one of the least successful, attempts to discover general laws which govern historical evolution, conceived on the then alluring analogy of biology and anatomy so triumphantly transformed by Darwin's new evolutionary theories. Like Marx (of whom at the time of writing *War and Peace* he apparently knew nothing), Tolstoy saw clearly that if history was a science, it must

[1] ibid.
[2] V. N. Nazariev, 'Lyudi bylogo vremeni', *L. N. Tolstoy v vospominaniyakh sovremennikov* (Moscow, 1955), vol. 1, p. 52.
[3] ibid., pp. 52–3.
[4] N. N. Gusev, *Dva goda s L. N. Tolstym* ... (Moscow, 1973), p. 188.

be possible to discover and formulate a set of true laws of history which, in conjunction with the data of empirical observation, would make prediction of the future (and 'retrodiction' of the past) as feasible as it had become, say, in geology or astronomy. But he saw more clearly than Marx and his followers that this had, in fact, not been achieved, and said so with his usual dogmatic candour, and reinforced his thesis with arguments designed to show that the prospect of achieving this goal was non-existent; and clinched the matter by observing that the fulfilment of this scientific hope would end human life as we knew it: 'If we allow that human life can be ruled by reason, the possibility of life [i.e. as a spontaneous activity involving consciousness of free will] is destroyed.'[1]

But what oppressed Tolstoy was not merely the 'unscientific' nature of history – that no matter how scrupulous the technique of historical research might be, no dependable laws could be discovered of the kind required even by the most undeveloped natural sciences. He further thought that he could not justify to himself the apparently arbitrary selection of material, and the no less arbitrary distribution of emphasis, to which all historical writing seemed to be doomed. He complains that while the factors which determine the life of mankind are very various, historians select from them only some single aspect, say the political or the economic, and represent it as primary, as the efficient cause of social change; but then, what of religion, what of 'spiritual' factors, and the many other aspects – a literally countless multiplicity – with which all events are endowed? How can we escape the conclusion that the histories which exist represent what Tolstoy declares to be 'perhaps only 0.001 per cent of the elements which actually constitute the real history of peoples'? History, as it is normally written, usually represents 'political' – public – events as the most important, while spiritual – 'inner' – events are largely forgotten; yet prima facie it is they – the 'inner' events – that are the most real, the most immediate experience of human beings; they, and only they, are what life, in the last analysis, is made of; hence the routine political historians are talking shallow nonsense.

Throughout the 1850s Tolstoy was obsessed by the desire to write a historical novel, one of his principal aims being to contrast the 'real' texture of life, both of individuals and communities, with the 'unreal' picture presented by historians. Again and again in the

[1] *War and Peace*, epilogue, part 1, chapter 1.

pages of *War and Peace* we get a sharp juxtaposition of 'reality' – what 'really' occurred – with the distorting medium through which it will later be presented in the official accounts offered to the public, and indeed be recollected by the actors themselves – the original memories having now been touched up by their own treacherous (inevitably treacherous because automatically rationalising and formalising) minds. Tolstoy is perpetually placing the heroes of *War and Peace* in situations where this becomes particularly evident.

Nikolay Rostov at the battle of Austerlitz sees the great soldier, Prince Bagration, riding up with his suite towards the village of Schöngrabern, whence the enemy is advancing; neither he nor his staff, nor the officers who gallop up to him with messages, nor anyone else, is, or can be, aware of what exactly is happening, nor where, nor why; nor is the chaos of the battle in any way made clearer either in fact or in the minds of the Russian officers by the appearance of Bagration. Nevertheless his arrival puts heart into his subordinates; his courage, his calm, his mere presence create the illusion of which he is himself the first victim, namely, that what is happening is somehow connected with *his* skill, *his* plans, that it is *his* authority that is in some way directing the course of the battle; and this, in its turn, has a marked effect on the general morale around him. The dispatches which will duly be written later will inevitably ascribe every act and event on the Russian side to him and his dispositions; the credit or discredit, the victory or the defeat, will belong to him, although it is clear to everyone that he will have had less to do with the conduct and outcome of the battle than the humble, unknown soldiers who do at least perform whatever actual fighting is done, that is, shoot at each other, wound, kill, advance, retreat and so on.

Prince Andrey, too, knows this, most clearly at Borodino, where he is mortally wounded. He begins to understand the truth earlier, during the period when he is making efforts to meet the 'important' persons who seem to be guiding the destinies of Russia; he then gradually becomes convinced that Alexander's principal adviser, the famous reformer Speransky, and his friends, and indeed Alexander himself, are systematically deluding themselves when they suppose their activities, their words, memoranda, rescripts, resolutions, laws and so forth, to be the motive factors which cause historical change and determine the destinies of men and nations; whereas in fact they are nothing: only so much self-important milling in the void. And so Tolstoy arrives at one of his celebrated paradoxes: the higher soldiers or statesmen are in the pyramid of authority, the farther they must be from its base, which consists of those ordinary men and women whose lives are the actual stuff of history; and, consequently, the smaller the effect of the words and acts of such remote personages, despite all their theoretical authority, upon that history.

In a famous passage dealing with the state of Moscow in 1812 Tolstoy observes that from the heroic achievements of Russia after the burning of Moscow one might infer that its inhabitants were absorbed entirely in acts of self-sacrifice – in saving their country or in lamenting its destruction, in heroism, martyrdom, despair – but that in fact this was not so. People were preoccupied by personal interests. Those who went about their ordinary business without feeling heroic emotions or thinking that they were actors upon the well-lighted stage of history were the most useful to their country and community, while those who tried to grasp the general course of events and wanted to take part in history, those who performed acts of incredible self-sacrifice or heroism, and participated in great events, were the most useless.[1] Worst of all, in Tolstoy's eyes, were those unceasing talkers who accused one another of the kind of thing 'for which no one could in fact have been responsible'; and this because 'nowhere is the commandment not to taste of the fruit of the tree of knowledge so clearly written as in the course of history. Only unconscious activity bears fruit, and the individual who plays a part in historical events never understands their significance. If he attempts to understand them, he is struck with sterility.'[2] To try to 'understand' anything by rational means is to make sure of failure. Pierre Bezukhov wanders about, 'lost' on the battlefield of Borodino, and looks for something which he imagines as a kind of set piece; a battle as depicted by the historians or the painters. But he finds only the ordinary confusion of individual human beings haphazardly attending to this or that human want.[3] That, at any rate, is concrete, uncontaminated by theories and abstractions; and Pierre is therefore closer to the truth about the course of events – at least as seen by men – than those who believe them to obey a discoverable set of laws or

[1] *War and Peace*, vol. 4, part 1, chapter 4.
[2] ibid.
[3] On the connection of this with Stendhal's *La Chartreuse de Parme* see p. 472 below, note 1.

rules. Pierre sees only a succession of 'accidents' whose origins and consequences are, by and large, untraceable and unpredictable; only loosely strung groups of events forming an ever-varying pattern, following no discernible order. Any claim to perceive patterns susceptible to 'scientific' formulae must be mendacious.

Tolstoy's bitterest taunts, his most corrosive irony, are reserved for those who pose as official specialists in managing human affairs, in this case the Western military theorists, a General Pfuel, or Generals Bennigsen and Paulucci, who are all shown talking equal nonsense at the Council of Drissa, whether they defend a given strategic or tactical theory or oppose it; these men must be impostors, since no theories can possibly fit the immense variety of possible human behaviour, the vast multiplicity of minute, undiscoverable causes and effects which form that interplay of men and nature which history purports to record. Those who affect to be able to contract this infinite multiplicity within their 'scientific' laws must be either deliberate charlatans or blind leaders of the blind. The harshest judgement is accordingly reserved for the master theorist himself, the great Napoleon, who acts upon, and has hypnotised others into believing, the assumption that he understands and controls events by his superior intellect, or by flashes of intuition, or by otherwise succeeding in answering correctly the problems posed by history. The greater the claim the greater the lie: Napoleon is consequently the most pitiable, the most contemptible of all the actors in the great tragedy.

This, then, is the great illusion which Tolstoy sets himself to expose: that individuals can, by the use of their own resources, understand and control the course of events. Those who believe this turn out to be dreadfully mistaken. And side by side with these public faces – these hollow men, half self-deluded, half aware of being fraudulent, talking, writing desperately and aimlessly in order to keep up appearances and avoid the bleak truths – side by side with all this elaborate machinery for concealing the spectacle of human impotence and irrelevance and blindness lies the real world, the stream of life which men understand, the attending to the ordinary details of daily existence. When Tolstoy contrasts this real life – the actual, everyday, 'live' experience of individuals – with the panoramic view conjured up by historians, it is clear to him which is real, and which is a coherent, sometimes elegantly contrived, but always fictitious construction. Utterly unlike her as he is in almost every other respect, Tolstoy is, perhaps, the first to propound the celebrated accusation which Virginia Woolf half a century later levelled against the public prophets of her own generation – Shaw and Wells and Arnold Bennett – blind materialists who did not begin to understand what it is that life truly consists of, who mistook its outer accidents, the unimportant aspects which lie outside the individual soul – the so-called social, economic, political realities – for that which alone is genuine, the individual experience, the specific relation of individuals to one another, the colours, smells, tastes, sounds and movements, the jealousies, loves, hatreds, passions, the rare flashes of insight, the transforming moments, the ordinary day-to-day succession of private data which constitute all there is – which are reality.

What, then, is the historian's task? To describe the ultimate data of subjective experience – the personal lives lived by men, the 'thoughts, knowledge, poetry, music, love, friendship, hates, passions'[1] of which, for Tolstoy, 'real' life is compounded, and only that? That was the task to which Turgenev was perpetually calling Tolstoy – him and all writers, but him in particular, because therein lay his true genius, his destiny as a great Russian writer; and this he rejected with violent indignation even during his middle years, before the final religious phase. For this was not to give the answer to the question of what there is, and why and how it comes to be and passes away, but to turn one's back upon it altogether, and stifle one's desire to discover how men live in society, and how they are affected by one another and by their environment, and to what end. This kind of artistic purism – preached in his day by Flaubert – this kind of preoccupation with the analysis and description of the experience and the relationships and problems and inner lives of individuals (later advocated and practised by Gide and the writers he influenced, both in France and in England) struck him as both trivial and false. He had no doubt about his own superlative skill in this very art, or that it was precisely this for which he was admired; and he condemned it absolutely.

In a letter written while he was working on *War and Peace* he said with bitterness that he had no doubt that what the public would like best would be his scenes of social and personal life, his ladies and his gentlemen, with their petty intrigues and entertaining conversations and marvellously described small idiosyncrasies.[2]

---

[1] *War and Peace*, vol. 2, part 3, chapter 1.

[2] Cf. the profession of faith in his celebrated – and militantly moralistic –

But these are the trivial 'flowers' of life, not the 'roots'. Tolstoy's purpose is the discovery of the truth, and therefore he must know what history consists of, and recreate only that. History is plainly not a science, and sociology, which pretends that it is, is a fraud; no genuine laws of history have been discovered, and the concepts in current use – 'cause', 'accident', 'genius' – explain nothing: they are merely thin disguises for ignorance. Why do the events the totality of which we call history occur as they do? Some historians attribute events to the acts of individuals, but this is no answer: for they do not explain how these acts 'cause' the events they are alleged to 'cause' or 'originate'.

There is a passage of savage irony intended by Tolstoy to parody the average school histories of his time, sufficiently typical to be worth reproducing in full:[1]

Louis XIV was a very proud and self-confident man. He had such and such mistresses, and such and such ministers, and he governed France badly. The heirs of Louis XIV were also weak men, and also governed France badly. They also had such and such favourites and such and such mistresses. Besides which, certain persons were at this time writing books. By the end of the eighteenth century there gathered in Paris two dozen or so persons who started saying that all men were free and equal. Because of this in the whole of France people began to slaughter and drown each other. These people killed the king and a good many others. At this time there was a man of genius in France – Napoleon. He conquered everyone everywhere, i.e. killed a great many people because he was a great genius; and, for some reason, he went off to kill Africans, and killed them so well, and was so clever and cunning, that, having arrived in France, he ordered everyone to obey him, which they did. Having made himself Emperor he again went to kill masses of people in Italy, Austria and Prussia. And there too he killed a great many. Now in Russia there was the Emperor Alexander, who decided to re-establish order in Europe, and therefore fought wars with Napoleon. But in the year '07 he suddenly made friends with him, and in the year '11 quarrelled with him again, and they both again began to kill a great many people. And Napoleon

introduction to an edition of Maupassant whose genius, despite everything, he admires ('Predislovie k sochineniyam Gyui de Mopassana', op. cit (p. 445 above, note 2), vol. 30, pp. 3–24). He thinks much more poorly of Bernard Shaw, whose social rhetoric he calls stale and platitudinous (diary entry for 31 January 1908, ibid., vol. 56, pp. 97–8).

[1] *War and Peace*, epilogue, part 2, chapter 1.

brought six hundred thousand men to Russia and conquered Moscow. But then he suddenly ran away from Moscow, and then the Emperor Alexander, aided by the advice of Stein and others, united Europe to raise an army against the disturber of her peace. All Napoleon's allies suddenly became his enemies; and this army marched against Napoleon, who had gathered new forces. The allies conquered Napoleon, entered Paris, forced Napoleon to renounce the throne, and sent him to the island of Elba, without, however, depriving him of the title of Emperor, and showing him all respect, in spite of the fact that five years before, and a year after, everyone considered him a brigand and beyond the law. Thereupon Louis XVIII, who until then had been an object of mere ridicule to both Frenchmen and the allies, began to reign. As for Napoleon, after shedding tears before the Old Guard, he gave up his throne, and went into exile. Then astute statesmen and diplomats, in particular Talleyrand, who had managed to sit down before anyone else in the famous armchair[1] and thereby to extend the frontiers of France, talked in Vienna, and by means of such talk made peoples happy or unhappy. Suddenly the diplomats and monarchs almost came to blows. They were almost ready to order their troops once again to kill each other; but at this moment Napoleon arrived in France with a battalion, and the French, who hated him, all immediately submitted to him. But this annoyed the allied monarchs very much and they again went to war with the French. And the genius Napoleon was defeated and taken to the island of St Helena, having suddenly been discovered to be an outlaw. Whereupon the exile, parted from his dear ones and his beloved France, died a slow death on a rock, and bequeathed his great deeds to posterity. As for Europe, a reaction occurred there, and all the princes began to treat their peoples badly once again.

Tolstoy continues:

The new history is like a deaf man replying to questions which nobody puts to him ... the primary question ... is, what power is it that moves the destinies of peoples? ... History seems to presuppose that this power can be taken for granted, and is familiar to everyone, but, in spite of every wish to admit that this power is familiar to us, anyone who has read a great many historical works cannot help doubting whether this power, which different historians understand in different ways, is in fact so completely familiar to everyone.

[1] Empire chairs of a certain shape are to this day called 'Talleyrand armchairs' in Russia.

He goes on to say that political historians who write in this way explain nothing; they merely attribute events to the 'power' which important individuals are said to exercise over others, but do not tell us what the term 'power' means: and yet this is the heart of the problem. The problem of historical movement is directly connected with the 'power' exercised by some men over others: but what is 'power'? How does one acquire it? Can it be transferred by one man to another? Surely it is not merely physical strength that is meant? Nor moral strength? Did Napoleon possess either of these?

General, as opposed to national, historians seem to Tolstoy merely to extend this category without elucidating it: instead of one country or nation, many are introduced, but the spectacle of the interplay of mysterious 'forces' makes it no clearer why some men or nations obey others, why wars are made, victories won, why innocent men who believe that murder is wicked kill one another with enthusiasm and pride, and are glorified for so doing; why great movements of human masses occur, sometimes from east to west, sometimes the other way. Tolstoy is particularly irritated by references to the dominant influence of great men or of ideas. Great men, we are told, are typical of the movements of their age: hence study of their characters 'explains' such movements. Do the characters of Diderot or Beaumarchais 'explain' the advance of the West upon the East? Do the letters of Ivan the Terrible to Prince Kurbsky 'explain' Russian expansion westward? But historians of culture do no better, for they merely add as an extra factor something called the 'force' of ideas or of books, although we still have no notion of what is meant by words like 'force'. But why should Napoleon, or Mme de Staël or Baron Stein or Tsar Alexander, or all of these, plus the *Contrat social*, 'cause' Frenchmen to behead or to drown each other? Why is this called 'explanation'? As for the importance which historians of culture attach to ideas, doubtless all men are liable to exaggerate the importance of their own wares: ideas are the commodity in which intellectuals deal – to a cobbler there's nothing like leather – the professors merely tend to magnify their personal activities into the central 'force' that rules the world. Tolstoy adds that an even deeper darkness is cast upon this subject by political theorists, moralists, metaphysicians. The celebrated notion of the social contract, for example, which some liberals peddle, speaks of the 'vesting' of the wills, in other words the power, of many men in one individual or group of individuals; but what kind of act is this 'vesting?' It may have a legal or ethical significance, it may be relevant to what should be considered as permitted or forbidden, to the world of rights and duties, or of the good and the bad, but as a factual explanation of how a sovereign accumulates enough 'power' – as if it were a commodity – which enables him to effect this or that result, it means nothing. It declares that the conferring of power makes powerful; but this tautology is too unilluminating. What is 'power' and what is 'conferring'? And who confers it and how is such conferring done?[1] The process seems very different from whatever it is that is discussed by the physical sciences. Conferring is an act, but an unintelligible one; conferring power, acquiring it, using it are not at all like eating or drinking or thinking or walking. We remain in the dark: *obscurum per obscurius*.

After demolishing the jurists and moralists and political philosophers – among them his beloved Rousseau – Tolstoy applies himself to demolishing the liberal theory of history according to which everything may turn upon what may seem an insignificant accident. Hence the pages in which he obstinately tries to prove that Napoleon knew as little of what actually went on during the battle of Borodino as the lowliest of his soldiers; and that therefore his cold on the eve of it, of which so much was made by the historians, could have made no appreciable difference. With great force he argues that only those orders or decisions issued by the commanders now seem particularly crucial (and are concentrated upon by historians) which happened to coincide with what later actually occurred; whereas a great many other exactly similar, perfectly good orders and decisions, which seemed no less crucial and vital to those who were issuing them at the time, are forgotten because, having been foiled by unfavourable turns of events, they were not, because they could not be, carried out, and for this reason now seem historically unimportant.

After disposing of the heroic theory of history, Tolstoy turns with even greater savagery upon scientific sociology, which claims

---

[1] One of Tolstoy's Russian critics, M. M. Rubinshtein, referred to above on p. 441, note 3, says that every science employs *some* unanalysed concepts, to explain which is the business of other sciences; and that 'power' happens to be the unexplained central concept of history. But Tolstoy's point is that no other science can 'explain' it, since it is, as used by historians, a meaningless term, not a concept but nothing at all – *vox nihili*.

to have discovered laws of history, but cannot possibly have found any, because the number of causes upon which events turn is too great for human knowledge or calculation. We know too few facts, and we select them at random and in accordance with our subjective inclinations. No doubt if we were omniscient we might be able, like Laplace's ideal observer, to plot the course of every drop of which the stream of history consists, but we are, of course, pathetically ignorant, and the areas of our knowledge are incredibly small compared to what is uncharted and (Tolstoy vehemently insists on this) unchartable. Freedom of the will is an illusion which cannot be shaken off, but, as great philosophers have said, it is an illusion nevertheless, and it derives solely from ignorance of true causes. The more we know about the circumstances of an act, the farther away from us the act is in time, the more difficult it is to think away its consequences; the more solidly embedded a fact is in the actual world in which we live, the less we can imagine how things might have turned out if something different had happened. For by now it seems inevitable: to think otherwise would upset too much of our world order. The more closely we relate an act to its context, the less free the actor seems to be, the less responsible for his act, and the less disposed we are to hold him accountable or blameworthy. The fact that we shall never identify all the causes, relate all human acts to the circumstances which condition them, does not imply that they are free, only that we shall never know how they are necessitated.

Tolstoy's central thesis – in some respects not unlike the theory of the inevitable 'self-deception' of the bourgeoisie held by his contemporary Karl Marx, save that what Marx reserves for a class, Tolstoy sees in almost all mankind – is that there is a natural law whereby the lives of human beings no less than that of nature are determined; but that men, unable to face this inexorable process, seek to represent it as a succession of free choices, to fix responsibility for what occurs upon persons endowed by them with heroic virtues or heroic vices, and called by them 'great men'. What are great men? They are ordinary human beings who are ignorant and vain enough to accept responsibility for the life of society, individuals who would rather take the blame for all the cruelties, injustices, disasters justified in their name than recognise their own insignificance and impotence in the cosmic flow which pursues its course irrespective of their wills and ideals. This is the central point of those passages (in which Tolstoy excelled) in which the actual course of events is described, side by side with the absurd, egocentric explanations which persons blown up with the sense of their own importance necessarily give to them; as well as of the wonderful descriptions of moments of illumination in which the truth about the human condition dawns upon those who have the humility to recognise their own unimportance and irrelevance. This is the purpose, too, of those philosophical passages where, in language more ferocious than Spinoza's, but with intentions similar to his, the errors of the pseudo-sciences are exposed.

There is a particularly vivid simile[1] in which the great man is likened to the ram whom the shepherd is fattening for slaughter. Because the ram duly grows fatter, and perhaps is used as a bell-wether for the rest of the flock, he may easily imagine that he is the leader of the flock, and that the other sheep go where they go solely in obedience to his will. He thinks this and the flock may think it too. Nevertheless the purpose of his selection is not the role he believes himself to play, but slaughter – a purpose conceived by beings whose aims neither he nor the other sheep can fathom. For Tolstoy Napoleon is just such a ram, and so to some degree is Alexander, and indeed all the great men of history. Indeed, as an acute literary historian has pointed out,[2] Tolstoy sometimes seems almost deliberately to ignore the historical evidence and more than once consciously distorts the facts in order to bolster up his favourite thesis.

The character of Kutuzov is a case in point. Such heroes as Pierre Bezukhov or Karataev are at least imaginary, and Tolstoy had an undisputed right to endow them with all the attributes he admired – humility, freedom from bureaucratic or scientific or other rationalistic kinds of blindness. But Kutuzov was a real person, and it is all the more instructive to observe the steps by which he transforms him from the sly, elderly, feeble voluptuary, the corrupt and somewhat sycophantic courtier of the early drafts of *War and Peace*, which were based on authentic sources, into the unforgettable symbol of the Russian people in all its simplicity and intuitive wisdom. By the time we reach the celebrated passage – one of the most moving in literature – in which Tolstoy describes the moment when the old man is woken in his camp at Fili to be told that the

---

[1] *War and Peace*, epilogue, part 1, chapter 2.
[2] See V. B. Shklovsky, op. cit. (p. 440 above, note 5), chapters 7 and 8, and also K. V. Pokrovsky, 'Istochniki romana "Voina i mir" ', in Obninsky and Polner, op. cit. (p. 441 above, note 3).

French army is retreating, we have left the facts behind us, and are in an imaginary realm, a historical and emotional atmosphere for which the evidence is flimsy, but which is artistically indispensable to Tolstoy's design. The final apotheosis of Kutuzov is totally unhistorical, for all Tolstoy's repeated professions of his undeviating devotion to the sacred cause of the truth.

In *War and Peace* Tolstoy treats facts cavalierly when it suits him, because he is above all obsessed by his thesis – the contrast between the universal and all-important but delusive experience of free will, the feeling of responsibility, the values of private life generally, on the one hand; and on the other the reality of inexorable historical determinism, not, indeed, experienced directly, but known to be true on irrefutable theoretical grounds. This corresponds in its turn to a tormenting inner conflict, one of many, in Tolstoy himself, between the two systems of value, the public and the private. On the one hand, if those feelings and immediate experiences upon which the ordinary values of private individuals and historians alike ultimately rest are nothing but a vast illusion, this must, in the name of the truth, be ruthlessly demonstrated, and the values and the explanations which derive from the illusion exposed and discredited. And in a sense Tolstoy does try to do this, particularly when he is philosophising, as in the great public scenes of the novel itself, the battle pieces, the descriptions of the movements of peoples, the metaphysical disquisitions. But, on the other hand, he also does the exact opposite of this, when he contrasts with this panorama of public life the superior value of personal experience, when he contrasts the concrete and multi-coloured reality of individual lives with the pale abstractions of scientists or historians, particularly the latter, 'from Gibbon to Buckle',[1] whom he denounces so harshly for mistaking their own empty categories for real facts. And yet the primacy of these private experiences and relationships and virtues presupposes that vision of life, with its sense of personal responsibility, and belief in freedom and the possibility of spontaneous action, to which the best pages of *War and Peace* are devoted, and which is the very illusion to be exorcised if the truth is to be faced.

This terrible dilemma is never finally resolved. Sometimes, as in the explanation of his intentions which he published before the

---

[1] *War and Peace*, vol. 4, part 2, chapter 1.

final part of *War and Peace* had appeared,[1] Tolstoy vacillates. The individual is 'in some sense' free when he alone is involved: thus, in raising his arm, he is free within physical limits. But once he is involved in relationships with others, he is no longer free, he is part of the inexorable stream. Freedom is real, but it is confined to trivial acts. At other times even this feeble ray of hope is extinguished: Tolstoy declares that he cannot admit even small exceptions to the universal law; causal determinism is either wholly pervasive or it is nothing, and chaos reigns. Men's acts may seem free of the social nexus, but they are not free, they cannot be free, they are part of it. Science cannot destroy the consciousness of freedom, without which there is no morality and no art, but it can refute it. 'Power' and 'accident' are but names for ignorance of the causal chains, but the chains exist whether we feel them or not. Fortunately we do not; for if we felt their weight, we could scarcely act at all; the loss of the illusion would paralyse the life which is lived on the basis of our happy ignorance. But all is well: for we never shall discover all the causal chains that operate: the number of such causes is infinitely great, the causes themselves infinitely small; historians select an absurdly small portion of them and attribute everything to this arbitrarily chosen tiny section. How would an ideal historical science operate? By using a kind of calculus whereby this 'differential', the infinitesimals – the infinitely small human and non-human actions and events – would be integrated, and in this way the continuum of history would no longer be distorted by being broken up into arbitrary segments.[2] Tolstoy expresses this notion of calculation by infinitesimals with great lucidity, and with his habitual simple, vivid, precise use of words. Henri Bergson, who made his name with his theory of reality as a flux fragmented artificially by the natural sciences, and thereby distorted and robbed of continuity and life, developed a very similar point at infinitely greater length, less clearly, less plausibly, and with an unnecessary parade of terminology.

It is not a mystical or an intuitionist view of life. Our ignorance of how things happen is not due to some inherent inaccessibility of the first causes, only to their multiplicity, the smallness of the ultimate units, and our own inability to see and hear and remember

---

[1] 'Neskol'ko slov po povodu knigi: "Voina i mir" ', *Russkii arkhiv* 6 (1868), columns 515–28.

[2] *War and Peace*, vol. 3, part 3, chapter 1.

and record and co-ordinate enough of the available material. Omniscience is in principle possible even to empirical beings, but, of course, in practice unattainable. This alone, and nothing deeper or more interesting, is the source of human megalomania, of all our absurd delusions. Since we are not, in fact, free, but could not live without the conviction that we are, what are we to do? Tolstoy arrives at no clear conclusion, only at the view, in some respects like Burke's, that it is better to realise that we understand what goes on as we do in fact understand it – much as spontaneous, normal, simple people, uncorrupted by theories, not blinded by the dust raised by the scientific authorities, do, in fact, understand life – than to seek to subvert such common-sense beliefs, which at least have the merit of having been tested by long experience, in favour of pseudo-sciences, which, being founded on absurdly inadequate data, are only a snare and a delusion. That is his case against all forms of optimistic rationalism, the natural sciences, liberal theories of progress, German military expertise, French sociology, confident social engineering of all kinds. And this is his reason for inventing a Kutuzov who followed his simple, Russian, untutored instinct, and despised or ignored the German, French and Italian experts; and for raising him to the status of a national hero, which he has, partly as a result of Tolstoy's portrait, retained ever since.

'His figures', said Akhsharumov in 1868, immediately on the appearance of the last part of *War and Peace*, 'are real and not mere pawns in the hands of an unintelligible destiny';[1] the author's theory, on the other hand, was ingenious but irrelevant. This remained the general view of Russian and, for the most part, foreign literary critics too. The Russian left-wing intellectuals attacked Tolstoy for 'social indifferentism', for disparagement of all noble social impulses as a compound of ignorance and foolish monomania, and an 'aristocratic' cynicism about life as a marsh which cannot be reclaimed; Flaubert and Turgenev, as we have seen, thought the tendency to philosophise unfortunate in itself; the only critic who took the doctrine seriously and tried to provide a rational refutation was the historian Kareev.[2] Patiently and mildly he pointed out that, fascinating as the contrast between the reality of personal life and the life of the social anthill may be,

---

[1] op. cit. (p. 441 above, note 1).
[2] N. I. Kareev, 'Istoricheskaya filosofiya v "Voine i mire"', *Vestnik evropy* 22 No 4 (July–August 1887), 227–69.

Tolstoy's conclusions did not follow. True, man is at once an atom living its own conscious life 'for itself', and at the same time the unconscious agent of some historical trend, a relatively insignificant element in the vast whole composed of a very large number of such elements. *War and Peace*, Kareev tells us, is 'a historical poem on the philosophical theme of the duality of human life'[1] – and Tolstoy was perfectly right to protest that history is not made to happen by the combination of such obscure entities as the 'power' or 'mental activity' assumed by naïve historians; indeed he was, in Kareev's view, at his best when he denounced the tendency of metaphysically minded writers to attribute causal efficacy to, or idealise, such abstract entities as 'heroes', 'historic forces', 'moral forces', 'nationalism', 'reason' and so on, whereby they simultaneously committed the two deadly sins of inventing non-existent entities to explain concrete events and of giving free reign to personal, or national, or class, or metaphysical bias.

So far so good, and Tolstoy is judged to have shown deeper insight – 'greater realism' – than most historians. He was right also in demanding that the infinitesimals of history be integrated. But then he himself had done just that by creating the individuals of his novel, who are not trivial precisely to the degree to which, in their characters and actions, they 'summate' countless others, who between them do 'move history'. This *is* the integrating of infinitesimals, not, of course, by scientific, but by 'artistic-psychological' means. Tolstoy was right to abhor abstractions, but this had led him too far, so that he ended by denying not merely that history was a natural science like chemistry – which was correct – but that it was a science at all, an activity with its own proper concepts and generalisations; which, if true, would abolish all history as such. Tolstoy was right to say that the impersonal 'forces' and 'purposes' of the older historians were myths, and dangerously misleading myths, but unless we were allowed to ask what made this or that group of individuals – who, in the end, of course, alone were real – behave thus and thus, without needing first to provide separate psychological analyses of each member of the group and then to 'integrate' them all, we could not think about history or society at all. Yet we did do this, and profitably, and to deny that we could discover a good deal by social

---

[1] ibid., p. 230. Cf. *War and Peace*, vol. 3, part 1, chapter 1 ('the two sides to the life of every man').

observation, historical inference and similar means was, for Kareev, tantamount to denying that we had criteria for distinguishing between historical truth and falsehood which were less or more reliable – and that was surely mere prejudice, fanatical obscurantism.

Kareev declares that it is men, doubtless, who make social forms, but these forms – the ways in which men live – in their turn affect those born into them; individual wills may not be all-powerful, but neither are they totally impotent, and some are more effective than others. Napoleon may not be a demigod, but neither is he a mere epiphenomenon of a process which would have occurred unaltered without him; the 'important people' are less important than they themselves or the more foolish historians may suppose, but neither are they shadows; individuals, besides their intimate inner lives, which alone seem real to Tolstoy, have social purposes, and some among them have strong wills too, and these sometimes transform the lives of communities. Tolstoy's notion of inexorable laws which work themselves out whatever men may think or wish is itself an oppressive myth; laws are only statistical probabilities, at any rate in the social sciences, not hideous and inexorable 'forces' – a concept the darkness of which, Kareev points out, Tolstoy himself in other contexts exposed with such brilliance and malice, when his opponent seemed to him too naïve or too clever or in the grip of some grotesque metaphysic. But to say that unless men make history they are themselves, particularly the 'great' among them, mere 'labels', because history makes itself, and only the unconscious life of the social hive, the human anthill, has genuine significance or value and 'reality' – what is this but a wholly unhistorical and dogmatic ethical scepticism? Why should we accept it when empirical evidence points elsewhere?

Kareev's objections are very reasonable, the most sensible and clearly formulated of all that ever were urged against Tolstoy's view of history. But in a sense he missed the point. Tolstoy was not primarily engaged in exposing the fallacies of histories based on this or that metaphysical schematism, or those which sought to explain too much in terms of some one chosen element particularly dear to the author (all of which Kareev approves), or in refuting the possibility of an empirical science of sociology (which Kareev thinks unreasonable of him) in order to set up some rival theory of his own. Tolstoy's concern with history derives from a deeper source than abstract interest in historical method or philosophical objections to given types of historical practice. It seems to spring from something more personal, a bitter inner conflict between his actual experience and his beliefs, between his vision of life and his theory of what it, and he himself, ought to be if the vision was to be bearable at all; between the immediate data, which he was too honest and too intelligent to ignore, and the need for an interpretation of them which did not lead to the childish absurdities of all previous views. For the one conviction to which his temperament and his intellect kept him faithful all his life was that all previous attempts at a rational theodicy – to explain how and why what occurred occurred as and when it did, and why it was bad or good that it should or should not do so – all such efforts were grotesque absurdities, shoddy deceptions which one sharp, honest word was sufficient to blow away.

The Russian critic Boris Eikhenbaum, who has written the best critical work on Tolstoy in any language, in the course of it develops the thesis that what oppressed Tolstoy most was his lack of positive convictions; and that the famous passage in *Anna Karenina* in which Levin's brother tells him that he – Levin – had no positive beliefs, that even communism, with its artificial, 'geometrical', symmetry, is better than total scepticism of his – Levin's – kind, in fact refers to Lev Nikolaevich himself, and to the attacks on him by his brother Nikolay Nikolaevich.[1] Whether or not the passage is literally autobiographical – and there is little in Tolstoy's writing that, in one way or another, is not – Eikhenbaum's theory seems, in general, valid. Tolstoy was by nature not a visionary; he saw the manifold objects and situations on earth in their full multiplicity; he grasped their individual essences, and what divided them from what they were not, with a clarity to which there is no parallel. Any comforting theory which attempted to collect, relate, 'synthesise', reveal hidden substrata and concealed inner connections, which, though not apparent to the naked eye, nevertheless guaranteed the unity of all things, the fact that they were 'ultimately' parts one of another with no loose ends – the ideal of the seamless whole – all such doctrines he exploded contemptuously and without difficulty. His genius lay in the perception of specific properties, the almost inexpressible individual quality in virtue of which the given object is uniquely different from all others. Nevertheless he longed for a universal explanatory principle; that is, the perception of resemblances or common

[1] B. M. Eikhenbaum, *Lev Tolstoy* (Leningrad, 1928–60), vol. 1, pp. 123–4.

origins, or single purpose, or unity in the apparent variety of the mutually exclusive bits and pieces which composed the furniture of the world.[1] Like all very penetrating, very imaginative, very clear-sighted analysts who dissect or pulverise in order to reach the indestructible core, and justify their own annihilating activities (from which they cannot abstain in any case) by the belief that such a core exists, he continued to kill his rivals' rickety constructions with cold contempt, as being unworthy of intelligent men, always hoping that the desperately-sought-for 'real' unity would presently emerge from the destruction of the shams and frauds – the knock-kneed army of eighteenth- and nineteenth-century philosophies of history. And the more obsessive the suspicion that perhaps the quest was vain, that no core and no unifying principle would ever be discovered, the more ferocious the measures to drive this thought away by increasingly merciless and ingenious executions and more and more false claimants to the title of the truth. As Tolstoy moved away from literature to polemical writing this tendency became increasingly prominent: the irritated awareness at the back of his mind that no final solution was ever, in principle, to be found, caused Tolstoy to attack the bogus solutions all the more savagely for the false comfort they offered – and for being an insult to the intelligence.[2] Tolstoy's purely intellectual genius for this kind of lethal activity was very great and exceptional, and all his life he looked for some edifice strong enough to resist his engines of destruction and his mines and battering-rams; he wished to be stopped by an immovable obstacle, he wished his violent projec-tiles to be resisted by impregnable fortifications. The eminent reasonableness and tentative methods of Kareev, his mild academic remonstrance, were altogether too unlike the final impenetrable, irreducible, solid bedrock of truth on which alone that secure interpretation of life could be built which all his life he wished to find.

---

[1] Here the paradox appears once more; for the 'infinitesimals', whose integration is the task of the ideal historian, must be reasonably uniform to make this operation possible; yet the sense of 'reality' consists in the sense of their unique differences.

[2] In our day French existentialists for similar psychological reasons have struck out against all explanations as such because they are a mere drug to still serious questions, short-lived palliatives for wounds which are unbearable but must be borne, above all not denied or 'explained'; for all explaining is explaining away, and that is a denial of the given – the existent – the brute facts.

The thin, 'positive' doctrine of historical change in *War and Peace* is all that remains of this despairing search, and it is the immense superiority of Tolstoy's offensive over his defensive weapons that has always made his philosophy of history – the theory of the minute particles, requiring integration – seem so threadbare and artificial to the average, reasonably critical, moderately sensitive reader of the novel. Hence the tendency of most of those who have written about *War and Peace*, both immediately on its appearance and in later years, to maintain Akhsharumov's thesis that Tolstoy's genius lay in his quality as a writer, a creator of a world more real than life itself; while the theoretical disquisitions, even though Tolstoy himself may have looked upon them as the most important ingredient in the book, in fact threw no light upon either the character or the value of the work itself, or on the creative process by which it was achieved. This anticipated the approach of those psychological critics who maintain that the author himself often scarcely knows the sources of his own activity: that the springs of his genius are invisible to him, the process itself largely unconscious, and his own overt purpose a mere rationalisation in his own mind of the true, but scarcely conscious, motives and methods involved in the act of creation, and consequently often a mere hindrance to those dispassionate students of art and literature who are engaged upon the 'scientific' – naturalistic – analysis of its origins and evolution.

Whatever we may think of the general validity of such an outlook, it is something of a historical irony that Tolstoy should have been treated in this fashion; for it is virtually his own way with the academic historians at whom he mocks with such Voltairian irony. And yet there is much poetic justice in it: for the unequal ratio of critical to constructive elements in his own philosophising seems due to the fact that his sense of reality (a reality which resides in individual persons and their relationships alone) served to explode all the large theories which ignored its findings, but proved insufficient by itself to provide the basis of a more satisfactory general account of the facts. And there is no evidence that Tolstoy himself ever conceived it possible that this was the root of the 'duality', the failure to reconcile the two lives lived by man.

The unresolved conflict between Tolstoy's belief that the attributes of personal life alone are real and his doctrine that analysis of them is insufficient to explain the course of history (that is, the behaviour of societies) is paralleled, at a profounder and more personal level, by the conflict between, on the one hand, his own gifts both as a writer and as a man and, on the other, his ideals – that which he sometimes believed himself to be, and at all times profoundly believed in, and wished to be.

If we may recall once again our division of artists into foxes and hedgehogs: Tolstoy perceived reality in its multiplicity, as a collection of separate entities round and into which he saw with a clarity and penetration scarcely ever equalled, but he believed only in one vast, unitary whole. No author who has ever lived has shown such powers of insight into the variety of life – the differences, the contrasts, the collisions of persons and things and situations, each apprehended in its absolute uniqueness and conveyed with a degree of directness and a precision of concrete imagery to be found in no other writer. No one has ever excelled Tolstoy in expressing the specific flavour, the exact quality of a feeling – the degree of its 'oscillation', the ebb and flow, the minute movements (which Turgenev mocked as a mere trick on his part) – the inner and outer texture and 'feel' of a look, a thought, a pang of sentiment, no less than of a specific situation, of an entire period, of the lives of individuals, families, communities, entire nations. The celebrated lifelikeness of every object and every person in his world derives from this astonishing capacity of presenting every ingredient of it in its fullest individual essence, in all its many dimensions, as it were: never as a mere datum, however vivid, within some stream of consciousness, with blurred edges, an outline, a shadow, an impressionistic representation; nor yet calling for, and dependent on, some process of reasoning in the mind of the reader; but always as a solid object, seen simultaneously from near and far, in natural, unaltering daylight, from all possible angles of vision, set in an absolutely specific context in time and space – an event fully present to the senses or the imagination in all its facets, with every nuance sharply and firmly articulated.

Yet what he believed in was the opposite. He advocated a single embracing vision; he preached not variety but simplicity, not many levels of consciousness but reduction to some single level – in *War and Peace*, to the standard of the good man, the single, spontaneous, open soul: as later to that of the peasants, or of a simple Christian ethic divorced from any complex theology or metaphysic; some simple, quasi-utilitarian criterion, whereby everything is interrelated directly, and all the items can be assessed in terms of one another by some simple measuring-rod. Tolstoy's genius lies in a capacity for marvellously accurate reproduction of the irreproducible, the almost miraculous evocation of the full, untranslatable individuality of the individual, which induces in the reader an acute awareness of the presence of the object itself, and not of a mere description of it, employing for this purpose metaphors which fix the quality of a particular experience as such, and avoiding those general terms which relate it to similar instances by ignoring individual differences – the 'oscillations' of feeling – in favour of what is common to them all. But then this same writer pleads for, indeed preaches with great fury, particularly in his last, religious phase, the exact opposite: the necessity of expelling everything that does not submit to some very general, very simple standard: say, what peasants like or dislike, or what the Gospels declare to be good.

This violent contradiction between the data of experience, from which he could not liberate himself, and which, of course, all his life he knew alone to be real, and his deeply metaphysical belief in the existence of a system to which they *must* belong, whether they appear to do so or not, this conflict between instinctive judgement and theoretical conviction – between his gifts and his opinions – mirrors the unresolved conflict between the reality of the moral life, with its sense of responsibility, joys, sorrows, sense of guilt and sense of achievement – all of which is nevertheless illusion – and the laws which govern everything, although we cannot know more than a negligible portion of them – so that all scientists and historians who say that they do know them and are guided by them are lying and deceiving – but which nevertheless alone are real. Beside Tolstoy, Gogol and Dostoevsky, whose abnormality is so often contrasted with Tolstoy's 'sanity', are well-integrated personalities, with a coherent outlook and a single vision. Yet out of this violent conflict grew *War and Peace*: its marvellous solidity should not blind us to the deep cleavage which yawns open whenever Tolstoy remembers, or rather reminds himself – fails to forget – what he is doing, and why.

IV

Theories are seldom born in the void. The question of the roots of Tolstoy's vision of history is therefore a reasonable one. Everything that Tolstoy writes on history has the stamp of his own original personality, a first-hand quality denied to most writers on abstract topics. On these subjects he wrote as an amateur, not as a professional; but let it be remembered that he belonged to the world of great affairs: he was a member of the ruling class of his country and his time, and knew and understood it completely; he lived in an environment exceptionally crowded with theories and ideas, he examined a great deal of material for *War and Peace* (though, as several Russian scholars have shown,[1] not as much as is sometimes supposed), he travelled a great deal, and met many notable public figures in Germany and France.

That he read widely, and was influenced by what he read, cannot be doubted. It is a commonplace that he owed a great deal to Rousseau, and probably derived from him, as much as from Diderot and the French Enlightenment, his analytic, anti-historical ways of approaching social problems, in particular the tendency to treat them in terms of timeless logical, moral and metaphysical categories, and not look for their essence, as the German historical school advocated, in terms of growth, and of response to a changing historical environment. He remained an admirer of Rousseau, and late in life still recommended *Émile* as the best book ever written on education.[2] Rousseau must have strengthened, if he did not actually originate, his growing tendency to idealise the soil and its cultivators – the simple peasant, who for Tolstoy is a repository of almost as rich a stock of 'natural' virtues as Rousseau's noble savage. Rousseau, too, must have reinforced the coarse-grained, rough peasant in Tolstoy, with his strongly moralistic, puritanical strain, his suspicion of, and antipathy to, the rich, the powerful, the happy as such, his streak of genuine vandalism, and occasional bursts of blind, very Russian rage against Western sophistication and refinement, and that adulation of 'virtue' and simple tastes, of the 'healthy' moral life, the militant, anti-liberal barbarism, which is one of Rousseau's specific contributions to the stock of Jacobin ideas. Perhaps Rousseau influenced him also in setting so high a value upon family life, and in his doctrine of the superiority of the heart over the head, of moral over intellectual or aesthetic virtues. This has been noted before, and it is true and

---

[1] For example, both Shklovsky and Eikhenbaum in the works cited above (p. 440, note 5, p. 463, note 1).

[2] 'On n'a pas rendu justice à Rousseau ... J'ai lu tout Rousseau, oui, tous les vingt volumes, y compris le *Dictionnaire de musique*. Je faisais mieux que l'admirer; je lui rendais une culte véritable ...' (see p. 472 below, note 3).

illuminating, but it does not account for Tolstoy's theory of history, of which little trace can be found in the profoundly unhistorical Rousseau. Indeed, in so far as Rousseau seeks to derive the right of some men to authority over others from a theory of the transference of power in accordance with the Social Contract, Tolstoy contemptuously refutes him.

We get somewhat nearer to the truth if we consider the influence upon Tolstoy of his romantic and conservative Slavophil contemporaries. He was close to some among them, particularly to Pogodin and Samarin, in the mid-1860s when he was writing *War and Peace*, and certainly shared their antagonism to the scientific theories of history then fashionable, whether the metaphysical positivism of Comte and his followers, or the more materialistic views of Chernyshevsky and Pisarev, as well as those of Buckle and Mill and Herbert Spencer, and the general British empiricist tradition, tinged by French and German scientific materialism, to which these very different figures all, in their various fashions, belonged. The Slavophils (and perhaps especially Tyutchev, whose poetry Tolstoy admired so deeply) may have done something to discredit for him historical theories modelled upon the natural sciences, which, for Tolstoy no less than for Dostoevsky, failed to give a true account of what men did and suffered. They were inadequate if only because they ignored man's 'inner' experience, treated him as a natural object played upon by the same forces as all the other constituents of the material world, and, taking the French Encyclopaedists at their word, tried to study social behaviour as one might study a beehive or an anthill, and then complained because the laws which they formulated failed to explain the behaviour of living men and women. These romantic medievalists may moreover have strengthened Tolstoy's natural anti-intellectualism and anti-liberalism, and his deeply sceptical and pessimistic view of the strength of non-rational motives in human behaviour, which at once dominate human beings and deceive them about themselves – in short that innate conservatism of outlook which very early made Tolstoy deeply suspect to the radical Russian intelligentsia of the 1850s and 1860s, and led them to think of him uneasily as being after all a count, an officer and a reactionary, not one of themselves, not genuinely enlightened or *révolté* at all, despite his boldest protests against the political system, his heterodoxies, his destructive nihilism.

But although Tolstoy and the Slavophils may have fought a

common enemy, their positive views diverged sharply. The Slavophil doctrine derived principally from German Idealism, in particular from Schelling's view (despite much lip-service to Hegel and
his interpreters) that true knowledge could not be obtained by the
use of reason, but only by a kind of imaginative self-identification
with the central principle of the universe – the soul of the world –
such as artists and thinkers have in moments of divine inspiration.
Some of the Slavophils identified this with the revealed truths of
the Orthodox religion and the mystical tradition of the Russian
Church, and bequeathed it to the Russian symbolist poets and
philosophers of a later generation. Tolstoy stood at the opposite
pole to all this. He believed that only by patient empirical
observation could any knowledge be obtained; that this knowledge
is always inadequate, that simple people often know the truth
better than learned men, because their observation of men and
nature is less clouded by empty theories, and not because they are
inspired vehicles of the divine afflatus. There is a hard cutting edge
of common sense about everything that Tolstoy wrote which
automatically puts to flight metaphysical fantasies and undisciplined tendencies towards esoteric experience, or the poetical or
theological interpretations of life which lay at the heart of the
Slavophil outlook, and (as in the analogous case of the anti-
industrial romanticism of the West) determined both its hatred of
politics and economics in the ordinary sense, and its mystical
nationalism. Moreover, the Slavophils were worshippers of historical method as alone disclosing the true nature – revealed only in its
impalpable growth in time – of individual institutions and abstract
sciences alike.

   None of this could possibly have found a sympathetic echo in
the very tough-minded, very matter-of-fact Tolstoy, especially the
realistic Tolstoy of the middle years; if the peasant Platon Karataev
has something in common with the agrarian ethos of the Slavophil
(and indeed pan-Slav) ideologists – simple rural wisdom as against
the absurdities of the over-clever West – yet Pierre Bezukhov in
the early drafts of War and Peace ends his life as a Decembrist and
an exile in Siberia, and cannot be conceived in all his spiritual
wanderings as ultimately finding comfort in any metaphysical
system, still less in the bosom of the Orthodox or any other
established Church. The Slavophils saw through the pretensions of
Western social and psychological science, and that was sympathetic
to Tolstoy; but their positive doctrines interested him little. He was

against unintelligible mysteries, against mists of antiquity, against any kind of recourse to mumbo-jumbo: his hostile picture of the Freemasons in *War and Peace* remained symptomatic of his attitude until the end. This can only have been reinforced by his interest in the writings of, and his visit in 1861 to, the exiled Proudhon, whose confused irrationalism, puritanism, hatred of authority and bourgeois intellectuals, and general Rousseauism and violence of tone evidently pleased him. It is more than possible that he took the title of his novel from Proudhon's *La Guerre et la paix*, published in the same year.

If the classical German Idealists had had no direct effect upon Tolstoy, there was at least one German philosopher for whom he did express admiration. Indeed it is not difficult to see why he found Schopenhauer attractive: that solitary thinker drew a gloomy picture of the impotent human will beating desperately against the rigidly determined laws of the universe; he spoke of the vanity of all human passions, the absurdity of rational systems, the universal failure to understand the non-rational springs of action and feeling, the suffering to which all flesh is subject, and the consequent desirability of reducing human vulnerability by reducing man himself to the condition of the utmost quietism, where, being passionless, he cannot be frustrated or humiliated or wounded. This celebrated doctrine reflected Tolstoy's later views – that man suffers much because he seeks too much, is foolishly ambitious and grotesquely overestimates his capacities. From Schopenhauer, too, may come the bitter emphasis laid on the familiar contrast of the illusion of free will with the reality of the iron laws which govern the world, in particular the account of the inevitable suffering which this illusion, since it cannot be made to vanish, must necessarily cause. This, for both Schopenhauer and Tolstoy, is the central tragedy of human life; if only men would learn how little the cleverest and most gifted among them can control, how little they can know of all the multitude of factors the orderly movement of which is the history of the world; above all, what presumptuous nonsense it is to claim to perceive an order merely on the strength of believing desperately that an order must exist, when all one actually perceives is meaningless chaos – a chaos of which the heightened form, the microcosm in which the disorder of human life is reflected in an intense degree, is war.

The best avowed of all Tolstoy's literary debts is, of course, that to Stendhal. In his celebrated interview in 1901 with Paul Boyer,[1] Tolstoy coupled Stendhal and Rousseau as the two writers to whom he owed most, and added that all he had learnt about war he had learnt from Stendhal's description of the battle of Waterloo in *La Chartreuse de Parme*, where Fabrice wanders about the battlefield 'understanding nothing'. He added that this conception – war 'without panache' or 'embellishments' – of which his brother Nikolay had spoken to him, he later had verified for himself during his own service in the Crimean War. Nothing ever won so much praise from active soldiers as Tolstoy's vignettes of episodes in the war, his descriptions of how battles appear to those who are actually engaged in them.

No doubt Tolstoy was right in declaring that he owed much of this dry light to Stendhal. But there is a figure behind Stendhal even drier, even more destructive, from whom Stendhal may well, at least in part, have derived his new method of interpreting social life, a celebrated writer with whose works Tolstoy was certainly acquainted and to whom he owed a deeper debt than is commonly supposed; for the striking resemblance between their views can hardly be put down either to accident, or to the mysterious operations of the *Zeitgeist*. This figure was the famous Joseph de Maistre; and the full story of his influence on Tolstoy, although it has been noted by students of Tolstoy, and by at least one critic of Maistre,[2] still largely remains to be written.

V

On 1 November 1865, in the middle of writing *War and Peace*, Tolstoy wrote down in his diary 'I am reading Maistre',[3] and on 7 September 1866 he wrote to the editor Bartenev, who acted as a kind of general assistant to him, asking him to send the 'Maistre archive', that is, his letters and notes. There is every reason why Tolstoy should have read this now relatively little-read author. Count Joseph de Maistre was a Savoyard royalist who had first made a name for himself by writing anti-revolutionary tracts during the last years of the eighteenth century. Although normally classified as an orthodox Catholic reactionary writer, a pillar of the

---

[1] See *Paul Boyer (1864–1949) chez Tolstoï* (Paris, 1950), p. 40.
[2] See Adolfo Omodeo, *Un reazionario* (Bari, 1939), p. 112, note 2.
[3] 'Chitayu "Maistre" ', quoted by B. M. Eikhenbaum, op. cit. (p. 463 above, note 1), vol. 2, p. 309.

Bourbon Restoration and a defender of the pre-revolutionary status quo, in particular of papal authority, he was a great deal more than this. He held grimly unconventional and misanthropic views about the nature of individuals and societies, and wrote with a dry and ironical violence about the incurably savage and wicked nature of man, the inevitability of perpetual slaughter, the divinely instituted character of wars, and the overwhelming part played in human affairs by the passion for self-immolation, which, more than natural sociability or artificial agreements, creates armies and civil societies alike. He emphasised the need for absolute authority, punishment and continual repression if civilisation and order were to survive at all. Both the content and the tone of his writings are closer to Nietzsche, d'Annunzio and the heralds of modern Fascism than to the respectable royalists of his own time, and caused a stir in their own day both among the legitimists and in Napoleonic France. In 1803 Maistre was sent by his master, the King of Piedmont-Sardinia, then living in exile in Rome as a victim of Napoleon and soon forced to move to Sardinia, as his semi-official representative to the Court of St Petersburg. Maistre, who possessed considerable social charm as well as an acute sense of his environment, made a great impression upon the society of the Russian capital as a polished courtier, a wit and a shrewd political observer. He remained in St Petersburg from 1803 to 1817, and his exquisitely written and often uncannily penetrating and prophetic diplomatic dispatches and letters, as well as his private correspondence and the various scattered notes on Russia and her inhabitants, sent to his government as well as to his friends and consultants among the Russian nobility, form a uniquely valuable source of information about the life and opinions of the ruling circles of the Russian Empire during and immediately after the Napoleonic period.

He died in 1821, the author of several theologico-political essays, but the definitive editions of his works, in particular of the celebrated *Soirées de Saint-Pétersbourg*, which in the form of Platonic dialogue dealt with the nature and sanctions of human government and other political and philosophical problems, as well as his *Correspondance diplomatique* and his letters, were published in full only in the 1850s and early 1860s by his son Rodolphe and by others. Maistre's open hatred of Austria, his anti-Bonapartism, as well as the rising importance of the Piedmontese kingdom before and after the Crimean War, naturally increased interest in his personality and his thought at this date. Books on him began to appear and excited a good deal of discussion in Russian literary and historical circles. Tolstoy possessed the *Soirées*, as well as Maistre's diplomatic correspondence and letters, and copies of them were to be found in the library at Yasnaya Polyana. It is in any case quite clear that Tolstoy used them extensively in *War and Peace*.[1] Thus the celebrated description of Paulucci's intervention in the debate of the Russian General Staff at Drissa is reproduced almost verbatim from a letter by Maistre. Similarly Prince Vasily's conversation at Mme Scherer's reception with the 'homme de beaucoup de mérite'[2] about Kutuzov is obviously based on a letter by Maistre, in which all the French phrases with which this conversation is sprinkled are to be found. There is, moreover, a marginal note in one of Tolstoy's early drafts, 'At Anna Pavlovna's J. Maistre', which refers to the raconteur who tells the beautiful Hélène and an admiring circle of listeners the idiotic anecdote about the meeting of Napoleon with the duc d'Enghien at supper with the celebrated actress Mlle Georges.[3] Again, old Prince Bolkonsky's habit of shifting his bed from one room to another is probably taken from a story which Maistre tells about the similar habit of Count Stroganov. Finally, the name of Maistre occurs in the novel itself,[4] as being among those who agree that it would be embarrassing and senseless to capture the more eminent princes and marshals of Napoleon's army, since this would merely create diplomatic difficulties. Zhikharev, whose memoirs Tolstoy is known to have used, met Maistre in 1807, and described him in glowing colours;[5] something of the atmosphere to be found in these memoirs enters into Tolstoy's description of the eminent émigrés in Anna Pavlovna Scherer's drawing-room, with which *War and Peace* opens, and his other references to fashionable Petersburg society at this date. These echoes and parallels have been collated carefully by Tolstoyan scholars, and leave no doubt about the extent of Tolstoy's borrowing.

Among these parallels there are similarities of a more important kind. Maistre explains that the victory of the legendary Horatius

---

[1] See Eikhenbaum, op. cit. (p. 463 above, note 1).

[2] *War and Peace*, vol. 3, part 2, chapter 6.

[3] ibid., vol. 1, part 1, chapter 3. For the note see op. cit. (p. 445 above, note 2), vol. 13, p. 687.

[4] *War and Peace*, vol. 4, part 3, chapter 19.

[5] S. P. Zhikharev, *Zapiski sovremennika* (Moscow, 1934), vol. 2, pp. 112–13.

over the Curiatii – like all victories in general – was due to the intangible factor of morale, and Tolstoy similarly speaks of the supreme importance of this unknown quantity in determining the outcome of battles – the impalpable 'spirit' of troops and their commanders. This emphasis on the imponderable and the incalculable is part and parcel of Maistre's general irrationalism. More clearly and boldly than anyone before him, Maistre declared that the human intellect was but a feeble instrument when pitted against the power of natural forces; that rational explanations of human conduct seldom explained anything. He maintained that only the irrational, precisely because it defied explanation and could therefore not be undermined by the critical activities of reason, was able to persist and be strong. And he gave as examples such irrational institutions as hereditary monarchy and marriage, which survived from age to age, while such rational institutions as elective monarchy, or 'free' personal relationships, swiftly and for no obvious 'reason' collapsed wherever they were introduced. Maistre conceived of life as a savage battle at all levels, between plants and animals no less than individuals and nations, a battle from which no gain was expected, but which originated in some primal, mysterious, sanguinary, self-immolatory craving implanted by God. This instinct was far more powerful than the feeble efforts of rational men who tried to achieve peace and happiness (which was, in any case, not the deepest desire of the human heart – only of its caricature, the liberal intellect) by planning the life of society without reckoning with the violent forces which sooner or later would inevitably cause their puny structures to collapse like so many houses of cards.

Maistre regarded the battlefield as typical of life in all its aspects, and derided the generals who thought that they were in fact controlling the movements of their troops and directing the course of the battle. He declared that no one in the actual heat of battle can begin to tell what is going on:

On parle beaucoup de batailles dans le monde sans savoir ce que c'est; on est surtout assez sujet à les considérer comme des points, tandis qu'elles couvrent deux ou trois lieues de pays: on vous dit gravement: Comment ne savez-vous pas ce qui s'est passé dans ce combat puisque vous y étiez? tandis que c'est précisément le contraire qu'on pourrait dire assez souvent. Celui qui est à la droite sait-il ce qui se passe à la gauche? sait-il seulement ce qui se passe à deux pas de lui? Je me représente aisément une de ces scènes épouvantables: sur un vaste terrain couvert de tous les apprêts du carnage, et qui semble s'ébranler sous les pas des hommes et des chevaux; au milieu du feu et des tourbillons de fumée; étourdi, transporté par le retentissement des armes à feu et des instruments militaires, par des voix qui command-ent, qui hurlent ou qui s'éteignent; environné de morts, de mourants, de cadavres mutilés; possédé tour à tour par la crainte, par l'espérance, par la rage, par cinq ou six ivresses différentes, que devient l'homme? que voit-il? que sait-il au bout de quelques heures? que peut-il sur lui et sur les autres? Parmi cette foule de guerriers qui ont combattu tout le jour, il n'y en a souvent pas un seul, et pas même le général, qui sache où est le vainqueur. Il ne tiendrait qu'à moi de vous citer des batailles modernes, des batailles fameuses dont la mémoire ne périra jamais, des batailles qui ont changé la face des affaires en Europe, et qui n'ont été perdues que parce que tel ou tel homme a cru qu'elles l'étaient; de manière qu'en supposant toutes les circonstances égales, et pas une goutte de sang de plus versée de part et d'autre, un autre général aurait fait chanter le *Te Deum* chez lui, et forcé l'histoire de dire tout le contraire de ce qu'elle dira.[1]

---

[1] *Les Soirées de Saint-Pétersbourg*, seventh conversation: op. cit. (p. 266 above, note 1), vol. 5, pp. 33–4. 'People talk a lot about battles without knowing what they are really like. In particular, they tend to consider them as occurring at one place, whereas they cover two or three leagues of country. They ask you seriously: *How is it that you don't know what happened in this battle, since you were there?* Whereas it is precisely the opposite that would often have to be said. Does the one on the right know what is happening on the left? Does he even know what is happening two paces from him? I can easily imagine one of these frightful scenes. On a vast field covered with all the apparatus of carnage and seeming to shudder under the feet of men and horses, in the midst of fire and whirling smoke, dazed and carried away by the din of firearms and cannon, by voices that order, roar, and die away, surrounded by the dead, the dying, the mutilated corpses, seized in turn by fear, hope, and rage, by five or six different passions, what happens to a man? What does he see? What does he know after a few hours? What can he know about himself and others? Among this crowd of warriors who have fought the whole day, there is often not a single one, not even the general, who knows who the victor is. I will restrict myself to citing modern battles, famous battles whose memory will never perish, battles that have changed the face of Europe and that were only lost because such and such a man thought they were lost; they were battles where all circumstances being equal and without a drop of blood more being shed on either side, the other general could have had a *Te Deum* sung in his own country and forced history to record the opposite of what it will say.' The translations in the notes are taken from Joseph de Maistre, *St Petersburg Dialogues*, trans. Richard A. Lebrun (Montreal etc., 1993): page references to this version in subsequent notes follow those to the French original, in parentheses. This passage appears on pp. 222–3.

And later:

N'avons-nous pas fini même par voir perdre des batailles gagnées? . . . Je crois en général que les batailles ne se gagnent ni ne se perdent point physiquement.[1]

And again, in a similar strain:

De même une armée de 40,000 hommes est inférieure physiquement à une autre armée de 60,000: mais si la première a plus de courage, d'expérience et de discipline, elle pourra battre la seconde; car elle a plus d'action avec moins de masse, et c'est ce que nous voyons à chaque page de l'histoire.[2]

And finally:

C'est l'opinion qui perd les batailles, et c'est l'opinion qui les gagne.[3]

Victory is a moral or psychological, not a physical, issue:

*qu'est ce qu'une bataille perdue?* . . . *C'est une bataille qu'on croit avoir perdue.* Rien n'est plus vrai. Un homme qui se bat avec un autre est vaincu lorsqu'il est tué ou terrassé, et que l'autre est debout; il n'en est pas ainsi de deux armées: l'une ne peut être tuée, tandis que l'autre reste en pied. Les forces se balancent ainsi que les morts, et depuis surtout que l'invention de la poudre a mis plus d'égalité dans les moyens de destruction, une bataille ne se perd plus matériellement; c'est-à-dire parce qu'il y a plus de morts d'un côté que de l'autre: aussi Frédéric II, qui s'y entendait un peu, disait: *Vaincre, c'est avancer.* Mais quel est celui qui avance? c'est celui dont la conscience et la contenance font reculer l'autre.[4]

---

[1] ibid., p. 35 (223). 'Have we not even seen won battles lost? . . . In general, I believe that battles are not won or lost physically.'

[2] ibid., p. 29 (220). 'In the same way, an army of 40,000 men is physically inferior to another army of 60,000, but if the first has more courage, experience, and discipline, it will be able to defeat the second, for it is more effective with less mass. This is what we can see on every page of history.'

[3] ibid., p. 31. 'It is opinion that loses battles, and it is opinion that wins them.'

[4] ibid., p. 32 (221). '*What is a lost battle?* . . . *It is a battle one believes one has lost.* Nothing is more true. One man fighting with another is defeated when he has been killed or brought to earth and the other remains standing. This is not the way it is with two armies; the one cannot be killed while the other remains on its feet. The forces are in equilibrium, as are the deaths, and especially since the invention of gunpowder has introduced more equality into the means of destruction, a battle is no longer lost materially, that is to say because there are

There is and can be no military science, for 'C'est l'imagination qui perd les batailles',[1] and 'peu de batailles sont perdues physiquement – vous tirez, je tire ... le véritable vainqueur, comme le véritable vaincu, c'est celui qui croit l'être'.[2]

This is the lesson which Tolstoy says he derives from Stendhal, but the words of Prince Andrey about Austerlitz – 'We lost because very early on we told ourselves we had lost'[3] – as well as the attribution of Russian victory over Napoleon to the strength of the Russian desire to survive, echo Maistre and not Stendhal.

This close parallelism between Maistre's and Tolstoy's views about the chaos and uncontrollability of battles and wars, with its larger implications for human life generally, together with the contempt of both for the naïve explanations provided by academic historians to account for human violence and lust for war, was noted by the eminent French historian Albert Sorel, in a little-known lecture to the École des Sciences Politiques delivered on 7 April 1888.[4] He drew a parallel between Maistre and Tolstoy, and observed that although Maistre was a theocrat, while Tolstoy was a 'nihilist', yet both regarded the first causes of events as mysterious, involving the reduction of human wills to nullity. 'The distance', wrote Sorel, 'from the theocrat to the mystic, and from the mystic to the nihilist, is smaller than that from the butterfly to the larva, from the larva to the chrysalis, from the chrysalis to the butterfly.'[5]

more dead on one side than the other. It was Frederick II, who understood a little about these things, who said: *To win is to advance*. But who is the one who advances? It is the one whose conscience and countenance makes the other fall back.'

[1] ibid., p. 33 (222). 'It is imagination that loses battles.'

[2] Letter of 14 September 1812 to Count de Front: ibid., vol. 12, pp. 220–1. 'Few battles are lost physically – you fire, I fire ... the real victor, like the real loser, is the one who believes himself to be so.'

[3] *War and Peace*, vol. 3, part 2, chapter 25.

[4] Albert Sorel, 'Tolstoï historien', *Revue bleue* 41 (January–June 1888), 460–9. This lecture, reprinted in revised form in Sorel's *Lectures historiques* (Paris, 1894), has been unjustly neglected by students of Tolstoy; it does much to correct the views of those (e.g. P. I. Biryukov and K. V. Pokrovsky in their works cited above (p. 439, note 2, and p. 457, note 2), not to mention later critics and literary historians who almost all rely upon their authority) who omit all reference to Maistre. Émile Haumant is almost unique among earlier scholars in ignoring secondary authorities and discovering the truth for himself; see his *La Culture française en Russie (1700–1900)* (Paris, 1910), pp. 490–2.

[5] op. cit. (note 4 above), p. 462. This passage is omitted from the 1894 reprint (p. 270).

Tolstoy resembles Maistre in being, above all, curious about first causes, in asking such questions as Maistre's '*Expliquez pourquoi ce qu'il y a de plus honorable dans le monde, au jugement de tout le genre humain sans exception, est le droit de verser innocemment le sang innocent?*',[1] in rejecting all rationalist or naturalistic answers, in stressing impalpable psychological and 'spiritual' – and sometimes 'zoological' – factors as determining events, and in stressing these at the expense of statistical analyses of military strength, very much like Maistre in his dispatches to his government at Cagliari. Indeed, Tolstoy's accounts of mass movements – in battle, and in the flight of the Russians from Moscow or of the French from Russia – might almost be designed to give concrete illustrations of Maistre's theory of the unplanned and unplannable character of all great events. But the parallel runs deeper. The Savoyard Count and the Russian are both reacting, and reacting violently, against liberal optimism concerning human goodness, human reason, and the value or inevitability of material progress: both furiously denounce the notion that mankind can be made eternally happy and virtuous by rational and scientific means.

The first great wave of optimistic rationalism which followed the Wars of Religion broke against the violence of the great French Revolution and the political despotism and social and economic misery which ensued: in Russia a similar development was shattered by the long succession of repressive measures taken by Nicholas I to counteract firstly the effect of the Decembrist revolt, and, nearly a quarter of a century later, the influence of the European revolutions of 1848–9; and to this must be added the material and moral effect, a decade later, of the Crimean débâcle. In both cases the emergence of naked force killed a great deal of tender-minded idealism, and resulted in various types of realism and toughness – among others, materialistic socialism, authoritarian neo-feudalism, blood-and-iron nationalism and other bitterly anti-liberal movements. In the case of both Maistre and Tolstoy, for all their unbridgeably deep psychological, social, cultural and religious differences, the disillusionment took the form of an acute scepticism about scientific method as such, distrust of all liberalism, positivism, rationalism, and of all the forms of high-minded

---

[1] op. cit. (p. 476 above, note 1), p. 10 (210). '*Explain why the most honourable thing in the world, according to the judgement of all of humanity, without exception, has always been the right to shed innocent blood innocently?*'

secularism then influential in Western Europe; and led to a deliberate emphasis on the 'unpleasant' aspects of human history, from which sentimental romantics, humanist historians and optimistic social theorists seemed so resolutely to be averting their gaze.

Both Maistre and Tolstoy spoke of political reformers (in one interesting instance, of the same individual representative of them, the Russian statesman Speransky) in the same tone of bitterly contemptuous irony. Maistre was suspected of having had an actual hand in Speransky's fall and exile; Tolstoy, through the eyes of Prince Andrey, describes the pale face of Alexander's one-time favourite, his soft hands, his fussy and self-important manner, the artificiality and emptiness of his movements – as somehow indicative of the unreality of his person and of his liberal activities – in a manner which Maistre could only have applauded. Both speak of intellectuals with scorn and hostility. Maistre regards them not merely as grotesque casualties of the historical process – hideous cautions created by Providence to scare mankind into a return to the ancient Roman faith – but as beings dangerous to society, a pestilential sect of questioners and corrupters of youth against whose corrosive activity all prudent rulers must take measures. Tolstoy treats them with contempt rather than hatred, and represents them as poor, misguided, feeble-witted creatures with delusions of grandeur. Maistre sees them as a brood of social and political locusts, as a canker at the heart of Christian civilisation, which is of all things the most sacred and will be preserved only by the heroic efforts of the Pope and his Church. Tolstoy looks on them as clever fools, spinners of empty subtleties, blind and deaf to the realities which simpler hearts can grasp, and from time to time he lets fly at them with the brutal violence of a grim, anarchical old peasant, avenging himself, after years of silence, on the silly, chattering, town-bred monkeys, so knowing, and full of words to explain everything, and superior, and impotent and empty. Both dismiss any interpretation of history which does not place at the heart of it the problem of the nature of power, and both speak with disdain about rationalistic attempts to explain it. Maistre amuses himself at the expense of the Encyclopaedists – their clever superficialities, their neat but empty categories – very much in the manner adopted by Tolstoy towards their descendants a century later, the scientific sociologists and historians. Both profess belief in the deep wisdom of the uncorrupted common people, although

Maistre's mordant *obiter dicta* about the hopeless barbarism, venality and ignorance of the Russians cannot have been to Tolstoy's taste, if indeed he ever read them.

Both Maistre and Tolstoy regard the Western world as in some sense 'rotting', as being in rapid decay. This was the doctrine which the Roman Catholic counter-revolutionaries at the turn of the century virtually invented, and it formed part of their view of the French Revolution as a divine punishment visited upon those who strayed from the Christian faith, and in particular that of the Roman Church. From France this denunciation of secularism was carried by many devious routes, mainly by second-rate journalists and their academic readers, to Germany and to Russia (to Russia both directly and via German versions), where it found a ready soil among those who, having themselves avoided the revolutionary upheavals, found it flattering to their *amour propre* to believe that they, at any rate, might still be on the path to greater power and glory, while the West, destroyed by the failure of its ancient faith, was fast disintegrating morally and politically. No doubt Tolstoy derived this element in his outlook at least as much from Slavophils and other Russian chauvinists as directly from Maistre, but it is worth noting that this belief is exceptionally powerful in both these dry and aristocratic observers, and governs their oddly similar outlooks. Both were *au fond* unyieldingly pessimistic thinkers, whose ruthless destruction of current illusions frightened off their contemporaries even when they reluctantly conceded the truth of what was said. Despite the fact that Maistre was fanatically ultramontane and a supporter of established institutions, while Tolstoy, unpolitical in his earlier work, gave no evidence of radical sentiment, both were obscurely felt to be nihilistic – the humane values of the nineteenth century fell to pieces under their fingers. Both sought for some escape from their own inescapable and unanswerable scepticism in some vast, impregnable truth which would protect them from the effects of their own natural inclinations and temperament: Maistre in the Church, Tolstoy in the uncorrupted human heart and simple brotherly love – a state he could have known but seldom, an ideal before the vision of which all his descriptive skill deserts him, so that he usually writes something inartistic, wooden and naïve; painfully touching, painfully unconvincing, and conspicuously remote from his own experience.

Yet the analogy must not be overstressed: it is true that both

Maistre and Tolstoy attach the greatest possible importance to war and conflict, but Maistre, like Proudhon after him,[1] glorifies war, and declares it to be mysterious and divine, while Tolstoy detests it and regards it as in principle explicable if only we knew enough of the many minute causes – the celebrated 'differential' of history. Maistre believed in authority because it was an irrational force, he believed in the need to submit, in the inevitability of crime and the supreme importance of inquisitions and punishment. He regarded the executioner as the cornerstone of society, and it was not for nothing that Stendhal called him *l'ami du bourreau* and Lamennais said of him that there were only two realities for him – crime and punishment – 'his works are all as though written on the scaffold'.[2] Maistre's vision of the world is one of savage creatures tearing each other limb from limb, killing for the sake of killing, with violence and blood, which he sees as the normal condition of all animate life. Tolstoy is far from such horror, crime and sadism;[3] and he is not, *pace* Albert Sorel and Vogüé, in any sense a mystic: he has no fear of questioning anything, and believes that some simple answer must exist – if only we did not insist on tormenting ourselves with searching for it in strange and remote places, when it lies all the time at our feet.

[1] Tolstoy visited Proudhon in Brussels in 1861, the year in which the latter published a work which was called *La Guerre et la paix*, translated into Russian three years later. On the basis of this fact Eikhenbaum tries to deduce the influence of Proudhon upon Tolstoy's novel. Proudhon follows Maistre in regarding the origins of wars as a dark and sacred mystery; and there is much confused irrationalism, puritanism, love of paradox, and general Rousseauism in all his work. But these qualities are widespread in radical French thought, and it is difficult to find anything specifically Proudhonist in Tolstoy's *War and Peace*, besides the title. The extent of Proudhon's general influence on all kinds of Russian intellectuals during this period was, of course, very large; it would thus be just as easy, indeed easier, to construct a case for regarding Dostoevsky – or Maxim Gorky – as a *proudhonisant* as to look on Tolstoy as one; yet this would be no more than an idle exercise in critical ingenuity; for the resemblances are vague and general, while the differences are deeper, more numerous and more specific.

[2] Letter of 8 October 1834 to the Comtesse de Senfft: Félicité de Lamennais, *Correspondance générale*, ed. Louis le Guillou (Paris, 1971–81), vol. 6, letter 2338, p. 307.

[3] Yet Tolstoy, too, says that millions of men kill each other, knowing that it is 'physically and morally evil', because it is 'necessary'; because 'in doing so men fulfilled an elemental, zoological law': op. cit. (p. 459 above, note 1), col. 526. This is pure Maistre, and very remote from Stendhal or Rousseau.

Maistre supported the principle of hierarchy and believed in a self-sacrificing aristocracy, heroism, obedience, and the most rigid control of the masses by their social and theological superiors. Accordingly he advocated that education in Russia be placed in the hands of the Jesuits; they would at least inculcate into the barbarous Scythians the Latin language, which was the sacred tongue of humanity if only because it embodied the prejudices and superstitions of previous ages – beliefs which had stood the test of history and experience – alone able to form a wall strong enough to keep out the terrible acids of atheism, liberalism and freedom of thought. Above all he regarded natural science and secular literature as dangerous commodities in the hands of those not completely indoctrinated against them, a heady wine which would dangerously excite, and in the end destroy, any society not used to it.

Tolstoy all his life fought against open obscurantism and artificial repression of the desire for knowledge; his harshest words were directed against those Russian statesmen and publicists in the last quarter of the nineteenth century – Pobedonostsev and his friends and minions – who practised precisely these maxims of the great Catholic reactionary. The author of *War and Peace* plainly hated the Jesuits, and particularly detested their success in converting Russian ladies of fashion during Alexander's reign – the final events in the life of Pierre's worthless wife, Hélène, might almost have been founded upon Maistre's activities as a missionary to the aristocracy of St Petersburg: indeed, there is every reason to think that the Jesuits were expelled from Russia, and Maistre himself was virtually recalled when his interference was deemed too overt and too successful by the Emperor himself.

Nothing, therefore, would have shocked and irritated Tolstoy so much as to be told that he had a great deal in common with this apostle of darkness, this defender of ignorance and serfdom. Nevertheless, of all writers on social questions, Maistre's tone most nearly resembles that of Tolstoy. Both preserve the same sardonic, almost cynical, disbelief in the improvement of society by rational means, by the enactment of good laws or the propagation of scientific knowledge. Both speak with the same angry irony of every fashionable explanation, every social nostrum, particularly of the ordering and planning of society in accordance with some man-made formula. In Maistre openly, and in Tolstoy less obviously, there is a deeply sceptical attitude towards all experts and all techniques, all high-minded professions of secular faith and efforts at social improvement by well-meaning but, alas, idealistic persons; there is the same distaste for anyone who deals in ideas, who believes in abstract principles: and both are deeply affected by Voltaire's temper, and bitterly reject his views. Both ultimately appeal to some elemental source concealed in the souls of men, Maistre even while denouncing Rousseau as a false prophet, Tolstoy with his more ambiguous attitude towards him. Both above all reject the concept of individual political liberty: of civil rights guaranteed by some impersonal system of justice. Maistre, because he regarded any desire for personal freedom – whether political or economic or social or cultural or religious – as wilful indiscipline and stupid insubordination, and supported tradition in its most darkly irrational and repressive forms, because it alone provided the energy which gave life, continuity and safe anchorage to social institutions; Tolstoy rejected political reform because he believed that ultimate regeneration could come only from within, and that the inner life was lived truly only in the untouched depths of the mass of the people.

VI

But there is a larger and more important parallel between Tolstoy's interpretation of history and Maistre's ideas, and it raises issues of fundamental principle concerning knowledge of the past. One of the most striking elements common to the thought of these dissimilar, and indeed antagonistic, *penseurs* is their preoccupation with the 'inexorable' character – the 'march' – of events. Both Tolstoy and Maistre think of what occurs as a thick, opaque, inextricably complex web of events, objects, characteristics, con-nected and divided by literally innumerable unidentifiable links – and gaps and sudden discontinuities too, visible and invisible. It is a view of reality which makes all clear, logical and scientific con-structions – the well-defined, symmetrical patterns of human reason – seem smooth, thin, empty, 'abstract' and totally ineffective as means either of description or of analysis of anything that lives, or has ever lived. Maistre attributes this to the incurable impotence of human powers of observation and of reasoning, at least when they function without the aid of the superhuman sources of knowledge – faith, revelation, tradition, above all the mystical vision of the great saints and doctors of the Church, their unanalysable, special sense of reality to which natural science, free criticism and the secular spirit are fatal. The wisest of the Greeks, many among the great Romans, and after them the dominant ecclesiastics and statesmen of the Middle Ages, Maistre tells us, possessed this insight; from it flowed their power, their dignity and their success. The natural enemies of this spirit are cleverness and specialisation: hence the contempt so rightly shown for, in the Roman world, experts and technicians – the *Graeculus esuriens* – the remote but unmistakable ancestors of the sharp, wizened figures of the modern Alexandrian Age – the terrible Eighteenth Century – all the *écrivasserie et avocasserie*, the miserable crew of scribblers and attorneys, with the predatory, sordid, grinning figure of Voltaire at their head, destructive and self-destructive, because blind and deaf to the true word of God. Only the Church understands the 'inner' rhythms, the 'deeper' currents of the world, the silent march of things; *non in commotione Dominus*; not in noisy democratic manifestos nor in the rattle of constitutional formulae, nor in revolutionary violence, but in the eternal natural order, governed by 'natural' law. Only those who understand it know what can and what cannot be achieved, what should and what should not be attempted. They and they alone hold the key to secular success as well as to spiritual salvation. Omniscience belongs only to God. But only by immersing ourselves in his word, his theological or metaphysical principles, embodied at their lowest in instincts and ancient superstitions which are but primitive ways, tested by time, of divining and obeying his laws – whereas reasoning is an effort to substitute one's own arbitrary rules – dare we hope for wisdom. Practical wisdom is to a large degree knowledge of the inevitable: of what, given our world order, could not but happen; and, conversely, of how things cannot be, or could not have been, done; of why some schemes must, cannot help but, end in failure, although for this no demonstrative or scientific reason can be given. The rare capacity for seeing this we rightly call a 'sense of reality' – it is a sense of what fits with what, of what cannot exist with what; and it goes by many names: insight, wisdom, practical genius, a sense of the past, an understanding of life and of human character.

Tolstoy's view is not very different; save that he gives as the reason for the folly of our exaggerated claims to understand or determine events not foolish or blasphemous efforts to do without special, that is, supernatural, knowledge, but our ignorance of too many among the vast number of interrelations – the minute determining causes of events. If we began to know the causal network in its infinite variety, we should cease to praise and blame, boast and regret, or look on human beings as heroes or villains, but should submit with due humility to unavoidable necessity. Yet to say no more than this is to give a travesty of his beliefs. It is indeed Tolstoy's explicit doctrine in *War and Peace* that all truth is in science – in the knowledge of material causes – and that we consequently render ourselves ridiculous by arriving at conclusions on too little evidence, comparing in this regard unfavourably with peasants or savages, who, being not so very much more ignorant, at least make more modest claims; but this is not the view of the world that, in fact, underlies either *War and Peace* or *Anna Karenina* or any other work which belongs to this period of Tolstoy's life. Kutuzov is wise and not merely clever as, for example, the time-serving Drubetskoy or Bilibin are clever, and he is not a victim to abstract heroes or dogma as the German military experts are; he is unlike them, and is wiser than they – but this is so not because he knows more facts than they and has at his fingertips a greater number of the 'minute causes' of events than his advisers or his adversaries – than Pfuel or Paulucci or Berthier or the King of Naples. Karataev brings light to Pierre, whereas the Freemasons did not, but this is so not because he happens to have scientific information superior to that possessed by the Moscow lodges; Levin goes through an experience during his work in the fields, and Prince Andrey while lying wounded on the battlefield of Austerlitz, but in neither case has there been a discovery of fresh facts or of new laws in any ordinary sense. On the contrary, the greater one's accumulation of facts, the more futile one's activity, the more hopeless one's failure – as shown by the group of reformers who surround Alexander. They and men like them are only saved from Faustian despair by stupidity (like the Germans and the military experts and experts generally) or by vanity (like Napoleon) or by frivolity (like Oblonsky) or by heartlessness (like Karenin).

What is it that Pierre, Prince Andrey, Levin discover? And what are they searching for, and what is the centre and climax of the spiritual crisis resolved by the experience that transforms their lives? Not the chastening realisation of how little of the totality of facts and laws known to Laplace's omniscient observer they – Pierre, Levin and the rest – can claim to have discovered; not a simple admission of Socratic ignorance. Still less does it consist in what is almost at the opposite pole – in a new, a more precise awareness of the 'iron laws' that govern our lives, in a vision of nature as a machine or a factory, in the cosmology of the great materialists, Diderot or La Mettrie or Cabanis, or of the mid-nineteenth century scientific writers idolised by the 'nihilist' Bazarov in Turgenev's *Fathers and Children*; nor yet in some transcendent sense of the inexpressible oneness of life to which poets, mystics and metaphysicians have in all ages testified. Nevertheless, something *is* perceived; there is a vision, or at least a glimpse, a moment of revelation which in some sense explains and reconciles, a theodicy, a justification of what exists and happens, as well as its elucidation. What does it consist in? Tolstoy does not tell us in so many words: for when (in his later, explicitly didactic works) he sets out to do so, his doctrine is no longer the same. Yet no reader of *War and Peace* can be wholly unaware of what he is being told. And that not only in the Kutuzov or Karataev scenes, or other quasi-theological or quasi-metaphysical passages – but even more, for example, in the narrative, non-philosophical section of the epilogue, in which Pierre, Natasha, Nikolay Rostov, Princess Marie are shown anchored in their new solid, sober lives with their established day-to-day routine. We are here plainly intended to see that these 'heroes' of the novel – the 'good' people – have now, after the storms and agonies of ten years and more, achieved a kind of peace, based on some degree of understanding: understanding of what? Of the need to submit: to what? Not simply to the will of God (not at any rate during the writing of the great novels, in the 1860s or 1870s), nor to the 'iron laws' of the sciences; but to the permanent relationships of things,[1] and the universal texture of human life, wherein alone truth and justice are to be found by a kind of 'natural' – somewhat Aristotelian – knowledge.

To do this is, above all, to grasp what human will and human reason can do, and what they cannot. How can this be known? Not by a specific enquiry and discovery, but by an awareness, not necessarily explicit or conscious, of certain general characteristics of human life and experience. And the most important and most pervasive of these is the crucial line that divides the 'surface' from

[1] Almost in the sense in which this phrase is used by Montesquieu in the opening sentence of *De l'esprit des lois*.

the 'depths' – on the one hand the world of perceptible, describable, analysable data, both physical and psychological, both 'external' and 'inner', both public and private, with which the sciences can deal, although they have in some regions – those outside physics – made so little progress; and, on the other hand, the order which, as it were, 'contains' and determines the structure of experience, the framework in which it – that is, we and all that we experience – must be conceived as being set, that which enters into our habits of thought, action, feeling, our emotions, hopes, wishes, our ways of talking, believing, reacting, being. We – sentient creatures – are in part living in a world the constituents of which we can discover, classify and act upon by rational, scientific, deliberately planned methods; but in part (Tolstoy and Maistre, and many thinkers with them, say much the larger part) we are immersed and submerged in a medium that, precisely to the degree to which we inevitably take it for granted as part of ourselves, we do not and cannot observe as if from the outside; cannot identify, measure and seek to manipulate; cannot even be wholly aware of, inasmuch as it enters too intimately into all our experience, is itself too closely interwoven with all that we are and do to be lifted out of the flow (it *is* the flow) and observed with scientific detachment, as an object. It – the medium in which we are – determines our most permanent categories, our standards of truth and falsehood, of reality and appearance, of the good and the bad, of the central and the peripheral, of the subjective and the objective, of the beautiful and the ugly, of movement and rest, of past, present and future, of one and many; hence neither these, nor any other explicitly conceived categories or concepts, can be applied to it – for it is itself but a vague name for the totality that includes these categories, these concepts, the ultimate framework, the basic presuppositions wherewith we function.

Nevertheless, though we cannot analyse the medium without some (impossible) vantage-point outside it (for there is no 'outside'), yet some human beings are better aware – although they cannot describe it – of the texture and direction of these 'submerged' portions of their own and everyone else's lives; better aware of this than others, who either ignore the existence of the all-pervasive medium (the 'flow of life'), and are rightly called superficial; or else try to apply to it instruments – scientific, metaphysical – adapted solely to objects above the surface, the relatively conscious, manipulable portion of our experience, and so achieve absurdities in their theories and humiliating failures in practice. Wisdom is ability to allow for the (at least by us) unalterable medium in which we act – as we allow for the pervasiveness, say, of time or space, which characterises all our experience; and to discount, less or more consciously, the 'inevitable trends', the 'imponderables', the 'way things are going'. It is not scientific knowledge, but a special sensitiveness to the contours of the circumstances in which we happen to be placed; it is a capacity for living without falling foul of some permanent condition or factor which cannot be either altered, or even fully described or calculated; an ability to be guided by rules of thumb – the 'immemorial wisdom' said to reside in peasants and other 'simple folk' – where rules of science do not, in principle, apply. This inexpressible sense of cosmic orientation is the 'sense of reality', the 'knowledge' of how to live.

Sometimes Tolstoy does speak as if science could in principle, if not in practice, penetrate and conquer everything; and if it did, then we should know the causes of all there is, and know we were not free, but wholly determined – which is all that the wisest can ever know. So, too, Maistre talks as if the schoolmen knew more than we, through their superior techniques: but what they knew was still, in some sense, 'the facts' – the subject-matter of the sciences. St Thomas knew incomparably more than Newton, and with more precision and more certainty, but what he knew was of the same kind. But despite this lip-service to the truth-finding capacities of natural science or theology, these avowals remain purely formal: and a very different belief finds expression in the positive doctrines of both Maistre and Tolstoy. Aquinas is praised by Maistre not for being a better mathematician than d'Alembert or Monge; Kutuzov's virtue does not, according to Tolstoy, consist in his being a better, more scientific theorist of war than Pfuel or Paulucci. These great men are wiser, not more knowledgeable; it is not their deductive or inductive reasoning that makes them masters; their vision is more 'profound', they see something the others fail to see; they see the way the world goes, what goes with what, and what never will be brought together; they see what can be and what cannot; how men live and to what ends, what they do and suffer, and how and why they act, and should act, thus and not otherwise.

This 'seeing' purveys, in a sense, no fresh information about the universe; it is an awareness of the interplay of the imponderable and the ponderable, of the 'shape' of things in general or of a specific situation, or of a particular character, which is precisely what cannot be deduced from, or even formulated in terms of, the laws of nature demanded by scientific determinism. Whatever can be subsumed under such laws scientists can and do deal with; that needs no 'wisdom'; and to deny science its rights because of the existence of this superior 'wisdom' is a wanton invasion of scientific territory, and a confusion of categories. Tolstoy, at least, does not go to the length of denying the efficacy of physics in its own sphere; but he thinks this sphere trivial in comparison with what is permanently out of the reach of science – the social, moral, political, spiritual worlds, which cannot be sorted out and described and predicted by any science, because the proportion in them of 'submerged', uninspectable life is too high. The insight that reveals the nature and structure of these worlds is not a mere makeshift substitute, an empirical *pis aller* to which recourse is had only so long as the relevant scientific techniques are insufficiently refined; its business is altogether different: it does what no science can claim to do; it distinguishes the real from the sham, the worthwhile from the worthless, that which can be done or borne from what cannot be; and does so without giving rational grounds for its pronouncements, if only because 'rational' and 'irrational' are terms that themselves acquire their meanings and uses in relation to – by 'growing out of' – it, and not vice versa. For what are the data of such understanding if not the ultimate soil, the framework, the atmosphere, the context, the medium (to use whatever metaphor is most expressive) in which all our thoughts and acts are felt, valued, judged, in the inevitable ways that they are?

It is the ever-present sense of this framework – of this movement of events, or changing pattern of characteristics – as something 'inexorable', universal, pervasive, not alterable by us, not in our power (in the sense of 'power' in which the progress of scientific knowledge has given us power over nature), that is at the root of Tolstoy's determinism, and of his realism, his pessimism, and his (and Maistre's) contempt for the faith placed in reason alike by science and by worldly common sense. It is 'there' – the framework, the foundation of everything – and the wise man alone has a sense of it; Pierre gropes for it; Kutuzov feels it in his bones; Karataev is at one with it. All Tolstoy's heroes attain to at least intermittent glimpses of it – and this it is that makes all the conventional explanations, the scientific, the historical, those of unreflective 'good sense', seem so hollow and, at their most pretentious, so shamefully false. Tolstoy himself, too, knows that the truth is there, and not 'here' – not in the regions susceptible to observation, discrimination, constructive imagination, not in the power of microscopic perception and analysis of which he is so much the greatest master of our time; but he has not, himself, seen it face to face; for he has not, do what he might, a vision of the whole; he is not, he is remote from being, a hedgehog; and what he sees is not the one, but always, with an ever-growing minuteness, in all its teeming individuality, with an obsessive, inescapable, incorruptible, all-penetrating lucidity which maddens him, the many.

## VII

We are part of a larger scheme of things than we can understand. We cannot describe it in the way in which external objects or the characters of other people can be described, by isolating them somewhat from the historical 'flow' in which they have their being, and from the 'submerged', unfathomed portions of themselves to which professional historians have, according to Tolstoy, paid so little heed; for we ourselves live in this whole and by it, and are wise only in the measure to which we make our peace with it. For until and unless we do so (only after much bitter suffering, if we are to trust Aeschylus and the Book of Job), we shall protest and suffer in vain, and make sorry fools of ourselves (as Napoleon did) into the bargain. This sense of the circumambient stream, defiance of whose nature through stupidity or overweening egotism will make our acts and thoughts self-defeating, is the vision of the unity of experience, the sense of history, the true knowledge of reality, the belief in the incommunicable wisdom of the sage (or the saint) which, *mutatis mutandis*, is common to Tolstoy and Maistre. Their realism is of a similar sort: the natural enemy of romanticism, sentimentalism and 'historicism' as much as of aggressive 'scientism'. Their purpose is not to distinguish the little that is known or done from the limitless ocean of what, in principle, could or one day will be known or done, whether by advance in the knowledge of the natural sciences or of metaphysics or of the historical sciences, or by a return to the past, or by some other method; what they seek to establish are the eternal frontiers of our knowledge and power, to demarcate them from what cannot in principle ever be known or altered by men. According to Maistre our destiny lies in original sin, in the fact that we are human – finite, fallible, vicious, vain – and that all our empirical knowledge (as opposed to the teachings of the Church) is infected by error and monomania. According to Tolstoy all our knowledge is necessarily empirical – there is no other – but it will never conduct us to true understanding, only to an accumulation of arbitrarily abstracted bits and pieces of information; yet that seems to him (as much as to any metaphysician of the Idealist school which he despised) worthless beside, and unintelligible save in so far as it derives from and points to, this inexpressible but very palpable kind of superior understanding which alone is worth pursuing.

Sometimes Tolstoy comes near to saying what it is: the more we know, he tells us, about a given human action, the more inevitable, determined it seems to us to be. Why? Because the more we know about all the relevant conditions and antecedents, the more difficult we find it to think away various circumstances, and conjecture what might have occurred without them; and as we go on removing in our imagination what we know to be true, fact by fact, this becomes not merely difficult but impossible. Tolstoy's meaning is not obscure. We are what we are, and live in a given situation which has the characteristics – physical, psychological, social – that it has; what we think, feel, do is conditioned by it, including our capacity for conceiving possible alternatives, whether in the present or future or past. Our imagination and ability to calculate, our power of conceiving, let us say, what might have been, if the past had, in this or that particular, been otherwise, soon reaches its natural limits, limits created both by the weakness of our capacity for calculating alternatives – 'might have beens' – and (we may add by a logical extension of Tolstoy's argument) even more by the fact that our thoughts, the terms in which they occur, the symbols themselves, are what they are, are themselves determined by the actual structure of our world. Our images and powers of conception are limited by the fact that our world possesses certain characteristics and not others: a world too different is (empirically) not conceivable at all; some minds are more imaginative than others, but all stop somewhere.

The world is a system and a network: to conceive of men as 'free' is to think of them as capable of having, at some past juncture, acted in some fashion other than that in which they did act; it is to think of what consequences would have come of such unfulfilled possibilities and in what respects the world would have been different, as a result, from the world as it now is. It is difficult enough to do this in the case of artificial, purely deductive systems, as for example in chess, where the permutations are finite in number, and clear in type – having been arranged so by us, artificially – so that the combinations are calculable. But if you apply this method to the vague, rich texture of the real world, and try to work out the implications of this or that unrealised plan or unperformed action – the effect of it on the totality of later events – basing yourself on such knowledge of causal laws and probabilities as you have, you will find that the greater the number of 'minute' causes you discriminate, the more appalling becomes the task of 'deducing' any consequence of the 'unhinging' of each of these, one by one; for each of the consequences affects the whole of the rest of the uncountable totality of events and things, which unlike chess is not defined in terms of a finite, arbitrarily chosen set of concepts and rules. And if, whether in real life or even in chess, you begin to tamper with basic notions – continuity of space, divisibility of time and the like – you will soon reach a stage in which the symbols fail to function, your thoughts become confused and paralysed. Consequently the fuller our knowledge of facts and of their connections the more difficult to conceive alternatives; the clearer and more exact the terms – or categories – in which we conceive and describe the world, the more fixed our world structure, the less 'free' acts seem. To know these limits, both of imagination and, ultimately, of thought itself, is to come face to face with the 'inexorable' unifying pattern of the world; to realise our identity with it, to submit to it, is to find truth and peace. This is not mere oriental fatalism, nor the mechanistic determinism of the celebrated German materialists of the day, Büchner and Vogt, or Moleschott, admired so deeply by the revolutionary 'nihilists' of Tolstoy's generation in Russia; nor is it a yearning for mystical illumination or integration. It is scrupulously empirical, rational, tough-minded and realistic. But its emotional cause is a passionate desire for a monistic vision of life on the part of a fox bitterly intent upon seeing in the manner of a hedgehog.

This is remarkably close to Maistre's dogmatic affirmations: we must achieve an attitude of assent to the demands of history which are the voice of God speaking through his servants and his divine institutions, not made by human hands and not destructible by them. We must attune ourselves to the true word of God, the inner 'go' of things; but what it is in concrete cases, how we are to conduct our private lives or public policies – of that we are told little by either critic of optimistic liberalism. Nor can we expect to be told. For the positive vision escapes them. Tolstoy's language – and Maistre's no less – is adapted to the opposite activity. It is in analysing, identifying sharply, marking differences, isolating concrete examples, piercing to the heart of each individual entity *per se* that Tolstoy rises to the full height of his genius; and similarly Maistre achieves his brilliant effects by pinning down and offering for public pillory – by a *montage sur l'épingle* – the absurdities committed by his opponents. They are acute observers of the varieties of experience: every attempt to represent these falsely, or to offer delusive explanations of them, they detect immediately and deride savagely. Yet they both know that the full truth, the ultimate basis of the correlation of all the ingredients of the universe with one another, the context in which alone anything that they, or anyone else, can say can ever be true or false, trivial or important – that resides in a synoptic vision which, because they do not possess it, they cannot express.

What is it that Pierre has learnt, of which Princess Marie's marriage is an acceptance, that Prince Andrey all his life pursued with such agony? Like Augustine, Tolstoy can say only what it is not. His genius is devastatingly destructive. He can only attempt to point towards his goal by exposing the false signposts to it; to isolate the truth by annihilating that which it is not – namely all that can be said in the clear, analytical language that corresponds to the all too clear, but necessarily limited, vision of the foxes. Like Moses, he must halt at the borders of the Promised Land; without it his journey is meaningless; but he cannot enter it; yet he knows that it exists, and can tell us, as no one else has ever told us, all that it is not – above all, not anything that art, or science or civilisation or rational criticism, can achieve.

So too Joseph de Maistre. He is the Voltaire of reaction. Every new doctrine since the ages of faith is torn to shreds with ferocious skill and malice. The pretenders are exposed and struck down one by one; the armoury of weapons against liberal and humanitarian doctrines is the most effective ever assembled. But the throne remains vacant, the positive doctrine is too unconvincing. Maistre sighs for the Dark Ages, but no sooner are plans for the undoing of the French Revolution – a return to the status quo ante – suggested by his fellow émigrés than he denounces them as childish nonsense

– an attempt to behave as if what has occurred and changed us all irretrievably had never been. To try to reverse the Revolution, he wrote, was as if one had been invited to drain the Lake of Geneva by bottling its waters in a wine-cellar.

There is no kinship between him and those who really did believe in the possibility of some kind of return – neo-medievalists from Wackenroder and Görres and Cobbett to G. K. Chesterton, and Slavophils and Distributists and Pre-Raphaelites and other nostalgic romantics; for he believed, as Tolstoy also did, in the exact opposite: in the 'inexorable' power of the present moment: in our inability to do away with the sum of conditions which cumulatively determine our basic categories, an order which we can never fully describe or, otherwise than by some immediate awareness of it, come to know.

The quarrel between these rival types of knowledge – that which results from methodical enquiry, and the more impalpable kind that consists in the 'sense of reality', in 'wisdom' – is very old. And the claims of both have generally been recognised to have some validity: the bitterest clashes have been concerned with the precise line which marks the frontier between their territories. Those who made large claims for non-scientific knowledge have been accused by their adversaries of irrationalism and obscurantism, of the deliberate rejection, in favour of the emotions or blind prejudice, of reliable public standards of ascertainable truth; and have, in their turn, charged their opponents, the ambitious champions of science, with making absurd claims, promising the impossible, issuing false prospectuses, undertaking to explain history or the arts or the states of the individual soul (and to change them too) when quite plainly they do not begin to understand what they are; when the results of their labours, even when they are not nugatory, tend to take unpredicted, often catastrophic, directions – and all this because they will not, being vain and headstrong, admit that too many factors in too many situations are always unknown, and not discoverable by the methods of natural science. Better, surely, not to pretend to calculate the incalculable, not to pretend that there is an Archimedean point outside the world whence everything is measurable and alterable; better to use in each context the methods that seem to fit it best, that give the (pragmatically) best results; to resist the temptations of Procrustes; above all to distinguish what is isolable, classifiable and capable of objective study and sometimes

of precise measurement and manipulation, from the most permanent, ubiquitous, inescapable, intimately present features of our
world, which, if anything, are over-familiar, so that their 'inexorable' pressure, being too much with us, is scarcely felt, hardly
noticed, and cannot conceivably be observed in perspective, be an
object of study.

This is the distinction that permeates the thought of Pascal and
Blake, Rousseau and Schelling, Goethe and Coleridge, Chateaubriand and Carlyle; of all those who speak of the reasons of the
heart, or of men's moral or spiritual nature, of sublimity and depth,
of the 'profounder' insight of poets and prophets, of special kinds
of understanding, of inwardly comprehending, or being at one
with, the world. To these latter thinkers both Tolstoy and Maistre
belong. Tolstoy blames everything on our ignorance of empirical
causes, and Maistre on the abandonment of Thomist logic or the
theology of the Catholic Church. But these avowed professions are
belied by the tone and content of what in fact the two great critics
say. Both stress, over and over again, the contrast between the
'inner' and the 'outer', the 'surface' which alone is lighted by the
rays of science and of reason, and the 'depths' – 'the real life lived
by men'. For Maistre, as later for Barrès, true knowledge – wisdom
– lies in an understanding of, and communion with, *la terre et les
morts* (what has this to do with Thomist logic?) – the great
unalterable movement created by the links between the dead and
the living and the yet unborn and the land on which they live; and
it is this, perhaps, or something akin to it, that, in their respective
fashions, Burke and Taine, and their many imitators, have attempted to convey.

As for Tolstoy, to him such mystical conservatism was peculiarly detestable, since it seemed to him to evade the central
question by merely restating it, concealed in a cloud of pompous
rhetoric, as the answer. Yet he, too, in the end, presents us with the
vision, dimly discerned by Kutuzov and by Pierre, of Russia in her
vastness, and what she could and what she could not do or suffer,
and how and when – all of which Napoleon and his advisers (who
knew a great deal but not of what was relevant to the issue) did not
perceive; and so (although their knowledge of history and science
and minute causes was perhaps greater than Kutuzov's or Pierre's)
were led duly to their doom. Maistre's paeans to the superior
science of the great Christian soldiers of the past and Tolstoy's
lamentations about our scientific ignorance should not mislead

anyone as to the nature of what they are in fact defending: awareness of the 'deep currents', the *raisons de coeur*, which they did not indeed themselves know by direct experience; but beside which, they were convinced, the devices of science were but a snare and a delusion.

Despite their deep dissimilarity and indeed violent opposition to one another, Tolstoy's sceptical realism and Maistre's dogmatic authoritarianism are blood brothers. For both spring from an agonised belief in a single, serene vision, in which all problems are resolved, all doubts stilled, peace and understanding finally achieved. Deprived of this vision, they devoted all their formidable resources, from their very different, and indeed often incompatible, positions, to the elimination of all possible adversaries and critics of it. The faiths for whose mere abstract possibility they fought were not, indeed, identical. It is the predicament in which they found themselves and that caused them to dedicate their strength to the lifelong task of destruction, it is their common enemies and the strong likeness between their temperaments that made them odd but unmistakable allies in a war which they were both conscious of fighting until their dying day.

VIII

Opposed as Tolstoy and Maistre were – one the apostle of the gospel that all men are brothers, the other the cold defender of the claims of violence, blind sacrifice, and eternal suffering – they were united by inability to escape from the same tragic paradox: they were both by nature sharp-eyed foxes, inescapably aware of sheer, *de facto* differences which divide and forces which disrupt the human world, observers utterly incapable of being deceived by the many subtle devices, the unifying systems and faiths and sciences, by which the superficial or the desperate sought to conceal the chaos from themselves and from one another. Both looked for a harmonious universe, but everywhere found war and disorder, which no attempt to cheat, however heavily disguised, could even begin to hide; and so, in a condition of final despair, offered to throw away the terrible weapons of criticism, with which both, but particularly Tolstoy, were over-generously endowed, in favour of the single great vision, something too indivisibly simple and remote from normal intellectual processes to be assailable by the instruments of reason, and therefore, perhaps, offering a path to peace and salvation.

Maistre began as a moderate liberal and ended by pulverising the new nineteenth-century world from the solitary citadel of his own variety of ultramontane Catholicism. Tolstoy began with a view of human life and history which contradicted all his knowledge, all his gifts, all his inclinations, and which, in consequence, he could scarcely be said to have embraced in the sense of practising it, either as a writer or as a man. From this, in his old age, he passed into a form of life in which he tried to resolve the glaring contradiction between what he believed about men and events, and what he thought he believed, or ought to believe, by behaving, in the end, as if factual questions of this kind were not the fundamental issues at all, only the trivial preoccupations of an idle, ill-conducted life, while the real questions were quite different. But it was of no use: the Muse cannot be cheated. Tolstoy was the least superficial of men: he could not swim with the tide without being drawn irresistibly beneath the surface to investigate the darker depths below; and he could not avoid seeing what he saw and doubting even that; he could close his eyes but not forget that he was doing so; his appalling, destructive sense of what was false frustrated this final effort at self-deception as it did all the earlier ones; and he died in agony, oppressed by the burden of his intellectual infallibility and his sense of perpetual moral error, the greatest of those who can neither reconcile, nor leave unreconciled, the conflict of what there is with what there ought to be.

Tolstoy's sense of reality was until the end too devastating to be compatible with any moral ideal which he was able to construct out of the fragments into which his intellect shivered the world, and he dedicated all of his vast strength of mind and will to the lifelong denial of this fact. At once insanely proud and filled with self-hatred, omniscient and doubting everything, cold and violently passionate, contemptuous and self-abasing, tormented and detached, surrounded by an adoring family, by devoted followers, by the admiration of the entire civilised world, and yet almost wholly isolated, he is the most tragic of the great writers, a desperate old man, beyond human aid, wandering self-blinded at Colonus.

# HERZEN AND HIS MEMOIRS

Alexander Herzen, like Diderot, was an amateur of genius whose opinions and activities changed the direction of social thought in his country. Like Diderot, too, he was a brilliant and irrepressible talker: he talked equally well in Russian and in French to his intimate friends and in the Moscow *salons* – always in an overwhelming flow of ideas and images; the waste, from the point of view of posterity (just as with Diderot), is probably immense: he had no Boswell and no Eckermann to record his conversation, nor was he a man who would have suffered such a relationship. His prose is essentially a form of talk, with the vices and virtues of talk: eloquent, spontaneous, liable to the heightened tones and exaggerations of the born story-teller, unable to resist long digressions which themselves carry him into a network of intersecting tributaries of memory or speculation, but always returning to the main stream of the story or the argument; but, above all, his prose has the vitality of spoken words – it appears to owe nothing to the carefully composed formal sentences of the French *philosophes* whom he admired or to the terrible philosophical style of the Germans from whom he learnt; we hear his voice almost too much – in the essays, the pamphlets, the autobiography, as much as in the letters and scraps of notes to his friends.

Civilised, imaginative, self-critical, Herzen was a marvellously gifted social observer; the record of what he saw is unique even in the articulate nineteenth century. He had an acute, easily stirred and ironical mind, a fiery and poetical temperament, and a capacity for vivid, often lyrical, writing – qualities that combined and reinforced each other in the succession of sharp vignettes of men, events, ideas, personal relationships, political situations and descriptions of entire forms of life in which his writings abound. He was a man of extreme refinement and sensibility, great intellectual energy and biting wit, easily irritated *amour propre*, and

a taste for polemical writing; he was addicted to analysis, investigation, exposure; he saw himself as an expert 'unmasker' of appearances and conventions, and dramatised himself as a devastating
discoverer of their social and moral core. Tolstoy, who had little
sympathy with Herzen's opinions, and was not given to excessive
praise of his contemporaries among men of letters, especially when
they belonged to his own class and country, said towards the end
of his life that he had never met anyone with 'so rare a combination
of scintillating depths and brilliance'.[1] These gifts make a good
many of Herzen's essays, political articles, day-to-day journalism,
casual notes and reviews, and especially letters written to intimates
or to political correspondents, irresistibly readable even today,
when the issues with which they were concerned are for the most
part dead and of interest mainly to historians.

Although much has been written about Herzen – and not only
in Russian – the task of his biographers has not been made easier
by the fact that he left an incomparable memorial to himself in his
own greatest work – *My Past and Thoughts* – a literary masterpiece
worthy to be placed by the side of the novels of his contemporaries
and countrymen, Tolstoy, Turgenev, Dostoevsky. Nor were they
altogether unaware of this. Turgenev, an intimate and lifelong
friend (the fluctuations of their personal relationship were important in the life of both; this complex and interesting story has never
been adequately told), admired him as a writer as well as a
revolutionary journalist. The celebrated critic Vissarion Belinsky
discovered, described and acclaimed his extraordinary literary gift
when they were both young and relatively unknown. Even the
angry and suspicious Dostoevsky excepted him from the virulent
hatred with which he regarded the pro-Western Russian revolutionaries, recognised the poetry of his writing, and remained well-
disposed towards him until the end of his life. As for Tolstoy, he
delighted both in his society and his writings: half a century after
their first meeting in London he still remembered the scene
vividly.[2]

---

[1] Reported by P. A. Sergeenko in his book on Tolstoy, *Tolstoy i ego
sovremenniki* (Moscow, 1911), p. 13.

[2] Sergeenko (ibid., pp. 13–14) says that Tolstoy told him in 1908 that he had a
very clear recollection of his visit to Herzen in his London house in March 1861.
'Lev Nikolaevich remembered him as a not very large, plump little man, who
generated electric energy. "Lively, responsive, intelligent, interesting," Lev

It is strange that this remarkable writer, in his lifetime a celebrated European figure, the admired friend of Michelet, Mazzini, Garibaldi and Victor Hugo, long canonised in his own country not only as a revolutionary but as one of its greatest men of letters, is, even today, not much more than a name in the West. The enjoyment to be obtained from reading his prose – for the most part still untranslated – makes this a strange and gratuitous loss.

Alexander Herzen was born in Moscow on 6 April 1812, some months before the great fire that destroyed the city during Napoleon's occupation after the battle of Borodino. His father, Ivan Alexandrovich Yakovlev, came of an ancient family distantly related to the Romanov dynasty. Like other rich and well-born members of the Russian gentry, he had spent some years abroad, and, during one of his journeys, met, and took back to Moscow with him, the daughter of a minor Württemberg official, Luiza Haag, a gentle, submissive, somewhat colourless girl, a good deal younger than himself. For some reason, perhaps owing to the disparity in their social positions, he never married her according to the rites of the Church. Yakovlev was a member of the Orthodox Church; she remained a Lutheran.[1] He was a proud, independent, disdainful man, and had grown increasingly morose and misanthropic. He retired before the war of 1812, and at the time of the French invasion was living in bitter and resentful idleness in his house in Moscow. During the occupation he was recognised by Marshal Mortier, whom he had known in Paris, and agreed – in return for a safe conduct enabling him to take his family out of the devastated city – to carry a message from Napoleon to the Emperor Alexander. For this indiscretion he was sent back to his estates, and only allowed to return to Moscow somewhat later.

In his large and gloomy house on the Arbat he brought up his son, Alexander, to whom he had given the surname Herzen, as if to stress the fact that he was the child of an irregular liaison, an affair

Nikolaevich explained (as usual illustrating every shade of meaning by appropriate movements of his hands), "Herzen at once began talking to me as if we had known each other for a long time. I found his personality enchanting ... I have never met a more attractive man. He stands head and shoulders above all the politicians of his own and of our time." '

[1] There is evidence, although it is not conclusive, that she was married to him according to the Lutheran rite, not recognised by the Orthodox Church.

of the heart. Luiza Haag was never accorded the full status of a wife, but the boy had every attention lavished upon him. He received the normal education of a young Russian nobleman of his time, that is to say, he was looked after by a host of nurses and serfs, and taught by private tutors, German and French, carefully chosen by his neurotic, irritable, devoted, suspicious father. Every care was taken to develop his gifts. He was a lively and imaginative child and absorbed knowledge easily and eagerly. His father loved him after his fashion: more, certainly, than his other son, also illegitimate, born ten years earlier, whom he had christened Egor (George). But he was, by the 1820s, a defeated and gloomy man, unable to communicate with his family or indeed anyone else. Shrewd, honourable, and neither unfeeling nor unjust, a 'difficult' character like old Prince Bolkonsky in Tolstoy's *War and Peace*, Ivan Yakovlev emerges from his son's recollections a self-lacerating, grim, shut-in, half-frozen human being, who terrorised his household with his whims and his sarcasm. He kept all doors and windows locked, the blinds permanently drawn, and, apart from a few old friends and his own brothers, saw virtually nobody. In later years his son described him as the product of 'the encounter of two such incompatible things as the eighteenth century and Russian life'[1] – a collision of cultures that had destroyed a good many among the more sensitive members of the Russian gentry in the reigns of Catherine II and her successors.

The boy escaped with relief from his father's oppressive and frightening company to the rooms occupied by his mother and the servants; she was kind and unassuming, crushed by her husband, frightened by her foreign surroundings, and seemed to accept her almost oriental status in the household with uncomplaining resignation. As for the servants, they were serfs from the Yakovlev estates, trained to behave obsequiously to the son and probable heir of their master. Herzen himself, in later years, attributed the deepest of all his social feelings (which his friend, the critic Belinsky, diagnosed so accurately), concern for the freedom and dignity of human individuals, to the barbarous conditions that surrounded him in childhood. He was a favourite child, and much spoiled, but the facts of his irregular birth and of his mother's

---

[1] A. I. Gertsen, *Sobranie sochinenii v tridtsati tomakh* (Moscow, 1954–66), vol. 8, p. 86. Subsequent references in this essay to Herzen's works are to this edition, hereafter called *Sobranie sochinenii*.

status were brought home to him by listening to the servants' gossip and, on at least one occasion, by overhearing a conversation about himself between his father and one of his old army comrades. The shock was, according to his own testimony, profound: it was probably one of the determining factors of his life.

He was taught Russian literature and history by a young university student, an enthusiastic follower of the new romantic movement, which, particularly in its German form, had then begun to dominate Russian intellectual life. He learned French (which his father wrote more easily than Russian) and German (which he spoke with his mother), and European, rather than Russian, history – his tutor was a French refugee who had emigrated to Russia after the French Revolution. The Frenchman did not reveal his political opinions, so Herzen tells us, until one day, when his pupil asked him why Louis XVI had been executed; to this he replied in an altered voice, 'Because he was a traitor to his country',[1] and finding the boy responsive, threw off his reserve and spoke to him openly about the liberty and equality of men. Herzen was a lonely child, at once pampered and cramped, lively and bored; he read voraciously in his father's large library, especially French books of the Enlightenment. He was fourteen when the leaders of the Decembrist conspiracy were hanged by the Emperor Nicholas I. He later declared that this event was the critical turning-point of his life; whether this was so or not, the memory of these aristocratic martyrs in the cause of Russian constitutional liberty later became a sacred symbol to him, as to many others of his class and generation, and affected him for the rest of his days. He tells us that a few years after this, he and his intimate friend Nick Ogarev, standing on the Sparrow Hills above Moscow, took a solemn 'Hannibalic' oath to avenge these fighters for the rights of man, and to dedicate their own lives to the cause for which they had died.

In due course he became a student in the University of Moscow. He was already steeped in Schiller and Goethe; he plunged into the study of German metaphysics – Kant, and particularly Schelling. And then the new French school of historians – Guizot, Augustin Thierry, and, in addition, the French Utopian socialists, Saint-Simon, Fourier, Leroux, and other social prophets smuggled into

[1] *Sobranie sochinenii*, vol. 8, p. 64: 'Parce qu'il a été traître à la patrie.'

Russia in defiance of the censorship, and became a convinced and passionate radical. He and Ogarev belonged to a group of students who read forbidden books and discussed dangerous ideas; for this he was, together with most other 'unreliable' students, duly arrested and, probably because he declined to repudiate the views imputed to him, condemned to imprisonment. His father used all his influence to get the sentence mitigated, but could not save his son from being exiled to the provincial city of Vyatka, near the borders of Asia, where he was not indeed kept in prison, but put to work in the local administration.

To his astonishment, he enjoyed this new test of his powers; he displayed administrative gifts and became a far more competent and perhaps even enthusiastic official than he was later prepared to admit, and helped to expose the corrupt and brutal governor, whom he detested and despised. In Vyatka he became involved in a passionate love-affair with a married woman, behaved badly, and suffered agonies of contrition. He read Dante, went through a religious phase, and began a long and passionate correspondence with his first cousin Natalie, who, like himself, was illegitimate, and lived as a companion in the house of a rich and despotic aunt. As a result of his father's ceaseless efforts, he was transferred to the city of Vladimir, and with the help of his young Moscow friends, arranged the elopement of Natalie. They were married in Vladimir against their relations' wishes. He was in due course allowed to return to Moscow and was appointed to a government post in Petersburg.

Whatever his ambitions at the time, he remained indomitably independent and committed to the radical cause. As a result of an indiscreet letter, opened by the censors, in which he had criticised the behaviour of the police, he was again sentenced to a period of exile, this time in Novgorod. Two years later, in 1842, he was once more permitted to return to Moscow. He was by then regarded as an established member of the new radical intelligentsia, and, indeed, as an honoured martyr in its cause, and began to write in the progressive periodicals of the time. He always dealt with the same central theme: the oppression of the individual; the humiliation and degradation of men by political and personal tyranny; the yoke of social custom, the dark ignorance, and savage, arbitrary misgovernment which maimed and destroyed human beings in the brutal and odious Russian Empire.

Like the other members of his circle, the young poet and

novelist Turgenev, the critic Belinsky, the future political agitators Bakunin and Katkov (the first in the cause of revolution, the second of reaction), the literary essayist Annenkov, his own intimate friend Ogarev, Herzen, with most of his intellectual contemporaries in Russia, became immersed in Hegel's philosophy. He composed arresting historical and philosophical essays, and stories dealing with social issues; they were published, widely read and discussed, and created a considerable reputation for their author. He adopted an uncompromising position. He was a leading representative of the dissident Russian gentry, and his socialist beliefs were caused less by a reaction against the cruelty and chaos of the *laissez-faire* economy of the bourgeois West – for Russia, then in its early industrial beginnings, was still a semi-feudal, socially and economically primitive society – than as a direct response to the agonising social problems in his native land: the poverty of the masses, serfdom and lack of individual freedom at all levels, and a lawless and brutal autocracy.[1] In addition there was the wounded national pride of a powerful and semi-barbarous society, whose leaders were aware of its backwardness, and suffered from mingled admiration, envy and resentment of the civilised West. The radicals believed in reform along democratic, secular, Western lines; the Slavophils retreated into mystical nationalism, and preached the need for return to native 'organic' forms of life and faith that, according to them, had been all but ruined by Peter I's reforms, which had merely encouraged a sedulous and humiliating aping of the soulless and, in any case, hopelessly decadent West. Herzen was an extreme 'Westerner', but he preserved his links with the Slavophil adversaries – he regarded the best among them as romantic reactionaries, misguided nationalists, but honourable allies against the tsarist bureaucracy – and later tended systematically to minimise his differences with them, perhaps from a desire to see all Russians who were not dead to human feeling ranged in a single vast protest against the evil regime.

In 1847 Ivan Yakovlev died. He left the greater part of his

---

[1] The historical and sociological explanation of the origins of Russian socialism and of Herzen's part in it cannot be attempted here. It has been treated in a number of (untranslated) Russian monographs, both pre- and post-revolutionary. The most detailed and original study of this topic to date [1968] is *Alexander Herzen and the Birth of Russian Socialism, 1812–1855* ([Cambridge, Massachusetts], 1961) by Martin Malia.

fortune to Luiza Haag and her son, Alexander Herzen. With immense faith in his own powers, and burning with a desire (in Fichte's words that expressed the attitude of a generation) to 'be and do something' in the world,[1] Herzen decided to emigrate. Whether he wished or expected to remain abroad during the rest of his life is uncertain, but so it turned out to be. He left in the same year, and travelled in considerable state, accompanied by his wife, his mother, two friends, as well as servants, and, crossing Germany, towards the end of 1847 reached the coveted city of Paris, the capital of the civilised world. He plunged at once into the life of the exiled radicals and socialists of many nationalities who played a central role in the fermenting intellectual and artistic activity of that city. By 1848, when a series of revolutions broke out in country after country in Europe, he found himself with Bakunin and Proudhon on the extreme left wing of revolutionary socialism. When rumours of his activities reached the Russian government, he was ordered to return immediately. He refused. His fortune in Russia and that of his mother were declared confiscated. Aided by the efforts of the banker James Rothschild, who had conceived a liking for the young Russian 'baron' and was in a position to bring pressure on the Russian government, Herzen recovered the major portion of his resources, and thereafter experienced no financial want. This gave him a degree of independence not then enjoyed by many exiles, as well as the financial means for supporting other refugees and radical causes.

Shortly after his arrival in Paris, before the revolution, he contributed a series of impassioned articles to a Moscow periodical controlled by his friends, in which he gave an eloquent and violently critical account of the conditions of life and culture in Paris, and, in particular, a devastating analysis of the degradation of the French bourgeoisie, an indictment not surpassed even in the works of his contemporaries Marx and Heine. His Moscow friends for the most part received this with disfavour: they regarded his analyses as characteristic flights of a highly rhetorical fancy, irresponsible extremism, ill suited to the needs of a misgoverned and backward country compared to which the progress of the middle classes in the West, whatever its shortcomings, was a notable step forward towards universal enlightenment. These early

---

[1] op. cit (p. 220 above, note 3), vol. 6, p. 383.

works – the *Letters from Avenue Marigny* and the Italian sketches that followed – possess qualities which became characteristic of all his writings: a rapid torrent of descriptive sentences, fresh, lucid, direct, interspersed with vivid and never irrelevant digressions, variations on the same theme in many keys, puns, neologisms, quotations real and imaginary, verbal inventions, gallicisms which irritated his nationalistic Russian friends, mordant personal observations and cascades of vivid images and incomparable epigrams, which, so far from either tiring or distracting the reader by their virtuosity, add to the force and swiftness of the narrative. The effect is one of spontaneous improvisation: exhilarating conversation by an intellectually gay and exceptionally clever and honest man endowed with singular powers of observation and expression. The mood is one of ardent political radicalism imbued with a typically aristocratic (and even more typically Muscovite) contempt for everything narrow, calculating, self-satisfied, commercial, anything cautious, petty or tending towards compromise and the *juste milieu*, of which Louis-Philippe and Guizot are held up to view as particularly repulsive incarnations.

Herzen's outlook in these essays is a combination of optimistic idealism – a vision of a socially, intellectually and morally free society, the beginnings of which, like Proudhon, Marx and Louis Blanc, he saw in the French working class; faith in the radical revolution which alone could create the conditions for their liberation; but, with this, a deep distrust (something that most of his allies did not share) of all general formulae as such, of the programmes and battle-cries of all the political parties, of the great, official historical goals – progress, liberty, equality, national unity, historic rights, human solidarity – principles and slogans in the name of which men had been, and doubtless would soon again be, violated and slaughtered, and their forms of life condemned and destroyed.

Like the more extreme of the left-wing disciples of Hegel, in particular like the anarchist Max Stirner, Herzen saw danger in the great magnificent abstractions the mere sound of which precipitated men into violent and meaningless slaughter – new idols, it seemed to him, on whose altars human blood was to be shed tomorrow as irrationally and uselessly as the blood of the victims of yesterday or the day before, sacrificed in honour of older divinities – Church or monarchy or the feudal order or the sacred customs of the tribe, that were now discredited as obstacles to the progress of mankind.

Together with this scepticism about the meaning and value of abstract ideals as such, in contrast with the concrete, short-term, immediate goals of identifiable living individuals – specific freedoms, reward for the day's work – Herzen spoke of something even more disquieting, a haunting sense of the ever widening and unbridgeable gulf between the humane values of the relatively free and civilised élites (to which he knew himself to belong) and the actual needs, desires and tastes of the vast voiceless masses of mankind, barbarous enough in the West, wilder still in Russia or the plains of Asia beyond. The old world was crumbling visibly, and it deserved to fall. It would be destroyed by its victims – the slaves who cared nothing for the art and the science of their masters; and indeed, Herzen asks, why should they care? Was it not erected on their suffering and degradation? Young and vigorous, filled with a just hatred of the old world built on their fathers' bones, the new barbarians will raze to the ground the edifices of their oppressors, and with them all that is most sublime and beautiful in Western civilisation; such a cataclysm might be not only inevitable but justified, since this civilisation, noble and valuable in the eyes of its beneficiaries, has offered nothing but suffering, a life without meaning, to the vast majority of mankind. Yet he does not pretend that this makes the prospect, to those who, like him, have tasted the riper fruits of civilisation, any less dreadful.

It has often been asserted by both Russian and Western critics that Herzen arrived in Paris a passionate, even Utopian idealist, and that it was the failure of the revolution of 1848 which brought about his disillusionment and a new, more pessimistic realism. This is not sufficiently borne out by the evidence.[1] Even in 1847, the sceptical note, in particular pessimism about the degree to which human beings can be transformed, and the still deeper scepticism about whether such changes, even if they were achieved by fearless and intelligent revolutionaries or reformers, ideal images of whom floated before the eyes of his Westernising friends in Russia, would in fact lead to a juster and freer order, or on the contrary to the rule

[1] The clearest formulation of this well-worn and almost universal thesis is to be found in E. H. Carr's lively and well-documented treatment of Herzen in his *The Romantic Exiles* (London, 1933). Malia's book (op. cit., p. 505 above, note 1) avoids this error.

of new masters over new slaves – that ominous note is sounded before the great débâcle. Yet, despite this, he remained a convinced, ultimately optimistic revolutionary. The spectacle of the workers' revolt and its brutal suppression in Italy and in France haunted Herzen all his life. His first-hand description of the events of 1848–9, in particular of the drowning in blood of the July revolt in Paris, is a masterpiece of 'committed' historical and sociological writing. So, too, are his sketches of the personalities involved in these upheavals, and his reflections upon them. Most of these essays and letters remain untranslated.

Herzen could not and would not return to Russia. He became a Swiss citizen, and to the disasters of the revolution was added a personal tragedy – the seduction of his adored wife by the most intimate of his new friends, the radical German poet Georg Herwegh, a friend of Marx and Wagner, the 'iron lark' of the German revolution, as Heine half ironically called him.[1] Herzen's progressive, somewhat Shelleyan, views on love, friendship, equality of the sexes, and the irrationality of bourgeois morality were tested by this crisis and broken by it. He went almost mad with grief and jealousy: his love, his vanity, his deeper assumptions about the basis of all human relationships suffered a traumatic shock from which he was never fully to recover. He did what few others have ever done: described every detail of his own agony, every step of his altering relationship with his wife, with Herwegh and Herwegh's wife, as they seemed to him in retrospect; he noted every communication that occurred between them, every moment of anger, despair, affection, love, hope, hatred, contempt and agonised, suicidal self-contempt. Every tone and nuance in his own moral and psychological condition is raised to high relief against the background of his public life in the world of exiles and conspirators, French, Italian, German, Russian, Austrian, Hungarian, Polish, who move on and off the stage on which he himself is always the central, self-absorbed, tragic hero. The account is not unbalanced – there is no obvious distortion – but it is wholly egocentric.

All his life Herzen perceived the external world clearly, and in proportion, but through the medium of his own self-romanticising personality, with his own impressionable, ill-organised self at the centre of his universe. No matter how violent his torment, he

[1] In 'An Georg Herwegh' (1841).

retains full artistic control of the tragedy which he is living through, but also writing. It is, perhaps, this artistic egotism, which all his work exhibits, that was in part responsible both for Natalie's suffocation and for the lack of reticence in his description of what took place: Herzen takes wholly for granted the reader's understanding and, still more, his undivided interest in every detail of his own, the writer's, mental and emotional life. Natalie's letters and desperate flight to Herwegh show the measure of the increasingly destructive effect of Herzen's self-absorbed blindness upon her frail and *exalté* temperament. We know comparatively little of Natalie's relationship with Herwegh: she may well have been physically in love with him, and he with her: the inflated literary language of the letters conceals more than it reveals; what is clear is that she felt unhappy, trapped and irresistibly attracted to her lover. If Herzen sensed this, he perceived it very dimly.

He appropriated the feelings of those nearest him as he did the ideas of Hegel or George Sand: that is, he took what he needed, and poured it into the vehement torrent of his own experience. He gave generously, if fitfully, to others; he put his own life into them, but for all his deep and lifelong belief in individual liberty and the absolute value of personal life and personal relationships, scarcely understood or tolerated wholly independent lives by the side of his own; his description of his agony is scrupulously and bitterly detailed and accurate, never self-sparing, eloquent but not sentimental, and remorselessly self-absorbed. It is a harrowing document. He did not publish the story in full during his lifetime, but now it forms part of his memoirs.

Self-expression – the need to say his own word – and perhaps the craving for recognition by others, by Russia, by Europe, were primary needs of Herzen's nature. Consequently, even during this, the darkest period of his life, he continued to pour out a stream of letters and articles in various languages on political and social topics; he helped to keep Proudhon going, kept up a correspondence with Swiss radicals and Russian émigrés, read widely, made notes, conceived ideas, argued, worked unremittingly both as a publicist and as an active supporter of left-wing and revolutionary causes. After a short while Natalie returned to him in Nice, only to die in his arms. Shortly before her death a ship on which his mother and one of his children, a deaf-mute, were travelling from Marseilles sank in a storm. Their bodies were not found. Herzen's life had reached its lowest ebb. He left Nice and the circle of

Italian, French and Polish revolutionaries to many of whom he was bound by ties of warm friendship, and with his three surviving children went to England. America was too far away and, besides, seemed to him too dull. England was no less remote from the scene of his defeats, political and personal, and yet still a part of Europe. It was then the country most hospitable to political refugees, civilised, tolerant of eccentricities or indifferent to them, proud of its civil liberties and its sympathy with the victims of foreign oppression. He arrived in London in 1851.

He and his children wandered from home to home in London and its suburbs, and there, after the death of Nicholas I had made it possible for him to leave Russia, his most intimate friend, Nikolay Ogarev, joined them. Together they set up a printing press, and began to publish a periodical in Russian called *The Pole Star* – the first organ wholly dedicated to uncompromising agitation against the imperial Russian regime. The earliest chapters of *My Past and Thoughts* appeared in its pages. The memory of the terrible years 1848–51 obsessed Herzen's thoughts and poisoned his bloodstream: it became an inescapable psychological necessity for him to seek relief by setting down this bitter history. This was the first section of his memoirs to be written. It was an opiate against the appalling loneliness of a life lived among uninterested strangers[1] while political reaction seemed to envelop the entire world, leaving no room for hope. Insensibly he was drawn into the past. He

---

[1] Herzen had no close English friends, although he had associates, allies and admirers. One of these, the radical journalist W. J. Linton, to whose *English Republic* Herzen had contributed articles, described him as 'short of stature, stoutly built, in his last days inclined to corpulence, with a grand head, long chestnut hair and beard, small, luminous eyes, and rather ruddy complexion. Suave in his manner, courteous, but with an intense power of irony, witty . . . clear, concise, and impressive, he was a subtle and profound thinker, with all the passionate nature of the "barbarian", yet generous and humane . . . Hospitable, and taking pleasure in society . . . a good conversationalist, with a frank and pleasant manner': *Memories* (London, 1895), pp. 146–7. And in his *European Republicans* (London, 1893) he said that the Spanish radical Emilio Castelar declared that Herzen, with his fair hair and beard, looked like a Goth, but possessed the warmth, vivacity, verve, 'inimitable grace' and 'marvellous variety' of a southerner (pp. 275–6). Turgenev and Herzen were the first Russians to move freely in European society. The impression that they made did a good deal, though perhaps not enough, to dispel the myth of the dark 'Slav soul', which took a long time to die; perhaps it is not altogether dead yet.

moved further and further into it and found it a source of liberty and strength.

This is how the book which he conceived on the analogy of *David Copperfield* came to be composed.[1] He began to write it in the last months of 1852. He wrote by fits and starts. The first three parts were probably finished by the end of 1853. In 1854 a selection which he called *Prison and Exile* – a title perhaps inspired by Silvio Pellico's celebrated *Le mie prigioni* – was published in English. It was an immediate success; encouraged by this, he continued. By the spring of 1855 the first four parts of the work were completed; they were all published by 1857. He revised Part IV, added new chapters to it and composed Part V; he completed the bulk of Part VI by 1858. The sections dealing with his intimate life – his love and the early years of his marriage – were composed in 1857: he could not bring himself to touch upon them until then. This was followed by an interval of seven years. Independent essays such as those on Robert Owen, the actor Shchepkin, the painter Ivanov, Garibaldi (*Camicia rossa*), were published in London between 1860 and 1864; but these, although usually included in the memoirs, were not intended for them. The first complete edition of the first four parts appeared in 1861. The final sections – Part VIII and almost the whole of Part VII – were written, in that order, in 1865–7.

Herzen deliberately left some sections unpublished: the most intimate details of his personal tragedy appeared posthumously – only a part of the chapter entitled 'Oceano nox' was printed in his lifetime. He omitted also the story of his affairs with Medvedeva in Vyatka and with the serf girl Katerina in Moscow – his confession of them to Natalie cast the first shadow over their relationship, a shadow that never lifted; he could not bear to see it in print while he lived. He suppressed, too, a chapter on 'The German Emigrants' which contains his unflattering comments on Marx and his followers, and some characteristically entertaining and ironical sketches of some of his old friends among the Russian radicals. He genuinely detested the practice of washing the revolutionaries' dirty linen in public, and made it clear that he did not intend to make fun of allies for the entertainment of the common enemy.

---

[1] '[*Copperfield*] is Dickens's *Past and Thoughts*,' he said in one of his letters in the early 1860s; humility was not among his virtues. *Sobranie sochinenii*, vol. 27, p. 394 (letter of 16 December 1863).

The first authoritative edition of the memoirs was compiled by Mikhail Lemke in the first complete edition of Herzen's works, which was begun before, and completed some years after, the Russian Revolution of 1917. It has since been revised in successive Soviet editions. The fullest version is that published in the exhaustive edition of Herzen's works, a handsome monument of Soviet scholarship.[1]

The memoirs formed a vivid and broken background accompaniment to Herzen's central activity: revolutionary journalism, to which he dedicated his life. The bulk of it is contained in the most celebrated of all Russian periodicals published abroad – *The Bell* (*Kolokol*) – edited by Herzen and Ogarev in London and then in Geneva from 1857 until 1867, with the motto (taken from Schiller) 'Vivos voco'.[2] *The Bell* had an immense success. It was the first systematic instrument of revolutionary propaganda directed against the Russian autocracy, written with knowledge, sincerity and mordant eloquence; it gathered round itself all that was uncowed not only in Russia and the Russian colonies abroad, but also among Poles and other oppressed nationalities. It began to penetrate into Russia by secret routes and was regularly read by high officials of State, including, it was rumoured, the Emperor himself. Herzen used the copious information that reached him in clandestine letters and personal messages, describing various misdeeds of the Russian bureaucracy, to expose specific scandals – cases of bribery, miscarriage of justice, tyranny and dishonesty by officials and influential persons. *The Bell* named names, offered documentary evidence, asked awkward questions and exposed hideous aspects of Russian life.

Russian travellers visited London in order to meet the mysterious leader of the mounting opposition to the Tsar. Generals, high officials and other loyal subjects of the Empire were among the many visitors who thronged to see him, some out of curiosity, others to shake his hand, to express sympathy or admiration. He reached the peak of his fame, both political and literary, after the defeat of Russia in the Crimean War and the death of Nicholas I. The open appeal by Herzen to the new Emperor[3] to free the serfs

---

[1] op. cit. (p. 502 above, note 1).

[2] Part of the inscription on the bell of the cathedral at Schaffhausen, used as the epigraph to Schiller's 'Das Lied von der Glocke' (1799).

[3] 'Pis'mo k Imperatoru Aleksandru vtoromu', *Sobranie sochinenii*, vol. 12, pp. 272–4.

and initiate bold and radical reforms 'from above', and, after the first concrete steps towards this had been taken in 1858, his paean of praise to Alexander II,[1] ending 'Thou hast conquered, O Galilean', created the illusion on both sides of the Russian frontier that a new liberal era was at last dawning, in which a degree of understanding – perhaps of actual co-operation – could be achieved between tsardom and its opponents. This state of mind did not last long. But Herzen's credit stood very high – higher than that of any other Russian in the West: in the late 1850s and early 1860s he was the acknowledged leader of all that was generous, enlightened, civilised, humane in Russia.

More than Bakunin and even Turgenev, whose novels formed a central source of knowledge about Russia in the West, Herzen counteracted the legend, ingrained in the minds of progressive Europeans (of whom Michelet was perhaps the most representative), that Russia consisted of nothing save only the government jackboot on the one hand, and the dark, silent, sullen mass of brutalised peasants on the other – an image that was the by-product of the widespread sympathy for the principal victim of Russian despotism, the martyred nation, Poland. Some among the Polish exiles spontaneously conceded this service to the truth on Herzen's part, if only because he was one of the rare Russians who genuinely liked and admired individual Poles, worked in close sympathy with them, and identified the cause of Russian liberation with that of all her oppressed subject nationalities. It was, indeed, this unswerving avoidance of chauvinism that was among the principal causes of the ultimate collapse of *The Bell* and of Herzen's own political undoing.

After Russia, Herzen's deepest love was for Italy and the Italians. The closest ties bound him to the Italian exiles Mazzini, Garibaldi, Saffi and Orsini. Although he supported every liberal beginning in France, his attitude towards her was more ambiguous. For this there were many reasons. Like Tocqueville (whom he personally disliked), he had a distaste for all that was centralised, bureaucratic, hierarchical, subject to rigid forms or rules; France was to him the incarnation of order, discipline, the worship of the State, of unity, and of despotic, abstract formulae that flattened all things to the same rule and pattern – something that had a family

---

[1] 'Cherez tri goda', *Kolokol*, 15 February 1858: *Sobranie sochinenii*, vol. 13, pp. 195–7.

resemblance to the great slave States – Prussia, Austria, Russia; with this he constantly contrasts the decentralised, uncrushed, untidy, 'truly democratic' Italians, whom he believed to possess a deep affinity with the free Russian spirit embodied in the peasant commune with its sense of natural justice and human worth. To this ideal even England seemed to him to be far less hostile than legalistic, calculating France: in such moods he comes close to his romantic Slavophil opponents. Moreover, he could not forget the betrayal of the revolution in Paris by the bourgeois parties in 1848, the execution of the workers, the suppression of the Roman revolution by the troops of the French Republic, the vanity, weakness and rhetoric of the French radical politicians – Lamartine, Marrast, Ledru-Rollin, Félix Pyat.

His sketches of the lives and behaviour of leading French exiles in England are masterpieces of amused, half-sympathetic, half-contemptuous description of the grotesque and futile aspects of every political emigration condemned to sterility, intrigue and a constant flow of self-justifying eloquence before a foreign audience too remote or bored to listen. Yet he thought well of individual members of it: he had for a time been a close ally of Proudhon, and despite their differences he continued to respect him; he regarded Louis Blanc as an honest and fearless democrat, he was on good terms with Victor Hugo, he liked and admired Michelet. In later years he visited at least one Paris political salon – admittedly, it was that of a Pole – with evident enjoyment: the Goncourts met him there and left a vivid description in their journal of his appearance and his conversation.[1]

---

[1] See entry in the *Journal* for 8 February 1865 – 'Dinner at Charles Edmund's [Cojecki] ... A Socratic mask with the warm and transparent flesh of a Rubens portrait, a red mark between the eyebrows as from a branding iron, greying beard and hair.

'As he talks there is a constant ironical chuckle which rises and falls in his throat. His voice is soft, melancholy, musical, without any of the harsh sonority one might have expected from his huge neck: the ideas are fine, delicate, pungent, at times subtle, always definite, illuminated by words that take time to arrive, but which always possess the felicitous quality of French as it is spoken by a civilised and witty foreigner.

'He speaks of Bakunin, of his eleven months in prison, chained to a wall, of his escape from Siberia by the Amur River, of his return by way of California, of his arrival in London, where, after a stormy, moist embrace, his first words [to Herzen] were "Can one get oysters here?"'

Herzen delighted the Goncourts with stories about the Emperor Nicholas

Although he was half German himself, or perhaps because of it, he felt, like his friend Bakunin, a strong aversion from what he regarded as the incurable philistinism of the Germans, and what seemed to him a peculiarly unattractive combination of craving for blind authority with a tendency to squalid internecine recriminations in public, more pronounced than among other émigrés. Perhaps his hatred of Herwegh, whom he knew to be a friend both of Marx and of Wagner, as well as Marx's onslaughts on Karl Vogt, the Swiss naturalist to whom Herzen was devoted, played some part in this. At least three of his most intimate friends were pure Germans. Goethe and Schiller meant more to him than any Russian writers. Yet there is something genuinely venomous in his account of the German exiles, quite different from the high-spirited sense of comedy with which he describes the idiosyncrasies of the other foreign colonies gathered in the 1850s and '60s in London – a city, if we are to believe Herzen, equally unconcerned with their absurdities and their martyrdoms.

As for his hosts, the English, they seldom appear in his pages. Herzen had met Mill, Carlyle and Owen. His first night in England was spent with English hosts. He was on reasonably good terms with one or two editors of radical papers (some of whom, like Linton and Cowen, helped him to propagate his views, and to preserve contact with revolutionaries on the Continent as well as with clandestine traffic of propaganda to Russia), and several radically inclined Members of Parliament, including minor ministers. In general, however, he seems to have had even less contact with Englishmen than his contemporary and fellow exile, Karl Marx. He admired England. He admired her constitution; the wild and tangled wood of her unwritten laws and customs brought the full resources of his romantic imagination into play. The entertaining passages of *My Past and Thoughts* in which he compares the French and the English, or the English and the Germans, display

walking in the night in his empty palace, after the fall of Eupatoria during the Crimean War, with the heavy, unearthly steps of the stone statue of the Commander in *Don Juan*. This was followed by anecdotes about English habits and manners – 'a country which he loves as the land of liberty' – to illustrate its absurd, class-conscious, unyielding traditionalism, particularly noticeable in the relations of masters and servants. The Goncourts quote a characteristic epigram made by Herzen to illustrate the difference between the French and English characters. They faithfully report the story of how James Rothschild managed to save Herzen's property in Russia.

acute and amused insight into the national characteristics of the English. But he could not altogether like them: they remained for him too insular, too indifferent, too unimaginative, too remote from the moral, social and aesthetic issues which lay closest to his own heart, too materialistic and self-satisfied. His judgements about them, always intelligent and sometimes penetrating, are distant and tend to be conventional. A description of the trial in London of a French radical who had killed a political opponent in a duel in Windsor Great Park is wonderfully executed, but remains a piece of genre-painting, a gay and brilliant caricature. The French, the Swiss, the Italians, even the Germans, certainly the Poles, are closer to him. He cannot establish any genuine personal relationship with the English. When he thinks of mankind he does not think of them.

Apart from his central preoccupations he devoted himself to the education of his children, which he entrusted in part to an idealistic German lady, Malwida von Meysenbug, afterwards a friend of Nietzsche and Romain Rolland. His personal life was intertwined with that of his intimate friend Ogarev, and of Ogarev's wife, who became his mistress; in spite of this the mutual devotion of the two friends remained unaltered – the memoirs reveal little of the curious emotional consequences of this relationship.

For the rest, he lived the life of an affluent, well-born man of letters, a member of the Russian, and more specifically Moscow, gentry, uprooted from his native soil, unable to achieve a settled existence or even the semblance of inward or outward peace, a life filled with occasional moments of hope and even exultation, followed by long periods of misery, corrosive self-criticism, and most of all overwhelming, omnivorous, bitter nostalgia. It may be this, as much as objective reasons, that caused him to idealise the Russian peasant, and to dream that the answer to the central 'social' question of his time – that of growing inequality, exploitation, dehumanisation of both the oppressor and the oppressed – lay in the preservation of the Russian peasant commune. He perceived in it the seeds of the development of a non-industrial, semi-anarchist socialism. Only such a solution, plainly influenced by the views of Fourier, Proudhon and George Sand, seemed to him free from the crushing, barrack-room discipline demanded by Western communists from Cabet to Marx; and from the equally suffocating, and, it seemed to him, far more vulgar and philistine ideals contained in moderate, half-socialist doctrines, with their faith in the progressive role of developing industrialism preached by the forerunners of social democracy in Germany and France and of the Fabians in England. At times he modified his view: towards the end of his life he began to recognise the historical significance of the organised urban workers. But all in all he remained faithful to his belief in the Russian peasant commune as an embryonic form of a life in which the quest for individual freedom was reconciled with the need for collective activity and responsibility. He retained to the end a romantic vision of the inevitable coming of a new, just, all-transforming social order.

Herzen is neither consistent nor systematic. His style during his middle years has lost the confident touch of his youth, and conveys the consuming nostalgia that never leaves him. He is obsessed by a sense of blind accident, although his faith in the values of life remains unshaken. Almost all traces of Hegelian influence are gone. 'It is as though someone (other than ourselves) had promised that everything in the world will be exquisitely beautiful, just and harmonious. We have marvelled enough at the deep wisdom of nature and history; it is time to realise that nature and history are full of the accidental and senseless, of muddle and bungling.'[1] This is highly characteristic of his mood in the 1860s; and it is no accident that his exposition is not ordered, but is a succession of fragments, episodes, isolated vignettes, a mingling of *Dichtung* and *Wahrheit*, facts and poetic licence.

His moods alternate sharply. Sometimes he believes in the need for a great, cleansing, revolutionary storm, even were it to take the form of a barbarian invasion likely to destroy all the values that he himself holds dear. At other times he reproaches his old friend Bakunin, who joined him in London after escaping from his Russian prisons, for wanting to make the revolution too soon; for not understanding that dwellings for free men cannot be con-structed out of the stones of a prison; that the average European of the nineteenth century is too deeply marked by the slavery of the old order to be capable of conceiving true freedom, that it is not the liberated slaves who will build the new order, but new men brought up in liberty. History has her own tempo. Patience and gradualism – not the haste and violence of a Peter the Great – can alone bring about a permanent transformation. At such moments he wonders whether the future belongs to the free, anarchic

---

[1] *Sobranie sochinenii*, vol. 10, p. 120.

peasant, or to the bold and ruthless planner; perhaps it is the industrial worker who is to be the heir to the new, unavoidable, collectivist economic order.[1] Then again he returns to his early moods of disillusionment and wonders whether men in general really desire freedom: perhaps only a few do so in each generation, while most human beings only want good government, no matter at whose hands. He anticipates Émile Faguet's bitter epigram about Rousseau's dictum that men who are born free are nevertheless everywhere in chains; 'it would be equally reasonable to say that sheep are born carnivorous, and everywhere nibble grass'.[2] Herzen uses a similar *reductio ad absurdum*.[3] Men desire freedom no more than fish desire to fly. The fact that a few flying fish exist does not demonstrate that fish in general were created to fly, or are not fundamentally quite content to stay below the surface of the water, for ever away from the sun and the light. Then he returns to his earlier optimism and the thought that somewhere – in Russia – there lives the unbroken human being, the peasant with his faculties intact, untainted by the corruption and sophistication of the West.

But this Rousseau-inspired faith, as he grows older, grows less secure. His sense of reality is too strong. For all his efforts, and the efforts of his socialist friends, he cannot deceive himself entirely. He oscillates between pessimism and optimism, scepticism and suspicion of his own scepticism, and is kept morally alive only by his hatred of all injustice, all arbitrariness, all mediocrity as such – in particular by his inability to compromise in any degree with either the brutality of reactionaries or the hypocrisy of bourgeois liberals. He is preserved by this, buoyed up by his belief that such evils will destroy themselves, by his love for his children and his devoted friends, and by his unquenchable delight in the variety of life and the comedy of human character.

On the whole, he grew more pessimistic. He began with an ideal vision of human life, and largely ignored the chasm which divided it from the present – whether the Russia of Nicholas, or the corrupt constitutionalism in the West. In his youth he glorified Jacobin radicalism and condemned its opponents in Russia – blind

---

[1] This is the thesis in which orthodox Soviet scholars claim to discern a belated approach to those of Marx.

[2] loc. cit. (p. 266 above, note 2).

[3] *Sobranie sochinenii*, vol. 6, p. 94.

conservatism, Slavophil nostalgia, the cautious gradualism of his friends Granovsky and Turgenev, as well as Hegelian appeals to patience and rational conformity to the inescapable rhythms of history, which seemed to him designed to ensure the triumph of the new bourgeois class. His attitude, before he went abroad, was boldly optimistic. There followed, not indeed a change of view, but a cooling-off, a tendency to a more sober and critical outlook. All genuine change, he began to think in 1847, is necessarily slow; the power of tradition (which he at once mocks at and admires in England) is very great; men are less malleable than was believed in the eighteenth century, nor do they truly seek liberty, only security and contentment; communism is but tsarism stood on its head, the replacement of one yoke by another; the ideals and watchwords of politics turn out, on examination, to be empty formulae in the name of which devout fanatics happily slaughter hecatombs of their fellows. He no longer feels certain that the gap between the enlightened élite and the masses can ever, in principle, be bridged (this becomes an obsessive refrain in later Russian thought), since the awakened people may, for unalterable psychological or socio-logical reasons, despise and reject the gifts of a civilisation which will never mean enough to them. But if all this is even in small part true, is radical transformation either practicable or desirable? From this follows Herzen's growing sense of obstacles that may be insurmountable, limits that may be impassable, his empiricism, scepticism, the latent pessimism and despair of the middle 1860s.

This is the attitude which some Soviet scholars interpret as the beginning of an approach on his part towards a quasi-Marxist recognition of the inexorable laws of social development – in particular the inevitability of industrialism, above all of the central role to be played by the proletariat. This is not how Herzen's left-wing Russian critics interpreted his views in his lifetime, or for the half century that followed. To them, rightly or wrongly, these doctrines seemed symptomatic of conservatism and betrayal. For in the 1850s and '60s a new generation of radicals grew up in Russia, then a backward country in the painful process of the earliest, most rudimentary beginnings of slow, sporadic, inefficient industrialisation. These were men of mixed social origins, filled with contempt for the feeble liberal compromises of 1848, with no illusions about the prospects of freedom in the West, determined on more ruthless methods; accepting as true only what the sciences can prove, prepared to be hard and, if need be, unscrupulous and cruel, in order to break the power of their equally ruthless oppressors; bitterly hostile to the aestheticism, the devotion to civilised values, of the 'soft' generation of the 1840s.

Herzen realised that the criticism and abuse showered upon him as an obsolete aristocratic dilettante by these 'nihilists' (as they came to be called after Turgenev's novel *Fathers and Children*, in which this conflict is vividly presented for the first time) was not altogether different from the disdain that he had himself felt in his own youth for the elegant and ineffective reformers of Alexander I's reign; but this did not make his position easier to bear. What was ill-received by the tough-minded revolutionaries pleased Tolstoy, who said more than once that the censorship of Herzen's works in Russia was a characteristic blunder on the part of the government; the government, in its anxiety to stop young men from marching towards the revolutionary morass, seized them and swept them off to Siberia or prison long before they were even in sight of it, while they were still on the broad highway; Herzen had trodden this very path, he had seen the chasm, and warned against it, particularly in his *Letters to an Old Comrade*. Nothing, Tolstoy argued, would have proved a better antidote to the 'revolutionary nihilism' which he condemned than Herzen's brilliant analyses. 'Our Russian life would not have been the same during the last twenty years if [Herzen] had not been kept from the younger generation.'[1] Suppression of his books, Tolstoy went on, was both a criminal and, from the point of view of those who did not desire a violent revolution, an idiotic policy.

At other times Tolstoy was less generous. In 1860, six months before they met, he had been reading Herzen's writings with mingled admiration and irritation: 'Herzen is a man of scattered intellect, and morbid *amour propre*,' he wrote in his diary, 'but his breadth, ability, goodness, elegance of mind are Russian.'[2] From time to time various correspondents record the fact that Tolstoy read Herzen, at times aloud to his family, with the greatest admiration. In 1896, during one of his angriest, most anti-rationalist moods, he said, 'In spite of his enormous talent, what did he say

---

[1] Letter to N. N. Gay senior of 13 February 1888. See also letter to V. G. Chertkov of 9 February 1888.

[2] Diary entry for 4 August 1860.

that was new or useful?'[1] – as for the argument that the generation of the 1840s could not say what it wanted to say because of the rigid Russian censorship, Herzen wrote in perfect freedom in Paris and yet managed to say nothing useful.

What irritated Tolstoy most was Herzen's socialism. In a letter to his aunt, Alexandra Tolstoy, he says that he despises Herzen's proclamations, which the Russian police suspect him of harbouring.[2] The fact that he believed in politics as a weapon was sufficient to condemn him in Tolstoy's eyes. From 1862 onwards, Tolstoy had declared his hostility to faith in liberal reform and improvement of human life by legal or institutional change. Herzen fell under this general ban. Moreover, Tolstoy seems to have felt a certain lack of personal sympathy for Herzen and his public position – even a kind of jealousy. When, in moments of acute discouragement and irritation, Tolstoy spoke (perhaps not very seriously) of leaving Russia for ever, he would say that whatever he did, he would not join Herzen or march under his banner: 'he goes his way, I shall go mine'.[3]

He seriously underrated Herzen's revolutionary temperament and instincts. However sceptical Herzen may have been of specific revolutionary doctrines or plans in Russia – and no one was more so – he believed to the end of his life in the moral and social need and the inevitability, sooner or later, of a revolution in Russia – a violent transformation followed by a just, that is a socialist, order. He did not, it is true, close his eyes to the possibility, even the probability, that the great rebellion would extinguish values to which he was himself dedicated – in particular, the freedoms without which he and others like him could not breathe. Nevertheless, he recognised not only the inevitability but the historic justice of the coming cataclysm. His moral tastes, his respect for human values, his entire style of life, divided him from the tough-minded younger radicals of the 1860s, but he did not, despite all his distrust of political fanaticism, whether on the right or on the left, turn into a cautious, reformist liberal constitutionalist. Even in his gradualist phase he remained an agitator, an egalitarian and a socialist to the end. It is this in him that both the Russian populists and the

[1] Diary entry for 17 May 1896. But on 12 October 1905 he writes in his diary that he is reading Herzen's *From the Other Shore*, and says 'Our intelligentsia has sunk so low that . . . it cannot understand him.'

[2] Letter of 22–3(?) July 1862.

[3] Letter to his aunt, Countess A. A. Tolstaya, 7 August 1862.

Russian Marxists – both Mikhailovsky and Lenin – recognised and saluted.

It was not prudence or moderation that led him to his unwavering support of Poland in her insurrection against Russia in 1863. The wave of passionate Russian nationalism which accompanied its suppression robbed him of sympathy even among Russian liberals. *The Bell* declined in circulation. The new, 'hard' revolutionaries needed his money, but made it plain that they looked upon him as a liberal dinosaur, the preacher of antiquated humanistic views, useless in the violent social struggle to come. He left London in the late 1860s and attempted to produce a French edition of *The Bell* in Geneva. When that too failed, he visited his friends in Florence, returning to Paris early in 1870, before the outbreak of the Franco-Prussian War. There he died of pleurisy, broken both morally and physically, but not disillusioned; still writing with concentrated intelligence and force. His body was taken to Nice, where he is buried beside his wife. A life-size statue still marks his grave.

Herzen's ideas have long since entered into the general texture of Russian political thought – liberals and radicals, populists and anarchists, socialists and communists have all claimed him as an ancestor. But what survives today of all that unceasing and feverish activity, even in his native country, is not a system or a doctrine but a handful of essays, some remarkable letters, and the extraordinary amalgam of memory, observation, moral passion, psychological analysis and political description, wedded to a major literary talent, which has immortalised his name. What remains is, above all, a passionate and inextinguishable temperament and a sense of the movement of nature and of its unpredictable possibilities, which he felt with an intensity which not even his uniquely rich and flexible prose could fully express.

He believed that the ultimate goal of life was life itself; that the day and the hour were ends in themselves, not a means to another day or another experience. He believed that remote ends were a dream, that faith in them was a fatal illusion; that to sacrifice the present or the immediate and foreseeable future to these distant ends must always lead to cruel and futile forms of human sacrifice. He believed that values were not found in an impersonal, objective realm, but were created by human beings, changed with the generations of men, but were none the less binding upon those who lived in their light; that suffering was inescapable, and infallible knowledge neither attainable nor needed. He believed in

reason, scientific methods, individual action, empirically discovered truths; but he tended to suspect that faith in general formulae,
laws, prescription in human affairs was an attempt, sometimes
catastrophic, always irrational, to escape from the uncertainty and
unpredictable variety of life to the false security of our own
symmetrical fantasies. He was fully conscious of what he believed.
He had obtained this knowledge at the cost of painful, and, at
times, unintended, self-analysis, and he described what he saw in
language of exceptional vitality, precision and poetry. His purely
personal credo remained unaltered from his earliest days: 'Art, and
the summer lightning of individual happiness: these are the only
real goods we have,' he declared in a self-revealing passage of the
kind that so deeply shocked the stern young Russian revolutionaries in the 1860s. Yet even they and their descendants did not and
do not reject his artistic and intellectual achievement.

Herzen was not, and had no desire to be, an impartial observer.
No less than the poets and the novelists of his nation, he created a
style, an outlook, and, in the words of Gorky's tribute to him, 'an
entire province, a country astonishingly rich in ideas',[1] where
everything is immediately recognisable as being his and his alone, a
country into which he transplants all that he touches, in which
things, sensations, feelings, persons, ideas, private and public
events, institutions, entire cultures are given shape and life by his
powerful and coherent historical imagination, and have stood up
against the forces of decay in the solid world which his memory,
his intelligence and his artistic genius recovered and reconstructed.
*My Past and Thoughts* is the Noah's ark in which he saved himself,
and not himself alone, from the destructive flood in which many
idealistic radicals of the 1840s were drowned. Genuine art survives
and transcends its immediate purpose. The structure that Herzen
built, in the first place, perhaps, for his own personal salvation,
built out of material provided by his own predicament – out of
exile, solitude, despair – survives intact. Written abroad, concerned
largely with European issues and figures, his reminiscences are a
great permanent monument to the civilised, sensitive, morally
preoccupied and gifted Russian society to which Herzen belonged;
their vitality and fascination have not declined in the hundred years
and more that have passed since the first chapters saw the light.

[1] M. Gorky, *Istoriya russkoi literatury* (Moscow, 1939), p. 206.

# CONVERSATIONS WITH AKHMATOVA AND PASTERNAK

I

IN THE SUMMER of 1945 the British Embassy in Moscow reported that it was short-handed, especially in the matter of officials who knew Russian, and it was suggested that I might fill a gap for four or five months. I accepted this offer eagerly, mainly, I must admit, because of my great desire to learn about the condition of Russian literature and art, about which relatively little was known in the West at that time. I knew something, of course, of what had happened to Russian writers and artists in the 1920s and '30s. The Revolution had stimulated a great wave of creative energy in Russia, in all the arts; bold experimentalism was everywhere encouraged: the new controllers of culture did not interfere with anything that could be represented as being a 'slap in the face' to bourgeois taste, whether it was Marxist or not. The new movement in the visual arts – the work of such painters as Kandinsky, Chagall, Soutine, Malevich, Klyun, Tatlin, of the sculptors Arkhipenko, Pevsner, Gabo, Lipchitz, Zadkine, of the theatre and film directors Meyerhold, Vakhtangov, Tairov, Eisenstein, Pudovkin – produced masterpieces which had a powerful impact in the West; there was a similar upward curve in the field of literature and literary criticism. Despite the violence and devastation of the Civil War, and the ruin and chaos brought about by it, revolutionary art of extraordinary vitality continued to be produced.

I remember meeting Sergei Eisenstein in 1945; he was in a state of terrible depression: this was the result of Stalin's condemnation of the original version of his film *Ivan the Terrible*, because that savage ruler, with whom Stalin identified himself, faced with the need to repress the treachery of the boyars, had, so Stalin complained, been misrepresented as a man tormented to the point of neurosis. I asked Eisenstein what he thought were the best years of his life. He answered without hesitation, 'The early '20s. That was the time. We were young and did marvellous things in the theatre. I remember once, greased pigs were let loose among the members of the audience, who leapt on their seats and screamed. It was terrific. Goodness, how we enjoyed ourselves!'

This was obviously too good to last. An onslaught was delivered on it by leftist zealots who demanded collective proletarian art. Then Stalin decided to put an end to all these politico-literary squabbles as a sheer waste of energy – not at all what was needed for Five Year Plans. The Writers' Union was created in the mid-1930s to impose orthodoxy. There was to be no more argument, no disturbance of men's minds. A dead level of conformism followed. Then came the final horror – the Great Purge, the political show trials, the mounting terror of 1937–8, the wild and indiscriminate mowing down of individuals and groups, later of whole peoples. I need not dwell on the facts of that murderous period, not the first, nor probably the last, in the history of Russia. Authentic accounts of the life of the intelligentsia in that time are to be found in the memoirs of, for example, Nadezhda Mandel'shtam, Lydia Chukovskaya, and, in a difference sense, in Akhmatova's poem *Requiem*. In 1939 Stalin called a halt to the proscriptions. Russian literature, art and thought emerged like an area that had been subjected to bombardment, with some noble buildings still relatively intact, but standing bare and solitary in a landscape of ruined and deserted streets.

Then came the German invasion, and an extraordinary thing happened. The need to achieve national unity in the face of the enemy led to some relaxation of the political controls. In the great wave of Russian patriotic feeling, writers old and young, particularly poets, whom their readers felt to be speaking for them, for what they themselves felt and believed – these writers were idolised as never before. Poets whose work had been regarded with disfavour by the authorities, and consequently published seldom, if at all, suddenly received letters from soldiers at the fronts, as often as not quoting their least political and most personal lines. Boris Pasternak and Anna Akhmatova, who had for a long time lived in a kind of internal exile, began to receive an astonishingly large number of letters from soldiers quoting from both published and unpublished poems; there was a stream of requests for autographs, for confirmation of the authenticity of texts, for expressions of the author's attitude to this or that problem. In the end this impressed itself on the minds of some of the Party's leaders. The status and personal security of these frowned-upon poets were, in consequence, improved. Public readings by poets, as well as the reciting from memory of poetry at private gatherings, had been common in pre-revolutionary Russia. What was novel was that when Pasternak and Akhmatova read their poems, and occasionally halted for a word, there were always, among the vast audiences gathered to hear them, scores of listeners who prompted them at once with lines from works both published and unpublished, and in any case not publicly available. No writer could help being moved by and drawing strength from this most genuine form of homage.

The status of the handful of poets who clearly rose far above the rest was, I found, unique. Neither painters nor composers nor prose writers, nor even the most popular actors or eloquent, patriotic journalists, were loved and admired so deeply and so universally, especially by the kind of people I spoke to in trams and trains and the underground, some of whom admitted that they had never read a word of their writings. The most famous and widely worshipped of all Russian poets was Boris Pasternak. I longed to meet him more than any other human being in the Soviet Union. I was warned that it was very difficult to meet those whom the authorities did not permit to appear at official receptions, where foreigners could meet only carefully selected Soviet citizens – the others had had it very forcibly impressed upon them that it was neither desirable nor safe for them to meet foreigners, particularly in private. I was lucky. By a fortuitous concatenation of circumstances, I did contrive, very early during my stay, to call upon Pasternak at his country cottage in the writers' village of Peredelkino, near Moscow.

II

I went to see him on a warm, sunlit afternoon in September 1945. The poet, his wife and his son Leonid were seated round a rough wooden table at the back of the dacha. Pasternak greeted me warmly. He was once described by his friend, the poet Marina Tsvetaeva, as looking like an Arab and his horse – he had a dark, melancholy, expressive, very *racé* face, familiar from many photographs and from his father's paintings. He spoke slowly in a low tenor monotone, with a continuous even sound, something between a humming and a drone, which those who met him almost always remarked upon: each vowel was elongated as if in some plaintive aria in an opera by Tchaikovsky, but with far more concentrated force and tension.

Almost at once Pasternak said, 'You come from England. I was in London in the '30s – in 1935, on my way back from the Anti-Fascist Congress in Paris.' He then said that during the summer of that year he had suddenly received a telephone call from the authorities, who told him that a congress of writers was in session in Paris and that he was to go to it without delay. He said that he had no suitable clothes – 'We will see to that,' said the officials. They tried to fit him out in a formal morning coat and striped trousers, a shirt with stiff cuffs and a wing collar, and black patent leather boots, which fitted perfectly. But he was, in the end, allowed to go in ordinary clothes. He was later told that André Malraux, the organiser of the congress, had insisted on getting him invited; Malraux had told the Soviet authorities that although he fully understood their reluctance to do so, yet not to send Pasternak and Babel' to Paris might cause unnecessary speculation; they were very well-known Soviet writers, and there were not many such in those days so likely to appeal to European liberals. 'You cannot imagine how many celebrities were there,' Pasternak said – 'Dreiser, Gide, Malraux, Aragon, Auden, Forster, Rosamond Lehmann, and lots of other terribly famous people. I spoke. I said to them "I understand that this is a meeting of writers to organise resistance to Fascism. I have only one thing to say to you: do not organise. Organisation is the death of art. Only personal independence matters. In 1789, 1848, 1917 writers were not organised for or against anything. Do not, I implore you, do not organise."

'I think they were surprised, but what else could I say? I thought I would get into trouble at home after that, but no one ever said a word to me about it, then or now. Then I went to London and travelled back in one of our boats, and shared a cabin with Shcherbakov, who was then the secretary of the Writers' Union, tremendously influential, and afterwards a member of the Politburo. I talked unceasingly, day and night. He begged me to stop and let him sleep. But I went on and on. Paris and London had awoken me. I could not stop. He begged for mercy but I was relentless. He must have thought me quite deranged: it may be that this helped me afterwards.' He meant, I think, that to be thought a little mad, or at least extremely eccentric, may have helped to save him during the Great Purge.

Pasternak then asked me if I had read his prose, in particular *The*

*Childhood of Lüvers.* 'I see by your expression', he said, most unjustly, 'that you think that these writings are contrived, tortured, self-conscious, horribly modernist – no, no, don't deny it, you do think this, and you are absolutely right. I am ashamed of them – not of my poetry, but of my prose – it was influenced by what was weakest and most muddled in the symbolist movement, fashionable in those years, full of mystical chaos – of course Andrey Bely was a genius – *Petersburg, Kotik Letaev* are full of wonderful things – I know that, you need not tell me – but his influence was fatal – Joyce is another matter – all that I wrote then was obsessed, forced, broken, artificial, no use [*negodno*]; but now I am writing something entirely different: something new, quite new, luminous, elegant, well-proportioned [*stroinoe*], classically pure and simple – what Winckelmann wanted, yes, and Goethe; and this will be my last word, my most important word, to the world. It is, yes, it is what I wish to be remembered by; I shall devote the rest of my life to it.'

I cannot vouch for the complete accuracy of all these words, but this is how I remember them. This projected work later became *Doctor Zhivago*. He had by 1945 completed a draft of a few early chapters, which he asked me to read, and send to his sisters in Oxford; I did so, but was not to know about the plan for the entire novel until much later. After that, Pasternak was silent for a while; none of us spoke. He then told us how much he liked Georgia, Georgian writers, Yashvili, Tabidze, and Georgian wine, how well received there he always was. After this he politely asked me about what was going on in the West; did I know Herbert Read and his doctrine of personalism? Here he explained that his belief in personal freedom was derived from Kantian individualism – Blok had misinterpreted Kant completely in his poem *Kant*. There was nothing here in Russia about which he could tell me. I must realise that the clock had stopped in Russia (I noticed that neither he nor any of the other writers I met ever used the words 'Soviet Union') in 1928 or so, when relations with the outer world were in effect cut off; the description of him and his work in, for instance, the Soviet Encyclopaedia bore no reference to his later life or writings.

He was interrupted by Lydia Seifullina, an elderly, well-known writer, who broke in while he was in mid-course: 'My fate is exactly the same,' she said: 'the last lines of the Encyclopaedia article about me say "Seifullina is at present in a state of psychological and artistic crisis" – the article has not been changed during the last twenty years. So far as the Soviet reader is concerned, I am still in a state of crisis, of suspended animation. We are like people in Pompeii, you and I, Boris Leonidovich, buried by ashes in mid-sentence. And we know so little: Maeterlinck and Kipling, I know, are dead; but Wells, Sinclair Lewis, Joyce, Bunin, Khodasevich – are they alive?' Pasternak looked embarrassed and changed the subject. He had been reading Proust – French Communist friends had sent him the entire masterpiece – he knew it, he said, and had reread it lately. He had not then heard of Sartre or Camus, and thought little of Hemingway ('Why Anna Andreevna [Akhmatova] thinks anything of him I cannot imagine,' he said).

He spoke in magnificent slow-moving periods, with occasional intense rushes of words. His talk often overflowed the banks of grammatical structure – lucid passages were succeeded by wild but always marvellously vivid and concrete images – and these might be followed by dark words when it was difficult to follow him – and then he would suddenly come into the clear again. His speech was at all times that of a poet, as were his writings. Someone once said that there are poets who are poets when they write poetry and prose-writers when they write prose; others are poets in everything that they write. Pasternak was a poet of genius in all that he did and was. As for his conversation, I cannot begin to describe its quality. The only other person I have met who talked as he talked was Virginia Woolf, who made one's mind race as he did, and obliterated one's normal vision of reality in the same exhilarating and, at times, terrifying way.

I use the word 'genius' advisedly. I am sometimes asked what I mean by this highly evocative but imprecise term. In answer I can only say this: the dancer Nijinsky was once asked how he managed to leap so high. He is reported to have answered that he saw no great problem in this. Most people when they leaped in the air came down at once. 'Why should you come down immediately? Stay in the air a little before you return, why not?' he is reported to have said. One of the criteria of genius seems to me to be precisely this: the power to do something perfectly simple and visible which ordinary people cannot, and know that they cannot, do – nor do they know how it is done, or why they cannot begin to do it. Pasternak at times spoke in great leaps; his use of words was the most imaginative that I have ever known; it was wild and very moving. There are, no doubt, many varieties of literary genius: Eliot, Joyce, Yeats, Auden, Russell did not (in my experience) talk like this. I did not wish to overstay my welcome. I left the poet, excited, and indeed overwhelmed, by his words and by his personality.

After Pasternak returned to Moscow I visited him almost weekly, and came to know him well. I cannot hope to describe the transforming effect of his presence, his voice and gestures. He talked about books and writers; he loved Proust and was steeped in his writings, and *Ulysses* – he had not, at any rate then, read Joyce's later work. He spoke about French symbolists, and about Verhaeren and Rilke, both of whom he had met; he greatly admired Rilke, both as a man and a writer. He was steeped in Shakespeare. He was dissatisfied with his own translations: 'I have tried to make Shakespeare work for me,' he said, 'but it has not been a success.' He grew up, he said, in the shadow of Tolstoy – for him an incomparable genius, greater than Dickens or Dostoevsky, a writer who stood with Shakespeare and Goethe and Pushkin. His father, the painter, had taken him to see Tolstoy on his deathbed, in 1910, at Astapovo. He found it impossible to be critical towards Tolstoy: Russia and Tolstoy were one. As for Russian poets, Blok was of course the dominant genius of his time, but he did not find him sympathetic. Bely was closer to him, a man of strange and unheard-of insights – magical and a holy fool in the tradition of Russian Orthodoxy. Bryusov he considered a self-constructed, ingenious, mechanical musical-box, a clever, calculating operator, not a poet at all. He did not mention Mandel'shtam. He felt most tenderly towards Marina Tsvetaeva, to whom he had been bound by many years of friendship.

His feelings towards Mayakovsky were more ambivalent: he had known him well, they had been close friends, and he had learned from him; he was, of course, a titanic destroyer of old forms, but, he added, unlike other Communists, he was at all times a human being – but no, not a major poet, not an immortal god like Tyutchev or Blok, not even a demigod like Fet or Bely. Time had diminished him. He was needed in his day, he was what those times had called for. There are poets, he said, who have their hour, Aseev, poor Klyuev – liquidated – Sel'vinsky – even Esenin. They fulfil an urgent need of the day, their gifts are of crucial importance to the development of poetry in their country, and then they are no more. Mayakovsky was the greatest of these – *The Cloud in Trousers* had its historical importance, but the shouting was unbearable: he inflated his talent and tortured it until it burst. The sad rags of the multi-coloured balloon still lay in one's path, if one was a Russian. He was gifted, important, but coarse and not grown up, and ended as a poster-artist. Mayakovsky's love-affairs had been disastrous for him as a man and a poet. He, Pasternak, had loved Mayakovsky as a man; his suicide was one of the blackest days of his own life.

Pasternak was a Russian patriot – his sense of his own historical connection with his country was very deep. He told me, again and again, how glad he was to spend his summers in the writers' village, Peredelkino, for it had once been part of the estate of that great Slavophil, Yury Samarin. The true line of tradition led from the legendary Sadko to the Stroganovs and the Kochubeys, to Derzhavin, Zhukovsky, Tyutchev, Pushkin, Baratynsky, Lermontov, Fet, Annensky, to the Aksakovs, Tolstoy, Bunin – to the Slavophils, not to the liberal intelligentsia, which, as Tolstoy maintained, did not know what men lived by. This passionate, almost obsessive, desire to be thought a true Russian writer, with roots deep in Russian soil, was particularly evident in his negative feelings towards his Jewish origins. He was unwilling to discuss the subject – he was not embarrassed by it, but he disliked it: he wished the Jews to disappear as a people.

His artistic taste had been formed in his youth and he remained faithful to the masters of that period. The memory of Scriabin – he had thought of becoming a composer himself – was sacred to him. I shall not easily forget the paean of praise offered by both Pasternak and Neuhaus (the celebrated musician, and former husband of Pasternak's wife Zinaida) to Scriabin, and to the symbolist painter Vrubel, whom, with Nicholas Roerich, they prized above all contemporary painters. Picasso and Matisse, Braque and Bonnard, Klee and Mondrian, seemed to mean as little to them as Kandinsky or Malevich.

There is a sense in which Akhmatova and her contemporaries Gumilev and Marina Tsvetaeva are the last great voices of the nineteenth century – perhaps Pasternak occupies an interspace between the two centuries, and so, perhaps, does Mandel'shtam. They were the last representatives of what can only be called the second Russian renaissance, basically untouched by the modern movement, by Picasso, Stravinsky, Eliot, Joyce, Schoenberg, even if they admired them; for the modern movement in Russia was aborted by political events (the poetry of Mandel'shtam is another story). Pasternak loved Russia. He was prepared to forgive his country all its shortcomings, all, save the barbarism of Stalin's reign; but even that, in 1945, he regarded as the darkness before the dawn which he was straining his eyes to detect – the hope expressed in the last chapters of *Doctor Zhivago*. He believed himself to be in communion with the inner life of the Russian people, to share its hopes and fears and dreams, to be its voice as, in their different fashions, Tyutchev, Tolstoy, Dostoevsky, Chekhov and Blok had been (by the time I knew him he conceded nothing to Nekrasov).

In conversation with me during my Moscow visits, when we were always alone, before a polished desk on which not a book or a scrap of paper was to be seen, he repeated his conviction that he lived close to the heart of his country, and sternly and repeatedly denied this role to Gorky and Mayakovsky, especially to the former, and felt that he had something to say to the rulers of Russia, something of immense importance which only he could say, although what this was – he spoke of it often – seemed dark and incoherent to me. This may well have been due to lack of understanding on my part – although Anna Akhmatova told me that when he spoke in this prophetic strain, she, too, failed to understand him.

It was when he was in one of these ecstatic moods that he told me of his telephone conversation with Stalin about Mandel'shtam's arrest, the famous conversation of which many differing versions circulated and still circulate. I can only reproduce the story as I remember that he told it me in 1945. According to his account he was in his Moscow flat with his wife and son and no one else when the telephone rang, and a voice told him that it was the Kremlin speaking, and that comrade Stalin wished to speak to him. He assumed that this was an idiotic practical joke, and put down his receiver. The telephone rang again, and the voice somehow convinced him that the call was authentic. Stalin then asked him whether he was speaking to Boris Leonidovich Pasternak. Pasternak said that it was indeed he. Stalin asked whether he was present when a lampoon about himself, Stalin, was recited by Mandel'shtam. Pasternak answered that it seemed to him of no importance whether he was or was not present, but that he was enormously happy that Stalin was speaking to him; that he had always known that this would happen; that they must meet and speak about matters of supreme importance. Stalin then asked whether Mandel'shtam was a master. Pasternak replied that as poets they were very different;

that he admired Mandel'shtam's poetry but felt no affinity with it; but that, in any case, this was not the point at all.

Here, in recounting the episode to me, Pasternak again embarked on one of his great metaphysical flights about the cosmic turning-points in the world's history; it was these that he wished to discuss with Stalin – it was of supreme importance that he should do so. I can easily imagine that he spoke in this vein to Stalin too. At any rate, Stalin asked him again whether he was or was not present when Mandel'shtam read the lampoon. Pasternak answered again that what mattered most was his indispensable meeting with Stalin, that it must happen soon, that everything depended on it, that they must speak about ultimate issues, about life and death. 'If I were Mandel'shtam's friend, I should have known better how to defend him,' said Stalin, and put down the receiver. Pasternak tried to ring back but, not surprisingly, failed to get through to the leader. The episode evidently preyed deeply upon him. He repeated to me the version I have just recounted on at least two other occasions, and told the story to other visitors, although, apparently, in different forms. His efforts to rescue Mandel'shtam, in particular his appeal to Bukharin, probably helped to preserve him at least for a time – Mandel'shtam was finally destroyed some years later – but Pasternak clearly felt, it may be without good reason, but as anyone not blinded by self-satisfaction or stupidity might feel, that perhaps another response might have done more for the condemned poet.[1]

He followed this story with accounts of other victims: Pil'nyak, who anxiously waited ('was constantly looking out the window') for an emissary to ask him to sign a denunciation of one of the men accused of treason in 1936, and because none came, realised that he, too, was doomed. He spoke of the circumstances of Tsvetaeva's suicide in 1941, which he thought might have been prevented if the literary bureaucrats had not behaved with such appalling heartlessness to her. He told the story of a man who asked him to sign an open letter condemning Marshal Tukhachevsky. When Pasternak refused and explained the reasons for his refusal, the man burst into tears, said that the poet was the noblest and most saintly human being whom he had ever met, embraced him fervently; and then went straight to the secret police, and denounced him.

---

[1] Akhmatova and Nadezhda Mandel'shtam agreed to give him four out of five for his behaviour in this case.

Pasternak went on to say that despite the positive role which the Communist Party had played during the war, and not in Russia alone, he found the idea of any kind of relationship with it increasingly repellent: Russia was a galley, a slave-ship, and the Party men were the overseers who whipped the rowers. Why, he wished to know, did a British Commonwealth diplomat then in Moscow, whom I surely knew, a man who knew some Russian and claimed to be a poet, and visited him occasionally, why did this person insist, on every possible and impossible occasion, that he, Pasternak, should get closer to the Party? He did not need gentlemen who came from the other side of the world to tell him what to do – could I tell the man that his visits were unwelcome? I promised that I would, but did not do so, partly for fear of rendering Pasternak's none too secure position still more precarious.

Pasternak reproached me, too; not, indeed, for seeking to impose my political or any other opinions on him – but for something that to him seemed almost as bad. Here we both were, in Russia, and wherever one looked, everything was disgusting, appalling, an abominable pigsty, yet I seemed to be positively exhilarated by it: 'You wander about', he said, 'and look at everything with bemused eyes' – I was no better (he declared) than other foreign visitors who saw nothing, and suffered from absurd delusions, maddening to the poor miserable natives.

Pasternak was acutely sensitive to the charge of accommodating himself to the demands of the Party or the State – he seemed afraid that his mere survival might be attributed to some unworthy effort to placate the authorities, some squalid compromise of his integrity to escape persecution. He kept returning to this point, and went to absurd lengths to deny that he was capable of conduct of which no one who knew him could begin to conceive him to be guilty. One day he asked me whether I had heard anyone speak of his wartime volume of poems *On Early Trains* as a gesture of conformity with the prevailing orthodoxy. I said truthfully that I had not heard this, that it was an absurd suggestion.

Anna Akhmatova, who was bound to him by the deepest friendship and admiration, told me that, at the end of the War, when she was returning from Tashkent, to which she had been evacuated from Leningrad, she stopped in Moscow and visited Peredelkino. Within a few hours of arriving she received a message from Pasternak that he could not see her – he had a fever – he was in bed – it was impossible. On the next day the message was repeated. On the third day he appeared before her looking unusually well, with no trace of any ailment. The first thing he did was to ask her whether she had read this, the latest book of his poems. He put the question with so painful an expression on his face that she tactfully said that she had not, not yet; at which his face cleared, he looked vastly relieved, and they talked happily. He evidently felt ashamed, needlessly, of these poems. It seemed to him a kind of half-hearted effort to write civic poetry – there was nothing he disliked more intensely than this genre.

Yet, in 1945, he still had hopes of a great renewal of Russian life as a result of the cleansing storm that the War had seemed to him to be – a storm as transforming, in its own terrible fashion, as the Revolution itself, a vast cataclysm beyond our puny moral categories. Such vast mutations cannot, he held, be judged. One must think and think about them, and seek to understand as much of them as one can, all one's life; they are beyond good and evil, acceptance or rejection, doubt or assent; they must be accepted as elemental changes, earthquakes, tidal waves, transforming events, which are beyond all ethical and historical categories. So, too, the dark nightmare of betrayals, purges, massacres of the innocents, followed by an appalling war, seemed to him a necessary prelude to some inevitable, unheard-of victory of the spirit.

I did not see him again for eleven years. By 1956 his estrangement from his country's political establishment was complete. He could not speak of it, or its representatives, without a shudder. By that time his friend Olga Ivinskaya had been arrested, interrogated, maltreated, sent to a labour camp for five years. 'Your Boris,' the Minister of State Security, Abakumov, had said to her, 'your Boris detests us, doesn't he?' 'They were right,' Pasternak said: 'she could not and did not deny it.' I had travelled to Peredelkino with Neuhaus and one of his sons by his first wife, who was now married to Pasternak. He repeated over and over again that Pasternak was a saint: that he was too unworldly – his hope that the Soviet authorities would permit the publication of *Doctor Zhivago* was plainly absurd – martyrdom of the author was far more likely. Pasternak was the greatest writer produced by Russia for decades, and he would be destroyed, as so many had been destroyed, by the State. This was an inheritance from the tsarist regime. Whatever the differences between the old and the new Russia, suspicion and persecution of writers and artists were common to both. His former wife Zinaida – now Pasternak's wife – had told him that Pasternak was determined to get his novel published somewhere. He had tried to dissuade him, but his words were in vain. If Pasternak mentioned the matter to me, would I – it was important – more than important – perhaps a matter of life and death, who could tell, even in these days? – would I try to persuade him to hold his hand? Neuhaus seemed to me to be right: Pasternak probably did need to be physically saved from himself.

By this time we had arrived at Pasternak's house. He was waiting for us by the gate and let Neuhaus go in, embraced me warmly and said that in the eleven years during which we had not met much had happened, most of it very evil. He stopped and added, 'Surely there is something you want to say to me?' I said, with monumental tactlessness (not to say unforgivable stupidity), 'Boris Leonidovich, I am happy to see you looking so well. But the main thing is that you have survived. This seemed almost miraculous to some of us' (I was thinking of the anti-Jewish persecution of Stalin's last years). His face darkened and he looked at me with real anger: 'I know what you are thinking,' he said. 'What am I thinking, Boris Leonidovich?' 'I know, I know it, I know exactly what is in your mind,' he replied in a breaking voice – it was very frightening – 'do not prevaricate. I can see more clearly into your mind than I can into my own.' 'What am I thinking?' I asked again, more and more disturbed by his words. 'You think – I know that you think – that I have done something for *them*.' 'I assure you, Boris Leonidovich,' I replied, 'that I never conceived of this – I have never heard this suggested by anyone, even as an idiotic joke.' In the end he seemed to believe me. But he was visibly upset. Only after I had assured him that admiration for him, not only as a writer, but as a free and independent human being, was, among civilised people, world-wide, did he begin to return to his normal state. 'At least', he said, 'I can say, like Heine, "I may not deserve to be remembered as a poet, but surely as a soldier in the battle for human freedom." '[1]

He took me to his study. There he thrust a thick envelope into my hands: 'My book,' he said, 'it is all there. It is my last word.

[1] Cf. op. cit. (p. 444 above, note 1), vol. 4, p. 306.

Please read it.' I read *Doctor Zhivago* during the following night and day, and when, two or three days later, I saw him again, I asked what he intended to do with it. He told me that he had given it to an Italian Communist, who worked in the Italian section of the Soviet radio, and at the same time was acting as an agent for the Communist Italian publisher Feltrinelli. He had assigned world rights to Feltrinelli. He wished his novel, his testament, the most authentic, most complete of all his writings – his poetry was nothing in comparison (although the poems in the novel were, he thought, perhaps the best he had written) – he wished his work to travel over the entire world, to lay waste with fire (he quoted Pushkin's famous biblical line), to lay waste the hearts of men.

After the midday meal was over, his wife, Zinaida Nikolaevna, drew me aside and begged me with tears in her eyes to dissuade him from getting *Doctor Zhivago* published abroad. She did not wish her children to suffer; surely I knew what 'they' were capable of? Moved by this plea, I spoke to the poet at the first opportunity. I promised to have microfilms of his novel made, to bury them in the four quarters of the globe, to bury copies in Oxford, in Valparaiso, in Tasmania, Cape Town, Haiti, Vancouver, Japan, so that copies might survive even if a nuclear war broke out – was he resolved to defy the Soviet authorities, had he considered the consequences?

For the second time during that week he showed a touch of real anger in talking to me. He told me that what I said was no doubt well-intentioned, that he was touched by my concern for his own safety and that of his family (this was said a trifle ironically), but that he knew what he was doing; that I was worse than that importunate Commonwealth diplomat eleven years ago. He had spoken to his sons. They were prepared to suffer. I was not to mention the matter again. I had read the book, surely I realised what it, above all its dissemination, meant to him. I was shamed into silence.

After an interval, we talked about French literature, as often before. Since our last meeting he had procured Sartre's *La Nausée*, and found it unreadable, and its obscenity revolting. Surely after four centuries of creative genius this great nation could not have ceased to generate literature? Aragon was a time-server, Duhamel, Guéhenno were inconceivably tedious; was Malraux still writing? Before I could reply, one of his guests, a gentle, silent woman, a teacher who had recently returned after fifteen years in a labour camp, to which she had been condemned solely for teaching English, shyly asked whether Aldous Huxley had written anything since *Point Counter Point*. Was Virginia Woolf still writing? – she had never seen a book by her; but from an account in an old French newspaper which in some mysterious fashion had found its way into her camp, she thought that she might like her work.

It is difficult to convey the pleasure of being able to bring news of art and literature of the outer world to human beings so genuinely eager to receive it, so unlikely to obtain it from any other source. I told her and the assembled company all that I could of English, American, French writing. It was like speaking to the victims of shipwreck on a desert island, cut off for decades from civilisation. All they heard they received as new, exciting and delightful. The Georgian poet Titsian Tabidze, Pasternak's great friend, had perished in the Great Purge. His widow, Nina Tabidze, who was present, wanted to know whether Shakespeare, Ibsen and Shaw were still great names in the Western theatre. I told her that interest in Shaw had declined, but that Chekhov was greatly admired and often performed, and added that Akhmatova had said to me that she could not understand this worship of Chekhov. His world was uniformly drab. The sun never shone. No swords flashed. Everything was covered by a horrible grey mist. Chekhov's universe was a sea of mud with wretched human creatures caught in it helplessly. It was a travesty of life. Pasternak said that Akhmatova was wholly mistaken. 'Tell her when you see her – we cannot go to Leningrad freely, as you probably can – tell her from all of us here, that all Russian writers preach to the reader: even Turgenev tells him that time is a great healer and that kind of thing; Chekhov alone does not. He is a pure artist – everything is dissolved in art – he is our answer to Flaubert.' He went on to say that Akhmatova would surely talk to me about Dostoevsky and attack Tolstoy. But Tolstoy was right about Dostoevsky, that his novels were a dreadful mess, a mixture of chauvinism and hysterical religion: 'Tell Anna Andreevna that, and from me!' But when I saw Akhmatova again, in Oxford in 1965, I thought it best not to report his judgement: she might have wished to answer him. But Pasternak was in his grave. In fact, she did speak to me of Dostoevsky with the most passionate admiration.

## III

This brings me to my meeting with the poet Anna Akhmatova. I had been introduced to her poems by Maurice Bowra, and longed to meet her. In November 1945 I went from Moscow to Leningrad. I had not seen the city since 1919, when I was ten years old and my family was allowed to return to our native city of Riga, the capital of a then independent republic. In Leningrad my recollections of childhood became fabulously vivid. I was inexpressibly moved by the look of the streets, the houses, the statues, the embankments, the market places, the suddenly familiar, still broken, railings of a little shop, in which samovars were mended, below the house in which we had lived. The inner yard of the house looked as sordid and abandoned as it had done during the first years of the Revolution. My memories of specific events, episodes, experiences came between me and the physical reality. It was as if I had walked into a legendary city, myself at once part of the vivid, half-remembered legend, and yet, at the same time, viewing it from some outside vantage-point. The city had been greatly damaged, but still in 1945 remained indescribably beautiful (it seemed wholly restored by the time I saw it again, eleven years later). I made my way to the Writers' Bookshop in the Nevsky Prospekt. While looking at the books I fell into casual conversation with a man who was turning over the leaves of a book of poems. He turned out to be a well-known critic and literary historian. We talked about recent events. He described the terrible ordeal of the siege of Leningrad and the martyrdom and heroism of many of its inhabitants, and said that some had died of cold and hunger, others, mostly the younger ones, had survived. Some had been evacuated. I asked him about the fate of writers in Leningrad. He said, 'You mean Zoshchenko and Akhmatova?' Akhmatova to me was a figure from the remote past. Maurice Bowra, who had translated some of her poems, spoke about her to me as someone not heard of since the First World War. 'Is Akhmatova still alive?' I asked. 'Akhmatova, Anna Andreevna?' he said: 'Why yes, of course. She lives not far from here on the Fontanka, in Fontanny Dom [Fountain House]; would you like to meet her?' It was as if I had suddenly been invited to meet Miss Christina Rossetti. I could hardly speak. I mumbled that I should indeed like to meet her. 'I shall telephone her,' my new acquaintance said. He returned to tell me that she would receive us at three that afternoon. I was to return to the bookshop, and we would go together.

I returned at the appointed hour. The critic and I left the bookshop, turned left, crossed the Anichkov Bridge, and turned left again, along the embankment of the Fontanka. Fountain House, the palace of the Sheremetevs, is a magnificent late baroque building, with gates of exquisite ironwork for which Leningrad is famous, and built around a spacious court – not unlike the quadrangle of a large Oxford or Cambridge college. We climbed up one of the steep, dark staircases, to an upper floor, and were admitted to Akhmatova's room. It was very barely furnished – virtually everything in it had, I gathered, been taken away – looted or sold – during the siege. There was a small table, three or four chairs, a wooden chest, a sofa, and, above the unlit stove, a drawing by Modigliani. A stately, grey-haired lady, a white shawl draped about her shoulders, slowly rose to greet us.

Anna Andreevna Akhmatova was immensely dignified, with unhurried gestures, a noble head, beautiful, somewhat severe features, and an expression of immense sadness. I bowed. It seemed appropriate, for she looked and moved like a tragic queen. I thanked her for receiving me, and said that people in the West would be glad to know that she was in good health, for nothing had been heard of her for many years. 'Oh, but an article on me has appeared in the *Dublin Review*,' she said, 'and a thesis is being written about my work, I am told, in Bologna.' She had a friend with her, an academic lady of some sort, and there was polite conversation for some minutes. Then Akhmatova asked me about the ordeal of London during the bombing: I answered as best I could, feeling acutely shy and constricted by her distant, somewhat regal manner. Suddenly I heard what sounded like my first name being shouted somewhere outside. I ignored this for a while – it could only be an illusion – but the shouting became louder and the word 'Isaiah' could be clearly heard. I went to the window and looked out, and saw a man whom I recognised as Randolph Churchill. He was standing in the middle of the great court, looking like a tipsy undergraduate, and screaming my name. I stood rooted to the floor for some seconds. Then I collected myself, muttered an apology, and ran down the stairs. My only thought was to prevent Churchill from coming to the room. My companion, the critic, ran after me anxiously. When we emerged into the court, Churchill came towards me and greeted me effusively: 'Mr X,' I said mechanically, 'I do not suppose that you have met Mr Randolph Churchill?' The critic froze, his expression changed from bewilderment to horror, and he left as rapidly as he could. I have no notion whether I was followed by agents of the secret police, but there could be no doubt that Randolph Churchill was. It was this untoward event that caused absurd rumours to circulate in Leningrad that a foreign delegation had arrived to persuade Akhmatova to leave Russia; that Winston Churchill, a lifelong admirer of the poet, was sending a special aircraft to take Akhmatova to England, and so on.

Randolph, whom I had not met since we were undergraduates at Oxford, subsequently explained that he was in Moscow as a journalist on behalf of the North American Newspaper Alliance. He had come to Leningrad as part of his assignment. On arriving at the Hotel Astoria, his first concern had been to get the pot of caviar which he had acquired into an icebox: but, as he knew no Russian, and his interpreter had disappeared, his cries for help had finally brought down a representative of the British Council. She saw to his caviar and, in the course of general conversation, told him that I was in the city. He said that I might make an excellent substitute interpreter, and unfortunately discovered from the British Council lady where I was to be found. The rest followed. When he reached Fountain House, he adopted a method which had served him well during his days in Christ Church (his Oxford college), and, I dare say, on other occasions; 'and', he said with a winning smile, 'it worked'. I detached myself from him as quickly as I could, and after obtaining her number from the bookseller, telephoned Akhmatova to offer an explanation of my precipitate departure, and to apologise for it. I asked if I might be allowed to call on her again. 'I shall wait for you at nine this evening,' she answered.

When I returned, a learned lady, an Assyriologist, was also present who asked me a great many questions about English universities and their organisation. Akhmatova was plainly uninterested and, for the most part, silent. Shortly before midnight the Assyriologist left, and then Akhmatova began to ask me about old friends who had emigrated – some of whom I might know. (She was sure of that, she told me later. In personal relationships, she assured me, her intuition – almost second sight – never failed her.) I did indeed know some of them. We talked about the composer Artur Lurié, whom I had met in America during the War. He had been an intimate friend of hers, and had set to music some of her, and of Mandel'shtam's, poetry. She asked about Boris Anrep, the mosaicist (whom I had never met): I knew little about him, only that he had decorated the floor of the entrance hall of the National Gallery with the figures of celebrated persons – Bertrand Russell, Virginia Woolf, Greta Garbo, Clive Bell, Lydia Lopokova and the like. Twenty years later I was able to tell her that an image of herself had been added to them by Anrep. She showed me a ring with a black stone which Anrep had given her in 1917.

She had, she said, met only one foreigner – a Pole – since the First World War. She asked after various other friends – Salomé Andronikova, to whom Mandel'shtam dedicated one of his most famous poems; Stravinsky's wife, Vera; the poets Vyacheslav Ivanov and Georgy Adamovich. I answered as best I could. She spoke of her visits to Paris before the First World War, of her friendship with Amedeo Modigliani, whose drawing of her hung over the fireplace – one of many (the rest had perished during the siege). She described her childhood on the shores of the Black Sea, a pagan, unbaptised land, she called it, where one felt close to an ancient, half-Greek, half-barbarian, deeply un-Russian culture. She spoke of her first husband, the celebrated poet Gumilev. She was convinced that he had not taken part in the monarchist conspiracy for which he had been executed; Gorky, who had been asked by many writers to intervene on his behalf, apparently did nothing to save him. She had not seen him for some time before his condemnation – they had been divorced some years before. Her eyes had tears in them when she described the harrowing circumstances of his death.

After a silence, she asked me whether I would like to hear her poetry. But before doing this, she said that she wished to recite two cantos from Byron's *Don Juan* to me, for they were relevant to what would follow. Even if I had known the poem well, I could not have told which cantos she had chosen, for although she read English fairly freely, her pronunciation of it made it impossible to understand more than a word or two. She closed her eyes and spoke the lines from memory, with intense emotion. I rose and looked out of the window to conceal my embarrassment. Perhaps, I thought afterwards, that is how we now read classical Greek and Latin. Yet we, too, are moved by the words, which, as we pronounce them, might have been wholly unintelligible to their authors and audiences. Then she read from her book of poems –

*Anno Domini, The White Flock, Out of Six Books* – 'Poems like these, but far better than mine,' she said, 'were the cause of the death of the best poet of our time, whom I loved and who loved me . . .' – whether she meant Gumilev or Mandel'shtam I could not tell, for she broke down in tears, and could not go on reading.

There are recordings of her readings, and I shall not attempt to describe them. She read the (at that time) still unfinished *Poem Without a Hero*. I realised even then that I was listening to a work of genius. I do not suppose that I understood that many-faceted and most magical poem and its deeply personal allusions any better than when I read it now. She made no secret of the fact that it was intended as a kind of final memorial of her life as a poet, to the past of the city – St Petersburg – which was part of her being, and, in the form of a Twelfth Night carnival procession of masked figures *en travesti*, to her friends, and to their lives and destinies and her own – a kind of artistic *nunc dimittis* before the inescapable end which would not be long in coming. It is a mysterious and deeply evocative work: a tumulus of learned commentary is inexorably rising over it. Soon it may be buried under its weight.

Then she read the *Requiem*, from a manuscript. She broke off and spoke of the years 1937–8, when both her husband and her son had been arrested and sent to prison camps (this was to happen again), of the queues of women who waited day and night, week after week, month after month, for news of their husbands, brothers, fathers, sons, for permission to send food or letters to them. No news ever came. No messages ever reached them. A pall of death in life hung over the cities of the Soviet Union, while the torture and slaughter of millions of innocents were going on. She spoke in a dry, matter-of-fact voice, occasionally interrupting herself with 'No, I cannot, it is no good, you come from a society of human beings, whereas here we are divided into human beings and . . .'. Then a long silence: 'And even now . . .'. She would once more be silent. I asked about Mandel'shtam: she paused, her eyes filled with tears, and she begged me not to speak of him: 'After he slapped Aleksey Tolstoy's face, it was all over . . .'. It took some time for her to collect herself. Then in a totally changed voice, she said, 'Aleksey Tolstoy wore lilac shirts *à la russe* when we were in Tashkent. He spoke of the marvellous time he and I would have together when we came back. He was a very gifted and interesting writer, a scoundrel, full of charm, and a man of stormy tempera-ment. He is dead now. He was capable of anything, anything. He was a wild adventurer. He liked only youth, power, vitality. He didn't finish his *Peter the First* because he said that he could only deal with Peter as a young man; what was he to do with all those people when they grew old? He was a kind of Dolokhov. He called me Annushka. That made me wince, but I liked him very much, even though he was the cause of the death of the best poet of our time, whom I loved, and who loved me.' (Her words were identical with those she had used earlier; it now seemed clear to me to whom, on both occasions, she was referring.)

It was, I think, by now about three in the morning. She showed no sign of wishing me to leave, and I was far too moved and absorbed to stir. She left the room and came back with a dish of boiled potatoes. It was all she had, and she was embarrassed at the poverty of her hospitality. I begged her to let me write down the *Poem Without a Hero* and *Requiem*: she said there was no need for that. A volume of her collected verse was due to appear the next February. It was all in proof. She would send me a copy. The Party, as we know, ruled otherwise. She was denounced by Zhdanov (in a phrase which he had not invented) as 'half nun, half harlot'. This put her beyond the official pale.

We talked about Russian literature. After dismissing Chekhov because of the absence in his world of heroism and martyrdom, of depth and darkness and sublimity, we talked about *Anna Karenina*. 'Why did Tolstoy make her commit suicide? As soon as she leaves Karenin, everything changes. She suddenly turns into a fallen woman, a *traviata*, a prostitute. Who punishes Anna? God? No, not God – society – that same society whose hypocrisies Tolstoy is constantly denouncing. In the end he tells us that Anna repels even Vronsky. Tolstoy is lying. He knew better than that. The morality of *Anna Karenina* is the morality of Tolstoy's Moscow aunts, of philistine conventions. It is all connected with his personal vicissitudes. When Tolstoy was happily married he wrote *War and Peace*, which celebrates the family. After he started hating Sophia Andreevna, but could not divorce her, because divorce is condemned by society, and maybe by the peasants too, he wrote *Anna Karenina*, and punished Anna for leaving her husband. When he was old, and no longer lusted so violently after peasant girls, he wrote *The Kreutzer Sonata* and forbade sex altogether.'

These were her words. I do not know how seriously they were meant, but Akhmatova's dislike of Tolstoy's sermons was genuine

– she regarded him as a monster of vanity, and an enemy of freedom. She worshipped Dostoevsky and, like him, despised Turgenev. And, after Dostoevsky, Kafka, whom she read in English translations. ('He wrote for me and about me,' she told me years afterwards in Oxford – 'Kafka is a greater writer than even Joyce and Eliot. He did not understand everything; only Pushkin did that.') She then spoke to me about Pushkin's *Egyptian Nights*, and about the pale stranger in that story who improvised verse on themes supplied by the audience. The virtuoso, in her opinion, was the Polish poet Adam Mickiewicz. Pushkin's relation to him became ambivalent. The Polish issue divided them. But Pushkin always recognised genius in his contemporaries. Blok was like that – with his mad eyes and marvellous genius, he too could have been an *improvisateur*. She said that Blok had never liked her, but that every schoolmistress in Russia believed, and would doubtless go on believing, that they had had a love-affair. Historians of literature believed this too. All this, in her opinion, was based on her poem *A Visit to the Poet*, dedicated to Blok; and, perhaps, also on the poem on the death of *The Grey-Eyed King*, although that was written more than ten years before Blok died. Blok liked none of the Acmeists, of whom she was one. He did not like Pasternak either.

She then spoke about Pasternak, to whom she was devoted. After Mandel'shtam's and Tsvetaeva's deaths, they were alone. The knowledge that the other was alive and at work was a source of infinite comfort to both of them. They criticised each other freely, but allowed no one else to do so. The passionate devotion of countless men and women in the Soviet Union who knew their verse by heart, and copied it and circulated it, was a source of pride to them. But they both remained effectively in exile. Yet the thought of emigration was hateful to both. They longed to visit the West, but not if it meant that they would be unable to return. Their deep patriotism was not tinged by nationalism. Akhmatova was not prepared to move. No matter what horrors might be in store, she would never abandon Russia.

She spoke of her childhood, her marriages, her relationships with others, of the rich artistic life in Petersburg before the First World War. She had no doubt that the culture of the West, especially now, in 1945, was far superior to it. She spoke about the great poet Annensky, who had taught her more even than Gumilev, and died largely ignored by editors and critics, a great forgotten master. She spoke about her loneliness and isolation. Leningrad, after the War, was for her nothing but the graveyard of her friends – it was like the aftermath of a forest fire, the few charred trees made the desolation still more desolate. She lived by translating. She had begged to be allowed to translate the letters of Rubens, not those of Romain Rolland. After unheard-of obstacles, permission was finally granted. I asked her what the Renaissance meant to her – was it a real historical past, or an idealised vision, an imaginary world? She replied that it was the latter. She felt nostalgia for it – that longing for a universal culture of which Mandel'shtam had spoken, as Goethe and Schlegel had thought of it – a longing for what had been transmuted into art and thought – nature, love, death, despair and martyrdom – a reality which had no history, nothing outside itself. She spoke in a calm, even voice, like a remote princess in exile, proud, unhappy, unapproachable, often in words of the most moving eloquence.

The account of the unrelieved tragedy of her life went beyond anything which anyone had ever described to me in spoken words; the recollection of it is still vivid and painful to me. I asked her whether she intended to compose a record of her literary life. She replied that her poetry was that, in particular the *Poem Without a Hero*, which she read to me again. Once more I begged her to let me write it down. Once again she declined. Our conversation, which touched on intimate details of both her life and my own, wandered from literature and art, and lasted until late in the morning of the following day. I saw her again when I was leaving the Soviet Union to go home by way of Leningrad and Helsinki. I went to say goodbye to her on the afternoon of 5 January 1946, and she then gave me one of her collections of verse, with a new poem inscribed on the flyleaf – the poem that was later to form the second in the cycle entitled *Cinque*. I realised that this poem, in this, its first version, had been directly inspired by our earlier meeting. There are other references and allusions to our meetings, in *Cinque* and elsewhere.

I did not see her on my next visit to the Soviet Union, in 1956. Her son, who had been re-arrested, had been released from his prison camp earlier that year, and Pasternak told me that she felt acutely nervous about seeing foreigners except by official order, but that she wished me to telephone her; this was far safer, for all her telephone conversations were monitored. Over the telephone she told me something of her experiences as a condemned writer;

of the turning away by some whom she had considered faithful friends, of the nobility and courage of others. She had reread Chekhov, and said that at least in *Ward No 6* he had accurately described her situation, and that of many others. Meanwhile her translations from the classical Korean verse had been published – 'You can imagine how much Korean I know; it is a selection; not selected by me. There is no need for you to read it.'

When we met in Oxford in 1965 Akhmatova told me that Stalin had been personally enraged by the fact that she had allowed me to visit her: 'So our nun now receives visits from foreign spies,' he is alleged to have remarked, and followed this with obscenities which she could not at first bring herself to repeat to me. The fact that I had never worked in any intelligence organisation was irrelevant. All members of foreign missions were spies to Stalin. Of course, she said, the old man was by then out of his mind, in the grip of pathological paranoia. In Oxford she told me that she was convinced that Stalin's fury, which we had caused, had unleashed the Cold War – that she and I had changed the history of mankind. She meant this quite literally and insisted on its truth. She saw herself and me as world-historical personages chosen by destiny to play our fateful part in a cosmic conflict, and this is reflected in her poems of this time. It was intrinsic to her entire historico-philosophical vision, from which much of her poetry flowed.

She told me that after her journey to Italy in the previous year, when she had been awarded a literary prize, she was visited by officials of the Soviet secret police, who asked her for her impressions of Rome. She replied that Rome seemed to her to be a city where paganism was still at war with Christianity. 'What war?' she was asked. 'Was the USA mentioned? Are Russian émigrés involved?' What should she answer when similar questions were put to her about England and Oxford? For to Russia she would return no matter what awaited her there. The Soviet regime was the established order of her country. With it she had lived, and with it she would die. This is what being a Russian meant.

We returned to Russian poetry. She spoke contemptuously of well-known young poets, favoured by the Soviet authorities. One of the most famous of these, who was in England at the time, had sent her a telegram to Oxford to congratulate her on her honorary doctorate. I was there when it arrived. She read it, and angrily threw it in the waste-paper basket – 'They are all little bandits, prostitutes of their gifts, and exploiters of public taste. Mayakov-sky's influence has been fatal to them all. Mayakovsky shouted at the top of his voice because it was natural to him to do so. He could not help it. His imitators have adopted his manner as a genre. They are vulgar declaimers with not a spark of true poetry in them.'

There were many gifted poets in Russia now: the best among them was Joseph Brodsky, whom she had, she said, brought up by hand, and whose poetry had in part been published – a noble poet in deep disfavour, with all that that implied. There were others, too, marvellously gifted – but their names would mean nothing to me – poets whose verses could not be published, and whose very existence was testimony to the unexhausted life of the imagination in Russia: 'They will eclipse us all,' she said, 'believe me, Pasternak and I and Mandel'shtam and Tsvetaeva, all of us are the end of a long period of elaboration which began in the nineteenth century. My friends and I thought we spoke with the voice of the twentieth century. But these new poets constitute a new beginning – behind bars now, but they will escape and astonish the world.' She spoke at some length in this prophetic vein, and returned again to Mayakovsky, driven to despair, betrayed by his friends, but, for a while, the true voice, the trumpet, of his people, though a fatal example to others; she herself owed nothing to him, but much to Annensky, the purest and finest of poets, remote from the hurly-burly of literary politics, largely neglected by avant-garde journals, fortunate to have died when he did. He was not read widely in his lifetime, but then this was the fate of other great poets – the present generation was far more sensitive to poetry than her own had been: who cared, who truly cared about Blok or Bely or Vyacheslav Ivanov in 1910? Or, for that matter, about herself and the poets of her group? But today the young knew it all by heart – she was still getting letters from young people, many of them from silly, ecstatic girls, but the sheer number of them was surely evidence of something.

Pasternak received even more of these, and liked them better. Had I met his friend Olga Ivinskaya? I had not. She found both Pasternak's wife, Zinaida, and his mistress equally unbearable, but Boris Leonidovich himself was a magical poet, one of the great poets of the Russian land: every sentence he wrote, in verse and prose, spoke with his authentic voice, unlike any other she had ever heard. Blok and Pasternak were divine poets; no modern Frenchman, no Englishman, not Valéry, not Eliot, could compare with them – Baudelaire, Shelley, Leopardi, that was the company to which they belonged. Like all great poets, they had little sense of the quality of others – Pasternak often praised inferior critics, discovered imaginary hidden gifts, encouraged all kinds of minor figures – decent writers but without talent – he had a mythological sense of history, in which quite worthless people sometimes played mysterious significant roles – like Evgraf in *Doctor Zhivago* (she vehemently denied that this mysterious figure was in any respect based on Stalin; she evidently found this impossible to contemplate). He did not really read contemporary authors he was prepared to praise – not Bagritsky or Aseev, not even Mandel'-shtam (whom he could not bear, though of course he did what he could for him when he was in trouble), nor her own work – he wrote her wonderful letters about her poetry, but the letters were about himself, not her – she knew that they were sublime fantasies which had little to do with her: 'Perhaps all great poets are like this.'

Paskernak's compliments naturally made those who received them very happy, but this was delusive; he was a generous giver, but not truly interested in the work of others: interested, of course, in Shakespeare, Goethe, the French symbolists, Rilke, perhaps Proust, but 'not in any of us'. She said that she missed Pasternak's existence every day of her life; they had never been in love, but they loved one another deeply and this irritated his wife. She then spoke of the 'blank' years during which she was officially out of account in the Soviet Union – from the mid-1920s until the late '30s. She said that when she was not translating, she read Russian poets: Pushkin constantly, of course, but also Odoevsky, Lermontov, Baratynsky – she thought Baratynsky's *Autumn* was a work of pure genius; and she had recently reread Velemir Khlebnikov – mad but marvellous.

I asked her if she would ever annotate the *Poem Without a Hero*: the allusions might be unintelligible to those who did not know the life it was concerned with; did she wish them to remain in darkness? She answered that when those who knew the world about which she spoke were overtaken by senility or death, the poem would die too; it would be buried with her and her century; it was not written for eternity, nor even for posterity: the past alone had significance for poets – childhood most of all – those were the emotions that they wished to re-create and re-live. Vaticination, odes to the future, even Pushkin's great epistle to Chaadaev, were a form of declamatory rhetoric, a striking of grandiose attitudes, the poet's eye peering into a dimly discernible future, a pose which she despised.

She knew, she said, that she had not long to live. Doctors had made it plain to her that her heart was weak. Above all, she did not wish to be pitied. She had faced horrors, and had known the most terrible depths of grief. She had exacted from her friends the promise that they would not allow the faintest gleam of pity for her to occur; hatred, insult, contempt, misunderstanding, persecution she could bear, but not sympathy if it was mingled with compassion. Her pride and dignity were very great.

The detachment and impersonality with which she seemed to speak only partially disguised her passionate convictions and moral judgements, against which there was plainly no appeal. Her accounts of personalities and lives were compounded of sharp insight into the moral centre of characters and situations (she did not spare her friends in this respect) together with fixed ideas, from which she could not be moved. She knew that our meeting had had serious historical consequences. She knew that the poet Georgy Ivanov, whom she accused of having written lying memoirs after he emigrated, had at one time been a police spy in the pay of the tsarist government. She knew that the poet Nekrasov in the nineteenth century had also been a government agent; that the poet Annensky had been hounded to death by his literary enemies. These beliefs had no apparent foundation in fact – they were intuitive, but they were not senseless, not sheer fantasies; they were elements in a coherent conception of her own and her nation's life and fate, of the central issues which Pasternak had wanted to discuss with Stalin, the vision which sustained and shaped her imagination and her art. She was not a visionary; she had, for the most part, a strong sense of reality. She described the literary and social scene in Petersburg before the First World War, and her part in it, with a sober realism and sharpness of detail which made it totally credible.

Akhmatova lived in terrible times, during which, according to Nadezhda Mandel'shtam, she behaved with heroism. She did not in public, nor indeed to me in private, utter a single word against the Soviet regime. But her entire life was what Herzen once described Russian literature as being – one continuous indictment of Russian reality. The worship of her memory in the Soviet Union today,[1] undeclared but widespread, has, so far as I know, no parallel. Her unyielding passive resistance to what she regarded as unworthy of her country and herself transformed her into a figure (as Belinsky once predicted about Herzen) not merely in Russian literature, but in the Russian history of our time.

My meetings and conversations with Boris Pasternak and Anna Akhmatova; my realisation of the conditions, scarcely describable, under which they lived and worked, and of the treatment to which they were subjected; and the fact that I was allowed to enter into a personal relationship, indeed, friendship, with them both, affected me profoundly and permanently changed my outlook. When I see their names in print, or hear them mentioned, I remember vividly the expressions on their faces, their gestures and their words. When I read their writings I can, to this day, hear the sound of their voices.

[1] This was written in 1980.

# THE APOTHEOSIS
# OF THE ROMANTIC WILL

*The Revolt against the Myth of an Ideal World*

I

THE HISTORY of ideas is a comparatively new field of knowledge, and still tends to be looked at with some suspicion in a good many academic quarters. Yet it has uncovered interesting facts. Among the most striking is the chronology of some of our most familiar concepts and categories, at any rate in the Western world. We discover with some surprise how recently some of them emerged: how strange some of our apparently most deeply rooted attitudes might have seemed to our ancestors. I do not mean by this ideas based upon specific scientific and technological discoveries and inventions unknown to them, or new hypotheses about the nature of matter, or the history of societies remote from us in time or space, or the evolution of the material universe, or the springs of our own behaviour, and the part played in it by insufficiently examined unconscious and irrational factors. I mean something at once more pervasive and less easily traceable to specific causes: changes in widely accepted, consciously followed, secular values, ideals, goals, at any rate in Western civilisation.

Thus no one today is surprised by the assumption that variety is, in general, preferable to uniformity – monotony, uniformity are pejorative words – or, to turn to qualities of character, that integrity and sincerity are admirable independently of the truth or validity of the beliefs or principles involved; that warm-hearted idealism is nobler, if less expedient, than cold realism; or tolerance than intolerance, even though these virtues can be taken too far and lead to dangerous consequences; and so on. Yet this has not long been so; for the notion that One is good, Many – diversity – is bad, since the truth is one, and only error is multiple, is far older, and deeply rooted in the Platonic tradition. Even Aristotle, who accepts that human types differ from each other, and that therefore elasticity in social arrangements is called for, accepts this as a fact, without regret but without any sign of approval; and, with very few exceptions, this view seems to prevail in the classical and medieval worlds, and is not seriously questioned until, say, the sixteenth century.

Again, what Catholic in, let us say, the sixteenth century would say, 'I abhor the heresies of the reformers, but I am deeply moved by the sincerity and integrity with which they hold and practise and sacrifice themselves for their abominable beliefs'? On the contrary, the deeper the sincerity of such heretics, or unbelievers – Muslims, Jews, atheists – the more dangerous they are, the more likely to lead souls to perdition, the more ruthlessly should they be eliminated, since heresy – false beliefs about the ends of men – is surely a poison more dangerous to the health of society than even hypocrisy or dissimulation, which at least do not openly attack the true doctrine. Only truth matters: to die in a false cause is wicked or pitiable.

Here, then, there is no common ground between views that prevailed even as late as the sixteenth or seventeenth century and modern liberal attitudes. Who in the ancient world or the Middle Ages even spoke of the virtues of diversity in life or thought? But when a modern thinker like Auguste Comte wondered why, when we do not allow freedom of opinion in mathematics, we should allow it in morals and politics, his very question shocked J. S. Mill and other liberals.[1] Yet most of these beliefs, which are part of modern liberal culture (and today under attack from both the right and the left on the part of those who have reverted to an older view) – these beliefs are relatively novel, and draw their plausibility from a deep and radical revolt against the central tradition of Western thought. This revolt, which seems to me to have become articulate in the second third of the eighteenth century, principally in Germany, has shaken the foundations of the old, traditional establishment, and has affected European thought and practice profoundly and unpredictably. It is perhaps the largest shift in European consciousness since the Reformation, to which, by twisting, circuitous paths, its origins can be traced.

[1] Cf. p. 222 above, note 3.

II

If I may be permitted an almost unpardonable degree of simplifica-
tion and generalisation, I should like to suggest that the central
core of the intellectual tradition in the West has, since Plato (or it
may be Pythagoras), rested upon three unquestioned dogmas:

(*a*) that to all genuine questions there is one true answer and one
only, all others being deviations from the truth and therefore false,
and that this applies to questions of conduct and feeling, that is, to
practice, as well as to questions of theory or observation – to
questions of value no less than to those of fact;

(*b*) that the true answers to such questions are in principle
knowable;

(*c*) that these true answers cannot clash with one another, for one
true proposition cannot be incompatible with another; that
together these answers must form a harmonious whole: according
to some they form a logical system each ingredient of which
logically entails and is entailed by all the other elements; according
to others the relationship is that of parts to a whole, or, at the very
least, of complete compatibility of each element with all the others.

There has, of course, been wide disagreement about the exact
path leading to these, often hidden, truths. Some have believed (and
believe) that they are to be found in sacred texts, or through their
interpretation by appropriate experts – priesthoods, inspired
prophets and seers, the doctrine and tradition of a Church. Some
put their faith in other kinds of experts: philosophers, scientists,
privileged observers of one kind or another, men who may,
perhaps, have undergone a special spiritual training, or alternatively
simple men, free from the corruption and sophistication of cities –
peasants, children, 'the people', beings whose souls are pure.
Others, again, have taught that these truths are accessible to all
men, provided their minds are not befuddled by wiseacres or
deliberate deceivers. As for the means of access to the truth, some
have appealed to nature, others to revelation; some to reason,
others to faith or intuition, or observation, or deductive and
inductive disciplines, hypothesis and experiment; and so on.

Even the most notorious sceptics accepted some part of this: the
Greek sophists distinguished between nature and culture and
believed that differences of circumstances, environment, temperament, accounted for the variety of laws and customs. But even they
believed that ultimate human ends were much the same every-

where, for all men seek to satisfy natural wants, desire security, peace, happiness and justice. Nor did Montesquieu or Hume, for all their relativism, deny this; the former's faith in absolute principles such as freedom and justice and the latter's faith in nature and custom led them to similar conclusions. Moralists, anthropologists, relativists, utilitarians, Marxists all assumed common experience and common ends in virtue of which human beings were human – too sharp a deviation from such standards pointed to perversion or mental sickness or madness.

Again, opinions differed about the conditions in which these truths were discoverable: some thought that men, because of original sin, or innate lack of ability, or natural obstacles, could never know the answers to every question, or perhaps any of them fully; some thought that there had been perfect knowledge before the Fall, or before the Flood or some other disaster that had befallen men – the building of the tower of Babel, or primitive accumulation of capital and the class war that resulted from it, or some other breach in the original harmony; others believed in progress – that the golden age lay not in the past but in the future; still others believed that men were finite, doomed to imperfection and error on this earth, but would know the truth in a life beyond the grave; or else that only the angels could know it; or only God himself. These differences led to deep divisions and destructive wars, since nothing less than the question of eternal salvation was at issue. But what none of the contending parties denied was that these fundamental questions were in principle answerable; and that a life formed according to the true answers would constitute the ideal society, the golden age, inasmuch as the very notion of human imperfection was intelligible only as a falling short of the perfect life. Even if we did not, in our fallen state, know of what it consisted, we knew that if only the fragments of the truth by which we lived could be fitted together like a jigsaw puzzle the resultant whole, translated into practice, would constitute the perfect life. This could not be so if the questions turned out to be in principle unanswerable, or if more than one answer to the same question was equally true, or, worse still, if some of the true answers proved to be incompatible with each other, if values clashed and could not, even in principle, be reconciled. But this would entail that the universe was in the end irrational in character – a conclusion which reason, and faith that wished to live in peace with reason, could not but reject.

All the Utopias known to us are based upon the discoverability and harmony of objectively true ends, true for all men, at all times and in all places. This holds of every ideal city, from Plato's Republic and his Laws, and Zeno's anarchist world community, and the City of the Sun of Iambulus, to the Utopias of Thomas More and Campanella, Bacon and Harrington and Fénelon. The communist societies of Mably and Morelly, the State capitalism of Saint-Simon, the Phalanstères of Fourier, the various combinations of anarchism and collectivism of Owen and Godwin, Cabet, William Morris and Chernyshevsky, Bellamy, Hertzka and others (there is no lack of them in the nineteenth century) rest on the three pillars of social optimism in the West of which I have spoken: that the central problems – the *massimi problemi* – of men are, in the end, the same throughout history; that they are in principle soluble; and that the solutions form a harmonious whole. Man has permanent interests, the character of which the right method can establish. These interests may differ from the goals which men actually seek, or think that they seek, which may be due to spiritual or intellectual blindness or laziness, or the unscrupulous machinations of self-seeking knaves – kings, priests, adventurers, power-seekers of all kinds – who throw dust in the eyes of fools and ultimately their own. Such illusions may also be due to the destructive influence of social arrangements – traditional hierarchies, the division of labour, the capitalist system – or again to impersonal factors, natural forces or the unintended consequences of human nature, which can be resisted and abolished.

Once men's true interests can be made clear, the claims which they embody can be satisfied by social arrangements founded on the right moral directions, which make use of technical progress or, alternatively, reject it in order to return to the idyllic simplicity of humanity's earlier days, a paradise which men have abandoned, or a golden age still to come. Thinkers from Bacon to the present have been inspired by the certainty that there must exist a total solution: that in the fullness of time, whether by the will of God or by human effort, the reign of irrationality, injustice and misery will end; man will be liberated, and will no longer be the plaything of forces beyond his control – savage nature, or the consequences of his own ignorance or folly or vice; that this springtime in human affairs will come once the obstacles, natural and human, are overcome, and then at last men will cease to fight each other, unite their powers, and co-operate to adapt nature to their needs (as the great materialist thinkers from Epicurus to Marx have advocated) or their needs to nature (as the Stoics and modern environmentalists have urged). This is common ground to the many varieties of revolutionary and reformist optimism, from Bacon to Condorcet, from the Communist Manifesto to modern technocrats, Communists, anarchists and seekers after alternative societies.

It is this great myth – in Sorel's sense of the word – that came under attack towards the end of the eighteenth century by a movement at first known in Germany as *Sturm und Drang*, and later as the many varieties of romanticism, nationalism, expressionism, emotivism, voluntarism and the many contemporary forms of irrationalism of both the right and the left familiar to everyone today. The prophets of the nineteenth century predicted many things – domination by international cartels, by collectivist regimes both socialist and capitalist, by military-industrial complexes, by scientific élites, preceded by *Krisen, Kriege, Katastrophen*, wars and holocausts – but what none of them, so far as I know, predicted was that the last third of the twentieth century would be dominated by a world-wide growth of nationalism, enthronement of the will of individuals or classes, and the rejection of reason and order as being prison-houses of the spirit. How did this begin?

III

It is customary to say that in the eighteenth century rational views and respect for coherent intellectual systems were succeeded by sentimentality and introspection and the celebration of feeling, as instanced by the bourgeois English novel, the *comédie larmoyante*, the addiction to self-revelation and self-pity of Rousseau and his disciples, and his onslaughts on the clever but morally empty or corrupt intellectuals of Paris, with their atheism and calculating utilitarianism, which did not take into account the need for love and free self-expression of the unperverted human heart; and that this discredited the hollow pseudo-classicism of the age and opened the gate to unbridled emotionalism. There is some truth in this, but on the one hand Rousseau, like the objects of his scorn, identified nature and reason, and condemned mere irrational 'passion'; and, on the other, emotion has never been absent from human relationships and art. The Bible, Homer, the Greek tragedians, Catullus, Virgil, Dante, French classical tragedy are full of profound emotion. It was not the human heart or human nature as such that were ignored or suppressed in the central tradition of European art, but this did not prevent continuous concern with form and structure, an emphasis on rules for which rational justification was sought. In art, as in philosophy and politics, there was for many centuries a conscious appeal to objective standards, of which the most extreme form was the doctrine of eternal prototypes, immutable Platonic or Christian patterns, in terms of which both life and thought, theory and practice, tended to be judged. The aesthetic doctrine of mimesis, which unites the ancient, medieval and Renaissance worlds with the Great Style of the eighteenth century, presupposes that there exist universal principles and eternal patterns to be incorporated or 'imitated'. The revolt which (at least temporarily) overthrew it was directed not merely against the decayed formalism and pedantry of chilly neo-classicism – it went much further, for it denied the reality of universal truths, the eternal forms which knowledge and creation, learning and art and life must learn to embody if they are to justify their claims to represent the noblest flights of human reason and imagination. The rise of science and empirical methods – what Whitehead once called the 'revolt of matter' – only substituted one set of forms for another; it shook faith in the a priori axioms and laws provided by theology or Aristotelian metaphysics, and put in their place laws and rules validated by empirical experience, in particular by a spectacularly increased capacity to fulfil Bacon's programme – to predict and control nature, and men as natural beings.

The 'revolt of matter' was not a rebellion against laws and rules as such, nor against old ideals – the reign of reason, of happiness and knowledge. On the contrary, the domination of mathematics and analogies made from it to other provinces of human thought, the faith in salvation by knowledge, were never so strong as they were during the Enlightenment. But by the end of the eighteenth century and the beginning of the nineteenth we find violent scorn for rules and forms as such – passionate pleas for the freedom of self-expression of groups, movements, individuals, whithersoever this might carry them. Idealistic students in German universities, affected by the romantic currents of the age, thought nothing of such goals as happiness, security or scientific knowledge, political and economic stability and social peace, and indeed looked upon such things with contempt. For the disciples of the new philosophy suffering was nobler than pleasure, failure was preferable to worldly success, which had about it something squalid and opportunist, and could surely be bought only at the cost of betraying one's integrity, independence, the inner light, the ideal vision within. They believed that it was the minorities, above all those who suffered for their convictions, that had the truth in them, and not the mindless majorities, that martyrdom was sacred no matter in what cause, that sincerity and authenticity and intensity of feeling, and, above all, defiance – which involved perpetual struggle against convention, against the oppressive forces of Church and State and philistine society, against cynicism and commercialism and indifference – that these were sacred values, even if, and perhaps because, they were bound to fail in the degraded world of masters and slaves; to fight, and if need be die, was brave and right and honourable, whereas to compromise and survive was cowardice and betrayal.

These men were champions not of feeling against reason, but of another faculty of the human spirit, the source of all life and action, of heroism and sacrifice, nobility and idealism both individual and collective – the proud, indomitable, untrammelled human will. If the exercise of it caused suffering, led to conflict, was incompatible with an untroubled, harmonious life, or the achievement of artistic perfection, serene and undisturbed by the dust and din of the battle for the fullness of life; if the revolt of Prometheus against the Olympian gods doomed him to eternal torment, then so much the worse for Olympus, down with the view of perfection which can be purchased only at the price of putting chains on the free, independent will, the unbridled imagination, the wild wind of inspiration which bloweth where it listeth. Independence, defiance by individuals and groups and nations, pursuit of goals not because they are universal but because they are mine, or those of my people, my culture – this was the outlook of a minority even among the German romantics, echoed by still fewer in the rest of Europe: nevertheless, they set their stamp on their time and on ours. No great artist, no national leader in the nineteenth century was wholly free from their influence. Let me return to some of its roots in the years before the French Revolution.

IV

No thinker was more opposed to undisciplined enthusiasm, emotional turbulence, *Schwärmerei* – vague, unfocused fervour and yearning – than Immanuel Kant. A scientific pioneer himself, he set himself to give a rational explanation and justification of the methods of the natural sciences, which he rightly looked upon as the major achievement of the age. Nevertheless, in his moral philosophy he did lift the lid of a Pandora's box, which released tendencies which he was among the first, with perfect honesty and consistency, to disown and condemn. He maintained, as every German schoolboy used to know, that the moral worth of an act depended on its being freely chosen by the agent; that if a man acted under the influence of causes which he could not and did not control, whether external, such as physical compulsion, or internal, such as instincts or desires or passions, then the act, whatever its consequences, whether they were good or bad, advantageous or harmful to men, had no moral value, for the act had not been freely chosen, but was simply the effect of mechanical causes, an event in nature, no more capable of being judged in ethical terms than the behaviour of an animal or a plant. If the determinism that reigns in nature – on which, indeed, the whole of natural science is based – determines the acts of a human agent, he is not truly an agent, for to act is to be capable of free choice between alternatives; and free will must in that case be an illusion. Kant is certain that freedom of the will is not illusory but real. Hence the immense emphasis that he places on human autonomy – on the capacity for free commitment to rationally chosen ends. The self, Kant tells us, must be 'raised above natural necessity', for if men are ruled by the same laws as those which govern the material world 'freedom cannot be saved', and without freedom there is no morality.[1]

Kant insists over and over again that what distinguishes man is his moral autonomy as against his physical heteronomy – for his body is governed by natural laws, not issuing from his own inner self. No doubt this doctrine owes a great deal to Rousseau, for whom all dignity, all pride rest upon independence. To be manipulated is to be enslaved. A world in which one man depends upon the favour of another is a world of masters and slaves, of bullying and condescension and patronage at one end, and obsequiousness, servility, duplicity and resentment at the other. But whereas Rousseau supposes that only dependence on other men is degrading, for no one resents the laws of nature, only ill will,[2] the

---

[1] *Critique of Pure Reason*, A466/B494; A536/B564.
[2] Cf. p. 195 above, note 2.

Germans went further. For Kant, total dependence on non-human nature – heteronomy – was incompatible with choice, freedom, morality. This exhibits a new attitude to nature, or at least the revival of an ancient Christian antagonism to it. The thinkers of the Enlightenment and their predecessors in the Renaissance (save for isolated antinomian mystics) tended to look upon nature as divine harmony, or as a great organic or artistic unity, or as an exquisite mechanism created by the divine watchmaker, or else as uncreated and eternal, but always as a model from which men depart at their cost. The principal need of man is to understand the external world and himself and the place that he occupies in the scheme of things: if he grasps this, he will not seek after goals incompatible with the needs of his nature, goals which he can follow only through some mistaken conception of what he is in himself, or of his relations to other men or the external world. This is equally true of rationalists and empiricists, Christian naturalists and pagans and atheists, both in the Renaissance and after – of Pico and Marsilio Ficino, of Locke and Spinoza, Leibniz and Gassendi. For them God is nature's God, nature is not, as it is for Augustine or Calvin, in conflict with the spirit, a source of temptation and debasement. This world-view reaches its clearest expression in the writings of the French philosophers of the eighteenth century, Helvétius and Holbach, d'Alembert and Condorcet, the friends of nature and the sciences, for whom man is subject to the same kind of causal laws as animals and plants and the inanimate world, physical and biological laws, and in the case of men psychological and economic too, established by observation and experiment, measurement and verification. Such notions as the immortal soul, a personal God, freedom of the will, are for them metaphysical fictions and illusions. But they are not so for Kant.

The German revolt against France and French materialism has social as well as intellectual roots. Germany in the first half of the eighteenth century, and for more than a century before, even before the devastation of the Thirty Years War, had little share in the great renaissance of the West – her cultural achievement after the Reformation is not comparable to that of the Italians in the fifteenth and sixteenth centuries, of Spain and England in the age of Shakespeare and Cervantes, of the Low Countries in the seventeenth century, least of all of France, the France of poets, soldiers, statesmen, thinkers, which in the seventeenth century dominated

Europe both culturally and politically, with only England and Holland as her rivals. What had the provincial German courts and cities, what had even Imperial Vienna, to offer? This sense of relative backwardness, of being an object of patronage or scorn to the French with their overweening sense of national and cultural superiority, created a sense of collective humiliation, later to turn into indignation and hostility, that sprang from wounded pride. The German reaction at first is to imitate French models, then to turn against them. Let the vain but godless French cultivate their ephemeral world, their material gains, their pursuit of glory, luxury, ostentation, the witty trivial chatter of the salons of Paris and the subservient court at Versailles. What is the worth of the philosophy of atheists or smooth, worldly abbés who do not begin to understand the true nature, the real purposes of men, their inner life, man's deepest concerns – his relation to the soul within him, to his brothers, above all to God – the deep, the agonising questions of man's being and vocation? Inward-looking German pietists abandoned French and Latin, turned to their native tongue, and spoke with scorn and horror of the glittering generalities of French civilisation, the blasphemous epigrams of Voltaire and his imitators. Still more contemptible were the feeble imitators of French culture, the caricature of French customs and taste in the little German principalities. German men of letters rebelled violently against the social oppression and stifling atmosphere of German society, of the despotic and often stupid and cruel German princes and princelings and their officials, who crushed or degraded the humbly born, particularly the most honest and gifted men among them, in the three hundred courts and governments into which Germany was then divided.

This surge of indignation formed the heart of the movement that, after the name of a play by one of its members, was called *Sturm und Drang*. Their plays are filled with cries of despair or savage indignation, titanic explosions of rage or hatred, vast destructive passions, unimaginable crimes which dwarf the scenes of violence even in Elizabethan drama; they celebrate passion, individuality, strength, genius, self-expression at whatever cost, against whatever odds, and usually end in blood and crime, their only form of protest against a grotesque and odious social order. Hence all these violent heroes – the *Kraftmenschen*, *Kraftschreiber*, *Kraftkerls*, *Kraftknaben* – who march hysterically through the pages of Klinger, Schubart, Leisewitz, Lenz, Heinse, and even the gentle Carl Philipp Moritz; until life began to imitate art, and the Swiss adventurer Christoph Kaufmann, a self-proclaimed follower of Christ and Rousseau, who so impressed Herder, Goethe, Hamann, Wieland, Lavater, swept through the German lands with a band of unkempt followers, denouncing polite culture, and celebrating anarchic freedom, transported by wild and mystical public exaltation of the flesh and the spirit.

Kant abhorred this kind of disordered imagination, and, still more, emotional exhibitionism and barbarous conduct. Although he too denounced the mechanistic psychology of the French Encyclopaedists as destructive of morality, his notion of the will is that of reason in action. He saves himself from subjectivism, and indeed irrationalism, by insisting that the will is truly free only so far as it wills the dictates of reason, which generate general rules binding on all rational men. It is when the concept of reason becomes obscure (and Kant never succeeded in formulating convincingly what this signified in practice), and only the independent will remains man's unique possession whereby he is distinguished from nature, that the new doctrine becomes infected by the 'stürmerisch' mood. In Kant's disciple, the dramatist and poet Schiller, the notion of freedom begins to move beyond the bounds of reason. Freedom is the central concept of Schiller's early works. He speaks of 'the legislator himself, the God within us', of 'high, demonic freedom', 'the pure demon within the man'. Man is most sublime when he resists the pressure of nature, when he exhibits 'moral independence of natural laws in a condition of emotional stress'.[1] It is will, not reason – certainly not feeling, which he shares with animals – that raises him above nature, and the very disharmony which may arise between nature and the tragic hero is not entirely to be deplored, for it awakens man's sense of his independence.

This is a clean break from Rousseau's invocations to nature and eternal values, no less than from Burke or Helvétius or Hume, with their sharply differing views. In Schiller's early plays it is the individual's resistance to external force, social or natural, that is celebrated. Nothing, perhaps, is more striking than the contrast

[1] *Schillers Werke* (op. cit., p. 260 above, note 3), vol. 20, p. 303, line 13; vol. 21, p. 46, line 30; ibid., p. 52, line 28; vol. 20, p. 196, line 6.

between the values of the leading champion of the German *Aufklärung*, Lessing, in the 1760s, and those of Schiller in the early '80s of the century. Lessing, in his play *Minna von Barnhelm*, written in 1768, describes a proud Prussian officer, accused of a crime of which he is innocent, who disdains to defend himself and prefers poverty and disgrace to fighting for his rights; he is high-minded, but also headstrong; his pride makes it impossible to stoop to quarrels with his detractors, and it is his mistress Minna who, by a display of skill, tact and good sense, manages to rescue him from his condition and cause him to be rehabilitated. Major Tellheim, because of his absurd sense of honour, is represented as heroic but somewhat ridiculous; it is the worldly wisdom of Minna that saves him and turns what might have been a tragic end into an amiable comedy. But Karl Moor in Schiller's *Robbers* is this same Tellheim lifted to a great tragic height: he has been betrayed by his unworthy brother, disinherited by his father, and is determined for his own sake, and that of other victims of injustice, to be avenged upon odious, hypocritical society. He forms a robber band, he pillages and murders, he kills the love he bears his mistress – he must be free to wreak his hatred, to pour destruction on the hateful world which has turned him into a criminal. In the end he gives himself up to the police for punishment, but he is a noble criminal, raised far above the degraded society which has ignored his personality, and Schiller writes a moving epitaph upon his tomb.

The distance which divides Karl Moor from Lessing's Tellheim is eighteen years: it was in that period that the revolt known as *Sturm und Drang* reached its height. In his later works Schiller, like Coleridge and Wordsworth and Goethe, came to terms with the world, and preached political resignation rather than revolt. Yet even in a later phase he returns to the notion of will as sheer defiance of nature and convention. Thus in discussing Corneille's *Médée* he tells us that when Medea, to avenge herself on Jason, who had abandoned her, killed her children by him, she is a true tragic heroine because with superhuman will-power she defied the force of circumstance and nature, crushed natural feeling, did not allow herself to become a mere animal, driven hither and thither by unresisted passion, but, in her very crime, exhibited the freedom of a self-directed personality, triumphant over nature, even though this freedom was turned to wholly evil ends. Above all, one must act and not be acted upon; Phaethon, he tells us, drove Apollo's horses wildly, to his doom, but he drove and was not driven. To surrender one's freedom is to surrender oneself, to lose one's humanity.

Rousseau says this too, yet he is sufficiently a son of the Enlightenment to believe that there are eternal truths graven on the hearts of all men, and it is only a corrupt civilisation that has robbed them of the ability to read them. Schiller too supposes that there was once a unity of thought and will and feeling – that man was once unbroken – then possessions, culture, luxury inflicted the fatal wound. This again is the myth of a paradise from which we are driven by some disastrous breach with nature, a paradise to which the Greeks were closer than we are. Schiller too struggles to reconcile the will, man's inborn freedom, his vocation to be his own master, with the laws of nature and history; he ends by believing that man's only salvation is in the realm of art, where he can achieve independence of the causal treadmill where, in Kant's image, man is a mere 'turnspit',[1] acted upon by external forces. Exploitation is evil inasmuch as it is the using of men as means to ends that are not their own, but those of the manipulator, the treatment of free beings as if they were things, tools, the deliberate denial of their humanity. Schiller oscillates between singing hymns to nature, which, in his Hellenic childhood, was at one with man, and an ominous sense of her as a destroyer; 'she treads them in the dust, the significant and the trivial, the noble and the base – she preserves a world of ants, but men, her most glorious creation, she crushes in her giant's arms . . . in one frivolous hour'.[2]

Nowhere was German *amour propre* more deeply wounded than in East Prussia, still semi-feudal and deeply traditionalist; nowhere was there deeper resentment of the policy of modernisation which Frederick the Great conducted by importing French officials who treated his simple and backward subjects with impatience and open disdain. It is not surprising, therefore, that the most gifted and sensitive sons of this province, Hamann, Herder, and Kant too, are particularly vehement in opposing the levelling activities of these morally blind imposers of alien methods on a pious, inward-looking culture. Kant and Herder at least admire the scientific achievements of the West: Hamann rejects these too. This is the

[1] op. cit. (p. 16 above, note 1), vol. 5, p. 97, line 19.
[2] *Schillers Werke* (op. cit., p. 260 above, note 3), vol. 21, p. 50, line 11.

very spirit in which Tolstoy and Dostoevsky, a century later, wrote about the West, and, as often as not, is a response of the humiliated, a form of sour grapes – a sublime form of it, perhaps, but still sour grapes – the pretence that what one cannot achieve oneself is not worth striving for.

This is the bitter atmosphere in which Herder writes: 'I am not here to think, but to be, feel, live!'[1] The sages of Paris reduce both knowledge and life to systems of contrived rules, the pursuit of external goods, for which men prostitute themselves, and sell their inner freedom, their authenticity; men, Germans, should seek to be themselves, instead of imitating – aping – strangers who have no connection with their own real natures and memories and ways of life. A man's powers of creation can be exercised fully only on his own native heath, living among men who are akin to him, physically and spiritually, those who speak his language, amongst whom he feels at home, with whom he feels that he belongs. Only so can true cultures be generated, each unique, each making its own peculiar contribution to human civilisation, each pursuing its own values in its own way, not to be submerged in some general cosmopolitan ocean which robs all native cultures of their particular substance and colour, of their national spirit and genius, which can flourish only on its own soil, from its own roots, stretching far back into a common past. Civilisation is a garden made rich and beautiful by the variety of its flowers, delicate plants which great conquering empires – Rome, Vienna, London – trample and crush out of existence.

This is the beginning of nationalism, and even more of populism. Herder upholds the value of variety and spontaneity, of the different, idiosyncratic paths pursued by peoples, each with its own style, ways of feeling and expression, and denounces the measuring of everything by the same timeless standards – in effect, those of the dominant French culture, which pretends that its values are valid for all time, universal, immutable. One culture is no mere step to another. Greece is not an antechamber to Rome. Shakespeare's plays are not a rudimentary form of the tragedies of Racine and Voltaire.

This has revolutionary implications. If each culture expresses its own vision and is entitled to do so, and if the goals and values of

[1] op. cit. (p. 252 above, note 1), vol. 29, p. 366.

different societies and ways of life are not commensurable, then it follows that there is no single set of principles, no universal truth for all men and times and places. The values of one civilisation will be different from, and perhaps incompatible with, the values of another. If free creation, spontaneous development along one's own native lines, not inhibited or suppressed by the dogmatic pronouncements of an élite of self-appointed arbiters, insensitive to history, is to be accorded supreme value; if authenticity and variety are not to be sacrificed to authority, organisation, centralisation, which inexorably tend to uniformity and the destruction of what men hold dearest – their language, their institutions, their habits, their form of life, all that has made them what they are – then the establishment of one world, organised on universally accepted rational principles – the ideal society – is not acceptable. Kant's defence of moral freedom and Herder's plea for the uniqueness of cultures, for all the former's insistence on rational principles and the latter's belief that national differences need not lead to collisions, shook – some might say undermined – what I have called the three pillars of the main Western tradition.

Undermined this tradition in favour of what? Not of the reign of feeling, but of the assertion of the will – the will to do what is universally right in Kant, but something which cuts even deeper in the case of Herder: the will to live one's own regional, local life, to develop one's own *eigentümlich* values, to sing one's own songs, to be governed by one's own laws in one's own home, not to be assimilated to a form of life that belongs to all and therefore to none. Freedom, Hegel once observed, is *Bei-sich-selbst-seyn*[1] – to be at home, not to be impinged upon by what is not one's own, by alien obstacles to self-realisation whether on the part of individuals or civilisations. The idea of the earthly paradise, of a golden age for the whole of mankind, of one life which all men live in peace and brotherhood, the Utopian vision of thinkers from Plato to H. G. Wells, is not compatible with this. This denial of monism was to lead, in due course, on the one hand to the conservatism of Burke and Möser; on the other, to romantic self-assertion, nationalism, the worship of heroes and leaders, and in the end to Fascism and brutal irrationalism and the oppression of minorities. But all that was still to come: in the eighteenth century the defence of variety,

[1] loc. cit. (p. 353 above, note 1).

opposition to universalism, is still cultural, literary, idealistic and humane.

V

Fichte drives this still further. Inspired both by Kant and less obviously by Herder, an admirer of the French Revolution, but disillusioned by the Terror, humiliated by the misfortunes of Germany, speaking in defence of 'reason' and 'harmony' – words used by now in more and more attenuated and elusive senses – Fichte is the true father of romanticism, above all in his celebration of will over calm, discursive thought. A man is made conscious of being what he is – of himself as against others or the external world – not by thought or contemplation, since the purer this is, the more a man's thought is in its object, the less conscious of itself it will be as a subject; self-awareness springs from encountering resistance. It is the impact on me of what is external to me, and the effort to resist it, that makes me know that I am what I am, aware of my aims, my nature, my essence, as opposed to what is not mine; and since I am not alone in the world, but connected by myriad strands, as Burke has taught us, to other men, it is this impact that makes me understand what my culture, my nation, my language, my historical tradition, my true home, have been and are. I carve out of external nature what I need, I see it in terms of my needs, temperament, questions, aspirations: 'I do not accept what nature offers because I must,' Fichte declares, 'I believe it because I will.'[1]

Descartes and Locke are evidently mistaken – the mind is not a wax tablet upon which nature imprints what she pleases, it is not an object, but a perpetual activity which shapes its world to respond to its ethical demands. It is the need to act that generates consciousness of the actual world: 'We do not act because we know, but we know because we are called upon to act.'[2] A change in my notion of what should be will change my world. The world of the poet (this is not Fichte's language) is different from the world of the banker, the world of the rich is not the world of the poor; the world of the Fascist is not the world of the liberal, the world of those who think and speak in German is not the world of the French. Fichte goes further: values, principles, moral and

---

[1] op. cit. (p. 220 above, note 3), vol. 2, p. 256.
[2] ibid., p. 263.

political goals, are not objectively given, not imposed on the agent by nature or a transcendent God. I am not determined by ends: ends are determined by me.[1] Food does not create hunger, it is my hunger that makes it food.[2] This is new and revolutionary.

Fichte's concept of the self is not wholly clear: it cannot be the empirical self, which is subject to the causal necessitation of the material world, but an eternal, divine spirit outside time and space, of which empirical selves are but transient emanations; at other times Fichte seems to speak of it as a super-personal self in which I am but an element – the Group – a culture, a nation, a Church. These are the beginnings of political anthropomorphism, the transformation of State, nation, progress, history, into super-sensible agents, with whose unbounded will I must identify my own finite desires if I am to understand myself and my significance, and be what, at my best, I could and should be. I can only understand this by action: 'Man shall be and do something',[3] we must be a 'quickening source of life', not an 'echo' of it or an 'annex' to it.[4] The essence of man is freedom, and although there is talk of reason, harmony, the reconciliation of one man's purpose to that of another in a rationally organised society, yet freedom is a sublime but dangerous gift: 'Not nature but freedom itself produces the greatest and most terrible disorders of our race; man is the cruellest enemy of man.'[5] Freedom is a double-edged weapon; it is because they are free that savages devour each other. Civilised nations are free, free to live in peace, but no less free to fight and make war; culture is not a deterrent of violence but its tool. He advocates peace, but if it is to be a choice between freedom, with its potentiality of violence, or the peace of subjection to the forces of nature, he unequivocally prefers – and indeed thinks it is the essence of man not to be able to avoid preferring – freedom. Creation is of man's essence; hence the doctrine of the dignity of labour, of which Fichte is virtually the author – labour is the impressing of my creative personality upon the material brought into existence by this very need, it is a means for expressing my inner self. The conquest of nature and the attainment of freedom

[1] ibid., pp. 264–5.
[2] ibid., p. 263.
[3] ibid., vol. 6, p. 383.
[4] ibid., vol. 7, p. 374.
[5] ibid., vol. 2, p. 269.

for nations and cultures is the self-realisation of the will: 'Sublime and living will! Named by no name, compassed by no thought!'[1]

Fichte's will is dynamic reason, reason in action. Yet it was not reason that seems to have impressed itself upon the imagination of his listeners in the lecture-halls of Jena and Berlin, but dynamism, self-assertion; the sacred vocation of man is to transform himself and his world by his indomitable will. This is something novel and audacious: ends are not, as had been thought for more than two millennia, objective values, discoverable within man or in a transcendent realm by some special faculty. Ends are not discovered at all, but made, not found but created. The Russian writer Alexander Herzen asked later in the nineteenth century: Where is the dance before I have danced it? Where is the picture before I have painted it? Where indeed? Joshua Reynolds thought that it dwelt in some super-sensuous empyrean of eternal Platonic forms which the inspired artist must discern and labour to embody as best he can in the medium in which he works – pigment, or marble, or bronze. But the answer Herzen implies is that before the work of art is created it is nowhere, that creation is creation out of nothing – an aesthetics of pure creation which Fichte applies to the realm of ethics, of all action. Man is not a mere compounder of pre-existent elements; imagination is not memory, it literally generates, as God generated the world. There are no objective rules, only what we make.

Art is not a mirror held up to nature, the creation of an object according to the rules, say, of harmony or perspective, designed to give pleasure. It is, as Herder taught, a means of communication, of self-expression for the individual spirit. What matters is the quality of this act, its authenticity. Since I, the creator, cannot control the empirical consequences of what I do, they are not part of me, do not form part of my real world. I can control only my own motives, my goals, my attitude to men and things. If another man causes me damage, I may suffer physical pain, but I shall not suffer grief unless I respect him, and that is within my control. Man is the inhabitant of two worlds, said Fichte, one of which, the physical, I can afford to ignore; the other, the spiritual, is in my power.[2] That is why worldly failure is unimportant, why worldly goods – riches,

[1] ibid., p. 303.
[2] ibid., p. 288.

security, success, fame – are trivial in contrast with what alone counts, my respect for myself as a free being, my moral principles, my artistic or human goals; to give up the latter for the former is to compromise my honour and independence, my real life, for the sake of something outside it, part of the empirical-causal treadmill, and this is to falsify what I know to be the truth, to prostitute myself, to sell out – for Fichte and those who followed him the ultimate sin.

From here it is no great distance to the worlds of Byron's gloomy heroes – satanic outcasts, proud, indomitable, sinister – Manfred, Beppo, Conrad, Lara, Cain – who defy society and suffer and destroy. They may, by the standards of the world, be accounted criminal, enemies of mankind, damned souls: but they are free; they have not bowed the knee in the House of Rimmon; they have preserved their integrity at a vast cost in agony and hatred. The Byronism that swept Europe, like the cult of Goethe's *Werther* half a century earlier, was a form of protest against real or imaginary suffocation in a mean, venal and hypocritical milieu, given over to greed, corruption and stupidity. Authenticity is all: 'The great object in life', Byron once said, 'is Sensation – to feel that we exist – even though in pain.'[1] His heroes are like Fichte's dramatisation of himself, lonely thinkers: 'There was in him a vital scorn of all ... He stood a stranger in this breathing world.'[2] The attack on everything that hems in and cramps, that persuades us that we are part of some great machine from which it is impossible to break out, since it is a mere illusion to believe that we can leave the prison – that is the common note of the romantic revolt. When Blake says 'A Robin Red breast in a Cage / Puts all Heaven in a

---

[1] He goes on: 'it is this "craving void" which drives us to Gaming – to Battle – to Travel – to intemperate but keenly felt pursuits of any description whose principal attraction is the agitation inseparable from their accomplishment.' *Byron's Letters and Journals*, ed. Leslie Marchand (London, 1973–94), vol. 3, p. 109. This was written in a letter of 1813 (6 September, to Annabella Milbanke). Half a century earlier the Scottish writer Adam Ferguson made of this 'craving void' and of the love of danger and of war, of hatred of *ennui*, one of the principal points of his attacks against contemporary morality and against the psychology of the French *raisonneurs*. His famous *Essay on the History of Civil Society* of 1767, which contrasted the Homeric virtues with the domesticated character of modern society, enjoyed widespread currency in Germany the following year in the translation made of it by Christian Garve.

[2] *Lara*, Canto I. 18, lines 313, 315.

Rage',[1] the cage is the Newtonian system. Locke and Newton are devils; 'Reasoning' is 'secret Murder';[2] 'Art is the Tree of Life ... Science is the Tree of Death.'[3] 'The tree of knowledge has robbed us of the fruit of life,' said Hamann a generation earlier,[4] and this is literally echoed by Byron. Freedom involves breaking rules, perhaps even committing crimes.

This note was earlier sounded by Diderot (and perhaps by Milton in his conception of Satan, and in Shakespeare's *Troilus*). Diderot conceived of man as the theatre of an unceasing civil war between an inner being, the natural man, struggling to get out of the outer man, the product of civilisation and convention. He drew analogies between the criminal and the genius, solitary and savage beings who break rules and defy conventions and take fearful risks, unlike the *hommes d'esprit* who scatter their wit elegantly and agreeably, but are tame and lack the sacred fire. Half a century before Byron, Lenz, the most authentic voice of the *Sturm und Drang*, wrote: 'Action – action is the soul of the world, not pleasure ... Without action all feeling and knowledge is nothing but postponed death.' And again, 'God brooded over the void and a world arose'; 'Clear a space! Destroy! Something will arise! Oh God-like feeling!'[5] What matters is the intensity of the creative impulse, the depth of nature from which it springs, the sincerity of one's beliefs, readiness to live and die for a principle, which counts for more than the validity of the conviction or the principle itself.

Voltaire and Carlyle both wrote about Muhammad. Voltaire's play is simply an attack on obscurantism, intolerance, religious fanaticism; when he speaks of Muhammad as a blind and destructive barbarian, he means, as everyone knew, the Roman Church, for him the greatest obstacle to justice, happiness, freedom, reason – universal goals which satisfy the deepest demands of all men at all times. When, a century later, Carlyle deals with the same subject, he cares only about Muhammad's character, the stuff of which he is made, and not his doctrines or their consequences: he calls him 'a fiery mass of life cast up from the great bosom of nature herself',

---

[1] loc. cit. (p. 260 above, note 1).
[2] 'Jerusalem', plate 64, line 20: ibid., vol. 1, p. 555.
[3] loc. cit. (p. 260 above, note 2).
[4] op. cit. (p. 250 above, note 4), vol. 6, p. 492, line 9.
[5] loc cit. (p. 257 above, note 1).

possessed of 'a deep, great, genuine sincerity'.[1] 'Heart! Warmth! Blood! Humanity! Life!' These are Herder's words.[2] The attack on Voltaire and the 'second-rate' shallow talk in France was mounted by the Germans in the last third of the eighteenth century. Half a century later the goal of rational happiness, especially in its Benthamite version, is rejected contemptuously by the new, romantic generation in continental Europe, for whom pleasure is but 'tepid water on the tongue'; the phrase is Hölderlin's,[3] but it could just as well have been uttered by Musset or Lermontov. Goethe, Wordsworth, Coleridge and even Schiller made their peace with the established order. So, in due course, did Schelling and Tieck, Friedrich Schlegel and Arnim and a good many other radicals. But in their earlier years these men celebrated the power of the will to freedom, to creative self-expression, with fateful consequences for the history and outlook of the years that followed.

One form of these ideas was the new image of the artist, raised above other men not only by his genius but by his heroic readiness to live and die for the sacred vision within him. It was this same ideal that animated and transformed the concept of nations or classes or minorities in their struggles for freedom at whatever cost. It took a more sinister form in the worship of the leader, the creator of a new social order as a work of art, who moulds men as the composer moulds sounds and the painter colours – men too feeble to rise by their own force of will. An exceptional being, the hero and genius to whom Carlyle and Fichte paid homage, can lift others to a level beyond any which they could have reached by their own efforts, even if this can be achieved only at the cost of the torment or death of multitudes.

For more than two millennia the view prevailed in Europe that there existed an unalterable structure of reality, and the great men were those who understood it correctly either in their theory or their practice – the wise who knew the truth, or the men of action, rulers and conquerors, who knew how to achieve their goals. In a sense the criterion of greatness was success based on getting the

---

[1] 'The Hero as Prophet': pp. 40 and 39 in Thomas Carlyle, *On Heroes, Hero-Worship, & the Heroic in History*, ed. Michael K. Goldberg and others (Berkeley etc., 1993).

[2] loc. cit. (p. 258 above, note 2).

[3] *Hyperion*, vol. 1, book 1: p. 118 in Hölderlin, *Sämtliche Werke*, ed. Norbert v. Hellingrath and others (Berlin, 1943), vol. 2.

answer right. But in the age of which I speak the hero is no longer the discoverer, or the winner in the race, but the creator, even, or perhaps all the more, if he was destroyed by the flame within him – a secularised image of the saint and martyr, of the life of sacrifice. For in the life of the spirit there were no objective principles or values – they were made so by a resolve of the will which shaped a man's or a people's world and its norms; action determined thought, not vice versa. To know is to impose a system, not to register passively, said Fichte; and laws are drawn not from facts, but from our own self. One categorises reality as the will dictates. If the empirical facts prove recalcitrant, one must put them in their place, in the mechanical treadmill of causes and effects, which have no relevance to the life of the spirit – to morality, religion, art, philosophy, the realm of ends, not means.

For these thinkers ordinary life, the common notion of reality, and in particular the artificial constructions of the natural sciences and practical techniques – economic, political, sociological – no less than that of common sense, are a baseless, utilitarian fabrication, what Georges Sorel later called 'la petite science',[1] something invented for their own convenience by technologists and ordinary men, not reality itself. For Friedrich Schlegel and Novalis, for Wackenroder and Tieck and Chamisso, above all for E. T. A. Hoffmann, the tidy regularities of daily life are but a curtain to conceal the terrifying spectacle of true reality, which has no structure, but is a wild whirlpool, a perpetual *tourbillon* of the creative spirit which no system can capture: life and motion cannot be represented by immobile, lifeless concepts, nor the infinite and unbounded by the finite and the fixed. A finished work of art, a systematic treatise, are attempts to freeze the flowing stream of life; only fragments, intimations, broken glimpses can begin to convey the perpetual movement of reality. The prophet of *Sturm und Drang*, Hamann, had said that the practical man was a somnambulist, secure and successful because he was blind; if he could see, he would go mad, for nature is a wild dance, and the irregulars of life – outlaws, beggars, vagabonds, the visionary, the sick, the abnormal – are closer to it than French philosophers, officials, scientists, sensible men, pillars of the enlightened bureaucracy: 'The tree of knowledge has robbed us of the fruit of life.'[2] The early German

---

[1] In *Réflexions sur la violence* (1908), chapter 4, section 3.
[2] loc. cit. (p. 573 above, note 4).

romantic plays and novels are inspired by an attempt to expose the concept of a stable, intelligible structure of reality which calm observers describe, classify, dissect, predict, as a sham and a delusion, a mere curtain of appearances designed to protect those not sensitive or brave enough to face the truth from the terrifying chaos beneath the false order of bourgeois existence. The irony of the cosmos plays with us all, wrote Tieck: the visible is about us like tapestries with shimmering colours and patterns. Beyond the tapestries is a region populated by dreams and delirium; none dares lift the tapestry and peer beyond the curtain.

Tieck is the originator of the Novel and the Theatre of the Absurd. In *William Lovell* everything turns out to be its opposite: the personal turns out to be impersonal; the living is discovered to be the dead; the organic, the mechanical; the real, the artificial; men seek freedom and fall into the blackest slavery. In Tieck's plays there is a deliberate attempt to confound the imaginary and the real: characters in the play (or in a play within the play) criticise the play, complain about the plot, and about the equipment of the theatre; members of the audience expostulate and demand that the illusion, on which all drama rests, be preserved; they are in turn answered sharply by the play's characters from the stage, to the bewilderment of the real audience; at times musical keys and dynamic tempi engage in dialogues with each other. In *Prince Zerbino*, when the Prince despairs of reaching the end of his journey he orders the play to be turned backwards – the events to be replayed in reverse order, to unhappen – the will is free to order what it pleases. In one of Arnim's plays an old nobleman complains that his legs are growing longer and longer: this is the result of boredom; the old man's inner state is externalised; moreover, his boredom itself is a symbol of the death-throes of the old Germany. As a perceptive contemporary Russian critic has remarked, this is full-blown expressionism long before its triumph a century later, in the Weimar period.

The attack upon the world of appearances at times takes surrealist forms: in one of Arnim's novels the hero finds that he has wandered into a beautiful lady's dreams, is invited by her to sit in one of her chairs, wishes to escape from the dream that is not his, sees that the chair remains empty, and feels great relief. Hoffmann carried this war upon the objective world, upon the very notion of objectivity, to its outer limits: old women who turn into brass door-knockers, or State Councillors who step into brandy-glasses,

are dissipated into alcoholic fumes, float over the earth, then re-
coagulate themselves and return to their armchairs and dressing-
gowns – these are not innocent flights of fancy but spring from a
deranged imagination in which the will is uncontrolled and the real
world proves to be a phantasmagoria. After this, the way lies clear
for Schopenhauer's world tossed hither and thither by a blind,
aimless, cosmic will, for Dostoevsky's underground man, and
Kafka's lucid nightmares, for Nietzsche's evocation of the *Kraftmenschen* condemned in Plato's dialogues – Thrasymachus, or
Callicles – who see no reason against sweeping aside the cobwebs
of laws and conventions if they obstruct their will to power, for
Baudelaire's 'enivrez-vous sans cesse!';[1] let the will become
intoxicated by drugs or pain, dreams or sorrow, no matter by
what, but let it break its chains.

Neither Hoffmann nor Tieck sets out, any more than Pascal or
Kierkegaard or Nerval, to deny the truths of science, or even those
of common sense, at their own level – that is, as categories required
for limited purposes, medical or technological or commercial. This
was not the world which mattered; they conceived true reality as
distinct from the irrelevant surface of things. The world without
frontiers or barriers, within or without, shaped and expressed by
art, by religion, by metaphysical insight, by all that is involved in
personal relationships – this was the world in which the will is
supreme, in which absolute values clashed in irreconcilable conflict,
the 'nocturnal world' of the soul, the source of all imaginative
experience, all poetry, all understanding, all that men truly live by.
It is when scientifically minded rationalists claimed to be able to
explain and control this level of experience in terms of their
concepts and categories, and declared that conflict and tragedy
arose only from ignorance of fact, inadequacies of method, the
incompetence or ill will of rulers and the benighted condition of
their subjects, so that in principle, at least, all this could be put
right, a harmonious, rationally organised society established, and
the dark sides of life be made to recede like an old, insubstantial,
scarcely remembered nightmare – is is then that the poets and the
mystics and all those who are sensitive to the individual, unorga-
nisable, untranslatable aspects of human experience tended to rebel.
Such men react against what appears to them to be the maddening

---

[1] 'Enivrez-vous' (1864), *Petits poèmes en prose* (*Le Spleen de Paris*) No 33.

dogmatism and smooth *bon sens* of the *raisonneurs* of the Enlightenment and their modern successors. Nor, despite the brilliant and heroic efforts of both Hegel and Marx to integrate the tensions, paradoxes and conflicts of human life and thought into new syntheses of successive crises and resolutions – the dialectic of history or cunning of reason (or of the process of production), leading to an ultimate triumph of reason and realisation of human potentialities – have the terrible doubts injected by these indignant critics ever been stilled.

I do not mean that these doubts have in fact prevailed, at least in the realm of ideology. Even if belief in the happy innocence of our first ancestors – *Saturnia regna* – has largely waned, faith in the possibility of a golden age still to come has remained unimpaired, and indeed spread far beyond the Western world. Both liberals and socialists, and many who put their trust in rational and scientific methods designed to effect a fundamental social transformation, whether by violent or gradual methods, have held this optimistic belief with mounting intensity during the last hundred years. The conviction that once the last obstacles – ignorance and irrationality, alienation and exploitation, and their individual and social roots – have been eliminated, true human history, that is, universal harmonious co-operation, will at last begin is a secular form of what is evidently a permanent need of mankind. But if it is the case that not all ultimate human ends are necessarily compatible, there may be no escape from choices governed by no overriding principle, some among them painful, both to the agent and to others. From this it would follow that the creation of a social structure that would, at the least, avoid morally intolerable alternatives, and at the most promote active solidarity in the pursuit of common objectives, may be the best that human beings can be expected to achieve, if too many varieties of positive action are not to be repressed, too many equally valid human goals are not to be frustrated.

But a course demanding so much skill and practical intelligence – the hope of what would be no more than a better world, dependent on the maintenance of what is bound to be an unstable equilibrium in need of constant attention and repair – is evidently not inspiring enough for most men, who crave a bold, universal, once-and-for-all panacea. It may be that men cannot face too much reality, or an open future, without a guarantee of a happy ending – providence, the self-realising spirit, the invisible hand, the cunning of reason or of history, or of a productive and creative social class. This seems borne out by the social and political doctrines that have proved most influential in recent times. Yet the romantic attack on the system-builders – the authors of the great historical libretti – has not been wholly ineffective. Whatever the political theorists may have taught, the imaginative literature of the nineteenth century, and of ours too, which expresses the moral outlook, conscious and unconscious, of the age, has (despite the apocalyptic moments of Dostoevsky or Walt Whitman) remained singularly unaffected by Utopian dreams. There is no vision of final perfection in Tolstoy, or Turgenev, in Balzac or Flaubert or Baudelaire or Carducci. Manzoni is perhaps the last major writer who still lives in the afterglow of a Christian-liberal, optimistic eschatology. The German romantic school and those it influenced, directly and indirectly – Schopenhauer, Nietzsche, Wagner, Ibsen, Joyce, Kafka, Beckett, the existentialists – whatever fantasies of their own they may have generated, do not cling to the myth of an ideal world. Nor from his wholly different standpoint does Freud. Small wonder that they have all been duly written off as decadent reactionaries by Marxist critics. Some indeed, and those not the least gifted or perceptive, are justly so described. Others were, and are, the very opposite: humane, generous, life-enhancing, openers of new doors.

One is not committed to applauding or even condoning the extravagances of romantic irrationalism if one concedes that, by revealing that the ends of men are many, often unpredictable, and some among them incompatible with one another, the romantics have dealt a fatal blow to the proposition that, all appearances to the contrary, a definite solution of the jigsaw puzzle is, at least in principle, possible, that power in the service of reason can achieve it, that rational organisation can bring about the perfect union of such values and counter-values as individual liberty and social equality, spontaneous self-expression and organised, socially directed efficiency, perfect knowledge and perfect happiness, the claims of personal life and the claims of parties, classes, nations, the public interest. If some ends recognised as fully human are at the same time ultimate and mutually incompatible, then the idea of a golden age, a perfect society compounded of a synthesis of all the correct solutions to all the central problems of human life, is shown to be incoherent in principle. This is the service rendered by romanticism, and in particular by the doctrine that forms its heart, namely, that morality is moulded by the will and that ends are created, not discovered. When this movement is justly condemned for the monstrous fallacy that life is, or can be made, a work of art, that the aesthetic model applies to politics, that the political leader is, at his highest, a sublime artist who shapes men according to his creative design – a fallacy that leads to dangerous nonsense in theory and savage brutality in practice – this at least may be set to its credit: that it has permanently shaken the faith in universal, objective truth in matters of conduct, in the possibility of a perfect and harmonious society, wholly free from conflict or injustice or oppression – a goal for which no sacrifice can be too great if men are ever to create Condorcet's reign of truth, happiness and virtue, bound 'by an indissoluble chain';[1] an ideal for which more human beings have, in our time, sacrificed themselves and others than, perhaps, for any other cause in human history.

[1] loc. cit. (p. 136 above, note 1).

# NATIONALISM

*Past Neglect and Present Power*

I

THE HISTORY of ideas is a rich but, by its very nature, an imprecise field, treated with natural suspicion by experts in more exact disciplines, but it has its surprises and rewards. Among them is the discovery that some of the most familiar values of our own culture are more recent than might at first be supposed. Integrity and sincerity were not among the attributes which were admired – indeed, they were scarcely mentioned – in the ancient or medieval worlds, which prized objective truth in matters of theory, and getting things right in matters of both theory and practice. The view that variety is desirable, whereas uniformity is monotonous, dreary, dull, a fetter upon the freely-ranging human spirit, 'Cimmerian, corpse-like',[1] as Goethe described Holbach's *Système de la nature*, stands in sharp contrast with the traditional view that truth is one, error many, a view scarcely challenged before – at the earliest – the end of the seventeenth century. The notion of toleration, not as a utilitarian expedient to avoid destructive strife, but as an intrinsic value; the concepts of liberty and human rights as they are discussed today; the notion of genius as the defiance of rules by the untrammelled will, contemptuous of the restraint of reason at any level – all these are elements in a great mutation in Western thought and feeling that took place in the eighteenth century, the consequences of which appear in various counter-revolutions all too obvious in every sphere of life today. This is a vast topic which I shall not directly discuss: I wish to draw attention to, at most, only one corner of it.

---

[1] loc. cit. (p. 258 above, note 3).

## II

The nineteenth century, as we all know, witnessed an immense growth of historical studies. There are many explanations of this: the revolutionary transformation of both life and thought brought about by the rapid and triumphant development of the natural sciences, in particular by technological invention and the consequent rise of large-scale industry; the rise of new States and classes and rulers in search of pedigrees; the disintegration of age-old religious and social institutions, at once the cause and the consequence of the Renaissance and the rise of secularism and the Reformation; all this riveted attention upon the phenomena of historical change and novelty. The fillip given to historical and, indeed, to all genetic studies, was incalculably great. There was a new sense of continuous advance, or at any rate of movement and change in the life of human society. It is not, therefore, surprising that major thinkers in this period set themselves to discover the laws which governed social change. It seemed reasonable to suppose that the new methods of the natural sciences, which proved capable of explaining the nature and the laws of the external world, could perform this service for the human world also. If such laws could be discovered at all, they must hold for the future as well as for the past. Prediction of the human future must be rescued from mystical prophets and interpreters of the apocalyptic books of the Bible, from the astrologers and dabblers in the occult, and become an organised province of scientific knowledge.

This hope spurred the new philosophies of history, and brought into being an entire new field of social studies. The new prophets tended to claim scientific validity for their statements about both the past and the future. Although much of what some of them wrote was the fruit of luxuriant and unbridled and sometimes egomaniacal imaginations, or at any rate highly speculative, the general record is a good deal more respectable than is commonly supposed. Condorcet may have been too optimistic in prophesying the development of a comprehensive and systematic natural science of man, and with it the end of crime and folly and misery in human affairs, due to indolence and ignorance and irrationality. In the darkness of his prison in 1794 he drew a glowing picture of a new, virtuous and happy world, organised by the application of scientific method to social organisation by intellectually and morally liberated men, leading to a harmonious society of nations, unbroken progress in the arts and sciences, and perpetual peace. This was plainly over-sanguine, yet the fruitfulness of applying mathematical, and in particular statistical, techniques to social problems was a prophecy at once original and important.

Saint-Simon was a man of genius who, as everyone knows, predicted the inevitable triumph of a technocratic order. He spoke of the coming union of science, finance and industrial organisation, and the replacement, in this new world of producers aided by scientists, of what amounted to clerical indoctrination by a new race of propagandists – artists, poets, priests of a new secular religion, mobilising men's emotions, without which the new industrial world could not be made to function. His disciple, Auguste Comte, called for and predicted the creation of an authoritarian élite to educate and control a rational, but not a democratic or liberal, society and its scientifically trained citizens. I will not enlarge upon the validity of this prophecy: the combination of technological skills and the absolute authority of a secular priesthood has been realised only too successfully in our day. And if those who believed that prejudice and ignorance and superstition, and their embodiment in irrational and repressive laws, economic, political, racial and sexual, would be swept away by the new enlightenment, have not had their expectations realised, this does not diminish the degree of their insight into the new paths which had opened in Western European development. This was the very vision of a rational, swept and garnered, new order, heralded by Bentham and Macaulay, which troubled Mill and Tocqueville and deeply repelled Carlyle and Disraeli, Ruskin and Thoreau, and, before them, some among the early German romantics at the turn of the nineteenth century. Fourier, in his turn, together with much nonsense, thundered against the evils of trade and industry, engaged in unbridled economic competition, tending to wanton destruction or adulteration of the fruits of human labour by those who wished to increase their own profits; he protested that the growth of centralised control over vast human groups led to servitude and alienation, and advocated the end of repression and the need for the rational canalisation of the passions by careful vocational guidance which would enable all human desires, capacities, inclinations to develop in a free and creative direction. Fourier was given to grotesque fantasies: but these ideas were not absurd, and much of what he predicted is now conventional wisdom.

Everyone has recognised the fatal accuracy of Tocqueville's uneasy anticipation of the conformity and the monotony of democratic egalitarianism, whatever may be thought of the nostrums by which he sought to modify its effects. Nor do I know of anyone who would deny that Karl Marx, whatever his errors, displayed unique powers of prognosis in identifying some of the central factors at work in his day that were not obvious to his contemporaries – the interdependence of technological change and culture, the concentration and centralisation of the means of production in private hands, the inexorable march of industrialisation, the rise and vast development of big business, then in its embryo, and the inevitable sharpening of social and political conflicts that this involved. Nor was he unsuccessful in unmasking the political and moral, philosophical and religious, liberal and scientific disguises under which some of the most brutal manifestations of these conflicts and their social and intellectual consequences were concealed.

These were major prophets, and there were others. The brilliant and wayward Bakunin predicted more accurately than his great rival Marx the situations in which great risings of the dispossessed would take place, and foresaw that they were liable to develop not in the most industrialised societies, on a rising curve of economic progress, but in countries in which the majority of the population was near subsistence level and had least to lose by an upheaval – primitive peasants in conditions of desperate poverty in backward rural economies where capitalism was weakest, such as Spain and Russia. He would have had no difficulty in understanding the causes of the great social upheavals in Asia and Africa in our own day. I could go on: the poet Heine, addressing the French in the early years of the reign of Louis-Philippe, saw that one fine day their German neighbours, spurred by a combination of historical memories and resentments with metaphysical and moral fanaticism, would fall upon them, and uproot the great monuments of Western culture: 'restrained neither by fear nor greed . . . like early Christians, whom neither physical torture nor physical pleasure could break',[1] these ideologically intoxicated barbarians would turn Europe into a desert. Lassalle preached, and perhaps foresaw, State socialism – the people's democracies of our day, whether one calls them State communism or State capitalism, a hybrid which Marx utterly condemned in his notes on the Gotha programme.

[1] op. cit. (p. 444 above, note 1), vol. 7, p. 351.

A decade or so later Jakob Burckhardt anticipated the military-industrial complexes which would inevitably control the decadent countries of the West; Max Weber had no doubts about the growing power of bureaucracy; Durkheim warned of the possibility of anomie; there followed all the nightmares of Zamyatin, Aldous Huxley, Orwell, half satirists, half prophets of our own time. Some remained pure prophecies, others, notably those of the Marxists and of Heine's new philosophical barbarians, who dominated the imagination of racialists and neo-pagan irrationalists, were, perhaps, to some degree self-fulfilling. The nineteenth century generated a great many other Utopias and prognoses, liberal, socialist, technocratic and those that were filled with neo-medieval nostalgia, a craving for a largely imaginary *Gemeinschaft* in the past – systems for the most part today justly forgotten.

In all this great array of elaborate, statistically supported mass of futurology and fantasy there is one peculiar lacuna. There was one movement which dominated much of the nineteenth century in Europe and was so pervasive, so familiar, that it is only by a conscious effort of the imagination that one can conceive a world in which it played no part: it had its partisans and its enemies, its democratic, aristocratic and monarchist wings, it inspired men of action and artists, intellectual élites and the masses; but, oddly enough, no significant thinkers known to me predicted for it a future in which it would play an even more dominant role. Yet it would, perhaps, be no overstatement to say that it is one of the most powerful, in some regions the most powerful, single movement at work in the world today; and that some of those who failed to foresee this development have paid for it with their liberty, indeed with their lives. This movement is nationalism. No influential thinker, to the best of my knowledge, foresaw its future – at any rate, no one clearly foretold it. The only exception known to me is the underrated Moses Hess, who, in 1862, in his book *Rome and Jerusalem*, affirmed that the Jews had the historic mission of uniting communism and nationality. But this was exhortation rather than prophecy, and the book remained virtually unread save by Zionists of a later day.

There is no need to emphasise the obvious fact that the great majority of the sovereign States represented at the Assembly of the United Nations today are actuated in a good deal of their behaviour by strong nationalist passions, even more than their predecessors of the League of Nations. Yet I suspect that this fact would have surprised most of the prophets of the nineteenth century, no matter how intelligent and politically intuitive. This is so because most social and political observers of that time, whether or not they were themselves nationalists, tended in general to anticipate the decline of this sentiment. Nationalism was, by and large, regarded in Europe as a passing phase. The desire on the part of most men to be citizens of a State coterminous with the nation which they regarded as their own was considered to be natural or, at any rate, brought about by a historical-political development of which the growth of national consciousness was at once the cause and the effect, at any rate in the West. Nationalism as a sentiment and an ideology was not (in my opinion, rightly) equated with national consciousness.

The need to belong to an easily identifiable group had been regarded, at any rate since Aristotle, as a natural requirement on the part of human beings: families, clans, tribes, estates, social orders, classes, religious organisations, political parties, and finally nations and States, were historical forms of the fulfilment of this basic human need. No one particular form was, perhaps, as necessary to human existence as the need for food or shelter or security or procreation, but some form of it was indispensable, and various theories were offered to account for the historical progression of these forms, from Plato and Polybius to Machiavelli, Bossuet, Vico, Turgot, Herder, Saint-Simon, Hegel, Comte, Marx and their modern successors. Common ancestry, common language, customs, traditions, memories, continuous occupancy of the same territory for a long period of time were held to constitute a society. This kind of homogeneity emphasised the differences between one group and its neighbours, the existence of tribal, cultural or national solidarity and, with it, a sense of difference from, often accompanied by active dislike or contempt for, groups with different customs and different real or mythical origins; and so was accepted as both accounting for and justifying national statehood. The British, French, Spanish, Portuguese and Scandinavian peoples had achieved this well before the nineteenth century; the German, Italian, Polish, Balkan and Baltic peoples had not. The Swiss had achieved a unique solution of their own. The coincidence of the territory of the State and nation was regarded as, on the whole, desirable, save by the supporters of the dynastic, multinational empires of Russia, Austria, Turkey, or by imperialists,

socialist internationalists, anarchists, and perhaps some ultramontane Catholics. The majority of political thinkers, whether they
approved of it or not, accepted this as an inevitable phase of social
organisation. Some hoped or feared that it would be succeeded by
other forms of political structure; some seemed to regard it as
'natural' and permanent. Nationalism – the elevation of the
interests of the unity and self-determination of the nation to the
status of the supreme value before which all other considerations
must, if need be, yield at all times, an ideology to which German
and Italian thinkers seemed particularly prone – was looked on by
observers of a more liberal type as a passing phase due to the
exacerbation of national consciousness held down and forcibly
repressed by despotic rulers aided by subservient Churches.

By the middle of the nineteenth century the aspirations for
political unity and self-rule of the Germans and Italians seemed
well on the way to realisation. Soon this dominant trend would
liberate the oppressed peoples of the multinational empires too.
After this, so it was believed, nationalism, which was a pathological
inflammation of wounded national consciousness, would abate: it
was caused by oppression and would vanish with it. This seemed
to be taking longer than the optimists anticipated, but by 1919 the
basic principle of the right to national self-government seemed
universally accepted. The Treaty of Versailles, recognising the right
to national independence, whatever else it might fail to achieve,
would at any rate solve the so-called national question. There was,
of course, the question of the rights of various national minorities
in the new national States, but these could be guaranteed by the
new League of Nations – surely if there was anything these States
could be expected to understand, if only from their own historical
experience, it was the need to satisfy the craving for autonomy on
the part of ethnic or cultural groups within their borders. Other
problems might still rack mankind – colonial exploitation, social
and political inequality, ignorance, poverty, injustice, hunger,
disease, corruption, privilege; but most enlightened liberals, and,
indeed, socialists, assumed that nationalism would decline, since
the deepest wounds inflicted upon nations were on the way to
being healed.

Marxists and other radical socialists went further. For them
national sentiment itself was a form of false consciousness, an
ideology generated, consciously or not, by the economic domination of a particular class, the bourgeoisie, in alliance with what was

left of the old aristocracy, used as a weapon in the retention and promotion of the class control of society, which, in its turn, rested on the exploitation of the labour power of the proletariat. In the fullness of time the workers, whom the process of production itself would inevitably organise into a disciplined force of ever-increasing size, political awareness and power, would overthrow their capitalist oppressors, enfeebled as they would be by the cut-throat competition among themselves that would undermine their capacity for organised resistance. The expropriators would be expropriated, the knell of capitalism would sound, and with it of the entire ideology of which national sentiment, religion and parliamentary democracy were so many particular aspects. National differences might remain, but they would, like local and ethnic characteristics, be unimportant in comparison with the solidarity of the workers of the world, associated producers freely co-operating in the harnessing of the forces of nature in the interests of all mankind.

What these views had in common was the belief that nationalism was the ephemeral product of the frustration of human craving for self-determination, a stage of human progress due to the working of impersonal forces and the ideologies thereby generated by them. On the nature of these forces theorists were not agreed, but for the most part they supposed that the phenomenon of nationalism itself would disappear with its causes, which in their turn would be destroyed by the irresistible advance of enlightenment, whether conceived in moral or technological terms – the victory of reason or of material progress or of both – identified with changes in the forces and relations of production, or with the struggle for social equality, economic and political democracy and the just distribution of the fruits of the earth; with the destruction of national barriers by world trade or by the triumphs of science, and of a morality founded on rational principles, and so the full realisation of human potentialities which sooner or later would be universally achieved.

In the face of all this, the claims and ideals of mere national groups would tend to lose importance, and would join other relics of human immaturity in ethnological museums. As for the nationalists among peoples who had achieved independence and self-government, they were written off as irrationalists, cases of regression or arrested development – and, with Nietzscheans, Sorelians, neo-romantics, out of account. It became more difficult to ignore mounting nationalism after national unity had been largely achieved – for instance, German chauvinism after 1871, or French integralism, or Italian *sacro egoismo* or the rise of racial theories and other anticipations of Fascism. None of these, however accounted for, were, so far as I know, regarded by the futurologists of the late nineteenth century or the early years of our own as harbingers of a new phase of human history; and this seems equally true of conservatives, liberals and Marxists. The age of *Krisen, Kriege, Katastrophen*, which, for instance, Karl Kautsky predicted,[1] he attributed to causes, and described in terms, in which nationalism, if it appears at all, figures only as a by-product, an element in the 'superstructure'. No one, so far as I know, so much as hinted that nationalism might dominate the last third of our own century to such a degree that few movements or revolutions would have any chance of success unless they came arm-in-arm with it, or at any rate not in opposition to it. This curious failure of vision on the part of otherwise acute social thinkers seems to me a fact in need of explanation, or, to say the least, of wider discussion than it has so far obtained. I am neither a historian nor a social psychologist, and do not volunteer an explanation of it: I should merely like to throw out a suggestion which may cast some light on this odd phenomenon.

III

Before doing so, however, I should like to say something on the origins of European nationalism as a state of mind. I do not mean by this national sentiment as such – that can probably be traced to tribal feeling in the earliest period of recorded history. I mean its elevation into the conscious doctrine, at once the product, articulation and synthesis of states of consciousness, that has been recognised by social observers as a force and a weapon. In this sense nationalism does not seem to exist in the ancient world, nor in the Christian Middle Ages. The Romans may have despised the Greeks, Cicero and Apion said disparaging things about the Jews, and Juvenal about Orientals in general; but this is mere xenophobia. There is passionate patriotism in Machiavelli or Shakespeare – and a long tradition of it long before them. I do not mean by nationalism a mere pride of ancestry – we are all sons of Cadmus,

[1] Karl Kautsky, *Der Weg zur Macht* (Berlin, 1909), esp. chapter 9.

we all come from Troy, we are descended from men who made a covenant with the Lord, we spring from a race of conquerors, Franks or Vikings, and rule over the progeny of Gallo-Romans or Celtic slaves by right of conquest.

By nationalism I mean something more definite, ideologically important and dangerous: namely the conviction, in the first place, that men belong to a particular human group, and that the way of life of the group differs from that of others; that the characters of the individuals who compose the group are shaped by, and cannot be understood apart from, those of the group, defined in terms of common territory, customs, laws, memories, beliefs, language, artistic and religious expression, social institutions, ways of life, to which some add heredity, kinship, racial characteristics; and that it is these factors which shape human beings, their purposes and their values.

Secondly, that the pattern of life of a society is similar to that of a biological organism; that what this organism needs for its proper development, which those most sensitive to its nature articulate in words or images or other forms of human expression, constitutes its common goals; that these goals are supreme; in cases of conflict with other values, which do not derive from the specific ends of a specific 'organism' – intellectual or religious or moral, personal or universal – these supreme values should prevail, since only so will the decadence and ruin of the nation be averted. Furthermore, that to call such patterns of life organic is to say that they cannot be artificially formed by individuals or groups, however dominating their positions, unless they are themselves penetrated by these historically developing ways of acting and thinking and feeling, for it is these mental and emotional and physical ways of living, of coping with reality, above all the ways in which human beings deal with one another, that determine everything else and constitute the national organism – the nation – whether it takes the form of a State or not. Whence it follows that the essential human unit in which man's nature is fully realised is not the individual, or a voluntary association which can be dissolved or altered or abandoned at will, but the nation; that it is to the creation and maintenance of the nation that the lives of subordinate units, the family, the tribe, the clan, the province, must, if they are fully themselves, be directed; for their nature and purpose, what is often called their meaning, are derived from its nature and its purposes; and that these are revealed not by rational analysis, but by a special awareness, which need not be fully conscious, of the unique relationship that binds individual human beings into the indissoluble and unanalysable organic whole which Burke identified with society, Rousseau with the people, Hegel with the State, but which for nationalists is, and can only be, the nation, whether its social structure or form of government.

Thirdly, this outlook entails the notion that one of the most compelling reasons, perhaps the most compelling, for holding a particular belief, pursuing a particular policy, serving a particular end, living a particular life, is that these ends, beliefs, policies, lives are *ours*. This is tantamount to saying that these rules or doctrines or principles should be followed not because they lead to virtue or happiness or justice or liberty, or are ordained by God or Church or prince or parliament or some other universally acknowledged authority, or are good or right in themselves, and therefore valid in their own right, universally, for all men in a given situation; rather they are to be followed because these values are those of *my* group – for the nationalist, of *my* nation; these thoughts, feelings, this course of action, are good or right, and I shall achieve fulfilment or happiness by identifying myself with them, because they are demands of the particular form of social life into which I have been born, to which I am connected by Burke's myriad strands, which reach into the past and future of my nation, and apart from which I am, to change the metaphor, a leaf, a twig, broken off from the tree which alone can give it life; so that if I am separated from it by circumstance or my own wilfulness, I shall become aimless, I shall wither away, being left, at best, with nostalgic memories of what it once was to have been truly alive and active and performing that function in the pattern of the national life understanding of which alone gave meaning and value to all I was and did.

Florid and emotive prose of this kind was used by Herder, Burke, Fichte, Michelet, and after them by sundry awakeners of the national souls of their dormant peoples in the Slav provinces of the Austrian or Turkish empires, or the oppressed nationalities (as well as the dominant majority population) ruled by the tsar; and then throughout the world. There is a distance between Burke's assertion that the individual may be foolish but the species is wise, and Fichte's declaration, a dozen or so years later, that the individual must vanish, must be absorbed, sublimated, into the species. Nevertheless the general direction is the same. This kind of value-laden language may at times affect to be descriptive, aimed only at illuminating the concept of nationhood or historical development. But its influence on conduct has been – and has by those who use it been intended to be – as great as that of the language of natural law or of human rights or of the class war or of any other idea which has shaped our world.

Finally, by a development which need cause no surprise, full-blown nationalism has arrived at the position that, if the satisfaction of the needs of the organism to which I belong turns out to be incompatible with the fulfilment of the goals of other groups, I, or the society to which I indissolubly belong, have no choice but to compel them to yield, if need be by force. If my group – let us call it nation – is freely to realise its true nature, this entails the need to remove obstacles in its path. Nothing that obstructs that which I recognise as my – that is, my nation's – supreme goal can be allowed to have equal value with it. There is no overarching criterion or standard in terms of which the various values of the lives, attributes, aspirations of different national groups can be ordered, for such a standard would be super-national, not itself immanent in, part and parcel of, a given social organism, but deriving its validity from some source outside the life of a particular society – a universal standard, as natural law or natural justice are conceived by those who believe in them. But since, on this view, all values and standards must of necessity be those intrinsic to a specific society, to a national organism, and its unique history, in terms of which alone the individual (like the other associations or groups to which he belongs), if he understands himself at all, conceives all values and purposes, such appeals to universality rest on a false view of the nature of man and of history. This is the ideology of organicism, loyalty, the *Volk* as the true carrier of the national values, integralism, historic roots, *la terre et les morts*, the national will: it is directed against the forces of disruption and decay categorised in the pejorative terms used to describe the application of methods of the natural sciences to human affairs – of critical, 'analytic' reason, 'cold' intellect, destructive, 'atomising' individualism, soulless mechanism, alien influences, shallow empiricism, rootless cosmopolitanism, abstract notions of nature, man, rights, which ignore differences of cultures and traditions – in short, the entire typology and catalogue of the enemy, which begins in the pages of Hamann and Burke, reaches a climax in Fichte and his romantic followers, is systematised by Maistre and Bonald, and reaches a new height in our own century in the propagandist writings of the First and Second World Wars, and the anathemas of irrationalist and Fascist writers, directed at the Enlightenment and all its works.

The language and the thought behind them, charged with emotion as they tend to be, are seldom wholly clear or consistent. The prophets of nationalism sometimes speak as if the superior, indeed, the supreme claims of his nation upon the individual are based on the fact that its life and ends and history alone give life and meaning to all that he is and does. But this seems to entail that other men stand in a similar relation to their own nations, with claims upon them equally valid and no less absolute, and that these may conflict with full realisation of the ends or 'mission' of another, for example, a given individual's own nation, and this in its turn appears to lead to cultural relativism in theory, which ill accords with the absolutism of the premise, even if it does not formally contradict it; as well as opening the door to war of all against all.

There are nationalists who seek to escape this conclusion by efforts to demonstrate that a given nation or race – say, the German – is intrinsically superior to other peoples, that its goals transcend theirs, or that its particular culture breeds beings in whom the true ends of men as such come closer to full realisation than in men outside its culture, as measured by some objective, trans-national standard. This is how Fichte speaks in his later writings (and the same thesis is to be found in Arndt and other German nationalists of this period). This, too, is entailed by the idea of the role played by the historic nations alone, each in its appointed time and place, to be found in the thought of Hegel. One can never feel completely certain whether these nationalist writers acclaim their own nation because it is what it is, or because its values alone approximate to some objective ideal or standard which, *ex hypothesi*, only those fortunate enough to be guided by them can even so much as understand, while other societies remain blind to them, and may always remain so, and are therefore objectively inferior. The line between the two conceptions is often blurred; but either leads to a collective self-worship, of which European, and perhaps American, nationalism has tended to be a powerful expression.

The nation is, of course, not the only focus of such worship. Similar language and rhetoric have historically been used in identifying the true interests of the individual with those of his

Church, his culture, his caste, his class, his party; sometimes these have overlapped or been fused into a unified ideal; at other times they have come into conflict. But the most powerful appeal of all these centres of devotion and self-identification has historically been the nation State. The revelation of its hold on its citizens in 1914, when it proved so much stronger than the class solidarity of the international working-class movement, exhibited this truth in a peculiarly devastating and tragic fashion.

Nationalism has assumed many forms since its birth in the eighteenth century, especially since its fusion with *étatisme*, the doctrine of the supremacy in all spheres of the State, in particular the nation State, and after its alliance with forces making for industrialisation and modernisation, once its sworn enemies. But it seems to me, in all its guises, to retain the four characteristics which I tried to outline above: the belief in the overriding need to belong to a nation; in the organic relationships of all the elements that constitute a nation; in the value of our own simply because it is ours; and, finally, faced by rival contenders for authority or loyalty, in the supremacy of its claims. These ingredients, in varying degrees and proportions, are to be found in all the rapidly growing nationalist ideologies which at present proliferate on the earth.

IV

It may be true that nationalism, as distinct from mere national consciousness – the sense of belonging to a nation – is in the first place a response to a patronising or disparaging attitude towards the traditional values of a society, the result of wounded pride and a sense of humiliation in its most socially conscious members, which in due course produce anger and self-assertion. This appears to be supported by the career of the paradigm of modern nationalism in the German reaction – from the conscious defence of German culture in the relatively mild literary patriotism of Thomasius and Lessing and their seventeenth-century forerunners, to Herder's assertion of cultural autonomy, until it leads to an outburst of aggressive chauvinism in Arndt, Jahn, Körner, Görres, during and after the Napoleonic invasion. But the story is plainly not so simple. Continuity of language, customs, occupation of a territory have existed since time immemorial. External aggression, not merely against tribes or peoples but against large societies unified by religion, or obedience to a single constituted authority, has, after all, occurred often enough in all parts of the globe. Yet neither in Europe, nor in Asia, neither in ancient times nor medieval, has this led to a specifically nationalist reaction: such has not been the response to defeat inflicted on Persians by Greeks, or on Greeks by Romans, or on Buddhists by Muslims, or on Graeco-Roman civilisation when it was overrun by Huns or Ottoman Turks, quite apart from all the innumerable smaller wars and destruction of native institutions by conquerors in either continent.

It seems clear, even to me who am not a historian or a sociologist, that while the infliction of a wound on the collective feeling of a society, or at least of its spiritual leaders, may be a necessary condition for the birth of nationalism, it is not a sufficient one; the society must, at least potentially, contain within itself a group or class of persons who are in search of a focus for loyalty or self-identification, or perhaps a base for power, no longer supplied by earlier forces for cohesion – tribal, or religious, or feudal, or dynastic, or military – such as was provided by the centralising policies of the monarchies of France or Spain, and was not provided by the rulers of German lands. In some cases these conditions are created by the emergence of new social classes seeking control of a society against older rulers, secular or clerical. If to this is added the wound of conquest, or even cultural disparagement from without, of a society which has at any rate the beginnings of a national culture, the soil for the rise of nationalism may be prepared.

Yet one more condition for it seems necessary: for nationalism to develop in it, a society must, in the minds of at least some of its most sensitive members, carry an image of itself as a nation, at least in embryo, in virtue of some general unifying factor or factors – language, ethnic origin, a common history (real or imaginary) – ideas and sentiments which are relatively articulate in the minds of the better educated and more socially and historically minded, and a good deal less articulate in, even absent from, the consciousness of the bulk of the population. This national image, which seems to make those in whom it is found capable of resentment if it is ignored or insulted, also unites some among them into a conscious ideological group or movement, particularly if they are faced by some common enemy, whether within the State or outside it – a Church or a government or foreign detractors. These are the men who speak or write to the people, and seek to make them conscious of their wrongs as a people – poets and novelists, historians and critics, theologians, philosophers and the like. Thus resistance to French hegemony in all spheres of life began in the apparently remote region of aesthetics and criticism (I do not here wish to go into the question of what it was in particular that stimulated the original reaction against French neo-classicism in England, or Switzerland). In the German lands it became a social and political force, a breeding-ground of nationalism. Among the Germans it took the form of a deliberate effort by writers to liberate them-selves – and others – from what they felt to be asphyxiating conditions – at first from the despotic dogmas of the French aesthetic legislators, which cramped the free development of the spirit.

But besides the arrogant French, there were domestic tyrants, social and not merely aesthetic. The great outburst of individual indignation against the rules and regulations of an oppressive and philistine society, which goes by the name of 'Storm and Stress', had as its direct objective the knocking down of all the walls and barriers of social life, obsequiousness and servility below and brutality, arbitrariness, arrogance and oppression above, lies and 'the cant and gibberish of hypocrisy',[1] as Burke calls it, at every level. What began to be questioned was the validity of any laws – the rules, supposedly enjoined by God or by nature or by the prince, that conferred authority and required universal obedi-ence. The demand was for freedom of self-expression, the free expression of the creative will, at its purest and strongest in artists, but present in all men. For Herder this vital energy was incarnated in the creations of the collective genius of peoples: legends, heroic poetry, myths, laws, customs, song, dance, religious and secular symbolism, temples, cathedrals, ritual acts – all were forms of expression and communication created by no individual authors or identifiable groups, but by the collective and impersonal imagina-tion and will of the entire community, acting at various levels of

[1] op. cit. (p. 256 above, note 2), p. 154.

consciousness; thus, he believed, were generated those intimate and impalpable bonds in virtue of which a society develops as a single organic whole.

The notion of a creative faculty, working in individuals and entire societies alike, replaced the notion of timeless objective truths, or unalterable models or rules, by following which alone men attain to happiness or virtue or justice or any proper fulfilment of their natures. From this sprang a new view of men and society, which stressed vitality, movement, change, respects in which individuals or groups differed rather than resembled each other, the charm and value of diversity, uniqueness, individuality, a view which conceived of the world as a garden where each tree, each flower, grows in its own peculiar fashion and incorporates those aspirations which circumstances and its own individual nature have generated, and is not, therefore, to be judged by the patterns and goals of other organisms. This cut athwart the dominant *philosophia perennis*, the belief in the generality, uniformity, universality, timeless validity of objective and eternal laws and rules that apply everywhere, at all times, to all men and things, the secular or naturalistic version of which was advocated by the leaders of the French Enlightenment, inspired by the triumph of the natural and mathematical sciences, in terms of which German culture, religious, literary, inward-looking, liable to mysticism, narrowly provincial, at best feebly imitative of the West, made such a poor showing.

I do not wish to imply that this crucial contrast was, at any rate at first, more than a vision in the heads of a small group of German poets and critics. But it was these writers who, in all probability, felt most acutely displaced by the social transformation through which Germany, and in particular Prussia, was passing under the Westernising reforms of Frederick the Great. Barred from all real power, unable to fit themselves into the bureaucratic organisation which was imposed on traditional ways of life, acutely sensitive to the incompatibility of their basically Christian, Protestant, moralistic outlook with the scientific temper of the French Enlightenment, harried by the petty despotism of three hundred princes, the most gifted and independent among them responded to the undermining of their world, which had begun with the humiliations inflicted upon their grandfathers by the armies of Louis XIV, by a growing revolt. They contrasted the depth and poetry of the German tradition, with its capacity for fitful but authentic insights into the inexhaustible, inexpressible variety of the life of the spirit, with the shallow materialism, the utilitarianism, and the thin, dehumanised shadow-play of the worlds of the French thinkers. This outlook is one of the well-springs of the romantic movement, which in Germany, at any rate, celebrated the collective will, untrammelled by rules which men could discover by rational methods, the spiritual life of the people in whose activity – or impersonal will – creative individuals could participate, but which they could not observe or describe. The conception of the political life of the nation as the expression of this collective will is the essence of political romanticism – that is, nationalism.

Let me repeat once again that even though nationalism seems to me in the first place to be a response to a wound inflicted upon a society, this, although it is a necessary, is not a sufficient cause of national self-assertion. The wounds inflicted upon one society by another, since time immemorial, have not in all cases led to a national response. For that something more is needed – namely, a new vision of life with which the wounded society, or the classes or groups which have been displaced by political and social change, can identify themselves, around which they can gather and attempt to restore their collective life. Thus both the Slavophil and the populist movements in Russia, like German nationalism, can be understood only if one realises the traumatic effect of the violent and rapid modernisation imposed on his people by Peter the Great, and, on a smaller scale, by Frederick the Great in Prussia – that is, the reaction against the effect of technological revolutions or the development of new markets and the decay of old ones, the consequent disruption of the lives of entire classes, the lack of opportunity for the use of their skills by educated men psychologically unfit to enter the new bureaucracy, and, finally, in the case of Germany, occupation or colonial rule by a powerful foreign enemy which destroyed traditional ways of life and left men, and especially the most sensitive and self-conscious among them – artists, thinkers, whatever their professions – without an established position, insecure and bewildered. There is then an effort to create a new synthesis, a new ideology, both to explain and justify resistance to the forces working against their convictions and ways of life, and to point in a new direction and offer them a new centre for self-identification.

This is a familiar enough phenomenon in our own time, which has not lacked in social and economic upheavals. Where ethnic ties and common historical experience are not strong enough to have created a sense of nationhood, this new focus can be a social class, or a political party, or a Church, or, most often, the centre of power and authority – the State itself, whether or not it is multinational – which raises the banner under which all those whose traditional modes of life have been disrupted – landless peasants, ruined landowners or shopkeepers, unemployed intellectuals, unsuccessful professionals in various spheres – can gather and regroup themselves. But none of these have, in fact, proved as potent, whether as a symbol or as a reality, as capable of acting as a unifying and dynamic force, as the nation; and when the nation is one with other centres of devotion – race, religion, class – its appeal is incomparably strong.

The first true nationalists – the Germans – are an example of the combination of wounded cultural pride and a philosophico-historical vision to stanch the wound and create an inner focus of resistance. First a small group of educated, discontented Francophobes, then, under the impact of the disasters at the hands of the French armies and Napoleon's *Gleichschaltung*, a vast popular movement, the first great upsurge of nationalist passion, with its wild student chauvinism and book-burnings and secret trials of traitors, a sorcerer's apprentice who got out of hand and excited the disgust of calm thinkers like Goethe and Hegel. Other nations followed, partly under the influence of German rhetoric, partly because their circumstances were sufficiently similar to create a similar malaise and generate the same dangerous remedy. After Germany, Italy and Poland and Russia, and in due course the Balkan and Baltic nationalities and Ireland, and after the débâcle the French Third Republic, and so to our own day, with its republics and dictatorships in Asia and Africa, the nationalist revolts of regional and ethnic groups in Belgium and Corsica, Canada and Spain and Cyprus, even in France and Britain, and who knows where else.

None of the prophets of the nineteenth century, so far as I can tell, anticipated anything of this kind. If anyone had suggested it, it would surely have been regarded as too improbable to be worth consideration. What is the reason for overlooking the likelihood of this cardinal development of our day?

V

Among the assumptions of rational thinkers of the liberal type in the nineteenth and for some decades in the twentieth century were these: that liberal democracy was the most satisfactory – or at least, the least unsatisfactory – form of human organisation; that the nation State was, or at least had historically come to be, the normal unit of independent, self-governing human society; and, finally, that once the multinational empires (which Herder had denounced as ill-assorted political monstrosities) had been dissolved into their constituent parts, the yearning for union of men with common language, habits, memories, outlooks would at last be satisfied, and a society of liberated, self-determined nation States – Mazzini's Young Italy, Young Germany, Young Poland, Young Russia – would come into existence, and, inspired by a patriotism not tainted by aggressive nationalism (itself a symptom of a pathological condition induced by oppression), would live at peace and in harmony with each other, no longer impeded by the irrational survivals of a servile past. The fact that a representative of Mazzini's movement was invited to, and attended, the meeting of the First International Working Men's Association, however little Marx may have liked it, is significant in this respect. This conviction was shared by the liberal and democratic founders of the succession States after the First World War, and was incorporated in the constitution of the League of Nations. As for Marxists, although they regarded nationalism as historically reactionary, even they did not demand the total abolition of national frontiers; provided that class exploitation was abolished by the socialist revolution, it was assumed that free national societies could exist side by side until, and after, the withering away of the State conceived as an instrument of class domination.

Neither of these ideologies anticipated the growth of national sentiment and, more than this, of aggressive nationalism. What, I think, was ignored was the fact which only, perhaps, Durkheim perceived clearly, namely, that the destruction of traditional hierarchies and orders of social life, in which men's loyalties were deeply involved, by the centralisation and bureaucratic 'rationalisation' which industrial progress required and generated, deprived great numbers of men of social and emotional security, produced the notorious phenomena of alienation, spiritual homelessness and growing anomie, and needed the creation, by deliberate social policy, of psychological equivalents for the lost cultural, political, religious bonds which served to maintain the older order. The socialists believed that class solidarity, the fraternity of the exploited, and the prospect of a just and rational society which the revolution would bring to birth, would provide this indispensable social cement; and, indeed, to a degree it did so. Moreover, some among the poor, the displaced, the deprived emigrated to the New World. But for the majority the vacuum was filled neither by professional associations, nor by political parties, nor by the revolutionary myths which Sorel sought to provide, but by the old, traditional bonds – language, the soil, historical memories real and imaginary – and by institutions or leaders functioning as incarnations of men's conceptions of themselves as a community, a *Gemeinschaft* – symbols and agencies which proved far more powerful than either socialists or enlightened liberals wished to believe. The idea, sometimes invested with a mystical or messianic fervour, of the nation as supreme authority, replacing the Church or the prince or the rule of law or other sources of ultimate values, relieved the pain of the wound to group consciousness, whoever may have inflicted it – a foreign enemy or native capitalists or imperialist exploiters or an artificially imposed, heartless bureaucracy.

This sentiment was, no doubt, deliberately exploited by parties and politicians, but it was there to be exploited, it was not invented by those who used it for ulterior purposes of their own. It was there, and possessed an independent force of its own, which could be combined with other forces, most effectively with the power of a State bent on modernisation, as a defence against other powers conceived of as alien or hostile, or with particular groups and classes and movements within the State, religious, political and economic, with which the bulk of the society did not instinctively identify itself. It developed, and could be used, in many different directions, as a weapon of secularism, industrialisation, modernisation, the rational use of resources, or in an appeal to a real or imaginary past, some lost, pagan or neo-medieval paradise, a vision of a braver, simpler, purer life, or as the call of the blood or of some ancient faith, against foreigners or cosmopolitans, or 'sophisters, oeconomists, and calculators',[1] who did not understand the

---

[1] loc. cit. (p. 256 above, note 2).

true soul of the people or the roots from which it sprang, and robbed it of its heritage.

It seems to me that those who, however perceptive in other respects, ignored the explosive power generated by the combination of unhealed mental wounds, however caused, with the image of the nation as a society of the living, the dead and those yet unborn (sinister as this could prove to be when driven to a point of pathological exacerbation), displayed insufficient grasp of social reality. This seems to me to be as true of the present as of the last two hundred years. Modern nationalism was indeed born on German soil, but it developed wherever conditions sufficiently resembled the impact of modernisation on traditional German society. I do not wish to say that this ideology was inevitable: it might, perhaps, not have been born at all. No one has yet convincingly demonstrated that the human imagination obeys discoverable laws, or is able to predict the movement of ideas. If this cluster of ideas had not been born, history might have taken another turn. The wounds inflicted on the Germans would have been there, but the balm which they generated, what Raymond Aron (who applied it to Marxism) has called the opium of the intellectuals, might have been a different one – and if this had happened, things might have fallen out otherwise. But the idea was born: and the consequences were what they were; and it seems to me to show a certain ideological obstinacy not to recognise their nature and importance.

Why was this, in general, not seen? Partly, perhaps, because of the 'Whig interpretation' so widely disseminated by enlightened liberal (and socialist) historians. The picture is familiar: on the one side, the powers of darkness: Church, capitalism, tradition, authority, hierarchy, exploitation, privilege; on the other, the *lumières*, the struggle for reason, for knowledge and the destruction of barriers between men, for equality, human rights (particularly those of the labouring masses), for individual and social liberty, the reduction of misery, oppression, brutality, the emphasis on what men had in common, not on their differences. Yet, to put it at its simplest, the differences were no less real than the generic identity, than Feuerbach's and Marx's 'species-being'. National sentiment, which sprang from them, fell on both sides of this division between light and darkness, progress and reaction, just as it has within the Communist camp of our own day; ignored differences assert themselves, and in the end rise against efforts to ride over them in favour of an assumed, or desired, uniformity. The ideal of a single, scientifically organised world system governed by reason was the heart of the programme of the Enlightenment. When Immanuel Kant, who can scarcely be accused of leanings towards irrationalism, declared that 'Out of the crooked timber of humanity no straight thing was ever made',[1] what he said was not absurd.

I have one more suggestion to offer. It seems to me that the thought of the nineteenth century, and the early twentieth, was astonishingly Europocentric. When even the most imaginative and the most radical political thinkers of those times spoke of the inhabitants of Africa or Asia, there was, as a rule, something curiously remote and abstract about their ideas. They thought of Asians and Africans almost exclusively in terms of their treatment by Europeans. Whether they were imperialists, or benevolent paternalists, or liberals and socialists outraged by conquest and exploitation, the peoples of Africa and Asia were discussed either as wards or as victims of Europeans, but seldom, if ever, in their own right, as peoples with histories and cultures of their own; with a past and present and future which must be understood in terms of their own actual character and circumstances; or, if the existence of such indigenous cultures was acknowledged, as in the case of, let us say, India or Persia, China or Japan, it tended to be largely ignored when the needs of these societies in the future were discussed. Consequently, the notion that a mounting nationalism might develop in these continents was not seriously allowed for. Even Lenin seemed to think of national movements in these continents solely as weapons against European imperialism; and of support of them only as being likely to accelerate or retard the march towards revolution in Europe. This is perfectly intelligible, since he and his fellow revolutionaries believed that this was where the centre of world power lay, that the proletarian revolution in Europe would automatically liberate the workers everywhere, that Asian or African colonial or semi-colonial regimes would thereby be swept away, and their subjects integrated into the new, socially emancipated international world order. Consequently Lenin was not interested in the life of various communities as such, in this respect following Marx, whose pages on, for example, India and China, or for that matter Ireland, expound no specific lessons for their future.

[1] loc. cit. (p. 16 above, note 1).

This wellnigh universal Europocentrism may at least in part account for the fact that the vast explosion not only of anti-imperialism but of nationalism in these continents remained so largely unpredicted. Until the enormous impact of the Japanese victory over Russia in 1904, no non-European people presented itself to the gaze of Western social or political theorists as, in the full sense of the word, a nation, whose intrinsic character, history, problems, potentialities for the future constituted a field of study of primary importance for students of public affairs, history, and human development in general. It is this, as much as anything else, that may help to explain this strange lacuna in the futurology of the past. It is instructive to bear in mind that while the Russian Revolution was genuinely free of any nationalist element, even after the Allied intervention – indeed, it is fair to describe it as wholly anti-nationalist in character – this did not last. The concessions which Stalin had to make to national sentiment before and during the invasion of Russia by Hitler, and the celebration thereafter of the heroes of purely Russian history, indicate the degree to which the mobilisation of this sentiment was required to promote the ends of the Soviet State. And this holds no less of the vast majority of States that have come into being since the end of the Second World War.

It would not, I think, be an exaggeration to say that no political movement today, at any rate outside the Western world, seems likely to succeed unless it allies itself to national sentiment. I must repeat that I am not a historian or a political scientist, and so do not claim to offer an explanation of this phenomenon. I only wish to pose a question, and indicate the need for greater attention to this particular offshoot of the romantic revolt, which has decisively affected our world.

# WINSTON CHURCHILL IN 1940

## I

IN THE now remote year 1928, an eminent English poet and critic published a book dealing with the art of writing English prose.[1] Writing at a time of bitter disillusion with the false splendours of the Edwardian era, and still more with the propaganda and phrasemaking occasioned by the First World War, the critic praised the virtues of simplicity. If simple prose was often dry and flat, it was at least honest. If it was at times awkward, shapeless and bleak, it did at least convey a feeling of truthfulness. Above all, it avoided the worst of all temptations – inflation, self-dramatisation, the construction of flimsy stucco façades, either deceptively smooth or covered with elaborate baroque detail which concealed a dreadful inner emptiness.

The time and mood are familiar enough: it was not long after Lytton Strachey had set a new fashion by his method of exposing the cant or muddleheadedness of eminent Victorians, after Bertrand Russell had unmasked the great nineteenth-century metaphysicians as authors of a monstrous hoax played upon generations eager to be deceived, after Keynes had successfully pilloried the follies and vices of the Allied statesmen at Versailles. This was the time when rhetoric and, indeed, eloquence were held up to obloquy as camouflage for literary and moral Pecksniffs, unscrupulous charlatans who corrupted artistic taste and discredited the cause of truth and reason, and at their worst incited to evil and led a credulous world to disaster. It was in this literary climate that the critic in question, with much skill and discrimination, explained why he admired the last recorded words spoken to Judge Thayer by the poor fish-pedlar Vanzetti[2] – moving, ungrammatical fragments uttered by a simple man about to die – more than he did

---

[1] Herbert Read, *English Prose Style* (London, 1928).
[2] ibid., p. 165.

the rolling periods of celebrated masters of fine writing widely read by the public at that time.

He selected as an example of the latter a man who in particular was regarded as the sworn enemy of all that the author prized most highly – humility, integrity, humanity, scrupulous regard for sensibility, individual freedom, personal affection – the celebrated but distrusted paladin of imperialism and the romantic conception of life, the swashbuckling militarist, the vehement orator and journalist, the most public of public personalities in a world dedicated to the cultivation of private virtues, the Chancellor of the Exchequer of the Conservative Government then in power, Winston Churchill.

After observing that 'These three conditions are necessary to Eloquence – firstly, an adequate theme; then a sincere and impassioned mind; and lastly a power of sustainment or pertinacity', the writer drove his thesis home with a quotation from the first part of Churchill's *World Crisis*, which had appeared some four years previously, and added: 'Such eloquence is false because it is artificial . . . the images are stale, the metaphors violent. The whole passage exhales a false dramatic atmosphere . . . a volley of rhetorical imperatives.' He went on to describe Churchill's prose as being high-sounding, redundant, falsely eloquent, declamatory, derived from undue 'aggrandisation of the self' instead of 'aggrandisation of the theme'; and condemned it root and branch.[1]

This view was well received by the young men who were painfully reacting against anything which appeared to go beyond the naked skeleton of the truth, at a time when not only rhetoric but even noble eloquence seemed outrageous hypocrisy. Churchill's critic spoke, and knew that he spoke, for a post-war generation; the psychological symptoms of the vast and rapid social transformation then in progress, from which the government in power so resolutely averted its gaze, were visible to the least discerning critics of literature and the arts; the mood was dissatisfied, hostile and insecure; the sequel to so much magnificence was too bitter, and left behind it a heritage of hatred for the grand style as such. The victims and casualties of the disaster thought they had earned the right to be rid of the trappings of an age which had heartlessly betrayed them.

Nevertheless the stern critic and his audience were profoundly

---

[1] ibid., pp. 191–2.

mistaken. What he and they denounced as so much tinsel and hollow pasteboard was in reality solid: it was this author's natural means for the expression of his heroic, highly coloured, sometimes over-simple and even naïve, but always genuine, vision of life. The critic saw only an unconvincing, sordidly transparent pastiche, but this was an illusion. The reality was something very different: an inspired, if unconscious, attempt at a revival. It went against the stream of contemporary thought and feeling only because it was a deliberate return to a formal mode of English utterance which extends from Gibbon and Dr Johnson to Peacock and Macaulay, a composite weapon created by Churchill in order to convey his particular vision. In the bleak and deflationary 1920s it was too bright, too big, too vivid, too unstable for the sensitive and sophisticated epigoni of the age of imperialism, who, living an inner life of absorbing complexity and delicacy, became unable and certainly unwilling to admire the light of a day which had destroyed so much of what they had trusted and loved. From this the critic and his supporters recoiled; but their analysis of their reasons was not convincing.

They had, of course, a right to their own scale of values, but it was a blunder to dismiss Churchill's prose as a false front, a hollow sham. Revivals are not false as such: the Gothic Revival, for example, represented a passionate, if nostalgic, attitude towards life, and while some examples of it may appear bizarre, it sprang from a deeper sentiment and had a good deal more to say than some of the thin and 'realistic' styles which followed; the fact that the creators of the Gothic Revival found their liberation in going back into a largely imaginary past in no way discredits them or their achievement. There are those who, inhibited by the furniture of the ordinary world, come to life only when they feel themselves actors upon a stage, and, thus emancipated, speak out for the first time, and are then found to have much to say. There are those who can function freely only in uniform or armour or court dress, see only through certain kinds of spectacles, act fearlessly only in situations which in some way are formalised for them, see life as a kind of play in which they and others are assigned certain lines which they must speak. So it happens – the last war afforded plenty of instances of this – that people of a shrinking disposition perform miracles of courage when life has been dramatised for them, when they are on the battlefield; and might continue to do so if they were constantly in uniform and life were always a battlefield.

This need for a framework is not 'escapism', not artificial or abnormal or a sign of maladjustment. Often it is a vision of experience in terms of the strongest single psychological ingredient in one's nature: not infrequently in the form of a simple struggle between conflicting forces or principles, between truth and false-hood, good and evil, right and wrong, between personal integrity and various forms of temptation and corruption (as in the case of the critic in question), or between what is conceived as permanent and what is ephemeral, or between the material and the immaterial, or between the forces of life and the forces of death, or between the religion of art and its supposed enemies – politicians or priests or philistines. Life may be seen through many windows, none of them necessarily clear or opaque, less or more distorting than any of the others. And since we think largely in words, they necessarily take on the property of serving as an armour. The style of Dr Johnson, which echoes so frequently in the prose of *Their Finest Hour*, particularly when the author indulges in a solemn facetiousness, was itself in its own day a weapon offensive and defensive; it requires no deep psychological subtlety to perceive why a man so vulnerable as Johnson – who belonged mentally to the previous century – had constant need of it.

II

Churchill's dominant category, the single, central, organising principle of his moral and intellectual universe, is a historical imagination so strong, so comprehensive, as to encase the whole of the present and the whole of the future in a framework of a rich and multicoloured past. Such an approach is dominated by a desire – and a capacity – to find fixed moral and intellectual bearings, to give shape and character, colour and direction and coherence, to the stream of events.

This kind of systematic 'historicism' is, of course, not confined to men of action or political theorists: Roman Catholic thinkers see life in terms of a firm and lucid historical structure, and so, of course, do Marxists, and so did the romantic historians and philosophers from whom the Marxists are directly descended. Nor do we complain of 'escapism' or perversion of the facts until the categories adopted are thought to do too much violence to the 'facts'. To interpret, to relate, to classify, to symbolise are those natural and unavoidable human activities which we loosely and conveniently describe as thinking. We complain, if we do, only when the result is too widely at variance with the common outlook of our own society and age and tradition.

Churchill sees history – and life – as a great Renaissance pageant: when he thinks of France or Italy, Germany or the Low Countries, Russia, India, Africa, the Arab lands, he sees vivid historical images – something between Victorian illustrations in a child's book of history and the great procession painted by Benozzo Gozzoli in the Riccardi Palace. His eye is never that of the neatly classifying sociologist, the careful psychological analyst, the plodding antiquary, the patient historical scholar. His poetry has not that anatomical vision which sees the naked bone beneath the flesh, skulls and skeletons and the omnipresence of decay and death beneath the flow of life. The units out of which his world is constructed are simpler and larger than life, the patterns vivid and repetitive like those of an epic poet, or at times like those of a dramatist who sees persons and situations as timeless symbols and embodiments of eternal, shining principles. The whole is a series of symmetrically formed and somewhat stylised compositions, either suffused with bright light or cast in darkest shadow, like a legend by Carpaccio, with scarcely any nuance, painted in primary colours, with no half-tones, nothing intangible, nothing impalpable, nothing half spoken or hinted or whispered: the voice does not alter in pitch or timbre.

The archaisms of style to which Churchill's wartime speeches accustomed us are indispensable ingredients of the heightened tone, the formal chronicler's attire, for which the solemnity of the occasion called. Churchill is fully conscious of this: the style should adequately respond to the demands which history makes upon the actors from moment to moment. 'The ideas set forth', he wrote in 1940 about a Foreign Office draft, 'appeared to me to err in trying to be too clever, to enter into refinements of policy unsuited to the tragic simplicity and grandeur of the times and the issues at stake.'

His own narrative consciously mounts and swells until it reaches the great climax of the Battle of Britain. The texture and the tension are those of a tragic opera, where the very artificiality of the medium, both in the recitative and in the arias, serves to eliminate the irrelevant dead level of normal existence and to set off in high relief the deeds and sufferings of the principal characters. The moments of comedy in such a work must necessarily conform to the style of the whole and be parodies of it; and this is Churchill's practice. When he says that he viewed this or that 'with stern and tranquil gaze', or informs his officials that any 'chortling' by them over the failure of a chosen scheme 'will be viewed with great disfavour by me', or describes the 'celestial grins' of his collabora-tors over the development of a well-concealed conspiracy, he does precisely this; the mock-heroic tone – reminiscent of *Stalky & Co.* – does not break the operatic conventions. But conventions though they be, they are not donned and doffed by the author at will: by now they are his second nature, and have completely fused with the first; art and nature are no longer distinguishable. The very rigid pattern of his prose is the normal medium of his ideas not merely when he sets himself to compose, but in the life of the imagination which permeates his daily existence.

Churchill's language is a medium which he invented because he needed it. It has a bold, ponderous, fairly uniform, easily recognis-able rhythm which lends itself to parody (including his own) like all strongly individual styles. A language is individual when its user is endowed with sharply marked characteristics and succeeds in creating a medium for their expression. The origins, the constitu-ents, the classical echoes which can be found in Churchill's prose are obvious enough; the product is, however, unique. Whatever the attitude that may be taken towards it, it must be recognised as a large-scale phenomenon of our time. To ignore or deny this would be blind or frivolous or dishonest. The utterance is always, and not merely on special occasions, formal (though it alters in intensity and colour with the situation), always public, Ciceronian, addressed to the world, remote from the hesitancies and stresses of introspection and private life.

III

The quality of Churchill's volumes on the Second World War is that of his whole life. His world is built upon the primacy of public over private relationships, upon the supreme value of action, of the battle between simple good and simple evil, between life and death; but, above all, battle. He has always fought. 'Whatever you may do,' he declared to the demoralised French ministers in the bleakest hour of 1940, 'we shall fight on for ever and ever and ever', and under this sign his own whole life has been lived.

What has he fought for? The answer is a good deal clearer than in the case of other equally passionate but less consistent men of action. Churchill's principles and beliefs on fundamental issues have never faltered. He has often been accused by his critics of inconstancy, of veering and even erratic judgement, as when he changed his allegiance from the Conservative to the Liberal Party, to and fro. But with the exception of the issue of protection, when he supported the tariff as Chancellor of the Exchequer in Baldwin's cabinet in the 1920s, this charge, which at first seems so plausible, is spectacularly false. Far from changing his opinions too often, Churchill has scarcely, during a long and stormy career, altered them at all. If anyone wishes to discover his views on the large and lasting issues of our time, he need only set himself to discover what Churchill has said or written on the subject at any period of his long and exceptionally articulate public life, in particular during the years before the First World War: the number of instances in which his views have in later years undergone any appreciable degree of change will be found astonishingly small.

The apparently solid and dependable Baldwin adjusted his attitudes with wonderful dexterity as and when circumstances required it. Chamberlain, long regarded as a grim and immovable rock of Tory opinion, altered his policies – more serious than Baldwin, he pursued policies, not being content with mere attitudes – when the Party or the situation seemed to him to require it. Churchill remained inflexibly attached to first principles.

It is the strength and coherence of his central, lifelong beliefs that have provoked greater uneasiness, more disfavour and suspicion, in the central office of the Conservative Party than his vehemence or passion for power, or what was considered his wayward, unreliable brilliance. No strongly centralised political organisation feels altogether happy with individuals who combine independence, a free imagination and a formidable strength of character with stubborn faith and a single-minded, unchanging view of the public and private good. Churchill, who believes that 'ambition, not so much for vulgar ends but for fame, glints in every mind', believes in and seeks to attain – as an artist his vision – personal greatness and personal glory. As much as any king conceived by a Renaissance dramatist or by a nineteenth-century historian or moralist, he thinks it a brave thing to ride in triumph through Persepolis; he knows with an unshakeable certainty what he considers to be big, handsome, noble and worthy of pursuit by someone in high station, and what, on the contrary, he abhors as being dim, grey, thin, likely to lower or destroy the play of colour and movement in the universe. Tacking and bending and timid compromise may commend themselves to those sound men of sense whose hopes of preserving the world they defend are shot through with an often unconscious pessimism; but if the policy they pursue is likely to slow the tempo, to diminish the forces of life, to lower the 'vital and vibrant energy' which he admires, say, in Lord Beaverbrook, Churchill is ready for attack.

Churchill is one of the diminishing number of those who genuinely believe in a specific world order: the desire to give it life and strength is the most powerful single influence upon everything which he thinks and imagines, does and is. When biographers and historians come to describe and analyse his views on Europe or America, on the British Empire or Russia, on India or Palestine, or even on social or economic policy, they will find that his opinions on all these topics are set in fixed patterns, set early in life and later only reinforced. Thus he has always believed in great States and civilisations in an almost hierarchical order, and has never, for instance, hated Germany as such: Germany is a great, historically hallowed State; the Germans are a great historic race and as such occupy a proportionate amount of space in Churchill's world picture. He denounced the Prussians in the First World War and the Nazis in the Second; the Germans scarcely at all. He has always entertained a glowing vision of France and her culture, and has unalterably advocated the necessity of Anglo-French collaboration. He has always looked on the Russians as a formless, quasi-Asiatic mass beyond the walls of European civilisation. His belief in and predilection for the American democracy are the foundation of his political outlook.

His vision in foreign affairs has always been consistently romantic. The struggle of the Jews for self-determination in Palestine engaged his imagination in precisely the way in which the Italian Risorgimento captured the sympathies of his Liberal forebears. Similarly his views on social policy conform to those Liberal principles which he received at the hands of the men he most admired in the great Liberal administration of the first decade of this century – Asquith, Haldane, Grey, Morley, above all Lloyd George before 1914 – and he has seen no reason to change them, whatever the world might do; and if these views, progressive in 1910, seem less convincing today, and indeed reveal an obstinate blindness to social and economic – as opposed to political –

injustice, of which Haldane or Lloyd George can scarcely be accused, that flows from Churchill's unalterable faith in the firmly conceived scheme of human relationships which he established within himself long ago, once and for all.

IV

It is an error to regard the imagination as a mainly revolutionary force – if it destroys and alters, it also fuses hitherto isolated beliefs, insights, mental habits, into strongly unified systems. These, if they are filled with sufficient energy and force of will – and, it may be added, fantasy, which is less frightened by the facts and creates ideal models in terms of which the facts are ordered in the mind – sometimes transform the outlook of an entire people and generation.

The British statesman most richly endowed with these gifts was Disraeli, who in effect conceived that imperialist mystique, that splendid but most un-English vision which, romantic to the point of exoticism, full of metaphysical emotion, to all appearances utterly opposed to everything most soberly empirical, utilitarian, anti-systematic in the British tradition, bound its spell on the mind of England for two generations.

Churchill's political imagination has something of the same magical power to transform. It is a magic which belongs equally to demagogues and great democratic leaders: Franklin Roosevelt, who as much as any man altered his country's inner image of itself and of its character and its history, possessed it in a high degree. But the differences between him and Churchill are greater than the similarities, and to some degree epitomise the differences of continents and civilisations. The contrast is brought out vividly by the respective parts which they played in the war which drew them so closely together.

The Second World War in some ways gave birth to less novelty and genius than the First. It was, of course, a greater cataclysm, fought over a wider area, and altered the social and political contours of the world at least as radically as its predecessor, perhaps more so. But the break in continuity in 1914 was far more violent. The years before 1914 look to us now, and looked even in the 1920s, as the end of a long period of largely peaceful development, broken suddenly and catastrophically. In Europe, at least, the years before 1914 were viewed with understandable nostalgia by those who after them knew no real peace.

The period between the wars marks a decline in the development of human culture if it is compared with that sustained and fruitful period which makes the nineteenth century seem a unique human achievement, so powerful that it persisted, even during the war which broke it, to a degree which seems astonishing to us now. The quality of literature, for example, which is surely one of the most reliable criteria of intellectual and moral vitality, was incomparably higher during the war of 1914–18 than it has been after 1939. In Western Europe alone these four years of slaughter and destruction were also years in which works of genius and talent continued to be produced by such established writers as Shaw and Wells and Kipling, Hauptmann and Gide, Chesterton and Arnold Bennett, Beerbohm and Yeats, as well as such younger writers as Proust and Joyce, Virginia Woolf and E. M. Forster, T. S. Eliot and Alexander Blok, Rilke, Stefan George and Valéry. Nor did natural science, philosophy and history cease to develop fruitfully. What has the more recent war to offer by comparison?

Yet perhaps there is one respect in which the Second World War did outshine its predecessor: the leaders of the nations involved in it were, with the significant exception of France, men of greater stature, psychologically more interesting, than their prototypes. It would hardly be disputed that Stalin is a more fascinating figure than Tsar Nicholas II; Hitler more arresting than the Kaiser; Mussolini than Victor Emmanuel; and, memorable as they were, President Wilson and Lloyd George yield in the attribute of sheer historical magnitude to Franklin Roosevelt and Winston Churchill.

History, we are told by Aristotle, is 'what Alcibiades did and suffered'.[1] This notion, despite all the efforts of the social sciences to overthrow it, remains a good deal more valid than rival hypotheses, provided that history is defined as that which historians actually do. At any rate Churchill accepts it wholeheartedly, and takes full advantage of his opportunities. And because his narrative deals largely in personalities and gives individual genius its full and sometimes more than its full due, the appearance of the great wartime protagonists in his pages gives his narrative some of the quality of an epic, whose heroes and villains acquire their stature not merely – or indeed at all – from the importance of the

[1] loc. cit. (p. 34 above, note 1).

events in which they are involved, but from their own intrinsic human size upon the stage of human history; their characteristics, involved as they are in perpetual juxtaposition and occasional collision with one another, set each other off in vast relief.

Comparisons and contrasts are bound to arise in the mind of the reader which sometimes take him beyond Churchill's pages. Thus Roosevelt stands out principally by his astonishing appetite for life and by his apparently complete freedom from fear of the future; as a man who welcomed the future eagerly as such, and conveyed the feeling that whatever the times might bring, all would be grist to his mill, nothing would be too formidable or crushing to be subdued and used and moulded into the pattern of the new and unpredictable forms of life into the building of which he, Roosevelt, and his allies and devoted subordinates would throw themselves with unheard-of energy and gusto. This avid anticipation of the future, the lack of nervous fear that the wave might prove too big or violent to navigate, contrasts most sharply with the uneasy longing to insulate themselves so clear in Stalin or Chamberlain. Hitler, too, in a sense, showed no fear, but his assurance sprang from a lunatic's violent and cunning vision, which distorted the facts too easily in his favour.

So passionate a faith in the future, so untroubled a confidence in one's power to mould it, when it is allied to a capacity for realistic appraisal of its true contours, implies an exceptionally sensitive awareness, conscious or half-conscious, of the tendencies of one's milieu, of the desires, hopes, fears, loves, hatreds of the human beings who compose it, of what are impersonally described as social and individual 'trends'. Roosevelt had this sensibility developed to the point of genius. He acquired the symbolic significance which he retained throughout his presidency largely because he sensed the tendencies of his time and their projections into the future to a most uncommon degree. His sense, not only of the movement of American public opinion but of the general direction in which the larger human society of his time was moving, was what is called uncanny. The inner currents, the tremors and complicated convolutions of this movement seemed to register themselves within his nervous system with a kind of seismographical accuracy. The majority of his fellow citizens recognised this – some with enthusiasm, others with gloom or bitter indignation. Peoples far beyond the frontiers of the United States rightly looked to him as the most genuine and unswerving spokesman of democracy of his time, the most contemporary, the most outward-looking, the boldest, most imaginative, most large-spirited, free from the obsessions of an inner life, with an unparalleled capacity for creating confidence in the power of his insight, his foresight, and his capacity genuinely to identify himself with the ideals of humble people.

This feeling of being at home not merely in the present but in the future, of knowing where he was going and by what means and why, made him, until his health was finally undermined, buoyant and gay: made him delight in the company of the most varied and opposed individuals, provided that they embodied some specific aspect of the turbulent stream of life, stood actively for the forward movement in their particular world, whatever it might be. And this inner *élan* made up, and more than made up, for faults of intellect or character, which his enemies – and his victims – never ceased to point out. He seemed genuinely unaffected by their taunts: what he could not abide was, before all, passivity, stillness, melancholy, fear of life or preoccupation with eternity or death, however great the insight or delicate the sensibility by which they were accompanied.

Churchill stands at almost the opposite pole. He too does not fear the future, and no man has ever loved life more vehemently and infused so much of it into everyone and everything that he has touched. But whereas Roosevelt, like all great innovators, had a half-conscious premonitory awareness of the coming shape of society, not wholly unlike that of an artist, Churchill, for all his extrovert air, looks within, and his strongest sense is the sense of the past.

The clear, brightly coloured vision of history in terms of which he conceives both the present and the future is the inexhaustible source from which he draws the primary stuff out of which his universe is so solidly built, so richly and elaborately ornamented. So firm and so embracing an edifice could not be constructed by anyone liable to react and respond like a sensitive instrument to the perpetually changing moods and directions of other persons or institutions or peoples. And, indeed, Churchill's strength (and what is most frightening in him) lies precisely in this: that, unlike Roosevelt, he is not equipped with numberless sensitive antennae which communicate the smallest oscillations of the outer world in all its unstable variety. Unlike Roosevelt (and unlike Gladstone and Lloyd George for that matter) he does not reflect a contemporary social or moral world in an intense and concentrated fashion; rather he creates one of such power and coherence that it becomes a reality and alters the external world by being imposed upon it with irresistible force. As his history of the war shows, he has an immense capacity for absorbing facts, but they emerge transformed by the categories which he powerfully imposes on the raw material into something which he can use to build his own massive, simple, impregnably fortified inner world.

Roosevelt, as a public personality, was a spontaneous, optimistic, pleasure-loving ruler who dismayed his assistants by the gay and apparently heedless abandon with which he seemed to delight in pursuing two or more totally incompatible policies, and astonished them even more by the swiftness and ease with which he managed to throw off the cares of office during the darkest and most dangerous moments. Churchill too loves pleasure, and he too lacks neither gaiety nor a capacity for exuberant self-expression, together with the habit of blithely cutting Gordian knots in a manner which often upset his experts; but he is not a frivolous man. His nature possesses a dimension of depth – and a corresponding sense of tragic possibilities – which Roosevelt's light-hearted genius instinctively passed by.

Roosevelt played the game of politics with virtuosity, and both his successes and his failures were carried off in splendid style; his performance seemed to flow with effortless skill. Churchill is acquainted with darkness as well as light. Like all inhabitants of inner worlds, and even transient visitors to them, he gives evidence of seasons of agonised brooding and slow recovery. Roosevelt might have spoken of sweat and blood, but when Churchill offered his people tears, he spoke a word which might have been uttered by Lincoln or Mazzini or Cromwell, but not by Roosevelt, great-hearted, generous and perceptive as he was.

V

Not the herald of the bright and cloudless civilisation of the future, Churchill is preoccupied by his own vivid world, and it is doubtful how far he has ever been aware of what actually goes on in the heads and hearts of others. He does not react, he acts; he does not mirror, he affects others and alters them to his own powerful measure. Writing of Dunkirk he says:

> There is no doubt that had I at this juncture faltered at all in the leading of the nation I should have been hurled out of office. I was

sure that every Minister was ready to be killed quite soon, and have all his family and possessions destroyed, rather than give in. In this they represented the House of Commons and almost all the people. It fell to me in these coming days and months to express their sentiments on suitable occasions. This I was able to do because they were mine also. There was a white glow, overpowering, sublime, which ran through our Island from end to end.[1]

And on 28 June of that year he told Lord Lothian, then ambassador in Washington, 'Your mood should be bland and phlegmatic. No one is down-hearted here.'[2]

These splendid sentences hardly do justice to his own part in creating the feeling which he describes. For Churchill is not a sensitive lens which absorbs and concentrates and reflects and amplifies the sentiments of others; unlike the European dictators, he does not play on public opinion like an instrument. In 1940 he assumed an indomitable stoutness, an unsurrendering quality on the part of his people, and carried on. If he did not represent the quintessence and epitome of what some, at any rate, of his fellow citizens feared and hoped in their hour of danger, this was because he idealised them with such intensity that in the end they approached his ideal and began to see themselves as he saw them: 'the buoyant and imperturbable temper of Britain which I had the honour to express' – it was indeed, but he had a lion's share in creating it. So hypnotic was the force of his words, so strong his faith, that by the sheer intensity of his eloquence he bound his spell upon them until it seemed to them that he was indeed speaking what was in their hearts and minds. Doubtless it was there; but largely dormant until he had awoken it within them.

After he had spoken to them in the summer of 1940 as no one has ever before or since, they conceived a new idea of themselves which their own prowess and the admiration of the world has since established as a heroic image in the history of mankind, like Thermopylae or the defeat of the Spanish Armada. They went forward into battle transformed by his words. The spirit which they found within them he had created within himself from his inner resources, and poured it into his nation, and took their vivid reaction for an original impulse on their part, which he merely had

---

[1] *Their Finest Hour* [*The Second World War*, vol. 2] (London, 1949), p. 88.
[2] ibid., p. 201.

the honour to clothe in suitable words. He created a heroic mood and turned the fortunes of the Battle of Britain not by catching the mood of his surroundings (which was not indeed, at any time, one of craven panic or bewilderment or apathy, but somewhat confused; stout-hearted but unorganised) but by being stubbornly impervious to it, as he has been to so many of the passing shades and tones of which the life around him has been composed.

The peculiar quality of heroic pride and a sense of the sublimity of the occasion arises in him not, as in Roosevelt, from delight in being alive and in control at a critical moment of history, in the very change and instability of things, in the infinite possibilities of the future whose very unpredictability offers endless possibilities of spontaneous moment-to-moment improvisation and large imaginative moves in harmony with the restless spirit of the time. On the contrary, it springs from a capacity for sustained introspective brooding, great depth and constancy of feeling – in particular, feeling for and fidelity to the great tradition for which he assumes a personal responsibility, a tradition which he bears upon his shoulders and must deliver, not only sound and undamaged but strengthened and embellished, to successors worthy of accepting the sacred burden.

Bismarck once said that there was no such thing as political intuition: political genius consisted in the ability to hear the distant hoofbeat of the horse of history – and then by superhuman effort to leap and catch the horseman by the coat-tails. No man has ever listened for this fateful sound more eagerly than Winston Churchill, and in 1940 he made the heroic leap. 'It is impossible', he writes of this time, 'to quell the inward excitement which comes from a prolonged balancing of terrible things', and when the crisis finally bursts he is ready, because after a lifetime of effort he has reached his goal.

The position of the Prime Minister is unique: 'If he trips he must be sustained: if he makes mistakes they must be covered; if he sleeps he must not be wantonly disturbed; if he is no good he must be pole-axed', and this because he is at that moment the guardian of the 'life of Britain, her message and her glory'. He trusted Roosevelt utterly, 'convinced that he would give up life itself, to say nothing about office, for the cause of world freedom now in such awful peril'. His prose records the tension which rises and swells to the culminating moment, the Battle of Britain – 'a time when it was equally good to live or die'. This bright, heroic vision of the mortal danger and the will to conquer, born in the hour when defeat seemed not merely possible but probable, is the product of a burning historical imagination, feeding upon the data not of the outer but of the inner eye: the picture has a shape and simplicity which future historians will find it hard to reproduce when they seek to assess and interpret the facts soberly in the grey light of common day.

VI

The Prime Minister was able to impose his imagination and his will upon his countrymen, and enjoy a Periclean reign, precisely because he appeared to them larger and nobler than life and lifted them to an abnormal height in a moment of crisis. It was a climate in which men do not usually like – nor ought they to like – living; it demands a violent tension which, if it lasts, destroys all sense of normal perspective, overdramatises personal relationships, and falsifies normal values to an intolerable extent. But, in the event, it did turn a large number of inhabitants of the British Isles out of their normal selves and, by dramatising their lives and making them seem to themselves and to each other clad in the fabulous garments appropriate to a great historic moment, transformed cowards into brave men, and so fulfilled the purpose of shining armour.

This is the kind of means by which dictators and demagogues transform peaceful populations into marching armies; it was Churchill's unique and unforgettable achievement that he created this necessary illusion within the framework of a free system without destroying or even twisting it; that he called forth spirits which did not stay to oppress and enslave the population after the hour of need had passed; that he saved the future by interpreting the present in terms of a vision of the past which did not distort or inhibit the historical development of the British people by attempting to make them realise some impossible and unattainable splendour in the name of an imaginary tradition or of an infallible, supernatural leader. Churchill was saved from this frightening nemesis of romanticism by a sufficiency of that libertarian feeling which, if it sometimes fell short of understanding the tragic aspects of modern despotisms, remained sharply perceptive – sometimes too tolerantly, but still perceptive – of what is false, grotesque, contemptible in the great frauds upon the people practised by totalitarian regimes. Some of the sharpest and most characteristic epithets are reserved for the dictators: Hitler is 'this evil man, this monstrous abortion of hatred and defeat'. Franco is a 'narrow-minded tyrant' of 'evil qualities' holding down a 'blood-drained people'. No quarter is given to the Pétain regime, and its appeal to tradition and the eternal France is treated as a repellent travesty of national feeling. Stalin in 1940–1 is 'at once a callous, a crafty, and an ill-informed giant'.

This very genuine hostility to usurpers, which is stronger in him than even his passion for authority and order, springs from a quality which Churchill conspicuously shared with President Roosevelt – uncommon love of life, aversion for the imposition of rigid disciplines upon the teeming variety of human relations, the instinctive sense of what promotes and what retards or distorts growth and vitality. But because the life which Churchill so loves presents itself to him in a historical guise as part of the pageant of tradition, his method of constructing historical narrative, the distribution of emphasis, the assignment of relative importance to persons and events, the theory of history, the architecture of the narrative, the structure of the sentences, the words themselves, are elements in an historical revival as fresh, as original and as idiosyncratic as the neo-classicism of the Renaissance or the Regency. To complain that this omits altogether too much by assuming that the impersonal, the dull, the undramatic are necessarily also unimportant may well be just; but to lament that this is not contemporary, and therefore in some way less true, less responsive to modern needs, than the noncommittal, neutral glass and plastic of those objective historians who regard facts and only facts as interesting and, worse still, all facts as equally interesting – what is this but craven pedantry and blindness?

## VII

The differences between the President and the Prime Minister were at least in one respect something more than the obvious differences of national character, education, and even temperament. For all his sense of history, his large, untroubled, easygoing style of life, his unshakeable feeling of personal security, his natural assumption of being at home in the great world far beyond the confines of his own country, Roosevelt was a typical child of the twentieth century and of the New World; while Churchill for all his love of the present hour, his unquenchable appetite for new knowledge, his sense of the technological possibilities of our time, and the restless roaming of his fancy in considering how they might be most imaginatively applied, despite his enthusiasm for Basic English, or the siren suit which so upset his hosts in Moscow – despite all this, Churchill remains a European of the nineteenth century.

The difference is deep, and accounts for a great deal in the incompatibility of outlook between him and the President of the United States, whom he admired so much and whose great office he held in awe. Something of the fundamental unlikeness between America and Europe, and perhaps between the twentieth century and the nineteenth, seemed to be crystallised in this remarkable interplay. It may perhaps be that the twentieth century is to the nineteenth as the nineteenth was to the eighteenth. Talleyrand once made the well-known observation that those who had not lived under the *ancien régime* did not know what true *plaisir de vivre* had been. And indeed, from our distant vantage-point, this is clear: the earnest, romantic young men of the early part of the nineteenth century seemed systematically unable to understand or to like the attitude to life of the most civilised representatives of the pre-revolutionary world, particularly in France, where the break was sharpest; the irony, the sharpness, the minute vision, the perception of and concentration upon fine differences in character, in style, the preoccupation with barely perceptible dissimilarities of hue, the extreme sensibility which makes the life of even so 'progressive' and forward-looking a man as Diderot so unbridgeably different from the larger and simpler vision of the romantics – this is something which the nineteenth century lacked the historical perspective to understand.

Suppose that Shelley had met and talked with Voltaire, what would he have felt? He would most probably have been profoundly shocked – shocked by the seemingly limited vision, the smallness of the field of awareness, the apparent triviality and finickiness, the almost spinsterish elaboration of Voltaire's malice, the preoccupation with tiny units, the subatomic texture of experience; he would have felt horror or pity before such wanton blindness to the large moral and spiritual issues of his own day – causes whose universal scope and significance painfully agitated the best and most awakened minds; he might have thought him wicked, but even more he would have thought him contemptible, too sharp, too small, too mean, grotesquely and unworthily obscene, prone to titter on the most sacred occasions, in the holiest places.

And Voltaire, in his turn, would very probably have been dreadfully bored, unable to see good cause for so much ethical eloquence; he would have looked with a cold and hostile eye on all this moral excitement: the magnificent Saint-Simonian vision of one world (which so stirred the left-wing young men half a century later), altering in shape and becoming integrated into a neatly organised man-made whole by the application of powerfully concentrated scientific, technical and spiritual resources, would to him have seemed a dreary and monotonous desert, too homogeneous, too flavourless, too unreal, apparently unconscious of those small, half-concealed but crucial distinctions and incongruities which give individuality and savour to experience, without which there could be no civilised vision, no wit, no conversation, certainly no art deriving from a refined and fastidious culture. The moral vision of the nineteenth century would have seemed to him a dull, blurred, coarse instrument unable to focus those pin-points of concentrated light, those short-lived patterns of sound and colour, whose infinite variety as they linger or flash past are comedy and tragedy – are the substance of personal relations and of worldly wisdom, of politics, of history, and of art.

The reason for this failure of communication was not a mere change in the point of view, but the kind of vision which divided the two centuries. The microscopic vision of the eighteenth century was succeeded by the macroscopic eye of the nineteenth. The latter saw much more widely, saw in universal or at least in European terms; it saw the contours of great mountain ranges where the eighteenth century discerned, however sharply and perceptively, only the veins and cracks and different shades of but a portion of the mountainside. The object of vision of the eighteenth century was smaller and its eye was closer to the object. The enormous moral issues of the nineteenth century were not within the field of its acutely discriminating gaze: that was the devastating difference which the great French Revolution had made, and it led to something not necessarily better or worse, uglier or more beautiful, profounder or more shallow, but to a situation which above all was different in kind.

Something not unlike this same chasm divides America from Europe (and the twentieth century from the nineteenth). The

American vision is larger and more generous; its thought transcends, despite the parochialism of its means of expression, the barriers of nationality and race and differences of outlook, in a big, sweeping, single view. It notices things rather than persons, and sees the world (those who saw it in this fashion in the nineteenth century were considered Utopian eccentrics) in terms of rich, infinitely mouldable raw material, waiting to be constructed and planned in order to satisfy a world-wide human craving for happiness or goodness or wisdom. And therefore to it the differences and conflicts which divide Europeans in so violent a fashion must seem petty, irrational and sordid, not worthy of self-respecting, morally conscious individuals and nations; ready, in fact, to be swept away in favour of a simpler and grander view of the powers and tasks of modern man.

To Europeans this American attitude, the large vista possible only for those who live on mountain heights or vast and level plains affording an unbroken view, seems curiously flat, without subtlety or colour, at times appearing to lack the entire dimension of depth, certainly without that immediate reaction to fine distinctions with which perhaps only those who live in valleys are endowed, and so America, which knows so much, to them seems to understand too little, to miss the central point. This does not, of course, apply to every American or European – there are natural Americans among the natives of Europe and vice versa – but it seems to characterise the most typical representatives of these disparate cultures.

## VIII

In some respects Roosevelt half-consciously understood and did not wholly condemn this attitude on the part of Europeans; and even more clearly Churchill is in many respects in instinctive sympathy with the American way of life. But by and large they do represent different outlooks, and the very high degree to which they were able to understand and admire each other's quality is a tribute to the extraordinary power of imagination and delight in the variety of life on the part of both. Each was to the other not merely an ally, the admired leader of a great people, but a symbol of a tradition and a civilisation; from the unity of their differences they hoped for a regeneration of the Western world.

Roosevelt was intrigued by the Russian sphinx; Churchill

instinctively recoiled from its alien and to him unattractive attributes. Roosevelt, on the whole, thought that he could cajole Russia
and even induce her to be assimilated into the great society which
would embrace mankind; Churchill, on the whole, remained
sceptical.

Roosevelt was imaginative, optimistic, episcopalian, self-confident, cheerful, empirical, fearless, and steeped in the ideas of social
progress; he believed that with enough energy and spirit anything
could be achieved by man; he shrank as much as any English
schoolboy from probing underneath the surface, and saw vast
affinities between the peoples in the world, out of which a new,
freer and richer order could somehow be built. Churchill was
imaginative and steeped in history, more serious, more intent, more
concentrated, more preoccupied, and felt very deeply the eternal
differences which could make such a structure difficult of attainment. He believed in institutions and the permanent characters of
races and classes and types of individuals. His government was
organised on clear principles; his personal private office was run in
a sharply disciplined manner. His habits, though unusual, were
regular. He believed in a natural, a social, almost a metaphysical
order – a sacred hierarchy which it was neither possible nor
desirable to upset.

Roosevelt believed in flexibility, improvisation, the fruitfulness
of using persons and resources in an infinite variety of new and
unexpected ways; his bureaucracy was somewhat chaotic, perhaps
deliberately so. His own office was not tidily organised, he
practised a highly personal form of government. He maddened the
advocates of institutional authority, but it is doubtful whether he
could have achieved his ends in any other way.

These dissimilarities of outlook went deep, but both were large
enough in scope and both were genuine visions, not narrowed and
distorted by personal idiosyncrasies and those disparities of moral
standard which so fatally divided Wilson, Lloyd George and
Clemenceau. The President and the Prime Minister often disagreed;
their ideals and their methods were widely different; in some of the
memoirs and gossip of Roosevelt's entourage much has been made
of this; but the discussion, at all times, was conducted on a level of
which both heads of government were conscious. They may have
opposed but they never wished to wound each other; they may
have issued contrary instructions but they never bickered; when
they compromised, as they so often did, they did so without a

sense of bitterness or defeat, but in response to the demands of history or one another's traditions and personality.

Each appeared to the other in a romantic light high above the battles of allies or subordinates: their meetings and correspondence were occasions to which both consciously rose; they were royal cousins and felt pride in this relationship, tempered by a sharp and sometimes amused, but never ironical, perception of the other's peculiar qualities. The relationship born during the great historical upheaval, somewhat aggrandised by its solemnity, never flagged or degenerated, but retained a combination of formal dignity and exuberant high spirits which can scarcely ever before have bound the heads of States. Each was personally fascinated not so much by the other as by the idea of the other, and infected him by his own peculiar brand of high spirits.

The relationship was made genuine by something more than even the solid community of interest or personal and official respect or admiration – namely, by the peculiar degree to which they liked each other's delight in the oddities and humours of life and their own active part in it. This was a unique personal bond, which Harry Hopkins understood and encouraged to the fullest degree. Roosevelt's sense of fun was perhaps the lighter, Churchill's a trifle grimmer. But it was something which they shared with each other and with few, if any, statesmen outside the Anglo-American orbit; their staffs sometimes ignored or misunderstood it, and it gave a most singular quality to their association.

Roosevelt's public utterances differ by a whole world from the dramatic masterpieces of Churchill, but they are not incompatible with them in spirit or in substance. Roosevelt has not left us his own account of his world as he saw it; and perhaps he lived too much from day to day to be temperamentally attracted to the performance of such a task. But both were thoroughly aware of their commanding position in the history of the modern world, and Churchill's account of his stewardship is written in full consciousness of this responsibility.

It is a great occasion, and he treats it with corresponding solemnity. Like a great actor – perhaps the last of his kind – upon the stage of history, he speaks his memorable lines with a large, unhurried and stately utterance in a blaze of light, as is appropriate to a man who knows that his work and his person will remain the object of scrutiny and judgement to many generations. His narrative is a great public performance and has the attribute of formal magnificence. The words, the splendid phrases, the sustained quality of feeling, are a unique medium which conveys his vision of himself and of his world, and will inevitably, like all that he has said and done, reinforce the famous public image, which is no longer distinguishable from the inner essence and the true nature of the author: of a man larger than life, composed of bigger and simpler elements than ordinary men, a gigantic historical figure during his own lifetime, superhumanly bold, strong and imaginative, one of the two greatest men of action his nation has produced, an orator of prodigious powers, the saviour of his country, a mythical hero who belongs to legend as much as to reality, the largest human being of our time.

# PRESIDENT
## FRANKLIN DELANO ROOSEVELT

I NEVER met Roosevelt, and although I spent more than three years in Washington during the War, I never even saw him. I regret this, for it seems to me that to see and, in particular, to hear the voice of someone who has occupied one's imagination for many years must modify one's impression in some profound way, and make it somehow more concrete and three-dimensional. However, I never did see him, and I heard him only over the wireless. Consequently I must try to convey my impression without the benefit of personal acquaintance, and without, I ought to add, any expert knowledge of American history or of international relations. Nor am I competent to speak of Roosevelt's domestic or foreign policies: or their larger political or economic effect. I shall try to give only a personal impression of the general impact of his personality on my generation in Europe.

When I say that some men occupy one's imagination for many years, this is literally true of Roosevelt and the young men of my own generation in England, and probably in many parts of Europe, and indeed the entire world. If one was young in the 1930s, and lived in a democracy, then, whatever one's politics, if one had human feelings at all, the faintest spark of social idealism, or any love of life whatever, one must have felt very much as young men in Continental Europe probably felt after the defeat of Napoleon during the years of the Restoration, that all was dark and quiet, a great reaction was abroad: and little stirred, and nothing resisted.

It all began with the great slump of 1931, which undermined the feeling, perhaps quite baseless, of economic security which a good many young people of the middle classes then had. There followed the iron '30s, of which the English poets of the time – Auden, Spender, Day Lewis – left a very vivid testament: the dark and leaden '30s, to which, alone of all periods, no one in Europe wishes to return, unless indeed they lament the passing of Fascism. There came Manchuria, Hitler, the Hunger Marchers, the Abyssinian War, the Peace Ballot, the Left Book Club, Malraux's political novels, even the article by Virginia Woolf in the *Daily Worker*, the Soviet trials and purges, the conversions of idealistic young liberals and radicals to Communism, or strong sympathy with it, often for no better reason than that it seemed the only force firm enough and strong enough to resist the Fascist enemy effectively; such conversions were sometimes followed by visits to Moscow or by fighting in Spain, and death on the battlefield, or else bitter and angry disillusionment with Communist practice, or some desperate and unconvinced choice between two evils of that which seemed the lesser.

The most insistent propaganda in those days declared that humanitarianism and liberalism and democratic forces were played out, and that the choice now lay between two bleak extremes, Communism and Fascism – the red or the black. To those who were not carried away by this patter the only light that was left in the darkness was the administration of Roosevelt and the New Deal in the United States. At a time of weakness and mounting despair in the democratic world Roosevelt radiated confidence and strength. He was the leader of the democratic world, and upon him alone, of all the statesmen of the '30s, no cloud rested – neither on him nor on the New Deal, which to European eyes still looks a bright chapter in the history of mankind. It is true that his great social experiment was conducted with an isolationist disregard of the outside world, but then it was psychologically intelligible that America, which had come into being in the reaction against the follies and evils of a Europe perpetually distraught by religious or national struggles, should try to seek salvation undisturbed by the currents of European life, particularly at a moment when Europe seemed about to collapse into a totalitarian nightmare. Roosevelt was therefore forgiven, by those who found the European situation tragic, for pursuing no particular foreign policy, indeed for trying to do, if not without any foreign policy at all, at any rate with a minimum of relationship with the outside world, which was indeed to some degree part of the American political tradition.

His internal policy was plainly animated by a humanitarian purpose. After the unbridled individualism of the 1920s, which had led to economic collapse and widespread misery, he was seeking to establish new rules of social justice. He was trying to do this without forcing his country into some doctrinaire strait-jacket, whether of socialism or State capitalism, or the kind of new social organisation which the Fascist regimes flaunted as the New Order. Social discontent was high in the United States, faith in business-men as saviours of society had evaporated overnight after the famous Wall Street Crash, and Roosevelt was providing a vast safety-valve for pent-up bitterness and indignation, and trying to prevent revolution and construct a regime which should provide for greater economic equality and social justice – ideals which were the best part of the tradition of American life – without altering the basis of freedom and democracy in his country. This was being done by what to unsympathetic critics seemed a haphazard collection of amateurs, college professors, journalists, personal friends, freelances of one kind or another, intellectuals, ideologists, what are nowadays called eggheads, whose very appearance and methods of conducting business or constructing policies irritated the servants of old-established government institutions in Wash-ington and tidy-minded conservatives of every type. Yet it was clear that the very amateurishness of these men, the fact that they were allowed to talk to their hearts' content, to experiment, to indulge in a vast amount of trial and error, that relations were personal and not institutional, bred its own vitality and enthusi-asm. Washington was doubtless full of quarrels, resignations, palace intrigues, perpetual warfare between individuals and groups of individuals, parties, cliques, personal supporters of this or that great captain, which must have maddened sober and responsible officials used to the slower tempo and more normal patterns of administration; as for bankers and businessmen, their feelings were past describing, but at this period they were little regarded, since they were considered to have discredited themselves too deeply, and indeed for ever.

Over this vast, seething chaos presided a handsome, charming, gay, very intelligent, very delightful, very audacious man, Franklin Delano Roosevelt. He was accused of many weaknesses. He had betrayed his class; he was ignorant, unscrupulous, irresponsible. He was ruthless in playing with the lives and careers of individuals. He was surrounded by adventurers, slick opportunists, intriguers. He made conflicting promises, cynically and brazenly, to individu-als and groups and representatives of foreign nations. He made up, with his vast and irresistible public charm, and his astonishing high spirits, for lack of other virtues considered as more important in the leader of the most powerful democracy in the world – the virtues of application, industry, responsibility. All this was said and some of it may indeed have been just. What attracted his followers were countervailing qualities of a rare and inspiring order: he was large-hearted and possessed wide political horizons, imaginative sweep, understanding of the time in which he lived and of the direction of the great new forces at work in the twentieth century – technological, racial, imperialist, anti-imperialist; he was in favour of life and movement, the promotion of the most generous possible fulfilment of the largest possible number of human wishes, and not in favour of caution and retrenchment and sitting still. Above all, he was absolutely fearless.

He was one of the few statesmen in the twentieth or any other century who seemed to have no fear at all of the future. He believed in his own strength and ability to manage, and succeed, whatever happened. He believed in the capacity and loyalty of his lieutenants, so that he looked upon the future with a calm eye, as if to say 'Let it come, whatever it may be, it will all be grist to our great mill. We shall turn it all to benefit.' It was this, perhaps, more than any other quality, which drew men of very different outlooks to him. In a despondent world which appeared divided between wicked and fatally efficient fanatics marching to destroy, and bewildered populations on the run, unenthusiastic martyrs in a cause they could not define, he believed in his own ability, so long as he was at the controls, to stem this terrible tide. He had all the character and energy and skill of the dictators, and he was on our side. He was, in his opinions and public action, every inch a democrat. All the political and personal and public criticism of him might be true; all the personal defects which his enemies and some of his friends attributed to him might be real; yet as a public figure he was unique. As the skies of Europe grew darker, in particular after war broke out, he seemed to the poor and the unhappy in Europe a kind of benevolent demigod who alone could and would save them in the end. His moral authority – the degree of confidence which he inspired outside his own country, and far more beyond America's frontiers than within them at all times – has no parallel. Perhaps President Wilson, in the early days, after the end of the First World War, when he drove triumphantly through Paris and London, may have inspired some such feeling; but it disappeared quickly and left a terrible feeling of disenchantment behind it. It was plain even to his enemies that President Roosevelt would not be broken as President Wilson was. But to his prestige and to his personality he added a degree of political skill – indeed virtuosity – which no American before him had ever possessed. His chance of realising his wishes was plainly greater; his followers would be less likely to reap bitter disappointment.

Indeed he was very different from Wilson. For they represent two contrasting types of statesman, in each of which occasionally men of compelling stature appear. The first kind of statesman is essentially a man of single principle and fanatical vision. Possessed by his own bright, coherent dream, he usually understands neither people nor events. He has no doubts or hesitations and by concentration of will-power, directness and strength he is able to ignore a great deal of what goes on outside him. This very blindness and stubborn self-absorption occasionally, in certain situations, enable him to bend events and men to his own fixed pattern. His strength lies in the fact that weak and vacillating human beings, themselves too insecure or incapable of deciding between alternatives, find relief and peace and strength in submitting to the leadership of a single leader of superhuman size, to whom all issues are clear, whose universe consists entirely of primary colours, mostly black and white, and who marches towards his goal looking neither to right nor to left, buoyed up by the violent vision within him. Such men differ widely in moral and intellectual quality, and, like forces of nature, do both good and harm in the world. To this type belong Garibaldi, Trotsky, Parnell, de Gaulle, perhaps Lenin too – the distinction I am drawing is not a moral one, not one of value but one of type. There are great benefactors, like Wilson, as well as fearful evil-doers, like Hitler, within this category.

The other kind of effective statesman is a naturally political being, as the simple hero is often explicitly anti-political and comes to rescue men, at least ostensibly, from the subtleties and frauds of political life. Politicians of this second type possess antennae of the greatest possible delicacy, which convey to them, in ways difficult or impossible to analyse, the perpetually changing contours of events and feelings and human activities round them – they are gifted with a peculiar, political sense fed on a capacity to take in minute impressions, to integrate a vast multitude of small evanescent unseizable detail, such as artists possess in relation to their material. Statesmen of this type know what to do and when to do it, if they are to achieve their ends, which themselves are usually not born within some private world of inner thought, or intro-verted feeling, but are the crystallisation, the raising to great intensity and clarity, of what a large number of their fellow citizens are thinking and feeling in some dim, inarticulate, but nevertheless persistent fashion. In virtue of this capacity to judge their material, very much as a sculptor knows what can be moulded out of wood and what out of marble, and how and when, they resemble doctors who have a natural gift for curing, which does not directly depend upon that knowledge of scientific anatomy which can be learned only by observation or experiment, or from the experiences of others, though it could not exist without it. This instinctive, or at any rate incommunicable, knowledge of where to look for what one needs, the power of divining where the treasure lies, is something common to many types of genius, to scientists and mathematicians no less than to businessmen and administrators and politicians. Such men, when they are statesmen, are acutely aware of which way the thoughts and feelings of human beings are flowing, and where life presses on them most heavily, and they convey to these human beings a sense of understanding their inner needs, of responding to their own deepest impulses, above all of being alone capable of organising the world along lines which the masses are instinctively groping for. To this type of statesman belonged Bismarck and Abraham Lincoln, Lloyd George and Thomas Masaryk, perhaps to some extent Gladstone, and to a minor degree Walpole. Roosevelt was a magnificent virtuoso of this type, and he was the most benevolent as well as the greatest master of his craft in modern times. He really did desire a better life for mankind. The great majorities which he obtained in the elections in the United States during his four terms of office, despite mounting hostility by the press, and perpetual prophecies on their part that he had gone too far, and would fail to be re-elected, were ultimately due to an obscure feeling on the part of the majority of the citizens of the United States that he was on their side, that he wished them well, and that he would do something for them. And this feeling gradually spread over the entire civilised world. He became a legendary hero – they themselves did not know quite why – to the indigent and the oppressed, far beyond the confines of the English-speaking world.

As I said before, he was, by some of his opponents, accused of betraying his class, and so he had. When a man who retains the manners, the style of life, the emotional texture and the charm of the old order of some free aristocratic upbringing revolts against his milieu and adopts the ideas and aspirations of the new, socially revolted class, and adopts them not out of expediency but out of genuine moral conviction, or from love of life, inability to remain on the side of what seems to him narrow, mean, restrictive – the result is fascinating and attractive. This is what makes the figures of such men as Condorcet or Charles James Fox, or some of the Russian, Italian and Polish revolutionaries in the nineteenth century, so attractive; for all we know this may have been the secret also of Moses or Pericles or Julius Caesar. It was this gentlemanly quality together with the fact that they felt him to be deeply committed to their side in the struggle and in favour of their way of life, as well as his open and fearless lack of neutrality in the war against the Nazis and the Fascists, that endeared him so deeply to the British people during the war years. I remember well how excited most people were in London, in November 1940, about the result of the Presidential election in the United States. In theory they should not have worried. Willkie, the Republican candidate, had expressed himself forcibly and sincerely as a supporter of the democracies. Yet it was absurd to say that the people of Britain were neutral in their feelings *vis-à-vis* the two candidates. They felt in their bones that Roosevelt was their lifelong friend, that he hated the Nazis as deeply as they did, that he wanted democracy and civilisation, in the sense in which they believed in it, to prevail, and that he knew what he wanted, and that his goal resembled their own ideals more than it did those of all his opponents. They felt that his heart was in the right place, and they did not, therefore, if they gave it a thought, care whether his political appointments were made under the influence of bosses or for personal reasons, or thoughtlessly; or whether his economic doctrines were heretical or whether he had a sufficiently scrupulous regard for the opinion of the Senate or the House of Representatives, or the prescriptions of the United States Constitution, or for the opinions of the Supreme Court. These matters were very remote from them. They knew that he would, to the extent of his enormous energy and ability, see them through. There is no such thing as long-lived mass hypnotism; the masses know what it is that they like, what genuinely appeals to them. What the Germans thought Hitler to be, Hitler, in fact, largely was, and what free men in Europe and in America and in Asia and in Africa and in Australia, and wherever else the rudiments of political thought stirred at all – what all these felt

Roosevelt to be, he in fact was. He was the greatest leader of democracy, the greatest champion of social progress in the twentieth century.

His enemies accused him of plotting to get America into the War. I do not wish to discuss this controversial issue, but it seems to me that the evidence for it is lacking. I think that when he promised to keep America at peace he meant to try as hard as he could to do so, compatibly with helping to promote the victory of the democracies. He must at one period have thought that he could win the War without entering it, and so, at the end of it, be in the unique position, hitherto achieved by no one, of being the arbiter of the world's fate without needing to placate those bitter forces which involvement in a war inevitably brings about, and which are an obstacle to reason and humanity in the making of the peace. He no doubt too often trusted in his own magical power of improvisation. Doubtless he made many political mistakes, some of them difficult to remedy: some would say about Stalin and his intentions, and the nature of the Soviet State; others might justly point to his coolness to the Free French movement, his cavalier intentions with regard to the Supreme Court of Justice in the United States, his errors about a good many other issues. He irritated his staunchest supporters and faithful servants because he did not tell them what he was doing; his government was highly personal and it maddened tidy-minded officials and humiliated those who thought the policy should be conducted in consultation with and through them. He sometimes exasperated his allies, but when these last bethought them of who his ill-wishers were in the USA and in the world outside, and what *their* motives were, their respect, affection and loyalty tended to return. No man made more public enemies, yet no man had a right to take greater pride in the quality and the motives of some of those enemies. He could justly call himself the friend of the people, and although his opponents accused him of being a demagogue, this charge seems to me unjust. He did not sacrifice fundamental political principles to a desire to retain power; he did not whip up evil passions merely in order to avenge himself upon those whom he disliked or wished to crush, or because it was an atmosphere in which he found it convenient to operate; he saw to it that his administration was in the van of public opinion and drew it on instead of being dragged by it; he made the majority of his fellow citizens prouder to be Americans than they had been before. He raised their status in their own eyes – immensely in those of the rest of the world.

It was an extraordinary transformation of an individual. Perhaps it was largely brought about by the collapse of his health in the early 1920s and his marvellous triumph over his disabilities. For he began life as a well-born, polite, not particularly gifted young man, something of a prig, liked but not greatly admired by his contemporaries at Groton and at Harvard, a competent Assistant Secretary of the Navy in the First World War; in short, he seemed embarked on the routine career of an American patrician with moderate political ambitions. His illness and the support and encouragement and political qualities of his wife – whose greatness of character and goodness of heart history will duly record – seemed to transform his public personality into that strong and beneficent champion who became the father of his people, in an altogether unique fashion. He did more than this: it is not too much to say that he altered the fundamental concept of government and its obligations to the governed. The Welfare State, so much denounced, has obviously come to stay: the direct moral responsibility for minimum standards of living and social services, which it took for granted, are today accepted almost without a murmur by the most conservative politicians in the Western democracies; the Republican Party victorious in 1952 made no effort to upset the basic principles – which seemed Utopian in the 1920s – of Roosevelt's social legislation.

But Roosevelt's greatest service to mankind (after ensuring the victory against the enemies of freedom) consists in the fact that he showed that it is possible to be politically effective and yet benevolent and human: that the fierce left- and right-wing propaganda of the 1930s, according to which the conquest and retention of political power is not compatible with human qualities, but necessarily demands from those who pursue it seriously the sacrifice of their lives upon the altar of some ruthless ideology, or the practice of despotism – this propaganda, which filled the art and talk of the day, was simply untrue. Roosevelt's example strengthened democracy everywhere, that is to say the view that the promotion of social justice and individual liberty does not necessarily mean the end of all efficient government; that power and order are not identical with a strait-jacket of doctrine, whether economic or political; that it is possible to reconcile individual liberty – a loose texture of society – with the indispensable minimum of organising and authority; and in this belief lies what Roosevelt's greatest predecessor once described as 'the last best hope of earth'.[1]

---

[1] Abraham Lincoln, Annual Message to Congress, 1 December 1862: p. 537 in *The Collected Works of Abraham Lincoln*, ed. R. P. Basler (New Brunswick, 1953), vol. 5.

# CONCISE BIBLIOGRAPHY OF ISAIAH BERLIN'S WRITINGS

*Henry Hardy*

## Writings by Berlin

With the exception of his biography of Marx, his anthology of the philosophers of the Enlightenment, and his study of J. G. Hamann, Isaiah Berlin's published work has taken the form of essays, often originating in lectures, and often somewhat inaccessibly published in the first instance. Fortunately most of these essays have now been collected, in seven volumes published between 1969 and 1990. The titles of these collected essays are listed below, under the titles of the volumes they comprise; an asterisk indicates inclusion in the present volume.

In chronological order of first publication, the books by Berlin that have so far appeared are these:

*Karl Marx: His Life and Environment* first appeared in 1939 (London: Thornton Butterworth; Toronto: Nelson); further editions were published by Oxford University Press in 1948, 1963 and 1978, and the latest, fourth, edition was reissued, with a new introduction by Alan Ryan, by Fontana in London in 1995 (with a revised guide to further reading by Terrell Carver) and by Oxford University Press in New York in 1996.

*The Age of Enlightenment: The Eighteenth-Century Philosophers* (New York, 1956: New American Library; reissued by Oxford University Press in 1979), is a selection, with commentary, from these philosophers' works.

*Four Essays on Liberty* (London and New York, 1969: Oxford University Press):

Introduction
Political Ideas in the Twentieth Century
* Historical Inevitability
* Two Concepts of Liberty
John Stuart Mill and the Ends of Life

*Vico and Herder: Two Studies in the History of Ideas* (London, 1976: Hogarth Press; New York, 1976: Viking):

Introduction
The Philosophical Ideas of Giambattista Vico
* Herder and the Enlightenment

*Russian Thinkers* (London, 1978: Hogarth Press; New York, 1978: Viking):

Introduction by Aileen Kelly
Russia and 1848
* The Hedgehog and the Fox
Herzen and Bakunin on Individual Liberty
A Remarkable Decade [1838–48]
    I    The Birth of the Russian Intelligentsia
    II   German Romanticism in Petersburg and Moscow
    III  Vissarion Belinsky
    IV   Alexander Herzen
Russian Populism
Tolstoy and Enlightenment
Fathers and Children: Turgenev and the Liberal Predicament

*Concepts and Categories: Philosophical Essays* (London, 1978: Hogarth Press; New York, 1979: Viking):

Introduction by Bernard Williams
The Purpose of Philosophy
Verification
Empirical Propositions and Hypothetical Statements
Logical Translation
Equality
* The Concept of Scientific History
* Does Political Theory Still Exist?
* 'From Hope and Fear Set Free'

*Against the Current: Essays in the History of Ideas* (London, 1979: Hogarth Press; New York, 1980: Viking):

Introduction by Roger Hausheer
* The Counter-Enlightenment
* The Originality of Machiavelli
* The Divorce between the Sciences and the Humanities
   Vico's Concept of Knowledge
   Vico and the Ideal of the Enlightenment
   Montesquieu
   Hume and the Sources of German Anti-Rationalism
     [Hume and Hamann]
* Herzen and his Memoirs
   The Life and Opinions of Moses Hess
   Benjamin Disraeli, Karl Marx and the Search for Identity
   The *'Naïveté'* of Verdi
   Georges Sorel
* Nationalism: Past Neglect and Present Power

*Personal Impressions* (London, 1980: Hogarth Press; New York, 1981: Viking; † = added in 2nd ed., London, 1998, Pimlico):

Introduction by Noel Annan
* Winston Churchill in 1940
* President Franklin Delano Roosevelt
   Chaim Weizmann
   Einstein and Israel
† Yitzhak Sadeh
   L. B. Namier
   Felix Frankfurter at Oxford
   Richard Pares
   Hubert Henderson at All Souls
   J. L. Austin and the Early Beginnings of Oxford Philosophy
   John Petrov Plamenatz
   Maurice Bowra
† David Cecil
† Memories of Virginia Woolf
† Edmund Wilson at Oxford
   Auberon Herbert
   Aldous Huxley
* Meetings with Russian Writers in 1945 and 1956[1]
† Epilogue: The Three Strands in My Life

[1] Reprinted here in a shorter version: see p. xviii above.

*The Crooked Timber of Humanity: Chapters in the History of Ideas* (London, 1990: John Murray; New York, 1991: Knopf):

* The Pursuit of the Ideal
  The Decline of Utopian Ideas in the West
  Giambattista Vico and Cultural History
  Alleged Relativism in Eighteenth-Century European Thought
  European Unity and its Vicissitudes
  Joseph de Maistre and the Origins of Fascism
* The Apotheosis of the Romantic Will:
    The Revolt against the Myth of an Ideal World
  The Bent Twig: On the Rise of Nationalism

The contents of the next two volumes were written during earlier decades, but (with one exception)[1] had not previously been published:

*The Magus of the North: J. G. Hamann and the Origins of Modern Irrationalism* (London, 1993: John Murray; New York, 1994: Farrar, Straus and Giroux).

*The Sense of Reality: Studies in Ideas and their History* (London, 1996: Chatto and Windus; New York, 1997: Farrar, Straus and Giroux):

Introduction by Patrick Gardiner
The Sense of Reality
Political Judgement
Philosophy and Government Repression
Socialism and Socialist Theories
Marxism and the International in the Nineteenth Century
The Romantic Revolution: A Crisis in the History of Modern Thought
Artistic Commitment: A Russian Legacy
Kant as an Unfamiliar Source of Nationalism
Rabindranath Tagore and the Consciousness of Nationality

Readers who wish to explore the many pieces not yet collected in volume form should consult the complete bibliography of Berlin's

---

[1] An earlier version of 'Socialism and Socialist Theories'.

writings by Henry Hardy, who has compiled and edited all the volumes published from 1978 onwards (jointly, in the case of *Russian Thinkers*, with Aileen Kelly). This bibliography appears in its currently most up-to-date published form in the 1997 Pimlico edition of *Against the Current*. Those interested in Berlin's unpublished lectures and broadcasts will find recordings of a number of them, including his 1965 Mellon Lectures on romanticism, at the National Sound Archive in London: the experience of listening to him speaking is highly recommended.

## Writings about Berlin

The list of publications stimulated by Berlin's ideas is growing steadily, in many languages. Here I confine myself to publications in English.

Three collections have been published in his honour:

Alan Ryan (ed.), *The Idea of Freedom: Essays in Honour of Isaiah Berlin* (Oxford and New York, 1979: Oxford University Press)

Avishai Margalit and others, *On the Thought of Isaiah Berlin: Papers Presented in Honour of Professor Sir Isaiah Berlin on the Occasion of his Eightieth Birthday* (Jerusalem, 1990: Israel Academy of Sciences and Humanities) (a 45-page pamphlet)

Edna and Avishai Margalit (eds), *Isaiah Berlin: A Celebration* (London, 1991: Hogarth Press; Chicago, 1991: University of Chicago Press)

Three book-length studies of Berlin's thought have so far appeared in English:

Robert Kocis, *A Critical Appraisal of Sir Isaiah Berlin's Political Philosophy* (Lewiston, NY, etc., 1989: Edwin Mellen Press)

Claude J. Galipeau, *Isaiah Berlin's Liberalism* (Oxford, 1994: Clarendon Press), with a specially valuable bibliography

John Gray, *Isaiah Berlin* (London, 1995: HarperCollins; New York, 1996: Princeton University Press; paperback, retitled *Berlin*, London, 1995: Fontana Modern Masters)

Among the many uncollected articles on Berlin, or on topics treated by him, the following may be of special interest:

Arnaldo Momigliano, 'On the Pioneer Trail' (review of *Vico and Herder*), *New York Review of Books*, 11 November 1976, 33–8

Patrick Gardiner, review of *Vico and Herder* in *History and Theory* 16 (1977), 45–51

Bhikhu Parekh, 'Isaiah Berlin', chapter 2 in his *Contemporary Political Thinkers* (Oxford, 1982: Martin Robertson)

Roger Hausheer, 'Berlin and the Emergence of Liberal Pluralism', in Pierre Manent and others, *European Liberty: Four Essays on the Occasion of the 25th Anniversary of the Erasmus Prize Foundation* (The Hague etc., 1983: Martinus Nijhoff)

John Gray, 'On Negative and Positive Liberty', chapter 4 in *Liberalisms: Essays in Political Philosophy* (London and New York, 1989: Routledge)

Eric Mack, 'Isaiah Berlin and the Quest for Liberal Pluralism', *Public Affairs Quarterly* 7 No 3 (July 1993), 215–30

George Crowder, 'Pluralism and Liberalism', *Political Studies* 42 (1994), 293–305 (reply by Berlin and Bernard Williams, ibid., 306–9)

Michael Walzer, 'Are there limits to liberalism?' (review of John Gray, *Isaiah Berlin*), *New York Review of Books*, 19 October 1995, 28–31

Ian Harris, 'Isaiah Berlin: *Two Concepts of Liberty*', in Murray Forsyth and Maurice Keens-Soper (eds), *The Political Classics: Green to Dworkin* (Oxford and New York, 1996: Oxford University Press)

In addition, many of the articles critical of 'Historical Inevitability' and 'Two Concepts of Liberty' are mentioned in Berlin's long and masterly introduction to *Four Essays on Liberty*.

Finally, there is a valuable book of interviews with Berlin:

Ramin Jahanbegloo, *Conversations with Isaiah Berlin* (London, 1992: Peter Halban; New York, 1992: Scribner's)

# INDEX

## Compiled by Douglas Matthews

Abakumov, V. S., 536
Abyssinia, 629
Accursius, 319n
Acton, John E. E. Dalberg Acton, 1st
    Baron, 176, 239, 356
Adamovich, Georgy Victorovich, 543
*Adrastea* (periodical), 376
Aeschylus, 491
aesthetics: and ideas, 64
Agathocles, tyrant of Syracuse, 296, 319
Agesilaus, 288, 296
Agrippa, Cornelius, 244, 331
Akhmatova, Anna Andreevna: post-war
    status, 526-7; appreciates Hemingway,
    530; as 19th-century writer, 532; on
    Pasternak, 533, 534n, 535-6, 546,
    549-50; on Chekhov, 539, 548; I. Berlin
    meets, 539, 540-52; praises Dostoevsky,
    539, 546; translations, 547-8; in Oxford,
    548; reputation, 552; *Cinque*, 547; *The
    Grey-Eyed King*, 546; *Poem Without a
    Hero*, 544-5, 547, 550; *Requiem*, 526,
    544-5; *A Visit to the Poet*, 546
Akhsharumov, Dmitry, 441, 460, 465
Aksakov, Sergey Timofeevich, Ivan
    Sergeevich and Konstantin Sergeevich,
    532
Alberti, Leon Battista, 320
Alcibiades, 34, 614
Alderisio, Felice, 272, 321n
Alembert, Jean Le Rond d', 134, 245, 346,
    359, 366, 489, 562
Alexander I, Tsar, 448, 452-3, 486, 521
Alexander II, Tsar, 513-14
Alexander the Great, 51, 141, 168, 336,
    373
Alfieri, Vittorio, 273
algebra, 86
Ambrose, St, 207n
anabaptists, 328

Anarchists, 220
Anaxagoras, 3
ancients and moderns controversy, 351,
    365
Andronikova, Salomé, 543
Annan, Noel, xxv
Annenkov, Pavel Vasil'evich, 439, 505
Annensky, Innokenty Fedorovich, 532,
    546, 551
Annunzio, Gabriele d', 473
Anrep, Boris, 543
Anti-Fascist Congress, Paris (1935), 528
Antigone, 11
Antiphon, 244
Antoni, Carlo: *Lo storicismo*, 362n
Apion, 589
Aquinas, St Thomas: and human purpose,
    71; and free will, 100; and moral
    responsibility, 159n; and Machiavelli,
    278; and necessity, 310; and unalterable
    human nature, 347, 350; doctrines, 367;
    on man as social, 417; Maistre praises,
    489
Aragon, Louis, 528, 538
archaeology: extrapolation in, 25
Archilochus, 436
Aristotelians: and science of politics, 69,
    71; and cosmic design, 178
Aristotle: and causation theory, xxvi, 99;
    on history, 17, 34, 614; and human
    purpose, 67, 71, 314; biology, 86;
    political philosophy, 86-7; on self-
    fulfilment, 92; and knowledge, 98; on
    different human institutions, 244, 247;
    on wicked, 270; and Machiavelli, 278,
    298, 300, 306, 384; and moral values,
    297; ethics, 309n; and single world-
    structure, 313, 392, 553; on society as
    organism, 364; and social units, 380,
    417, 586; and isolated man, 384;

historical place, 399; as 'fox', 437;
    Politics, 294, 319
Arkhipenko, A., 525
Arminius, 369, 407
Arndt, Ernst Moritz, 376n, 399, 593–4
Arnim, Achim von, 574, 576
Arnold, Gottfried, 363
Aron, Raymond, 602
art: Herder on commitment in, 417–23;
    objective standards in, 559
asceticism (self-denial), 211
Aseev, Nikolay Nikolaevich, 531, 550
Asquith, Herbert Henry, 1st Earl of
    Oxford and Asquith, 612
astronomy, 26, 63
Astruc, Jean, 365
Athens: Machiavelli on, 287, 291, 303, 307,
    312; achievements, 336; and Roman law,
    354; Herder admires, 409; see also
    Greece (ancient)
Attila the Hun, 141
Auden, Wystan Hugh, 528, 530, 628
Auerbach, Erich, 356n
Aufklärung see Enlightenment
Augustine, St, 270, 341, 494, 562
Augustus Caesar, 336
authority: in political theory, 64–5;
    objective, 70; and liberty, 71–2, 220,
    234, 237, 305; and law, 75; obedience
    to, 78; choice and acceptance of, 231–3;
    opposed by romantics, 264–5; Maistre
    on, 266–8, 482–3, 497; and nationalism,
    596
autocracy: and liberty, 201, 211 & n
autonomy see self-determination
Auvergne, Pierre d', 319
axioms, 60
Ayer, Alfred Jules, 100, 141n, 156

Babbitt, Irving, 87
Babel', Isaac Emmanuilovich., 528
Bach, Johann Sebastian, 8
Bacon, Francis: Utopianism, 136–7, 557,
    558; and Machiavelli, 276, 285; and
    unified reality, 328; and scientific
    method, 329, 334; and myths, 351n
Baglioni, Giovanpaolo, 300, 303, 311, 321n
Bagration, Prince Petr Ivanovich, 448
Bagritsky, Eduard Georgievich (pseudonym
    of Eduard Georgievich Dzyubin), 550
Bakunin, Mikhail Aleksandrovich: and
    destructive forces, 138; reads Hegel,
    505; and 1848 revolutions, 506;
    reputation, 514; and Herzen, 515n, 516,
    518; social predictions, 584

Baldwin, Stanley, 611
Balzac, Honoré de, 437, 579
Baratynsky, Evgeny Abramovich, 532, 550
Barnard, Frederick M., 374n
Baron, Hans, 300
Barrès, Maurice, 155, 496
Bartenev, Victor V., 473
Batteux, abbé Charles, 262, 389, 418n
Baudelaire, Charles, 550, 579
Baudoin, François, 333
Bayle, Pierre, 331, 337, 365, 408
Beaumarchais, Pierre Augustin Caron de,
    454
Beaverbrook, William Maxwell Aitken, 1st
    Baron, 612
Beckett, Samuel, 579
Beerbohm, Max, 614
Beethoven, Ludwig van, 8
behaviour, human: understanding of, 42–5,
    52–3, 84; and rationality, 92–4;
    compulsive and uncontrollable, 93–4,
    97, 101–2; and outside forces, 95–7,
    99–100, 150–3, 160–1; and self-
    determination, 99–102, 105–6, 135, 140,
    146–9; and individual character and
    endeavour, 122–3
belief: understanding of, 89
Belinsky, Vissarion Grigorievich, 197, 440,
    500, 502, 505, 552
Bell, The (Kolokol; periodical), 513–14, 523
Bellamy, Edward, 557
Bellarmino, Roberto F. R., Cardinal, 310
Belloc, Hilaire, 143, 163
Bely, Andrey (pseudonym of Boris
    Nikolaevich Bugaev), 529, 531, 549
Bengel, Johann Albrecht, 253
Ben-Gurion, David, xii
Bennett, Arnold, 441n, 451, 614
Bennigsen, General Levin August T.,
    Count, 450
Bentham, Jeremy: on human relationships,
    75; mocks natural law, 79; Marx rejects
    political morality, 81; on human
    enslavement to passions, 209; on liberty,
    219n; on law as restraint, 220; on
    individual interests, 242n; Mill criticises,
    318; and Machiavelli, 320; doctrines,
    367, 574; rationalism, 583
Berenson, Bernard, 119
Bergson, Henri, 72, 251, 261, 459
Berkeley, George, Bishop, 330, 382n
Berlin, Isaiah: ideas and principles, ix–xv,
    xxiv–xxxvi; background, xxiii–xxiv; at
    British Embassy in Moscow, 525, 527;
    meets Pasternak, 527–31, 533, 536–8,

552; meets Akhmatova, 539, 540–52
Bernal, John Desmond, 328
Bible: on wicked, 270; criticisms of, 365; metaphor in, 404; emotion in, 558
Biryukov, Pavel Ivanovich, 439n, 441, 478n
Bismarck, Prince Otto von, xiv, 22, 50, 183, 619, 633
Blackwell, Thomas, the younger, 365, 389
Blake, William: radical protest in, 257, 421; attacks constrictions of science, 259–60, 573; on knowledge, 496
blame see praise and blame
Blanc, Louis, 507, 515
Blok, Aleksandr Aleksandrovich, 437, 529, 531, 533, 546, 549–50, 614
Boccalini, Traiano, 276
Bodin, Jean: on freedom and obedience, 72; on family and political life, 75; on universal truths, 244; on Machiavelli, 279; and cultural history, 333, 351–2, 355, 362
Bodmer, Johann Jacob, 362–3, 389
Boeckh, August, 355
Bogoslovsky, E. I., 439n
Boileau-Despréaux, Nicolas, 262, 330, 389, 418n
Bollandists, 330
bon sens, le, 327, 338, 428
Bonald, Louis Gabriel Ambroise, vicomte de, 264, 267–8, 592
Bonnard, Pierre, 532
Borgia, Cesare, Duke of Valentino, 273, 284, 296, 299
Borodino, Battle of (1812), 448–9, 455
Bosanquet, Bernard H., 221
Bossuet, Jacques Bénigne: and social activities, 19; on objective march of history, 126, 428; and structure of history, 181, 410; on Christian achievement, 336, 364; on social group, 586
Botkin, Vasily Petrovich, 440, 442
Boulainvilliers, Henri, comte de, 333, 363, 407, 430n
Bowra, Maurice, 540
Boyer, Paul, 472
Boyle, Robert, 51
Bradley, Francis Herbert, 110, 221
Brandeis, Louis D., 189n
Braque, Georges, 532
Breitinger, Johann Jacob, 355, 362–3, 389
Brinton, Crane, 219n
Britten, Benjamin, 412
Brodsky, Joseph, 549

Bruni, Leonardo, 355
Brutus, Marcus Junius, 288, 307
Bryusov, Valery Yakovlevich, 531
Büchner, Georg, 121, 264, 493
Buckle, Henry Thomas: materialism, 19, 366; and science of history, 20, 21n, 34, 37, 39, 355–6; and unified reality, 328; Tolstoy criticises, 458, 469; History of Civilization in England, 21n
Budé, Guillaume, 333
Bukharin, Nikolay Ivanovich, 209n, 534
Bunin, Ivan Alekseevich, 530, 532
Burckhardt, Jakob, 278, 301, 356, 380n, 585
Burd, L., 274–5
Burke, Edmund: metaphors, 76; and patterns of history, 155; on individual in society, 198, 219, 228, 232n, 242n, 569; on compromise, 240; anti-intellectualism, 251, 256; on society as organism, 364, 591–2; opposes Enlightenment, 380, 394; and Herder, 393, 428; on understanding, 460; and knowledge, 496; on nature, 564; conservatism, 568; attacks hypocrisy, 596
Burton, Sir Richard, 402
Bury, John Bagnell, x
Butler, Joseph: Fifteen Sermons, 127n
Butterfield, Herbert: on 'human predicament', 158, 160n, 162n; on Machiavelli, 186, 275
Byron, George Gordon, 6th Baron, 8n, 262, 264, 572–3; Don Juan, 543

Cabanis, Pierre Jean Georges, 487
Cabet, Étienne, 137, 517, 557
Caesar, Julius, 51, 141, 288, 373, 634
Calepio, Count Pietro, 362
Callicles, 270
Calvin, Jean, 562
Camillus, 296
Campanella, Tommaso, 137, 557
Camus, Albert, 530
capitalism: and nationalism, 588
Capponi, Gino: Storia della repubblica di Firenze, 321n
Caprariis, Vittorio de, 274
Carducci, Giosuè, 579
Carlyle, Thomas: and creative spirit, xii, 72; and abstract forces in history, 125; historical view, 159, 356; and authoritarianism, 222; anti-rationalism, 261, 328; on lifelessness of modern man, 395; influence on Germans, 400; and

knowledge, 496; Herzen meets, 516; on
Muhammad, 573; on heroes, 574;
repelled by rational order, 583
Carneades, 270, 317, 425
Carpaccio, Vittorio, 609
Carr, Edward Hallett, x, 157n, 162n, 508n
Carritt, E. F., 116
Cassirer, Ernst, 273–4, 275n, 277n
Castelar, Emilio, 511n
Cathars, 328
Catherine II (the Great), Empress of
Russia, 445, 502
Catholic Church see Roman Catholic
Church
Catullus, 558
causation, xxvi, 99–101; see also
determinism
Cesarotti, Melchior, 362, 365
Chaadaev, Petr Yakovlevich, 551
Chabod, Federico, 274, 297, 299
Chagall, Marc, 525
Chamberlain, Houston Stewart, 125
Chamberlain, Neville, 615
Chamisso, Adelbert von, 575
Charlemagne, Emperor, 187, 373
Charron, Pierre, 244, 331
Chateaubriand, François René, vicomte de,
264, 496
Châtelet, Gabrielle Emile, marquise du,
335
Chaucer, Geoffrey, 421
Chekhov, Anton Pavlovich, 423, 437, 533,
539, 545
Chernyshevsky, Nikolai Gerasimovich, 14,
469, 557
Chertkov, Vladimir Grigor'evich, 521n
Chesterton, Gilbert Keith, 495, 614
children: and obedience, 218, 220;
compulsory education of, 240
China: Voltaire on, 362
choice (individual): and freedom, xxvii,
95–7, 100–1, 105–8, 111, 116, 141n, 203,
205; and march of history, 128, 140,
141n, 145–6; and responsibility, 141n,
147; and determinism, 149, 186–7;
under threat, 202n; freedom of, 239,
456, 458, 471; of values, 242; Kant and,
433; Tolstoy disbelieves in, 456, 458,
485, 489–90
Christian Democrats, 85
Christianity: and revealed truth, 4; virtues,
7; Machiavelli and values of, 289–94;
297–9, 306, 308, 309n, 310–12, 321–3;
and unity of world, 313; and rise of
science, 329; Herder on, 372, 397n;

mysticism, 382n
Chrysippus, 99–101
Chukovskaya, Lydia, 526
Churchill, Randolph, 541–2
Churchill, Sir Winston: qualities, xii, xiv,
xxxv, 614, 616–22, 627; and Akhmatova,
542; prose style, 606–10, 619, 626–7;
historical imagination, 608–9, 614–17,
621, 625; beliefs and principles, 610–13,
625; relations with Roosevelt, 613–17,
619, 622, 624–6; and American
viewpoint, 624
Cicero: and free will, 100; as lawyer, 142;
on Carneades, 270; Machiavelli and,
283, 295, 300, 309; and political
method, 319; Herder on, 404n; on man
as social, 417; disparages Jews, 589
Clark, Robert T., Jr: Herder, 435n
class (social): in Marxist theory, 34, 124–5,
457, 587–8; and nationalism, 594
classicism: and formulation of values, 262
Clemenceau, Georges, 625
Cobbett, William, 263, 495
Cochrane, Eric, 297
coercion: limits of, 193–203, 209; and
individual freedom, 204–5, 211 & n,
218–23, 229, 232, 235; and education,
220–1; and power, 234; consent to, 235
Cojecki, Charles Edmund, 515n
Coke, Sir Edward, 333
Coleridge, Samuel Taylor: anti-rationalism,
261, 263; on purpose in natural activity,
263; historical sense, 356; and
knowledge, 496; rejects revolt, 565, 574
Collingwood, Robin G., 7, 355
common good: Machiavelli on, 304–5, 308
Communists: operational ideas, 89;
Pasternak on, 535; reformist ideals, 558;
popular appeal, 629; see also Marxism
compulsion see coercion
Comte, Auguste: materialism, 19; and
scientific history, 21, 25, 39, 120, 166,
182; classification of sciences, 36; and
political philosophy, 66; on empirical
knowledge, 77; and free will, 117;
achievements and influence, 119–21;
optimism, 137, 154, 178, 188; on
understanding, 154; and founding of
sociology, 185–6, 446; on free thinking
in politics and morals, 222–3, 554; and
unified reality, 328; and Herder, 360;
Tolstoy's hostility to, 469; calls for
authoritarian élite, 583; on social group,
586
Condillac, Étienne Bonnot de: materialism,

19; and scientific method, 80, 134; and sociological history, 120; on uniform reality, 248, 370; on origins of language, 383

Condorcet, M. J. A. N. Caritat, marquis de: on naturalistic sociology, xxv; optimistic view of world, 4–5, 136–7, 154, 558, 582; materialism, 19–20; on empirical knowledge, 77; on lack of individual rights in classical times, 201; on natural bonds, 238; on attaining human ends, 245, 580; belief in universal civilisation, 255; historical sense, 356; and progress, 408, 428; on benevolent nature, 562; qualities, 634; *Esquisse d'un tableau historique*, 136, 238n

Confucius, 8n

Constant, Benjamin: on personal freedom, 196, 198, 232, 236; on popular sovereignty, 234–5; criticises Rousseau, 235; and the State, 305

Corneille, Pierre, 350, 363; *Médée*, 565

Cowen, Joseph, 516

creativity: Fichte on, 72, 422, 570–1; and rules, 261–2; and art, 341, 571; Herder on, 383, 417–23; and spontaneity, 568

Creighton, Mandell, Bishop of London, 163

Crimean War, 513, 516n

Critias, 244

Croce, Benedetto: on Machiavelli, 272, 278–9, 288–9, 297–300, 315, 317; on positivists, 356; and feeling, 389

Cromwell, Oliver, xii, 51, 141, 163, 617

Cujas, Jacques, 333

cultures, plurality of *see* pluralism

Cyrus the Great, 188, 295, 300, 307, 309

Daniel, *Père* Gabriel, 333

Danilevsky, Nikolay Yakovlevich, 441

Dante Alighieri: dates, 23; Machiavelli and, 295, 310; and necessity, 310; literary style, 350; celebrated, 389; as 'hedgehog', 437; Herzen reads, 504; emotion in, 558

Darwin, Charles, 167, 182, 360, 446

Day Lewis, Cecil, 628

Decembrists, 479, 503

deduction, 62

Deffand, marquise Marie du, 8n

deism, 23

democracy: and oppression, 234–6

Derzhavin, Gavrila Romanovich, 532

Descartes, René: disdains history, 17, 24,

127, 332, 353, 365; and scientific method, 42, 166, 262, 329, 332; physics, 86, 87n; on unified knowledge, 245, 328; categorisations, 381, 390–1; and nature, 393; Fichte rejects, 569; *Discourse on Method*, 329; *Meditations*, 329

despotism, 201 & n, 208, 225, 228, 236

determinism: I. Berlin opposes, x–xi, xxvii–xxviii; in human behaviour, 98–109, 135, 140, 146–9, 493; and existence of world, 135–6; and historical change, 139–40, 146; distinct from fatalism, 141n, 493; and historical judgement, 160–3; as dogma, 179–80; and scientific observation, 179; sociological, 186; Kant on compatibility with morality, 258–9, 561; Herder and, 432; Tolstoy's belief in, 456, 458, 485, 489–90

Dickens, Charles, 445, 531; *David Copperfield*, 512

Diderot, Denis: belief in universal civilisation, 255, 359; Herder's sympathy for, 255; dismisses Homer, 365; and uniformity, 370; on actor and role, 406; scepticism over progress, 408; Tolstoy and, 454, 468; materialism, 487; qualities, 499; on individual freedom, 573; sensibility, 622

Dilthey, Wilhelm, 56, 356, 389

Dio Cassius, 293

Dionysius, tyrant, 296

Disraeli, Benjamin, 583, 613

Dostoevsky, Fedor Mikhailovich: as 'hedgehog', xiv, 437; rejects Encyclopaedists, 80; satirises nihilists, 196; and great sinner, 309; and human fantasies, 317; and Tolstoy, 467, 469; and Proudhon, 482n; praises Herzen, 500; Pasternak on, 531, 533, 539; Akhmatova praises, 539, 546; rejects Western values, 567; and underground man, 577; pessimism, 579; *The Idiot*, 294

Doughty, Charles Montagu, 402

dreams, 174

Dreiser, Theodore, 528

Dubos, abbé Jean Baptiste, 362–3, 418n

du Châtelet, marquise *see* Châtelet, Gabrielle Emilie, marquise du

du Deffand, marquise *see* Deffand, marquise Marie du

Dufresnoy, Nicolas Lenglet, 333

Duhamel, Georges, 538

Dumoulin, Charles, 333
Durkheim, Emile, 183n, 281, 435, 585, 600

economics: scientific procedure in, 33,
    35–6; history, 37
education: purpose of, 220
Egidio da Viterbo, 282
Eikhenbaum, Boris Mikhailovich, 441n,
    463, 468n, 474n, 482n
Einfühlung see empathy
Eisenstein, Sergey Mikhailovich, 525
Eliot, Thomas Stearns, 276n, 530, 532, 546,
    550, 614
emotion: expression of, 558–9
empathy (Einfühlung), 389, 405, 426, 428
empiricism: I. Berlin's belief in, xxv; ideals,
    4; and scientific method, 18; and
    political theory, 60–3, 81–2, 84–5; and
    history, 182; and liberal rationality,
    225n; and rise of science, 559
Encyclopaedists: Herder's attitude to, 80,
    360, 394, 432; and benevolent nature,
    313; and unified reality, 328; on social
    behaviour, 469; see also Enlightenment,
    French
Engels, Friedrich: and scientific history, 21,
    39; and march of history, 126n;
    idealism, 155; and administration of
    things, 191; on Machiavelli, 277
England: political idealism in, 212n;
    sovereignty in, 237n; Herzen in, 511,
    516–17; imperialism, 613
Enlightenment, French: opposition to, x,
    xxxiv, 243, 248–55, 260–8, 351n, 355,
    566–7; I. Berlin's interest in, xxv–xxvi,
    xxxiii; Voltaire on, 8n, 339; central
    doctrines, 243–4, 261–3, 426, 597; Vico
    on, 248; Herder and, 254–7, 359–435;
    Möser on, 256; and French Revolution,
    268; on nature as divine harmony, 562;
    and German nationalism, 597
Entrèves, Alexandre Passerin d', 276n
Epictetus, 112–13, 207n, 211
Epicureans: on self-control and will, 92,
    99; on human ends, 314; Vico reads,
    340
Epicurus, 214, 558
equality: I. Berlin on, xii; as human goal,
    10; in political theory, 64; and liberty,
    196–7, 205n, 226, 230; in sight of God,
    201n
Erasmus, Desiderius, 200, 437
Erigena, Johannes Scotus, 63, 393
Esenin, Sergey Alexandrovich, 531
étatisme, 594

ethics: and ideas, 1–3, 64; Greek, 297–8;
    see also morality
Euclid, 51
Euripides, 426
evil: and liberty, 219n; Maistre on man as,
    265–7, 473, 492
existentialists: discount objective standards,
    70, 74; achievements, 73; on importance
    of individual choice, 187; oppose
    explanations, 464n; reject Utopianism,
    579
experience: and knowledge, 29
expressionism: Herder's doctrine of, 361,
    367–8, 380–97

Faguet, Émile, 266, 519
Faraday, Michael, 20
Fascism: and nationalism, xxxi, 589, 593;
    operational ideas, 89; historical theory,
    182; and authority, 268; and denial of
    monism, 568; Communist opposition
    to, 629; and New Order, 630
Feltrinelli (Italian publishing house), 538
Fénelon, François de Salignac de la Mothe,
    333, 557
Ferdinand I of Aragon, King of Spain,
    294, 306
Ferguson, Adam, 355, 393; Essay of the
    History of Civil Society, 364, 572n
Festugière, A. J., 91
Fet, Afanasy Afanasievich (pseudonym of
    Afanasy Afanasievich Shenshin), 440,
    442, 531–2
Feuerbach, Ludwig, 602
Fichte, Johann Gottlieb: and creative spirit,
    xxx, 72, 422, 570–1; power of ideas,
    192; on rationalism in society, 216,
    221–3; on education, 220–1; anti-
    rationalism, 261; on Machiavelli, 272,
    274, 292, 307; patriotism, 371, 591, 593;
    social ideals, 398; and community, 424n;
    on ambition and achievement, 506; and
    beginnings of romanticism, 569–72; on
    dignity of labour, 570; on self and will,
    570–2, 574–5
Ficino, Marsilio, 281, 562
Figgis, John Neville, 280
final solutions, 12–14
Fisch, M. H., 330n
Flaubert, Gustave, 440, 451, 460, 539, 579
Florence, 8, 336
Fontenelle, Bernard le Bovier de, 339,
    344n, 364
formal method (of answering questions),
    60–3

Forster, Edwin Morgan, 154, 528, 614
Forster, Georg, 371
Foscolo, Ugo, 271
Fourier, François Charles Marie: optimism, 137, 393; Herzen reads, 503, 517; and ideal state, 557; opposes trade and industry, 583
Fox, Charles James, 634
France: political commitment in, 212n; Herzen's view of, 514–15; cultural dominance, 562–3, 597–8; Churchill on, 612; *ancien régime*, 622
France, Anatole, 137
Francesca, Piero della, 276
Francke, August Hermann, 253
Franco, General Francisco, 172–3, 621
Franklin, Benjamin, 380n
fraternity: and liberty, 226, 230
Frederick II (the Great), King of Prussia: Carlyle praises, xii; attacks Holbach, 141; tolerance, 201n; promotes Enlightenment values and reforms, 249, 251, 566, 597–8; uniformity of system, 256; on Machiavelli, 279, 304; authoritarianism, 305; Herder and, 373, 397; Maistre on, 477
freedom *see* liberty
Freemasons: Tolstoy attacks, 471, 486
free will *see* choice
French Revolution: Condorcet's influence on, xxvi; causes explained, 46–7, 166; evaluation of, 168–9; aims for positive freedom, 233; and end of Enlightenment, 268; welcomed in Germany, 371; principles, 434; Roman Catholic view of, 481; Maistre on, 494–5; moral effect, 623
Freud, Sigmund, 48, 155, 182, 435, 579
Friedrich, Carl Joachim, 278
Fritzsche, Robert Arnold, 428n

Gabo, Naum, 525
Galileo Galilei: achievements, 20, 79; and rational method, 262; and Machiavelli, 285; and unified reality, 328
Gardiner, Patrick L., 109
Garibaldi, Giuseppe, 501, 512, 514, 632
Gassendi, Pierre, 562
Gatterer, J. C., 361
Gaulle, Charles de, xiv, 632
Gay, N. N., Sr, 521n
*Geisteswissenschaften*, 48
Genghis Khan, 23, 50, 156, 168, 187
genius, 530
Gentili, Alberico, 271

Gentillet, Innocent, 270, 279–80
Gentz, Friedrich von, 371
George, Stefan, 614
German language, 365, 366
Germany: reacts against foreign domination, xi, 597–9; inner life in, xxx, 211, 366; historical writing in, 339; nationalism, 371–2, 563, 586–7, 589, 593–4, 596–600, 602; Herder on spirit of, 375–6, 397–9, 403, 413–14, 433; Moser on as victim, 395n; Herzen on, 516; romantic movement in, 559–65, 569, 574–6, 579; cultural backwardness, 562–3, 566; Churchill on, 612
Gerstenberg, Heinrich Wilhelm von, 257
Gibbon, Edward: as historian, 143, 159, 339, 407; Tolstoy criticises, 458; prose style, 607
Gide, André, 451, 528, 614
Gilbert, Allan H., 271
Gilbert, Felix, 322
Gladstone, William Ewart, 616, 633
Gleim, Johann Wilhelm Ludwig, 370
Gnostics, 155, 183
Gobineau, Joseph Arthur, comte de, 125
Godwin, William, 154, 557
Goethe, Johann Wolfgang von: on individual experience, 250; attacks Holbach, 258; anti-rationalism, 261; Herder and, 370, 377, 380, 411, 417, 428, 432; principles, 371; on cultural decline, 395n; social ideals, 398, 403; admires ancient Athens, 409; and unity of man, 421; and artistic creation, 422; on Herder's personality, 424n; disclaims models for Faust, 435; as 'fox', 437; and knowledge, 496; Herzen reads, 503, 516; influence on Pasternak, 529, 531, 550; on Renaissance, 547; praises Kaufmann, 564; rejects revolt, 565, 574; on Holbach's *Système de la nature*, 581; and German chauvinism, 599; *Werther*, 572; *Xenien* (with Schiller), 377
Gogol, Nikolay Vasil'evich, 437, 467
Goncourt, Edmond and Jules, 515
Gorky, Maxim (*pseudonym of* Aleksey Maksimovich Peshkov), 482n, 524, 533, 543
Görres, J. Joseph von, 361n, 371, 376n, 399, 495
Gothic architecture, 411
Gothic Revival, 607
Gottsched, Johann Christoph, 404
Gozzoli, Benozzo, 609
Gracchi, 142

Gramsci, Antonio, 275n, 278
Granovsky, Timofey Nikolaevich, 520
Great Chain of Being, 312
Greece (ancient): achievements, 7–9; and personal constraints, 211; ethics, 297; Plutarch glorifies, 331; and origins of art, 396; Maistre on, 485; emotion in, 558; see also Athens
Green, Thomas Hill: ix, 88–9, 221; *Lecture on Liberal Legislation and Freedom of Contract*, 205n
Gregorio, Pietro de, 333
Grey, Edward, Viscount, 612
Grimm, Jakob, 361n
Grotius, Hugo, 347, 350, 417
Gryphius, Andreas, 365
Guéhenno, Jean, 538
Guicciardini, Francesco, 276, 286, 292, 319
Guizot, François Pierre Guillaume, 503, 507
Gumilev, Nikolay Stepanovich, 532, 543–4, 546
Gusev, Nikolay Nikolaevich, 446

Haag, Luiza, 501–2, 506
Haldane, Richard Burdon, Viscount, 612–13
Hale, Matthew, 333
Halévy, Élie, 163
Haller, Carl Ludwig von, 432
Hamann, Johann Georg: I. Berlin champions, xi, xxxi; attacks Enlightenment doctrines, xxix, 248–52, 368, 380, 566; on language and symbols, xxix–xxx, 252–3, 365, 381–2, 386; historical view, 355, 357, 370; and Vico's ideas, 357; and spirit of nation, 363, 397, 592; teaches Herder, 364, 370, 373, 379, 381–2, 409; anti-theory stance, 366; and German tradition, 366, 413n, 566; hatred of State, 373; criticises Kant, 378; on thought and feeling, 381–2; and alienation, 396n; on unity of man, 421; on artistic commitment, 422–3; on Kaufmann, 564; on effects of knowledge, 573, 575; criticises practical man, 575
Hampshire, Stuart N., 103, 105–6, 110, 116–17, 141n
Hancock, Sir William Keith, 273
Hannibal, 296
happiness: as attainable end, 136–7
Hare, Richard M., 100
Harrington, James, 319, 557
Hart, Herbert Lionel Adolphus, 117

Haumant, Émile, 441n, 478n
Hauptmann, Gerhart, 614
Haydn, Hiram, 271
Hayek, Friedrich von: xii; *The Counter-Revolution of Science*, 126n
health: and value judgements, 64, 69
Hearn, Lafcadio, 402
Hegel, Georg Wilhelm Friedrich: on freedom, ix, 417, 568; on historical change, 5, 50, 76, 126, 137–8, 578; and historical laws, 33, 41, 56, 435; on reason and understanding, 57; and creative spirit, 72, 124, 137, 422; and self-knowledge, 95, 116, 213–14; and structure of history, 181; and laws of institutions, 214; on rationalism in society, 217; on obedience of rationality, 221; and individual in society, 232n, 371, 586; anti-rationalism, 261; views of, 269; and Machiavelli, 271, 274–6, 307, 308; ethics, 309n; on history and morality, 317; and Vico's ideas, 353; Herder's influence on, 361n; doctrines, 367; on progress, 378; social ideals, 398; admires ancient Athens, 409; Ranke criticises, 431; as 'hedgehog', 437; Tolstoy reads, 444; influence on Slavophils, 470; Herzen studies, 505, 507, 510, 518, 520; on State, 591; and nationalism, 593, 599; *Grundlinien der Philosophie des Rechts*, 433n
Hegelians: anti-individualism, 123, 125n; and cosmic design, 178; historical theory, 182; and slavery to nature, 204, 296; determinism, 222; and abandonment of final harmony, 238
Heine, Heinrich, 192, 407, 506, 509, 537, 584–5; 'Zum Lazarus', 445n
Heinse, Johann Jacob Wilhelm, 419, 564; *Ardinghello und die glückseligen Inseln*, 258
Helvétius, Claude Adrien: and empiricism of political thought, 73, 77, 414; on freedom, 194n; on human enslavement to passions, 209; belief in universal civilisation, 255, 355, 359, 370; on benevolent nature, 264, 562, 564
Hemingway, Ernest, 530
Hemsterhuis, Frans, 364
Heraclitus, 12
Herder, Caroline, 388
Herder, Johann Gottfried: I. Berlin champions, xi, xxx–xxxi, xxxv; on plurality of cultures, xxx, 8–9, 14, 254–7, 361, 368, 378–9, 398–401,

403–12, 415–17, 424–32, 567;
nationalism, xxxi, 371–8, 384, 397–8,
591, 594, 596; and belonging,
xxxii–xxxiv, 412–17, 586; concept of
history, 24, 56, 120, 165n, 355, 361–2,
368, 405–7, 410–12, 427; compares
family and political life, 75; rejects
Encyclopaedists, 80, 360; and individual
in society, 125, 214, 405; Prussian
cultural background, 249, 366, 566;
attacks Voltaire, 252, 255, 362; opposes
Enlightenment doctrines, 253–4,
359–435; advocates relativism, 255, 390,
407n, 427–9; on importance of feeling,
258, 367–8, 370, 389, 567; influence on
Goethe, 258; on Machiavelli, 274–5; and
historical writing, 339, 362, 405; and
Vico's ideas, 347, 357, 361, 405; anti-
rationalism, 359–60; attitude to natural
science, 360–1, 364; beliefs and
doctrines, 360–9, 432–5; and populism,
361, 367, 370–80, 399–403, 414, 417; on
society as organism, 364; defends
German language and culture, 365–6,
398–400, 403, 413–14, 433, 566–7, 596;
and self-expression, 367–8; on unity of
fact and value, 369–70, 412–13, 419; and
progress, 378, 407–10, 429;
expressionism, 380–97, 417–18; on
language, 381–8; sea voyage to France,
387–8; attacks Kant, 391; *Kräfte*
doctrine, 393–4, 400, 414, 424n; social
ideals, 397–8; and *Humanität*, 410, 423,
426–9, 433; empiricism, 414; aesthetics,
417–22; influence, 417; on unity of man,
419–23; character, 423n; assessed, 432–5;
praises Kaufmann, 564; and
Muhammad, 574; denounces multinational empires, 600; *Adrastea*, 413,
422; *German National Glory*, 376n;
*God: Some Conversations*, 432n; *Ideas
about the Philosophy of History of
Mankind* (*Ideen*), 368, 393, 395, 413,
426–7; *Kalligone*, 413, 422; *Letters on
the Advancement of Mankind*, 375;
*Metakritik*, 391; *On Hebrew Poetry*,
413; *Stimmen der Völker in Liedern*,
418; *Yet Another Philosophy of History*
(*Auch eine Philosophie der Geschichte*),
361n, 362, 375, 396n, 403, 405, 408,
424, 427
heresy: sincerity in, 554
hero, the, 564, 574–5
Herodotus, 270, 331, 336, 437
Hertzka, Theodor, 557

Herwegh, Georg, 509–10, 516
Herzen, Alexander (Aleksandr Ivanovich
Gertsen): I. Berlin champions, xi;
eloquence, 499; qualities of mind,
499–500; Belinsky on, 500, 502, 552;
memoirs, 500, 511–24; birth and
upbringing, 501–3; reading, 503–4;
career, 504; exiled, 504; love-affairs, 504,
512, 517; marriage, 504; revolutionary
views, 504–8, 522; inheritance and
financial independence, 506; in Paris,
506, 508; literary style, 507, 518; artistic
egotism, 509–10; and wife's infidelity
and death, 509–10; loses mother and
child, 510; appearance, 511n; in
England, 511, 516–17; political and
social ideas, 514–15, 517–19, 522–4;
reputation, 514; friendships and private
life, 516–18; later beliefs, 519–21; death
in Paris, 523; achievements and
influence, 524; on Russian literature,
551; and works of creation, 571; *From
the Other Shore*, 13–14; *Letters from
Avenue Marigny*, 507; *Letters to an Old
Comrade*, 521; *My Past and Thoughts*,
500, 511–13, 516, 524
Herzen, Nataliya (A.H.'s wife), 504, 506,
509–10
Hess, Moses: xi; *Rome and Jerusalem*, 585
heteronomy, 208–10, 220–1, 562
Hilbert, David, 167
history: as natural science, x, xxxviii,
17–58, 120–1, 164–6, 171, 182–3, 331–2,
335; supposed laws and patterns of,
xxvii, 28–37, 40–3, 53–6, 129–34,
139–40, 144–5, 151–2, 180–1, 266; and
progress towards ideal, 6; Aristotle on,
17; nature and purpose of, 17–18, 152;
and cultural differences, 22–3, 50–4,
127–8, 142–3, 157, 176; Herder on, 24,
56, 120, 165n, 355, 361–2, 368, 405–7,
410, 427; Vico on, 24, 48, 50, 56, 165n,
340, 342–3, 349–58; reasoning in, 31–3,
40–5; kinship to art, 47–8; explanation
and judgement in, 48–50, 56–8, 178,
187–8; accident in, 70; inevitability in,
119–90; Comte's view of, 120–1; and
individual endeavour, 122–4, 160–1;
impersonal forces in, 123–7, 150–3, 161,
183–5, 187, 189; perceived purpose in,
132; objectivity and bias in, 143–4,
161–5, 169–75, 177–8, 187–8; moral
judgement in, 158–66, 170–2, 176–8,
188–90; and basic assumptions, 166–7;
ideology in, 175; and metaphysics, 182;

relevance of, 335–7; Voltaire on role of, 335–9; Tolstoy's philosophy of, 439–69, 484–8, 491–2, 498; Maistre on, 484–5; Churchill's view of, 608–9

Hitler, Adolf: character, xiv, 614–15, 632; and final solution, 12; and national self-assertion, 125; in historical process, 141; and historical determinism, 156; actions judged, 163, 168, 187; invades Russia, 604; Churchill on, 621; as threat, 629

Hobbes, Thomas: on lack of purpose in nature, 71; and empiricism of political thought, 73; Rousseau rejects political obligation, 80–1; and free will, 141n, 195n; on knowing reality, 155; on social safeguards, 198; on oppression by sovereign, 235; and Machiavelli, 271, 293, 308, 318–19; on moral values, 290, 293; revolutionary thinking, 315; on self-preservation, 318; on knowledge, 341; on human nature, 350; Leviathan, 195n

Hoffmann, Ernst Theodor Amadeus, 575–7

Holbach, Paul H. Dietrich, Baron von: and knowledge, 117; and science of human behaviour, 134; belief in universal civilisation, 255, 359; on benevolent nature, 264, 562; dismisses rites, 346; anti-clericalism, 377; Herder and, 411; Système de la nature (System of Nature), 141, 258, 581

Hölderlin, Johann Christian Friedrich, 409, 574

Homer, 347, 350, 365, 388–9, 399, 558
Hooker, Richard, 364, 417
Hopkins, Harry, 626
Horace, 404n
Horneck, Philipp Wilhelm von, 365
Hotman, François, 279, 333
Hugo, Victor, 262, 501, 515
human behaviour: scientific study of, 19–20
human nature: variability, 214, 347; and freedom, 266
'human predicament', 158, 160
humanism: Machiavelli and, 289, 293, 313
Humanität, 410, 423, 426–9, 433
humanities: divorce from sciences, 326–58
Humboldt, Wilhelm von, 371, 398
Hume, David: as 'fox', xiv; in linguistic analytical tradition, ix; on empirical knowledge, 77, 82; and scientific method, 80; on descriptive and value statements, 84; and free will, 100, 141n;

denies absolute truth, 245, 249; accepts rational method, 262; and benevolent nature, 264, 313, 564; Machiavelli and, 278; and necessity, 319; and Enlightenment spirit, 339; on historical studies, 361; Herder and, 368, 390, 406, 412, 428; on limits of reason, 382; condemns Middle Ages, 407; scepticism over progress, 408; Tolstoy reads, 445; faith in nature and custom, 556

Huovinen, Lauri, 275
Hurd, Richard, Bishop of Worcester, 363, 389
Huxley, Aldous, 168, 539, 585

Iambulus, 557
Ibsen, Henrik, 437, 539, 579
Idealist movement, 422, 470–1, 492, 559
ideas: power of, 191–3
ideologies, 61, 72–3, 89, 175
Il'in, Ivan Aleksandrovich, 441n
imagination (fantasia): Vico on, 346, 351n, 354–6; Herder and, 369; see also empathy (Einfühlung)
Impressionism, 8
individual, the: in society, 226–7
induction, 62
International Working Men's Association, 600
Ionian philosophers, 76, 86
Iselin, J. C., 408
Isidore of Seville, 350
Italy: nationalism in, 587, 589, 600
Ivan IV (the Terrible), Tsar, 454
Ivan the Terrible (film), 525
Ivanov, Alexander Andreevich, 512
Ivanov, Georgy Vladimirovich, 551
Ivanov, Vyacheslav Ivanovich, 549
Ivinskaya, Olga, 536, 549

Jacobi, Friedrich Heinrich, 251, 260, 432n
Jacobins, 219n, 233, 271
Jacoby, Günter: Herder als Faust, 435n
Jahn, Friedrich Ludwig, 376n, 399, 594
James, William, 206
Jansenism, 244
Japan, 604
Jefferson, Thomas, 198
Jesuits: on Machiavelli, 279; Tolstoy's hatred of, 483
Jews: sense of alienation, xi; and revealed truth, 4; Herder on, 374, 399, 403–4, 433; Hamann and, 382; unifying role, 585; disparaged by classical writers, 589
Job, Book of, 491

John of Salisbury, 364
Johnson, Samuel, 142n, 607–8
Joly, Maurice, 289n
Joseph II, Emperor of Austria, 201n
Joyce, James, 437, 529–30, 532, 546, 579, 614; *Ulysses*, 531
judgement: faculty of, 31
Julius II, Pope, 303
Justinian: *Digest*, 319n
Juvenal, 289, 316, 589

Kaegi, Werner, 272
Kafka, Franz, 546, 577, 579
Kamenev, Lev Borisovich, 277n
Kandinsky, Vassily, 525, 532
Kant, Immanuel: on 'crooked timber of humanity', xv, 16, 241, 603; and boundaries of natural world, xxvii; explanations of history, 48, 52, 378; and political philosophy, 65, 73, 371; on freedom and obligation, 72, 142n, 207n; rejects Encyclopaedists and *lumières*, 80, 394; dismisses naturalistic tradition, 81; and empiricism, 82, 148n, 414; validity, 88; and personal freedom and autonomy, 116, 187, 207n, 208–9, 223–4, 227n, 561–2, 566–8; on values, 209; on rationalism in society, 216, 561; on political liberty, 219; on paternalism as despotism, 228; Prussian cultural background, 249, 366, 566; hatred of matter, 250; on determinism and morality, 258–9, 561; accepts rational method, 262, 564; and hypothetical imperatives, 297; and Herder, 366, 369, 378–9, 390–1, 407, 429; categorisations, 386, 390–1; and artistic creation, 422; on human imperfectibility, 430; and free will, 433, 561, 564; Herzen reads, 503; Pasternak on, 529; abhorrence of disordered imagination, 564; *Anthropologie*, 378–9; *Critique of Pure Reason*, 192; 'Idee zu einer allgemeinen Geschichte in weltbürgerlicher Absicht', 224n; *Zum ewigen Frieden*, 379
Kareev, Nikolay Ivanovich, 441n, 460–2, 464
Katkov, Mikhail Nikiforovich, 505
Kaufmann, Christoph, 564
Kautsky, Karl, 589
Keotz, Christian Adolph, 411
Kepler, Johannes, 21n, 187
Keynes, John Maynard, Baron, 51, 605
Khlebnikov, Velemir Vladimirovich, 550
Khodasevich, Vladislav Felitsianovich., 530

Kierkegaard, Søren, 95, 263, 328, 577
Kipling, Rudyard, 530, 614
Klee, Paul, 532
Kleist, Christian Ewald, 388
Klinger, Friedrich Maximilian von, 257, 419, 564
Klopstock, Friedrich Gottlieb, 370, 397, 407, 422
Klyuev, Nikolay Alekseevich, 531
Klyun, I. V., 525
knowledge: and attainment of freedom, xxvii, 91, 93–8, 102, 104, 110–17, 213–15; and experience, 29; intuitive, 52; and general propositions, 54; sociology of, 89; and choice, 101–2; and prediction of events, 101, 104–7, 109, 116; and moral judgements, 135–6, 178; and optimism, 154–5; dominance of scientific method, 341–2; and historical understanding, 352–3; Tolstoy on, 486–96; Hamann on, 573, 575
Knutzen, Martin, 366
Kochubeys, the, 532
*Kolokol* see *Bell, The*
Körner, Karl Theodor, 376n, 594
Kropotkin, Prince Peter, 398
Kurbsky, Prince Andrey Mikhailovich, 454
Kutuzov, Marshal Mikhail Golenishchev, 457–8, 460, 474, 486–7, 489–90, 496

Lafitau, *Père* Joseph F., 364
La Fontaine, Jean de, 330
Lamartine, Alphonse Marie Louis de, 515
Lamennais, Félicité de, 398, 482
La Mettrie, Julien Offray de, 121, 487
La Mothe le Vayer, François de, 331
language: Hamann on nature of, 252–3, 381–2; universal, 266; perfect, 330; Vico on shaping effect of, 340, 344–7, 349, 354–5, 381; Herder on, 381–8
Laplace, Pierre Simon, marquis de, 20, 145, 456, 486
La Popelinière, Henri Lancelot Voisin, sieur de, 333
Laski, Harold J., 364n
Lassalle, Ferdinand J. G., 75, 199, 276, 584
Lavater, Johann Kaspar, 250, 364, 366, 385, 564
Lavoisier, Antoine Laurent, 51
law: in political theory, 64; as restraint, 220; acceptance of, 224
Lawrence, David Herbert, 424n
League of Nations, 585, 587, 600
Le Caron, Louis (Charondas), 333
Ledru-Rollin, Alexandre Auguste, 515

Lehmann, Rosamond, 528
Leibniz, Gottfried Wilhelm von: and science of history, 41, 134, 332; and free will, 100; on liberating value of knowledge, 155; on uniform reality, 248; on Machiavelli, 323; on perfect language, 330; and cosmic nature, 364, 393, 562; supports German language, 365; Herder admires, 390–1, 399, 405, 432; and empiricism, 414; and communal life, 424n; and plurality of values, 425; *Nouveaux Essais*, 419, 432
Leisewitz, Johann Anton, 257, 564
Lemke, Mikhail, 513
Lenin, Vladimir Il'ich: on achieving final solution, 13–14; outlook, 51; factory image, 75; on knowing reality, 155; as dominant figure, 183; Europocentrism, 603; qualities, 632
Leningrad: I. Berlin revisits, 540–4; Akhmatova on, 547
Lenz, Jakob Michael Reinhold, 257, 564, 573
Leo X, Pope, 295, 321n
Leon, Derrick, 441
Leont'ev, Konstantin, 441
Leopardi, Giacomo, Count, 550
Lermontov, Mikhail Yurevich, 532, 550, 574
Leroux, Pierre, 503
Le Roy, Louis, 333
Lessing, Gotthold Ephraim: Utopianism, 137; and Herder, 362, 370, 428; supports German language, 365; nationalist value-judgements, 404, 594; and progress, 428; and romantic movement, 565; *Minna von Barnhelm*, 565; *Nathan the Wise*, 428
Lewis, Sinclair, 530
Lewis, Wyndham, 430n
liberal humanism, 210
liberalism: and rationality, 224n; and coercion, 235–6
liberty (freedom): and coercion and interference ('negative'), ix, xxxii, 193–203, 204, 211–12, 219–25, 229, 232, 235–6, 241; I. Berlin on, ix–x, xii, xxviii; 'positive', ix–x, xxxii, 203–6, 233–4, 237; knowledge as agent for, xxvii, 91–8, 102–3, 106–7, 110–17, 213–16; as human goal, 10–11; concept of, 65, 108–10, 236–7, 568; and obedience, 71–2; and self-determination, 100–1, 107–8, 140–7, 150, 156, 187, 203–17, 223–4, 237, 241; possibilities of and obstacles to, 111–15;

as delusion, 156; equality of, 196–7, 205n; and choice, 202n, 242; compatibility with authority and law, 220, 231–2; and individual, 226; and recognition, 229–30; minimum, 235–6; Hegel on, 417
Lincoln, Abraham, xiv, 617, 633, 637n
Linton, W. J., 511n, 516
Lipchitz, Jacques, 525
Lipsius, Justus, 273
Livy, Titus, 283, 289, 305, 309, 404n
Lloyd George, David, xiv, 612–14, 616, 625, 633
Locke, John: achievements, 73, 367; on government as trustee, 76; and scientific method, 80; and free will, 100, 141n; on personal freedom, 196; optimism, 198; on law and freedom, 218; Blake attacks, 260, 573; on confusions from misuse of language, 330; on human nature, 347, 350; and 'essences', 384; on man as social, 417; on nature and God, 562; Fichte rejects, 569
Logau, Friedrich, Baron von, 365
logic: as formal discipline, 60
logical positivism, xi
Lothian, Philip Henry Kerr, 11th Marquess of, 618
Louis XIV, King of France, 256, 267, 336, 363, 397, 598
Louis XVI, King of France, 46, 265, 267, 503
Louis XVIII, King of France, 453
Louis-Philippe, King of the French, 507, 584
Lovejoy, Arthur O., 389
Lowth, Robert, Bishop of London, 355, 365, 389, 403
Lubbock, Percy, 441
Lucretius, 340, 351, 404n, 437
Lurié, Artur, 542–3
Luther, Martin, 51, 72
Lycurgus, 281

Mably, abbé Gabriel Bonnot de, 245, 395, 430, 557
Macaulay, Thomas Babington, Baron: historical attitudes, 143, 159, 163; on Machiavelli, 274–5, 277, 305; rationalism, 583; prose style, 607
Machiavelli, Niccolò: and plurality of values, xiii, xxix, 316–17, 320–1, 324, 425; and incompatible ideals, 6–8, 14, 320, 322–4; political philosophy, 73, 86, 301–2, 304–5; originality of, 269–325;

varied interpretations of, 269–83, 307–8, 315; positive beliefs and teachings, 283–99, 305–11, 313–16; and moral values, 288–9, 297–8, 300, 302–4, 308, 311, 317; and Christian values, 289–94, 298–9, 306, 308, 309n, 310–12, 321–3; on political method and practice, 299–303, 308–9, 319–20; and *raison d'état*, 299, 308, 310–11, 319; arouses horror, 305, 307–10; patriotism, 307, 589; assessed, 313–25; non-Utopian, 325; Herder and, 369; and classical values, 430; on social group, 586; *Discourses*, 269–70, 272, 291, 293, 300–1, 305, 307, 320, 321n, 323; *Histories*, 270; *History of Florence*, 277; *Mandragola*, 318n, 320; *The Prince*, 269–71, 276, 278–9, 283, 285, 300, 301, 305, 308, 319–20, 323

Machon, Canon Louis, 272

madness, 83

Maeterlinck, Maurice, 530

Maistre, Joseph de: doctrines, xi–xii, xxxi; image of executioner, 75, 267; attacks Enlightenment, 264, 380; on men as evil, 265–7, 473, 492; on authority, 266–8, 482–3, 497; draws moral lessons, 435; background and views, 472–5, 480–1, 483, 493–4, 496–8; influence on Tolstoy, 472–84, 491, 497; view of history, 484–5, 488–91; destructive power, 493–5, 498; and knowledge, 496; and nationalism, 592; *Correspondance diplomatique*, 473; *Soirées de Saint-Pétersbourg*, 473–4, 476n, 477n

Maistre, Rodolphe de, 473

Malebranche, Nicolas de, 332

Malevich, Kazimir Severinovich, 525, 532

Malia, Martin, 505n, 508n

Mallet du Pan, Jacques, 363, 407

Malraux, André, 528, 538, 629

Mandel'shtam, Nadezhda, 526, 534n, 551

Mandel'shtam, Osip Emilievich, 531–4, 543–4, 546–7, 549–50

Mannheim, Karl, 89

Manzoni, Alessandro, 579

Mao Tse-tung, 13

Marcus Aurelius, Roman Emperor, 287, 296

Maritain, Jacques, 279, 308n

Marrast, Armand, 515

Marsilio of Padua, 270, 280, 308, 320

Marx, Karl: and need for leaders, xii; I. Berlin writes on, xxv–xxvi; on historical change, 5, 48, 126, 137–8, 578, 584–5; knowledge of human behaviour, 53; and historical sense, 56, 182, 353, 356, 446–7, 456; and political philosophy, 66, 73; and creative spirit, 72, 422; rejects Encyclopaedists, 80; discards Bentham's morality, 81; Tolstoy disdains, 81; and self-knowledge, 95, 214; and moral freedom, 110; and social class, 124, 138, 456; materialism, 137, 558; and idealism, 155; and historical relativism, 157; and growth of sociological mythology, 183n; on obstructive nature of social institutions, 214–15; on understanding, 215; on rationalism in society, 217; appeal to colonial subjects, 231; views of, 269; and Machiavelli, 277, 308; revolutionary thinking, 315; doctrines, 367; on oppression, 376; on cultural decline, 395n; and alienation, 420; and Herzen, 506–7, 512, 517; friendship with Herwegh, 516; on State socialism, 584; on social group, 586; and generic identity, 602; Europocentrism, 603; *German Ideology*, 420n

Marxism: decline, xxxvi; on finding solutions, 12; and class struggle, 34, 124–5; and science of politics, 69; and human purpose, 70, 556; historical theory, 182, 608; and withering of State, 191; on material deprivation, 195n; and abandonment of final harmony, 238; and false consciousness, 317, 587; Herzen's supposed leanings towards, 519n, 520; rejects pessimistic writers, 579; opposes nationalism, 587, 600; Aron attacks, 602

Masaryk, Thomas, 633

mathematics: as model, 35; as formal science, 60; progress of, 73; and reasoning, 212–13; Vico on, as human invention, 246, 341

Matisse, Henri, 532

Mattingly, Garrett, 271, 273

Maude, Aylmer, 441

Maupassant, Guy de, 452n

Maupertuis, Pierre Louis Moreau de, 383

Maurists, 330

Mayakovsky, Vladimir Vladimirovich, 531–3, 549

Mazarin, Jules, Cardinal, 337

Mazzei, Lapo, 301

Mazzini, Giuseppe, 398, 402, 501, 514, 600, 617

Meinecke, Friedrich: on Machiavelli, 276, 278, 282, 322, 325; on Voltaire, 337; on

historism, 427n
Mencke, J. B., 365
Mendelssohn, Moses, 404
Merezhkovsky, Dmitry Sergeevich, 441
metaphor: in political philosophy, 75–6; in historical discourse, 131; Vico on, 344–5; in Bible, 404
metaphysics: and history, 182
Meyerhold, Vsevolod Emilievich, 525
Meysenbug, Malwilda von, 517
Michaelis, Johann David, 365
Michelet, Jules: historical viewpoint, 120, 159; restores Vico, 248; and national achievements, 398, 591; friendship with Herzen, 501, 515; view of Russians, 514
Mickiewicz, Adam, 546
Mikhailov, Mikhail Larionovich, 444n
Mikhailovsky, Nikolay Konstantinovich, 523
Milbanke, Annabella (later Lady Byron), 572n
Mill, John Stuart: doctrines, ix, 88–9; achievements, 73; and social pressures, 95; and free will, 100; on personal freedom and compulsion, 196, 198–200, 211, 221, 232–3, 236; private and social life, 226; on deprivation of human rights, 229; on self-assertion, 231; on government by the people, 234; and experiments in living, 240; on Bentham, 318; on lifelessness of modern man, 395; on Herder's influence, 417; Tolstoy on, 469; Herzen meets, 516; shocked by Comte's freedom of opinion in morals, 554; wariness of rationalism, 583; Auguste Comte and Positivism, 222n; On Liberty, ix, 199n
Millar, John, 363
Milton, John, 350, 362, 389, 573
mimesis, 559
Modigliani, Amedeo, 541, 543
Moleschott, J., 493
Molière, Jean Baptiste Poquelin de, 330, 437
Momigliano, Arnaldo, 9, 390n
Mondrian, Piet, 532
Monge, Gaspard, 489
monism, xxviii–xxix, xxxi–xxxii, 66, 69, 241, 312–13, 322, 553–5, 568
Monod, Gabriel-Jean-Jacques, 37
Montaigne, Michel Eyquem, seigneur de: on universal truths, 244; and cultural history, 351, 353; scepticism over progress, 408; and pluralism, 425; as 'fox', 437; and historical study, 361
Montesquieu, Charles Louis de Secondat,

baron de: and spirit of the laws, 53, 363; materialist view of history, 182, 339, 351, 353; on political liberty, 219; on variety of values, 244, 248, 362, 380; accepts rational method, 262; and climate, 384; categorisations, 392–3; and historical judgement, 407; ethical relativism, 428; influence on Catherine the Great, 445; belief in absolute principles, 556; De l'esprit des lois, 380n, 487n
morality: and ideal, 5, 11; and judgement, 135–6, 156–7, 179, 188–90; and specialised knowledge, 223; Kant on compatibility with determinism, 258–9, 561; and human ends, 315
More, Sir Thomas, 313, 557
Morelli, Giovanni di Pagolo, 301
Morelly, 557
Moritz, Carl Philipp, 564
Morley, John, Viscount, 612
Morris, William, 398, 557
Mortier, Marshal Adolphe Edouard Casimir Joseph, duc de Trévise, 501
Moscherosch, Johann Michael, 365
Moser, Friedrich Karl von, 363, 395, 398; Von dem deutschen Nationalgeist, 395n
Möser, Justus: anti-rationalism, 251, 394; on cultural variety, 256–7, 363–4, 568; historical view, 355; on traditions, 373; on German depression, 375; and Herder, 393
Moses: Machiavelli and, 281, 288, 295, 300, 307, 309; Herder and, 399; Tolstoy and, 494; personality, 634
Mosheim, Johann Lorenz von, 365
Mozart, Wolfgang Amadeus: The Magic Flute, 225
Muhammad the Prophet, 141, 573
Müller, Adam, 263
Muralt, Beat Ludwig von, 355, 362–3
Muralt, Leonard von, 273
Muslims: and revealed truth, 4
Musset, Alfred de, 574
Mussolini, Benito, 189n, 614
Mussorgsky, Modest Petrovich, 402
mysticism, 328
myths: as vision of world, 247; Fontenelle rejects, 344n; Vico on, 344, 348–9, 351n; Voltaire dismisses, 344, 346, 348, 351n; Herder on, 411

Namier, Lewis B., 53, 56, 146
Napoleon I (Bonaparte), Emperor of the French: historical importance, 169;

achievements, 183; massacres, 187; imposes force, 222; authoritarianism, 305; victories in Germany, 371; Tolstoy on, 450, 452–5, 457, 462, 474, 486, 491, 496

nation: and identity, xxxii–xxxiii, 590–4; as term, 131n

nationalism, 581–603; Herder and, xxxi, 197–9, 371–8, 384, 401; rise of, 558–9, 567, 574, 585–6, 589, 593–4, 598–9; as conscious doctrine, 586–9, 591; defined, 590–1; and loyalty, 592; and relativism, 593; and injured pride, 594–5, 597–9, 602; and unifying image, 595–6; spread of, 599–601, 604; and group consciousness, 600–1; ideology of, 602–4; Europocentrism, 603–4; see also State, the

National Socialism, xxxi

natural law: and obedience, 78, 204, 208; and historical inevitability, 134; in Enlightenment thinking, 244–6, 264; unmentioned by Machiavelli, 280; and human ideals, 322; Vico denies, 350; empirical rules, 559

natural science: influence, xxv; history as, xxviii, 17–58, 133, 331–2; and general laws, 28–30, 40, 45, 55–6; models in, 30, 35, 39; reasoning in, 31, 41–2, 45, 62; and answering questions, 60–2; progress of, 73, 326, 582–3; supplants theology and metaphysics, 80; and moral judgement, 188–9; divorce from humanities, 326–58; and single reality, 326–8; Vico opposes, 334; Herder's attitude to, 360–1, 364, 433

nature: controllability, 217; wildness of, 252, 257; Schelling on, as living organism, 261; harmony in, 264, 313, 562; limited human understanding of, 342; Leibniz on, 364; Herder on, 389, 393; human adaptation of, 558; romantic resistance to, 564–6

Navalikhin, S., 440n

Nazariev, V. N., 446

Nekrasov, Nikolay Alekseevich, 533, 551

neoclassicism, 559

Neoplatonism, 183, 382n, 393

Nerva, Roman Emperor, 287

Nerval, Gérard de, 577

Neuhaus, G. G., 532, 536–7

New Deal (USA), xxxv, 629

Newton, Isaac: general scientific laws, 19, 36; achievements, 20, 21n, 26, 79, 133, 167; general outlook, 51; Blake attacks, 259–60, 573; and unified reality, 328

Nicholas I, Tsar, 479, 503, 511, 513, 515n

Nicholas II, Tsar, 614

Niebuhr, Barthold Georg, 355

Nietzsche, Friedrich: doctrines, xii; and creative spirit, 72; and human relationships, 75; and destructive forces, 138; on cosmic purposelessness, 263, 577, 579; and Machiavelli, 292, 316; anti-rationalism, 328; hatred of State, 377; personality, 424n; as 'hedgehog', 437; and Maistre, 473; and Malwilda von Meysenbug, 517

nihilists, 521

Nijinsky, Vatslav Fomich, 530

Nisbet, H. B., 361n, 391n, 414n

nomothetic sociology, 186

Norov, A. S., 440n

Novalis (pseudonym of F. L. von Hardenberg), 263, 371, 575

novels: and scientific writing, 167–8

Nowell-Smith, Patrick H., 100, 141n

Numa, 281

Oakeshott, Michael, xiii

obedience: rationale of, 64–5, 71, 78, 193, 207–8, 221; in children, 218, 220; in ignorant, 221

objective pluralism see pluralism

observation: of data, 60, 62, 73

Occam, William, 200, 201n, 384

occultism, 328

Odoevsky, Prince Aleksandr Ivanovich, 550

Oenamaus, 99n

Ogareva, Nataliya, 517

Ogarev, Nikolay Platonovich, 503–5, 511, 513, 517

Oliverotto da Fermo, 296, 300, 319

Olschki, Leonardo, 273

oppression see coercion

optimism, 136, 154

Origen, 165n

original sin, 69, 264, 492, 556

Orsini, Felice, 514

Orwell, George, 316, 585

Ossian (pseudonym of James Macpherson), 363, 386, 388, 395n

Owen, Robert, 137, 512, 516, 557

Paine, Thomas, 198

palaeontology: extrapolation in, 25

Palmieri, Matteo, 317

Paolucci, Henry, 318n

Pareto, Vilfredo, 182, 317, 435

Paris: 1848 revolution, 506, 508–9, 515;

Herzen in, 506, 508, 523
Parnell, Charles Stewart, 632
Pascal, Blaise: on society as organism, 364; as 'hedgehog', 437; on knowledge, 496; and scientific truths, 577
Pascal, Roy, 395n, 521n
Pasquier, Étienne, 333
Pasternak, Boris Leonidovich: post-war status, 526–7; I. Berlin meets, 527–31, 533, 536–8, 552; eloquence, 530; patriotism, 532–3, 536; Akhmatova on, 533, 534n, 535–6, 546, 549–50; conversation with Stalin, 533–4, 551; disavows Communist Party, 535; *The Childhood of Lüvers*, 529; *Dr Zhivago*, 423, 529, 533, 536–8, 550; *On Early Trains*, 535–6
Pasternak, Leonid Borisovich, 527
Pasternak, Zinaida (Boris's wife), 527, 532, 537–8, 549–50
Pasteur, Louis, 163
paternalism, 208, 228, 395
patriotism: and German romantics, 371, 377, 403; Herder and, 371–2; and nationalism, 589
Patrizi, Francesco, 305n, 331
Paulucci, General Filipp Osipovich, marquis, 450, 474, 486, 489
Peacock, Thomas Love, 607
Pears, David F. (ed.): *Freedom and the Will*, 105n
Pellico, Silvio: *Le mie prigioni*, 512
Percy, Thomas, 389
Pericles, 289, 299, 307, 322, 634
Pertinax, 306
Pertsev, V. N., 441n
Pétain, Marshal Philippe, 621
Peter I (the Great), Tsar, 3, 265, 505, 518, 598
Pevsner, A., 525
Pfuel, General Ernst von, 450, 486, 489
Philip of Macedon, 296, 302, 321n
*philosophes*: aim for empiricism in moral philosophy, 79; on morality, 223; and future perfection, 241; *see also* Enlightenment, French
philosophy: status and nature of, 62–3; doctrines, 86–8; and politics, 192–3
physics: and purposelessness, xxvi; as model, 35
Picasso, Pablo, 532
Pico della Mirandola, Giovanni, 281, 320, 562
pietism, 248
Pisarev, Dmitry Ivanovich, 469

Pisistratus, 287–8, 296
Plato: and world picture, xxvi; on rule by élite, 4; influence, 9; and objectivity in ethics and aesthetics, 64; and obedience, 72; political philosophy, 86–8; and causation theory, 99; and moral freedom, 110; on Sophocles, 210; and abandonment of final harmony, 238; on uniform reality, 248, 312–13, 326–7, 392, 555; views of, 269; on wicked, 270; on human ends, 314, 431; revolutionary thinking, 315; on political power, 319; on mathematics, 341; on good and evil, 392; Herder on, 405; as 'hedgehog', 437; and ideal city, 557, 568; and will to power, 577; and social group, 586
Platonic ideal, 5, 557
Platonists, 69, 178, 204
Plekhanov, Georgy Valentinovich, 21, 155
pluralism: I. Berlin's belief in, xii, xxxii, xxxiv–xxxv; objective, xxv, xxxii, xxxv, 390n; Herder's idea of, xxx, 361, 368, 398–401, 403–12, 415–17, 424–32, 567–8; and social values, xxxi, 7–10, 68, 242; defined, 9; and negative liberty, 241; Machiavelli and, 316–17, 320–4; and romantic movement, 559–60
Plutarch, 331
Pobedonostsev, Konstantin Petrovich, 483
poetry: as vision of world, 247, 251; Herder on, 421–2
Poggio Bracciolini, Gian Francesco, 281
Pogodin, Mikhail Petrovich, 469
Pokrovsky, K. V., 457n, 478n
Pol Pot, 13
Poland, 363, 523, 600
Pole, Reginald, Cardinal, 270, 279
*Pole Star, The* (periodical), 511
*polis*, 297–8, 372, 398
political philosophy: as ethics, 1; and human purpose, 66–70
political theory: question of existence, 59–90; concerns, 74; and philosophical ideas, 192
Polybius, 309, 351, 586
Pontano, Giovanni (or Jovianus Pontanus), 282, 317, 425
Popper, Karl: denounces Plato's political philosophy, 87; on self-knowledge, 105–6; on 'essentialism', 125n, 281; criticises metaphysical historicism, 126n; and Machiavelli, 278, 281; *The Open Society and its Enemies*, 126n; *The Poverty of Historicism*, 126n
populism: Herder's doctrine of, 361, 367,

370–80, 399–403, 414, 417; rise of, 567
Posidonius, 116
positivists, 69, 328; *see also* Comte,
   Auguste
power: and oppression, 234
praise and blame, xxviii, 127–8, 135–6, 140,
   141n, 146–7, 156, 159–60, 171, 175, 177;
   *see also* morality
predictability, 101, 104–7, 109, 116
Preen, Friedrich von, 380n
Prezzolini, Giuseppe, 271, 285n, 289n, 292,
   321n, 323n
Priam, King of Troy, 92
privacy, 201
progress: and ideal, 6; Herzen on, 13; Vico
   on, 348, 351; Herder on, 378, 407–10,
   428, 429; and natural sciences, 582
Prometheus, 560
Protagoras, 244
*Protocols of the Learned Elders of Zion*,
   289n
Proudhon, Pierre Joseph: anarchism, 398;
   Tolstoy visits, 482n; Herzen and, 506–7,
   510, 515, 517; *La Guerre et la Paix*, 471
Proust, Marcel, 167, 437, 530–1, 550, 614
Prussia, 249, 366, 566; *see also* Germany
psychology: as natural science, 19–20, 61,
   63
Ptolemy, 35
Publilius Syrus, 319n
Pudovkin, Vsevolod Illarionovich, 525
Pufendorf, Samuel, Baron von, 338, 365
purpose (human), 66–72, 84, 92, 129–30
Pushkin, Alexander Sergeevich, 196, 437,
   531–2, 546, 550–1
Pyat, Félix, 515
Pyatkovsky, A. P., 440n
Pythagoras, 341, 555


questions: answering, 60–7, 79; legitimacy
   of, 62
quietism, 211n, 212n


Racine, Jean, 8, 167, 330, 350, 363
Rainborow, Thomas, 227n
*raison d'état*, 299, 308, 310–11, 319
Ramat, Raffaello, 275, 286
Ranke, Leopold von, 54n, 120, 163, 274,
   431
rationalism and reason: I. Berlin's attitude
   to, xiii–xiv, xxv, xxxi, xxxiii; Herder
   attacks, xxxi, 360; and reorganisation of
   society, 4–6, 213–18, 220; and
   answering questions, 60–1; and

understanding, 89, 104; and human
   freedom, 93, 213–16, 218–19, 225n,
   577–8; and human behaviour, 103–4;
   and Enlightenment doctrines, 244;
   opposed by anti-Enlightenment
   thinkers, 249–51, 256–8, 261–6;
   Machiavelli on, 313; and human ends,
   314; and scientific method, 327, 334;
   and unified reality, 328
Read, Herbert, 529; *English Prose Style*,
   605n
reason *see* rationalism and reason
recognition: human need for, 227–31
Reformation: Machiavelli and, 292; and
   mystical movements, 328; and
   beginnings of diversity, 554
Reimarus, Hermann Samuel, 359
relativism: cultural, 9–10; in political
   theory, 64; and inevitability, 171; and
   collapse of ideals, 179–80; opposition to
   Enlightenment, 243, 248; Herder
   advocates, 255, 390, 407n, 427–9; Vico
   propounds, 351; and differing
   objectives, 425; and nationalism, 593
*Religious Maxims . . . from . . . Machiavelli*,
   272
Remus, 307
Renaissance: art in, 8; cultural
   individuality, 50; on nature as divine
   harmony, 562
Renan, Ernest, 21, 37
Renaudet, Augustin, 273–4
responsibility: and choice, 95–6, 108,
   145–6, 156; and determinism, 99, 135,
   140–5, 149–61, 182; seen as delusion,
   179
revolution of 1848, 506, 508–9, 515
Reynolds, Sir Joshua, 261, 571
Ricci, Luigi, 271
Richelieu, Cardinal Jean Armand du
   Plessis, duc de, 22, 50
Ridolfi, Roberto, 272–4, 321n
rights, 64, 201, 236
Rilke, Rainer Maria, 531, 550, 614
rites: Vico on, 344, 346–7
Ritter, Gerhard, 302, 432
Robertson, William, 406
Robespierre, Maximilien, 51, 169, 192, 267
Roerich, Nicholas, 532
Rolland, Romain, 517, 547
Roman Catholic Church: and rational
   language, 330; and Western decadence,
   481; historicism, 608
romanticism: and human purpose, 70,
   579–80; anti-rationality, 251, 256–7,

577–9; and self-expression, 261; and creativity, 262; anti-authoritarianism, 264; German beginnings, 559–65, 569–76, 579, 598

Rome (ancient): and personal constraints, 211; Machiavelli on, 287–9, 291, 300, 303, 307, 312, 322–3; Plutarch on, 331; achievements, 336; and Athenian law, 354; Herder on, 374–5, 433; Maistre on, 485

Romulus, 288, 295, 300, 307, 309

Roosevelt, Eleanor, 636

Roosevelt, Franklin Delano: political achievements, xii, xxxv, 629–30, 632, 635–6; personality and qualities, xiv, 615, 628–36; relations with Churchill, 613–17, 619, 621–2, 624–6; illness, 636

Rossetti, Christina, 545

Rossini, Gioacchino Antonio, 402

Rothschild, James, 506, 516n

Rouché, Max, 361n, 397n, 407n, 427

Rousseau, Jean-Jacques: on true freedom, x, 210; ideals, 3, 73; influence on French Revolution, 46; rejects Hobbes's political obligation, 80–1; Babbitt denounces, 87; on cultural inhibitions and innocence, 114; Heine attacks ideas, 192; on ill will, 195; on obedience to law, 208; influence on liberal humanism, 210; on rationalism in society, 216, 219, 366, 394, 558; on universality of self-direction, 223; on austerity of laws of liberty, 233; Constant opposes, 235; on corrupting effect of civilisation, 245, 327, 566; pleads for natural feeling, 252, 558; on will, 259; accepts rational method, 262; demands revolutionary change, 264; Faguet ridicules, 266, 519; Maistre denounces, 266, 484; views of, 269; and Machiavelli, 271, 292; revolutionary thinking, 315; letter to Poles, 363; denounces stage, 366; doctrines, 367; on State, 377; and social units, 380; praises primitive societies, 389; and populism, 401; personality, 424n; and plurality of values, 425; on man's imperfectibility, 430; Tolstoy and, 445, 455, 468–9, 472; on knowledge, 496; idealises independence and freedom, 561–2, 566; on people as organic whole, 591; Discourses, 366, 395; Émile, 195n, 259, 264, 468; Social Contract, 208n

Royal Society of London, 330

Rubens, Peter Paul, 547

Rubinshtein, M. M., 441n, 445n

rules (socio-political), 64, 78

Ruskin, John, 395, 398, 583

Russell, Bertrand Arthur William: in linguistic analytical tradition, ix; and human purpose, 67; and empirical knowledge, 82; and free will, 100, 141n; on uniform reality, 248; on Machiavelli, 279; talking, 530; attacks Victorian metaphysicians, 605

Russia: 1917 Revolution, xxvi, 169, 434–5, 604; novelists and writers in, 2–3, 423, 526–7; Herder's influence in, 402; intelligentsia in, 420; repression in, 479; radicalism in, 505–6; image in West, 511n, 514; nationalism in, 523, 600, 604; Soviet art in, 525–6; Great Terror, 526; Pasternak on, 532–3, 535–6; reaction against modernisation, 598; 1904 defeat by Japan, 604; Churchill's view of, 612, 624–5; Roosevelt and, 624–5; trials and purges, 629

Russo, Luigi, 297, 300

Ryle, Gilbert, 52

Sabine, George H., 277–8

Sade, Donatien Alphonse François, marquis de, 258, 389

Sadko, 532

Saffi, Aurelio, 514

Saint-Evremond, Charles de Saint-Denis, sieur de, 362–3

Saint-Réal, abbé César Vichard de, 333

Saint-Simon, Claude-Henri, comte de: and political philosophy, 66; and human goals, 68; optimism, 137, 154, 583; historical theory, 182, 435; and administration, 191; and Machiavelli, 281; and unified reality, 328, 623; and creative epochs, 395; Comte and, 446; Herzen reads, 503; and State capitalism, 557; on social group, 586

Sainte-Beuve, Charles-Augustin, 380n

Samarin, Yury Fedorovich, 469, 532

Sanctis, Francesco de, 275, 276, 289n

Sand, George, 264, 510, 517

Sartre, Jean-Paul: xiii, 11, 530; La Nausée, 538

Sasso, Gennaro, 274

Savigny, Friedrich Karl von, 361n, 393

Savonarola, Girolamo, 286, 294, 306, 309, 369

Schelling, Friedrich Wilhelm Joseph von: and creative spirit, 72, 124, 422; theodicy, 182; power of ideas, 192;

romantic anti-rationalism, 251; on primal nature, 260–1; on purpose in natural activity, 263; patriotism, 371, 403; Herder and, 432; influence on Slavophils, 470; and knowledge, 496; accepts established order, 574

Schiller, Johann Christoph Friedrich von: patriotism, 371, 377; on cultural decline, 395n; admires ancient Athens, 409; on naïve manner, 414; influence on Russian radicals, 421; Herzen reads, 503, 516; Herzen takes motto from, 513; and freedom beyond reason, 564–6; accepts established order, 574; *Die Räuber (The Robbers)*, 260, 565; *Xenien* (with Goethe), 377

Schlegel, August Wilhelm von, 361n, 371

Schlegel, Friedrich: irrationalism, 263; and Herder, 361n; patriotism, 371; influence on Russian radicals, 421; on Renaissance, 547; accepts established order, 574; on obscuring reality, 575

Schleiermacher, Friedrich E. D., 371, 421

Schlick, Moritz, 100, 141n

Schlözer, Kurd von, 361, 403

Schmid, Karl, 273

Schoenberg, Arnold, 532

Scholastics: and cosmic design, 178

Schopenhauer, Arthur: and free will, 100, 117, 148n, 471; and moral freedom, 110; pessimism, 178; on liberation by death, 212; anti-rationalism, 261; on cosmic purposelessness, 263, 577, 579; influence on Tolstoy, 471

Schubart, Christian Friedrich Daniel, 257, 564

Schumpeter, Joseph A.: *Capitalism, Socialism, and Democracy*, 242n

Schütze, Martin, 391n

*Schwärmerei*, 561

science *see* natural science

Scipio, 288, 295, 296, 299

Scotus Erigena *see* Erigena, Johannes Scotus

Scriabin, Aleksandr Nikolaevich, 532

Seifullina, Lydia, 529

self: understanding of, 94–5, 105; and freedom, 203–6; noumenal, 207

self-denial *see* asceticism

self-determination (autonomy), xxvii, 98–102, 110, 203–18, 223–4

self-fulfilment, 92

self-realisation, 212–16

Sel'vinsky, Il'ya L'vovich, 531

semantics: as science, 63

Seneca, 8n

Sereno, Renzo, 277

Sergeenko, P. A., 500n

Severus, Lucius Septimus, Roman Emperor, 296, 306

Sextus Empiricus, 316

Sforza, Francesco, 300

Shaftesbury, Anthony Ashley Cooper, 3rd Earl of: anti-intellectualism, 251, 366; on artists, 362; influence on Germans, 400; and historical judgement, 406; and nature, 421

Shakespeare, William: literary style, 350–1; reputation, 362, 389; Herder and, 369, 399, 421; and plurality of values, 426; as 'fox', 437; Pasternak's knowledge of, 531, 550; Russian interest in, 539; patriotism, 589; *Hamlet*, 23, 50; *Troilus and Cressida*, 573

Shaw, George Bernard, 137, 451, 452n, 539, 614

Shchepkin, Mikhail Semenovich, 512

Shcherbakov, Aleksandr Sergeevich, 528

Shelgunov, Nikolay Vasil'evich, 440

Shelley, Percy Bysshe, 264, 550, 622

Shklovsky, Viktor Borisovich, 440n, 457n, 468n

Simmons, E. J., 441

Simon, *Père* Richard, 365

sincerity: as virtue, 553–4

Singleton, Charles S., 278

Sismondi, Jean Charles Léonard de, 305, 398

Skinner, Burrhus Frederick, 328

slavery: and freedom, 112–13

Slavophils (Russian): on freedom and obedience, 72; compare family and political life, 75; and Tolstoy, 469–70, 481; Maistre and, 495; Herzen and, 505, 520; Pasternak on, 532; reaction against modernisation, 598

Smith, Adam, 51, 198, 313

social Darwinism, 292, 378

social sciences: scientific procedure in, 33

society: rational organisation of, 3–5, 216–17; institutional obstructiveness, 214–15; individual in, 226–7; conflicts of values in, 238; as organism, 364

sociology: as natural science, 18–19, 41, 185; beginnings, 183, 185–6

Socrates, 3–4, 225, 399

Soderini, Piero, 286, 303, 306, 309

Solon, 354

Sophists (Greek), 244, 314, 555

Sophocles, 8 & n, 11, 210, 426; *Antigone*,

xii–xiii
Sorel, Albert, 441n, 443, 478, 482
Sorel, Charles, 333
Sorel, Georges, 182, 558, 575, 601
Soutine, Chaim, 525
sovereignty, 65, 233–4, 237n
Soviet Union see Russia
Spanish Civil War, 629
Sparre, Erik, 333
Sparta, 233, 287, 307, 312
Spencer, Herbert: materialism, 19; and
    social sciences, 25; and human
    relationships, 75; idealism, 155;
    evolutionary doctrines, 378; Tolstoy on,
    469
Spender, Stephen, 628
Spener, Philipp Jacob, 253
Spengler, Oswald: typology, 9; and
    historical laws, 33; and impersonal
    historical forces, 124, 126
Spenser, Edmund, 421
Speransky, Mikhail Mikhailovich, 448, 480
Spinoza, Benedictus de: and lack of
    purpose in nature, 71; and empiricism
    of political thought, 73; and liberating
    value of knowledge, 98, 154, 155, 213,
    334; and free will, 100, 103, 110, 117;
    and autonomy, 116; on rationalism, 217,
    329, 333–4; on obedience in children,
    218; Jacobi on, 260; and Machiavelli,
    271, 276, 293, 308; on moral values,
    290, 293; political theory, 333; on
    human nature, 347, 350; questions
    Bible, 365; Herder and, 391, 432;
    Tolstoy and, 457; on nature and God,
    562; Ethics, 103, 329; Treatise on the
    Improvement of the Understanding, 329
spontaneity: as human quality, xii, 11
Stadelmann, Rudolf, 428n
Staël, Anne Louise Germaine, baronne de,
    454
Stalin, Josef V., 172–3, 187, 525–6, 533–4,
    548, 550–1, 604, 614–15, 621, 635
Stassov, Vladimir Vasil'evich, 402
State, the: and interference, ix, 198–9,
    201–2, 206; and minority interests, xii;
    goal of perfection, 12; and authority, 75;
    242, 265–6; views of, 85; as term, 131n;
    Marxist ideal of withering away, 191;
    and rationalism, 216–17; Machiavelli
    and, 278, 288, 294, 301, 304–5, 307, 309;
    Herder deplores, 373, 376–7, 396–7,
    400, 428; and socialism, 584; Hegel on,
    591; and self-identification, 594; as unit,
    600; see also nationalism

status: as human goal, 227–31
Stein, Karl, Baron vom, 454
Stendhal (pseudonym of Marie-Henri
    Beyle), 167, 472, 478, 482
Stephen, James: Liberty, Equality,
    Fraternity, 200
Stephen, Leslie, 364n
Stern, Fritz (ed.): The Varieties of History,
    54n
Sterne, Laurence, 445
Stirner, Max, 263, 507
Stoics: ideals, 4, 211, 558; and science of
    politics, 69, 85; and human
    relationships, 75; logic, 86; on liberating
    value of knowledge, 91, 95, 98; on self-
    control, 92; and causation theory, 99;
    and acceptance, 103, 115, 179; and self-
    determination, 110, 223; on inner
    integrity, 209n; and rise of autocracy,
    211; and Machiavelli, 284; and divine
    Logos, 313; and absolute principles, 350
Strachey, Lytton, 605
Strauss, Leo, 279
Stravinsky, Igor, 532
Stravinsky, Vera, 543
Stroganovs, the, 532
Sturm und Drang movement, xxix, 252,
    257–8, 328, 388, 419, 558, 563, 565, 573,
    575, 596
subjectivism, 64, 70, 171, 429; see also
    relativism
suffering: avoidance of, 14–15
Sulzer, Johann Georg, 415, 424n
Süssmilch, Johann Peter, 383
symbols: and words, 381

Tabidze, Nina, 539
Tabidze, Titsian Yustinovich, 529, 539
Tacitus, 51, 289, 293, 319
Taine, Hippolyte: materialism, 19; and
    scientific history, 21, 34, 37–9, 55, 155;
    and study of human and social samples,
    38–9, 43; historical view, 159; and
    knowledge, 496
Tairov, Aleksandr Yakovlevich, 525
Talleyrand, Charles Maurice de, 453, 622
Tamerlane, 273
Tatlin, Vladimir Evgrafovich, 525
Tawney, Richard Henry, 240; Equality,
    196n
teleology, 23, 129–30, 132–4
Thayer, Judge Webster, 605
theory: and formulation of doctrines, 27
Theseus, 288, 295, 300, 307, 309
Thierry, Augustin, 503

Thiers, Adolphe, 445
Thirty Years War, 211, 562
Thomasius, Christian, 365, 594
Thomists: and science of politics, 69, 71,
    85; see also Aquinas, St Thomas
Thoreau, Henry David, 398, 583
Thrasymachus, 270
Thucydides, 51, 173, 270, 309, 319
Tieck, Johann Ludwig, 263, 371, 574,
    575–7; Prince Zerbino, 576; William
    Lovell, 576
time: as moving river, 22
Timoleon, 288, 295–6
Tocqueville, Alexis de, 196, 236, 514,
    583–4
Toffanin, Giuseppe, 272
Tolstoy, Aleksey Nikolaevich, 544
Tolstoy, Countess Aleksandra, 522
Tolstoy, Count Lev Nikolaevich: and need
    for leaders, xii; I. Berlin on, xiv; ideals,
    3; on truth, 16; parodies historical
    explanations, 46; dismisses Marx's
    doctrines, 81; on understanding and
    knowledge, 154, 327, 470, 486–96; and
    historical judgement, 158, 159n;
    difficulty of categorising, 437–8;
    philosophy of history, 439–69, 484–8,
    491–2, 498; reading, 444–5; disbelieves
    in free will, 456, 458–60, 485, 489–90;
    creative genius, 465; and personal
    conflict, 465–7; advocates simplicity,
    466–8; influences on, 468–79; anti-
    intellectualism, 469, 480; and Slavophils,
    469–70; Maistre and, 472–91, 497–8;
    rejects political reform, 484; destructive
    force, 493–4; isolation, 498; on Herzen,
    500, 521–2; Pasternak on, 531–3;
    Akhmatova attacks, 539, 545–6; rejects
    Western values, 567; discounts
    Utopianism, 579; Anna Karenina, 463,
    486, 545; The Kreutzer Sonata, 545;
    Sevastopol in May, 16; War and Peace,
    2, 439–43, 446, 448–50, 457–61, 465–8,
    470–1, 474, 482n, 486–7, 502, 545
Tolstoy, Nikolay Nikolaevich (Lev's
    brother), 463, 472
Tolstoy, Countess Sof'ya Andreevna
    (Lev's wife), 545
Tommasini, Oreste, 275
Tönnies, Ferdinand Julius, 75, 424n
totalitarianism: and authority, 268
Toynbee, Arnold, 33, 124, 130–1, 182
Treitschke, Heinrich von, 143, 307, 399
Trevor-Roper, Hugh, 307n
Trotsky, Leon, x, 13, 159, 632

truth: as ideal, 16; and history, 17; and
    knowledge, 91–118
Tsvetaeva, Marina Ivanovna, 527, 531–2,
    534, 546, 549
Tukhachevsky, Marshal Mikhail
    Nikolaevich, 534
Turgenev, Ivan Sergeevich: as 'fox', xiv; as
    'pure' writer, 423; and Pushkin, 437; on
    Tolstoy, 439–40, 451, 460, 466; on
    Herzen, 500; reads Hegel, 505;
    reputation, 511n, 514; gradualism, 520;
    Pasternak on, 539; Akhmatova despises,
    546; discounts Utopianism, 579; Fathers
    and Children, 487, 521
Turgot, Anne Jacques Robert, baron de
    l'Aulne, 178, 408, 586
tyranny, xxxii, 233–4
Tyutchev, Fedor Ivanovich, 469, 531–3

United Nations: and nationalism, 585
United States of America: political idealism
    in, 212n; Churchill on, 612; vision,
    623–4; Roosevelt's New Deal in, 629
unity: search for, 180
utilitarianism, 15, 223
Utopias: and belief in attainable happiness,
    xxxii, xxxv, 137, 191, 313–14, 556, 568,
    579; value of, 12; and fantasy, 58;
    nineteenth-century, 585
Uz, Johann Peter, 370

Vaihinger, Hans, 148n
Vakhtangov, Evgeny Bagrationovich, 525
Valentino, Duke of see Borgia, Cesare
Valéry, Paul, 550, 614
Valla, Laurentius, 330
value judgements, 63–5
value pluralism see pluralism
values (cultural and moral): incompatibility
    and plurality, 7, 9–12, 14–16, 238–9,
    244, 248, 425–6, 556–7; and human
    purpose, 67–8; and empirical fact, 80;
    and defining man, 83; Kant on, 209;
    determination of, 240, 242, 262–3
Vanini, Lucilio, 323
Vanzetti, Bartolomeo, 605
Verdi, Giuseppe, 402
Verhaeren, Émile, 531
Verne, Jules, 137
Versailles, Treaty of (1919), 587
Vesterling, Hermann, 428n
Vettori, Francesco, 283, 299
Vico, Giambattista: I. Berlin champions, xi;
    concept of history, xxix–xxx, 24, 48, 50,
    56, 165n, 340, 342–3, 349–58; opposes

scientific method, xxix, 334, 352, 357;
and cultural succession, 7–9, 14, 247–8,
350–1, 354–5; and social activities, 19;
on 'inner' and 'outer', 53; rediscovery
of, 120, 393; on mathematics as human
invention, 246, 341; denies doctrine of
timeless law, 247–8; on understanding,
253; background, 340; on language,
myths and rites, 344–9, 355, 381, 387;
on *fantasia* (imagination), 346, 351n,
354–6; Herder and, 361–2, 405; and
spirit of nation, 363; and Homeric
scholarship, 365; on nature, 389; and
artistic creation, 418n; on social group,
586; *Scienza nuova* (*New Science*), 7,
246, 248, 345n, 347n, 353
Victor Emmanuel III, King of Italy, 614
Viennese positivists, 328
Vignier, Nicolas, 333
Villari, Pasquali, 278
Villey, Michel: *Leçons d'histoire de la
philosophie du droit*, 201n
Vincent of Lérins, 327n
Virgil, 404n, 558
virtues: diversity of, 553–4
Vitmer, A., 440n
Vögelin, Eric, 273
Vogt, Karl, 493, 516
Vogüé, Eugène Melchior, vicomte de, 441,
482
Voltaire, François Marie Arouet de: on
Enlightenment, 8n; influence on French
Revolution, 46; and toleration, 142; on
attaining human ends, 245; Herder
attacks, 252, 255, 362, 406, 411–12, 415,
434; mocks variations in laws, 256;
Maistre on, 267, 284–5; and Machiavelli,
320; and unified reality, 328, 359; on
history, 334–9, 352, 355, 361; and
scientific method, 334–5; dismisses
mythology and rites, 344n, 346, 348,
351n; literary style, 350; absolutism,
355; praises foreign civilisations, 362–3,
431; anti-clericalism, 377; and Wolff's
syllogisms, 394; condemns Middle Ages,
407, 411; on progress, 408; on cultural
differences, 415; on artistic creativity,
419; and *bon sens*, 428; Tolstoy rejects,
484; German reaction against, 563, 574;
on Muhammad, 573; and spirit of time,
622–3; *Essai sur les moeurs*, 335, 362,
415; *La Philosophie d'histoire par feu
l'abbé Bazin*, 408
Vranck, François, 333
Vrubel, Mikhail Aleksandrovich, 532

Vyatka (Russia), 504, 512
Vyazemsky, Prince Petr Andreevich, 443

Wackenroder, Wilhelm Heinrich, 495, 575
Wagner, Richard, 360, 407, 516, 579
Walder, E., 272
Walker, Leslie, 272
Walpole, Robert, 633
Warton, Thomas (senior) and Joseph, 365,
400
Weber, Max: on explanation of actions, 41;
and sense of history, 56; social order,
75; and sociology of knowledge, 89; and
growth of sociological mythology,
183n; on power of bureaucracy, 585
Wegelin, Jakob von Daniel, 362, 430n
Weil, Simone, 87
Weizmann, Chaim, xxiv
Wells, G. A., 361n, 386n, 427n, 433n
Wells, Herbert George, 137, 168, 328, 334,
451, 530, 568, 614
*Weltanschauung*, 23
Whitehead, Alfred North, 559
Whitfield, John Humphreys, 293
Whitman, Walt, 579
Wieland, Christoph Martin, 403, 424n, 564
Wilhelm II, Kaiser, 614
will: and causation theory, 99–100; and
moral freedom, 259; Rousseau on, 259;
Fichte on, 570–2, 574–5; freedom and
supremacy of, 577
Willkie, Wendell, 634
Wilson, Woodrow, 614, 625, 631–2
Winckelmann, Johann Joachim, 347, 363,
396, 430, 529
*Wirkungszusammenhang*, 55
Wittgenstein, Ludwig, 84
Wolf, Friedrich August, 355, 365
Wolff, Christian, Baron von, 359, 386, 394
Wolin, Sheldon S., 311
Wood, Robert, 388
Woolf, Virginia, 451, 530, 539, 614, 629
Wordsworth, William, 261, 565, 574
World War II, 613–14
Writers' Union (USSR), 526
Wundt, Wilhelm Max, 25

Xenophon, 305

Yakovenko, Professor, 441n
Yakovlev, Ivan Aleksandrovich (Herzen's
father), 501–6
Yashvili, Pavle (known as Paolo)
Dzhibraelovich, 529
Yeats, William Butler, 530, 614

Yggdrasil, 312
Young, Edward, 355, 389, 400

Zadkine, Ossip, 525
Zamyatin, Evgeny Ivanovich, 585
Zenkovsky, V. V., 441n
Zeno, 155, 557
Zhdanov, Andrey Aleksandrovich, 545

Zhikharev, S. P., 474
Zhukovsky, Vasily Andreevich, 532
Zimmermann, J. G. Ritter von, 363
Zinzendorf, Nikolaus Ludwig, Count von, 363
Zola, Émile, 167
Zoshchenko, Mikhail Mikhailovich, 540
Zweig, Stefan, 441